Comparative Perspectives on E-government

Serving Today and Building for Tomorrow

Edited by

Peter Hernon
Rowena Cullen
Harold C. Relyea

The Scarecrow Press, Inc.
Lanham, Maryland • Toronto • Oxford
2006

SCARECROW PRESS, INC.

Published in the United States of America
by Scarecrow Press, Inc.
A wholly owned subsidary of
The Rowman & Littlefield Publishing Group, Inc.
4501 Forbes Boulevard, Suite 200, Lanham, Maryland 20706
www.scarecrowpress.com

PO Box 317
Oxford
OX2 9RU, UK

British Library Cataloguing in Publication Information Available

Library of Congress Cataloging-in-Publication Data

Comparative perspectives on e-government : serving today and building for
tomorrow / edited by Peter Hernon, Rowena Cullen, Harold C. Relyea.
p. cm.
Includes bibliographical references and index.
ISBN-13: 978-0-8108-5735-3 (alk. paper)
ISBN-13: 978-0-8108-5357-7 (pbk. : alk. paper)
ISBN-10: 0-8108-5735-9 (alk. paper)
ISBN-10: 0-8108-5357-4 (pbk. : alk. paper)
1. Internet in public administration.   2. Internet in public administration—Cross-
cultural studies.   I. Hernon, Peter.   II. Cullen, Rowena.   III. Relyea, Harold.
JF1525.A8C62   2006
352.3′802854678—dc22   2005033580

Contents

Figures and Tables

FIGURES

TABLES

Preface

Peter Hernon

*S*tarting in the 1990s, many governments began to use information and communications technologies, especially Internet applications, to improve the efficiency and economy of government operations and to provide their citizens, the business community, and government officials (perhaps representing different levels of government) with information and services. Today, government Web sites in a number of countries are more sophisticated but they still continue to evolve, and the members of the public and business community they serve might reside anywhere in the world. There are differences in e-government offerings between developed and developing countries and, even in developed nations, from country to country. Some countries primarily emphasize service provision; others might be less involved in such provision, preferring to concentrate on conveying information; and some might be trying to advance e-democracy. Each facet of e-government that is important to a government evolves from a simple stage to more advanced stages and is linked to a planning process intended to promote efficiency and economy, as well as to satisfy the needs of the audiences served. Clearly, the goal of e-government is to become entrenched in the everyday lives of citizens, members of the business community, and government officials so that they become reliant on Internet access to government.

Comparative Perspectives on E-government draws upon the expertise of a number of contributors who have conducted research and policy analyses related to government information policy and e-government, and who have published previously in these areas. The focus of coverage is on five countries (Australia, Canada, New Zealand, the United Kingdom, and the United States) and topical issues such as the digital divide, the balance between access and security in the aftermath of 9/11, trust in government, the citizen's perspective on e-government, and the evaluation of government Web sites. More specifically, chapter 1, which introduces e-government, provides a framework characterizing it. Chapters 2–6 discuss the development of e-government in the five countries, while chapters 7–9 cover trust in government, access and security, and trends in archiving information and records. Based on direct discussions with citizens of one country, chapters 10 and 11 present the public's perspective on e-government. Public opinion polls in other countries suggest that those findings have application beyond that one country, New Zealand.

Chapter 12 focuses on government portals and makes comparisons across selected countries. It explains what certain countries are trying to accomplish and the challenges they face. Chapter 13 suggests ways to frame evaluation results for use in continuous quality improvement and furthering best practices. Agencies are quantifying the amount of material they offer through their Web sites, the number of hits they encounter for a specified time period, and the amount of money they generate through the sale of products and services. As the chapter illustrates, there are other types of metrics and methods, not all of which produce simple indicators or benchmarks.

Chapters 14 and 15 focus on broadband Internet access and the digital divide. Chapter 16, which returns to the topic of the first chapter, highlights e-government worldwide and summarizes developments in the United States. Chapter 17 revisits some of the key issues raised in the various chapters and offers suggestions for the future as e-government advances and becomes better integrated with the non-Internet environment.

The origin of this book dates back to winter 2004 when I spent a five-month sabbatical leave at the School of Information Management, Victoria University (Wellington, New Zealand). I taught a course on information policy emphasizing government information policy and, together with Rowena Cullen, conducted the research culminating in chapters 10 and 11. Both experiences reinforced the need for a multi-country, in-depth examination of e-government for the purposes of creating a book for graduate students in various disciplines. Other intended audiences include scholars researching e-government and government information policy, public officials wanting to review and advance e-government, information resource managers seeking to review the layout and effectiveness of the Web sites under their purview, archivists seeking to preserve the accomplishments of e-government, librarians contemplating their role in the age of e-government, and, as a matter of fact, anyone interested in the topic.

There is a need to understand the phenomenon of e-government better—its development, mission and goals, success in achieving those goals, and future plans. This understanding should extend to both developed and developing countries and should consist of more detailed cross-country analyses and comparisons. E-government is a dynamic topic in which the expectations of government and the public may be in conflict, and many members of the public may still be unfamiliar with the availability and value of online government information and services. Furthermore, these individuals may not have an everyday need for such information or services. Clearly, e-government presents both challenges and opportunities.

I

INTRODUCTION

E-government: Transforming Government

Peter Hernon and Rowena Cullen

$\mathscr{I}$n the 1990s with the construction of the so-called information superhighway, governments at the national and subnational levels began to develop a presence on the Internet and the World Wide Web. Initially that presence might have been equated with a minor road but, over time, it has become a significant part of that highway. However, the public has not always been aware of (or appreciated) the government section of the superhighway, oftentimes preferring to take a bypass. They might even come to an intersection and discover that the road choices for government (choices highlighting each department and agency, the legislature, and the courts) are overwhelming. They might encounter a portal—a multifunctional Web site that usually includes Web directories, indexes, and links to other appropriate Web-based resources—and, in some (not all) instances, might find it useful in navigating that portion of the superhighway labeled "government."

The presence of government on the information superhighway has become known as e-government or e-gov. However, as Harold C. Relyea notes,

> The conditions contributing to the e-government phenomenon were recognized at least three decades ago. Observations offered by the authors of a report of the Commission on the Year 2000 of the American Academy of Arts and Sciences are informative in this regard. Concerning the executive branch [of the U.S. government], the report proffered that "[b]y the year 2000, despite the growth in the size and complexity of federal programs, the technological improvement of the computer, closed-circuit TV, facsimile transmission, and so on, will make it possible for the federal bureaucracy to carry out its functions much more efficiently and effectively than it can today, with no increase in total manpower."[1]

E-government, it is commonly pointed out, links government to information and communications technologies (ICT) for the purpose of enhancing access to government information and the delivery of government services; making more efficient purchases of goods and services; and improving the internal effectiveness, efficiency, and innovativeness of government. The World Bank Group, which expands on these purposes, explains that these technologies

> serve a variety of different ends: better delivery of government services to citizens, improved interactions with business and industry, citizen empowerment through access to

information, or more efficient government management. The resulting benefits can be less corruption, increased transparency, greater convenience, revenue growth, and/or cost reductions.[2]

The report notes, "The Bank has identified corruption as the single greatest obstacle to economic and social development," and it maintains "that an effective anticorruption strategy builds on five key elements: (1) increasing political accountability, (2) strengthening civil society participation, (3) creating a competitive private sector, (4) institutional restraints on power, [and] (5) improving public sector management."[3]

Relyea reminds us,

New information technologies have affected government operations in the past, as the following comment, penned in 1910, attests: "Public officials, even in the United States, have been slow to change from the old-fashioned and more dignified use of written documents and uniformed messengers; but in the last ten years there has been a sweeping revolution in this respect. Government by telephone! This is a new idea that has already arrived in the more efficient departments of the Federal service. And as for the present Congress, that body has gone so far as to plan for a special system of its own, in both Houses, so that all official announcements may be heard by wire."[4]

Against this background, this chapter links e-government to information management and offers a model depicting the various facets of e-government, noting that different governments emphasize some facets over others. The chapter also discusses the stages through which e-government has evolved and makes some preliminary comparisons beyond the countries highlighted in this book (Australia, Canada, New Zealand, the United Kingdom, and the United States), showing, for instance, how developing countries fit into e-government. The purpose is to provide a framework for the discussion provided in the other chapters. The concluding chapter revisits this chapter and the model of e-government.

INFORMATION MANAGEMENT

Governments manage the information, records, images, and datasets that they generate or collect. They create *records* in the course of conducting their official business and share some of those records with the parties to that business. A record may be a matter, physically, of defined space in a medium such as a piece of paper. It may also be undefined, as in some electronic records. A record should be recognized less for its form or format and more for its context and content. In brief, in a policy context, a record is "what the government says it is" (i.e., a document or format that contains information that is a matter of record or information in need of preservation).

Information management relates to the information life cycle and its six stages: (1) creation, (2) production, (3) transmission (viewed in terms of distribution and dissemination), (4) transmission (viewed this time in terms of access, retrieval, and use), (5) review, and (6) retirement or retention. The information that has been accessed, used, or even retired might lead to the creation of new information and the subsequent stages. In an electronic environment, the stages need not be sequential. Stage 4, for instance, might involve the use of a geographic information system (GIS), which might lead directly to the creation of new information. Furthermore, planning and security influence all six stages.

One purpose of e-government, such as in the United Kingdom and the United States, is to improve the management of government resources and the delivery of services. This purpose is reflected in the call for greater efficiency and effectiveness in that management and in service delivery. The Organisation for Economic Co-operation and Development (OECD) offers a more complete rationale for e-government. The OECD sees e-government as "more about government than about 'e'"[5] because it seeks to improve services and efficiency, contributes to public management modernization and reform, helps to build trust between government and citizens, helps government achieve specific policy outcomes, and contributes to economic policy objectives, such as "reduced government spending through more effective programmes, and efficiencies and improvements in business productivity through IT [information technology]–enabled administrative simplification and enhanced government information."[6]

Stage 4 of the life cycle for e-government refers to the mixture of information (aimed at different age groups and audiences), documents, records, images (e.g., photographs and satellite imagery), and datasets (e.g., GIS applications and data provided by the agency conducting the official census of a country) that government Web sites contain. Given the resources available—many of which may lack a paper counterpart—a question becomes, "Do government Web sites constitute a record?" In the case of New Zealand,

> Archives New Zealand considers a record to be "information created, received, and maintained as evidence or information by an organization or person, in pursuance of legal obligations or in the transaction of business" (International Standard on Information and Documentation—Records Management, ISO 15489) no matter what its medium of support: paper, magnetic tape, digital or other. Websites are therefore already considered to be records and we are in fact shortly about to publish a "Guide to Developing Record-keeping Strategies for Websites."[7]

MODEL OF E-GOVERNMENT

Figure 1.1 offers a generalized model of e-government that depicts seven facets:

1. information provision and access;
2. delivery of services;
3. e-commerce;
4. emergency response (natural disasters or reporting terrorist threats);
5. procurement;
6. governance or e-engagement;
7. e-compliance (for large and small businesses and for individuals).

E-government is minimally understood as the provision of government services and information via the Internet for businesses and citizens. In increasingly competitive markets, the quality and efficiency of those services are often aimed at businesses (domestic and international). Nonetheless, with access to more and presumably better information, citizens become more empowered and can hold governments accountable for their services and actions. However, in a number of countries certain facets might be downplayed or ignored. For example, some countries would not support governance as a way to encourage public participation in the development of public policy. In other countries (e.g., the United States), government officials hold online chats with the public on a regular basis. The U.S. Patent and Trademark Office, for instance, holds regular Web-based question-and-answer forums with the public. The public can type questions and submit them via the Web, and government officials, in turn, reply and post the answers on the agency Web site. In New Zealand, the E-government Unit of the State Services Commission (SSC) encourages government agencies to notify citizens on their Web site of policies on which they are currently consulting, to make those documents freely available on the Web, and to accept submissions by e-mail.

In one-party dominant regimes, the effectiveness and efficiency of government may be measured differently than it is in a democracy (for the purposes of this book defined as a state in which the government has been freely elected by the people). In either a one-party dominant regime or a democracy, information dissemination could become a means to reinforce the official government position, and the public might prefer to use Web sites of the private sector and individuals. In some countries, such Web sites might represent the cutting edge of the struggle between an authoritarian state and those seeking more freedom.

Complicating any depiction such as the one in figure 1.1 is the fact that any of the facets might contain developmental stages, and those stages might differ depending on the audience. In other words, there might be differences between services developed for citizens, business and industry, and other government agencies. Furthermore, the evaluation framework might vary according to audience; that shift might be determined

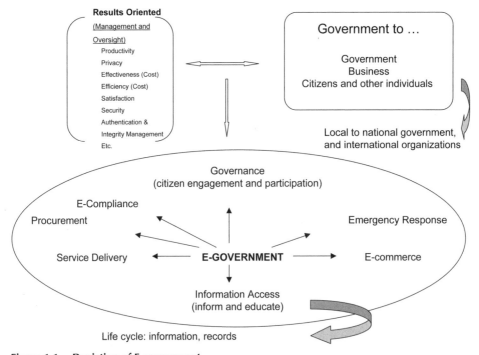

Figure 1.1.   Depiction of E-government

by statutory or administrative acts and policies. The public, for example, would be interested in matters related to satisfaction, service quality, efficiency, location of relevant information and services, and so on. Government, on the other hand, might have other priorities, but it should not slight the public's perspective.

Table 1.1, based on the seven facets depicted in the figure, offers some examples of each. The countries discussed in this book vary in the extent to which each government fully supports each facet. The greatest number of examples exists for information access and service delivery. There are also numerous instances of e-commerce. As already noted, governance may not be something that a government wants to promote, and e-compliance is probably the newest and least-developed facet.

In many of these countries, it might be possible to pull up a form but difficult to download it. In some instances, the public might have to download the form, complete it, and mail it back. In other instances, the font size used for the form is too small for people with disabilities and others to easily read. The inability of the public to conduct transactions entirely online likely impacts the extent of its satisfaction with e-government.

Government resources on the Web are becoming so extensive that most countries employ some form of organizational principle. In most developed countries, individual government agencies develop their own Web sites, with varying degrees of oversight and control from an outside body (e.g., the SSC in New Zealand, the Office of Management and Budget in the United States, the Cabinet Office in the United Kingdom) and various systems of centralized access, as through some form of central portal. Agency Web sites are then structured according to the internal activities and divisions of the parent department. Increasingly in some countries, government departments and agencies arrange access to resources on their home pages according to audience: whether the person is a member of the public, business community, or government (local to national), and in a few countries this same approach is taken on the central portal as well.

Such an approach, focusing on the needs of users, their reasons for visiting a Web site, and the activities they wish to carry out when there, is better aligned with the widely held principles of effective use of the Web for business, educational, or government purposes, as articulated by Web industry leaders.[8] Furthermore, in some countries, the government imposes a management perspective (emphasizing outcomes and a results orientation) and relates the use of the Web by government agencies to planning, evaluation, and the improved delivery of information and services.

That management context should not focus exclusively on the needs of the executive branch government as it tries to promote itself as innovative, effective, and efficient regarding e-government internally (e.g., to the legislature). Clearly, all branches of government should participate in creating and executing a vision and strategy for e-government. In functioning democracies, the context should go beyond the internal needs of government and reflect the expectations and extent of satisfaction of the user or customer group (these concerns are addressed in chapter 13).

E-government also has the potential to build collaboration within the central government and between that government and subnational authorities such as state, provincial, regional, and city governments. Given the widespread lack of public understanding of the structure of government, and the different functions and roles that the various departments and agencies perform, transparent access to government infor-

Table 1.1.   Examples of Web Sites and Pages Illustrating the Different Facets of E-government

Facet	Purpose
E-commerce	Online bookstore for U.S. Government publications (Government Printing Office), http://bookstore.gpo.gov/
	Electronic Commerce (Australian Government Information and Services), http://www.australia.gov.au/index.php?195
E-compliance	Environmental Protection Agency (seeks "to maximize compliance and reduce threats to public health and the environment by employing an integrated approach of compliance assistance, compliance incentives and innovative civil and criminal enforcement"), http://www.epa.gov/compliance/
Emergency Response	"The FBI encourages the public to report any suspected violations of U.S. federal law. You can do so by calling your local FBI office, Legal Attaché office, or by submitting a tip via the FBI Tips and Public Leads form," http://www.fbi.gov/contactus.htm.
Governance	Rulemaking.gov ("makes it easier for you to participate in federal rulemaking—an essential part of the American democratic process"), http://www.regulations.gov/
	Inspector General of Intelligence and Security: Complaints ("allegation of unlawful 'bugging' of telephones, inappropriate surveillance, delays in security assessments of asylum seekers, inappropriate involvement in court matters, poor recruitment practices, etc."), http://www.igis.gov.au; http://www.igis.gov.au/complaints.cfm
Information Access	Interactive Feature—Explore: Earth, Moon, Mars and Beyond (National Aeronautics and Space Administration), http://www.nasa.gov/home/index.html
	Online Photos (Franklin D. Roosevelt Presidential Library and Museum: photographs of the president and first lady, the Great Depression, and World War II), http://www.fdrlibrary.marist.edu/photos.html
	Learning section for disabled people and caregivers ("Information on learning for people with special educational needs, learning difficulties or other disabilities"), http://www.direct.gov.uk/Topics/Learning/fs/en
	Bureau of Land Management ("HISTORICAL PHOTOGRAPHS View more than 2,500 historic photo images taken across the United States from 1890–1970"), http://www.photos.blm.gov/
Procurement	OMB's Office of Federal Procurement Policy, http://www.whitehouse.gov/omb/procurement/index.html
	FedBizOpps ("the single government point-of-entry for federal government procurement opportunities over $25,000"), http://www.fedbizopps.gov/
	AcqNet (a gateway to information and information resources related to procurement), http://www.acqnet.gov/
	Syndicated Procurement ("Provide ways for government agencies to collaborate in buying goods and services through syndicated procurement, adoption of best practice processes and sharing knowledge"), http://www.e-government.govt.nz/procurement/index.asp
Service Delivery	Top 100 Forms (available through Firstgov.gov), http://www.forms.gov/bgfPortal/citizen.portal. These forms require Acrobat Reader to read.
	Science.gov provides access to more than 47 million pages of government science information, and it offers personalized e-mail alerts, http://www.science.gov/

Chat with a Librarian (American Memory of the Library of Congress: "Chat is available from Monday through Friday 2:00-4:00 PM Eastern Time (except Federal Holidays)." To contact a librarian during another time, please use our Ask a Librarian web form"), http://www.loc.gov/rr/askalib/chat-memory.html

MyNASA ("sign up to customize your own MyNASA page with specific and up-to-date news and features"), http://mynasa.nasa.gov/portal/site/mynasa/index.jsp? bandwidth = high

MyUSDA (create a customizable Web portal via a personal account that stores content and alert preferences). The U.S. Department of Agriculture has more than nine million Web pages behind its home page, http://www.usda.gov/wps/portal/usda home

Export.gov ("the portal to all export-related assistance and market information offered by the federal government. Whether you're looking for trade leads, free export counseling, or help with the export process"), http://www.export.gov/

Department of Commerce (Gold Key Matching Services—Arranges one-on-one appointments with carefully selected potential business partners in a targeted export market. The Gold Key Matching Services offer customized market and industry briefings with our trade specialists, timely and relevant market research, appointments with prospective trade partners in key industry sectors, post-meeting debriefing with our trade specialists and assistance in developing appropriate follow-up strategies, help with travel, accommodations, interpreter service, and clerical support), http://www.commerce.gov/contracts.html

The Disaster Assistance Process for Individuals (Federal Emergency Management Agency), http://www.fema.gov/about/process/

El IRS en español (Internal Revenue Service), http://www.irs.gov/espanol/index.-html

Licensing (Bureau of Industry and Security: assists "visitors through the export licensing process and provides important information that individuals and firms need to know before exporting"), http://www.bis.doc.gov/licensing/index.htm

Food Safety.Gov (serves as a centralized hub gathering information from various government agencies about how to protect your food and water supplies against potential terrorist threats), see http://www.foodsafety.gov/

U.S. Government Graphics and Photos (current and historical ones across the federal government), http://www.firstgov.gov/Topics/Graphics.shtml

New Zealand Customs Service ("This section of our website is to help you with Customs requirements if you are exporting goods"), http://www.customs.govt.nz/ exporters/default.asp

Unclaimed Monies Online Search facility (Australian Securities and Investments Commission), http://www.asic.gov.au/fido/fido.nsf/byheadline/Looking + for + lost + money%F?openDocu . . .

Service Canada ("one-stop access to government services—helping Canadians get to the services they need quickly, easily and conveniently"), http://www.service canada.gc.ca/en/home.html

The Canadian Business Network (offers Canadian businesses a single access point to key government services and information), http://canadabusiness.gc.ca/gol/cbec/ site.nsf/en/index.html mation and services, from whichever department or agency is responsible, and seamless access to any of the seven facets of e-government become desirable goals. This requires a whole-of-government approach to the Web from central and regional governments, a common sense of purpose, and a commitment to e-government that is necessary to underpin the elements of infrastructure (common architecture, design, and metadata) needed to facilitate seamless access and effective navigation across government sites at all levels. This approach requires a political commitment from central government down to the smallest local agency.

An example of the level of confusion that can exist is shown in the terminology used to characterize the types of government publications (e.g., in the United States an executive order versus a National Security Presidential Directive, a Memorandum of Notification, or a presidential finding; or a congressional hearing versus a congressional report). Retrieving government information and records from Web sites or a print environment requires an understanding of such terminology, and some of these types include records that are withheld from public scrutiny for a period of time or, in some instances, permanently.

DEVELOPMENTAL STAGES OF E-GOVERNMENT

The presence of government on the Internet has evolved considerably since the time when governments first placed some basic information on their home pages. That information could be hard to locate and there were few portals (or well-functioning ones) to aid the public in navigating different Web sites and locating the information needed. Naturally, both portals and the government Web sites in many countries have improved over time.

Darrell M. West suggests that there are four separate stages of e-government development: (1) the billboard stage; (2) the partial-service-delivery stage; (3) the portal stage, with fully executable and integrated service delivery; and (4) interactive democracy with public outreach and accountability enhancing features.[9] The first stage is a static mechanism for posting publications, legislation, and policy documents, mostly available also in print form for the public to view. Members of the public can only view and download information; they can neither manipulate nor interact with it (e.g., through GIS applications). In the second stage, they can request and use online services and manipulate informational databases to a limited extent. Still, the offering of online services is sporadic and their number is limited. Furthermore, there is infrequent posting of privacy and security statements on home pages, and accessibility of Web sites to people with either disabilities or poor English-language skills is limited.

In the third stage, online services are widely available and integrated into the offerings that Web sites provide. Government departments and agencies pay attention to the public's privacy and security concerns, and, if they rely on cookies,[10] they should acknowledge this practice and post their policies on their Web sites. The needs and preferences of those with disabilities and limited English-language skills are likely to be addressed at this stage, through the creation and application of government Web guidelines for accessibility,[11] if their needs and preferences had not been covered in stage 2.

For some countries, stage 4 enables the public to customize service delivery (e.g., regarding electronic subscription services) and engage in two-way communication with government officials (e.g., through e-mail and Webcasts—audiovisual presentations such as a news conference that can be viewed online in real time or archived for later viewing).

Although the four stages show that e-government evolves or transforms a government's presence on the Web, they represent a simplistic characterization. Use of the word "portal" to characterize the third stage is misleading and misses the point that what is being described is a change of activities that can be carried out online. Arguably, portals could be used in all four stages of e-government development. The four stages confuse e-government with e-democracy; e-government focuses on the function of government, which can be (but does not have to be) unrelated to the exercise of citizens' rights and responsibilities online (e-democracy).

Different stages can occur simultaneously, and West's stages do not fully address figure 1.1. Surely, there are other stages. Governance might also include e-voting at some point, and stages should cover the integration of different levels of sub- or regional government into a single Web portal, such as through FirstGov in the United States. Furthermore, given the official nature of records, the need for archival policies and procedures, especially concerning retirement and relocation of government Web pages, merits a separate stage or at least inclusion within interactive democracy.

Andrew Chadwick and Christopher May view e-government as being informed by an understanding of the nature and roles of government. They define three *heuristic* models of the interaction between states and citizens, based on a key set of questions that include:

- What role does government play?
- Who are the principal actors and what are their interests?
- What is the dominant perspective on the flow of information?
- What are the principal mechanisms for interaction between government and citizens?
- What attention is paid to the ability of citizens to interact electronically?
- What is the defining logic of each model?

From these questions they advance three models of e-government: managerial, consultative, and participatory.[12] The managerial model, they suggest, distinguishes between *citizens* and citizens as *customers* of government information and services. The model focuses on the use of e-government to improve the efficiency of government, increasing flows of information to break down unhelpful departmental boundaries and entrenched vertical hierarchies, and transforming government to give people information and services where and when they want them. This model, they suggest, "treats information as relatively simple, and unilinear rather than complex and discursively generated. Information will be *delivered* and will empower those previously unable to access it."[13] The managerial model not only characterizes information as unilinear but also tends to perceive the citizens as either a single body of consumers or individuals making up a single body.

The consultative model, by contrast, allows governments to seek voter opinion on particular issues to guide policymaking. Direct access to government, unmediated by "special interest groups," can be facilitated by placing publicly available computers in such locations as public libraries to ensure more representative polling. While still based on a direct question-and-answer communication and quantifiable responses to policy innovations, this direct access is critical to the development of e-democracy and represents a stage on the way to participatory e-government.

It is only in the third model, the participatory model, that any sense of the multiple constituencies of government emerges and the unilinear model of information flow is abandoned. A model of participatory democracy based on a multiplicity of *communities of interest*—the participatory model—"conceives of a more complex, horizontal, and multidirectional interactivity."[14] Despite ongoing rhetoric from governments about the potential for participatory e-government and e-democracy, the authors contend that "achievements to date fall far short of anything approaching 'electronic democracy.'"[15]

Despite the fact that most governments remain at the managerial stage of e-government, Marc Holzer, Lung-Teng Hu, and Seok-Hwi Song provide examples of attempts by several levels of governments in the United States to introduce consultative, if not fully participatory, e-government, as envisaged by Chadwick and May. They define "best practice" in e-government as the citizen's ability to participate in the affairs of the state and through government Web sites to "capably participate in setting the policy agenda and [influence] policy decisions."[16] However, the authors note that in the consultative processes on government Web sites citizens are not actually engaging with government officials but more commonly with a Webmaster, and with each other. In order to build a more encompassing consensus of citizens' views, a more effective way of managing this process will be needed. Furthermore, if citizens are to develop trust in the new forms of participatory e-government, a more effective form of "digital citizenship" will need to be created.[17]

USABILITY AND AUTHENTICITY ISSUES

A number of additional issues must be considered in relation to the development of e-government. Later chapters will address issues of physical and intellectual access to e-government in more detail, and in the context of the development of e-government in each of the countries covered. Nonetheless, it is important to note here that usability remains a key issue for all governments to consider. Government Web site developers have improved their understanding of good Web site design and architecture and the effective use of metadata in recent years to create some outstanding examples of effective use of the Web. Many of them have made good use of usability and other forms of user studies to reorganize Web site content so that the public can more easily locate the information and services they need and want. However, many sites in both developed and developing countries still fall behind commercial Web sites in exploiting the potential of the Web to maximize user satisfaction, to foster access to information and services, and to facilitate consultative and participatory government.

Another issue relates to the question of the statutory authority of the information provided on government Web sites and the assumption that the informational matter provided on those sites is the official version; in other words, does the government stand behind the authority and reliability of all information presented? This is often not the case, although this varies from jurisdiction to jurisdiction. A government body may retain a presentation copy of a print publication as the authentic version or the source of record and retain printed statutes and regulations as the authoritative version of the law. If there is no paper counterpart and if different versions exist, the question becomes, "What version of an online document does the government stand behind?" The answer is often not apparent from visiting a Web site. More than that, a government body may not have developed a satisfactory answer to the question and may not have archived earlier versions in an accessible format.

A further concern relates to the potential for a so-called official Web document to be altered by another party. Digital watermarking, which is already used to ensure the security and authenticity of digital photographs by embedding an encrypted image in the photographic image, is one means of ensuring the integrity of official documents whose authenticity is critical. The information presented on the Web is not so protected, and thus, in some instances, the integrity of that information has been questioned.[18]

Other ways to combat fraud and enhance security exist and apply mostly to e-commerce. However, all governments that are developing electronic services (in addition to providing information) grapple with the problem of authenticating online users, through methods ranging from electronic signatures and certificates, to more esoteric methods such as electronic fingerprinting or iris recognition, where the image of a user's eye is captured and compared with a preregistered image. Widespread concern about the integrity of information provided by government, or personal information that users supply, would erode public confidence in government on the Internet. This concern is a key issue addressed in subsequent chapters.

EFFICIENCY

Policymakers view efficiency in terms of cost cutting (e.g., reducing the number of personnel necessary to complete a task), more efficient procurement, and increased speed and accuracy of transactions. E-government thus offers the potential for improved efficiency in terms of enhanced government-to-government exchange of information and payments, along with government-to-citizen, government-to-business, and government-to-employee exchanges. Initiatives currently being explored in many jurisdictions to improve internal and external efficiency include:

- Syndicated procurement, or e-procurement, in which agencies are encouraged to collaborate in buying goods and services and to adopt best-practice processes and share knowledge of suppliers. E-procurement benefits both agencies and suppliers.
- Shared online workspace, in which agencies are expected to work online, sharing work between agencies and their partners outside government.

Such initiatives require the development of interoperability standards within and between agencies and government and subgovernment levels. Interoperability helps government agencies work together electronically and makes systems, knowledge, and experience reusable from one agency to another. For citizens and businesses interacting with government, it reduces the effort required to deal with government online by encouraging a consistency of approach, and it simplifies online tendering for government contracts—common in many jurisdictions—and filing tax and import/export returns—a key element of e-compliance.

In summary, e-government efficiency is not viewed merely in terms of cost savings related to the accomplishment of department and agency goals and objectives, or improving the management of government or government information technology (IT). The identification and application of best practices from other areas of the public and private sectors have influenced the development of e-government initiatives.

Efficiency also assumes a customer component as it can focus on the ability of the public to find the information or service desired quickly. For example, some agencies such as the U.S. Government Accountability Office (GAO), formerly called the General Accounting Office, have adopted the three-click rule, also adopted by the FirstGov Web site, whereby visitors to their Web site should be able to find the information needed within three clicks of the mouse. GAO officials think that this rule "will result in a significant increase in the number of users" of its home page. To assist customers and increase efficiency, the agency publishes documents on its Web site within twenty-four hours of receipt. As a result, it has seen the "average weekly hits to its home page" increase from 760,000 in May 2003 to 1.2 million in May 2004. The "average weekly downloads of PDF documents" went from 440,000 in May 2003 to 700,000 the following May.[19]

One problem with e-government that all jurisdictions face is that Web statistics are not always standardized or comparable. Interoperability standards that also standardize Web metrics software packages will help resolve this problem. A further complication is that Web transaction data, for example, from a central portal, may not be linked to other datasets, showing, for instance, the topics on which the public sought information, the paths they traveled to find the information, and whether, when they arrived at a particular agency site, they were able to find the information. Innumerable studies, cited in later chapters, show users constantly frustrated in their attempts to find information, and solutions require close attention to the appropriate use and integration of metrics. Chapter 13, which covers evaluation, builds on this observation and discusses the types of metrics used to gauge the success or continued maturity of Web sites.

ORGANIZATIONAL CULTURE AND E-GOVERNMENT

A complication in achieving the potential of e-government is that institutions, organizations, and societal groups have different cultures and respond differently to the possibilities that new ICT provides. Institutional culture refers to the assumptions, norms, values, rituals, traditions, philosophies, and ideologies that characterize an institution. Institutions consist of subunits, each with its own culture. Organizational culture reflects the personality of the organization. One categorization of organizational culture often used in the management literature is clan, hierarchical, and market; these categories are not mutually exclusive. A market culture focuses on the projection of an institutional image, and the changes in that image may be more cosmetic than substantive. Hierarchical and clan cultures maintain the status quo and provide an enjoyable work atmosphere. Hierarchical cultures have a strong sense of mission, are less innovative than other institutions, and rate lower than other institutional cultures on organizational effectiveness.

Because culture is so firmly rooted in an organization's history and collective experience, working to change it requires a major investment of leadership, time, resources, and planning. Those policymakers, leaders, and planners seeking to manage organizational change must pay careful attention to the interaction between the planning and development of public sector reform and the achievement of a vision or strategy for a digital information society. These groups must encourage departments and agencies to explore innovation in the digital age and to maximize the potential of the Web and e-government. The development of collaborative relationships within the organization and with other departments and agencies to provide seamless Web access to citizens is a major culture change that must be well led and managed. For example, e-government in the United Kingdom has explored ways to address this issue and to get government agencies to participate in a centralized portal and to deliver services digitally.

Problems can arise when departments and agencies assume they know what their publics want and need and organize the content of their Web sites around these assumptions. Failure to manage digital information in terms of the needs, wants, and expectations of citizens will have an adverse impact on e-government. However, achieving a culture change of this magnitude, from what has been seen as a distant, inflexible, print-bound, and unresponsive bureaucracy to a dynamic, digital, participatory environment, will require, as Chadwick and May point out, a radical change of policy and direction for most governments and their bureaucracies.[20]

Common problems that many countries experience in relation to management of Web projects relate to compliance with accessibility and content guidelines, applications of metadata and other infrastructural systems for full interoperability and seamless searching, and problems in implementing government-to-government and government-to-business initiatives (e.g., e-procurement and shared workspace). Key issues that an OECD report into the failure of IT and e-government projects highlighted include the need for the involvement and commitment of top management (rather than delegating to the IT department) to ensure project success and the shortage of skilled IT staff to implement projects. E-government projects carry risks, not least the failure to deliver on their promises and citizens turning away from those projects; this risk must be managed and dealt with on an ongoing basis. The key principles advocated in the report include:

- Establish appropriate governance structures.
- Think small.
- Use known technologies.
- Identify and manage risk.
- Ensure compliance with best practices for project management.
- Hold business managers accountable.
- Recruit and retain talent.
- Prudently manage knowledge.
- Establish environments of trust with private vendors.
- Involve end users.

The general lesson is not that governments should not take any risks; rather, governments must identify risks, determine which risks they are willing to take, and manage the relevant risk within appropriate governance structures.[21]

Failure to manage these projects efficiently may make oversight bodies such as legislatures less willing to fund new or planned ICT projects. The result may be to undermine future efforts to implement new e-government services and technologies and to create specialized portals. Without progress and innovation, e-government may not evolve or mature; those facets depicted in figure 1.1 that a particular government highlights in its national vision or strategy may not continue to improve.

E-GOVERNMENT GLOBALLY

Countries vary as to their stage of development and how they interpret the term *e-government*. According to the United Nations' *Global E-governance Readiness Report 2004*, 178 of the United Nations' 191 member states had Web sites (a significant increase since 2001 when 143 states had Web sites), but only 15 governments in the world invited comment on government policy on their Web sites, and only 33 supported transactions such as filing forms or paying fines, fees, or taxes online.[22]

An analysis of the e-government literature by Adrienne Muir and Charles Oppenheim from 1997 to 2001 showed that in the early stages, the targets set for e-government by governments worldwide were vague, that "few governments seem to have addressed in any thoughtful manner the problems citizens might have with use of the technology," and that "the risks of exacerbating the digital divide are also rarely explicitly expressed."[23] The authors considered Australia, New Zealand, the United States, and Canada to be leading the field at that time and commended the New Zealand government's efforts to ensure that its Web sites are useful for citizens who have difficulty spelling. They also praised the Canadian government for its use of minority languages and noted that the emergence of government portals "is without doubt the most significant development observed in our research."[24]

In its annual survey of e-government globally, Accenture, a management consulting and technology services company (see www.accenture.com), charts changes in the e-government landscape.[25] In this report, Accenture offers a better characterization of the development of e-government than West's four stages, and one more closely aligned with the Chadwick and May model. E-government, the report suggests, evolves through a series of plateaus in an effort to transform government from an agency-centric to a citizen-centric (or customer-focused) operation capable of delivering information and services to citizens, businesses, and other government departments and agencies 24/7/365. "Moving to a higher stage of maturity requires more than . . . incremental progress." It requires governments to rethink their e-government strategies and to "focus on ways of adding value."[26] The plateaus range from "online presence," which "is a passive presentation of general information,"[27] to "basic capability," to "service availability," to "mature delivery," and ultimately to "service transformation," which transforms "how government functions are conceived, organized, and executed."[28]

The report shows that a number of governments are shifting their efforts on e-government to consultation with citizens and suggests that people who use online government services have a much higher satisfaction rate than those who use traditional mechanisms, such as the phone or in-person visits.[29] Undoubtedly, with the release of future reports, the range and grouping of plateaus will continue to develop as e-government becomes more sophisticated or mature. Accenture rates Canada, Singapore, and the United States as achieving the highest overall maturity scores. In effect, these countries are the leaders in approaching service transformation.

EXAMPLES OF INDIVIDUAL COUNTRIES

Although the book examines selected democracies, this section highlights e-government in selected other countries. It indicates that countries interpret e-government differently, have different foci, and are at different stages of development. The picture portrayed in this book and the five countries highlighted are not typical of practices in every country. As a result, figure 1.1 represents an aspiration that some countries are closer to meeting, while others might let it serve as a guide to their evolution of e-government.

One reason for Singapore's high position in the development of e-government, as Weiling Ke and Kwok Kee Wei note, is its "ability to capitalize on the benefits offered by a reasonably small, well-informed, and well-wired public. It has a stable government with a long-term commitment to ensure the benefits of technology are maximized."[30] The e-government transformation there can be attributed to "strong leadership with vision," government's acceptance of that vision, formulation of "a strategic action plan that provides clear guidelines for agencies to follow in implementing e-government initiatives," developing an information infrastructure, bridging the digital divide, and working toward "business process integration among agencies" for the services provided.[31]

Finland is another example of "an e-government pioneer" for its inclusion of e-government as "an explicit component of public sector reform." Finland "is at the forefront in the development of e-engagement. E-engagement focuses on improving online access to government information and public participation in policymaking."[32] The centralized government promotes e-government while regional and local governments serve as the primary service providers. Under parliamentary authority, the independent central agencies provide important services, as do the private and nonprofit sectors through an Information Society Advisory Board. Within this context, problems relate to a failure to communicate a clear e-government vision for an information society, to foster more interagency collaboration, and to ensure ownership of e-government initiatives. Furthermore, ministries that do not have central coordination responsibilities "have been passive in developing and encouraging e-government initiatives in the agencies under them."[33] Another complication is that "in Finland, as in other OECD countries, little is known about actual citizen demand."[34]

Taiwan, like Singapore, is a small, densely populated country with a highly literate and IT-skilled population. Ranked as a world leader in e-government, it has implemented key platforms of e-government, including the provision of most government information online, a one-stop-shop portal, and a wide range of e-services, including certificate-based authentication, online filing and payment of taxes, electronic official-documents exchange, electronic disbursement, and electronic motor vehicle registration. Government agencies have implemented e-management projects such as e-procurement, e-project management, e-personnel management, e-publishing, and e-learning for staff development. Taiwan recently implemented an electronic tendering system "for digitizing the procurement procedure in government agencies where inefficiency and even corruption have been underlying problems."[35]

Other Asian countries fare less well. The development of e-government in Japan is hampered by the failure to include citizen needs in planning improved access to government information. Other weaknesses are the lack of effective leadership, poor coordination among the various e-government initiatives, a government monopoly over its information, and "poor management over the flow and storage of government information."[36] Hong Kong, however, "has made considerable progress in developing online service delivery, notably for the business sector, but . . . needs to adopt a broader strategy that goes beyond service delivery to encompass citizen engagement and participation."[37] This may be difficult to achieve, given the role played by the government of the People's Republic of China in the governance of Hong Kong.

At the other end of the scale lie developing countries that have a very different focus in their approach to e-government. Subhajit Basu shows that developing countries are making progress at the initial stages of developing e-government but face significant obstacles in achieving the full advantage of e-government. The governments, for example, must be willing to decentralize some responsibilities and processes and to use electronic means of disseminating information and services. More information would then have to be digitized, more computers would have to be accessible to the public, and a broad spectrum of the public would have to be literate and see the value of using those information resources and services. Furthermore, many members of the public may fail to understand what e-government is or could become.[38]

Indonesia is an example of a country that is undergoing significant change as it moves beyond democracy as "merely a tool of rhetorical politics" and as the system of government transforms from centralization to decentralization.[39] E-government is envisioned as a way to promote good governance through more efficient, effective, and transparent regional government. Clearly, Indonesia, which has 385 regions, is at the lower end of the plateaus and has many problems to resolve if its e-government intends to advance.

Bangladesh, which is in a similar position, is in the first stages of developing e-government. It has significant technical, infrastructure, and political obstacles to overcome. "The government continues to struggle in its efforts to provide current information on governmental activities electronically. Not all government agencies possess web sites," and only one government agency offers electronic services to the public.[40] In these (and other) developing countries, the potential for e-government to help eliminate corruption and advance the growth of democracy will play a major role in economic growth.[41]

CONCLUSION

E-government is a term that does not have the exact same meaning or application worldwide. Different components or facets characterize the approach that a particular government takes to disseminating information, delivering services, conducting business, and communicating with the public. Yet, according to the U.S. GAO, as e-government evolves and matures, there are ten challenges to resolve: government must (1) "minimize the risk associated with the dissemination of personal information," (2) "maintain a focus on the needs of citizens accessing government Web sites," (3) "sustain committed executive [political] leadership," (4) build "effective E-Government business cases," (5) implement "appropriate security controls," (6) maintain "electronic records," (7) maintain "a robust technical infrastructure," (8) address "IT human capital concerns," (9) ensure "uniform service to the public," and (10) determine and periodically review the scope of e-government to ensure that e-government accomplishes its mission, vision, and documented strategy while continuing to mature.[42]

An eleventh challenge related to disparities in access to e-government encompasses the digital divide (addressed in chapters 14 and 15) and accessibility for people with disabilities. A twelfth challenge covers government information technology management and funding, and it "includes issues such as government information technology worker recruitment, retention, and compensation; the establishment of a CIO [chief information officer] at the national level; and cooperation across levels of government."[43]

Perhaps there is an additional challenge, namely, ensuring that the public does not equate e-government with George Orwell's vision of society depicted in the novel *1984*.[44] The intent of e-government is to neither consolidate the flow of information under government direction or censorship, nor have the message that governments deliver through misinformation or disinformation accepted by the public as truth. Nor is the intent to collect inappropriate information about citizens. A government must ensure that the public, business community, and other governments trust the information and services provided. In a democracy, the public should not come to regard the provision of personal information in terms of a loss of personal privacy or an intrusion of government into their personal lives. Governments should not arbitrarily decide which records to preserve and fail to maintain an audit trail that the public or any group interested in accountability could follow. Clearly, there are some risks in the continued transformation to e-government; however, with diligent care and proper oversight, the benefits outweigh the disadvantages, and the portrait of "big brother" and the "ministry of truth" depicted in *1984* will largely remain a myth—from the perspective of both government and the governed. E-government therefore is a process or a means to an end, not an end in itself. It is critical to examine e-government, therefore, in the context of a government's future plans for its development and evolution into new stages (see chapter 16).

NOTES

1. Harold C. Relyea, "E-Gov Comes to the Federal Government," in *U.S. Government on the Web: Getting the Information You Need*, ed. Peter Hernon, Robert E. Dugan, and John A. Shuler (Westport, CT: Libraries Unlimited, 2003), 379. For the quote see William M. Capron, "The Executive Branch in the Year 2000," in *The Future of the U.S. Government: Toward the Year 2000*, ed. Harvey S. Perloff (New York: George Brazziller, 1971), 307.

2. World Bank Group, "E★Government: A Definition of E★Government" (Washington, DC: World Bank, n.d.). Available at www1.worldbank.org/publicsector/egov/definition.htm, accessed July 15, 2004.

3. World Bank Group, "The Anticorruption Home Page: 'Anticorruption'" (Washington, DC: World Bank, n.d.). Available at www.worldbank.org/anticorruption, accessed July 20, 2004.

4. Relyea, "E-Gov Comes to the Federal Government," 380. For the quote see Herbert N. Casson, *The History of the Telephone* (Chicago: A. C. McClurg, 1910), 2012.

5. Organisation for Economic Co-operation and Development (OECD), "Policy Brief: Checklist for E-Government Leaders," *OECD Observer* (2003), 1. Available at www.oecd.org/dataoecd/62/58/11923037.pdf, accessed July 20, 2004.

6. OECD, "Checklist for E-Government Leaders," 3.

7. E-mail correspondence to Peter Hernon from Mary Neazor, Archives New Zealand, March 17, 2004. The guide appears at www.archives.govt.nz/continuum/index.html.

8. Vanessa Donnelly, *Designing Easy-to-Use Web Sites: A Hands-on Approach to Structuring Successful Web Sites* (Harlow, UK: Addison-Wesley, 2001).

9. Darrell M. West, "E-government and the Transformation of Service Delivery and Citizen Attitudes," *Public Administration Review* 64, no. 1 (January/February 2004): 15–27.

10. Cookies are small computer files placed on a Web site visitor's hard drive that track that user's travels on the Web to determine who visited the site recently and how that person got there. A cookie should neither gather invasive information about the public and its online behavior nor track behavior without user consent.

11. Most governments base guidelines for accessibility for users with disabilities that inhibit their use of Web sites (e.g., sight impairment) on the World Wide Web Consortium's *Web Content Accessibility Guidelines* (Cambridge, MA: W3C, 1999), 9. Available at www.w3c.org/TE/WAI-WEB CONTENY/, accessed March 1, 2005. These guidelines also enable access for users with low bandwidth or low-level browsers, or those using mobile technology such as handheld or cell phones.

12. Andrew Chadwick and Christopher May, "Interaction between States and Citizens in the Age of the Internet: 'e-Government' in the United States, Britain, and the European Union," *Governance: An International Journal of Policy, Administration and Institutions* 16 (April 2003): 271–300.

13. Chadwick and May, "Interaction between States and Citizens," 278.

14. Chadwick and May, "Interaction between States and Citizens," 280.

15. Chadwick and May, "Interaction between States and Citizens," 296.

16. Marc Holzer, Lung-Teng Hu, and Seok-Hwi Song, "Digital Government and Citizen Participation in the United States," in *Digital Government: Principles and Best Practices*, ed. D. G. Garson and A. Pavlichev (Hershey, PA: Ideas Group, 2004), 312.

17. Holzer, Lung-Teng Hu, and Seok-Hwi Song, "Digital Government," 312.

18. It has been charged that the Bush administration has removed information from executive branch Web sites that contradicts its social philosophy. See, e.g., "Office of Special Counsel Scrubs Website," *OMB Watcher* 5 (February 23, 2004). Available at www.ombwatch.org/article/articleview/2060/1/208, accessed March 9, 2004.

19. Florence Olsen, "GAO Web Site Redesign Improves Efficiency," *Federal Computer Week* 18, no. 24 (July 19, 2004): 44.

20. Chadwick and May, "Interaction between States and Citizens."

21. For an excellent discussion of cultures, especially those in the UK, see OECD, "The Hidden Threat to E-Government: Avoiding Large Government IT Failures," *OECD Public Management Policy Brief no. 8* (Paris: OECD, 2001). Available at www.oecd.org/dataoecd/19/12/1901677.pdf, accessed July 19, 2004.

22. United Nations, *Global E-governance Readiness Report 2004: Toward Access for Opportunity* (New York: United Nations, 2004). See also Nick Swartz, "E-government around the World," *Information Management Journal* 38 (January/February 2004): 12.

23. Adrienne Muir and Charles Oppenheim, "National Information Policy Developments World-Wide 1: Electronic Government," *Journal of Information Science* 28, no. 3 (2002): 173–86.

24. Muir and Oppenheim, "National Information Policy Developments," 183.

25. Since the year 2000, Accenture has produced the annual report as part of its Government Executive Series (www.accenture.com). The title changes each year to reflect where the company thinks

e-government is going. For example, *eGovernment Leadership* was produced in 2003 and *eGovernment Leadership: High Performance, Maximum Value* (see n. 26) was released in 2004.

26. Accenture, *eGovernment Leadership: Engaging the Customer*, Government Executive Series 3 (New York: Accenture, 2004). Available at www.accenture.com, accessed July 15, 2004. In another report, Accenture divides countries into three groups: "low-maturity countries," "medium-maturity countries," and "high-maturity countries." See Accenture, *eGovernment Leadership: High Performance, Maximum Value* (New York: Accenture, 2004). Available at www.accenture.com, accessed July 15, 2004.

27. G. Matthew Bonham, Jeffrey W. Seifert, and Stuart J. Thorson, "The Transformational Potential of e-Government: The Role of Political Leadership," 6 (paper presented at the panel on Electronic Governance and Information Policy, Fourth Pan European International Relations Conference of the European Consortium for Political Research, University of Kent, Canterbury, UK, September 9, 2001). Available at www.maxwell.syr.edu/maxpages/faculty/gmbonham/ecpr.htm, accessed July 20, 2004. Instead of adopting Darrell M. West's conceptualization of the stages of e-government development, they use the more commonly known characterization, namely, presence, interaction, transaction, and transformation. See Darrell M. West, "E-government and the Transformation of Service Delivery and Citizen Attitudes," *Public Administration Review* 64, no. 1 (January/February 2004): 15–27.

28. Bonham, Seifert, and Thorson, "Transformational Potential of e-Government." For a discussion of the plateaus see Accenture, *eGovernment Leadership*, 8.

29. Bonham, Seifert, and Thorson, "Transformational Potential of e-Government." See also *Government: The Next American Revolution*, Reports Based on Findings of Surveys Conducted by Hart-Teeter (Washington, DC: Council for Excellence in Government, 2004). Available at www.excelgov .org, accessed June 1, 2004.

30. Weiling Ke and Kwok Kee Wei, "Successful E-government in Singapore," *Communications of the ACM* 47, no. 6 (June 2004): 95.

31. Weiling Ke and Kwok Kee Wei, "Successful E-government in Singapore," 98–99.

32. OECD, Policy Brief: "E-Government in Finland: An Assessment," *OECD Observer* (2003), 6. Available at www.oecd.org/dataoecd/20/50/13314420.pdf, accessed July 20, 2004.

33. OECD, "E-Government in Finland," 2.

34. OECD, "E-Government in Finland," 2. The report identifies other barriers impeding the development of e-government, including legislative and regulatory barriers, budgetary barriers, technical barriers, and the digital divide.

35. Pin-Yu Chu, Naiyi Hsiao, Fung-Wu Lee, and Chun-Wei Chen, "Exploring Success Factors for Taiwan's Government Electronic Tendering System: Behavioral Perspectives from End Users," *Government Information Quarterly* 21, no. 2 (2004): 220.

36. Takashi Koga, "Access to Government Information in Japan: A Long Way toward Electronic Government?" *Government Information Quarterly* 20, no. 1 (2003): 47.

37. Ian Holliday and Rebecca C. W. Kwok, "Governance in the Information Age: Building E-Government in Hong Kong," *New Media & Society* 6, no. 4 (August 2004): 549.

38. Subhajit Basu, "E-government and Developing Countries: An Overview," *International Review of Law Computers & Technology* 18, no. 1 (March 2004): 109–32.

39. Meithya Rose, "Democratizing Information and Communication by Implementing E-government in Indonesian Regional Government," *International Information & Library Review* 36 (2004): 219–26.

40. Hasan Sadik, "Introducing E-government in Bangladesh: Problems and Prospects," *International Social Science Review* 78, nos. 3 and 4 (2003): 121.

41. World Bank Group, The Anticorruption Home Page.

42. General Accounting Office, *Electronic Government: Challenges Must Be Addressed with Effective Leadership and Management*, GAO-01-959T (Washington, DC: General Accounting Office, 2001), 1–2.

43. Bonham, Seifert, and Thorson, "Transformational Potential of e-Government," 18.

44. George Orwell, *1984* (New York: New American Library, 1950).

II

INDIVIDUAL COUNTRIES

2

E-government in the United States

Jeffrey W. Seifert

$\mathscr{T}$he image of tectonic plates shifting is frequently invoked by scholars to describe various types of shifts and changes related to government. Whether being used to explain changes in the political, policy, or administrative landscape, it is an apt (even if perhaps overused) analogy. Government is supposed to be deliberative and stable and not easily swayed by the most recent passing fancy of public opinion. Change can and does happen, though major changes can often, in retrospect, be traced to a long period of preceding events. Government reform, in particular, can take a long time to carry out because it presents change, and organizations are often resistant to change. So it should not be surprising that attempts to reform government through the integration of information technology (IT) into various government processes have not already resulted in the wholesale transformation of government. Yet, many people have expected electronic government (e-government) to revolutionize government as we know it. Perhaps the speed associated with changing technology, especially IT, leads to unrealistic expectations of this speed of change being transferred to changes in government. However, what we are actually experiencing is more of an evolution of government.

While e-government is frequently viewed as a very recent phenomenon, some scholars have documented the antecedents of today's e-government initiatives in the United States back to at least the 1960s.[1] It was at this time that J. C. R. Licklinder wrote about the potential for computers to move beyond being storage units to having interactive capabilities. In a 1968 article written with Robert W. Taylor, which was based on some of Licklinder's earlier writings,[2] they considered the idea of "interactive multi-access computer communities."[3] Licklinder and Taylor posited the possibility of then interconnecting these communities to create a "super community" for the purpose of sharing data resources and programs. Although it would be twenty-five years before the Web browser Mosaic, the forerunner to Netscape, was developed, thirty years before a beta version of Google appeared on the Internet,[4] and thirty-two years before the U.S. government's portal, FirstGov,[5] was launched, these earlier thoughts helped plant the seed of today's attempt to integrate IT into government processes, which we now commonly refer to as e-government.

The views in this chapter are those of the author and do not necessarily reflect the position of either the Congressional Research Service or the Library of Congress.

This development begs the question, then, what is e-government? The concept of e-government conjures different images for different people.[6] For some, it is submitting a form online. For others, it might be sending an e-mail message to their member of Congress. A 2000 Gartner Group report described e-government as "the continuous optimization of service delivery, constituency participation, and governance by transforming internal and external relationships through technology, the Internet, and new media."[7] A year later, Mark Forman, the first associate director for Information Technology and E-Government at the Office of Management and Budget (OMB), defined e-government as "the use of Internet technology and protocols to transform agency effectiveness, efficiency, and service quality."[8] For the U.S. government, the current official definition of e-government comes from the E-Government Act of 2002, which defines e-government as

> the use by the Government of web-based Internet applications and other information technologies, combined with processes that implement these technologies, to (A) enhance the access to and delivery of Government information and services to the public, other agencies, and other Government entities; or (B) bring about improvements in Government operations that may include effectiveness, efficiency, service quality, or transformation.[9]

Just as e-government has evolved as a concept, so too it is evolving as a practice. Development of e-government can be represented on a continuum, ranging from simpler to more complex undertakings. In a 2004 report, Accenture, a global marketing company, suggested that e-government in many developed countries, including the United States, has reached a plateau in recent years.[10] This slowdown is what Accenture refers to as the "maturation" of e-government, which reflects the fact that many of the leading governments have addressed most of the simpler e-government goals, leaving a number of more difficult tasks for resolution. Indeed, in a 2003 speech before government IT administrators, Karen Evans, the OMB administrator for E-Government and Information Technology, reportedly referred to a group of twenty-five e-government initiatives as "low-hanging fruit," and added that "the next set of projects will be harder."[11]

A similar characterization could be used to describe some of the reform efforts of the Clinton administration. On March 3, 1993, two months after taking office, President Clinton announced the National Performance Review (NPR). The NPR was to start as a six-month review of the federal government by a task force led by Vice President Albert Gore Jr. The purpose of the review was to identify ways to "reinvent government." The task force produced a report containing 380 major recommendations for government reform and reorganization.[12] Although the NPR encouraged reducing personnel, it also emphasized that people (federal employees) were not the problem, but that they were hindered by outdated and rigid structures and processes.[13] The NPR explicitly tried to change how government worked from being a top-down bureaucracy to encouraging entrepreneurial government that empowers citizens. The term "electronic government" appears approximately four times throughout more than three hundred pages, and then only in the context of electronic payments.[14] The NPR's twin missions were to "work better" and "cost less."[15] These twin missions were guided by four key principles:

- cutting red tape;
- putting customers first;
- empowering employees to get results; and
- cutting back to basics—producing better government for less by reinventing systems.[16]

One year later, a status report found that 90 percent of the original recommendations had been implemented and that $46.9 billion of the $108 billion in projected savings had been achieved.[17] Additional status reports and recommendations continued throughout the eight years of the Clinton presidency.[18] However, political and policy conflicts between the president and Congress muted most of the more ambitious efforts.[19]

It is not until 1997 that the concept of "electronic government" seemed to take a recognizable focus in the NPR. In February of that year, a new report was released, *Access America: Reengineering through Technology*, in which a wide range of services are considered under the rubric of electronic government. The report speculates that citizens who are members of "this new government" would be able to carry out activities such as householders checking the environmental conditions in the area around their home, police verifying fingerprints and criminal records electronically, students applying for and receiving education loans online, and companies visiting a "one stop government shop" for export assistance.[20]

In 1998, the National Performance Review was renamed the National Partnership for Reinventing Government.[21] At that time, the NPR was reorganized into eight teams, one of which was to "technologically transform America."[22] Up until this point, while IT had an intended role in reforming government, it was mostly diffuse, and the degree of government-wide IT planning was generally less coordinated. Concentrated modernization efforts became more prominent closer to the end of the NPR. Also, around this time, Web-based technology began to become considerably more sophisticated, and e-commerce started growing exponentially. Federal e-government got started, but its overall progress was limited. However, as this chapter will demonstrate, the United States has since moved far beyond these earlier notions of using IT to reform government.

This chapter examines the ongoing development, evolution, and maturation of e-government at the national level in the United States. Placed in the context of a common model of developmental stages of e-government, this chapter looks at how e-government in the federal government was in its infancy during the waning years of the Clinton administration and then assumed a new direction and greater importance at the start of the George W. Bush administration as one of the key tools of government reform. This examination includes a review of the role of the Expanding E-Government initiative within the President's Management Agenda, the launch and development of the more than twenty Quicksilver e-government initiatives, the creation and revision of the Bush administration's e-government strategy, the passage of the E-Government Act, and the growing importance of the Federal Enterprise Architecture in shaping the future of federal e-government, including the emergence of a second generation of e-government initiatives organized around the government's Lines of Business. The chapter concludes with a discussion of some of the most critical challenges facing the U.S. government as it prepares to enter the transformation stage of e-government.

DEVELOPMENTAL STAGES OF E-GOVERNMENT

Although different e-government initiatives strive to accomplish different goals, some observers argue that one of the overarching themes of e-government is to realize fully the capabilities of available IT in an effort to transform government from an agency-centric, limited-service operation into an automated, citizen-centric operation capable of delivering government services to citizens, businesses, and other government agencies twenty-four hours a day, seven days a week. However, for a variety of technical, economic, and political reasons, it takes time for these initiatives to evolve into their full potential. Consequently, some observers use a common schema for classifying the stages of evolution of e-government projects.[23] The schema is based on the degree to which the properties of information technology have been utilized to enable the delivery of services electronically. Using this schema, four stages of evolution can be identified: presence, interaction, transaction, and transformation.[24]

Presence

Presence is the first stage of development and is the establishment of a placeholder for delivering information in the future. It represents the simplest and least expensive entrance into e-government, and it also offers the fewest options for citizens. A typical example is a basic Web site that lists cursory information about an agency, such as hours of operation, a mailing address, and/or phone numbers, but has no interactive capabilities. It is a passive presentation of general information. Some observers refer to these types of sites as *brochureware*, suggesting they are the electronic equivalent of a paper brochure.

Interaction

The second stage is interaction. Although interactive Web-based initiatives offer enhanced capabilities, efforts in this group are still limited in their ability to streamline and automate government functions. Interactions are relatively simple and generally revolve around information provision. These types of initiatives are designed to help the customer avoid a trip to an office or a phone call by making commonly requested information and forms available around the clock. These resources may include instructions for obtaining services, downloadable forms to be printed and mailed back to an agency, or perhaps e-mail contact to respond to simple questions.

Transaction

The third stage in the evolution of e-government initiatives is transaction. These initiatives are more complex than simple information provision and embody the types of activities popularly associated with e-government. They enable clients to complete entire tasks electronically at any time of the day or night. These initiatives effectively create self-service operations for tasks such as license renewals, paying taxes and fees, and submitting bids for procurement contracts. Although the level of interactivity is of a higher magnitude than second-stage initiatives, the activities still involve a flow of information that is primarily one-way (either to government or to the client, depending on the activity). The electronic responses are generally highly regularized and create predictable outcomes (e.g., approving a license renewal, creating a receipt, or acknowledging a bid).

Transformation

The highest order of evolution for e-government initiatives is transformation. Initiatives at this level utilize the full capabilities of the technology to transform how government functions are conceived, organized, and executed. Such initiatives would have the robust customer relationship management capabilities required to handle a full range of questions, problems, and needs. Currently, there are very few examples of this type of initiative, in part due to administrative, technical, and fiscal constraints. One of the distinctions of these initiatives is that they facilitate the seamless flow of information and collaborative decision making between federal, state, local, public, and private partners. In other words, transformative e-government initiatives often seek to remove the organizational barriers that promote agency-centric solutions and, instead, promote customer-centric solutions. Some advocates suggest that, at its most advanced level, e-government could potentially reorganize, combine, and/or eliminate existing agencies and replace them with virtual organizations.[25]

It is important to note that an e-government initiative does not necessarily have to start at the first stage and work its way through all of the stages. Instead, a project can skip levels, either from its inception or as it develops. This is especially true of more recent e-government initiatives, which have had the benefit of being able to take advantage of the lessons learned from earlier initiatives, as well as the most recent technology developments. In the case of the United States, viewed at a national level, its longer history of e-government experimentation and time spent working its way through the beginning stages of e-government reflects its experience as an early innovator and adopter of e-government, as well as its investment in developing a sophisticated IT infrastructure. As a result, the time the United States has taken to develop its e-government capacity, both philosophically and practically, seems comparatively longer than the efforts of more recent converts to e-government.

PRESIDENT CLINTON'S MEMORANDUM ON E-GOVERNMENT

On December 17, 1999, nearly a year before the end of his administration, President Clinton released a memorandum directed to the heads of executive departments and agencies on the subject of electronic government. The memorandum laid out some general guiding principles, as well as a list of eleven actions to be carried out. The memorandum was at once broad and far-reaching in its scope and somewhat ambiguous on the details of how some of the outlined objectives were to be achieved. One of its primary guiding principles was that government information should be organized "by category of information and service—rather than by agency—in a way that meets people's needs."[26] Implicitly embedded in this principle was the idea that government should be citizen focused, or citizen centered, in a way that matches the manner in which citizens approach government for information and services, rather than in a way that reinforces the boundaries between different departments and agencies. A second guiding principle was that government should be open and convenient in communicating with, and providing information to, citizens. In other words, government officials were expected to use technology to facilitate two-way communication and access to information, rather than reinforcing stereotypes of government being overly bureaucratic and unresponsive. As a third guiding principle, it was considered critical that citizens "have confidence that their online communications with the Government are secure and their privacy protected."[27]

The eleven actions outlined in the memorandum included items that were to be applied across the federal government, as well as activities directed at specific departments. Some of the government-wide actions included promoting "access to Government information organized not by agency, but by the type of service or information that people may be seeking" within a year of the memorandum being issued, making "the forms needed for the top 500 Government services used by the public" available online; promoting the use of electronic commerce (e-commerce) to improve procurement efficiency; posting privacy policies on government Web sites and taking actions to protect information on sites geared toward children; creating public e-mail addresses so that citizens can contact agencies electronically; and developing strategies for integrating the Internet as a means of improving how agencies carry out their individual missions. Some of the department-specific actions included directing the National Science Foundation to carry out a study regarding the feasibility of online voting; directing the departments of Health and Human Services, Education, Veterans Affairs, and Agriculture, as well as other government entities, such as the Social Security Administration and the Federal Emergency Management Agency, to "make a broad range of benefits and services available through private and secure electronic use of the Internet"; and directing a group of agencies to work together to develop the means to use digital signature certificates to enhance the security of communications between the government and citizens.[28]

In many ways, the December 1999 memorandum represented the Clinton administration's first concrete attempts to begin implementing e-government government-wide. The actions called for in the memorandum reflected the activities and findings learned over the past six years through the National Performance Review (renamed the National Partnership for Reinventing Government in 1998), as well as the growth of a critical mass of citizens now using the Internet. The development and proliferation of various technological enhancements, such as better Web browsers, public key encryption, and multimedia Web features, also contributed by offering a reason and a means for citizens to go online. However, two factors affected the longer-term implementation of the actions called for in the memorandum. First, with only a year remaining in office, the Clinton administration faced the limitations inherent in the twilight of a lame-duck administration that wished to complete a number of initiatives begun throughout the previous seven years. Second, the memorandum vested leadership for many of these activities with Vice President Albert Gore Jr., who was already very publicly associated as the champion of the NPR and who would ultimately lose to George

W. Bush in the 2000 presidential election. As a result, the NPR shut down its operations with the inauguration of the new Bush administration, which had its own plans
for government reform in the form of the President's Management Agenda.

PRESIDENT'S MANAGEMENT AGENDA

About halfway through the first year of its first term, the Bush administration, in August
2001, unveiled the President's Management Agenda (PMA), which has served as the
administration's primary vehicle for government-reform efforts. The PMA, which
emphasizes the application of businesslike practices and principles, is frequently referred
to by administration officials as an explanation or justification for various efforts to
change how government works. Three guiding principles are cited in the PMA as integral to "the President's vision for government reform," which states that government
should be:

- citizen-centered, not bureaucracy-centered;
- results-oriented; and
- market-based, actively promoting rather than stifling innovation through competition.[29]

When it was first introduced, the PMA included five government-wide initiatives
and nine agency-specific program initiatives.[30] Agencies' progress on both sets of initiatives is measured using a quarterly "scorecard," which utilizes a "stoplight scoring system." In this scoring system, green indicates success, yellow indicates mixed results, and
red indicates unsatisfactory results in attempting to achieve program goals.[31]

The five government-wide initiatives of the PMA are strategic management of
human capital, competitive sourcing, improved financial performance, expanded electronic government, and budget and performance integration. Within the description of
the expanded electronic government initiative, one can find a number of the core ideas
and values that have influenced, and continue to influence, the development of
e-government at its most formative stages in the U.S. government. Specifically, the
PMA underscores the need to improve IT management, simplify business processes,
and unify information flows between agencies. Also emphasized is the value of making
government citizen centered and not agency centered, the importance of breaking
down bureaucratic barriers, or the so-called stovepipes that separate agencies, to
develop government-wide solutions, and the need to use technology to transform government, rather than simply automate existing processes.[32] To achieve this vision of
e-government, the PMA outlines a range of potential e-government projects that the
federal government could decide to undertake, pending the findings of an interagency
task force (discussed below). The PMA calls for the task force to focus on projects that
encourage the creation of single points of access to government services (one-stop shopping), streamline the processes that businesses must follow to fulfill their government
reporting requirements, facilitate the sharing of information between and within various
levels of government, and automate common internal processes through the sharing of
best practices. Some of the initiatives suggested in the PMA include e-procurement,
e-grants, e-regulation, e-signatures, and the expansion of the FirstGov Web site,[33]

which first went online on September 22, 2000, and serves as the portal to the U.S. government. Commensurate with the PMA's general promotion of applying business principles to government, the PMA also anticipates the use of business cases to "manage E-government projects more effectively by using the budget process to insist on more effective planning of IT investments by government agencies."[34]

QUICKSILVER INITIATIVES

Pursuant to the July 18, 2001, OMB Memorandum M-01-28, issued by director Mitchell Daniels Jr., an e-government (Quicksilver) task force was established to create a strategy for achieving the Bush administration's e-government goals.[35] The task force, which began its work on August 9, 2001, and is referred to in the PMA published that same month, included eighty-one individuals from forty-six different agencies and bureaus. The task force initially identified more than 350 potential projects through interviews with agency officials and e-mail responses to a solicitation for suggestions. These project ideas were then organized into approximately forty-five basic project concepts to filter out duplicates and combine similar suggestions. A steering committee of the task force then selected approximately thirty initiatives for further consideration. Mini business cases for each of these initiatives were then prepared by members of the task force to evaluate their potential costs, benefits, and risks.[36] Special attention was also paid to the initiatives' potential to reduce redundancy and transform the way government interacts with citizens. In its initial assessment of e-government opportunities, the task force discovered that the federal government's business architecture, the organization and function of its core processes, was characterized by excessive duplication and overlap. Specifically, the task force concluded that, "of 28 lines of business found in the federal government, the assessment revealed that, on average, 19 Executive Departments and agencies are performing each line of business."[37] Such overlap, it was noted, can contribute to duplicative spending on staff, technology, and administration, as well as create unnecessary complexity and bureaucracy.[38] With that in mind, three primary criteria were used to select the final projects:

- the value to citizens;
- the potential for improvement in agency efficiency; and
- the likelihood of deploying the initiative within eighteen to twenty-four months.[39]

On September 25, 2001, the task force selected twenty-three interagency initiatives designed to integrate better agency operations and IT investments. These initiatives, sometimes referred to as the Quicksilver projects, were originally grouped into five categories: government-to-citizen, government-to-government, government-to-business, internal effectiveness and efficiency, and addressing barriers to e-government success. The final category was later dropped in favor of the other four categories. Examples of these initiatives include an e-authentication project led by the General Services Administration (GSA) to increase the use of digital signatures, the eligibility assistance online project (also referred to as GovBenefits.gov) led by the Department of Labor to create a common access point for information regarding government benefits available to citizens, and the Small Business Administration's One-Stop Business Compliance project, being designed to help businesses navigate legal and regulatory requirements. A twenty-fourth initiative, a government-wide payroll process project, was subsequently added by the President's Management Council.[40] In 2002, the e-clearance initiative, originally included as part of the Enterprise Human Resources Integration project, was established as a separate project, for a total of twenty-five initiatives. Since that time the Bush administration has reclassified the e-authentication initiative as "a separate initiative that provides secure and robust authentication services to the 24 [i]nitiatives," bringing the official tally again to twenty-four initiatives.[41] Table 2.1 summarizes the initiatives and their goals.

As the initial round of e-government projects has continued to develop and become fully operational, OMB has stated it plans to focus attention on initiatives that consolidate IT systems in six functional areas, or lines of business. These include financial management, human resource management, grants management, case management, federal health architecture, and information security. This attempt to develop a second generation of e-government initiatives is discussed at the end of the chapter.

E-GOVERNMENT STRATEGY—2002

In February 2002, OMB released the Bush administration's first e-government strategy, suggesting that it "presents the federal government's plan for E-Government."[42] For the most part, this document served to explain the work of the task force (described above) in selecting the Quicksilver initiatives as part of the strategy and reinforce the idea that these initiatives are intended to help carry out the goals of all five of the government-wide initiatives of the PMA, as well as support homeland security efforts. The e-government strategy also served to further elaborate on the ideas originally presented in the PMA.

While echoing the increasingly familiar refrain that the Bush administration's government reform efforts are driven by the principles of government being citizen centered, results oriented, and market based, the e-government strategy also presented a somewhat more specific description of the goals of the "Expanding E-Government" initiative of the PMA. These goals were listed as:

- Make it easy for citizens to obtain service and interact with the federal government.
- Improve government efficiency and effectiveness.
- Improve government's responsiveness to citizens.[43]

However, the document also enumerates a longer list of "significant improvements in the federal government" that are expected to result from carrying out the e-government strategy. These more tangible actions include:

- simplifying delivery of services to citizens;
- eliminating layers of government management;
- making it possible for citizens, businesses, other levels of government, and federal employees to easily find information and get service from the federal government;

Table 2.1.   Quicksilver Presidential E-government Initiatives

Initiative Name (Managing Partner)	Goals
Government-to-Citizen (G2C)	
Recreation One-Stop (Dept. of the Interior) http://www.recreation.gov	• Reduce amount of time citizens expend searching for information about recreation sites and reservations • Eliminate task duplication across government agencies, which will decrease operational costs, while improving customer service and increasing use at underutilized facilities
GovBenefits.gov (Dept. of Labor) http://www.govbenefits.gov	• Reduce the amount of time citizens spend trying to identify and access relevant information about government benefit programs that match their specific needs • Reduce the number of incorrect benefits submittals from citizens
E-Loans (ED) http://www.govloans.gov	• Provide citizens with quick and easy access to federal loan program information on the Web • Provide agencies and lenders with quicker and easier access to risk mitigation data
USA Services (General Services Administration) http://www.usaservices.gov 1-800-FedInfo (333-4636) Publications Center in Pueblo, CO	• Improve customer service to citizens across the federal government • Reduce costs in labor, information technology, and citizen service contact centers by providing best value and practices to federal agencies in citizen customer service
IRS Free File (Treasury) http://www.irs.gov/app/freeFile/welcome.jsp	• Reduce burden and costs to taxpayers
Government-to-Business (G2B)	
E-Rulemaking (Environmental Protection Agency) http://www.regulations.gov	• Enhance public access and participation in the regulatory process through electronic systems • Reduce burden for citizens and businesses in finding relevant regulations and commenting on proposed rulemaking actions • Consolidate redundant docket systems • Improve agency regulatory processes and more timely regulatory decisions
Expanding Electronic Tax Products for Businesses (Treasury) http://www.irs.gov	• Reduce burden for tax forms filed by businesses • Reduce total processing time required for processing of accurate tax information
Federal Asset Sales (General Services Administration) http://www.firstgov.gov	• Provide substantial benefit to the federal government through maximizing net proceeds from asset sales, reducing selling expenses, and improving utilization and donation processes • Reduce the expense and difficulty of doing business with the government

International Trade Process Streamlining (Dept. of Commerce)
http://www.export.gov
http://www.export.gov/china

- Create a seamless environment for exporters to research markets, gather trade leads, and conduct a majority of their export transactions online
- Provide more timely and accurate export information
- Reduce the amount of time spent by U.S. exporters in collecting information and filling out forms
- Continue to expand forms available in One Stop, One Form

Business Gateway (Small Business Administration)
http://www.business.gov

- Consolidate redundant investments in e-forms systems
- Increase federal agencies' GPEA* compliance to at least 75% by 9/04
- Reduce amount of redundant data and forms submitted to the federal government
- Reduce burden on small businesses

Consolidated Health Informatics (Dept. of Health and Human Services)
http://www.whitehouse.gov/omb/egov/c-3-6-chi.html

- Enable agencies to improve patient safety, which will reduce error rates, lower administrative costs, and strengthen national public health and disaster preparedness

Government-to-Government (G2G)

Geospatial One-Stop (Dept. of the Interior)
http://www.geodata.gov
http://www.geo-one-stop.gov

- Reduce burden on public entities by creating consistency, compatibility, and easy access to geospatial data
- Stimulate vendor development of geospatial tools and reduce technology risk for geospatial data users
- Reduce total processing time to gain access to geospatial data, which will improve decision making and the delivery of government services
- Provide shared access to spatial data and resources

Disaster Management (Dept. of Homeland Security)
http://www.disasterhelp.gov

- Save lives and reduce property loss
- Provide federal, state, and local emergency managers better online access to disaster-management-related information, planning, and response tools

SAFECOM (Dept. of Homeland Security)
http://www.safecomprogram.gov

- Reduce the unnecessary loss of life and property during emergency incidents by facilitating public safety communications and interoperability
- Reduce costs to local, tribal, state, and federal public safety agencies through coordinating standards for communications equipment
- Reduce costs to local, tribal, state, and federal public safety agencies through coordinated planning and guidance

(continues)

Table 2.1.   Continued

Initiative Name (Managing Partner)	Goals
E-Vital (Social Security Administration) http://www.whitehouse.gov/omb/egov/c-2-4-evital.html	• Reduce administrative, program, and customer costs associated with vital records • Enhance the ability of state and federal agencies to provide quality customer service by improving the accuracy and speed of access to vital records data • Reduce frequency and amount of benefits fraud and erroneous payments as a result of untimely and inaccurate vital records
Grants.gov (Dept. of Health and Human Services) http://www.grants.gov	• Minimize the burden of finding and applying for grants • Minimize time spent looking up procedures and filling out redundant information, while maximizing time on actual grant-related work • Facilitate the review process and enable agencies to make awards more efficiently • Avoid the cost of building and maintaining redundant agency grant systems

Internal Efficiency and Effectiveness (IEE)

Initiative Name (Managing Partner)	Goals
E-Training (Office of Personnel Management) http://www.golearn.gov	• Avoid/decrease costs of tuition fee, travel expenses, and software license fees • Compress learning times through use of online coursework versus instructor-led courses
Recruitment One-Stop (Office of Personnel Management) http://www.usajobs.gov	• Increase public satisfaction with the federal hiring process • Expedite agencies' identification of qualified candidates • Improve quality of new hires
Enterprise HR Integration (Office of Personnel Management) http://www.opm.gov/egov	• Reduce dependencies on paper-based processes • Provide single source of official employee information • Provide single set of analytical tools supporting workforce analysis, forecasting, and strategic management of human capital
E-Clearance (Office of Personnel Management) http://www.opm.gov/egov	• Reduce time to locate previous investigations, which enhances the opportunities for reciprocity • Reduce data entry burden and time
E-Payroll (Office of Personnel Management) http://www.opm.gov/egov	• Reduce modernization costs by consolidating payroll systems • Reduce cost per payroll transaction per employee
E-Travel (General Services Administration) http://egov.gsa.gov	• Improve the government's internal efficiency, administrative performance, and regulatory compliance relative to travel • Eliminate redundant and stovepipe travel-management systems through a buy once/use many shared services approach

	• Minimize capital investment, operations, and maintenance costs for travel-management services
	• Bring world-class travel management and superior customer service to the federal travel process
Integrated Acquisition Environment (General Services Administration) http://www.BPN.gov http://www.FedBizOpps.gov http://www.FedTeDS.gov http://www.PPIRS.gov http://www.wdol.gov https://fpds.gov http://www.epls.gov http://www.contractdirectory.gov	• Reduce burden for vendors • Achieve cost savings through consolidated vendor information, procurement data systems, and common processes • Reduce cycle time of procurement process
E-Records Management (National Archives and Records Administration) http://www.archives.gov/records_management/initiatives/erm_overview.html	• Increase percentage of eligible data archived/preserved electronically • Provide consistency in approach to implementing e-records management applications • Improve ability of agencies to access/retrieve records

Cross-Cutting

E-Authentication (General Services Administration) http://www.cio.gov/eauthentication	• Reduce authentication system development and acquisition costs • Reduce burden of conducting secure transactions with government • Eliminate the need for federal agencies to establish independent authentication systems • Protect privacy by ensuring that individuals can control their own personal information

Source: GPO Access, "Budget of the United States Government: Main Page: Fiscal Year 2006 Budget (FY06)" (Washington, DC: GPO, 2005). Available at http://www.gpoaccess.gov/usbudget/fy06/pdf/ap_cd_rom/9_3.pdf, accessed July 1, 2005.
*GPEA = Government Paperwork Elimination Act

• simplifying agencies' business processes and reducing costs through integrating and eliminating redundant systems;
• enabling achievement of the other elements of the President's Management Agenda; and
• streamlining government operations to guarantee rapid response to citizen needs.[44]

As a mode of government reform, e-government is heavily reliant on the successful implementation of IT solutions. However, up to this point, the U.S. federal government's track record was dismal. Although it is the world's largest purchaser of IT, spending $50.4 billion in fiscal year 2002[45] (and a projected amount of more than $65 billion in FY 2006), there was a belief that the government "has not experienced commensurate improvements in productivity, quality and customer service."[46] In previous decades, there were instances in which millions of dollars were lost on ineffective and/ or obsolete solutions. While legislation, such as the Clinger–Cohen Act,[47] had been passed in recent years in an attempt to address this problem, there was evidence to suggest that more could be done. In response, the e-government strategy attempted to address some of the structural problems. Four such problems have been identified in particular:

- Program performance value: Agencies typically evaluate their IT systems according to how well they serve the agency's processes and needs—not how well they respond to citizens' needs. Systems are often evaluated by the percentage of time they are working rather than the internal and external performance benefit they deliver to the programs they support.
- Technology leverage: In the 1990s, government agencies used IT to automate existing processes rather than to create more efficient and effective solutions that are now possible because of commercial e-business lessons learned.
- Islands of automation: Agencies generally buy systems that address internal needs, and rarely are the systems able to interoperate or communicate with those in other agencies. Consequently, citizens have to search across multiple agencies to get service, businesses have to file the same information multiple times, and agencies cannot easily share information.
- Resistance to change: Budget processes and agency cultures perpetuate obsolete bureaucratic divisions. Budgeting processes have not provided a mechanism for investing in cross-agency IT. Moreover, agency cultures and fear of reorganization create resistance to integrating work and sharing use of systems across several agencies.[48]

Although the e-government strategy focused heavily on technology, it did not ignore the fact that government is composed of people, organized into various departments and agencies, who in many ways pose far greater challenges than those associated with technology. Drawing on the work of the e-government task force, the e-government strategy includes a list of five "recurring barriers," paired with mitigation actions "endorsed by the President's Management Council for overcoming each chronic barrier."[49] These barriers included agency culture, the lack of a federal architecture, trust, resources, and stakeholder resistance.

One noticeable difference between the PMA and the e-government strategy is that while the former focuses mostly on laying out a philosophy of government reform, the latter focuses mostly on the actual steps being taken, or to be taken, to implement one part of the PMA (namely, the Expanding E-Government initiative). In this respect, one can begin to see U.S. federal e-government developing a much more cohesive and demonstrable character to a degree that the NPR efforts of the previous administration arguably did not quite reach.

PRESIDENT BUSH'S MEMORANDUM ON E-GOVERNMENT

On July 10, 2002, five months following the release of the Bush administration's e-government strategy, President Bush issued a brief, two-paragraph memorandum directed to the heads of executive departments and agencies on the subject of electronic government. The memorandum reinforced and clarified the role e-government was to have in carrying out the administration's plans for government reform, as one of the five government-wide initiatives in the President's Management Agenda. Specifically, e-government was portrayed as "important in making Government more responsive and cost-effective." The memorandum also reiterated the three principles guiding the administration's government reform efforts, that "[g]overnment should be citizen-centered, results-oriented, and market-based." Perhaps most important, though, was the memorandum's emphasis on "cross-agency teamwork." Although the PMA did promote e-government projects that would span traditional agency boundaries, these projects were to be selected by a task force, in coordination with OMB, suggesting a top-down approach without explicit reference to how agencies would be expected to carry out these initiatives. In contrast, the memorandum emphasized the administration's expectation that agencies would work together to break down the "stovepipes" that separated them and would look past individual agency interests. The resistance of organizational cultures to change is frequently one of the biggest challenges for e-government initiatives, especially those initiatives that result in a reallocation of resources, decision-making authority, and/or personnel. The U.S. government is no exception. However, by emphasizing the importance of, and praising those agencies that were already engaged in, "cross-agency teamwork," the memorandum provided both a mandate and political cover for agency heads to participate in e-government initiatives that an entrenched bureaucracy may be resistant to embracing.

E-GOVERNMENT ACT OF 2002

On December 17, 2002, President Bush signed the E-Government Act of 2002 (P.L. 107-347) into law. Building upon the Clinger-Cohen Act, the E-Government Act serves as the primary legislative vehicle to guide evolving federal IT management practices and to promote initiatives to make government information and services available online. In doing so, it also represents a continuation of efforts to realize greater efficiencies and reduce redundancies through improved intergovernmental coordination and by aligning IT investments. The law contains a variety of provisions related to federal government IT management, information security, and the provision of services and information electronically. One of the most recognized provisions involves the creation of an Office of Electronic Government (OEG) within OMB. The office is headed by an administrator, who is responsible for carrying out a variety of information resources management (IRM) functions, as well as administering the interagency E-Government Fund authorized by the law.

In addition, while the Bush administration's Quicksilver initiatives are separate from, and predate, the E-Government Act, some of the goals of the Quicksilver initiatives are statutorily affirmed by the act's provisions. For example, section 216 addresses the development of common protocols for geographic information systems, which is also one of the objectives of the Geospatial One-Stop project.[50] Section 203 directs agencies to adopt electronic signature methods. Likewise, the e-authentication initiative strives to develop a government-wide approach to electronic identity systems.[51] In addition, some of the act's broader provisions, such as those related to the development of privacy guidelines, information security standards, and the identification of means to bridge disparities in Internet access among citizens, contribute to the technological and regulatory infrastructure needed to support e-government generally.

The stated purposes of the E-Government Act include establishing effective leadership of federal information technology projects, requiring the use of Internet-based IT initiatives to reduce costs and increase opportunities for citizen participation in government, transforming agency operations, promoting interagency collaboration for e-government processes, and making the federal government more transparent and accountable. The seventy-two-page law is divided into five titles and incorporates the language from at least four other bills that had been introduced separately in Congress. It also amends different parts of the *United States Code* in the areas of federal information policy and information security.

Title I establishes the Office of Electronic Government in OMB. This new office is headed by an administrator, who is to be appointed by the president of the United States. As head of the OEG, the administrator is tasked with assisting the director of OMB, and the OMB deputy director of management, in coordination with the efforts of the administrator of the Office of Information and Regulatory Affairs, another OMB unit, to carry out relevant OMB responsibilities for prescribing guidelines and regulations for agency implementation of the Privacy Act,[52] the Clinger-Cohen Act, IT acquisition pilot programs, and the Government Paperwork Elimination Act.[53] It also requires the GSA to consult with the administrator of the Office of Electronic Government on any efforts by GSA to promote e-government.

Title I also amends Title 44 of the *United States Code* by adding a chapter titled "Management and Promotion of Electronic Government Services," which focuses on issues related to the functions of the administrator of the OEG, the Chief Information Officers (CIO) Council, and the E-Government Fund (discussed below). The chapter makes the administrator of OEG responsible for carrying out a variety of IRM functions. Some of these responsibilities include advising the director on IRM resources and strategies; providing "overall leadership and direction on electronic government"; promoting the effective and innovative use of IT by agencies especially through multiagency collaborative projects; administering and distributing funds from the E-Government Fund; consulting with GSA "to promote electronic government and the efficient use of information technologies by agencies"; leading activities on behalf of the OMB deputy director of management, who serves as the chair of the CIO Council; assisting the OMB director "in establishing policies which shall set the framework for information technology standards" to be developed by the National Institute for Standards and Technology; sponsoring an ongoing dialogue with federal, state, local, and tribal leaders to encourage collaboration and enhance consultation on IT best practices and innovation; promoting electronic procurement initiatives; and implementing accessibility standards.

In addition, Title I establishes the CIO Council by law,[54] with the OMB deputy director of management as chair, and details its organizational structure and mandate. Furthermore, Title I establishes an E-Government Fund for interagency information technology projects. The fund is to be administered by the GSA administrator, with the assistance of the administrator of OEG. The provision authorizes appropriations for the E-Government Fund in the following amounts: $45 million for FY 2003, $50 million for FY 2004, $100 million for FY 2005, $150 million for FY 2006, and "such sums as necessary for fiscal year 2007." The provision also allows funds to be made available until expended and requires the OMB director to submit annual reports to the president and Congress regarding the operation of the fund.

Title II focuses on enhancing a variety of e-government services, establishing performance measures, and clarifying OMB's role as the leader and coordinator of federal e-government services. The responsibilities of the OEG are also described in greater detail. Among its provisions, Title II requires agencies to participate in the CIO Council and to submit annual agency e-government status reports; requires executive agencies to adopt electronic signature methods; directs the federal courts and regulatory agencies to establish Web sites containing information useful to citizens; outlines the responsibilities of the OMB director for maintaining accessibility, usability, and preservation of government information; establishes privacy requirements regarding agency use of personally identifiable information and requires privacy guidelines be established for federal Web sites; creates a public–private exchange program for midlevel IT workers between government agencies and private sector organizations; amends a chapter of Title 10 of the *United States Code* by adding a new section regarding the facilitation of new incentives and procedures to encourage agencies to use share-in-savings procurement techniques; amends a section of Title 40 of the *United States Code* by allowing state or local governments to use federal supply schedules for IT purchases; and mandates the development of common protocols for geographic information systems.

In addition, several studies are mandated, including a feasibility study on integrating federal information systems across agencies and implementing up to five pilot projects; an interagency study on the best practices of federally funded community technology centers; a study "on using information technology to enhance crisis response and consequence management of natural and manmade disasters"; and a study to examine disparities in Internet access based on demographic characteristics.

Title III, better known as the Federal Information Security Management Act (FISMA) of 2002, supersedes similar language as it appeared in the Homeland Security Act of 2002[55] and reauthorizes and amends the Government Information Security Reform Act (GISRA).[56] Among its provisions, FISMA amends a subchapter of Title 44 of the *United States Code* by stipulating the general authority, functions, and responsibilities of the OMB director and individual agencies relating to developing and maintaining federal information security policies and practices. It also requires agencies to conduct annual independent evaluations of their information security programs and practices. Agencies operating or controlling national security systems are also responsible for maintaining the appropriate level of information security protections for these systems. In addition, FISMA amends the Clinger-Cohen Act by requiring the secretary of commerce, on the basis of proposals developed by the National Institute of Standards and Technology (NIST), to promulgate information security standards for federal information systems. It also amends section 20 of the National Institute of Standards and Technology Act[57] by affirming the role of NIST to develop standards, guidelines, and minimum requirements for information systems used by federal agencies or by contractors on behalf of an agency. It also directs NIST to carry out these activities in consultation and coordination with the relevant agencies and offices, including but not limited to the OMB director, the National Security Agency, the GAO,[58] and the secretary of homeland security. FISMA amends the National Institute of Standards and Technology Act[59] by replacing the existing Computer System Security and Privacy Advisory Board with the new Information Security and Privacy Advisory Board. It directs the Information Security and Privacy Advisory Board to advise NIST and the OMB director on information security and privacy issues relating to government information systems.

Title IV authorizes appropriations for the bill through fiscal 2007 and makes the bill effective 120 days after enactment. Title V is referred to as the Confidential Information Protection and Statistical Efficiency Act of 2002. It designates the OMB director as being responsible for coordinating and overseeing the confidentiality and disclosure policies established in the title and establishes limitations on the use and disclosure of data and information by government agencies. Title V identifies the Bureau of the Census, the Bureau of Economic Analysis, and the Bureau of Labor Statistics each as a "Designated Statistical Agency" and outlines their responsibilities regarding the use, handling, and sharing of data.

E-GOVERNMENT STRATEGY—2003

A little over one year after it first unveiled its e-government strategy, the Bush administration released an updated version in April 2003. This updated version recounted the achievements of the past year, while laying out the challenges and plans for action in 2003 and 2004. It also provided an intended timetable for fulfilling the mandates of the E-Government Act.

Three major themes were prominent in the April 2003 e-government strategy. One theme was the emphasis on citizen-focused e-government. Throughout the document, references were made to concepts such as "one-stop, on-line access to information and services to individuals,"[60] redesigning government Web sites "to provide government services with '3 clicks,' "[61] and reorganizing the development of IT investments around "groups of citizens."[62] Another theme was the emphasis on government-wide solutions. The revised e-government strategy spoke of both modernizing agencies from within, using *"principles of e-business,"* such as "buy once, use many," and "collect once, use many,"[63] and "integrating IT investments *across* agencies."[64] The revised strategy also elaborated on the importance of the federal enterprise architecture (FEA) initiative to e-government, and the anticipated efforts to develop new e-government initiatives centered on the Lines of Business,[65] both of which had been discussed in less detail in the earlier version of the e-government strategy. A third theme was the importance of leadership to the success of e-government. The CIO Council and OMB, as well as various intergovernmental groups, are frequently mentioned for their roles in managing and guiding complex initiatives. The importance of support from agency leaders and the need to recruit and retain a qualified IT workforce, especially project managers, are highlighted as critical to the future of federal e-government.[66]

In the year following the release of the original version of the e-government strategy, the federal government had made notable progress on most of the twenty-four Quicksilver initiatives, as well as other reforms needed to facilitate the advancement of e-government. Most of these efforts revolved around the creation of various thematically organized portals, such as Volunteer.gov, Recreation.gov, GovBenefits.gov, BusinessLaw.gov, and Regulations.gov, and agency-specific modernization efforts.[67] While most of the e-government activities up to this point required relatively little integration, consolidation, and transformation of the government's technical infrastructure, these activities were important for laying the groundwork for integration and collaboration between agencies in the future. Indeed, one of the major challenges identified for 2003 and beyond was "to physically migrate agency-unique solutions to each cross-agency E-Government solution, reducing costs and generating more citizen-centered results."[68] Other challenges included "leadership support, parochialism, funding, and communication."[69]

To overcome these challenges and achieve its goals for e-government, OMB cited five broad strategies it would pursue:

1. Simplify work processes to improve service to citizens.
2. Use the annual budget process and other OMB requirements to support e-government implementation.
3. Improve project delivery through development, recruitment, and retention of a qualified IT workforce.
4. Continue to modernize agency IT management around citizen-centered Lines of Business.
5. Engage agency leadership to support e-government project implementation.[70]

OMB also enumerated several specific goals, or "measures of success," it would use to gauge the effectiveness of federal e-government efforts:

- Agencies are focusing IT spending on high priority modernization initiatives.
- Major IT projects are within 10 percent of cost/schedule/performance objectives.
- Major IT systems have been certified, accredited, or otherwise authorized as being properly secured.
- Twenty-four presidential e-government initiatives are operational and yield benefits (e.g., cost reduction, response time, burden reduction, and improved citizen service).
- Negotiate government-wide Enterprise Software licenses.
- Reduce redundant IT spending in the six overlapping Lines of Business identified in the FY 2004 budget, by defining government-wide solutions.[71]

FEDERAL ENTERPRISE ARCHITECTURE INITIATIVE

Prompted by the findings of the task force in 2001, the federal enterprise architecture was started in February 2002 by OMB and continues to be developed today. An enterprise architecture (EA) serves as a blueprint of the business operations of an organization, and the information and technology needed to carry out these functions, both currently and prospectively. As such, it is an IT management and planning tool. It is designed to be comprehensive and scalable, to account for future growth needs. EA planning represents a business-driven approach to IT management that emphasizes interoperability and information sharing.

The creation of EAs long predates the development of the Quicksilver initiatives, however. In the mid-1980s, John Zachman developed the Zachman Framework, which was designed to serve as a blueprint, or an architecture, to facilitate the integration of IT systems.[72] The "enterprise" for which an architecture is created refers to either a "single organization or mission area that transcends more than one organizational boundary (e.g., financial management, homeland security)."[73]

Since the development of the Zachman Framework, various parts of the federal government have attempted to work with EAs. More recently, the Clinger-Cohen Act, passed in 1996, tasked agency CIOs with, among other responsibilities, "developing, maintaining, and facilitating the implementation of a sound and integrated information technology architecture for the executive agency."[74] The Clinger-Cohen Act defined information technology architecture as "an integrated framework for evolving or maintaining existing information technology and acquiring new information technology to achieve the agency's strategic goals and information resources management goals."[75]

In September 1999, the federal CIO Council issued its FEA Framework.[76] In the glossary of the document, the FEA is defined as

> a strategic information asset base, which defines the business, the information necessary to operate the business, the technologies necessary to support the business operations, and the transitional processes necessary for implementing new technologies in response to the changing business needs. It is a representation or blueprint.[77]

The E-Government Act, passed in 2002, tasked the administrator of OEG with overseeing the development of EAs both within and across agencies. The act defined enterprise architecture as

> (A) means—(i) a strategic information asset base, which defines the mission; (ii) the information necessary to perform the mission; (iii) the technologies necessary to perform the mission; and (iv) the transitional processes for implementing new technologies in response to changing mission needs; and (B) includes—(i) a baseline architecture; (ii) a target architecture; and (iii) a sequencing plan.[78]

The FEA is composed of five reference models: Performance, Business, Service, Data, and Technical. Each of the reference models represents specific aspects of the FEA and provides a "common language" for departments and agencies to use in developing common technology solutions. The reference models are updated to reflect changes in applications and services. Brief descriptions of the five reference models, drawn from the FEA Web site, follow:

- Performance Reference Model: a framework for measuring the output of major IT investments and their contributions toward achieving organizational goals.[79]
- Business Reference Model: a framework for describing the federal government business operations independent of the agencies that perform them.[80]
- Service Components Reference Model: a framework to identify information technology service components (applications) used to support government business functions.[81]
- Data Reference Model: describes, at an aggregate level, the data and information used to support government program and business operations.[82]
- Technical Reference Model: a framework used to describe the standards, specifications, and technologies used to support and facilitate the delivery of service components (applications).[83]

The 2003 e-government strategy emphasizes the role of the FEA in developing a comprehensive IT management strategy and supporting e-government initiatives. As e-government initiatives become more complex (more transformative in nature) and the FEA reference models become more detailed, it is anticipated that IT management decisions will become increasingly centralized, reversing a trend of decentralized IT management that began to occur in the federal government with the passage of the Clinger-Cohen Act in 1996.[84] While such centralization of decision making can dampen entrepreneurialism and sometimes lead to one-size-fits-all solutions that are not always appropriate, it can also provide benefits, such as improved efficiency and cost savings. The 2003 e-government strategy favors the latter view, citing the "value to IT management." This includes:

- improves decisions about IT system investments (e.g., enables an agency to determine if a system is redundant);
- aligns IT support with business objectives;
- aligns IT investments with business drivers;
- reduces redundancy;
- improves interoperability between processes and systems;
- supports realization of economies of scale.[85]

LINES OF BUSINESS INITIATIVES

In attempting to develop a second generation of e-government projects, there is an interest in moving beyond the somewhat limited nature of the cross-agency collaboration of some of the Quicksilver projects toward initiatives that have a potentially truly government-wide character. To that end, in spring 2004, after reviewing data collected from agencies for the development of the FEA and formulating the annual federal budget, OMB identified "five major collaborative initiatives to transform government, improve services to citizens, and deliver substantial savings."[86] The five areas include financial management, human resources management, grants management, case management, and federal health architecture. These initiatives were chosen, in part, because they represent core business functions common to many departments and agencies, and/or have the potential to reap significant efficiency and efficacy gains. Hence, they are strong candidates for utilizing some of the more transformative e-government practices, such as "buy once, use many," breaking down the so-called stovepipes, and contributing to a shared infrastructure. These Lines of Business (LoB) initiatives, currently in their operational phases, are anticipated to create $5 billion in savings over ten years. The initiatives and their primary objectives, as drawn from the LoB Web site, are:

- Financial management: to develop a government-wide financial management solution that is efficient and improves business performance while ensuring integrity in accountability, financial controls, and mission effectiveness.[87]
- Human resource management: to develop government-wide, modern, cost-effective, standardized, and interoperable human resource solutions providing common core functionality to support the strategic management of human capital.[88]

- Grants management: to develop a government-wide solution to support end-to-end grants management activities that promote citizen access, customer service, and agency financial and technical stewardship.[89]
- Case management: to facilitate the management and sharing of information between federal and local law enforcement agencies, and with citizens, using common solutions and data standards.[90]
- Federal health architecture: to improve the health and safety of citizens through access to reliable health-related information and services, and through greater interoperability of health information and technology between medical providers.[91]

In March 2005, OMB established a task force for a sixth project, the information technology security LoB initiative. This new IT security initiative is intended to address common security weaknesses faced by many agencies and generally improve the state of federal information security. At the time of this writing, this initiative is currently in the planning phase, but it is anticipated that government-wide solutions will be developed to enhance agencies' abilities to carry out critical security practices including training, information sharing on threats and defenses, threat awareness and incident response, program management, and risk management.[92]

As OMB continues to collect and analyze information from the departments and agencies, it will be able to further develop the FEA and, in turn, likely identify additional opportunities for e-government initiatives based around the LoB. However, while developing initiatives focused around the various lines of business represents a critical organizational and technological step for U.S. e-government, it also has the potential to challenge some of the constitutional principles that underlie the country's system of governance. Some of these challenges are discussed below.

IMPLICATIONS FOR FEDERALISM

One area where the implications for implementing e-government initiatives may have a significant effect relates to the concerns of federalism. The U.S. Constitution established a federal system of governance granting certain powers to the national government while reserving others to the states and the people. Throughout the history of the country, the nature of American federalism has evolved, reflecting the political, economic, and social changes that have occurred.[93] However, one of the hallmarks of a federal system of governance is the emphasis on vertical divisions of power. In contrast, e-government initiatives utilize information technologies that emphasize a horizontal, or networked, model of communication and interaction. While e-government is designed, in part, to break down the barriers separating different agencies, it could also have a similar effect on the boundaries of federal governance.

In light of the divergent properties of federalism and e-government, the advent of e-government has the potential to affect significantly the power relationship between the national and state governments. An example includes initiatives to create "one-stop-shopping" Web sites to obtain government services and information, such as the FirstGov site. In addition to its original role of providing access to all federal government Web sites, FirstGov has added links to most state Web sites as well.[94] One of the goals of these types of sites is to create an experience that attenuates the agency-centric approach to providing services. Although this usually refers to agencies at the same level of government, it could also include services that are provided through some form of national, state, and/or local cooperation, such as welfare, transportation, or law enforcement activities. However, these same efforts to improve the delivery of government services could also diffuse political responsibility and credit, making it less clear from where the funding and direction are originating.

CONCLUSION

Taking into account the speed of technological change and the inherently fluid nature of politics, predictions about the future of e-government are made at one's own peril. However, absent a crystal ball, there are still some signs that suggest that the United States is approaching a potentially critical point in its e-government maturation. If the United States can successfully address a handful of key challenges, then it is likely that the federal government will begin to undergo a slow, but distinguishable, process of transformation. The failure to address these challenges successfully, however, would suggest a delay in the transformation process, although not necessarily a halt to the continued development of e-government. Instead, e-government would continue to evolve, but in a more fractured way that could introduce new IT management challenges (e.g., divergent data standards, duplicative investments, and incompatible systems), which will make full transformation harder to achieve further down the road. Choices being made regarding the design of EAs, the selection of new initiatives, and the technological solutions to use reflect the values, priorities, and needs of the government. For these reasons, it is important to be aware that the decisions being made now will likely have a lasting impact on the options and opportunities for the future development of e-government in the United States.

The challenges facing the federal government are formidable but not insurmountable. They include both technology-related and non-technology-related challenges. Arguably, the technology-related challenges are easier to address than the nontechnology challenges, which reflect long-standing institutional dynamics. The list below is not comprehensive. One could easily add dozens of other problems to the list, both specific and general. However, these six challenges represent some of the most critical junctures of e-government, points upon which the future development of e-government is most dependent. They include:

- Organizational culture: Organizational culture issues have been a long-running concern for government reform. The resistance of organizational cultures to change is frequently one of the biggest challenges for e-government initiatives, especially those initiatives that result in a reallocation of resources, decision-making authority, and/or personnel. A lack of buy-in on the part of both agency managers and rank-and-file employees and/or the absence of a project champion can significantly undermine the potential benefits of an e-government initiative. Resistance can also come from citizens. The "build it and they will come" philosophy rarely works in practice. Citizens need to be convinced of the value of an e-government initiative before they will embrace it. Concerns about privacy and security, as well as the speed, reliability, and accuracy of activities conducted online, must also be adequately assuaged.

- Project management and IT leadership: As IT projects have become more integrated into the function of a department or agency, the role of CIOs has evolved as well. CIOs are reportedly being called upon not only for their technological expertise but also to provide strategic leadership in the areas of policy, budget, and contract oversight. The CIO's relationship with top-level department decision makers can also be critical to successfully implementing e-government initiatives. This suggests that, in selecting a department-level CIO, one needs to select an individual who has a deep contextual understanding of the mission and functions of an organization, but who also brings a wider range of experiences and perspectives to the position. Similarly, the increased size and complexity of IT projects has further underscored the need for strong project managers to carry out these initiatives. While it is not uncommon for IT project management to be just one of several duties assigned to an individual, some observers have suggested that IT projects with budgets of $5 million or larger should have dedicated, full-time managers. The possibility of requiring federal IT project managers to obtain some form of professional certification has also been raised.[95]

- Cross-agency funding (E-government Fund): The problem of cross-agency funding highlights the clash between the horizontal nature of government-wide e-government initiatives and the vertical organization of government. Congressional authorizing committees are organized by department and/or agency. The allocation of resources and the oversight of activities are likewise jurisdictionally defined. There are relatively few mechanisms to facilitate cross-agency collaboration regarding the spending of funds. Although the E-Government Act authorizes a significant sum that can be spent on e-government initiatives in the form of the E-Government Fund, concerns regarding oversight have prompted Congress to appropriate no more than $5 million in any given fiscal year since the passage of the E-Government Act. In the longer term, solutions that adequately address the needs of collaborative initiatives with appropriate oversight will be needed.

- Enterprise architecture: As a blueprint of the business functions of an organization, and the technology used to carry out these functions, the EA is the means to develop government-wide initiatives. As such, it is also the means to address the problem of interoperability, the ability of a computer system or data to work with other systems or data using common standards or processes. Interoperability is an important part of the larger effort to improve interagency collaboration and information sharing. It also represents a significant challenge as the federal government implements cross-agency initiatives, such as the E-Payroll and Gov-Benefits.gov projects, to eliminate redundant systems and facilitate a "one-stop service delivery" approach to e-government. Decisions made early in the development of the federal enterprise architecture can have significant implications for future IT projects, suggesting that regular assessments of this process may be necessary to help minimize any potential complications.

- Information security: In a series of evaluations published since 1997, the GAO has repeatedly reported that the largest federal agencies have made only limited progress in addressing computer security vulnerabilities, citing information security as a government-wide high-risk issue. Specifically, GAO has identified six areas of weakness: lack of senior management attention to information security; inadequate accountability for job and program performance related to IT security; limited security training for general users, IT professionals, and security professionals; inadequate integration of security into the capital planning and investment control process; poor security for contractor-provided services; and limited capability to detect, report, and share information on vulnerabilities or to detect intrusions, suspected intrusions, or virus infections.[96] For e-government activities, service continuity is considered critical not only for the availability and service delivery" approach to e-government. Decisions made early in the devel-fraud and misuse of sensitive data are concerns as well.

- Authentication: To achieve the goal of true one-stop shopping for the citizen and "collect once, use many" for agencies, a workable authentication system will be needed. The ability to accurately authenticate the identity of a user online is critical to carrying out the higher-order e-government activities. To be convenient, it will need to allow citizens to access information and carry out activities using one set of information. To be workable, it will need to be secure, with interoperable standards, but not so complex or bulky that it adversely affects the application's performance and the user's experience. With the rapidly growing awareness of identity theft and the growing number of data thefts, the need for an authentication solution grows more acute.

Although the U.S. government continues to move forward with a second generation of e-government projects, and beyond, the path to transforming government remains a work in progress. On the one hand, e-government provides new opportunities to enhance governance, which can include improved efficiency, new services, increased citizen participation, and a more robust continuity of government capability. On the other hand, e-government also presents new challenges to governance, including information security, privacy, disparities in computer access, and management and funding requirements. Together, all of these issues are complicated by their combined intra- and intergovernmental nature, while also crosscutting the various stages of e-government development. However, they also share a number of recurring themes often associated with previous, less technologically dependent approaches to improving government, such as jurisdictional authority, procedures for the appropriate handling of information, building and maintaining infrastructures, providing services, and citizens' rights. The multidimensional nature of e-government suggests that there are no quick fixes for the concerns raised but, rather, that issues will need to be addressed with careful attention to context and precedent.

NOTES

1. Harold C. Relyea and Henry B. Hogue, "A Brief History of the Emergence of Digital Government in the United States," in *Digital Government: Principles and Best Practices*, ed. Alexei Pavlichev and G. David Garson (Hershey, PA: Idea Group Publishing, 2004), 16–33.

2. J. C. R. Licklinder, "Man-Computer Symbiosis," *IRE Transactions on Human Factors in Electronics* 1 (1960): 4–11; J. C. R. Licklinder and W. E. Clark, "On-line Man-Computer Communication," *Proceedings of the American Federation of Information Processing Societies* 21 (1962): 113–28.

3. J. C. R. Licklinder and Robert W. Taylor, "The Computer as a Communication Device," *Science and Technology* 76 (1968): 21–31.

4. For a historical time line of Google's development, see Google, "The Google Timeline." Available at www.google.com/intl/en/corporate/timeline.html, accessed July 1, 2005.

5. For more information about the history of the FirstGov portal, see www.firstgov.gov/About .shtml, accessed July 1, 2005.

6. Jeffrey W. Seifert and Harold C. Relyea, "Considering E-government from the Federal Perspective: An Evolving Concept, a Developing Practice," *Journal of E-Government* 1 (2004): 7–15.

7. Gartner Group, "Key Issues in E-Government Strategy and Management," in *Research Notes, Key Issues* (Stamford, CT: Gartner Group, Inc., May 23, 2000).

8. Stephen Barr, "President Searching for a Few Good E-government Ideas," *Washington Post*, August 10, 2001, B2.

9. 116 Stat. 2899, at 2902.

10. Accenture, *eGovernment Leadership: High Performance, Maximum Value* (New York: Accenture, May 2004). Available at www.accenture.com/xdoc/en/industries/government/gove_egov_value .pdf, accessed July 1, 2005.

11. Jason Miller, "Next Wave of Egov Projects Coming Soon," *Government Computer News*, December 18, 2003. Available at www.washingtontechnology.com/news/1_1/daily_news/22380-1 .html, accessed July 1, 2005.

12. Office of the Vice President, *From Red Tape to Results: Creating a Government That Works Better and Costs Less, Report of the National Performance Review* (Washington, DC: Office of the Vice President, 1993).

13. Office of the Vice President, *From Red Tape to Results*, 96.

14. Office of the Vice President, *From Red Tape to Results*, 181–82.

15. Office of the Vice President, *From Red Tape to Results*, xxiii.

16. Office of the Vice President, *From Red Tape to Results*, xxxviii–xl.

17. Office of the Vice President, *Creating a Government That Works Better and Costs Less, Status Report September, 1994, Report of the National Performance Review* (Washington, DC: Office of the Vice President, 1994), 5–6.

18. For an archive of the NPR Web site and all of its reports see University of North Texas, Cyber-Cemetery (Denton: University of North Texas Libraries, 2005). Available at http://govinfo.library .unt.edu/npr/library/review.html, accessed July 1, 2005.

19. Harold C. Relyea, Maricele J. Cornejo, and Henry B. Hogue, *The National Performance Review and Other Government Initiatives: An Overview, 1993–2001,* CRS Report RL30596 (Washington, DC: CRS, June 4, 2001).

20. Office of the Vice President, *Access America: Reengineering through Information Technology, Report of the National Partnership for Reinventing Government and the Government Information Technology Services Board* (Washington, DC: Office of the Vice President, 1997), 2–3.

21. For a detailed time line of the history of NPR, see http://govinfo.library.unt.edu/npr/whowe are/historypart4.html (see note 18).

22. Anne Laurent, "Revamping Reinvention," *Government Executive* 30 (April 1998): 31–32.

23. Christopher Baum and Andrea Di Maio, *Gartner's Four Phases of E-Government Model* (Stamford, CT: Gartner Group, November 21, 2000).

24. While the exact terminology and number of stages used to distinguish stages of e-government development can vary significantly from study to study, the common element among these schemas is to highlight the developmental aspect most governments go through as they attempt to integrate information technology into their administrative practices and processes.

25. Baum and Di Maio, *Gartner's Four Phases of E-Government Model.*

26. White House, Memorandum for the Heads of Executive Departments and Agencies: *Electronic Government* (Washington, DC: White House, December 17, 1999), 1.

27. White House, Memorandum.

28. White House, Memorandum, 1–3.

29. Office of Management and Budget (OMB), *The President's Management Agenda, FY 2002* (Washington, DC: OMB, 2001), 4.

30. The number of program initiatives would ultimately grow to ten. The original nine program initiatives included faith-based and community initiative, privatization of military housing, better research and development investment criteria, elimination of fraud and error in student aid programs and deficiencies in financial management, housing and urban development management and performance, broadened health insurance coverage through state initiatives, a "right-sized" overseas presence, reform of food aid programs, and coordination of veterans affairs and defense programs and systems. However, in an August 2004 OMB report to federal employees detailing the status of the PMA, the reform of food aid initiative was not carried forward, and two new program initiatives were added. The new program initiatives included strengthening real property management and optimizing the use of federal property, and eliminating improper payments. Virginia A. McMurty, *The President's Management Agenda: A Brief Introduction*, CRS Report RS21416 (Washington, DC: Congressional Research Service [CRS], February 14, 2005), 1; U.S. GAO, *Financial Management: Challenges in Meeting Requirements of the Improper Payments Information Act*, GAO-05-417 (Washington, DC: GAO, March 2005), 7n8. Available at www.gao.gov/new.items/d05417.pdf, accessed July 1, 2005; U.S. OMB, "The Federal Government Is Results-Oriented: A Report to Federal Employees" (Washington, DC: OMB, August 2004), 9–10. Available at www.whitehouse.gov/omb/pma/2004_pma_report.pdf, accessed July 1, 2005.

31. For more details on the scoring system, and an archive of the quarterly scorecards, see www.whitehouse.gov/results/agenda/scorecard.html.

32. OMB, *The President's Management Agenda*, 23.

33. The FirstGov Web site is available at www.firstgov.gov.

34. OMB, *The President's Management Agenda,* 24.

35. OMB, "Citizen-Centered E-Government: Developing the Action Plan," Memorandum for the Heads of Executive Departments and Agencies, M-01-28 (Washington, DC: OMB, July 18, 2001).

36. GAO, *Electronic Government: Selection and Implementation of the Office of Management and Budget's 24 Initiatives*, GAO Report GAO-03-229 (Washington, DC: GAO, November 2002), 14; OMB, *Implementing the President's Management Agenda for E-Government, E-Government Strategy, Simplified Delivery of Services to Citizens* (Washington, DC: OMB, February 2002), 6. Available at www.whitehouse.gov/omb/inforeg/egovstrategy.pdf, accessed July 1, 2005; OMB, *Implementing the President's Management Agenda for E-Government, E-Government Strategy, Simplified Delivery of Services to Citizens* (Washington, DC: OMB, April 2003), 21. Available at www.whitehouse.gov/omb/egov/2003egov_strat.pdf, accessed July 1, 2005.

37. OMB, *Implementing the President's Management Agenda for E-Government, E-Government Strategy*, 2.

38. OMB, *Implementing the President's Management Agenda for E-Government, E-Government Strategy*, 7.

39. OMB, *Implementing the President's Management Agenda for E-Government, E-Government Strategy*, 9.

40. OMB, *Implementing the President's Management Agenda for E-Government, E-Government Strategy*, 10.

41. OMB, "E-GOV: About E-GOV" (Washington, DC: OMB, n.d.). Available at www.whitehouse.gov/omb/egov/c-presidential.html, accessed July 1, 2005.

42. OMB, *Implementing the President's Management Agenda for E-Government, E-Government Strategy*, 1.

43. OMB, *Implementing the President's Management Agenda for E-Government, E-Government Strategy*, 1.

44. OMB, *Implementing the President's Management Agenda for E-Government, E-Government Strategy*, 4.

45. See OMB, *Budget of the United States Government, Fiscal Year 2006* (Washington, DC: OMB, 2005). Available at www.whitehouse.gov/omb/budget/fy2004/sheets/itspending.xls, accessed July 1, 2005. This table was published on CD-ROM (no print version) as supplemental materials [www.whitehouse.gov/omb/budget/fy2006/spec.html] of this volume of the President's FY2006 proposed budget: Analytical Perspectives, Budget of the United States Government, Fiscal Year 2006, www.whitehouse.gov/omb/budget/fy2006/.

46. OMB, *Implementing the President's Management Agenda for E-Government, E-Government Strategy*, 5.

47. Jeffrey W. Seifert, *Government Information Technology Management: Past and Future Issues (The Clinger-Cohen Act)*, CRS Report RL30661 (Washington, DC: CRS, January 15, 2002).

48. OMB, *Implementing the President's Management Agenda for E-Government, E-Government Strategy*, 5.

49. OMB, *Implementing the President's Management Agenda for E-Government, E-Government Strategy*, 11.

50. The Geospatial One-Stop project Web site is available at www.geo-one-stop.gov/.

51. The e-authentication project Web site is available at www.cio.gov/eauthentication/.

52. 5 U.S.C. 552a.

53. 112 STAT. 2681–749.

54. The CIO Council was originally established by Executive Order 13011 *Federal Information Technology* on July 16, 1996, to serve as "the principal interagency forum to improve agency practices on such matters as the design, modernization, use, sharing, and performance of agency information resources."

55. P.L. 107-296; 116 STAT. 2229.

56. GISRA was passed as part of the Floyd D. Spence National Defense Authorization Act for FY 2001 (P.L. 106-398, Title X, Subtitle G).

57. 15 U.S.C. 278g–3.

58. The General Accounting Office was renamed the Government Accountability Office effective July 7, 2004.

59. 15 U.S.C. 278g–4.

60. OMB, *Implementing the President's Management Agenda for E-Government, E-Government* Strategy (2003), 9.

61. OMB, *Implementing the President's Management Agenda for E-Government, E-Government Strategy* (2003) 11.

62. OMB, *Implementing the President's Management Agenda for E-Government, E-Government Strategy* (2003) 3.

63. OMB, *Implementing the President's Management Agenda for E-Government, E-Government Strategy* (2003) 16.

64. OMB, *Implementing the President's Management Agenda for E-Government, E-Government Strategy* (2003), 3 (italics in original).

65. OMB, *Implementing the President's Management Agenda for E-Government, E-Government Strategy* (2003), 17.

66. OMB, *Implementing the President's Management Agenda for E-Government, E-Government Strategy* (2003), 15–16.

67. OMB, *Implementing the President's Management Agenda for E-Government, E-Government Strategy* (2003), 12–13.

68. OMB, *Implementing the President's Management Agenda for E-Government, E-Government Strategy* (2003), 5.

69. OMB, *Implementing the President's Management Agenda for E-Government, E-Government Strategy* (2003), 5.

70. OMB, *Implementing the President's Management Agenda for E-Government, E-Government Strategy* (2003), 16–17.

71. OMB, *Implementing the President's Management Agenda for E-Government, E-Government Strategy* (2003), 18.

72. J. A. Zachman. "A Framework for Information Systems Architecture," *IBM Systems Journal* 26, no. 3 (1987): 276–92.

73. GAO, *Information Technology: The Federal Enterprise Architecture and Agencies' Enterprise Architectures are Still Maturing,* GAO Testimony GAO-04-798T (Washington, DC: GAO, May 19, 2004), 4.

74. 110 STAT. 685.

75. 110 STAT. 686.

76. Chief Information Officers Council, *Federal Enterprise Architecture. Version 1.1* (Washington, DC: CIO Council, 1999). Available at www.cio.gov/archive/fedarch1.pdf, accessed July 1, 2005.

77. CIO Council, *Federal Enterprise Architecture. Version 1.1,* C-5.

78. 116 STAT. 2902.

79. For more detail on the Performance Reference Model, see OMB, "E-GOV: Performance Reference Model" (Washington, DC: OMB, n.d.). Available at www.whitehouse.gov/omb/egov/a-2-prm.html, accessed July 1, 2005.

80. For more detail on the Business Reference Model, see OMB, "E-GOV: Business Reference Model" (Washington, DC: OMB, n.d.). Available at www.whitehouse.gov/omb/egov/a-3-brm.html, accessed July 1, 2005.

81. For more detail on the Service Components Reference Model, see OMB, "E-GOV: Service Components Reference Model" (Washington, DC: OMB, n.d.). Available at www.whitehouse.gov/omb/egov/a-4-srm.html, accessed July 1, 2005.

82. For more detail on the Data Reference Model, see OMB, "E-GOV: Data Reference Model" (Washington, DC: OMB, n.d.). Available at www.whitehouse.gov/omb/egov/a-5-drm.html, accessed July 1, 2005.

83. For more detail on the Technical Reference Model, see OMB, "E-GOV: Technical Reference Model" (Washington, DC: OMB, n.d.). Available at www.whitehouse.gov/omb/egov/a-6-trm.html, accessed July 1, 2005.

84. The Clinger-Cohen Act repealed the Brooks Act of 1965 (P.L. 89-306). The goal of the Brooks Act was to reform federal information technology procurement by concentrating purchasing authority within the GSA. However, prolonged acquisition cycles and rapid changes in technology eventually diminished the effectiveness of the "one-size-fits-all" approach of the Brooks Act.

85. OMB, *Implementing the President's Management Agenda for E-Government, E-Government Strategy* (2003), 13.

86. OMB, *Enabling Citizen-Centered Electronic Government 2005–2006 FEA PMO Action Plan* (Washington, DC: OMB, March 2005), 11.

87. For more detailed information, see OMB, "E-GOV: Financial Management" (Washington, DC: OMB, n.d.). Available at www.whitehouse.gov/omb/egov/c-6-2-financial.html, accessed July 1, 2005.

88. For more detailed information, see OMB, "E-GOV: Human Resources Management" (Washington, DC: OMB, n.d.). Available at www.whitehouse.gov/omb/egov/c-6-4-human.html, accessed July 1, 2005.

89. For more detailed information, see OMB, "E-GOV: Grants Management" (Washington, DC: OMB, n.d.). Available at www.whitehouse.gov/omb/egov/c-6-3-grants.html, accessed July 1, 2005.

90. For more detailed information, see OMB, "E-GOV: Case Management" (Washington, DC: OMB, n.d.). Available at www.whitehouse.gov/omb/egov/c-6-1-case.html, accessed July 1, 2005.

91. For more detailed information, see OMB, "E-GOV: Federal Health Architecture" (Washington, DC: OMB, n.d.). Available at www.whitehouse.gov/omb/egov/c-6-5-federal.html, accessed July 1, 2005.

92. OMB, *Implementing the President's Management Agenda for E-Government, E-Government Strategy* (2003), 12.

93. Eugene Boyd and Michael K. Fauntroy, *American Federalism, 1776 to 2000: Significant Events,* CRS Report RL31057 (Washington, DC: CRS, November 30, 2000).

94. William Matthews, "FirstGov to Add State Links," *Federal Computer Week,* May 21, 2001, 13.

95. Sara Michael, "Do Your Project Managers Measure Up?" *Federal Computer Week,* November 3, 2003, 28; Sara Michael, "Execs Call for Full-Time Project Managers," *Federal Computer Week,* November 5, 2003. Available at www.fcw.com/fcw/articles/2003/1103/web-egov-11-05-03.asp, accessed July 1, 2005.

96. GAO, *Information Security: Continued Efforts Needed to Fully Implement Statutory Requirements,* GAO Testimony GAO-03-852T (Washington, DC: GAO, June 24, 2003), 8.

3

E-government in the United Kingdom

Peter Hernon

$\mathscr{T}$he central government in the United Kingdom has taken a two-pronged approach to the Internet and e-government. First, it encourages the public and the business community to use the Internet and to recognize the advantages of communicating and conducting transactions, including engaging in e-commerce, over it. The government maintains that members of the public will not alter their present information-gathering behaviors until they are comfortable with, and competent in, using computers and navigating the World Wide Web. To encourage use and transform information-gathering behavior, the government has increased the opportunities for the public to gain access to the Internet more effectively and efficiently from their home, work, or school, or nearby online center (over six thousand of them exist in shops, community centers, libraries, and so forth) and to receive training in the use of computers. Second, the central government has encouraged the public, business community, and local government to interact with it over the Internet and for local governments to have a presence on the Web, providing both information and services.

The central government considers e-government as a means to exploit information and communication technologies (ICT) for the benefit of society, the economy, and public services; modernize public services; and make those services electronic and more responsive to a knowledge economy in which higher education, businesses, and other segments of the UK society are able to compete more successfully in a global electronic economy. "It is envisioned that the extra cost invested in providing additional electronic channels will eventually allow substantial savings through the scale back of a more costly physical channel and the reallocation of resources to other areas of public services."[1]

The purpose of this chapter is to provide an overview of the two-pronged approach and to discuss the historical development of UK government on the Web and the policy framework behind e-government. Coverage concludes with late 2004 and the entrance of a new policy initiative and personnel.

DEVELOPMENT OF E-GOVERNMENT

In its green paper, *Government Direct*, of November 1996, the Conservative government viewed citizens and businesses as customers of government services and endorsed improved services to those customers, more efficient and open government administration, and a substantial cost savings for the taxpayer. Echoing the same themes, the Labour government, which was elected the following May, shifted some of the emphasis, adopted the phrase "joined-up government," and produced the *Modernising Government* white paper of 1999. This white paper offered an agenda for public sector reform and recommended that ICT become a means to encourage innovation in information and knowledge management. The Cabinet Office led the movement to develop e-government.[2]

In September 1999, the government created the Office of the e-Envoy as part of the Cabinet Office to advance the UK's online capability, encourage public use of the Internet, assist the nation in becoming a leading knowledge economy, and improve operational efficiency across the public sector. The goal for government has been "to create modern, customer focused and efficient public services that stand comparison with those offered by the private sector," while the goal for the economy has been "to increase the productivity and competitiveness of UK business and to maintain macroeconomic stability." Expressed another way, "the role of government has been to create a world-class market environment for electronic business." Finally, the goal for society has been to ensure universal access to the Internet that is both fair and equitable.[3]

Also in 1999, information-age government champions, who were thirty-six senior officials and local government representatives from across government, emerged to

- support the e-envoy in implementing and developing strategy;
- help in winning and sustaining commitment to the [e-government] program across the public sector;
- assist the e-envoy in identifying cross-cutting initiatives;
- champion the delivery of departmental and sectoral e-business strategies; and
- sustain a network for sharing knowledge and experience in e-government programs.[4]

In the summer of 2004, the Office of the e-Envoy became the e-Government Unit, which "works with departments to deliver efficiency savings while improving the delivery of public services by joining up electronic government services around the needs of customers."[5] The position of e-envoy was replaced with a head of e-government, which is a cabinet-level position that "gives strategic leadership and drive to the application of ICT within central government and to support the reform and modernization of Britain's public services."[6] Like the Office of the e-Envoy, the e-Government Unit supports Directgov (www.direct.gov.uk), a portal that was launched in March 2004 to make it easier for the public to locate electronic government information and services. Directgov arranges information and services by audience ("parents," "motorists," "disabled people and carers"), identifies the five most requested topics, and provides news headlines and additional information. The unit also issues assorted publications (e.g., on the interoperability framework; see, for instance, http://e-government.cabinetoffice.gov.uk/EStrategy/EStrategy/fs/en) and statistics. The statistics include monthly "site traffic figures" for Directgov and the office of the e-Envoy (see http://e-government.cabinetoffice.gov.uk/MediaCentre/Current PressReleaseArticle/fs/en?C...). Those statistics indicate the number of "unique users," "total visits," and "page views."

Four principles guide "citizen-focused" e-government. The first one, "building services around citizens' choices," refers to innovative services that meet the needs of a public that wants "high quality services which are accessible, convenient and secure. People should not need to understand how government is organized, or to know which department or agency does what, or whether a function is exercised by central or local government." The second principle, "making government and its services more accessible," encourages the electronic delivery of services; recognizes that access to records is established under the Freedom of Information Act 2000, which went fully into force in January 2005; and expects government organizations to be more responsive to citizens' views. At the same time, "it will be vital to make sure that people can trust the systems . . . [that government] use[s], by ensuring that their personal data is protected and that systems are secure." The third principle, "social inclusion," requires services to be "available to all and easy to use." It also recognizes that "Digital TV and mobile phones will become increasingly important as a means of accessing the Internet." Furthermore, "the telephone will remain a preferred means of contact for many. Call centres must be improved by giving their staff access to information networks that will enable them to provide better service. Better information systems will support the work of those who have face to face contact with the public." And the final principle, "using information better," refers to the responsibility of government to manage information, knowledge, and change.[7]

These four principles recognize that the information government collects and produces is a valuable resource. In effect, e-government involves the dissemination of information and services, supporting e-commerce and online transactions, and serving democracy through this dissemination. In a speech before a summit of e-envoys from different countries, Prime Minister Tony Blair illustrated how access to information supports democracy by noting, "One million people from all over the world accessed the Government's dossier on Iraq within hours of its release on the No10 website, just one simple example of the democratisation of information that was unimaginable until very recently."[8]

To advance these principles, the central government has published "a range of new frameworks across government" that covers the following:

- Data structures: The Government Secure Intranet will contain "standard definitions and programming tools to allow government departments to develop new systems in a consistent and standardized way, and to present the data they already hold in a common way."
- Digital signatures: The purpose is to combine e-business with e-government by ensuring proper identification and authentication. The government wants to "ensure legal equivalence between digital and paper and pen signatures and work with financial institutions and others so that their digital signature products can be used to enable government transactions."
- Call centers: These enable the public to talk directly with government and to identify themselves and their exact needs.
- Smartcards: These can carry digital signatures and support varied functions.
- Digital TV: The government wants to develop and deliver services, and convey information, using digital TV.

- Web sites: The government has produced guidelines for government Web sites to follow.
- Use of government portals: In essence, these function as one-stop shopping or provide a place for those unfamiliar with the structure of government to find the types of information and services they need.[9]

In essence, the government's e-government strategy enables the public to interact with government through different channels: in person, by telephone, or through the Internet. The strategy recognizes that data protection and the ability of government to handle financial transactions in a safe and secure environment are essential to the success of e-commerce. Furthermore, members of the public must be willing to conduct business with government electronically; in this regard, they should not distinguish between online banking or purchasing from reputable companies and providing some personal information to government online.

MEASUREMENT FRAMEWORK

The framework focuses on data collection to reflect how the UK's position in the e-economy compares (benchmarks) internationally regarding readiness, take-up, and the long-term impact of policies. The government tracks data about individuals, business, and government and compares those data to selected countries.[10] In addition, the UK relies on best practices and the e-Government Unit (as well as the former Office of the e-Envoy) encourages departments and agencies to have their Web managers be able to answer three questions:

- Does it contain the information people seek?
- How easy is it to find the information?
- How often is the site used?[11]

The e-Government Unit wants Webmasters to "judge the effectiveness of the Web site's content, design, navigation and underlying technology," to analyze Web server logs, and to determine the number of unique users, visitor duration and traffic pattern, visitor origin (including country), visitor IP (Internet provider) address, and visitor preference for browser type and version. They should also identify from those logs "error message counts (indicating that pages and other content were not served successfully) and traffic analysis focusing on peak times (to assess bandwidth requirements) and 'dead' times (should it be necessary to switch the site off while maintenance is carried out)." Furthermore, they should collect information about requests that were successfully and unsuccessfully resolved, the most and least frequently visited pages, top entry pages, and top referring Web sites. The e-Government Unit points out that the information derived from Web server logs will enable Webmasters to

> identify the most popular content; review the navigation system for example, identifying orphaned pages; identify referring websites (the sites from which users arrive at your website); audit the level of response to electronic forms; assess the effectiveness of marketing/ PR [public relations] campaigns in bringing traffic to the website; provide information on

users' platforms and browsers; [and] identify users DNS domains and their visits from abroad or from within government.[12]

The data highlighted through comparison of best practices comprise inputs and occasionally outputs, and they focus more on Internet use than on use of government home pages or on the satisfaction and service expectations of the public, and how well those services and information resources resolved their information needs. In their examination of Web server logs, Webmasters might use transactional log analyses and conduct usability tests to see what information the public seeks, how they seek it, and how better to organize resources on a home page to simplify access to information and services.

In the United States, the Bush administration supports three-click access to information and services contained in FirstGov, a U.S. government portal. A similar expectation might be applied to UK portals. However, customer satisfaction and expectations should not be ignored or assumed to be ascertainable through an analysis of Web server logs.

CHALLENGES

In 2002, it was estimated that "around 7 million adults in Britain lack functional literacy and numeracy skills. The number of adults with poorly developed ICT skills exceeds this."[13] To address these problems, the central government initiated programs such as the provision of free ICT training through learning centers for people who are unemployed or possess few computer and navigation skills. The government also funds high-speed broadband connectivity in schools. Yet, it should not be assumed that increased training and connectivity necessarily result in increased demand for online information and services from the public sector.

In its annual report for 2003, the Office of the e-Envoy noted that "the UK now enjoys some of the lowest Internet access prices in the world, and levels of use have grown rapidly as a result." The report proclaimed that "with 61% of the population now reporting that they have used the Internet at some time, 'e-citizens' now make up a majority of the adult population."[14] However, this claim of success should be tempered by the fact that 39 percent has not yet been captured and that "some time" reflects a wide range from "seldom" to "quite frequently." Furthermore, e-government depends on public use of official government sites and not to the Internet in general.

In response to these criticisms, the annual report notes that over half of that 39 percent has a general lack of interest in using the Internet as well as a lack of understanding of the benefits of Internet use.[15] In essence, the implication is that these individuals seem to be satisfied with their present means of information gathering and use. However, as the e-Envoy noted, "the challenge is how we can continue to encourage those who remain disengaged to take advantage of the opportunities for access that now exist, and how we can help expand the activity of those who are already online so that the full potential of the Internet may be harnessed for users, businesses and public service providers alike."[16]

The goal of the central government was to make all government services available online by 2005 for the public's use 24/7/365. However, to create transparency and to generate the maximum impact, the government has concentrated on enabling a set of key e-services in areas such as benefits, education, health care, and personal tax that will likely have the largest impact in terms of user benefit, government efficiency, and alignment with overall policy priorities.

As the prime minister recognizes, "British businesses and citizens are not yet using government services online in the numbers that match the best in the world."[17] His plan is to make these services not only more convenient for the public to find and use, but also to invest in their improved delivery. An example of the direction in which services are moving can be found in the health care industry, where an electronic appointment-booking service in x-ray clinics is expected to reduce the number of missed appointments, save staff time, and reduce waiting times for other patients. Still, to achieve its goal of getting the public to rely on electronic services, the government needs to convince those groups that traditionally make heavy use of government services to continue to do so electronically. At the same time, "the devolution of government authority from the central to the regional and local levels implies that the local authorities will remain the key drivers for the development and implementation of" electronic service delivery.[18]

Despite the e-service priorities, critics such as George Kuk charge that the 2005 deadline means that government agencies rushed to create services without adequately considering the needs, expectations, and information-gathering behavior of those people they want to attract. Furthermore, "from the inception of e-government, the aim of encouraging disadvantaged groups (those with low incomes, the elderly, and individuals with disabilities) to take up the online services is more rhetoric than a reality. Unfortunately, there is still much to be done to fulfill the promise of e-government."[19] In addition, the critics question the extent to which service targets are achievable.

LOOKING TO THE FUTURE

As previously mentioned, one function of e-government in the United Kingdom is to promote communication between the public and government. With improved access to information and services, e-participation might occur. This refers to the involvement of the public in the policymaking process, whereby they express their views and share knowledge with government policymakers. At the same time, government needs to find new and innovative ways for that communication to occur.

In September 2004, Ian Watmore, the UK managing director of Accenture, a consulting and technology services company, became the first head of the Cabinet Office's e-Government Unit. This office is tasked with ensuring that ICT supports the government's business transactions and improves the efficiency and the delivery of public services to the public. The office is charged with seeing that government transforms service delivery and improves efficiency in the public service at a time when the government has a large percentage of its services online. The complication will be to ensure that those services are less departmental centric and more citizen centric—built around the information needs of the public.

Because the prime minister directed information technology professionals in government to ensure "that IT supports the business transformation of Government itself so that we can provide better, more efficient, public services," the specific responsibilities of the unit are to

- stimulate joined-up business-led IT strategies and policies;
- support citizen-centered public service reform;
- maximize the reuse and consistent application of common ICT components and systems across government;
- promote and assist joined-up identification and authentication across the public sector;
- enable corporate service transformation;
- be an IT change agent;
- sponsor cost-effective IT security;
- increase IT-enabled change capability/capacity;
- support mission-critical projects;
- build partnerships with IT suppliers;
- engage in stakeholder management;
- engage in local government stakeholder management;
- improve confidence in government IT;
- engage in common infrastructure development;
- support Directgov; and
- deliver knowledge network products.[20]

Undoubtedly, the new office of e-government will convert these responsibilities into goals and measurable objectives, outcomes, and targets. That office must also deal with stagnation in the public acceptance and the expectation of widespread use of e-government services. Complicating matters, most government services "only provide information rather than letting people carry out transactions." According to a report of the National Audit Office, "the public may show little interest in e-government unless it is cheaper, faster, and easier for people to carry out important tasks online than by traditional methods."[21] The report calls for government to pass cost saving for online services on to the public. Some incentives for using electronic services might be a lower cost for paying for a driver's license or a passport, access to free services, or faster service delivery.

After 2006, the government is also interested in holding e-enabled general elections. To that end, it is currently conducting pilot programs to test e-voting in local elections. Both e-participation and e-voting contribute to e-democracy, which is guided by five principles:

1. inclusion: a voice for all;
2. openness: electronic provision of information;
3. security and privacy: a safe place;
4. responsiveness: listening and responding to people;
5. deliberation: making the most of people's ideas.[22]

GOVERNMENT WEB SITES

With the existence of more than three thousand gov.uk domain-name Web sites and nine hundred central government Web sites, the public wants a portal that promotes one-stop shopping or at least guides them in their search for relevant information and services. They expect that any portal will be "clearly branded and heavily promoted."[23]

The Government Gateway (www.gateway.gov.uk/) is a centralized registration location for e-government services that fosters end-to-end transactions among agencies as well as their customers. "This means that in the future [through it], electronic transactions involving many different departments at once would be possible, ensuring a truly joined-up electronic public service. Over time, it is anticipated that the Gateway will handle a substantial part of the estimated 5–6 billion of annual government-related transactions."[24]

GovTalk (www.govtalk.gov.uk), which the Office of the e-Envoy created, provides key documents about the foundation of the UK's government strategy. It also aims to help government and industry leaders collaborate on e-government policies and standards.

The Office of Government Commerce (www.ogc.gov.uk), which deals with excellence in procurement, works with government departments to improve procurement and procurement management. It even maintains a Web page entitled "eProcurement Home," which covers news, events, projects, tools, useful Web links, resources, and more. Among the resources is the *eProcurement Strategy for Central Civil Government*.

> eProcurement is the term to describe the use of electronic methods in every stage of the purchasing process from identification of requirement through payment, and potentially to contract management. Electronic enablement of the purchasing process can be more specifically identified as sourcing for contractual processes . . .[;] eProcurement for transactional processes . . .[; and] ePayment (e.g., e-invoicing and self-billing).[25]

The Office of the Deputy Prime Minister provides a local home page (www.local gov.gov.uk/page.cfm?pageID = 74&Language = eng) that conveys a vision for the placement of local government within e-government. A complementary site, IDeA (www.idea.gov.uk), covers local e-government activities in the United Kingdom; however, it also encourages local governments worldwide to put e-government into practice.

The Freedom of Information Web site (www.foi.gov.uk) provides a forum for the public to request government records and for government to recognize the types of resources covered by the 2000 Freedom of Information Act. A good companion site is that of the Office of the Information Commission (www.informationcommissioner .gov.uk), which covers data protection, freedom of information, and privacy and electronic communications.

BARRIERS

The central government recognizes that e-government becomes a way to

- expand services, move more of them to the Internet, and make them more effective and efficient;
- provide the public with information useful to improve their lives and those of others;

- provide for e-procurement;
- foster e-democracy;[26] and
- promote e-commerce.

Despite such a broad involvement in e-government, Andrew Chadwick and Christopher May argue that the United Kingdom has been timid in the development of projects to realize each of these facets. They attribute the timidity to the cost of high-profile projects and the fact that a number of them have gone over budget. They also see e-government as managerially directed (i.e., focused on accountability and regulatory measures). Although access to current information advances the democratic processes, this is more of a by-product than a central thrust of e-government.[27] Explained another way, e-government in the United Kingdom has the above-mentioned five purposes; however, not all are of the same importance and at the same level of development.

E-government, combined with ICT, can help government modernize the economy and transform society, businesses, and public services. As Wilson Wong and Eric Welch argue, "more information delivered in a more timely fashion to citizens is expected to increase transparency of government, empowering citizens to more closely monitor government performance."[28] The result should be improved government accountability. However, a complication is that public opinion polls indicate that the public does not fully trust government and the information presented. Distrust impacts the extent to which the public will rely on e-government and its provision of services and information.

The United Kingdom, a constitutional monarchy with a parliamentary system of government, is not merely moving existing government functions and services to an electronic format. In some instances, it is rethinking those services, but that reconceptualization does not always reflect the public's service expectations and information-gathering behaviors. At times, citizens are unaware of which government services are available online, and many of the electronic services are vastly underutilized.

CONCLUSION

To realize the potential of e-government and to promote Internet use, the UK government has instigated campaigns (e.g., Get Started) to motivate the public to use the Internet and has combined those campaigns with the formation of a network of nearby online centers and training programs. Although the goal is to make the public feel more comfortable in using the Internet, at present use centers solely or largely on sending and receiving e-mail messages.[29] Yet, as some surveys indicate, despite the considerable effort of the central government to develop and market its vision of e-government, the public's perception of e-government is limited. The public prefers to use electronic services that do not require an extensive disclosure of personal information.

The United Kingdom is not currently considered to be one of the leading countries regarding the public's use of e-government.[30] In effect, use of e-government has peaked and slowed down in comparison to a number of other countries; however, there is optimism that the newly created head of e-government might develop a new strategy that reverses the trend and produces services that go beyond information provision and that embrace customer preferences and expectations. Nonetheless, e-government in the United Kingdom will not replace other means of public and government interaction.

NOTES

1. George Kuk, "The Digital Divide and the Quality of Electronic Service Delivery in Local Government in the United Kingdom," *Government Information Quarterly* 20, no. 4 (2003): 353.

2. Andrew Chadwick and Christopher May, "Interaction between States and Citizens in the Age of the Internet: 'e-Government' in the United States, Britain, and the European Union," *Governance: An International Journal of Policy, Administration and Institutions* 16, no. 2 (April 2003): 271–300. This article provides a historical overview of the emergence of e-government in Britain.

3. Cabinet Office, Office of the e-Envoy, *UK Online: Annual Report 2003* (London: Office of the e-Envoy), 3. Available at www.e-envoy.gov.uk, accessed July 8, 2004.

4. Cabinet Office, E-Government Unit, "Strategic Framework for Public Services," 1. Available at http://e-government.cabinetoffice.gov.uk/Estrategy/StrategicFrameworkArticle/fs/en?CON..., accessed July 12, 2004.

5. Cabinet Office, E-Government Unit, "Our Responsibilities" (London: E-Government Unit, n.d.), 1. Available at http://e-government.cabinetoffice.gov.ul/Home/Homepage/fs/en, accessed July 8, 2004.

6. Cabinet Office, Office of the e-Envoy, *UK Online*, 3.

7. Cabinet Office, E-Government Unit, "Strategic Framework for Public Services," 1–2. Available at http://e-government.cabinetoffice.gov.uk/EStrategy/StrategicFrameworkArticle/fs/en? CON..., accessed July 9, 2004.

8. "Prime Minister's Keynote Speech to e-Summit" (London: Prime Minister's Office, 2004), 2. Available at www.number10.gov.ukl/output/Page1734.asp, accessed July 8, 2004. For additional examples, see "Information Age Government," in *Modernising Government White Paper* (London: Cabinet Office, E-Government Unit, 1999). Available at www.archive.official-documents.co.uk/document/cm43/4310/4310-05.htm, accessed July 9, 2004.

9. "Information Age Government," 8–9. See also UKGovTalk, "e-Services Documents: e-Government Schema Guidelines for XML" (London: Cabinet Office, 2004). Available at www.govtalk.gov.uk/schemasstandards/eservices_document2.asp?docnum=859, accessed July 9, 2004. For other Web guidelines, see Cabinet Office, E-Government Unit, "Index of Web Guidelines Related Publications" (London: Cabinet Office, n.d.). Available at: http://e-government.cabinet office.gov.ukl/Resources/WebGuidelines/fs/en, accessed July 9, 2004.

10. See Cabinet Office, "Measurement Framework for the e-Economy" (London: Cabinet Office, 2004). Available at http://e-government.cabinetoffice.gov.uk/Resources/EStatmap/fs/en, accessed July 9, 2004.

11. See Cabinet Office, E-Government Unit, *Illustrated Handbook for Web Management Teams* (London: Cabinet Office, 2004). Available at http://e-government.cabinetoffice.gov.uk?resources/Web GuidelinesArticle/fs/en? CONTE..., accessed July 12, 2004. This guide explains different metrics that Webmasters might consider in their evaluation of their Web sites. It advises that cookies do not comprise a reliable method for determining the number of users or for identifying repeat users.

12. Cabinet Office, e-Government Unit, "Web Handbook Checklist" (London: Cabinet Office, n.d.), 1–3. Available at http://e-government.cabinetoffice.gov.uk/Resources/WebHandbookIndex 1Article/fs/en?C..., accessed July 12, 2004. Additional performance metrics apply to the Web sites of local government; see Office of the Deputy Prime Minister, "News Release" (London: Office of the Deputy Prime Minister, April 2004). Available at www.odm.gov.uk/pns/DisplayPN.cgi?pn_id =2004_0112, accessed July 12, 2004.

13. "Information Age Government," 5.

14. Cabinet Office, Office of the e-Envoy, *UK Online*, 6.

15. Cabinet Office, Office of the e-Envoy, *UK Online*, 7.

16. Cabinet Office, Office of the e-Envoy, *UK Online*, 8.

17. "Information Age Government," 6.

18. Kuk, "Digital Divide and Quality of Electronic Service Delivery," 354.

19. Kuk, "Digital Divide and Quality of Electronic Service Delivery," 361.

20. Cabinet Office, E-Government Unit, "Responsibilities" (London: Cabinet Office, 2005). Available at www.cabinetoffice.gov.uk/e-government/responsibilities/, accessed June 11, 2005.

21. "Public Should Benefit from E-government Savings," *ZDNet UK News,* April 5, 2002. Available at http://news.zdnet.co.uk/internet/0,39020369,2107816,00.htm, accessed September 13, 2004. The National Audit Office report is entitled *Better Public Services through E-government* (www.nao.org .uk/).

22. Accenture, *eGovernment Leadership: High Performance, Maximum Value* (New York: Accenture, 2004), 34. Available at www.accenture.com, accessed July 8, 2004.

23. Accenture, *eGovernment Leadership*, 30.

24. Cabinet Office, E-Government Unit, *The Government Gateway* (London: Cabinet Office, 2004), 1. Available at www.iagchampions.gov/uk/Briefings/BriefingsArticle/fs/en?CONTENT _ID = 40000..., accessed July 12, 2004.

25. Office of Government Commerce, "What Is eProcurement?" (London: Office of Government Commerce, 2004). Available at www.ogc.gov.uk/index.asp?id = 2363, accessed July 12, 2004.

26. See Cabinet Office, "In the Search of Democracy" (London: Cabinet Office, 2004). Available at www.democracy.gov.uk, accessed July 10, 2004.

27. Chadwick and May, "Interaction between States and Citizens."

28. Wilson Wong and Eric Welch, "Does E-Government Promote Accountability? A Comparative Analysis of Website Openness and Government Accountability," *Governance: An International Journal of Policy, Administration and Institutions* 17, no 2 (April 2004): 276.

29. For additional initiatives, see Cabinet Office, Office of the e-Envoy, *UK Online*, 10–11.

30. RAND Europe, *Benchmarking e-Government in Europe and the US.* Prepared in cooperation with SIBIS [Statistical Indicators Benchmarking the Information Society] (Bonn, Germany, 2003), 38, 50. Available at www.sibis-eu.org, accessed July 8, 2004. See also Accenture's *eGovernment Leadership* series. The annual report labels the UK among those countries that are above average in Internet penetration but have below-average use of e-government (see www.accenture.com).

• *4* •

E-government in Canada

Kirsti Nilsen

$\mathcal{C}$anada's e-government program has ranked first every year since Accenture began to rank the e-government landscape in 2001. In its first annual report,[1] this global marketing company ranked Canada first in overall maturity and as first of three "Innovative Leaders" because of its coordinated approach across the whole of government, its depth and breadth of service maturity, its adoption of customer relationship management techniques, and its portal, the Canada Site. In 2005, Canada continued to maintain its lead through "impressive accomplishments," including the redesign of the Canada Site with gateways and clusters tailored to users and by providing most-commonly used services online, ensuring transaction security, and scoring high in customer service maturity.[2] The e-government program is customer centered, takes a whole-of-government approach, and has transformed service delivery to gain better operational efficiencies.

E-government developed in an incremental manner, progressing through various stages:

- The first encouraged the use of information and communication technologies (ICTs) in government.
- The second considered how the government's role on the Internet ought to work.
- The third developed computer and Internet skills among Canadians.
- The fourth encouraged electronic commerce.
- The fifth connected Canadians to the government through a structured e-government initiative, which is still evolving.

This chapter discusses these stages by showing how Canada became an e-government leader. It includes a short history of e-government development, examines the extent to which Canadians embrace e-government, and looks at the future for e-government in Canada. The focus is on the federal government level—neither the ten provinces and two territories nor metropolitan or regional e-government developments. At all levels, e-government, to some extent, is encouraged and expedited through federal initiatives such as the Canada Site's portal, which provides horizontal access to government information and services.[3]

DEVELOPMENTAL PHASES OF E-GOVERNMENT

E-government development occurred in two broad phases. The first one involved making information available online, and the second phase was initiated by the Governor-General's 1999 Speech from the Throne,[4] which committed the government to making all public services available online by 2004 and spawned the Government On-Line (GOL) initiative.[5] Budgetary restrictions influenced these developments and motivated government interest through the 1990s. Departments were expected to operate "like businesses," and there was considerable incentive to reduce the workforce and expand the use of ICTs.[6]

Phase One: Information Availability

The intensity and speed of development of the first phase of e-government from 1990 to 1999 suggest that, in the late 1980s and early 1990s, there had been considerable policy discussion. By April 1994, Treasury Board Secretariat (the central agency that manages the federal government's financial, personnel, and administrative responsibilities, including coordination of information policy and information management) issued *Blueprint for Renewing Government Services Using Information Technology*, which it began to implement in late 1995.[7] Focusing on the role of ICTs within government, the *Blueprint* was the first document that specifically called for a move from an organization-centric to a citizen-centric perspective. It envisioned "government services that were affordable, accessible and responsive," and called for direct single-window access for multiple services, transparent and seamless service delivery using departmental clusters, shared information and computing resources, and a paperless environment. Except for the hopeful (but doomed) call for a "paperless environment," one can look at the current state of e-government in Canada and see that the government moved forward quite successfully in reaching this ambitious vision.

Though the term *e-government* or *electronic government* did not appear in the *Blueprint,* it is evident that this was a truly significant policy directive on the road to e-government in Canada. It provides an excellent example of what Andrew Chadwick and Christopher May call the "managerial model," which calls for an improvement in the flow of information within government. Information becomes something that can be "delivered" to empower those previously unable to access it.[8]

The Role of the Information Highway Advisory Council   Motivated, to some extent, by how e-government in the United States was emerging and by the unfolding World Wide Web, the government wanted to ensure that the development of the so-called information highway[9] would contribute to Canada's goals and objectives. It established the Information Highway Advisory Council (IHAC) in early 1994, which issued reports in both 1995 and 1997.[10] The first report endorsed the *Blueprint* and made a number of recommendations that the council thought would result in significant savings and improved quality of service to the public. It urged the government to act as a "persuasive model user" of ICT, suggesting that governments at all levels in Canada "should "re-engineer themselves.""[11]

The second report, which focused on the growth of the Internet, urged government to "play a vital role in promoting both the Internet and electronic commerce."[12] Given that the *Blueprint* document predated the formation of the council and had already laid the groundwork for government action, the council is perhaps best remembered for producing a consultative model that generated support and provided justification for action, rather than direction.

Moving from Silos toward Portals   At the same time as the council was considering the implications of the information highway, individual government departments were promoting the use of ICTs in various ways. Industry Canada, which was in the forefront, actively encouraged the use of the technology to spur economic growth. Beginning in 1994, through its Community Access Program, Industry Canada created "CAP sites" where Canadians could develop skills and access computers and the Internet. Through the SchoolNet program, it also placed computers in schools and public libraries. In 1996, it launched *Strategis,* a comprehensive Web site designed to provide business and consumer information and to encourage Internet use by small and medium-sized businesses. Departmental adoption of ICTs was viewed in the mid-1990s as a money-saving measure that would streamline government and save on labor costs. Human Resources and Development Canada, for example, replaced five thousand frontline workers with self-service kiosks.[13]

During this time, the federal government encouraged cross-departmental initiatives. In March 1995, a government-wide Internet strategy was approved. It called for the creation of standards to guide the development of government Web pages and the establishment of "a primary Government of Canada Internet site to provide a corporate-wide federal presence on the Internet."[14] The bilingual Canada Site opened in December 1995; by March 1996, seventy federal government institutions had World Wide Web sites accessible from the Canada Site.

A government report responding to IHAC's first report identified "getting government right" as a goal, and to get government "right," it needed to ensure "better services and more affordable, accessible and responsive government" as well as to make government a "model user and catalyst" for ICT developments across Canada. The report argued that providing government services electronically would "bring about a qualitative improvement in the responsiveness and accessibility of government."[15] Underlying "Getting Government Right" was the need to control government deficits and debt,[16] and the financial imperative behind the agenda pushed the country forward in the development of e-government.

The Most-Connected Nation   The Governor-General's Throne Speech in September 1997 committed Canada to making its "information and knowledge infrastructure accessible to all Canadians . . . [and to] making Canada the most connected nation in the world" by 2000.[17] This commitment led to the "Connecting Canadians" initiative, with Industry Canada as the lead department. In various ways each program within the initiative sought to bring Internet access to a variety of communities, particularly in rural and remote areas.

Electronic Commerce   The Treasury Board identified electronic commerce as a "key initiative" in implementing the *Blueprint* and set the goal of making e-commerce the "preferred way of doing government business by 1998."[18] It was assumed that the emergence of e-commerce would lead to "a marked improvement in government effectiveness and efficiency,"[19] and, in 1998, Industry Canada's Electronic Commerce Task Force argued that government could play a key role, by "demonstrating the advantages of electronic service delivery, building critical mass and trust among users, and piloting new technologies."[20]

Throughout this period, and still today, the term *electronic commerce* was used without clear definition. Sometimes it referred to all electronic transactions and at other times only to the government's internal and external money transactions. The auditor general added to the ambiguity: "For the government, [it] involves using computers and telecommunications systems for a wide range of activities . . . they can be financial such as transferring funds, or non-financial, such as providing or exchanging data and information,"[21] thus covering a spectrum of activities for what has become known as e-government.

By the End of Phase One   At the end of 1998, the Canadian federal government was still using a managerial model with individual departments providing information through their Web presence over the Internet. The Canada Site was beginning to act as a portal, but there was very limited interaction capability. However, there had been much activity behind the scenes and a move toward a more consultative model exemplified by IHAC. The government was ready to move on to a structured e-government initiative.

Phase Two: Government On-Line

The second phase began with the October 1999 Speech from the Throne, which expanded the 1997 most-connected-nation goal to cover government's connection to Canadians.[22] This commitment led to the launch of the Government On-Line (GOL) initiative in 2000, to deliver government's programs, services, and information over the Internet.

This speech was the first time e-government was specifically and clearly supported on the Canadian federal government agenda. An important question is, What motivated the government to move in this direction? An October 2000 report on the government's online activities suggests an answer that included three factors: ICTs were changing the expectations of citizens and businesses in their relationships with government; globalization (and the growing global e-marketplace) meant that public policy could not be made in isolation of the global context; and there was a drive within government to provide for citizen-centered service delivery.[23] Treasury Board claimed that e-government would "transform the fundamental relationship between government and citizens."[24] Outside observers cite the budgetary crisis of the early 1990s, labor costs, the influence of the ICT industry, the push for public–private partnerships, and other such factors as more likely motivators.[25]

In August 2000, Treasury Board, which oversaw the GOL initiative, touted the benefits of e-government (better service, better government, and stimulation of e-commerce) and described GOL as a multiyear project[26] that would bring federal organizations "on-line in stages, with all commonly used programs and services on-line" by the deadline, with the goal of using ICTs "to provide Canadians with enhanced access to improved citizen-centred, integrated services, anytime, anywhere and in the official language of their choice."[27]

First-Generation Government On-Line Strategy   Just days after the 1999 Throne Speech, Treasury Board announced a strategy for making government more responsive and affordable through its "Electronic Service Delivery Vision" for "citizen-centered government."[28] By December 1999, the "first generation" Government On-Line

Strategy had been created to meet the 2004 objective (in 2001 the deadline was moved to 2005). The strategy set out three tiers that were intended to build on one another to create a fully secure system for electronic service delivery for the government:

1. Tier 1 would establish a strong federal presence on the Internet by December 31, 2000 (with departmental and program information, basic search, and online availability of forms);
2. Tier 2 would deliver secure, interactive electronic services by 2005 (with full electronic delivery of key services featuring e-commerce, e-payments, supply chain management, customer service, and so on); and
3. Tier 3, with no fixed deadline, would extend service delivery with external partners (through leading edge pilot projects featuring multi-jurisdictional services, a citizen-centric approach, and customer relationship management.).[29]

As Sunny Marche and James D. McNiven write, this "articulation is more practical and less ambitious than the sweeping vision of the original Throne Speech. Gone is the notion of providing all services anytime, anywhere, which has been replaced with a more specific list." They point out that the idea of online communities was present in the objectives of both Tier 2 and Tier 3, the "only element of the plan that potentially begins to move in the direction of e-governance instead of e-government."[30]

A distinction has always been made in Canada between governance and government—"the delivery of a service is a function of government, while determining whether or not to provide a service relates to governance."[31] By the time the first-generation e-government strategy was developed, a related distinction was beginning to be made in Canadian discourse between the terms *e-government* and *e-governance*. The former refers to "the provision of routine government information and transactions using . . . Internet technologies," while e-governance is a "technology-mediated relationship between citizens and their governments" with the potential for "electronic deliberation over civic communication, over policy evolution, and in democratic expressions of civic will."[32]

In March 2000, the Clerk of the Privy Council (who heads the federal public service in Canada) committed the public service to modernized service delivery using e-government, with information on programs and services and with key forms online the end of that year.[33] In order to present a unified face to the world on their Internet sites, Canadian federal organizations were encouraged to implement consistent "common look and feel" (CLF) standards that were originally issued in May 2000, and a new version of the Canada Site was launched incorporating the CLF guidelines.[34]

By December 2000, the government declared that the Tier 1 objective had been met, with "100% of identified information services and forms" online.[35] This claim, however, raises the question of what percentage of the total had been "identified."

The Years 2001–2003, Moving Forward on Several Fronts   The government recommitted itself, in January 2001, to connecting Canadians to the Internet and to e-government by developing and strengthening its information infrastructure; by closing the digital divide, particularly in rural, remote, northern, and Aboriginal communities; and by improving privacy and copyright protections on the Internet.[36] In December 2001, in a Federal Budget announcement, the deadline for achieving GOL was moved from 2004 to the end of 2005 "to make way for the heightened security agenda."[37]

Two guiding principles for GOL were enunciated in 2001: (1) organizing services and information around the needs and expectations of citizens, and (2) taking a whole-of-government approach. These principles suggest that GOL was meant to be citizen-centric rather than organization-centric and that it should be responsive to citizen wants, rather than organizational priorities. According to its Web site, GOL was designed to be centrally coordinated, providing services collaboratively across government departments and agencies and across jurisdictions, including the involvement of the private and not-for-profit sectors. Furthermore, GOL was meant to be transformative "by encouraging the re-engineering, consolidation and integration of services."[38] One means to achieve citizen-centric service was the *clustering* of services, which had been instituted on the Canada Site in January 2001. Clustering meant that information and services were grouped together under three main headings: "Services for Canadians," "Services for Non-Canadians," and "Services for Canadian Business." The goal was to "ensure seamless, one-stop access to various information areas and a range of functionality, based on users' needs and regardless of their knowledge of the government's organizational structure."[39]

Canadian government officials later claimed that clustering was the right starting point because it brought a cultural change of working horizontally and provided a platform for integrated government services. It also served to highlight horizontal issues such as governance, partnerships, content management, and service standards.[40] The "clusters" are now often called "audience-based gateways."

Broadband   The 2001 Throne Speech called for ensuring that broadband access would be available to all Canadian communities by 2004, including in rural and remote regions that were not well served by the private sector.[41] Industry Canada immediately established a (mostly private sector) National Broadband Task Force to map out a strategy to achieve the government's goal. The task force's final report claimed that broadband would have a significant impact on e-governance, in particular in the operation of the political system, in public service delivery, and on the relationship among government, the private sector, and civil society. The report also maintained that it is the role of government to ensure effective utilization of broadband networks through e-government, as well as e-health, e-learning, and e-research.[42]

When the task force completed its work, it was assumed that the government would quickly implement the strategy. However, progress has been slow; funding was not immediately available owing to increased security requirements following September 11, 2001. In early 2003, the Conference Board of Canada warned that broadband was not accessible to "72 per cent of Canadian communities, mostly in rural and remote regions,"[43] and in fall 2004, the government made a commitment to ensuring affordable high-speed Internet access for all Canadian communities by 2005.[44] Because this did not occur, in April 2005 a Telecommunications Review Panel was asked to submit a report by the end of the year recommending mechanisms to ensure access for all Canadians to high-speed networks.[45]

Government Online Advisory Panel   In 2001, an independent (mostly private sector) Government Online Advisory Panel was established to provide advice over the next two years on issues related to the government online objectives. In its 2002 report, the panel argued that government should immediately change the way it operated and adopt a client-driven approach. The panel urged the government to "commit to citizen-centric service as an urgent priority," transforming its "organizational 'silos' into an integrated, multi-channel, multi-service delivery network operating across programs, departments and jurisdictions."[46] However, it warned that transformation was not possible under the current governance structure of the GOL initiative. In its 2003 final report, the panel pointed out that if the government did not transform its services as recommended in the 2002 report, the services would deteriorate and government would "lose its relevance to Canadians." The panel urged the government to implement "an integrated service delivery network that offers a similar quality of service over the Internet, on the phone, in person, or through the mail, and that operates seamlessly across different programs, departments and orders of government."[47]

The Auditor General's Critique   Each year, the auditor general of Canada "audits federal government operations and provides Parliament with independent information, advice and assurance to help hold the government to account for its stewardship of public funds" and issues no more than three reports on varying departments or issues, along with an annual report.[48]

In November 2003, the focus was on Government On-Line. While the auditor general, Sheila Fraser, found much to praise in Canada's e-government program, several problems in achieving the 2005 deadline were identified. The report warned that with "two years remaining in the six-year . . . GOL . . . initiative, the government needs to devote immediate attention to dealing with some important risks. If it does not, GOL could become an expensive and underused vehicle." The report noted that, while the planning process was successful, it "did not fully establish specific outcomes that are expected to be achieved by 2005 in terms of the overall GOL objective of full service transformation."[49] The failure to define specific outcomes was one of the main points raised in the report, along with governance and the need to provide greater direction and leadership to government departments, and the consequent failure to develop detailed plans for service transformation within departments.

With respect to funding of the GOL initiative, the initial authorization for implementing services by 2005 was $880 million to be administered by the GOL Management Office, with additional costs to be funded by departments and agencies. The auditor general's report noted the lack of planning within departments for this funding and that the actual cost by 2005 would be "much greater than $880 million, given that departments are spending large amounts of money on their own internal on-line projects." The report noted that in 2001, "the government estimated that the cost of putting all key services on-line may be over $2 billion, based on department and agency projections" and that "the full cost of delivering all services electronically is not known."[50]

A December 2003 reorganization of public services moved responsibility for implementation and operation of GOL from Treasury Board to the Department of Public Works and Government Service Canada (PWGSC). Policymaking and overall service delivery remained with Treasury Board.[51] The restructuring that led to this shift in responsibility occurred just after the auditor general's report was prepared—but before it was officially released. It is difficult to know whether the report had any influence on this decision on GOL governance, but it does appear that some of the questions raised in her report (and by the advisory panel) were addressed by the reorganization.

Responding to the Auditor General's Critique   An examination of the first two GOL annual reports (covering 2001 and 2002)[52] illustrates the problem of fuzzy objectives. In the first report there is no mention of objectives or goals or measurable outcomes; rather there are "commitments" to make government more accessible, to make online service better and more responsive, to build trust and confidence in online delivery, and to serve all Canadians, ensuring choice of channels, formats, and language. The second report stated that one of the key goals of GOL is "to increase satisfaction with government services by providing on-line access to the most commonly used federal services." None of these commitments or goals was measurable without the collection and reporting of baseline data.

Not long after the auditor general's report was published, there was a significant attempt to address outcomes. In the spring of 2004, a "performance measurement regime" was established to improve the quality of the data collected and assess better "progress being made."[53] An October 2004 performance measurement document listed a set of outcomes that it stated had been in place since 2000 but went on to list a revised set of expected outcomes and outline methodology and data sources for measurement.[54] These outcomes are no less fuzzy than earlier "commitments." And none are measurable in any quantitative sense. For example, one expected outcome is "convenience," which is described as "Federal Web sites are easily identifiable and easy to navigate. Relevant on-line information and services are put together in ways that make sense from a citizen/client perspective."[55] However, the 2005 annual report (covering 2004) is replete with data and notes that "key performance indicators across service delivery channels" (Internet, phone, fax, post, and in-person) are being developed to help efficiently and cost-effectively assess how services are meeting citizen and client needs.[56]

Transaction Security   Security and legitimacy of transactions have been an ongoing concern, and in the mid-1990s the government instituted a number of public key infrastructure (PKI) projects to demonstrate secure electronic delivery. The result was Secure Channel, which is dedicated to ensuring the security and privacy of online transactions with the federal government. While the auditor general described the channel as "one of the world's first such services for mass use by individuals that incorporate the 'digital signature certificate' concept," she questioned how much progress had been made on this "highly complex and costly" project and the work still needed before "all clients can fully complete a binding transaction in real time without leaving the department's Web site."[57] Nevertheless, by autumn 2004, PWGSC described Secure Channel as the "common electronic infrastructure of the Government of Canada" and "a prime enabler of GOL" to which all government agencies had migrated by the fall of 2003.[58] The auditor general's continuing concerns about government-wide security of information technology were expressed in a February 2005 report. With respect to GOL, that report warned that "before departments and agencies can deliver their services, either by wireless devices or on-line on the Secure Channel network, they will need to meet stringent baseline IT security standards."[59]

Pulling Back in 2004   Canada never did become the most-connected nation, though it has ranked second behind the United States for several years. In early 2003, the government began a review of all its programs that connected Canadians "to information and knowledge."[60] An evaluation of Industry Canada's Community Access Program (CAP) concluded that because there had been much progress, it was no longer relevant to help provide affordable Internet access, except in order to address the digital divide among underprivileged Canadians and those in rural, remote, and northern regions and to improve accessibility for persons with disabilities.[61] It is clear that except in the digital-divide areas, the government saw the basic objectives of the Connecting Canadians initiative as having been met.

GOL in 2004   The December 2003 transfer of responsibility for GOL administration and operation to PWGSC resulted in a shift in priorities. For the first time, guiding principles were clearly enunciated for GOL. Its services were to be

- bilingual and client driven;
- accessible from home, the workplace, or public access points twenty-four hours a day, seven days a week;
- intuitive, easy to use, and easy to navigate;
- accessible to citizens with special needs;
- respectful of privacy, security, and confidentiality; and
- implemented to ensure Canadians have choices in how they access government.[62]

In 2004, the focus was on the development of an efficient, cost-effective, and sustainable way to deliver online services. PWGSC further narrowed the original service targets, which had moved from putting online *all* government information and services, to putting "over 130" and then "all 130" commonly used services online.[63] PWGSC maintained that "recent international studies" recommended that "governments need to focus on services that are suitable for on-line delivery and that deliver value to the user, as opposed to simply putting all their services on-line." PWGSC further emphasized that "traditional ways of obtaining services, that is by telephone, by mail and in person, will continue and are constantly being improved so all citizens have better access to Government of Canada information and services."[64]

HOW SUCCESSFUL IS E-GOVERNMENT TODAY?

PWGSC described GOL as "a government-wide initiative with each department having responsibility for implementing its own on-line services while maintaining access for clients to traditional modes of service delivery." It stated that GOL was launched because of demand and because it would "eventually save the government money." PWGSC provided figures that suggest that the cost of Internet transactions are one-tenth of those by telephone, one-twentieth of those by mail, and one-thirtieth of those conducted in person and, since "the federal government conducts about 400 million transactions each year, savings will accrue as Canadians and businesses increasingly use the Internet to complete transactions."[65] Gilles Paquet maintains that providing services online "may entail a shift of the cost burden of service delivery toward the citizen."[66]

One wonders how much saving money has driven the entire GOL initiative. Nevertheless, the initiative has accomplished a good deal,[67] and any examination of the many government portals and individual Web sites finds an impressive range of information and transactional services. The GOL initiative was the driving force behind e-government development beginning in 1999, and this initiative is slated to end in 2005.

Although Canada is first on the Accenture rankings, the company's 2005 report notes that the country needs to progress further in "customer" service.[68] Canada is second, behind the United States, on the Conference Board's 2004 Connectedness Index, which ranks countries that are members of the Organisation for Economic Cooperation and Development (OECD) on availability of ICT and the price, reach, and use of ICT. On this index Canada led on *price* "because Canadian charges for Internet access, phone connections, local and long-distance calls are low," but the United States led on *availability* and *use* (because of e-business indicators: Internet purchases and business-to-business e-commerce), and Sweden led on *reach* indicators.[69]

Departments can use these external rankings to generate support and increased funding, but internal evaluation is essential for long-term success of any e-government program. As the report of the auditor general noted, the GOL program did not have

> appropriate (specific, measurable, achievable, and relevant) expected outcomes [and,] without specifying clear outcomes to work toward, the government would not be able to say whether GOL as a whole, or individual projects associated with it, could be considered successful. . . . Accordingly, the government could declare victory in 2005 without having to measure its accomplishments against a set of clear expected outcomes.[70]

Treasury Board developed outcomes for the end of 2005, and it benchmarked the level of service maturity and transformation expected. Convenience and credibility were to be assessed by departments using self-assessment tools.[71] There is no mention of three-click access—as emphasized by the Bush administration in the United States—as an aim. The oft-repeated goal of having the 130 most commonly used information and transactional services (provided by departments and agencies) online has yet to fully materialize. There are varying degrees of functionality among these services,[72] and the rationale for selecting these particular 130 services is unclear.

Suggesting that most citizens use the Internet for information, Tom Mitchinson and Mark Ratner believe the government has focused primarily on making transactional services available and has "not been proactive in thoroughly evaluating . . . [its] record holdings and making the appropriate records available in a format that allows for easy accessibility by the public."[73]

HOW WELL HAVE CANADIANS EMBRACED E-GOVERNMENT?

The 2004 Accenture report states that, unlike that of many countries, Canada's e-government action plan is built on "a remarkably solid foundation of fact—based on known information from its customer base."[74] Over the years, the government established an Internet Research Panel and conducted five online surveys and two sets of national online focus groups with Canadian Internet users.[75]

Almost 600 million interactions (out of a total of 853.1 million interactions—both informational and transactional services—with government) occurred on the Internet. An independent survey firm found that 71 percent of Internet users had used a government of Canada Web site in the past twelve months; on average there were 1.2 million visits to the Canada Site every month, and 81 percent of users of government services reported being satisfied or very satisfied; GOL itself reports that 94 percent were satisfied or very satisfied, based on departmental data.[76] The data on number of monthly visits to the Canada Site are probably based on the number of hits, and it is difficult to know what percentage of these hits represents users who are proactively seeking information and what percentage is random or accidental hits.[77] Data on transactional uses are more robust.

Online filing of tax returns has provided the breakthrough that brings many Canadians to the transactional level of e-government. Forty percent of individual tax returns for 2003 were filed electronically, and this percentage is predicted to increase to 70 percent for the 2007 tax year. In addition, 90 percent of applications for federal jobs were received online. However, these levels of usage of electronic transactions represents only 30 percent of clients, and "the number of clients completing their transaction on traditional, more costly channels remained relatively static."[78] These findings raise concern that not enough Canadians are accessing the online services, and the government needs to develop "a strategy to ensure on-line services are more widely used" and to encourage citizens to migrate "from traditional service channels such as the telephone, mail or in-person service to the electronic channel."[79] A migration strategy, however, seems at cross-purposes with the advisory panel's recommendations and the program's own support for multiple channels of communication. Furthermore, the 2005 Accenture citizen survey found that "only 41 percent of Canadians felt that government services and departments were effective at working together"; citizens want "integrated and seamless service regardless of the channel they choose."[80]

FUTURE DEVELOPMENT FOR E-GOVERNMENT

The Government On-Line Initiative ended in 2005, but that does not mean the demise of e-government in Canada. The funding will shift to another centralized initiative. "In the years ahead, expertise and best practices gained through the GOL Initiative will be channelled to other government-wide initiatives that will transform government to be more accessible and responsive to the needs of Canadians."[81] PWGSC claims it will continue its efforts "to ensure a successful conclusion to the GOL initiative, and build on its experience for the delivery of next generation services."[82]

Service Canada

In late 2003, the prime minister established the Expenditure Review Committee (ERC) to review all government spending and recommend cuts for the 2005 budget. The committee reviewed horizontal policies and programs, the management and use of ICT, and service delivery infrastructure. It then stated that the delivery of federal services and programs to Canadians could be "substantially improved—while also reducing overhead cost to the taxpayer" through implementation of Service Canada, part of a whole-of-government service transformation agenda initiated by Treasury Board, to provide "one-stop service to meet the full range of client needs."[83] The goal, as Lucienne Robillard, then president of Treasury Board, pointed out in 2003, is to make e-government simply government.[84]

Service Canada is the projected next step in Canadian e-government development. The Service Canada concept of creating a completely separate agency to deliver all citizen-centered services and benefits, through all appropriate channels, is not new, and there have been previous efforts in this direction.[85] The ERC stated that the "Service Canada model fits perfectly with its mandate of finding ways to improve the delivery of federal programs and also lowering costs." According to ERC,

> Service Canada will provide Canadians with simpler, more convenient and higher-quality services with increased options. Benefits will include better coordination of the delivery of federal services; a more accessible and effective federal presence in regions; and the elimination of waste, overlap and duplication. Net savings over the five years will be $3.05 billion.[86]

ERC considers Service Canada to be one of the biggest single reforms in federal operations and projects that the reform will be accomplished over a three-year period on a government-wide basis.

Alden Cuddihey of Accenture believes that Service Canada "points to a multi-channel approach and personalized, two-way relationships," and focuses on "outcomes in terms of client satisfaction, cost savings and efficiencies, policy outcomes and compliance, and accountability and transparency." Its success will require horizontal and vertical implementation and "partnerships across government and with the private sector, non-governmental organizations and volunteer groups." He sees Canada as "still playing catch-up to its citizen's expectations" and says that "what we have not seen yet is the radical reinvention of service delivery in the government sector. . . . [N]ow is . . . [the time] to move from driving the development of e-government for its own sake, to driving public sector value through transformed service delivery—giving citizens better service."[87]

Problems in Realizing Service Canada

Canada has succeeded in the implementation of a comprehensive e-government initiative. Yet, for Service Canada to be successful, it will have to overcome political, financial, and structural barriers. Politically there are no guarantees that the proposals for Service Canada, or for the envisioned service transformation, will be sustained. The earmarked funding might disappear if there is an election that brings in a more conservative government. If the underlying purpose of Service Canada is actually to save money, then the goal of better serving Canadians through enhanced service delivery might be undermined.

The structural barriers may be even greater. By breaking down boundaries of authority and accountability, e-government and the forthcoming "service transformation" create particular problems in Canada, where accountability flows vertically to a single minister. This verticality frustrates horizontal action, and it is argued that "already the integrative nature of Internet portals and the manner in which services are delivered by them highlights the need for different and multiple forms of accountability."[88] These problems are not unique to Canada but are complicated because of the nature of Canadian federalism. As one observer points out, "e-government makes the territorial segmentation of government . . . increasingly irrelevant."[89]

CONCLUSION

While GOL succeeded in providing electronic service delivery, it failed "to generate fundamental change in the governance regime."[90] E-government requires a shift in the authority and accountability structures. Yet, "even the notion of a government-wide citizen-centric portal causes interdepartmental problems."[91] Service Canada is the next likely step for e-government in Canada, but it is not the ultimate goal. It is simply part of a broader vision of "Next Generation Public Services" that encompasses a "whole-of-government service transformation agenda."[92] Thus, despite the barriers, Canada is forging ahead with its new approach to public service transformation, which it argues is "not fiscally driven" but intended to "reach more Canadians with the right services at the right time."[93] This agenda may well address Accenture's concerns about "customer" service, but whether this focus will transform the fundamental relationship between government and citizens is another question.[94] For this to happen, government needs to move beyond a focus on e-government that is defined "solely by information technology, service delivery and methods of operation" to a broader definition of e-government that grows out of and serves an information society.[95] Canada is moving in this direction. Clearly, though it is not yet ready to make the leap, Canada is poised to move toward a reconceptualization of the model in figure 1.1 that would place e-governance at the center.

NOTES

1. Accenture, *e-Government Leadership: Rhetoric vs Reality—Closing the Gap* (New York: Accenture, 2001), 22–23. Available at www.accenture.com/xdoc/en/industries/government/2001FullReport.pdf, accessed May 16, 2005.

2. Accenture, *Leadership in Customer Service: New Expectations, New Experiences* (New York: Accenture 2005), 11, 60–61. Available at www.accenture.com/xdoc/en/industries/government/insights/leadership_customerservice.pdf, accessed May 16, 2005.

3. Canada Site [portal]. Available at www.canada.gc.ca, accessed May 7, 2005.

4. In Canada, a Speech from the Throne (commonly referred to as the Throne Speech) is given by the governor general (who is the Queen's representative in Canada) at the beginning of each new parliamentary session, announcing the government's agenda and setting out the policies and legislation that the government intends to introduce.

5. Barbara Ann Allan, Luc Juillet, Gilles Paquet, and Jeffrey Roy, "E-Governance and Government On-line in Canada: Partnerships, People, and Prospects," *Government Information Quarterly* 18 (2001): 95.

6. Graham Longford, "Rethinking the Virtual State: A Critical Perspective on E-Government," in *Seeking Convergence in Policy and Practice: Communications in the Public Interest*, ed. Marita Moll and Leslie Regan Shade (Ottawa: Canadian Centre for Policy Alternatives, 2004), 2:109–40.

7. Treasury Board Secretariat, *Blueprint for Renewing Government Services Using Information Technology*, Executive Summary (Ottawa: Treasury Board, 2004), ix, xiii. Available at www.tbs-sct.gc.ca/pubs_pol/ciopubs/tb_oimp/uit-ati/uit-ati_e.asp, accessed May 7, 2005.

8. Andrew Chadwick and Christopher May, "Interaction between States and Citizens in the Age of the Internet: 'e-Government' in the United States, Britain, and the European Union," *Governance: An International Journal of Policy, Administration and Institutions* 16, no. 2 (April 2003): 277–78.

9. The term *information superhighway* was not used in Canada.

10. The Information Highway Advisory Council is generally identified as either IHAC1 or

IHAC2. In IHAC1 it gathered advice on fifteen policy issues beginning in 1994 and published several interim reports until submission of a final report in September 1995. IHAC2 refers to the period after it was revived in June 1996 when IHAC members were asked to devote another year to giving further advice on how to carry forward the policy agenda, and ended with submission of a final report in September 1997.

11. Information Highway Advisory Council (IHAC), *Connection, Community, Content: The Challenge of the Information Highway,* Final Report [Phase 1] (Ottawa: Industry Canada, 1995), xi, 135–39. Available at www.hc-sc.gc.ca/ohih-bsi/pubs/1995_connect/rpt_e.html, accessed May 7, 2005.

12. IHAC, *Preparing Canada for a Digital World,* Final Report [Phase 2] (Ottawa: Industry Canada, 1997), 23, 36. Available at www.iigr.ca/pdf/documents/768_Preparing_Canada_for_a_D.pdf, accessed May 7, 2005.

13. Longford, "Rethinking the Virtual State," 115.

14. Treasury Board Secretariat, "Government of Canada's Internet Strategy," in *Government of Canada Internet Guide* (Ottawa: Treasury Board, 1995). The first edition was titled *The Internet: A Guide to Internet Users,* published on the TBS Web site earlier in 1995. These early documents are no longer available on the Treasury Board Web site. The current *Government of Canada Internet Guide* (Ottawa: Treasury Board, last updated March 2004) does not include the Internet strategy. Available at www.cio-dpi.gc.ca/ig-gi/index_e.asp, accessed April 8, 2005.

15. IHAC, *Building the Information Society: Moving Canada into the 21st Century* (Ottawa: Supply and Services, 1996), 1, 2, 27. Available at www.ifla.org/documents/infopol/canada/ihac9601.pdf, accessed May 9, 2005.

16. Privy Council, *Getting Government Right: A Progress Report* (Ottawa: Privy Council Office, 1996), 19–20. Available at www.tbs-sct.gc.ca/est-pre/19961997/gettinge.pdf, accessed May 7, 2005.

17. Parliament, Speech from the Throne to Open the First Session of the Thirty-sixth Parliament of Canada (Ottawa: Parliament, September 23, 1997). Available at www.parl.gc.ca/information/about/process/info/throne/index.asp?lang=E&parl=36&sess=1, accessed May 7, 2005.

18. Auditor General, *E Commerce: Conducting Government Business via the Internet* (Ottawa: Auditor General, 1998), sec. 19.17. Available at www.oag-bvg.gc.ca/domino/reports.nsf/html/9819ce.html, accessed May 7, 2005.

19. IHAC, *Building the Information Society,* 28.

20. Industry Canada, Electronic Commerce Task Force, *Canadian Electronic Commerce Strategy* (Ottawa: Industry Canada, 1998), 2, 38. Available at http://strategis.ic.gc.ca/epic/internet/inecic -ceac.nsf/vwapj/ecom_eng.pdf/$file/ecom_eng.pdf, accessed May 7, 2005.

21. Auditor General, *E Commerce,* sec. 19.9.

22. Parliament, Speech from the Throne to Open the Second Session of the Thirty-sixth Parliament of Canada (Ottawa: Parliament, October 12, 1999). Available at www.parl.gc.ca/information/about/process/info/throne/index.asp?lang=E&parl=36&sess=2, accessed May 7, 2005.

23. Canada, *Report on Canadian Government On-Line Activities,* Country report presented by Christine Poirier at the Government On-Line International Network meeting in Leiden, October 8–11, 2000 (Leiden, The Netherlands, October 2000). Available at www.governments-online.org/documents/Canada_Leiden.pdf, accessed April 11, 2005.

24. Treasury Board, Speaking Notes for the Honourable Lucienne Robillard, President of the Treasury Board, to the International Council for Information Technology in Government Administration (Ottawa: Treasury Board, September 18, 2000). Available at www.tbs-sct.gc.ca/media/ps-dp/2000/0918_e.asp, accessed May 16, 2005.

25. See, e.g., Longford, "Rethinking the Virtual State"; Sunny Marche and James D. McNiven, "E-government and E-governance: The Future Isn't What It Used to Be," *Canadian Journal of Administrative Sciences* 20 (2003): 83.

26. Treasury Board Secretariat, *Government On-Line: Serving Canadians in a Digital World* (Ottawa: Treasury Board, last updated February 2004). Available at www.gol-ged.gc.ca/pub/serv-can/serv -can00_e.asp, accessed May 7, 2005.

27. Canada, Government On-Line: Serving Canadians Better [Web site] (Ottawa, updated May 13, 2004). Available at www.gol-ged.gc.ca/index_e.asp, accessed April 10, 2005.

28. Treasury Board Secretariat, *Strategic Directions for Information Management and Information Technology: Enabling 21st Century Service to Canadians* (Ottawa: Treasury Board, 1999). Available at www.tbs-sct.gc.ca/pubs_pol/ciopubs/TB_OIMP/sdimit_e.asp, accessed May 7, 2005.

29. Marche and McNiven, "E-government and E-governance"; Public Works and Government Services Canada (PWGSC), Government On-Line [Web site], *Priorities* (Ottawa: PWGSC, last updated April 1, 2004). Available at www.communication.gc.ca/gol_ged/gol_overview.html, accessed May 7, 2005.

30. Marche and McNiven, "E-Government and E-Governance," 83.

31. Marche and McNiven, "E-Government and E-Governance," 75.

32. Marche and McNiven, "E-Government and E-Governance," 75.

33. Privy Council, *Seventh Annual Report to the Prime Minister on the Public Service of Canada,* by Mel Cappe, Clerk of the Privy Council and Secretary to the Cabinet (Ottawa: Privy Council Office, March 31, 2000). Available at www.pco-bcp.gc.ca/default.asp?Page = Publications&Language = E& doc = 7rept2000/7rept2000cover_e.htm, accessed April 11, 2005.

34. Treasury Board Secretariat, Chief Information Officer Branch, Common Look and Feel for the Internet [Web site] (Ottawa: Treasury Board, last updated March 2004). Available at www.cio-dpi.gc.ca/clf-nsi/index_e.asp, accessed May 7, 2005.

35. PWGSC, Government On-Line [Web site], *Government On-Line History.*

36. Parliament, Speech from the Throne to Open the First Session of the Thirty-seventh Parliament of Canada (Ottawa: Parliament, January 30, 2001). Available at www.parl.gc.ca/information/about/process/info/throne/index.asp?lang = E&parl = 37&sess = 1, accessed May 7, 2005.

37. Auditor General, *Information Technology: Government On-Line,* Report of the Auditor General (Ottawa: Auditor General, 2003), sec. 1.20. Available at www.oag-bvg.gc.ca/domino/reports.nsf/html/20031101ce.html, accessed May 1, 2005.

38. Canada, Government On-Line: Serving Canadians Better [Web site], *Guiding Principles.*

39. PWGSC, Government On-Line [Web site], *Government On-Line History.*

40. Michael Turner and Christine Desloges, "Strategies and Framework for Government On-Line: A Canadian Experience," PowerPoint presentation, June 18, 2002, World Bank e-Government Learning Workshop, Washington, DC. Available at www.comnet-it.org/e-government/cdn experience.pdf, accessed May 7, 2005.

41. Parliament, Speech from the Throne to Open the First Session of the Thirty-seventh Parliament of Canada.

42. National Broadband Task Force, *The New National Dream: Networking the Nation for Broadband Access* (Ottawa: Industry Canada, 2001), 1, 9, 20. Available at http://broadband.gc.ca/pub/program/NBTF/broadband.pdf, accessed May 7, 2005.

43. Conference Board of Canada, "Canada Still Holds Second Place in Connectedness Index—But Slipping," News Release 04-23 (Toronto: Conference Board of Canada, April 27, 2004). Available at www.conferenceboard.ca/press/2004/connectedness.asp, accessed May 7, 2005.

44. Industry Canada, *Industry Canada: Making a Difference* (Ottawa: Industry Canada, October 2003), sec. 5: Connectedness. Available at www.ic.gc.ca/cmb/welcomeic.nsf/532340a8523f337185 25649d006b119d/012bffa29fcb623885256dc200424073!OpenDocument, accessed May 7, 2005.

45. Industry Canada, "Minister Emerson Appoints Members of Telecommunications Policy Review Panel," Backgrounder, News Release (Ottawa: Industry Canada, April 11, 2005). Available at www.ic.gc.ca/cmb/welcomeic.nsf/0/85256a5d006b972085256fe0005b8149?OpenDocument, accessed April 11, 2005.

46. Government On-Line Advisory Panel, *Transforming Government to Serve Canadian Better,* Report to the President of the Treasury Board of Canada (Ottawa: Treasury Board, December 2002), Recommendations. Available at www.gol-ged.gc.ca/pnl-grp/reports/second/transform/transform00 _e.asp, accessed May 4, 2005.

47. Government On-Line Advisory Panel, *Connecting with Canadians: Pursuing Service Transformation,* Final Report to the President of the Treasury Board of Canada (Ottawa: Treasury Board, December 2003), Introduction. Available at www.gol-ged.gc.ca/pnl-grp/reports/final/final00_e.asp, accessed May 4, 2005.

48. Auditor General [Web site]. Available at www.oag-bvg.gc.ca/domino/oag-bvg.nsf/tml/menue.html, accessed May 9, 2005.

49. Auditor General, *Information Technology: Government On-Line,* sec. 1.1, 1.2.

50. Auditor General, *Information Technology: Government On-Line,* sec. 1.5, 1.7.

51. Treasury Board Secretariat, Chief Information Officer Branch, "Our Responsibilities Have Changed!" (Ottawa: Treasury Board, March 29, 2004). Available at www.cio-dpi.gc.ca/cio-dpi/resp_e.asp, accessed April 12, 2005.

52. Canada, *Government On-Line and Canadians* (First Annual Report) (Ottawa: March 2002). Available at www.gol-ged.gc.ca/rpt/2002rpt_e.asp, accessed April 30, 2005; Canada, *Government On-Line 2003* (Second Annual Report) (Ottawa: March 2003). Available at www.gol-ged.gc.ca/rpt2003/rpt03_e.asp, accessed April 30, 2005.

53. Canada, *Government On-Line 2004:* "This Report: What's Next" (Third Annual Report) (Ottawa, March 2004). Available at www.gol-ged.gc.ca/rpt2004/rpttb_e.asp, accessed April 30, 2005.

54. Treasury Board Secretariat, Chief Information Officer Branch, *Performance Measurement for the Government On-Line Initiative: Performance Measurement Methodology: Expected Outcomes* (Ottawa: Treasury Board, October 2004). Available at www.cio-dpi.gc.ca/si-as/performance/performance00_e.asp, accessed April 12, 2005.

55. Treasury Board Secretariat, Chief Information Officer Branch, *Performance Measurement for the Government On-Line Initiative.*

56. Canada, *Government On-Line 2005: From Vision to Reality and Beyond* (Fourth Annual Report) (Ottawa, March 2005). See "Integrated Performance Measurement." Available at www.gol-ged.gc.ca/rpt2005/rpttb_e.asp, accessed April 30, 2005.

57. Auditor General, *Information Technology: Government On-Line,* sec. 1.77.

58. PWGSC, "What Is Government On-Line?" (and its fact sheet, "Secure Channel") (Ottawa: PWGSC, last updated October 8, 2004). Available at www.pwgsc.gc.ca/text/factsheets/secure_channel-e.html, accessed April 17, 2005.

59. Auditor General, *Information Technology Security,* chap. 1 of 2005 Status Report (Ottawa: Auditor General, February 2005), sections 1.1, 1.11–1.16. Available at www.oag-bvg.gc.ca/domino/reports.nsf/html/05menu_e.html, accessed May 1, 2005.

60. Department of Finance, *Budget 2003—Budget Plan,* chap. 5, "Investing in a More Productive, Sustainable Economy" (Ottawa: Department of Finance, February 2003). Available at www.fin.gc.ca/budget03/bp/bpc5e.htm, accessed May 7, 2005.

61. Industry Canada, *Evaluation Study of the Community Access Program* (Ottawa: Industry Canada, January 16, 2004). Available at www.ic.gc.ca/cmb/welcomeic.nsf/0/ffd2e3755d7f251585256e9800510b66?OpenDocument, accessed May 7, 2005.

62. PWGSC, Government On-Line [Web site], *Priorities,* "Guiding Principles."

63. Canada, *Government On-Line 2005,* "Information Services" and "Transactional Services."

64. PWGSC, Government On-Line [Web site], *Priorities.*

65. PWGSC, "What Is Government On-Line?" (and the fact sheet) (Ottawa: PWGSC, last updated March 2005). Available at www.pwgsc.gc.ca/text/factsheets/what_is_gov-e.html, accessed May 1, 2005.

66. Gilles Paquet, "There Is More to Governance than Public Candelabras: E-governance and Canada's Public Service," in *E-Government Reconsidered: Renewal of Governance for the Knowledge Age,* ed. E. Lynn Oliver and Larry Sanders (Regina: Canadian Plains Research Center, University of Regina and Saskatchewan Institute of Public Policy, 2004), 193.

67. See charts in Canada, *Government On-Line 2005.* See "Information Services" and "Transactional Services."

68. Accenture, *Leadership in Customer Service,* 60–61.

69. Conference Board of Canada, "Canada Still Holds Second Place."

70. Auditor General, *Information Technology,* sec. 1.36.

71. Treasury Board Secretariat, Chief Information Officer Branch, *Performance Measurement for the Government On-Line Initiative,* app. 1, 2, 3; Canada, *Government On-Line 2005,* app. D.

72. Canada, *Government On-Line 2005.* See "Introduction: From Vision to Reality . . . and Beyond," "Better and More Responsive Services," "Information Services," and "Transactional Services."

73. Tom Mitchinson and Mark Ratner, "Promoting Transparency through the Electronic Dissemination of Information," in *E-Government Reconsidered,* 89–105, quote on 91.

74. Accenture, *E-Government Leadership: High Performance, Maximum Value* (New York: Accenture, 2004), 68. Available at www.accenture.com/xdoc/en/industries/government/gove_egov_value.pdf, accessed May 16, 2005.

75. Canada, *Government On-Line 2005,* see "Measuring Progress."

76. Canada, *Government On-Line 2005,* see "Measuring Progress."

77. Some hits will result from Internet users surfing the Web for pleasure or interest, without actually searching for "information" from the government. Others might be using a search engine such as Google and come across links to government sites that they open and do not peruse.

78. Canada, *Government On-Line 2005.*

79. Canada, *Government On-Line 2005.*

80. Accenture, *Leadership in Customer Service,* 61.

81. Canada, *Government On-Line 2005.*

82. PWGSC, *Report on Plans and Priorities: 2005-2006 Estimates,* sect. III Supplementary Information, Horizontal Initiative C, "Government On-Line" (Ottawa: PWGSC Canada, 2005). Available at www.pwgsc.gc.ca/reports/text/rpp_2005-2006_sct3_tbl20_c-e.html, accessed May 6, 2005.

83. Canada, Department of Finance, *Expenditure Review for Sound Financial Management* (Ottawa: Department of Finance, February 23, 2005). Available at www.fin.gc.ca/budget05/booklets/bkexpe .htm, accessed May 6, 2005. See also PWGSC, *Report on Plans and Priorities.*

84. Treasury Board, "Crossing Boundaries Conference: When E-government Becomes Simply Government; Making the Case for Radical Incrementalism in Public Service Governance," speech by Lucienne Robillard, president of the Treasury Board (Ottawa: Treasury Board, May 8, 2003). Available at www.tbs-sct.gc.ca/media/ps-dp/2003/0508_e.asp, accessed May 16, 2005.

85. A pre-Internet example was Information Canada, which existed from 1970 to 1976. Marche and McNiven note the Service New Brunswick model "appears to be catching on in other provinces and it may spread to the federal government"; see Marche and McNiven, "E-government and E-governance," 9.

86. Department of Finance, *Expenditure Review for Sound Financial Management.*

87. Alden Cuddihey, " 'No. 1 with a But': E-Government Legal and Policy Issues," *IT World Canada* [Web site] (May 5, 2005). Available at www.itworldcanada.com, accessed May 6, 2005.

88. E-Government Policy Network, "Transforming Government and Governance for the 21st Century: A Conceptual Framework," in *E-Government Reconsidered,* 13.

89. Roger Gibbins, "Federalism and the Challenge of Electronic Portals," in *E-Government Reconsidered,* 39.

90. Paquet, "There Is More to Governance than Public Candelabras," 193.

91. Marche and McNiven, "E-government and E-governance."

92. Treasury Board, Serving Canadians Better: Moving Forward with Service Transformation at the Enterprise Level [Web site]: "Canada's Strategic Approach to e-Government" (Ottawa: Treasury Board, 2004). Available at www.cio-dpi.gc.ca/cio-dpi/2004/canada/canadatb_e.asp, accessed May 16, 2005.

93. Privy Council, *Twelfth Annual Report to the Prime Minister on the Public Service of Canada*, by Alex Himmelfarb, Clerk of the Privy Council and Secretary to the Cabinet (Ottawa: Privy Council Office, March 31, 2005). Available at www.pco-bcp.gc.ca/docs/Report/12_report-rapport_e.pdf, accessed May 17, 2005.

94. See Longford, "Rethinking the Virtual State," for a good discussion of the difficulties of relying on ICT to accomplish government transformation.

95. E-Government Policy Network, "Transforming Government and Governance," 5.

• 5 •

E-government in Australia

Sue Burgess and Jan Houghton

*O*ver the last decade, Australian governments at all levels have been planning and implementing broad policies for the application and use of information and communication technologies (ICTs) by the general public and the business community. Central to these plans has been the role of the government in guiding the development of the infrastructure, initiating and/or funding projects, and coordinating strategies across agency and sectoral boundaries and interests. Equally important has been the role of government agencies in leading the use of ICTs for improving their own information management and for delivering services. This leadership role has been one of the key strategies of e-government development in Australia. That development has followed a steady, although somewhat fragmented, path to a point where it is consistently ranked very highly against other countries on international indices of e-government development. The path is fragmented because, as will emerge from the outline of the progress of e-government in Australia, there have been a number of public sector agencies involved, with changing functions and responsibilities for policy planning, implementation, and monitoring.

One constant has been the objective of making government "an exemplar in the use of ICT to improve citizen engagement, efficiency, and effectiveness of service delivery."[1] The three broad goals of e-government reflected in this statement are present in the major ICT policies of all tiers of government in Australia,[2] that is, to improve the efficiency of information management practices within and across government agencies and jurisdictions; to deliver fast, timely, and appropriate information and services electronically for business and the wider community; and to allow greater opportunities for citizen interaction with government and government processes progressing from more access to full participation in government or e-democracy. To date, most emphasis has been on the first two goals, although more attention is now being paid to the third.[3]

This chapter includes a brief outline of some important historical developments; an overview of current e-government approaches, policies, and achievements; and coverage of future developments. The focus is on the policies and strategies of the Australian federal government, although information and examples will also be provided from state and local governments as appropriate. To help in understanding the political and social context for policymaking in the information and communications area, the chapter unfolds with some general background information on Australia.

CHALLENGES FOR E-GOVERNMENT

Australia's three-tier (federal, state, and local) system of government creates a major challenge as, at each level, there are separate but complementary functions and responsibilities, and inevitably there are crossovers. Within the same level of government there are territorial issues related to responsibilities across agencies and competing priorities. For ICT planning generally, cooperation and coordination are essential to avoid duplication, the incompatibility of systems, and wasted resources. Australian governments, like those around the world, are following a "whole-of-government approach" to electronic government described by the federal government as creating "seamless, responsive and citizen-focused government for the benefit of all Australians" and "broader and faster access to integrated, flexible and more customized services."[4]

There are additional challenges for online service delivery arising from Australia's geography and vast distances with some areas sparsely populated and others with high population concentrations.[5] Politically, if governments in Australia do not provide for "the bush" as well as the cities, they face an electoral backlash. There have been cost and technical accessibility issues for rural and remote areas. Although the Australian population is relatively homogeneous, within the wider community there are socially and economically disadvantaged groups with differing needs for information and other services and differing levels of ability in accessing those services. These include indigenous citizens, older people, and those with disabilities. Australia is a multicultural country, so there are also language and ethnic differences to be addressed in information and service provision.

Although, overall, there is a high take-up rate of new technology generally and the Internet in particular, there has been less take-up by individuals according to a range of socioeconomic indicators (e.g., those related to indigenous Australians; those who are older, unemployed, and looking to join the labor force; those on low income; and those with less education or with poor English skills). Australians living and working in regional and remote areas also have less access to the Internet.[6]

DEVELOPMENTS IN E-GOVERNMENT

In 1993, the then Labor government under Prime Minister Paul Keating established an expert group to investigate and report on the development and use of broadband technology across all spheres of domestic and economic life in Australia. The government's vision as presented in the 1994 report *Networking Australia's Future*[7] recommended a national broadband strategy based on three key elements: education and community access, industry development, and the role of government. As well as establishing the necessary regulatory environment, coordinating policies across all sectors, and improving efficiency through better information management, government agencies would lead in using the network for service delivery to demonstrate "the benefits of the new communications services to the private sector and the wider community."[8]

The major push toward e-government began three years later with the change to the more conservative coalition government that is still in power. In 1997, Prime Minister John Howard's industry policy statement, *Investing For Growth*,[9] committed the federal government to:

- delivering all appropriate services electronically on the Internet by 2001;
- establishing a government information center as a main point of access to information about government services; and, in consultation with the states, developing a "single window access" to government information and services in Australia;
- establishing electronic payment as the normal means for commonwealth payments by 2000; and
- establishing a government-wide intranet for secure online communication.

There was now a greater focus on building an information economy through fostering electronic commerce, with the government leading by example in the development of online service provision. There was also recognition that this should be seen clearly as a "transformative" process for the public sector agencies responsible for providing information and services.

Also in 1997, the National Office of the Information Economy (NOIE) was established as a separate government agency to implement and coordinate the federal government's online and Internet policies and to develop strategies for reducing the "digital divide." NOIE's first task was to develop the government's overall ICT policy, *A Strategic Framework for the Information Economy: Identifying Priorities for Action*, which was subsequently released in December 1998.[10] In this policy, the government presented its vision and guiding principles and outlined ten key strategic priorities and related action areas for building Australia's information economy. One of these priorities was to "implement a world class model for delivery of all appropriate government services online" by "providing as many affordable, equitable and accessible government services as is practical online."[11] Key action areas associated with this priority were to:

- continue with a whole-of-government approach;
- ensure consistency, cost effectiveness, interoperability, and transparency within government;
- work toward cross-jurisdictional agreement on minimum standards;
- facilitate seamless and integrated electronic service delivery; and
- develop information management standards for the digitization of public records, publications, and archives.

NOIE was within the portfolio of the minister for communications, information technology and the arts. However, there was a division of responsibility as a second agency, the Office of Government Information Technology (OGIT) in the Department of Finance and Administration (DOFA), was responsible for coordinating the use of technology by the government to ensure high-quality services and consistency, cost effectiveness, and interoperative systems. In 1988, OGIT developed the first single federal government entry point, www.fed.gov.au (now www.australia.gov.au).[12]

In 1999, the Australian National Audit Office (ANAO) undertook a survey of government agencies[13] and concluded that the majority were likely to meet the 2001 commitment for delivering services online, although ANAO noted that there was no clear definition of "appropriate" services. This determination was left to the agencies, and for the most part they favored client-service information and support, procurement and payment services, public relations and advertising, and general services. The ANAO identified four stages for progressive achievement of online delivery and grouped agencies accordingly. The stages were:

- having a "presence" where the agency puts information on a Web site and allows downloading;
- providing for some basic interaction (e.g., submitting queries and e-mailing forms); and
- allowing completed transactions to be performed.

The final stage of transformation involves the complete integration of the service and enables online users to move seamlessly from agency to agency. By 2001, only 2 percent were expected to be at the last stage, although more than half of the agencies would have an established Web presence.

ANAO's survey also found that there were some impediments that agencies needed to address. These included current legislative restrictions on electronic formats, legal liabilities relating to information on Web sites, the shortage of IT skills, and issues of data security and privacy, particularly problems in using the public key infrastructure (PKI) to encrypt, decrypt, and verify data. The survey also suggested that agencies review costs and benefits of keeping both electronic and traditional services and reassess the way in which they performed their functions for online delivery.

In April 2000 the federal government released its more detailed e-government strategy, *Government Online,*[14] which set out eight priorities to be implemented and monitored through the Office of Government Online (OGO), an agency within the Department of Communications, Information Technology and the Arts (DCITA). Priorities included assisting agencies to take full advantage of opportunities provided by the Internet to deliver high-quality, low-cost, easy-to-use, and accessible services; putting government businesses online; enhancing online services for regional Australia; and facilitating the development of cross-agency services. The premise was that users should be able to find the information and services they needed without having to understand the structure of government. The OGO was given the responsibility for monitoring progress and documenting best practice, including compliance with the Online Information Service Obligations (OISOs; www.agimo.gov.au/information/oiso), which mandated a minimum set of information that agencies must provide on Web sites and required agencies to use metadata developed for the Australian Government Locator Service (AGLS; www.naa.gov.au/recordkeeping/gov_online/agls/summary.html).

Also in 2000, the government released policies on specific aspects of e-government. One was the *Customer Focussed Portals Framework,* which was intended to simplify access to government information and provide the "platform for integrated service delivery."[15] It brought together a number of Web sites (e.g., HealthInsite, www.healthinsite.gov.au/, and the Business Entry Point, www.business.gov.au/ Business + Entry + Point/) and allowed searching by subject area as well as for specific government agencies and services. Another procedural policy was the Commonwealth Electronic Procurement Implementation Strategy (www.agimo.gov.au/publications/ 2000/04/eproc_strategy), which was developed to facilitate the way in which the government did business with its suppliers.

The *Better Services, Better Government* strategy, released in November 2002,[16] marked the next stage in progress toward e-government from the initial focus on putting government information and services online to developing a more "comprehensive and integrated" system for information service delivery and administration. The title of the strategy reflects the government's view that "better services" equals "better government." The focus was primarily on the transformation of internal processes and with achieving and demonstrating "tangible returns" from ICT investment (e.g., cost reductions through increased efficiency and improved service delivery to customers as well as continuing the emphasis on a whole-of-government approach to counter separate planning by individual agencies and to ensure better access to government services and information).[17] To assist with this objective, the *Interoperability Technical Framework for the Australian Government,*[18] released in 2003, sets technical standards for Australian government agencies to allow them to communicate and exchange information.

Since 2002, the Information Management Strategy Committee (IMSC; www .imsc.gov.au), which was established following a recommendation by the Management Advisory Committee's report *Australian Government Use of Information and Communication Technology,*[19] undertook the broad coordinating role for e-government. This high-level committee, made up of the heads of major departments and agencies, facilitates whole-of-government and multiagency approaches to ICT investment, governance, and management. This means changing organizational cultures, encouraging agencies to work across boundaries and across jurisdictions through data sharing and interoperability of systems, using common metadata and following common Web design and other technical protocols, and transforming internal processes to lower transaction costs and operate more efficiently. One approach is to encourage the development of clusters for information sharing on relevant social and economic indicators (e.g., health, education, and trade) and environmental indicators (e.g., climate).[20] The IMSC provides specific guidance and best-practice models on these matters to public sector agencies. A Chief Information Officer Committee reports to the IMSC on issues related to architecture, standards, and shared services.

A revised strategic framework, *Australia's Strategic Framework for the Information Economy 2004–2006: Opportunities and Challenges for the Information Age,* was released in 2004. It streamlined the broad priorities of the 1998 policy from sixteen to four:[21]

1. to ensure that all Australians have the capabilities, networks, and tools to participate in the information economy;
2. to ensure the security and interoperability of Australia's information infrastructure and support confidence in digital services;
3. to develop Australia's innovation system as a platform for productivity growth and industry transformation;
4. to raise Australian public sector productivity, collaboration, and accessibility through the effective use of information, knowledge, and ICT.

A range of supporting strategies was also identified; these address the key challenges of equity of access, privacy, and security; cross-agency and cross-sector collaboration; and so on. Better governance was again emphasized, as was the need to develop partnerships with the private sector. All of these issues are integral to the further development of e-government and e-commerce.

By 2004, Australia, in the government's view,[22] was now one of the world's lead-ing information economies overall and a role model of best practice for e-government. Strategies put in place first through the implementation of *Government Online,*[23] and later through *Better Services, Better Government,*[24] continued to be implemented. A range of issues still had to be addressed; examples include increasing the spread of ICTs and skills development across the community and industry to reduce economic, social, and geographic barriers to full participation; security and interoperability issues particularly related to authentication, privacy, and consumer protection to promote confidence in online transactions; fostering collaborations across government, community, and busi-ness sectors; and improvements in public service productivity and efficiency. The focus remained on better information management and the provision of more efficient e-services, as well as establishing the legal and technological environment for e-commerce within the national and global context. In early 2004, the federal govern-ment decided on a major change in the governance framework for e-government activ-ities in order to achieve these goals.

MANAGEMENT OF E-GOVERNMENT

In March 2004 the federal government announced that NOIE would cease to operate as a separate agency and its functions and responsibilities related to broad policy, research, and programs would be transferred to an Office for the Information Economy (OIE; www.dcita.gov.au/ie) to be established within the Department of Communica-tions, Information Technology and the Arts. A separate agency, the Australian Govern-ment Information Management Office (AGIMO; www.agimo.gov.au), would also be established under the minister for communications, information technology and the arts to focus on promoting and coordinating the use of ICTs for delivering Australian gov-ernment policies, programs, and services and maintaining the government's leadership role.[25] The rationale for this change was to allow the AGIMO to concentrate on gaining benefits from the use of ICTs for the delivery of Australian government programs and services while the new Office for the Information Economy handled the broader policy and research functions. Subsequently in October 2004 it was announced that the AGIMO would be incorporated within the Department of Finance and Administra-tion.[26] This was a return to the earlier division of responsibilities for e-government between separate government departments (DCITA and DOFA) and a recognition that e-government is now a well-established area of government administration.

Overall responsibility for coordination of federal e-government activities remains with the IMSC, and a ministerial forum, the Online Council, has representatives from the states as well as the federal government. The council considers policies and proce-dures for services involving multiple agencies and across jurisdictions, and it is currently implementing a series of initiatives under its Integrated Service Delivery Framework.[27] More broadly, two other agencies, the Australian National Audit Office and the Man-agement Advisory Committee (MAC), also monitor progress and issue reports from time to time. (Findings from their reports are referred to later in the chapter.)

At the state/territory level, as would be expected, developments and governance arrangements have followed a similar path with each government having a main ICT policy and a central agency to implement strategies, including those for e-government, and to monitor progress. In New South Wales (NSW), for example, the government released its *Information Management and Technology Blueprint* and *Connect NSW* reports in 1997.[28] The Government Chief Information Office (previously the Office of Information and Communications Technology) within the Department of Commerce (www.oit.nsw.gov.au/) manages e-government. In Victoria, the current policy is contained in *Connecting Victoria*,[29] released in 1999 and managed by Multimedia Victoria (www.mmv.vic.gov.au/). In Western Australia, the Office of E-government administers the *E-government Strategy for the Western Australian Public Sector.*[30]

MEASURING ACHIEVEMENTS

As outlined below, the focus of the federal government has been primarily on collecting data and measuring performance and progress against key indicators. Both the 1998 Strategic Framework[31] and the Government Online[32] strategy included policies on monitoring progress toward specific objectives. NOIE delivered three progress reports on achievements related to the broad Strategic Framework priorities.[33] For e-government activities, under the Online Reporting Framework developed by NOIE, agencies were required to report twice yearly to the Office of Government Online on activities such as cross-agency integration of services, compliance with procedural requirements, and outcomes for the intended beneficiaries of online initiatives.[34]

NOIE also commissioned the *E-government Benefits Study*[35] in 2003, which investigated the demand for and benefits of e-government for both the government and the user. The study found there was a strong demand particularly for preliminary information, which typically was followed up through more traditional channels. Benefits to the government that were identified included cost reduction and greater efficiency, whereas the benefits to users included improvements in finding information, in service quality, and in their ability to conduct business and make decisions. The study identified a number of barriers to the development of e-government, including the need for higher take-up rates for the Internet, improved design and navigation for Web sites, and greater security and privacy. It also found a need for better mechanisms to track online service delivery and its value for citizens. In the final phase, the return on investment from implementing online services was examined in order to determine a benchmark for agencies when they planned new services. A number of case studies were developed as part of this study to provide examples for agencies.

In the Better Services, Better Government[36] strategy, the emphasis was also on assessing the costs and benefits of online service delivery and measuring how agencies were doing in terms of meeting the broad e-government agenda. There were regular review mechanisms for assessing progress on key performance indicators, and NOIE was in the process of developing appropriate evaluation frameworks and benchmarks.[37] Under the current governance framework, the AGIMO is now responsible for reporting on developments in e-government, and it does so through its annual report.[38] AGIMO's specific responsibility is for reporting on "[s]trategic advice, activities and representation relating to the application of new technologies to government administration, information and services."[39] Other aspects of progress under the Strategic Framework 2004–2006 are reported by the Office for the Information Economy (OIE), for example, in the National Information Economy Index.[40]

As mentioned earlier, the ANAO has an important role in monitoring government investment and processes for the use of ICTs and has developed *Internet Delivery Decisions: A Government Program Manager's Guide*[41] to assist agencies. The ANAO has undertaken a number of evaluations, the latest for the period 2004/2005, in which it examined how agencies are measuring the efficiency and effectiveness of services delivered through the Internet.[42] Measuring Internet take-up, levels of accessibility, and tangible returns on ICT investment was an important objective of the Better Services, Better Government strategy. ANAO concluded after its latest evaluation that overall, although there had been improvements in some aspects (e.g., Web site management), agencies did not have adequate systems in place to assess whether their use of the Internet to deliver services and programs was efficient and effective either for users or for the government in the form of tangible returns on investment.

Australia has performed well on a number of international surveys on e-government, which measure e-government developments against a range of indicators.[43] The *United Nations Global E-Readiness Report 2004*[44] reports performance on a series of measures. On the "Web measure index," which measures progress against a Web presence model that covers emerging, enhanced, interactive, transactional, and networked stages, Australia ranks eighth, down from third in 2003.[45] On the "global e-government readiness" measure, which is a composite measure based on the Web measure index, an assessment of past spending on telecommunications, and levels of education and literacy, Australia is ranked sixth (from third in 2003).[46] This change in Australia's ranking is primarily reflective of the greatly improved performance of Denmark and Korea. Australia ranks eighth (same as in 2003) on the UN's "e-participation index,"[47] which measures governments' use of ICTs to engage citizens more in consultation than decision making. It assumes the existence of e-participation at a rather rudimentary level.

In the 2004 Accenture survey, Australia was rated fourth (with several other countries) on an e-government maturity index.[48] Accenture, an international management consulting and technology services company, noted that there was a lack of integration across government agencies although there were high levels of service breadth. Concern was expressed at the lack of a central e-government action plan due to the federated approach adopted by the federal government whereby each agency develops its own plan and approach. Accenture praised the valuable leadership role played by NOIE, particularly through the Better Services, Better Government strategy and the *E-government Benefits Study*,[49] which emphasized greater efficiency and a return on investment. Accenture also conducted a survey of Australian citizens, which showed that they are mostly using government Web sites to look for information (75 percent), rather than for conducting transactions (15 percent); 10 percent said that they used it for both equally.[50]

PROGRESS TOWARD ACHIEVING E-GOVERNMENT GOALS

In relation to the broad goal of better information management, it is difficult to assess whether the federal government's changes to governance over the last ten years have increased efficiency and effectiveness, particularly from the perspective of those seeking to access and use government information and services. The establishment of the National Office of the Information Economy in 1997 was certainly a key factor in putting in place the legal and regulatory framework necessary for the provision of online information and services and in providing leadership across a very large and diverse range of functions. The governance framework now in place is clearer, with key functions split between the Australian Government Information Management Office and the Office for the Information Economy. The role of the Information Management Strategy Committee is to facilitate a big picture or whole-of-government approach. The AGIMO sees itself as supporting the work of the IMSC by "identifying and progressing solutions to whole-of-government issues." In its latest annual report, AGIMO claimed increased collaboration between agencies and the development of more integrated services as an indication that progress was being made.[51] For example, it reported on the implementation of the Technology Interoperability Framework (www.agimo .gov.au/publications/2003/08/framework), the release of a draft paper for an Australian Government Authentication Framework (www.agimo.gov.au/infrastructure/ authentication), and the rollout of the FedLink encryption system (www.fedlink.gov.au) for increasing the security of communications among agencies.[52] Activities more relevant to the digital divide (e.g., Internet access and use) are reported by DCITA in its *Information Economy Index* and *Current State of Play.*[53]

Projects being implemented under the National Service Improvement Framework[54] that cross jurisdictions include a pilot program with Centrelink and local governments in Western Australia and Queensland. This project provides Centrelink's Customer Confirmation Service to the participant local governments, thereby delivering a more efficient and seamless service to their customers by providing real-time advice on customers' eligibility for a concession, with the customers' consent. The aim of the TIGERS (Trials of Innovative Government Electronic Regional Services) Program in Tasmania is to develop integrated services involving multiple agencies and multiple jurisdictions. A number of pilot projects were implemented, including an online student bus pass application system (https://eform.dier.tas.gov.au/sbpoaf/) with online eligibility validation provided by Centrelink and Fishonline, a service for recreational fishers (www.fishonline.tas.gov.au/).[55]

This seamless, whole-of-government approach is also exemplified by the development of single-access portals that allow for searching by subject as well as by specific functions and agencies. Examples include Multiservice Express, now Victoria Online Portal (www.vic.gov.au/index.jsp), and the federal government's intergovernmental portal (www.australia.gov.au). The "look and feel" throughout the latter site is not consistent, and individual portals are also being developed around customer groupings (e.g., seniors and indigenous people) and subjects or topics (e.g., environment and employment). This system of portals upon portals is likely to be somewhat confusing to users. It is intended that the site be further developed to allow full search and retrieval capabilities across all levels of government and all government sites, as opposed to the current functionality, which merely points to the portal for each level of government.

Cross-agency examples that have internal effiencies as well as a user focus as their aim include Jobsearch (www.jobsearch.gov.au/), which is a product of the Department of Employment and Workplace Relations. It provides job seekers and their intermediaries with a suite of online employment services and involves cooperation between several federal government agencies and businesses for current job notifications. The e-tax program developed by the Australian Taxation Office (http://ato.gov.au/individuals/) is a much-touted example of effective user-centered product and service design in response to individual taxpayer feedback on the complexity of the TaxPack (the instruction booklet produced by the ATO to assist individuals to complete their own tax returns) as well as an example of increased internal efficiency. According to the ATO, internal efficiencies achieved include lower customer inquiry rates and increased accuracy of income tax returns, which in turn lower the error-correction rate and reduce TaxPack printing requirements.[56] (Raelene Vivian details the collaborative design processes used by the ATO.[57])

In order to ensure that people with disabilities and people using older equipment or assistive technology can use Web sites, the federal government requires its Web sites to follow the World Wide Web Consortium's Web Accessibility Standards.[58] Priority 1 ("single" A) level appears to be mandated, although the wording is ambiguous, that is, "all websites were to follow the W3C guidelines to a sufficient extent that they pass recognized tests of accessibility."[59] AGIMO's *Access and Equity Issues for Websites*[60] is also concerned with making federal government Web sites accessible to people from diverse cultures as well as to those whose first language is not English. Examples of Web sites providing high levels of access include the Australian Human Rights and Equal Opportunity Commission (www.hreoc.gov.au/) and Centrelink (www.centrelink.gov.au/).

The extent to which federal government Web sites generally meet these guidelines is another matter. There have been some independent evaluations of government Web sites, and these have not been complimentary of the sites' user friendliness in general and their accessibility in particular, although the situation is constantly improving.[61] One study by the Hiser Group,[62] in 2002, focused on the user experience of government portal sites, comparing cross-agency portal sites within a single tier of local, state, and federal government (i.e., the earlier versions of the federal government portal, fed.gov.au and vic.gov.au) with portals that provide access to multiple tiers of government. The study findings indicate that the new-generation portals are repeating many of the mistakes of the earlier portals. Examples of these mistakes include categorization of information that requires knowledge of the structure and functions of government, a lack of a common look and feel across government sites, insufficient location cues, and lack of cross-linking to related information across government Web sites.

Sue Burgess and Jan Houghton,[63] who evaluated a number of NSW government Web sites, found a lack of clarity as to the purpose and audience of a site as one of several common factors making government sites frustrating and difficult for users. Other factors included inadequacies in online searching and help options, and a lack of provision for access by those with disabilities or with lower levels of technology or with older browsers. There were minimal information and services available in languages other than English, a major shortcoming in a multicultural country like Australia. According to Andrew Arch and Brian Hardy,[64] the current Australian approach of specifying minimum requirements but asking for higher levels of conformance has not delivered accessibility that is sufficient to meet the needs of e-government. This is despite the case of *Maguire v. Sydney Organising Committee for the Olympic Games* (SOCOG) in 2000, in which SOCOG was successfully taken to court for its failure to provide an accessible site. This example provides a clear indication that the Australian Disability Discrimination Act 1992 also applies to online services and publications.[65] A particular concern with the provision of government services online is to ensure that every stage in the delivery chain is accessible.

Other accessibility issues relate to access to the Internet itself. While Australia is ranked high on the UN's "e-readiness" index, there are still significant areas and groups within the Australian population that have little or no access to the Internet. This indicates that many Australians do not participate in the information economy and are unable to access and use government information and services on the Internet. As Anni Dugdale et al. note,[66] many of those with low Internet access or use are those who receive significant government support. In other words, they constitute an important target group if access to electronic government services is to be increased, and they also constitute an important target group to reach for consultation on service improvements and policy developments. Access to computers and the Internet via community access centers and public libraries is one means of improving access, as are programs aimed at improving skill and confidence in using the Internet; see, for example, the federal government's Community Connectivity programs (www.dcita.gov.au/ie/community _connectivity) and the Victorian government's Public Internet Access Program (www .egaps.vicnet.net.au/). The National Communications Fund is aimed at using ICTs to improve the delivery of government services (e.g., health and education, particularly in rural and remote areas); see, for example, Network WA (www.egov.dpc.wa.gov.au/ index.cfm?fuseaction = projects.network).

PROGRESS TOWARD ACHIEVING E-DEMOCRACY

It is apparent from the outline of e-government developments in Australia, that there has been less emphasis on the third theme of the broad government vision, that is, for greater citizen interaction with government and involvement in the processes of government (e.g., online consultations, involvement in policymaking, and petitioning government). All four stages of electronic government expressed in the model developed by the Australian National Audit Office[67] (referred to earlier) equate to the "managerial" ideal type of Andrew Chadwick and Christopher May,[68] where the concern is primarily with improving efficiency (backroom administration) and service delivery.

In the revised *Strategic Framework* published in 2004, the federal government, under its fourth priority, refers to citizen interaction with the processes of government as a guiding principle. It implies that this priority will be achieved through improved service delivery and the creation of "efficient links with customers."[69] In the *Better Services, Better Government* strategy, this goal had received some attention; for example, one aim is "to enhance closer citizen engagement" in policy formulation and processes.[70] However, citizen engagement occupies only half of one page in the twenty-five-page document, and whereas there are very detailed proposals for improvements to internal processes and technologies, the section dealing with closer citizen engagement merely explains the term and refers generally to the existence of consultation practices used by federal agencies with their stakeholders, including some use of online consultation. State governments have moved more rapidly on this front, as discussed further in the following section.

This concern with community engagement on the part of the federal government is a reflection of what Meredith Edwards[71] sees as the changing role of government to that of an enabler or facilitator of services that are delivered (outsourced) by third parties. It is also seen as government's response to increased cynicism toward government by citizens. Governance (i.e., how an organization conducts itself and the processes and structures used to achieve its goals) has become more of an issue. This includes those outside government who deliver and use services becoming involved in the development and monitoring of policy and programs.

The federal government's view on community engagement is more fully articulated in the Management Advisory Committee report *Connecting Government: Whole of Government Responses to Australia's Priority Challenges.*[72] It places strong emphasis on the importance in a democracy of maintaining two-way communication between the government and various external groups and individuals, and the report acknowledges the need to engage with citizens to improve design, responsiveness, and quality of policies and programs. One of its chapters is devoted to engagement with groups and individuals outside the public service where more that one level of government is involved.[73] There is, however, little or no focus on the use of information technology to foster the actual engagement process. *Connecting Government* also identified the importance of public servants developing increasingly sophisticated professional skills and techniques to manage this interaction.[74]

The 2004 "State of the Service" agency survey conducted by the Public Service Commission included a new question that explored the extent to which agencies are conducting formal consultations on program delivery and the development of government policy. The results indicated that there is much more consultation by agencies related to program delivery than to policy development and that the consultation is primarily with industry stakeholders and nongovernment organizations and much less frequently with members of the public. The forms of consultation were not specified, but it is clear from the text that few involved the use of ICTs and that all were within contexts defined by the government as opposed to by citizens.[75]

This thread has also been picked up by AGIMO in its *Better Practice Checklist: Online Policy Consultation,* which was developed with the assistance of the WA Office of E-Government and which draws on the consultation guidelines of the United Kingdom and the Organisation for Economic Co-operation and Development (OECD).[76] AGIMO also provides federal government examples of better practice in policy consultation using information technology (www.agimo.gov.au/practice/delivery/examples/consultation). None of the examples provided showed the use of online discussion or engagement. The technology was being used primarily to provide access to government documents and the resultant submissions from individuals and groups (e.g., Department of Defence community consultation, see www.defence.gov.au/consultation2/index.htm). The citizen-engagement theme has been further explored through a conference and series of papers initiated by NOIE and jointly published by AGIMO/Institute of Public Administration, ACT Division under the title *Future Challenges for E-government.*[77]

Examples of the use of information technology to facilitate citizen interaction with governments at the state government level include the Queensland government's three-year pilot e-democracy program, which is designed to test the use of the Internet in opening up democratic processes and enhancing the community's access to and participation in decision making. Among the initiatives being trialed are e-petitions, Internet broadcast of Parliament, and online community consultations.[78] The practical difficulties of engaging in online community dialogue and consultation and its impact on the work of public servants is illustrated by Kerrie Oakes[79] in her discussion of the day-to-day issues arising out of the operation of the Generate youth Web site, which is part of the community consultation initiative. This site (www.generate.qld.gov.au) provides a forum for active two-way engagement between young people and the Queensland government. The issues identified by Oakes include skill development for public servants to enable them to moderate online discussions and summarize contributions; integration of offline and online activities; content management and record keeping processes; the relative roles and responsibilities of public servants and politicians; and the necessity for the provision of timely feedback on the progress of the matter to participants.

The e-government efforts of the Victorian state government have widened to include a concern for governance and ways to encourage citizen initiatives and interaction with government. In 1999, this government set up a Democracy Online initiative, including a reference to a parliamentary committee (now the Subcommittee on Electronic Democracy), which has produced a substantial discussion paper on electronic democracy[80] and conducted public hearings (www.victorianedemocracy.info/). The focus is on netcasting of parliamentary proceedings; online interactive and collaborative approaches to policy discussion, including citizen e-mail and online forums; and other technology solutions to promote access and participation.

In New South Wales early support by government for the development of networked communities, especially for those isolated by distance or social dislocation, evolved into the Community Builders site (www.communitybuilders.nsw.gov.au/), which has assisted those working in community development by providing an avenue for sharing knowledge and resources. The emphasis here has been on building capacity in civil society by using the forums on the community builders' Web site to facilitate communication between and among communities rather than between community and government.

Online voting was introduced for the first time at state or territory level in the 2001 Australian Capital Territory election when some seventeen thousand voters availed themselves of the opportunity. The subsequent election in 2004 also provided this option. Voting was via personal computers located at the prepolling voting centers and at several of the polling booths on election day. A report on the 2001 experience from the ACT Electoral Commission indicated few problems with its use and a range of advantages (e.g., eliminating the need for manual counting of electronic votes, reducing the number of informal votes, allowing blind and sight-impaired people to vote without assistance and in secret through use of headphones and recorded voice instructions, and providing on-screen voting instructions in twelve different languages).[81]

At the local government level in Australia, there has been some interest shown in developing ICT-based options for engaging with local residents. Brisbane City Council's Your City Your Say (YCYS; http://ycys.brisbane.qld.gov.au/) provides an extended example of community consultation on issues of broad strategic importance. It draws on several thousand members of the community who have registered on the site. Topics range widely and have included sustainability, water sprinkler systems, and homelessness. The YCYS consultation process also includes provision of relevant information on the issues under discussion.

Beginning in February 2005, Warringah (in Sydney, NSW) Council's fortnightly meetings have been broadcast live over the Internet (www.warringah.nsw.gov.au). Local residents can see the administrator[82] and council staff responding to questions from the public forum at the beginning of each council meeting, as well as dealing with council reports and decisions arising.

LOOKING TO THE FUTURE

With the incorporation of AGIMO into the Department of Finance and Administration, there will be an increased emphasis on improving internal agency efficiency through the use of information technology and on agencies more carefully assessing the value and benefits of proposed online services. The number of transactional services is likely to increase with greater attention being paid to ease of use and accessibility issues. Because most users of government Web sites currently use them primarily to look for information rather than to conduct a transaction, significant progress here will be difficult. The push to implement cross-agency and cross-sector programs requiring interoperability between systems and the transformation of business processes is likely to continue, but the complexities involved mean that progress will be slower. What is not so clear is what emphasis, despite the rhetoric, will be placed on initiatives at the federal government level to increase the level of community engagement. There are few initiatives specifically addressing this objective. It is at state and local government levels that there is likely to be greater use of information technologies to engage the community.

CONCLUSION

Australia is clearly an e-government leader when measured against global benchmarks, although the rate of increase is slowing as more complex e-government activities and problems are addressed. With Australia's federated structure of government, vertical integration of electronic government remains one of the key challenges if seamless government is to be achieved. The goal of increased citizen interaction with government may also conflict with the provision of the most efficient online services, and digital-divide issues will continue to be an issue in a large country with a small population.

NOTES

1. Department of Communications, Information Technology and the Arts (DCITA), *Australia's Strategic Framework for the Information Economy, 2004–2006* (Canberra: DCITA, 2004), 9. Available at www.dcita.gov.au/ie/framework, accessed March 10, 2005.

2. See, e.g., New South Wales, Office of Information and Communications Technology, *Information Management and Technology Blueprint* (Sydney: Office of Information and Communications Technology, 1997). Available at www.gcio.nsw.gov.au/content/1.2.4.content.asp, accessed January 5, 2005; New South Wales, Office of Information and Communications Technology, *Connect NSW: An Internet Strategy for NSW* (Sydney: Office of Information and Communications Technology, 1997); John Brumby, *Connecting Victoria* (Melbourne: Minister for State and Regional Development, 1999). Available at www.mmv.vic.gov.au/connectingvictoria, accessed January 20, 2005; Western Australia, *E-government Strategy for the Western Australian Public Sector* (Perth: Office of E-government, 2004).

3. National Office of the Information Economy (NOIE), *Better Services, Better Government* (Canberra: NOIE, 2002), 10. Available at www.agimo.gov.au/__data/assets/pdf_file/35503/Better _Services-Better_Gov.pdf, accessed January 30, 2005; Australian Public Service Commission, *State of the Service Report, 2003–2004* (Canberra: Australian Public Service Commission, 2004), 51. Available at www.apsc.gov.au/stateoftheservice/0304/chaper4.pdf, accessed March 20, 2005.

4. NOIE, *Better Services, Better Government,* 1.

5. See, e.g., DCITA, *Tel: Info: The Regional Landscape.* Available at www.telinfo.gov.au/, accessed March 25, 2005.

6. Rachel Lloyd and Anthea Bill, *Australia Online: How Australians Are Using Computers and the Internet 2001,* ABS Catalog No. 2056.0 (Canberra: Australian Bureau of Statistics, Australian Census Analytic Program, 2004). Available at www.abs.gov.au, accessed February 10, 2005; Australian Bureau of Statistics, *Household Use of Information Technology, Australia 2003*, ABS Catalog No. 8146.0 (Canberra: Australian Bureau of Statistics, 2004). Available at www.abs.gov.au/Ausstats/abs@.nsf/0/ acc2d18cc958bc7bca2568a9001393ae?OpenDocument, accessed February 10, 2005; Australian Bureau of Statistics, *Household Use of Information Technology;* DCITA, *Current State of Play 2004* (Canberra: DCITA, 2004). Available at www.dcita.gov.au/ie, accessed March 10, 2005.

7. Broadband Services Expert Group, *Networking Australia's Future, Final Report* (Canberra: Australian Government Publishing Service, 1995), x.

8. Broadband Services Expert Group, *Networking Australia's Future,* 93.

9. John Howard, *Investing for Growth: The Howard Government's Plan for Industry* (Canberra: Department of the Prime Minister, 1997), 69–70. Available at www1.industry.gov.au/archive/ growth/html/statement.html, accessed March 19, 2005.

10. DCITA, *A Strategic Framework for the Information Economy: Identifying Priorities for Action* (Canberra: DCITA, 1998).

11. DCITA, *Strategic Framework for the Information Economy,* 26.

12. John Fahey, *Media Release:Towards an Australian Strategy for the Information Economy* (Canberra: Minister for Finance and Administration, 1998).

13. Australian National Audit Office (ANAO), *Electronic Service Delivery, Including Internet Use, by Commonwealth Government Agencies,* ANAO Report No.18, 1999/2000 (Canberra: ANAO, 1999).

14. DCITA, *Government Online: The Commonwealth Government's Strategy* (Canberra: DCITA, 2000). Available at www.agimo.gov.au/publications/2000/04/govonline, accessed February 1, 2005.

15. DCITA, *Customer Focussed Portals Framework* (Canberra: DCITA, 2000). Available at www .agimo.gov.au/services/portals, accessed February 1, 2005).

16. NOIE, *Better Services, Better Government.*

17. NOIE, "Executive Summary," *Better Services, Better Government.*

18. NOIE, *Interoperability Technical Framework for the Australian Government* (Canberra: NOIE, 2003). Available at www.agimo.gov.au/publications/2003/08/framework, accessed February 10, 2005.

19. Management Advisory Committee, *Australian Government Use of Information and Communication Technology* (Canberra: Management Advisory Committee, 2002).

20. Management Advisory Committee, *Connecting Government: Whole of Government Responses to Australia's Priority Challenges* (Canberra: Management Advisory Committee, 2004), 4. Available at www.apsc.gov.au/mac/connectinggovernment.htm, accessed February 8, 2005.

21. DCITA, *Australia's Strategic Framework.*

22. Daryl Williams, *News Release: Strategic Framework for the Information Economy* (Canberra: Minister for Communications, Information Technology and the Arts, 2004).

23. DCITA, *Government Online: The Commonwealth Government's Strategy.*

24. NOIE, *Better Services, Better Government.*

25. Daryl Williams, *News Release: Maximising the Benefits of the Information Economy* (Canberra: Minister for Communications, Information Technology and the Arts, 2004).

26. John Howard, *Media Release: Fourth Howard Ministry* (Canberra: Office of the Prime Minister,

2004). Available at www.pm.gov.au/news/media_releases/media_Release1134.html, accessed March 1, 2005.

27. DCITA, *Australia's Strategic Framework,* 46.

28. New South Wales, Office of Information and Communications Technology, *Information Management and Technology Blueprint*; New South Wales, Office of Information and Communications Technology, *Connect NSW.*

29. Brumby, *Connecting Victoria.*

30. Western Australia, *E-government Strategy for the Western Australian Public Sector.*

31. DCITA, *Strategic Framework for the Information Economy.*

32. DCITA, *Government Online.*

33. NOIE, *Advancing Australia: The Information Economy Progress Report* (Camberra: NOIE, July 1999, May 2000, November 2002). Available at www.dcita.gov.au/ie/publications/2002/november/advancing_australia_-_the_information_economy_progress_report_2002, accessed March 15, 2005; www.dcita.gov.au/ie/publications/2000/may/strategic_framework_for_the_information_economy_-_second_progress_report, accessed March 10, 2005.

34. DCITA, *Government Online,* 7.

35. NOIE, *E-government Benefits: Agency Case Studies* (Canberra: NOIE, 2003). Available at www.agimo.gov.au/government/benefits_study, accessed November 1, 2004.

36. NOIE, *Better Services, Better Government.*

37. NOIE, *Better Services, Better Government,* 23.

38. The latest is Australian Government Information Management Office (AGIMO), *Annual Report 2003–2004* (Canberra: AGIMO, 2004). Available at www.agimo.gov.au/publications/2004/10/annrep03-04, accessed December 10, 2004.

39. AGIMO, *Annual Report 2003–2004,* parts 2, 13.

40. DCITA, *Information Economy Index* (Canberra: DCITA, 2004). Available at www.dcita.gov.au/__data/assets/pdf_file/23454/IE_Index_2004.pdf, accessed March 10, 2005.

41. ANAO, *Internet Delivery Decisions: A Government Program Manager's Guide* (Canberra: ANAO, 2001). Available at www.anao.gov.au/WebSite.nsf/Publications/4A256AE90015F69B4A256A3E0025D82A, accessed December 1, 2004.

42. ANAO, *Quality Internet Services for Government Clients: Monitoring and Evaluation by Government Agencies,* Report No. 30 (Canberra: ANAO, 2004). Available at www.anao.gov.au/WebSite.nsf/Publications/2A51AE59FB11AA5ECA256E40000DCC32, accessed March 5, 2005.

43. Organization for Economic Co-operation and Development (OECD), *E-Government Imperative* (Paris: OECD, 2003), 169–81; United Nations, Division for Public Administration and Development Management, *Global E-Government Readiness Report 2004: Towards Access for Opportunity,* UNPAN 2004/11 (New York: United Nations, 2004), 43–44. Available at www.unpan.org/egovernment4.asp, accessed March 1, 2005; Accenture, *eGovernment Leadership: High Performance, Maximum Value* (New York: Accenture, 2004), 61–62, 23ff. Available at www.accenture.com/xd/xd.asp?it=enweb&xd=industries%5Cgovernment%5Cgove_egov_value.xml, accessed March 12, 2005.

44. United Nations, Division for Public Administration and Development Management, *Global E-Government Readiness Report 2004.*

45. United Nations, "Web Measure Index," in *Global E-Government Readiness Report,* 52.

46. United Nations, "E-readiness Index," in *Global E-Government Readiness Report,* 23.

47. United Nations, "E-participation Index," in *Global E-Government Readiness Report,* 66.

48. Accenture, "E-government Maturity Index," in *eGovernment Leadership,* 7.

49. NOIE, *Better Services, Better Government*; NOIE, *E-government Benefits.*

50. Accenture, *eGovernment Leadership,* 25.

51. AGIMO, *Annual Report 2003–2004,* 4.

52. AGIMO, *Annual Report 2003–2004,* 4–5.

53. DCITA, *Information Economy Index 2004*; DCITA, *Current State of Play 2004* (Canberra: Author, 2005).

54. AGIMO, *Annual Report 2003–2004*, 28–29.

55. Croger Associates, *TIGERS Report: Program Summary* (Canberra: NOIE, 2003). Available at www.agimo.gov.au/publications/2003/09/tigers_report/case_studies, accessed March 10, 2005.

56. NOIE, "Australian Taxation Office," in *E-government Benefits*, 8–13.

57. Raelene Vivian, "Elements of Good Government Community Collaboration," in *Future Challenges for E-government,* vol. 1 (Canberra: AGIMO, 2004), 27–46.

58. World Wide Web Consortium, *Web Content Accessibility Guidelines* (Cambridge, MA: W3C, 1999). Available at www.w3.org/TR/WAI-WEBCONTENT/, accessed March 1, 2005.

59. NOIE, *Guide to Minimum Website Standards, April 2003* (Canberra: NOIE, 2003), 22.

60. AGIMO, *Access and Equity Issues for Websites*, Better Practice Checklist no. 19 (Canberra: AGIMO, 2004). Available at www.agimo.gov.au/practice/delivery/checklists/web_access, accessed March 9, 2005.

61. Hiser Group, *The User Experience of Government Online: Recommendations for a Citizen-centric Future* (Melbourne: Hiser Group, 2002). Available at www.egov.vic.gov.au/pdfs/HiserUsability Report.pdf, accessed March 10, 2005; Accenture, *eGovernment Leadership,* 61–62, 23ff; Sue Burgess and Jan Houghton, "Evaluation of Selected NSW Government Websites: A User Perspective," in *Performance Audit Report: E-government: User-friendliness of Websites* (Sydney: Audit Office of New South Wales, 2002), 23–46. Available at www.audit.nsw.gov.au/publications/reports/performance/2002/websites/Websites-Contents.html.

62. Hiser Group, *The User Experience of Government Online.*

63. Burgess and Houghton, "Evaluation of Selected NSW Government Websites."

64. Andrew Arch and Brian Hardy, "E-government Accessible to All," in *Future Challenges for E-government* (Canberra: AGIMO, 2004), 2:65.

65. Human Rights and Equal Opportunity Commission, *Bruce Lindsay Maguire v. Sydney Organising Committee for the Olympic Games*, H99/115 (Sydney: Human Rights and Equal Opportunity Commission, 2000). Available at www.hreoc.gov.au/disability_rights/decisions/comdec/2000/DD000120.htm, accessed March 10, 2005.

66. Anni Dugdale, Anne Daly, Franco Papandrea, and Maria Maley, "Connecting the Dots: Accessing E-government," in *Future Challenges for E-government* (Canberra: AGIMO, 2004), 2:75–91. Available at www.agimo.gov.au/publications/2004/05/egovt_challenges/, accessed April 15, 2005.

67. ANAO, *Electronic Service Delivery.*

68. Andrew Chadwick and Christopher May, "Interaction between States and Citizens in the Age of the Internet: E-government in the United States, Britain and the European Union," *Governance: An International Journal of Policy, Administration and Institutions* 16, no. 2 (April 2003): 271–300.

69. DCITA, *Australia's Strategic Framework,* 49.

70. NOIE, *Better Services, Better Government*, 10.

71. Meredith Edwards, "Public Sector Governance: Future Issues for Australia," *Australian Journal of Public Administration* 61, no. 2 (June 2002): 51–61.

72. Management Advisory Committee, *Connecting Government.*

73. Management Advisory Committee, "Making Connections outside the APS: The Nature of Engagement in Whole of Government Activities," in *Connecting Government*, chap. 6.

74. Management Advisory Committee, "Making Connections outside the APS," chap. 6.

75. Australian Public Service Commission, "Public Consultation and Communication," in *State of the Service Report, 2003–2004,* 71–72.

76. AGIMO, *Online Policy Consultation: Better Practice Checklist 12* (Canberra: AGIMO, 2004). Available at www.agimo.gov.au/practice/delivery/checklists/online_policy, accessed March 5, 2005.

77. AGIMO and Institute of Public Administration Australia, ICT Division, *Future Challenges for E-government,* 2 vols. (Canberra: AGIMO, 2004).

78. Michael Hogan, Natalie Cook, and Monika Henderson, "The Queensland Government's

E-democracy Agenda" (paper presented at the Australian Electronic Governance Conference 2004, Melbourne: University of Melbourne, Centre for Public Policy, April 2004). Available at www .public-policy.unimelb.edu.au/egovernance/ConferenceContent.html#michaelhogan, accessed March 1, 2005; Queensland Government, "Get Involved" Web site (Brisbane: Department of Communities, Community Engagement and Development Policy Unit). Available at www.getinvolved .qld.gov.au, accessed March 10, 2005.

79. Kerrie Oakes, "The Impact of Electronic Governance on the Public Sector" (paper presented at the Australian Electronic Governance Conference 2004). Available at www.public-policy.unimelb .edu.au/egovernance/ConferenceContent.html#kerrieoakes, accessed March 1, 2005.

80. Trinitas Proprietary Limited, *Inquiry into Electronic Democracy: Scrutiny of Acts and Regulations Committee, Discussion Paper* (Melbourne: Parliament of Victoria, 2002). Available at www.parliament .vic.gov.au/sarc/E-Democracy/Discussion%20Paper.htm, accessed March 1, 2005.

81. Australian Capital Territory Electoral Commission, *The 2001 ACT General Assembly Election Electronic Voting and Counting System Review* (Canberra: Australian Capital Territory, 2002). Available at www.elections.act.gov.au/CompExecSumm.htm, accessed March 25, 2005.

82. The previous council was dismissed owing to a lack of transparency in decision making and an administrator put in place for five years.

• 6 •

E-government in New Zealand

Rowena Cullen

$\mathcal{E}$-government within New Zealand is part of an overall government-led Digital Strategy intended to ensure that New Zealanders benefit from the power of information and communications technology (ICT). The vision of the recently released Digital Strategy is to make New Zealand "a world leader in using information and technology to realise its economic, social, environmental, and cultural goals, to the benefit of all its people." The government has defined three specific areas for action: content, confidence, and connection that will link government, business, and communities to achieve certain benefits: "instant access to national knowledge resources (whether cultural, scientific, heritage, archival, broadcasting or community); government services that are customised to our individual needs; and the economic benefits that flow from higher productivity."[1] This chapter examines the development and implementation of e-government in New Zealand over the past decade, the strategies and instruments that have been seen as critical to that development, and the extent to which these have delivered e-government information and services that meet individual needs.

In terms of e-government development, New Zealand has a natural advantage over other countries, with its small population, single national government, and limited number of levels of local and regional bodies with jurisdiction at the city or district level. However, in the crucial decade during which many nations advanced considerably in e-government, several factors retarded the development of e-government in New Zealand. First, a wide-ranging program of public sector reform through the 1980s and 1990s focused on clarifying the outputs of government departments, the separation of policy development, and the delivery of services.[2] Service agencies were established as state-owned enterprises (SOEs) and crown entities (state-funded hospitals became Crown Health Enterprises), some of which were categorized as crown companies, depending on the degree to which they charged for services, and could be expected to operate in a commercial framework. Although most SOEs and crown entities are heavily dependent on state funding, these structures were designed to remove them from direct government intervention. Their accountability was managed through *purchase agreements* made with government for the services they provide, and the requirement to report annually to Parliament.[3]

This politically engineered "distance from government" also gave crown entities and SOEs some distance from the direct control of central government agencies such as the State Services Commission, the Treasury, and the Cabinet Office, which have jurisdiction over core government departments and ministries. The state services commissioner is the government's principal adviser on the role and structure of government departments and other agencies and, in the words of the State Sector Act, "on management systems, structures and organizations" as well as overseeing personnel policies and management within the state sector, and setting minimum standards and codes of conduct. Although the State Services Commission therefore has *some* authority over the application of information and communications technologies, and therefore the implementation of e-government in the broader state sector, it is not always sufficient to ensure that these agencies comply with guidelines and standards, even though they offer specific services, and charge for such services, that are integral to the more advanced phases of e-government, where the emphasis is on transactions rather than just information transfer.

The second factor that impacted the development of e-government in New Zealand, one closely related to the public sector reforms, was the introduction of accountability in the public sector through narrowly defined and closely audited outputs for which government agencies and their chief executives were responsible, leaving little room for flexibility and experimentation with new forms of communications or office management. Changes in 1994 to the departmental reporting process, introducing departmental Statements of Intent as the vehicle for articulating and assessing achievement against departmental objectives, and which may include reference to outcomes as well as more narrowly defined outputs, have since allowed more flexibility in departmental activities.

E-government in New Zealand began with a set of Cabinet papers in the mid-1990s that articulated some of the principles that would emerge in the early vision statements concerning the development of e-government in this country. The *Discussion Paper for Information Sharing*, published in 1995 by the Interdepartmental Committee on Information Technology, raised some key issues about the government's responsibility for the dissemination of information, including electronic information, in a democracy. These included:

- What government information should be available, and to whom, particularly in a proportional representation environment?
- What explicit principles guide government information?
- Is the provision of electronic information about government part of a national infrastructure such as roads or commercial services?
- Should equity of access to specified government information be consistent across the Public Service for all New Zealanders?[4]

The key issues raised in this discussion paper, the answers to which seem so obvious a decade later, were eventually addressed in a brief statement adopted by the New Zealand Cabinet in 1997. The *Policy Framework for Government-Held Information* put forward core principles that were intended to cover all government information, regardless of the medium or the channel of delivery. The two principles stated:

1. Government departments should make information available easily, widely, and equitably to the people of New Zealand, except where reasons preclude such availability as specified in legislation.

2. Government departments should make the following information increasingly available on an electronic basis:
   * all published material or material already in the public domain;
   * all policies that could be released publicly;
   * all information created or collected on a statutory basis (subject to commercial sensitivity and privacy considerations);
   * all documents that the public may be required to complete; and
   * corporate documentation in which the public would be interested.[5]

Central government agencies within New Zealand still do not fully comply with these principles, although, increasingly, as documents are born digital, it is easier to ensure their availability through electronic channels. However, the principle of making information "widely and equitably available" was never abandoned, although it was obscured for some years by overoptimistic estimates of the potential and impact of electronic information and service delivery during the early years of e-government. It is only now reemerging as a formally adopted multichannel policy, in which the reality that citizens will continue to want face-to-face and telephone contact with government and access to print publications is recognized.

On September 28, 1999, Maurice Williamson, minister of communications in the National government party of 1996–1999, and a vocal champion of e-government, released *Vision Statement: Electronic Government for New Zealand*, which stated that "E-government will harness people and technology to revolutionise the delivery of government services to New Zealanders. The new services will be tailored, inexpensive, easy to use, personal and friendly."[6] This vision statement was developed in conjunction with the State Services Commission and a group of chief executives of central government departments that had been meeting for two years as the Chief Executives' Group on Information Management and Technology. The vision embraced open government and cheaper government, promised privacy and greater equality, and promulgated the development of a "one-stop shop" for citizens to transact their business with government and meet their personal needs. It anticipated many of the developments that have since taken place in the development of e-government in New Zealand: registering a company, payment of employee and goods and services taxes online (for companies and institutions), online consultation over policy, a national health intranet, an online land information service, and the development of protocols for the use of digital signatures.

However, Williamson's vision was developed against a background of "less government" and a culture embodying a significant lack of cooperation, even the promotion of competition, between government agencies. Although the majority of central government departments and related agencies (including state-owned enterprises and commercial services) had by this time developed Web sites, there was a lack of standardization and central management. E-government development was therefore piecemeal, and there was some competition between key agencies as to which would be the driving (and controlling) agency.

The Chief Executives' Group provided a briefing to the incoming Labour government in December 1999 that emphasized the need for a number of factors to be addressed in order to deliver the anticipated benefits of e-government. These ranged from "well-developed and articulated vision through to building an appropriate technical and organizational infrastructure."[7] The briefing acknowledges the declared intent of many countries to use e-government to reinvent government, simplifying and streamlining it, as well as enabling greater participation of citizens and enhancing democratic process. The document advocates making use of

> the power of information and communication technologies (ICTs) to rebuild government from the outside in. Here, emphasis is generally placed upon focusing on the needs of citizens, communities and businesses, not those of government agencies. In New Zealand there has been discussion around using an e-government initiative to move government from what is best described as a "silo" model to a networked model.[8]

The briefing noted, "A concerted effort has been made to get all Public Service chief executives to agree to adopt inter-agency collaboration in the use of information and technology as a desirable way of operating in the future. Effective collaboration will be a key success factor in any e-government strategy." The briefing identified eight key issues that needed to be addressed to achieve e-government in New Zealand: leadership, from cabinet and the chief executives; a clear overarching strategy; a focus on citizens; avoiding increasing the already identified digital divide; an overarching governance mechanism; integration across agencies; resources; and effective communication with all New Zealanders.

E-GOVERNMENT UNIT ESTABLISHED

In July 2000, a formal e-government program was announced, and the E-government Unit was established within the State Services Commission to develop and manage the delivery of an overarching e-government strategy, facilitate uptake by government agencies of the e-government vision, identify opportunities for collaboration across government agencies, and provide advice to the minister of state services on e-government policy. Although the E-government Unit was given a central role in defining and achieving the government's objectives for e-government, "the delivery of e-government, in which people can meet the majority of their information and services needs from government online, is the responsibility of all the government agencies in partnership with the Unit."[9]

In April 2001, the unit released its first e-government strategy, which established as its operational vision the statement "New Zealand is a world leader in e-government"[10] and the supporting mission: "*By 2004 the Internet will be the dominant means of enabling ready access to government information, services and processes.*" The focus of the strategy was on:

- better services: more convenient and reliable, with lower compliance costs, higher quality and value;
- cost effectiveness and efficiency: cheaper, better information and services for customers and better value for taxpayers;
- improved reputation: building an image of New Zealand as a modern nation, an attractive location for people and business;
- greater participation by people in government: making it easier, for those who wish to, to contribute; and
- leadership: supporting the knowledge society through public sector innovation.

The strategy outlined some key deliverables for the current year and the succeeding two years, starting with the development of some foundation deliverables in the area of standards and policies covering investment in information technology (IT) across the government sector; the development of a secure electronic environment; a government metadata framework; a Web-portal strategy and standards; a framework for common data standards to ensure interoperability; and a National Information Infrastructure Protection strategy (NIIPS) to protect against cyber attack. Immediate deliverables included as many government forms online as was possible, a pilot program investigating e-billing capability, and an e-procurement strategy to develop government purchasing online. Deliverables over the ensuing year included the development of a government Web portal as the primary entry point to government online, a common change-of-address strategy, and an authentication policy to ensure appropriate identification and protection to the government's online customers.[11]

A PORTAL STRATEGY ESTABLISHED

The portal strategy that was developed at the same time was one of the first public successes of the E-government Unit. In 1995, the Ministry of Commerce had launched an online government directory, and this was merged in 1997 with the Department of Internal Affair's Online Blue Pages (so named after that section of the telephone book that lists government agencies). The Online Blue Pages provided brief descriptive and contact information about individual government agencies but had its own e-mail address for inquiries. This developed into "NZGO—Gateway to the New Zealand Government Online," a set of pages developed over 1999/2000 (some of which can still be viewed at the Wayback archive of Web sites, www.nzgo.govt.nz),[12] which provided an overview of the structure of the New Zealand government, listed government agencies and their online contacts, and offered brief news and news releases, as well as recent publications available online. The site also listed issues that the government was "currently consulting on" and linked to discussion documents.

Following the establishment of the E-government Unit and the initial New Zealand E-government program on July 1, 2000, a formal portal strategy was developed with an imaginative, forward-looking, and highly ambitious vision. This vision again projected the portal as "a world leader in electronic delivery of government information and services via the Internet" and "the preferred mechanism for customers to access central and local government information." The portal was to reflect the New Zealand people and land, the country's history and values, culture, and heritage. It was also to be able to categorize customers by their age, gender, nationality, location, expertise, and other factors. A series of scenarios outlined how the "one-stop-shop" concept would work, one scenario depicting how a citizen was able to register the birth of a baby, secure home help, and request an enhanced benefit and a larger state house, all on the night of the birth, from the maternity hospital. The key elements needed to achieve this were identified as a governance framework; enhancing, securing, and operating the existing NZGO; establishing a Customer Advisory Group to develop appropriate relationships with customers and proxies for service delivery; developing and publishing a Quality of Service Charter, Trust Charter, and Infomediary Code of Conduct; providing input to the service inventory and portal planning for enabling shared/integrated services delivery; implementation of metadata standards and collection of metadata; and development of search capabilities to use metadata to find government services.[13]

Many of these early ambitions have been modified by the complexities of implementation and have been tempered by the need to secure cooperation and compliance from central government agencies, as well as local government agencies and state-owned enterprises not within the jurisdiction of the State Services Commission. Strategies have been modified over the years and emphases in implementation changed. The extent to which these early visions have been realized can be assessed by a consideration of the issues with which the E-government Unit is currently grappling, its own assessment of its achievement so far, and independent research that highlights which parts of the e-government program and strategy have been successful in reaching citizens and which have not.

IMPACTS OF NEW ZEALAND LAW AND GOVERNANCE STRUCTURES ON THE DEVELOPMENT OF E-GOVERNMENT

A number of other aspects of New Zealand law, and initiatives in the New Zealand public service, have had an impact on the development of e-government within the country. Access to government information had been improving since the passing of the Official Information Act in 1982, which made all but commercially sensitive information or information concerning individuals disclosable, and a culture of information dissemination and consultation was slowly developing. While Peter Hernon commented in 1996 that the culture was one of "information on request . . . and not on information dissemination,"[14] the *Discussion Paper for Information Sharing* of 1995 signaled a change in the government's approach to information disclosure that has continued to inform e-government developments and helps to reinforce the transformation of government to the citizen-centric model promoted in these early discussion papers. The Privacy Act, passed in 1993, which was an innovative and leading piece of legislation within the commonwealth at the time, provided for the protection of personal information that set a useful framework for developments in e-government and for parallel developments within the health sector as more and more patient information was stored in electronic health records. (In countries with a state-provided primary, secondary, and tertiary health care system, health remains an integral part of e-government. The benefits of better patient record management and greater efficiency through data exchange in the health sector were thus included in the initial vision statement of 2000.)

At the same time, in 2001 a ministerial advisory group, which included public service chief executives and external commentators, conducted a review of the core operations of the New Zealand public service. The *Review of the Centre* focused on the public management system and how well it responded to "the needs and expectations of ministers and of citizens, be they individuals, communities, businesses, or Maori."[15] Issues identified that needed to be addressed included "the interface of government with citizens, particularly on cross-cutting issues where multiple agencies are involved" and "fragmentation, and the loss of focus on the big picture that fragmentation can cause. . . . Fragmentation makes coordinated service delivery more complicated, adds to the costs of doing business, and blurs accountability for some issues." This fragmentation was perceived to extend to local government and community organizations. Suggested solutions, which were piloted over the next three years, included cross-agency teams, revision of departmental accountability systems, change management, and leadership development. These were couched within a framework of "achieving better integrated, citizen focused, service delivery."[16] Although e-government was not highlighted as the solution to these problems, awareness of its potential informs the whole-of-government approach of the *Review of the Centre* initiative. Its cross-cutting approach to solutions was a considerable impetus to make progress on key e-government initiatives that were being put on the agenda (projects such as interoperability and shared workspace).

E-GOVERNMENT AT THE
LOCAL GOVERNMENT LEVEL

Although citizens may not make a distinction between central or national government and local governments, and see their relationship with government as pertaining to both types of institutions; the degree of authority central government has over local governments is limited in New Zealand. Local government is an institution comprising a number of separate and autonomous organizations (local authorities) in a political system over which Parliament is supreme.[17] Parliament provides the authority for both central and local government and the constraints within which each institution and its constituent organizations function.

The distinction between Parliament and central government is fundamental but is sometimes overlooked. This oversight may have originated in earlier times when the distinction between the two was somewhat blurred. This blurring could have led to the assumptions that central government possesses authority over local government or that local authorities are properly regarded as agents of central government.[18]

The State Services Commission and the E-government Unit, which were in a position to regulate and require the introduction of various e-government initiatives in central government agencies, could only attempt to persuade and lead by example at the local body level. Initiatives at this level are entirely dependent on each local body making its own commitment to e-government and the use of the Internet to communicate and interact with its citizens. Some of these bodies have been successful, although smaller, less well-resourced local bodies such as some regional councils needed assistance to deal with e-government and its potential. In one study a wide range in the quality and functionality of the Web sites of city, district, and regional councils was shown when these councils were measured against standard criteria for assessing e-government Web sites.[19] However, their performance on many criteria was better than that of a similar assessment of central government agency Web sites conducted less than two years earlier.[20]

Through cooperative organizations such as Local Government New Zealand, the Association of Local Government Information Management (ALGIM), and the Society of Local Government Officers (SOLGM), e-government was placed firmly on the agenda for local bodies, and an increasingly productive relationship with the E-government Unit resulted. In 1997, the Local Government Online (LGOL) Web site was established under a joint initiative from ALGIM and SOLGM to offer Internet-related services to the local government sector. These services consisted of a template Web site and Web site hosting facilities, targeted to smaller councils without a large IT department, plus online resources and Web links to assist councils with their business. (The LGOL Web site also operates as a local government portal to local body news and services.)

In May 2003 a local e-government strategy, developed by all these bodies, was launched. The strategy is focused on providing easy online access to council information and services, developing innovative products, enhancing people's participation in local democracy (planning and decision making), and providing community leadership on e-business initiatives. LGOL continues to offer some standard information and service transactions that can be customized to each council, and it strongly endorses the standards developed by the E-Government Unit, including the metadata thesauri being developed and the online authentication standards.[21] In 2004, Local Government New Zealand and the E-government Unit signed an agreement to promote cooperation and encourage councils to add information about core council services to the All of Government portal.[22]

MANY ASPECTS OF E-HEALTH
INVOLVE E-GOVERNMENT

There are other areas in which state-funded services might come under the heading of e-government, one such being health services. Improved services and cost savings are envisaged in the Digital Strategy for the health sector, through wireless and broadband access to patient records and the evidence-based knowledge sources. The Ministry of Health has an evolving IT strategy, the most significant expression of which was the WAVE project (Working to Add Value through E-information), whose eight workstreams and the WAVE Board came up with ten priorities, which until mid-2005 dominated the strategic thinking in the health sector. These included the establishment of a separate unit within the Ministry of Health to manage health IT; improve the collection of ethnicity data from the existing health statistics; implement a national Health Provider Index; improve the accuracy of the National Patient Index; gather electronic information from primary health care providers; facilitate the transfer of information between pharmacy and laboratory service providers and the primary health care sector; improve messaging standards; develop data dictionaries and other health IT standards to capture health events more accurately; establish a health portal; and develop interoperability standards for data exchange, security, and network infrastructure.[23] While progress has been made on many of these fronts, especially in the improvement of the quality of data collected from a variety of agencies and in the development of the national indexes, many of these goals have not yet been achieved to the desired level, and the same issues make up key planks in the current health information strategy that is currently under development. The focus is still on infrastructure to support interoperability and quality of data throughout the sector.

The health sector is unique in that although most of the funding is provided from government, most of the providers in the sector (e.g., family practitioners, pharmacists, and health IT vendors) are private providers, and establishing networks and interoperability is therefore problematic. However, through its support for organizations (e.g.,

Health Informatics New Zealand [www.hinz.org.nz/] and the Health Information Standards Organization [HISO]),[24] the Ministry of Health is having some success in fostering interoperability, standards, and networking throughout the sector. Although secondary (hospital-based) care is managed through twenty-one individual district health boards, which as crown entities have a considerable degree of autonomy, the newly formed District Health Boards New Zealand (DHBNZ)[25] will operate in the way that LGNZ does to encourage uptake of standards (e.g., the HL7 health messaging standard) that are being adopted throughout the sector.[26] Many of the e-government projects outlined below, such as online authentication, digital signatures and certificates, and the geospatial data project are also critical to effective development of IT in the health sector.

CURRENT INITIATIVES IN E-GOVERNMENT

The E-government Unit groups its current policies and implementation initiatives under five main principles that determine key areas of activity. These are accessibility, cooperation, security, and participation.

Accessibility

The e-government portal is one of the main ways in which the E-government Unit hopes to achieve accessibility. It is intended to provide structured single-point access to information and services provided by government agencies through their Web sites. With a simple memorable URL (www.govt.nz) and a plain but functional design, the portal offers access to information and services under a series of headings: for example, "Services," which link to a range of services listed alphabetically by topic; "Contacts," which links to an alphabetical list of contacts with all central and local government agencies; "Things to know when . . . ," which are services related to specific life events; "Maori," or services for Maori people and communities; "Participate in Government," which links to a range of alternatives (e.g., how to contact your member of Parliament, make a submission to Parliamentary Select Committee hearings, or how to present a petition); and "About New Zealand," which links to online information about the country from a range of agencies—Statistics, Conservation—and the official online encyclopedia, *Te Ara*. At the home page level, and in some parts of the pages for Maori, headings are also in Maori, the language of the indigenous people and an official language of the country (alongside English). By providing access through these various headings, the portal aims to fulfill the objectives of the first portal strategy: "to categorise customers by their age, gender, nationality, location, expertise and other factors."

The portal does not provide information or services directly, and it is not intended to replace individual government Web sites or prevent people going directly to those sites. The portal intentionally provides information about how to find out about services, or where information is available, before linking the customer to the information sought. The portal has been labeled "the model of a 'classic' portal, which contains little stand-alone information or services, but rather guides citizens to useful government links and services in an easy-to-find manner."[27] The portal handles a range of anticipated questions well, provided they are stated in the expected way, but is less adept at answering more complex queries or suggesting an appropriate place to seek their answers. The research findings discussed in chapters 10 and 11 show that the portal has had limited use so far, is not yet well known, and has not yet realized its objective of becoming "the preferred mechanism for customers to access central government and local government information." A clear statement of what it does and does not offer and some advice to users in how to execute a successful search would not go amiss.

A series of subject portals—the first of many intended such portals—supplements the main portal with online information about government services. A set of education portals, described by the *E-Government Readiness Report* as representing "a model approach to further access to education and skill development," includes Studylink (www.studylink.govt.nz), which allows students to apply online for financial assistance in the form of loans or allowances (Maori version of the page is available); Te Kete Ipurangi, the online learning center (www.tki.org.nz); the tertiary education portal (www.ted.govt.nz/); and the tertiary e-learning portal (www.eLearn.govt.nz), another bilingual site that links to resources designed to support the primary and secondary education curricula. The business portal (www.biz.org.nz) and the Department of Labour's WorkSite portal (www.worksite.govt.nz/) support business and employment. The E-government Unit's own Web site acts as a portal and repository for current and historical information on the development of e-government in New Zealand, thus exemplifying its own principles and values.

The infrastructure of the main government portal (www.govt.nz) incorporates a well-developed system of metadata, the New Zealand Government Locator System (NZGLS), which is based on a set of metadata standards and a thesaurus. The NZGLS metadata standard for creating discovery-level metadata is itself closely based on two well-established standards: the Dublin Core Metadata Element Set and the Australian Government Locator Service. Archives New Zealand, with support from an expert NZGLS Working Group, which consists of representatives from across government, oversees the management of the standard.[28] The NZGLS metadata standard includes a thesaurus that consists of the Functions of New Zealand (FONZ) and the Subjects of New Zealand (SONZ) thesauri. Terms from both these thesauri are combined to describe government information, services, and other resources in a consistent manner. The National Library of New Zealand, which is the custodian of the NZGLS thesauri, is responsible for maintaining the data.[29]

The portal's infrastructure also includes an e-service delivery architecture that has been developed to

- identify and prioritize how government services will be brought online and made available via the portal;
- develop guidelines, procedures, and methodologies to assist agencies and clusters of agencies to integrate services delivered electronically; and
- share best practice in successful electronic service delivery.

Information about the architecture on the E-government Web site specifically notes, "Integrated and well-coordinated e-services promise efficiency gains for agencies and outcomes that align with the recommendations of the Report of the Advisory Group on the Review of the Centre."[30] The architecture is intended to support shared technology components, developed in a whole-of-government way, where these are applicable, "to avoid duplication of effort and wasted public funding, as well as to enable more seamless integration of services across agencies."[31]

A critical element of accessibility relates, not to the portal, but to the government Web guidelines, which make up the other plank in the E-government Unit's accessibility policy. These are mandatory, through a Cabinet Minute passed in December 2003 for all central government agencies, and were originally based on the guidelines for government Web sites developed in the United Kingdom. The UK guidelines closely reflected the Web accessibility guidelines of the World Wide Web Consortium (W3C) of the time.[32] The first version, developed by the Government Information Systems Managers Forum (GOVIS),[33] and adopted and issued by the E-government Unit in February 2001, have been updated and localized over time, and the current version, version 2.1, includes guidelines on the use of cascading style sheets (CSS2); how the Maori language can be represented on Web pages with macrons while remaining accessible to text-only and low-level browsers; and the use of access keys, used by many people in the disability communities for rapid navigation. The guidelines also provide practical ways to provide economical and equitable access to trustworthy information and services, reflecting the core values of the public service in New Zealand. Version 2.1 of the guidelines is a whole-of-government standard for the development, management, and delivery of public sector Web sites. Although they are voluntary beyond the core public sector, a number of local authorities and crown entities have adopted the guidelines.

Cooperation

Several current initiatives of the E-government Unit enhance cooperation, a key plank of the *Review of the Centre*. Under this category, projects on interoperability (e-GIF), geospatial information, and shared workspace have been developed, as well as policies concerning governance and funding, e-government people networks, and vendor relationships. The e-GIF, or e-Government Interoperability Framework project, underpins many of the other e-government projects. Along with the E-government strategy, Web guidelines and NZGLS metadata, and the authentication project, the New Zealand e-government interoperability standards form the required elements of the e-government infrastructure in New Zealand. All other policies and requirements are discretionary at this stage.

Based on the e-GIF of the UK, and international standards bodies such as W3C and OASIS, the e-GIF is a collection of policies and standards endorsed for New Zealand government IT systems, each of which an expert working group oversees and recommends for inclusion in the e-GIF. The policies and standards focus on specific aspects of the online publishing environment such as:

- xNAL (eXtensible Name and Address Language);
- ESA (Emergency Services and Government Administration);
- NZGMS (New Zealand Geospatial Metadata standard);
- RSS (RDF Site Summary) news standards;
- CVL (controlled value lists); and
- Namespaces (XML Namespaces).

The e-GIF strategy and policies are also required to address standards developing in other areas (e.g., health, where international standards such as HL7 are being adopted). Standardization of geospatial information, used for a variety of purposes (e.g., emergency services, health services, electoral boundaries, mapping services, land-use decisions, and legislation), relies on compliance with International Standards Organization (ISO) standards and is closely linked to work on the New Zealand Geospatial Metadata standard. The geospatial metadata standard is viewed as part of the broader NZGLS.

Interagency collaboration is also enhanced by the development of a secure public sector intranet (psi.govt.nz) and the shared workspace project, a modular toolbox intended to support interagency collaboration and groups sharing work in progress. While the intranet and shared workspace are intended to be a repository for information resources of value to the whole state sector and provide valuable experience in using online collaboration tools, they will not function as an all-of-government document management and archiving service. Long-term vendors and contractual partners with government agencies will also have secure access to parts of the shared workspace. Also derived from the principles of the *Review of the Centre* is the establishment of formal people networks within public service departments and some other government organizations and the nomination of e-government agency leaders to drive the implementation of e-government in their organizations. The development of appropriate governance structures for shared projects is also part of the cooperation plan.

Finally, syndicated online procurement to optimize purchasing power is managed through the Syndicated Procurement Unit, which has already resulted in significant savings to some agencies.

Security

Many of these developments require a secure electronic environment. Aware that there is public concern about trust and security, the online authentication project and secure electronic environment projects are addressing this concern from the point of view of both government agencies and citizens. The secure electronic environment (SEE) project aims to develop and implement a secure electronic environment for exchange of government e-mail and to govern access to repositories of government information for authorized public servants. This will be managed through a directory (the SEE directory), which will act as the definitive reference point for information about people, organizations, services, and other objects of interest. Authorization of public servants to access various domains in the SEE will be managed through the directory and assigned SEE keys, which will authenticate users with digital certificates, allow access to sensitive across-agency repositories of information, and create audit logs when users access the system.

SecureMail is an extension of an existing e-government initiative, known as SEE-Mail, which has been operating since 2000 and is used by over forty government agencies as a means for the secure exchange of e-mail and attachments using the Internet. Many communications among government, businesses, and people include personal in-confidence information. Communicating such information over the Internet requires sufficient security to protect the privacy and rights of an individual as well as the integrity of an organization. SecureMail has been designed to meet this additional need. Used appropriately, SecureMail will provide a high level of assurance that the "from" address has not been faked (spoofed) and no unauthorized person has read or altered the message.

An analogy used by the E-government Unit to explain the SecureMail service to customers is that SecureMail provides the option to send a message on letterhead paper in a sealed envelope, where previously all messages were typically sent as postcards. Currently, the SEE is used to develop shared applications, business processes, and workflow systems for internal government activities (e.g., shared workspace). This environment is currently designed to facilitate the sharing of data and information that is classified up to the level of *sensitive*. Although there are no immediate plans for the higher security level, *confidential* data, the environment has been designed to support it should there be a need in future.

Attacks from outside the system, especially cyber attacks, are addressed by the National Information Infrastructure Protection (NIIP) program, managed through the Government Communication Security Bureau, which covers all communications networks affecting critical national infrastructure. Protection against computer misuse and hackers is still a shared responsibility with each agency being required to adopt relevant IT security standards in both software and staff practice.

Secure communication from citizens to government will be managed through the authentication project, which has been the subject of widespread consultation, and has been developed as an all-of-government (i.e., mandatory) e-government program. Initiated in 2002 to facilitate the increasing volume of transactions between citizens and agencies, it is now at the stage of initial implementation,[34] focused on the concept of a shared or common log-on service and the development of standards (e.g., data and messaging standards) for the overall authentication process, as well as policies governing privacy and legal implications. Current research focuses on ways in which electronic identity can be managed, although legislation authorizing the use of digital signatures and digital certificates in both business and government has been in place for some years.[35] Conceived as a two-stage process whereby individuals provide evidence to register their identity and then are given or establish an "associated identifier" (e.g., a username and password), the authentication project still envisages a "one-stop-shop" approach to government agencies, in which citizens will have "a unique key that opens many government service doors."[36]

Although authentication will be a centralized activity, through an identity management service managed by the Department of Internal Affairs (which already manages passports), authorization to gain access to various kinds of information and the assignment of specific roles to individuals (e.g., a citizen paying for a service, a registered contractor tendering a service, or another agency exchanging data) will still be the responsibility of individual agencies. Privacy remains an ongoing concern in the authentication project, and privacy impact assessments are made at each stage of development.

The E-government Unit has ongoing concerns about trust and security discussed in a report that summarizes a range of issues believed to represent threats to Internet security within the New Zealand government, and which may deter users from making full use of e-government information and services.[37] These threats range from spam, virus attacks, and phishing (e-mail fraud involving attempts to obtain a person's bank account number and password), to breaches of personal privacy. The possibility of a reduction in Internet use, and therefore e-government use, as a result of citizens' concerns about these threats was raised by participants in various surveys of e-government use in New Zealand (although none of the participants suggested they would reduce their Internet use for this reason).[38]

The paper by Cate Curtis, Jack Vowles, and Bruce Curtis focuses on assets the E-government Unit wishes to protect, namely, Internet infrastructure; public confidence in the Internet and e-government; agency confidence in the e-government program; and confidence in the information being transmitted (the integrity of the information provided, its long-term availability, and privacy of personal information).[39] While all possible threats (including pornography and child abuse) are seen as having an impact on public and agency confidence, some threats have an impact on information integrity or on infrastructure. Inadequate government IT security and denial-of-service attacks may have an impact on all four dimensions of trust: infrastructure, public confidence, agency confidence, and information integrity. Actions and policies proposed to combat these threats include education (of citizens and agency staff), policy development, and enforcement. Specific actions being considered include a centralized Internet gateway for government agencies (no direct access to agency Web sites); antispam legislation; rapid development of secure log-ons; encouragement of authentication in the private sector (e.g., banks); introduction of laws to clarify software licenses and expose spyware; increased protection of intellectual property through copyright and digital rights legislation; government involvement in Internet governance; review of arrangements for cyber security; vigorous prosecution of breaches of acceptable practice (including spamming, promoting viruses, and identity theft); and education programs for Internet users and agencies. Although this report contains some firm recommendations on these actions, they have not yet been adopted as government policy.

Participation

The last major project the E-government Unit is working on is participation. The issues here are also still being actively researched, and a series of policy papers outlines current E-government Unit thinking on the issues. The participation project is closely aligned with the people-centric principles of the original vision statement, the founding e-government strategy, and the more recent digital strategy. It includes a range of initiatives already discussed: the portal, the use of metadata to improve access to government information and services, the promotion on the portal of issues on which the government is currently consulting citizens, and the availability of legislation online. E-voting, which is already being tried in Australia, the United States, and the United Kingdom, related initiatives (e.g., online voter registration and e-petitions), and a highly successful initiative of the Scottish Parliament are not yet on the agenda, although notice is taken of such developments.

The main issue addressed in relation to participation is how the Internet should be integrated into the way in which government interacts with citizens in comparison to other channels (e.g., counter services, mail, and call centers). *The Channel Strategy: Scoping Study* was one of three related studies commissioned to help the E-government Unit develop a channel strategy (the other two looked at the existence of policies and legislation in New Zealand that might impact the issue and how other countries had dealt with the issue). The scoping study reported that there was clear evidence that New Zealanders continue to demand access to government information and services through a variety of channels (e.g., telephone and face-to-face meetings) and that future demand for online services is most likely to come from young people, well-educated higher-income groups, special interest groups (e.g., genealogists), and the business sector. The study noted, "In some cases there is not a strong match between some of these groups and the delivery of government services. For example, the government is more likely to deliver services to the socially disadvantaged than those with higher education and higher incomes, except where the latter operate businesses."[40] Counteracting this to some extent is the research reported in *Wired for Well-Being*[41] (which comprises chapters 10 and 11), which suggests that in many other cases young people and the well-educated higher income groups make considerable use of a wide variety of government services in relation to higher education, recreational pursuits, and awareness of policy issues. The scoping study notes similar patterns (of high demand for a small range of services from nonwired disadvantaged groups) in other countries and concludes that despite apparent efficiencies for government agencies in shifting to an electronic environment, a variety of channels will be required for the foreseeable future to deliver citizen-centric e-government.

A channel strategy is thus seen as an integral part of promoting citizen participation in e-government and, indeed, in all government. A number of higher-level issues related to participation are canvassed in *Participation through E-government,* which identifies a number of enablers and barriers to participation, many of which have been identified in studies of the digital divide in a range of countries. Access barriers that need to be, or are being, addressed include infrastructure (broadband connections into all communities, and all citizens with at least community-based access to the Internet). Accessibility is a more difficult problem that involves social and cultural issues, many of which are further defined in the report *Wired for Well-Being.*[42] In addition, there is a culture within some agencies that is resistant to change and reluctant to encourage citizen participation in policy development and the design of service delivery. *Participation through E-government* connects these social and institutional barriers with some of the major planks of the e-government strategy and implementation program—authentication, for example, is seen as supporting trust, which is now defined in terms closer to those emerging in the e-commerce domain; trust is about "being credible (being open, honest and accessible), being reliable (being fair and responsive, doing what you say), and being trustworthy (through a partnership that operates for best mutual interest and exchanged value)."[43]

Participation is emerging as a complex social issue and as one linked to the most advanced stages of e-government development. While the E-government Unit is focused on "providing government information to people in ways that make it accessible and relevant, and creating opportunities for people to be actively involved in the design and delivery of government policies and services,"[44] the paper notes that

> increased participation by public and businesses is not intended to replace our representative system. The Government is still expected to take the initiative and to lead. Such leadership can, however, take advantage of referring to wider resources to inform policies, service design and delivery, and to improve trust in democracy through increased transparency and accountability.[45]

This level of active participation is related to the third level of e-government, the transformational level, which is part of the e-government strategy and is directly referred to in the mission for 2010. The clarification of the concepts of participation and transformation from the point of view of the New Zealand government and the E-government Unit is helpful in defining the common ground for discussion surrounding the development of e-government in New Zealand and for harnessing the cooperation of government agencies, business, and citizens.

THE ACHIEVEMENT OF E-GOVERNMENT

After some eight years of formal development of e-government (although many government agencies had well-developed Web sites long before this), the government paused to assess its achievement in e-government to date, using the targeted outcomes set in the e-government strategy for 2004: convenience and satisfaction, integration and efficiency, and participation. The achieving e-government project used five approaches to measure progress toward these performance metrics: analysis of recent e-government surveys to measure the demand for e-government; an assessment of agency Web sites; an appraisal of the quality of metadata records used on the government portal; extensive consultation with agencies; and a review of the E-government Unit's contribution to the strategy's outcomes and targets.[46]

According to the report *Achieving E-government 2004*, agencies are making considerable progress in meeting performance metrics. On convenience and satisfaction, almost without exception agencies are putting considerable focus on using Internet and network technologies to improve public access to information. The report highlights the findings of the *Channel-Surfing* telephone survey of five thousand respondents commissioned by the E-government Unit in 2004 that 28 percent of respondents gained access to government information or services online because it was "convenient, faster, easy, and a good source of information."[47] *Achieving E-government 2004* also notes that 67 percent of the government Web sites evaluated as part of the assessment effort received a rating of *good* or *high* against a wide range of criteria, and that all of the sties provided ready access to information. It also notes that the portal "enables ready access to a wide range of agencies' information and services, whether available online or offline. Metadata records are generally of a high quality."[48]

The report also notes,

> Most agencies are improving back-office systems such as re-vamping intranets to provide more relevant and tailored information for staff; introducing electronic document management system; and sharing information and data with other agencies. Some agencies are introducing mobile computing, dramatically improving access to information for staff working away from their office. Agencies are using internet technologies to improve traditional service delivery channels.[49]

The portal had not achieved all its goals of integration between agencies, thereby offering customers a "one-stop shop." Measuring achievement so far against criteria set for integration and efficiency, the *Achieving E-government 2004* report notes that "online services for the public still tend to be strongly based around individual agencies, requiring customers to contact several agencies to complete related transactions or processes."[50] Nevertheless, it notes that agencies are increasingly designing services around the needs of the customer. Portals enable information to be tailored to the needs of the user, and are increasingly used to integrate services and information for individuals. . . . Several initiatives are underway to provide integrated online services to enable people to contact multiple agencies or web sites to complete transactions, and that this is supported by the number of agencies adopting the interoperability (eGIF) standards. This helps them to share information and data more effectively and enables different agencies to bundle services together to meet peoples' needs.[51]

The quality of metadata that agencies supply to the portal also affects integrated online services, and this was an area of performance of agencies that the report rates highly. "A number of agencies have exemplary metadata that is accurate, well-written, up-to-date and provides good coverage of the agencies' information and services via the government portal . . . most agencies are providing good metadata records."[52] At the same time, the report notes, the Web site evaluation found that many agencies were using links to other agency Web sites to enable users to gain access to related information.[53] Continuation of this practice and the use of multiple Web sites and customizing information for specific groups of users would make the sites more responsive to user needs. (This was an issue that several respondents in the *Wired for Well-Being* report had raised.)

On the other performance metric, participation, *Achieving E-government 2004* concludes that there are now more opportunities for agencies to use the Internet to enable people to gain access to consultation documents, find news, and be informed of the current activities of government. This was perhaps the second area (after integration of services through the portal) on which the E-government Unit found achievement most lacking.

In the evaluation of thirty-nine individual government Web sites that makes up a large section of the report, there are many examples of best practice in providing services and facilitating online interaction, with resulting efficiency and satisfaction for both agencies and citizens.[54] This evaluation suggests that there is still considerable variation in the level of information and services offered by the New Zealand government Web sites, sometimes because of their different functions and audiences, and variations in usability. Listed as examples of best practice for their overall Web sites are Inland Revenue (www.ird.govt.nz), Statistics New Zealand (www.stats.govt.nz), and Archives New Zealand (www.archives.govt.nz). The Ministry of Agriculture and Forestry (MAF; www.maf.govt.nz), which has been positively cited in earlier studies,[55] and the Ministry for the Environment (www.MfE.govt.nz) are cited for best practice in required government content. In particular, the MAF site offers advanced online services in some areas where there has been commercial demand, such as in the area of electronic certification of agricultural exports, managed by MAF subsidiary the New Zealand Food Safety Authority, or the commercially advantageous data sharing between the New Zealand Customs Service's CusMod system and MAF's QuanCargo program.

These are good examples of the benefits of focusing on a particular group of citizens and their needs and providing integrated services to meet these needs. Initiatives (e.g., plans for an e-census in 2006, projects based on interagency data exchange such as the ability for international students to make application to a tertiary institution of their choice and secure a student visa online through the Department of Labour's Web site) are highlighted that will provide models for other agencies. The online provision of New Zealand–based information to all citizens through their public libraries, as exemplified in the National Library's New Zealand full-text database, EPIC, and the digital library, Matapihi, are cited as developments toward that part of the vision that expressly addresses the information needs of New Zealanders, providing access to their own history and culture online.

Achieving E-government 2004, as it openly acknowledges, is written primarily from a supply perspective, that is, the perspective of government, the E-government Unit carrying out one of its mandatory roles of "monitoring progress toward achieving the e-government vision."[56] The report makes good use of the independent user evaluations conducted under contract to the E-government Unit during the year: *Wired for Well-Being* and *Channel Surfing.* Integrating the formal evaluations with comments and feedback from users from these two research reports, *Achieving E-government 2004* concludes that despite the high overall ratings of 67 percent of the Web sites evaluated, and the recognition of some sites as outstanding, overall New Zealand government Web sites still need to address the following issues:

- usability and navigation;
- use and quality of the Web site search function;
- accessibility features (e.g., style sheets and navigation aids) missing;
- contact e-mail addresses missing or not responded to;
- broken links, and lack of links to relevant content;
- too many documents in pdf format that are not accessible to users with sight problems;
- policies covering privacy, copyright, and other feedback missing;
- home page not indicating content clearly;
- lack of consultation documents.[57]

The research reports themselves paint a slightly more complex picture. *Wired for Well-Being* also highlights issues on which citizens routinely contacted government and why they needed to do so, their preference for using multiple channels for making contact, and the general lack of awareness of what information and services were available on government Web sites. There was little knowledge of what e-government is and equally little knowledge of the portal, and those who did know of the portal made little use of it. Unless the URL of a government department was known, the search engine Google was the most common approach to finding government information on the Internet.[58]

Many of the findings in *Wired for Well-Being* were confirmed in a telephone survey conducted in 2005. It was found that participants still preferred telephone, in-person contact, and contact by letter to making use of the Internet or e-mail (only 10 percent used electronic channels). Fifteen percent of those who did use the Internet to contact government made use of the portal. Thirty-five percent of those who had not used the Internet to contact government did not know they could do so, and those who did make use of e-government channels had little knowledge of what was available in this format—listing many items they believed would be of value but were not yet available that are already available.[59]

Among specific groups and communities, however, there is evidence of greater knowledge and uptake, most notably in the business and agricultural sector, where clear gains in efficiency and a reduction in the costs of compliance with regulations and procedures have resulted from the development of integrated online services and transactions. These integrated developments and the level of participation and consultation across all sites have led the *Global E-government Readiness Report* to conclude:

> New Zealand has taken extra efforts to actively encourage and promote its use to citizens and does so not only at the national site . . . but across all ministries and sub-sites. This kind of integrated implementation and promotion puts the online consultation section in an altogether different league, one shared by only a few other innovators and leaders.[60]

CONCLUSION

The achievement to date of e-government in New Zealand would seem to be mixed. New Zealand has focused on a public management approach, in which a well-developed strategy and a coherent approach across agencies have enabled it to make considerable progress on e-government infrastructure and, to a lesser extent, the connectivity with citizens that underpins widespread adoption of e-government among the public. It has now redressed the lack of control by central agencies over government services outside the core state services, through the Crown Entities Act 2004, which allows the minister of state services and the minister of finance jointly to direct crown entities (e.g., Housing New Zealand Corporation, Land Transport New Zealand, the Tertiary Education Commission, and the district health boards) to give effect to a government policy or support a whole-of-government approach (e.g., complying with e-government requirements).[61] This will further facilitate the development and integration of online services across the sector.

The E-government Unit has not yet managed to communicate its message to all citizens or to develop a strong, centralized, citizen-centric focus in all agencies, despite its vision. While the development of infrastructure and systems has been critical to its success so far, it is now perhaps time for an e-citizens charter and a more demand-side approach to development.[62] There is a considerable way to go to meet the expectations for 2004 of the mission statement of 2003, let alone those for 2007:

- By June 2004 the Internet will be the dominant means of enabling ready access to government information, services, and processes.
- By June 2007, networks and Internet technologies will be integral to the delivery of government information, services, and processes.
- By June 2010, the operation of government will have been transformed through its use of the Internet.[63]

These expectations have been absorbed into the State Services Commission's new "Development Goals for All of the State Services," which are also expressed in the 2007/2010 time frame. These include to

- be an employer of choice, especially for high achievers;
- develop a culture of excellence and leaning throughout the sector;

- use technology and the Internet to manage processes and service delivery throughout the sector, leading to a transformation of the operation of government;
- ensure coordination of the sector and the joint pursuit of joint outcomes;
- enhance accessibility, responsiveness, and effectiveness in the sector, pointing citizens to "right doors in the right places" and through a variety of channels; and
- improve the level of trust New Zealanders place in the agencies of the state services.[64]

In this way the State Services Commission sees that it has effectively "mainstreamed" the goals of e-government across all the operations of the state sector.

As the E-Government Unit faces closer integration into the routine work of the State Services Commission and its director takes up a new post as deputy commissioner, information and communication technologies, it will be important not to lose the momentum that e-government has built up in New Zealand, and to keep focused on the task that lies ahead. As the new deputy commissioner indicates, this is "to ensure that there is progress on all of government 'e' initiatives, without constraining individual agency innovation and that in part and in total the 'e' initiatives contribute to the ongoing development of the Public Management system."[65] New Zealand has made its greatest e-government gains in the area of public management. The government is now seeking to take the people with it into its vision of the future of e-government and focus on some of its early goals and the real benefits to citizens that e-government can bring.

NOTES

1. Ministry for Economic Development, *The Digital Strategy: Creating Our Digital Future* (Wellington: Ministry for Economic Development, 2005). Available at www.digitalstrategy.govt.nz/, accessed May 16, 2005.

2. The public sector in New Zealand comprises the state sector (central government) and all local authorities (local government), including local authority trading enterprises (LATEs). The public sector is wider than the state sector, which is wider than the public service.

3. Richard Mulgan, "Public Sector Reform in New Zealand: Issues of Public Accountability," *Asia Pacific School of Economics and Government Discussion Papers* (Canberra: Asia Pacific School of Economics and Government, Australian National University, 2004).

4. Peter Hernon, "Government Information Policy in New Zealand: Businesslike but Evolving?" *Government Information Quarterly* 13 (1996): 215.

5. State Services Commission, *Policy Framework for Government-Held Information* (Wellington: State Services Commission, 1997). Available at www.ssc.govt.nz/display/document.asp?NavID=82& DocID=2934, accessed April 18, 2005.

6. Maurice Williamson, *Vision Statement: Electronic Government for New Zealand* (Wellington: Parliament, 1999). Available at www.executive.govt.nz/96-99/minister/williamson/egovernment/vision.html, accessed April 10, 2005.

7. Chief Executives' Group on Information Management and Technology, *Electronic Government: Briefing to Minister of State Services and Minister of Information Technology, December 1999* (Wellington: Chief Executives' Group on Information Management and Technology, 1999). Available at www.e.govt.nz/archive/services/networks/info-tech-briefing/info-tech-briefing. pdf, accessed April 11, 2005.

8. Chief Executives' Group on Information Management and Technology, *Electronic Government*, 3.

9. State Services Commission, E-government Unit, *Overview of the E-government Programme* (Wellington: State Services Commission, 2000). Available at www.e.govt.nz/about-egovt/programme, accessed April 9, 2005.

10. In 2003, the mission was extended to include goals for 2007 and 2010; see State Services Commission, E-government Unit, "E-government Vision, Mission, Goals, and Outcome" (Wellington: State Services Commission, 2003). Available at www.e.govt.nz/about-egovt/strategy/strategy-june-2003, accessed April 10, 2005.

11. State Services Commission, E-government Unit, *Government@your.service: E-government Strategy* (Wellington: State Services Commission, April 2001). Available at www.e.govt.nz/archive/about-egovt/programme/e-gov-strategy-apr-01/e-govt-strategy-apr-01.pdf, accessed April 8, 2005.

12. See *The Internet Archive*, available at www.archive.org, accessed April 10, 2005.

13. State Services Commission, E-government Unit, *New Zealand Government Portal Strategy for a Customer-Centric Portal: Part B, High-Level Implementation Plan, 2001–2004* (Wellington: State Services Commission, 2000). Available at www.e.govt.nz/archive/standards/nzgls/nz-gov-portal-strategy/listing_archives, accessed April 6, 2005.

14. Hernon, "Government Information Policy in New Zealand," 215.

15. State Services Commission, *Report of the Advisory Group on the Review of the Centre*, presented to the Ministers of State Services and Finance (Wellington: State Services Commission, November 2001). Available at www.ssc.govt.nz/display/document.asp?NavID = 105, accessed April 10, 2005.

16. State Services Commission, *Review of the Centre*, 6.

17. There are two main types of local authority: regional councils and territorial authorities (comprising city and district councils).

18. Jo Crib and Tom Berthold, *Roles of Central and Local Government in Joint Problems,* Working Papers no. 1 (Wellington: State Services Commission, 1999).

19. Rowena Cullen, Deborah O'Connor, and Anna Veritt, "An Evaluation of Local Government Websites in New Zealand," *Journal of Political Marketing* 2, no. 2/3 (2003), special issue, *The World of E-government*, 185–211.

20. Rowena Cullen and Caroline Houghton, "Democracy Online: An Assessment of New Zealand Government Web Sites," *Government Information Quarterly* 17 (2000): 243–67.

21. *Strategic Plan for E-Local Government* (Wellington: Local Government New Zealand, 2003). Available (as a pdf file) at http://library.lgnz.co.nz/cgi-bin/koha/opac-detail.pl?bib = 201, accessed April 11, 2005.

22. Local government information on the All of Government Project—the Big Ask Project (Wellington: Local Government New Zealand). Available at www.lgnz.co.nz/projects/archive/Bigask, accessed April 10, 2005.

23. WAVE Advisory Board to Director-General of Health, *From Strategy to Reality: The WAVE Project; Kia Hopu te Ngaru* (Wellington: Ministry of Health, 2001). Available at www.moh.govt.nz/publications, accessed April 12, 2005.

24. Ministry of Health, Health Information Standards Organization (Wellington: Ministry of Health). Available at www.hiso.govt.nz, accessed April 11, 2005.

25. District Health Boards New Zealand. Available at www.dhbnz.org.nz, accessed April 27, 2005.

26. Health Level Seven. Available at www.hl7.org/, accessed April 13, 2005.

27. United Nations, *Global E-government Readiness Report 2004: Toward Access for Opportunity* (New York: United Nations, 2004), 45.

28. State Services Commission, E-government Unit, "NZGLS Metadata Standard" (Wellington, State Services Commission, n.d.). Available at www.e.govt.nz/standards/nzgls/standard, accessed April 6, 2005.

29. State Services Commission, E-government Unit, "NZGLS Thesaurus (FONZ and SONZ)"

(Wellington, State Services Commission, n.d.). Available at www.e.govt.nz/standards/nzgls/thesauri, accessed April 6, 2005.

30. State Services Commission, E-government Unit, *E-services: Electronic Service Delivery* (Wellington: State Services Commission, n.d.). Available at www.e-government.govt.nz/e-services/index.asp, accessed April 10, 2005.

31. State Services Commission, E-government Unit, *@your.service: Updated E-government Strategy Incorporates Service Delivery Architecture* (Wellington: State Services Commission, n.d.). Available at www.e.govt.nz/archive/about-egovt/programme/e-gov-strategy-apr-01/e-govt-strategy-apr-01 .pdf, accessed April 12, 2005.

32. W3C, *W3C Accessibility Initiative* (Cambridge, MA: MIT, n.d.). Available at www.w3.org/ WAI/, accessed April 18, 2005.

33. See the GOVIS Web site (Wellington: GOVIS). Available at www.govis.org.nz, accessed April 16, 2005.

34. A tender process is under way, and the initial trial will be conducted in the Ministry of Economic Development.

35. New Zealand, Electronic Transactions Act 2002.

36. State Services Commission, E-government Unit, *Authentication for E-government: Government Logon Service Development Overview* (Wellington: State Services Commission, April 2005). Available (as a pdf file) at www.e.govt.nz/services/authentication/authent-blueprint-0605, accessed April 12, 2005.

37. State Services Commission, E-government Unit, *Trust and Security of the Internet: Keeping the Internet Safe for E-government in New Zealand* (Wellington: State Services Commission, November 24, 2004). Available at www.e.govt.nz/policy/trust-security/trust-security-2004, accessed April 15, 2005.

38. Taylor Nelson Sofres, *GO2003* (Wellington: State Services Commission, December 2003). Available at www.e.govt.nz/resources/research/go-survey-2003, accessed April 15, 2005; Cate Curtis, Jack Vowles and Bruce Curtis, *Channel-Surfing: How New Zealanders Access Government* (Wellington: State Services Commission, 2004). Available at www.e.govt.nz/resources/research/research/ channel-surfing-200409, accessed April 10, 2005.

39. Curtis, Vowles, and Curtis, *Channel-Surfing*.

40. State Services Commission, E-government Unit, *The Channel Strategy: Scoping Study* (Wellington: State Services Commission, June 2004). Available at www.e.govt.nz/policy/participation/chan nel/cs-scoping-0104, accessed April 10, 2005.

41. Rowena Cullen and Peter Hernon, *Wired for Well-Being: Citizens' Response to E-government* (Wellington: State Services Commission, E-government Unit, June 2004). Available at www.e.govt .nz/resources/research/research/vuw-report-200406, accessed April 12, 2005.

42. Cullen and Hernon, *Wired for Well-Being*.

43. State Services Commission, E-government Unit, *Participation through E-government: The Context* (Wellington: State Services Commission, 2004). Available atwww.e.govt.nz/participation/participa-tion-0305, accessed April 20, 2005.

44. State Services Commission, E-government Unit, *Participation through E-government*, 7.

45. State Services Commission, E-government Unit, *Participation through E-government*, 4.

46. State Services Commission, E-government Unit, *Achieving E-government 2004: A Report on Progress towards the New Zealand E-government Strategy* (Wellington: State Services Commission, 2004), 14. Available at www.e.govt.nz/resources/research/research/ready-access-2004, accessed April 20, 2005.

47. State Services Commission, E-government Unit, *Achieving E-government 2004*, 2.

48. State Services Commission, E-government Unit, *Achieving E-government 2004*, 3.

49. State Services Commission, E-government Unit, *Achieving E-government 2004*, 3.

50. State Services Commission, E-government Unit, *Achieving E-government 2004*, 3.

51. State Services Commission, E-government Unit, *Achieving E-government 2004*, 3.

52. State Services Commission, E-government Unit, *Achieving E-government 2004*, 19.

53. State Services Commission, E-government Unit, *Achieving E-government 2004*, 23.

54. State Services Commission, E-government Unit, *Achieving E-government 2004*, 23.

55. Cullen and Houghton, "Democracy Online."

56. See New Zealand Government, Cabinet Minute, May 2000. Cab (00)M14 1F(1).

57. New Zealand Government, Cabinet Minute, May 2000, 31.

58. Cullen and Hernon, *Wired for Well-Being.*

59. Curtis, Vowles, and Curtis, *Channel-Surfing.*

60. United Nations, *Global E-Government Readiness Report*, 45.

61. New Zealand, Crown Entities Act 2004.

62. Matt Poelmans, "Making E-government Work: The Content and Significance of an e-Citizens' Charter," in *Connected Government: Thought Leaders. Essays from Innovators*, ed. Willi Kaczorowski (London: Premium Publishing, 2004), 78–89.

63. State Services Commission, E-government Unit, "E-government Vision, Mission, Goals, and Outcomes."

64. State Services Commission, "Development Goals for All of the State Services" (Wellington: State Services Commission, 2005). Available at www.ssc.govt.nz/display/document.asp?DocID= 4730, accessed April 28, 2005.

65. Laurence Millar, "Connected Government: The New Zealand Story," in *Connected Government,* 25–41.

III

FOUNDATIONAL ISSUES

• 7 •

Trust in Government

Peter Hernon

$\mathcal{T}$he literature dealing with the public's confidence and trust in government indicates that "citizens are likely to trust government only to the extent that they believe that it will act in their interests, that its procedures are fair, and that their trust of the state and others is reciprocated."[1] Still, it is important to remember that "the American republic was born in a climate of suspicion that persists to this day."[2] Such a climate is not unique to the United States. For example, one reason for the erosion of public trust in Tony Blair's Labour government relates to the prime minister's claims, which were subsequently disproved, about the existence of weapons of mass destruction in Iraq.[3] Although the public in New Zealand tends to rate trust in government high, this is not true for all segments of society. The seabed issue—a vigorous debate over whether the indigenous Maori, with their claim to customary rights, or the Crown are the proper stewards of the nation's coastline—illustrates that for the Maori there is great distrust (see chapter 11).

An excellent example of distrust in government in the United States occurred with the 2000 presidential election. Both Al Gore Jr. and George W. Bush received 48 percent of the popular vote (50,996,116 to 50,456,169), but Bush received 271 of the 537 electoral votes. The awarding of the electoral votes of Florida to him was controversial and raised questions about the accuracy of the process for counting votes, regardless of whether they are recorded electronically or manually (punch cards). While there has been considerable discussion regarding the viability of Internet voting, to date no Internet systems have been certified for national use. For the foreseeable future, Internet voting at the national level seems like an unlikely addition to e-government as envisioned in figure 1.1.

Although not widely known, another issue of distrust in government in the United States has emerged. In late fall 2001, a federal judge shut down the home pages of the Department of Interior and still has not allowed the home page of the Bureau of Indian Affairs to reopen. For years, the department has collected money on oil and gas leases on lands in the public domain for American Indians; however, the inability of the department to account adequately for the money held in the trust system resulted in the court taking action against the department, including the shutdown of its home pages. At the time that this chapter was written, the court was still very critical of the progress that the department has made in resolving the matter. Undoubtedly, this issue has resulted in American Indians having less confidence in the ability of the department to protect their financial interests and to abide by the law. As chapter 11 indicates, indigenous peoples may believe there is a significant gap between government statements (promises) and actions.

The purpose of this chapter is to provide a general overview of trust and to relate that issue briefly to e-government. The success of e-government, in part, depends on the public's perception that the information provided is accurate, is not intended to deceive them, and does not unduly reflect the philosophy of the ruling political party. As well, distrust might discourage the public from engaging in e-commerce and other facets of e-government depicted in figure 1.1.

UNITED STATES

Public trust and confidence in government comprise complex issues, and some of the distrust is generational. Still, the public may distinguish between government in general and those facets appearing in e-government. Segments of the population are changing the ways in which they gather information, stay informed, and conduct business. Clearly, the literature on public trust and confidence in government is limited and does not adequately consider the impact of e-government on the public and business community. There is a lack of empirical evidence about whether e-government influences public attitudes about government and, if it does have some effect, how and in what manner. Although e-government may not influence general attitudes and behavior, trust and confidence are essential if the public is to rely on a digital environment in which a government offers information, services, and online compliance and documents its accountability.

Overview

Public confidence and trust in the national government to do what is right and to tell the truth "most of the time" were high during Franklin D. Roosevelt's New Deal and remained so during and following World War II. Except in the aftermath of 9/11 and on the issues of national and homeland security, trust in the government has declined for decades as is evidenced from polls reflecting public opinion, for instance, on the Johnson and Nixon administrations' handling of the Vietnam War and the Watergate affair, and the 2000 presidential election. Those polls also attribute the decline to the George W. Bush administration's venture into Iraq—its rationale for going to war and the controversial effort to rebuild the devastated nation and to turn it into a democracy.

Some of the other factors that have eroded public trust in the national government include spending priorities perceived as misguided, inefficiencies and waste in carrying out departmental and agency responsibilities, and concern over issues such as racial profiling. Furthermore, the issue of trust applies to negative perceptions of the economy, escalation in the number and types of crime, scandals within government and involving public figures, the bureaucracy, and politicians, and even the quality of the information that governments provide both domestically and internationally. The lack of trust might even have an impact on declining voting rates.[4]

In one of the public opinion surveys related to trust, the Pew Research Center, in

April 2000, found that "a majority of Americans have said they can seldom trust the government to do the right thing." The survey did find that the public placed greater trust in some agencies (e.g., the Federal Aviation Administration, the Food and Drug Administration, the Environmental Protection Agency, and the Social Security Administration) than they did in the federal government as a whole. A favorable percentage also existed for the Internal Revenue Service, but that percentage was smaller than it was for the above-mentioned agencies.[5] A positive aspect is that the nation's youth are more optimistic and have given Congress higher approval ratings. Although they are more optimistic than other age groups, much public distrust in the national government still remains.[6]

Elections

Beginning with the 1996 presidential and congressional elections in the United States, candidates used the Web to organize campaign events, send supporters e-mail updates, advance their positions, and define their opposition. In that contest, the Pew Research Center "discovered that about 20 million Americans (12% of the voting population) used the Internet to keep up with the campaign, and 2% listed the Internet as their primary source of political information."[7] With the 2004 presidential primaries, Howard Dean, former governor of Vermont, used the Web to energize his supporters, recruit volunteers in his campaign, and solicit campaign contributions. He targeted those people who felt apathetic about being involved in a political contest and made them think they had a stake in the outcome. The question is, "To what extent will they remain involved, or will they return to their old ways?"

Although a recent study did not answer the questions, it did note that

> political trust is highest among voters who voted either for both the presidential and congressional winners or the presidential winner and congressional losers; trust is lowest among those who voted for both the presidential and congressional losers or congressional winners and the presidential loser.[8]

Today, campaign Web sites for both presidential and congressional candidates are likely to identify a candidate's position on numerous issues, to offer press releases and news articles, to provide surveys so that site visitors can express their views on various issues, to offer photo opportunities and schedules for public events, to encourage people to work for the candidate, to enable visitors to sign up for e-mail update and make campaign contributions, to report the candidate's campaign schedule, and to present press information and opportunities for visitors to discuss issues. Clearly, no serious candidate—or political party—would forgo the use of the Internet as part of a campaign strategy. Once elected or reelected, these individuals regard the Internet as an essential means of communicating with their constituents.

Interestingly, in his acceptance speech as presidential nominee for the Democratic Party (July 2004), Sen. John F. Kerry directed the televised audience to his Web site (JohnKerry.com) for information about his position on issues. With the creation of GeorgeWBush.com., both political parties then asked the public to bypass the mass media and approach their home pages directly as a way to follow issues, without receiving commentary from the media. Equally as interesting is the fact that in the October

2004 vice presidential debate, Vice President Dick Cheney pointed listeners to a Web site where they could find information about what he said were misstatements made by Senators Kerry and John Edwards. However, he referred to the site as factcheck.com instead of factcheck.org. This example reinforces the intent of those running for political office to deal directly with the public, but they must be careful about the correct URL for the Web site they advance, including its extension. In the case of factcheck .com, it was a site of a political activist who opposed the reelection of President Bush.

Removal of Information from Web Sites

Following 9/11, numerous government departments and agencies reviewed the content of their home pages in the belief that some of it might be useful to terrorists or hackers. As chapter 8 notes, removal might have a legitimate function (blocking access to information truly helpful to terrorists), but it also might shape the message the public receives.

The issue of trust arises when government hides information of no conceivable use to terrorists; rather, the information is politically damaging to those in government. A relevant example dates back to the Cold War and focuses on *Openness: Human Radiation Experiments* of the Department of Energy. This project exists because

> throughout our nation's history, the government has needed to operate with some secrecy to protect our nation's security. At the same time, Americans have recognized that the government's power to act in secret conflicts with core democratic principles. Misuse of secrecy feeds a sense of mistrust in government that can undermine our cohesion as a nation.
>
> During the Cold War, the government funded human radiation experiments, some of which were secret. It is imperative that the public have access to the record of the government's activities. The [Clinton] Administration has opened the record . . . , and has changed rules that kept documents secret for many years after it was necessary. These changes, along with other safeguards in place already, will help to ensure that the government does not repeat the wrongs of the human radiation experiments.[9]

On the Department's Web site, there is also mention that

> a large and growing body of documents collected by the Federal agencies is available for online searching through the Internet at the Human Radiation Experiments Interagency Web Site. This site currently allows citizens to examine nearly 300,000 pages of material and will contain approximately half a million pages when completed later this year. The database provides both document images and sophisticated full text searching capabilities. Many of these documents were originally unclassified, but approximately 7,000 were specifically declassified for this project.[10]

However, when an interested party investigates the Human Radiation Experiments (HREX) and the Web site, that person discovers

> the HREX website is currently closed down for two reasons [the site was still down on June 11, 2005]: (1) After the events of September 11, 2001, the Federal Government undertook a review of all information on its websites to determine the appropriateness of the information on the websites. The database for the HREX website is currently under-

going a review in light of the events of 9/11 to determine whether all of the information in the database is appropriate. (2) The HREX website was hosted by antiquated technology. After the review of the information in the database is complete, it will be moved to the OpenNet website which is a platform composed of current technologies. The timing of when the HREX information will be available on OpenNet is unknown, therefore you may wish to periodically visit the OpenNet website at http://www.osti.gov/opennet.[11]

The removal of content and, in some cases, shrouding science in greater secrecy inhibit scientific progress, which depends on the open and frank exchange of information and building on the work of others, and the accountability of government to the electorate. In essence, scholarly communication—the way that scientists and scholars gather information and communicate among themselves—is impeded. The difficult challenge is to find the proper balance between access and withholding information.

Information Quality

Supporters of the Information Quality Act (P.L. 106-554), also known as the Data Quality Act (DQA), primarily industry groups, claim the law keeps the government from using bad data, while opponents (e.g., environmental and citizens groups) maintain that the law expands industrial influence over the regulatory process. Interested stakeholders, including industry associations, have filed data quality challenges to federal regulations, whereas public interest groups seek repeal of the act. Agencies believe in the importance of and principles behind the law—maximizing the quality of data they use.

The legislation has generated controversy since the Office of Management and Budget (OMB) produced DQA guidelines for agencies in 2002. The DQA does not sufficiently address the issue of open scientific dialogue, free from political interference. How free are government-employed scientists to express scientific opinions that differ from the administration's political agenda?[12] The impact of the act on public trust is unknown. Most likely, the public is unaware of the act and the controversies surrounding it.

THE OFFICIAL OR UNOFFICIAL VERSION

The quantity of information available through government Web sites is voluminous. Complicating matters, there may be different versions of an electronic record on the same or different Web sites, and the government may not stand behind the authority of those electronic versions. Paper copy, if it exists, may constitute the presentation or official version. For electronic documents, when they constitute *records* (see 44 U.S.C. 3301),

- Are they the "official" version?
- How likely are they to be preserved and retained?
- By whom?

A related question is, How can agencies maintain an audit trail documenting the development, implementation, and enforcement of policy for which there are no (or few) paper records? Such questions have been raised for more than a decade, but have not been resolved.

Should the contents of a government publication or image presented on government home pages be accepted at face value? Perhaps a better phrased question is, How often and under what circumstances can the integrity of a document—in either print or electronic form—be taken for granted? Those concerned about the erosion of privacy in the digital information age warn that there should be no automatic acceptance of content and that data overlays through the use of geographic information systems (GISs), in some instances, could erode privacy rights. An extensive array of publicly available information profiles individual households and reveals much about people living there. Furthermore, it is easy to alter information content and to pass a forgery as genuine.

MISINFORMATION AND DISINFORMATION

Navigation of the Internet might involve having to deal with hazards such as digital bandits. Digital technology enables people to manipulate images, thereby subverting the certainty of photographic evidence.[13] Tom Raum notes that text itself is easily altered. According to him, the Clinton White House "deleted the word 'lie' four times in issuing a sanitized electronic version of a press release attacking a critic of President Clinton's health plan."[14]

Inaccurate information might result from either a deliberate attempt to deceive or mislead *(disinformation),* or an honest mistake *(misinformation).* Either way, incorrect information is released. Clearly, "authenticating and verifying the integrity of a document is . . . [more than] simply obtaining [and using] a copy of the document."[15] There are increased opportunities for disinformation and misinformation to occur, and for the public unknowingly to reference them. Some key questions become, For what information and under what circumstances do people verify the authenticity of the information and data they use? How trusting are they (and should they be) of information content received via the Internet? Should individuals be any more or less trusting of information in a digital format? Is liability associated with information in electronic formats?

In 1995, I reported an exploratory study into disinformation that still has application to today.[16] Updating the conclusion to that paper, I now ask, Does the vulnerability of government information available through the Internet reduce the credibility of that information and the public's view of e-government? As chapters 10 and 11 indicate, members of the New Zealand public surveyed believed that disinformation is more likely to occur with general Internet use and less so with government home pages. However, if the popular press reported numerous and serious problems with the information content of those home pages, public confidence in e-government would likely erode.

TRUST: GLOBAL IMPLICATIONS

In *Against All Enemies,* Richard A. Clarke, former national coordinator for security, infrastructure protection, and counterterrorism in the Clinton administration and part of the subsequent Bush administration, notes that, by 2003, the invasion of Iraq cost the United States many friends worldwide. As he wrote, "the U.S. was not trusted or liked by majorities in Islamic countries. After the invasion, those numbers hit all-time highs not only in Muslim countries but around the world. . . . [W]e were now seen as a super-bully more than a superpower, not just for what we did but for the way we did it, disdaining international mechanisms that we would later need."[17]

As this example illustrates, the audiences of e-government are not confined to the public of the government maintaining its digital presence. E-government might also be intended for the world's population and other countries doing business with the one country or interested in its policies and information. Such people might dismiss the information, say, of the U.S. government, as inaccurate and intended to deceive—or solely to justify the position of the U.S. government. The question becomes, Do the world's populations, in Muslim and other countries, trust and use U.S. government information? Do they even believe what the government claims on its Web sites, especially ones such as that of the White House? Does the distrust extend to information and policies of a country's allies? Negative answers to such questions have direct implications for e-government when the e-citizen is viewed in a global context and when a government wants to expand the role of the business community in world markets.

INSPIRING PUBLIC TRUST

The Organisation for Economic Co-operation and Development (OECD) issued a report, *Trust in Government: Ethics Measures in OECD Countries,* that views "public service" as "a public trust." Public trust refers to the public's interaction with public servants in person, over the telephone, or via e-mail contact. The public expects to be treated fairly and to receive reliable service. The report concludes that "public ethics are a prerequisite to public trust and a keystone of good governance."[18]

In a separate policy brief, the OECD elaborated on the report and noted that "fair and reliable public services . . . create a favorable environment for businesses, thus contributing to well-functioning markets and economic growth."[19] Expanding on the criteria critical for obtaining public trust, the policy brief emphasized the

- integrity, efficiency, and effectiveness of public servants;
- objectivity and impartiality of the information content;
- rationality and quality of the service provision; and
- transparency in navigating government structures to locate the right public servant, information, or service. Transparency requires the development, implementation, and enforcement of Web standards and guidelines.[20]

However, impartiality is the top core public service value, and all of these core values relate to e-government. "A growing number of [OECD] countries" have laws to punish corruption (e.g., bribery of public servants) and are "seeking to punish breaches of core public service values and principles (such as impartiality in decision-making) and the use of public office for private gain."[21] Corruption might apply to e-commerce, digital service provision, and e-procurement (see figure 1.1). It might also influence the extent to which governments want to become involved in e-government; opportunities for corruption are perhaps greater when the public has face-to-face communication with public servants. Furthermore, does the government provide for whistleblowing on government Web sites regarding fraud? In many instances the answer is yes; however, in those situations, how are whistleblowers treated, and do their complaints lead to change and improved agency performance?

To the above list of values, one might add openness and privacy protection and, when government departments and agencies engaged in e-commerce collect personal information, there should be standards to protect privacy. Those standards should be monitored and enforced. Furthermore, there should be clear explanations on Web sites about how the information gathered will be used.

Finally, as the list below indicates, "Citizens trust public institutions if they know that public offices are used for the public good." The OECD has identified eight "steps for building trust in public institutions":

1. Defining a clear mission for the public service: Adapting the mission of the public service to current needs and ensuring that its core values and standards meet changing public expectations are key challenges in a rapidly changing world.

2. Safeguarding values while adapting to change: The changing socioeconomic environment, especially the growing demand for transparency, requires that governments review and adjust mechanisms to ensure that public servants' behavior corresponds to expected standards.

3. Empowering both public servants and citizens to report misconduct: Clear and known procedures that facilitate the reporting of wrongdoing and provide protection of whistleblowers assist the detection of individual cases of misconduct.

4. Integrating integrity measures into overall management: Integrity measures are not a distinct activity, but rather an integral part of all management systems in which integrity measures provide complementary support for the overall management environment.

5. Coordinating integrity measures: A precondition for success. Successful integrity measures consist of a combination of actions that are consistent and take into account the wider public service environment. Assessing the effectiveness of measures provides feedback to policymakers on their implementation and also lays the groundwork for future policies.

6. Shifting emphasis from enforcement to prevention: Sound ethics management policy adequately combines enforcement and prevention measures. However, there is a growing recognition that increased attention to prevention reduces the need for enforcement. Prevention is a less expensive investment in the long term, with a more positive impact on the public service culture and on the relationship between the public service and civil society.

7. Anticipating problems: By anticipating situations that might weaken adherence to public service values and standards of behavior, governments can prepare suitable responses to prevent adverse effects. For example, how can governments meet increasing public demands for more information on private interests that affect public decisions?

8. Taking advantage of new technology: Exploring ways to harness new technolo-

gies can help governments find new ways to internalize integrity and inform citizens on standards expected of officials serving the public.[22]

Although those steps do not center on e-government, they help to create an environment essential for e-government to function. E-government cannot be successful unless the public and business community place trust in the information and services provided, as well as in the institutions and public servants providing them with access to the information and services.

SOME USEFUL WEB SITES DEALING WITH ASPECTS OF TRUST

Some U.S. government Web sites of interest to readers interested in the issue of trust include:

- The Computer Incident Advisory Capacity (CIAC) of the Department of Energy (http://hoaxbusters.ciac.org), which discusses hoax Internet viruses and stories about them.
- Federal Election Commission (http://www.fec.gov/), where the public can file complaints over alleged violations of election laws and regulations.
- Federal Trade Commission (http://www.ftc.gov/), which provides information about scams and rip-offs. It also maintains the national do-not-call registry.
- Food and Drug Administration (http://www.fda.gov/), which covers clinical trials and the areas that the agency regulates (e.g., food, drugs, medical devices, and radiation-emitting products).
- Department of Health and Human Services (http://www.os.dhhs.gov/), which provides information related to diseases, safety and wellness, and much more. In some cases (e.g., Healthfinder, http://www.healthfinder.gov/), the government stands behind the authority of the information it provides.
- Office of Research Integrity (http://ori.hhs.gov/), which is an office within the Public Health Service that deals with scientific misconduct (fraudulent and falsified research). It investigates those cases brought to its attention and publicizes the cases in which misconduct was and was not found. It also covers the responsibilities of research mentors, the protection of human subjects, conflicts of interest, and much more.

CONCLUSION

Without information about what the government is doing and why, citizens residing in democracies cannot exercise accountability over government institutions. Trust is fundamental to good governance and creating public confidence in public servants, the services and information provided, and open and accountable government. E-government requires public trust and confidence in the information and services provided and in the transactions completed.

Although the public may increasingly turn to government Web sites to gather information, they regard the Internet as only one means of contacting government.[23] It has been claimed that, during 2003, sixty-eight million Americans used government Web sites.[24] As well, in that year, government departments and agencies sold more than $3.6 billion in products and property (e-commerce) over the Internet.[25] As a consequence, the e-citizen is emerging. That person most likely gathers information from different channels but believes that access to government information is a key component of accountability. E-citizens want to see how a government develops policies and the actual language of those policies, how those policies affect them, and how to make government performance more responsive to the needs and expectations of the governed. E-citizens might also seek information and services from governments of other countries, as well as assistance from their own government in competing more effectively globally.

Further development in e-citizenship will require that the public place greater trust in the digital information and services that governments provide, make repeated use of government Web sites, and believe that the information and services have value and relevance to their lives—both work and personal. The insertion of a political or social agenda into the public service role of e-government, of course, will create a formidable obstacle to realizing the potential of e-government.

Despite the many strides made in getting the public to use government Web sites, the public typically is not as familiar with these sites as they are with the home pages of the business community and news media. Empirical evidence, however, is lacking. There is a need for studies of the public's information-seeking behavior for government information in a digital environment beyond that reported in chapters 10 and 11.

Although e-government will not eliminate the public's distrust of government, the government can seek to build the confidence and trust of the members of the public who use services and information delivered via a portal or government home page. The New Zealand government, for instance, offers a series of strategies to build that confidence and trust (see chapters 6, 10, and 11). Clearly, governments must be aware of that need and work to achieve the support and satisfaction of the online public.[26] Ultimately the success of e-government depends on the public having sufficient confidence and trust in the information and services provided digitally that they use them on a recurring basis.

NOTES

1. Valerie Braithwaite, Margaret Levi, and other contributors show that trust is a complex concept. They also present an analytical, philosophical, and historical discussion of trust from different disciplinary perspectives (e.g., economics and anthropology). See Valerie Braithwaite and Margaret Levi, eds., *Trust and Governance* (New York: Russell Sage Foundation, 1998), 88.

2. See Joseph S. Nye Jr., Philip D. Zelikow, and David C. King, *Why People Don't Trust Government* (Cambridge, MA: Harvard University Press, 1997), 88. The authors provide an excellent historical context to the present-day discussion of mistrust. Mistrust is not confined to government. It also shapes the public's view of corporations, the media, and so forth.

3. See, e.g., Clifton Coles, "Britons Distrust Government on Key Risk Issues: Providing Technical Information Is Not Enough to Instill Trust," *Futurist* 37 (July–August 2003): 10. In a survey, Coles reports that "about a quarter to a third of Britons queried . . . believe that the government is acting in the best public interest regarding such issues as radioactive waste and genetic testing."

4. For coverage of the types of issues highlighted in this section, see sources such as Council for Excellence in Government, *Partnership for Trust in Government.* A project with the Ford Foundation (Washington, DC: Council for Excellence in Government), www.trustingov.org/, accessed October 17, 2004.

5. "What Americans Think: Trust in Government," *Spectrum* 73, no. 2 (Spring 2000): 19.

6. Jeffrey M. Jones, "Congressional Approval: Better or Worse with Age?" *Gallup Poll: Tuesday Briefing* (May 18, 2004). Available at www.gallup.com/content/login.aspx?ci = 11731, accessed July 28, 2004.

7. Barbara K. Kaye and Thomas J. Johnson, "Online and in the Know: Uses and Gratifications of the Web for Political Information," *Journal of Broadcasting & Electronic Media* 46 (March 2002): 9. Available in *General Reference Center Gold.* Retrieved December 21, 2005, from http://0-find.galegroup .com.library.simmons.edu/itx/retrieve.do?contentSet = IAC-Documents&qrySerId = Locale(en,US,): FQE = (JN,None,44)"Journal + of + Broadcasting + & + Electronic + Media":And:LQE = (DA,None ,8)20020301$&inPS = true&tabID = T002&prodId = GRGM&searchId = R1&retrieveFormat = PDF&currentPosition = 4&srcprod = GRGM&userGroupName = mlin_b_simmcol&resultList Type = RESULT_LIST&sort = DateDescend&docId = A84971981&noOfPages = 18&isAcrobat Available = true.

8. Christopher J. Anderson and Andrew J. LoTemplo, "Winning, Losing, and Political Trust in America," *British Journal of Political Science* 32 (April 2002): 335.

9. See Department of Energy (DOE), Roadmap (Washington, DC: DOE, n.d.). Available at www.eh.doe.gov/ohre/roadmap/whitehouse/part1.html, accessed October 17, 2004.

10. DOE, Roadmap.

11. See DOE, Human Radiation Experiment, Home page (Washington, DC: DOE). Available at http://hrex.dis.anl.gov/, accessed October 17, 2004. (Note: no other information about the site was provided.)

12. One of the charges against the Bush administration is that it has inserted its social and religious positions into the policies, information content, and positions stated on government Web sites.

13. William J. Mitchell, "When Is Seeing Believing?" *Scientific American,* February 1994, 68.

14. Tom Raum, "Memo Tests Honesty as Best Policy," *Middlesex News* [Framingham, Massachusetts], February 11, 1994, A4. See also William P. Cheshire, "Hoaxing along the Infobahn," *Arizona Republic,* October 30, 1994, E1. He discusses H.R. 5904, Sniper Prevention and Firearms Collection Act, supposedly introduced by Rep. Karen English. The "bill is a hoax, one of countless bogus documents circulating among the patrons of the nation's computer networks."

15. Office of Technology Assessment, *Accessibility and Integrity of Networked Information Collections,* background paper (Washington, DC: Office of Technology Assessment, 1993), 65–66.

16. Peter Hernon, "Disinformation and Misinformation through the Internet: Findings of an Exploratory Study," *Government Information Quarterly* 12, no. 2 (1995): 133–39. See also Anne P. Mintz, ed., *Web of Deception: Misinformation on the Internet* (Medford, NJ: Information Today, 2002); Peter Hernon, Robert E. Dugan, and John A. Shuler, *U.S. Government on the Web: Getting the Information You Need,* 3rd ed. (Westport, CT: Libraries Unlimited, 2003), 18.

17. Richard A. Clarke, *Against All Enemies: Inside America's War on Terror* (New York: Free Press, 2004), 273.

18. Organisation of Economic Co-operation and Development (OECD), *Trust in Government: Ethics Measures in OECD Countries* (Paris: OECD, 2000). Quotes taken from abstract appearing at http:// 217.26.192.119/cgi-bin/OECDBookShop,storefront/4106839700edf940273fc0a8 011 . . . , accessed July 28, 2004.

19. OECD, *Building Public Trust: Ethics Measures in OECD Countries,* OECD Public Management Policy Brief 7 (Paris: OECD, 2000), unpaged.

20. OECD, *Building Public Trust,* 5, 7.

21. OECD, *Building Public Trust,* 2.

22. OECD, *Building Public Trust,* 5.

23. Pew Internet & American Life Project, *How Americans Get in Touch with Government* (Washington, DC: Pew Internet & American Life Project, 2004). Available at www.pewinternet.org, accessed July 28, 2004.

24. Pew Internet & American Life Project, *The Rise of the E-Citizen: How People Use Government Agencies' Web Sites* (Washington, DC: Pew Internet & American Life Project, 2004). Available at www.pewinternet.org, accessed July 28, 2004.

25. Pew Internet & American Life Project, *Dot-gov Goes Retail* (Washington, DC: Pew Internet & American Life Project, 2004). Available at www.pewinternet.org, accessed July 28, 2004.

26. New Zealand, State Services Commission, *New Zealand Government Portal Strategy for a Customer-Centric Portal: Part B—High-Level Implementation Plan, 2001–2004* (Wellington: State Services Commission, 2001). Available at www.e-government.govt.nz/docs/nz-gov-portal-strategy-b/index.html, accessed October 18, 2004.

• 8 •

Access and Security

Harold C. Relyea

$\mathcal{I}$mproved public access to government information, both for informative and transactional purposes, is a major objective in the realization of e-government. In the United States, for instance, the E-Government Act of 2002, enacted in the closing days of the 107th Congress, avows two purposes in this regard: (1) "To promote access to high quality Government information and services across multiple channels," and (2) "To make the Federal Government more transparent and accountable."[1] The latter consideration is particularly important for maintaining the sovereignty of the citizenry in democracies and near democracies. The public is not merely informed; the operations of government are transparent—evident and understandable—and the decisions and actions of government officials affecting those operations are subject, directly or indirectly, to question, prompting justification, and disapproval.

Immediately following these stated purposes, however, the E-Government Act offers a qualifying expectation: "To provide enhanced access to Government information and services in a manner consistent with laws regarding protection of privacy, national security, records retention, access for persons with disabilities, and other relevant laws."[2] Thus, the realization of e-government, at least as envisioned or mandated by this statute, is not to occur to the neglect or detriment of other interests—security, in all of its dimensions, being a primary one. Among those dimensions are security of the person, including both the individual and the corporate body; security of the state, including its relationship to other nations and transborder entities; and security of the homeland. This latter consideration received heightened attention in the United States in the aftermath of the September 11, 2001, attacks on the World Trade Center and the Pentagon, but its antecedents may be traced at least to earlier civil defense and internal security efforts, if not ultimately to the American colonial experience with organizing militia for community protection.[3] For those legislating the E-Government Act, this dimension of security was very fresh in their thinking as the 107th Congress had struggled from June through November with crafting the omnibus Homeland Security Act of 2002, which mandated the Department of Homeland Security, a presidentially headed Homeland Security Council, and a variety of security precautions and conditions "to prevent terrorist attacks within the United States, reduce America's vulnerability to terrorism, and minimize the damage and recover from attacks that do occur."[4]

As defined in the E-Government Act, electronic government means "the use by the Government of web-based Internet applications and other information technologies, combined with processes that implement these technologies, to (A) enhance the access to and delivery of Government information and services to the public, other agencies, and other Government entities; or (B) bring about improvements in Government operations that may include effectiveness, efficiency, service quality, or transformation."[5] The first prong of this conceptualization, embracing the delivery of federal government information and services to not only the public but also "other agencies, and other Government entities" suggests that security will be a factor in the delivery owing to the subject matter and/or to guarantee the integrity of the information. Turning, in this regard, to the Homeland Security Act, subtitle I of Title VIII, denominated the Homeland Security Information Sharing Act, directs the president, among other requirements, to

> prescribe and implement procedures under which relevant Federal agencies . . .
> (A) share relevant and appropriate homeland security information with other Federal agencies, including the Department [of Homeland Security], and appropriate State and local [government] personnel;
> (B) identify and safeguard homeland security information that is sensitive but unclassified; and
> (C) to the extent such information is in [security] classified form, determine whether, how, and to what extent to remove classified information, as appropriate, and with which such personnel it may be shared after such information is removed.[6]

Specifying that the mandated information sharing system shall "have the capability to transmit unclassified or classified information," "ensure the security and confidentiality of such [shared] information," and "protect the constitutional and statutory rights of any individuals who are subjects of such information," the act leaves no doubt about the need for security arrangements.[7]

A NEUTRAL CONCEPT

Understood basically as government use of Web-based Internet applications and other information technologies to enhance the accessibility and delivery of government information with a view to efficiency, economy, and service quality, e-government may be regarded as a politically neutral concept, which is realizable in regimes ranging from the democratic to the authoritarian.[8] E-government may appear to flourish (i.e., be more fully realized) within democracies and near democracies, and to enjoy a more reciprocal relationship with these forms of government. Nonetheless, it has been lately observed that the "much-vaunted promise of the Internet to extend governance and democracy has yet to be brought to fruition, and its potential to do so to date represents something of a mixed bag."[9]

In another effort at definition, which resulted in the neutral explanation that e-government "is the use of electronic processes by citizens, businesses, and the government to communicate, to disseminate and gather information, to facilitate payments, and to carry out permitting in an online environment," the observation was offered that such attempts "will, at some point in the not too distant future, be a moot point . . . because it is inevitable that *e-government* will simply become government."[10] This comment suggests that e-government may be adaptable to, or realizable by, almost any form of government, the possible exception being the totalitarian regime. The discussion in this chapter draws largely upon the American federal experience, which has a long history of open government, balanced with security concerns, and is currently evolving as one of the leading e-government countries.

Wherever and whenever e-government occurs, it arrives in, and is adapted to, a preexisting governmental environment with its own legal and policy legacy.[11] That it can occur in a variety of governmental environments has implications, of course, for realizing access and applying security within the e-government context. These considerations are explored in the paragraphs below.

ACCESS

Prior to discussing information access, a cautionary consideration might be offered: information, as such, is not necessarily reliable or unreliable, but, because it is not always verified, it is not knowledge. When governments provide information through publication, it may take the form of propaganda or, a somewhat new term of late, disinformation. The concept of access arises when someone wants government information that the government did not publish. When access is realized, however, the record or document obtained must still be assessed regarding the validity or reliability of the information it contains. The English philosopher and lawyer Sir Francis Bacon was likely virtuous, but certainly accurate, when he famously wrote that "knowledge is power."

Publication

Long before the e-government phenomenon, governments made information available to the public through publication programs. Primary documents so printed and distributed included statutes, ordinances, and other administrative law instruments. These were often produced individually in leaflet or pamphlet form; cumulatively in subsequent bound volumes; and in facsimile in selected newspapers. Other materials that came to be printed and made available for public examination included the official messages, speech texts, and directives of the primary executive leader; the proceedings of legislative bodies, minimally as minutes and more elaborately as verbatim transcripts; and the decisions of courts, beginning usually with the higher level and, perhaps, specialized tribunals.

Such publication policy evolution may be seen in the experience of the United States, where the federal government has a long and rich history in this regard. With the commencement of constitutional governance in the spring of 1789, Congress quickly provided for the printing and distribution of both the laws and treaties,[12] the preservation of state papers,[13] and the maintenance of official files in the new departments.[14] The printing and distribution of both the Senate and House journals were authorized in 1813.[15] Congress arranged for a contemporary summary of legislative floor proceedings to be published in the *Register of Debates* in 1824, then switched in 1833 to the weekly *Congressional Globe,* which sought to chronicle every step in the legislative process of the two chambers, and then established a daily publication schedule for the *Globe* in 1865.[16] Subsequently, the *Congressional Record* succeeded the *Globe* in March 1873 as the official congressional gazette.[17] Unlike its predecessors, which were produced by private printers on contract to the government, the *Record* was published by the newly established Government Printing Office (GPO).

Provision was initially made in 1846 for the routine printing of all congressional reports, special documents, and bills.[18] Disappointing experience with contract printers to fulfill printing needs prompted Congress to establish the GPO in 1860 to produce all of its literature and to serve, as well, the printing needs of the executive branch.[19] Additional aspects of government-wide printing and publication policy were set with the Printing Act of 1895, which is the source of much of the basic policy still found in the printing chapters of Title 44 of the *United States Code*.[20]

To make government publications more widely available for public use, Congress, in 1857, extended a depository library program, originally launched in 1813 with congressional materials, to include other federal literature.[21] The Printing Act of 1895 vested the superintendent of documents, located within the GPO, with responsibility for distributing documents to, and otherwise managing, the depositories.[22] The superintendent was authorized to reprint departmental publications for public sale in 1904[23] and to do the same regarding congressional documents in 1922.[24]

In the judiciary, the publication of Supreme Court decisions began in 1790 as a private venture. In March 1817, the Court was statutorily authorized to designate and compensate a reporter to manage the compilation and publication of its decisions, with a specified number of copies being supplied without cost for use by the federal government.[25] This arrangement continued until 1922 when the GPO was given responsibility for securing the Court's printing, including publication of the *United States Reports,* its opinion series, and the superintendent of documents was authorized to sell volumes of the series to the public.[26] By contrast, the decisions of the lower federal courts have long been compiled and produced by commercial publishers. These decisions, however, as rendered, remain available for public inspection in docket files at the courthouses where the litigation occurred.

Executive branch printing, as noted above, was initially produced as congressional literature. Presidential messages and departmental reports, for example, were printed as House or Senate documents. Throughout the nineteenth century, both the branch—consisting of the president, vice president, a few departments, and a couple of independent agencies—and its volume of published information remained relatively small. The rise of the administrative state during the second decade of the twentieth century, however, produced a crisis in executive information availability. Powerful new administrative authorities were created to intervene in, and regulate, various sectors of American society. An autonomous Department of Labor was established in 1913, along with the Federal Reserve System, which serves as the nation's central bank. The Federal Trade Commission was mandated the following year to promote competition through the prevention of general trade restraints, monopolies, and price discrimination. With the entry of the United States into World War I in April 1917, regulatory activities further expanded and the number of federal administrative agencies increased. In the immediate postwar era, this government expansion momentarily slowed but began again with the onset of the Great Depression in 1929 and the arrival of President Franklin D. Roosevelt and his New Deal in 1933.

As federal regulatory powers and administrative entities grew dramatically during the 1930s, there was a concomitant increase in both the number and the variety of controlling directives, regulations, and requirements. While a contemporary observer characterized the situation in 1920 as one of "confusion,"[27] another described the deteriorating conditions in 1934 as "chaos."[28] During the early months of the New Deal, administrative law pronouncements were in such disarray that, on one occasion, government attorneys arguing a lawsuit before the Supreme Court were embarrassed to find that their case was based on a nonexistent regulation;[29] at another time, they discovered that they were pursuing litigation under a revoked executive order.[30]

To improve information availability, Congress authorized an executive branch gazette, the *Federal Register,* in 1935.[31] Produced in a now familiar magazine format, it contains various presidential directives and agency regulations and has come to be published each workday. In 1937, Congress inaugurated the *Code of Federal Regulations,* a useful supplement to the *Register.*[32] This accumulation of the instruments and authorities appearing in the gazette contains almost all operative agency regulations in a codified format and is now updated annually.

This history reflects the experience of one national government in proactively making government information available to the public. Ultimately, the decision as to what information will be published is made by the government, or by one arm of the government, such as the legislature, for itself or other segments of the government. The mirror opposite of this situation concerns access: the obtaining of government information by the public on its own volition. Understood in this way, access traditionally has been realized in two ways regarding government information.

Presumptive Procedure

One way to establish public access to unpublished government information is through the creation of so-called freedom of information (FOI) or access-to-information laws. Usually statutory, such laws embody a presumption of public access; prescribe a procedure for requesting access to unpublished, existing, identifiable records; establish qualifying conditions, such as the inapplicability of the law to some government institutions and categories of information exempt from the rule of disclosure; and specify where disputes over the availability of requested records may be ultimately settled. Administrative factors may be included, such as prescribing fees for search, review, and duplication of requested records and time frames in which requests must be processed. Use of such laws may be limited to citizens, which may be cumbersome if surrogates, such as native attorneys, are engaged to stand in for otherwise nonqualifying requesters.

Such access laws date to 1766 in Sweden, followed by a 1951 version in Finland, and the U.S. Freedom of Information Act of 1966. Thereafter, among those embracing such laws were Denmark and Norway in 1970, France and Holland in 1978, Australia and New Zealand in 1982, and Canada in 1983. With the collapse of the Union of Soviet Socialist Republics, several nations freed from that regime successfully adopted such laws, as have various other nations for a number of reasons, not the least of which are enhanced democracy, extension of human rights, control of the administrative state, modernization and adaptation to the postindustrial information society, and exposing corruption. "Over fifty countries around the world have now adopted comprehensive Freedom of Information Acts to facilitate access to records held by government bodies," it has recently been reported, "and over thirty more have pending efforts." It also was noted that "over half of the FOI laws have been adopted in just the last ten years."[33]

Records Management

Another way to establish public access to unpublished government information is through life cycle records management, with the result that historically valuable materials, regardless of format, will be available in archived form. In the United States, life cycle management of the records of the federal government probably began in earnest after the creation of the National Archives and Records Administration in 1934, which brought the archives and records of all three branches "under the charge and superintendence of the Archivist" of the United States.[34] Since 1789, the Department of State, in addition to its diplomacy and foreign relations responsibilities, had fulfilled the housekeeping duties of collecting and preserving the highest-level official documents of the government, such as presidentially signed enrolled legislation, ratified treaties, and similar state papers. Lesser records generated within the departments remained within their files. The need for a National Archives with its simple "records management" mission was prompted by two developments. The first of these was the growing volume of records being produced by an expanding federal government. Between 1861, when the Civil War erupted, and 1916, the year before the United States entered World War I, the accumulated total of federal records swelled from 108,000 to 1,031,000 cubic feet. Many of these were records that had long outlived their usefulness, and many managers within the departments and agencies of the executive branch clamored for an orderly and systematic process for disposing of useless records and properly storing those worthy of retention. Proper storage included considerations for safety, because fire—another experience prompting improved conditions—had sporadically claimed some important materials, as well as maintenance of a suitable atmosphere and relatively easy retrieval arrangements. Congress did not give attention to the matter until 1896, when interest in a general storage facility, a "hall of records," was evidenced. Over the next three decades, many historians, archivists, and patriotic organizations became advocates for a national archival institution, and such a facility came to be regarded as a central repository for the historically valuable, permanent records of the federal government, which, once accessioned, would no longer be under the control of the individual agencies. In 1926, Congress allocated $1 million toward "the construction of an extensible archives building and the acquisition of a site" for the edifice. Although complications slowed the process, and additional funds had to be appropriated, a site was selected, ground was broken in September 1931, the cornerstone of the facility was laid in February 1933, and the agency to manage the building was mandated in June 1934.[35]

The immediate work of the newly established National Archives largely focused on records at the end of the management life cycle—those awaiting some final disposition. The archivist and his staff were empowered to inspect any and all federal records, wherever located, with a view to requisitioning such materials for transfer to the National Archives for permanent retention and public availability. In conducting this activity, Archives personnel were able to eliminate backlogs of inactive records within the agencies by removing the historically valuable materials for permanent preservation, destroying the useless papers, and temporarily storing others for later, final disposition.

In the course of this work, they also could identify active records having historical value. Out of these early efforts, there emerged the various regulations, handbooks, and schedules that have evolved into the versions that currently govern records disposition.[36]

There are a few government archives that, despite wars and other national calamities, have collections that reach back many years. The National Archives of England, Wales, and the United Kingdom, for instance, was formed in April 2003 from the Public Records Office and the Historical Manuscripts Commission, both of which had a durable lineage, with the result that its holdings span a thousand years of British history. Responsible for the preservation of the records of the central government and the courts of law, the Archives also advises government entities and the wider public sector on best practices in records management and selecting records of enduring historical value.

In the People's Republic of China (PRC), the State Archives Bureau in Beijing directly manages two so-called historical archives, one for Ming and Qing dynasty records and another for the national governments of the 1911–1949 period, and the national or Central Archives has holdings dating from 1949 to recent times. There are, as well, subnational archives in provinces, autonomous regions, special municipalities, and subprovincial cities, counties, townships, and districts. The Bureau provides policy guidance, standards, and instructions for operations by archival entities at the subnational level, as well as the central government entities, and provides professional leadership for the latter regarding life cycle records management. The total archival system is of very broad scope, embracing a huge quantity of records concerning Chinese society, no matter what the origin (public or private), and considered to be of such national value (the property of the people of China) that they must be in the custody of, and management by, the state. The observation has been offered, however, that the "Chinese archival lexicon does not include a concept of 'access' as a scholar's or citizen's right to examine original documents directly." Instead, "Chinese archivists persistently translate 'access' as 'archives-use services.'" What this means in practice is that those seeking to use archival materials, including users on assignment from government entities, must justify their need to archivists, who decide, based upon the scope of the user's research and focus as explained in their application, what materials are pertinent for examination.[37]

For many government archives, records are withheld from public access for thirty years from the date of their creation. Some may adhere to the older fifty-year standard or reserve that longer period for security-sensitive materials. The National Archives in Great Britain follows the thirty-year rule, but may, like the United States, substitute the access arrangements of its FOI Act, adopted in November 2000, for the temporal limitation. Archival law in the PRC permits, but does not require, that records in government archives be opened thirty years after their creation. Furthermore, materials concerning state security and "national interest" may be restricted for fifty years or more. Those depositing records in which they have a proprietary interest may control examination by requiring their consent to do so, and, it has been noted, "in practice depositing state agencies have first use privileges to the documents they deposited."[38]

Finally, it should be noted that life cycle records management is important not only for making historically valuable records available for public access in archived form but also for supporting public access to agency records pursuant to FOI laws. Undoubtedly, during the past thirty years, nations implementing such information access laws have quickly become aware of the extent to which the management of government records was in disarray. Failure to locate quickly records responsive to an FOI request usually results in failure to meet established deadlines for such access. As these miscarriages continue to occur, request backlogs can mount, overseers may intervene, hapless managers may be reprimanded or dismissed, and scarce resources may, of necessity, have to be committed to remedy the situation. Technology has brought some notable improvements in this regard as more and more records during the past dozen years have been produced or otherwise stored in electronic form, and sophisticated search engines have made their retrieval much easier.

SECURITY

The concept of security may be understood in various ways, such as freedom from danger or as the end result of making something—a form of government, a state, a regime, a document, an electronic information system—safe against adverse contingencies. At the outset of this chapter, security was viewed as having at least three dimensions: security of the person, including both the individual and the corporate body; security of the state, including its relationship to other nations and transborder entities; and security of the homeland. Reviewed below are the primary policies and practices for realizing information security.

Statutory Protection

In many jurisdictions, statutory provisions identify types of information to be secured. Sometimes the information may be narrowly or specifically designated, and sometimes conditions concerning its management may be provided. A wide variety of types of information—business, commercial, trade, financial, banking, law enforcement, personally identifiable, intelligence, defense, foreign relations—might be so secured. The degree of discretion officials exercise regarding such provisions may become an issue if they are viewed as improperly overextending such security protection to defeat access requests. When originally enacted in 1966, the U.S. FOI Act permitted the withholding of information "specifically exempted from disclosure by statute."[39] After the Supreme Court ruled that this exemption allowed the administrator of the Federal Aviation Administration to withhold any records of the agency when he considered their disclosure "not required in the interest of the public,"[40] Congress amended the provision to except information "specifically exempted from disclosure by statute . . . , provided that such statute (A) requires that the matters be withheld from the public in such a manner as to leave no discretion on the issue, or (B) establishes particular criteria for withholding or refers to particular types of matters to be withheld."[41]

Some jurisdictions may have so-called official secrets laws, which, for reasons of state security, prescribe that all government information, or at least that of the executive sector, is protected against unauthorized disclosure and provide criminal punishments for government personnel disclosing any government information without authorization and, perhaps, also for any recipient of such information who knew its disclosure was unauthorized. Such law in Great Britain dates to 1889 and had been replicated in Commonwealth countries like Australia and Canada but has been ameliorated in the past few years by FOI laws. In the United States, since 1946 certain atomic energy information—"all data concerning (1) design, manufacture, or utilization of atomic weapons; (2) the production of special nuclear material [such as plutonium and isotopes 233 and 235 enriched uranium]; or (3) the use of special nuclear material in the production of energy"—has been denominated "Restricted Data," which is subject to security requirements.[42] Such information, regardless of who produces it, is "born" in a protected status without the necessity of any affirmative action by the government. Anyone producing such information who is not authorized to possess it or does not properly protect it must surrender it to the government.[43]

Many nations have laws regulating exports, including not only products of science and technology having armament and weaponry application and dual civilian-military use, but also related scientific and technical data. During the early 1980s, attempts by the Reagan administration to regulate scientific and technological communication more vigorously resulted in considerable controversy. The dispute subsided with the departure of some key defense officials and the administration's adoption of a trade stance supporting American competitiveness, particularly regarding the overseas sale of goods and services utilizing dual-use technologies.[44]

Security Regulations

In some jurisdictions, official secrecy policy may be established by administrative regulations. This was the case in the People's Republic of China when, in 1951, the initial Provisional Regulations for the Preservation of State Secrets were promulgated. Designed to prevent "spies inside or outside the country, counter-revolutionary elements and subversive elements from prying into, stealing, or selling state secrets," the regulations, in the absence of a definition of "state secrets," provided a long list of examples, concluding with "all other state affairs that must be kept secret." In the aftermath of the PRC becoming open to foreign investment in 1979, the regulations made it difficult for potential entrepreneurs to obtain legal, economic, and other government information relative to conducting and establishing business.[45]

A few years later, a new Law of the People's Republic of China on the Preservation of State Secrets was enacted in September 1988 and became effective in May 1989, replacing the 1951 regulations. The statute established a tripartite hierarchy of categories of harm that would result from the improper disclosure of state secrets. Information within these categories is marked accordingly and has a specific period of protection, which, however, may be extended at the discretion of officials. In addition to defining a state secret, the law contains a list of secret matters, but these are sufficiently general as to require administrative interpretations and implementing regulations.[46]

In the United States, classification arrangements for protecting state secrets concerning national security are presidentially prescribed in executive orders, the first of which was issued by President Franklin D. Roosevelt in March 1940.[47] This development was probably prompted somewhat by desires to clarify the authority of civilian personnel in the national defense community to classify information, to establish a broader basis for protecting military information in view of growing global hostilities, and to better manage a discretionary power seemingly of increasing importance to the entire executive branch. Prior to this 1940 order, information had been designated officially secret by armed forces personnel pursuant to army and navy general orders and regulations. The first systematic procedures for the protection of national defense information, devoid of special markings, were established by War Department General Orders No. 3 of February 1912. Records determined to be "confidential" were to be kept under lock, "accessible only to the officer to whom intrusted." Serial numbers were issued for all such "confidential" materials, with the numbers marked on the documents and lists of same kept at the offices from which they emanated. With the enlargement of the armed forces after the entry of the United States into World War I, the registry system was abandoned and a tripartite system of classification markings was inaugurated in November 1917 with General Orders No. 64 of the General Headquarters of the American Expeditionary Force.

During World War II, in addition to the president's order and prevailing armed forces directives on marking and handling classified information, the Office of War Information, in September 1942, issued a government-wide regulation on creating and managing classified materials. Among other ad hoc arrangements of the era, personnel cleared to work on the Manhattan Project for the production of the atomic bomb, in committing themselves not to disclose protected information improperly, were "required to read and sign either the Espionage Act or a special secrecy agreement," establishing their awareness of their secrecy obligations and a fiduciary trust which, if breached, constituted a basis for their dismissal.[48]

A few years after the conclusion of World War II, President Harry S. Truman issued an order in February 1950 reiterating the text of the Roosevelt directive, but adding a fourth, "Top Secret," classification designation and making American information-security categories consistent with those of American allies. This was followed by a September 1951 directive from Truman introducing three sweeping innovations in security classification policy. First, the order indicated the chief executive was relying upon "the authority vested in me by the Constitution and statutes, and as President of the United States" in issuing the directive. This formula appeared to strengthen the president's discretion to make official secrecy policy by intertwining his responsibility as commander in chief with the constitutional obligation to "take care that the laws be faithfully executed."[49] Second, information was now classified in the interest of "national security," a somewhat new, but nebulous, concept, which, in the view of some, conveyed more latitude for the creation of official secrets. It replaced the previously relied upon "national defense" standard for classification. Third, the order extended classification authority to nonmilitary entities, to be exercised by, presumably, but not explicitly limited to, those having some role in "national security" policy.

The broad discretion to create official secrets granted by Truman's new order engendered widespread criticism from the public and the press. In response, President Dwight D. Eisenhower, shortly after his election to office, instructed his attorney general to review the order with a view to revising or rescinding it. The subsequent recommendation was for a new directive, which was issued in November 1953. It withdrew classification authority from twenty-eight entities, limited this discretion in seventeen other units to the agency head, returned to the national defense standard for applying secrecy, eliminated the "Restricted" category, which was the lowest level of protection, and explicitly defined the remaining three classification areas to prevent their indiscriminate use.

Thereafter, the Eisenhower order, with slight amendment, prescribed operative security classification policy and procedure for the next two decades. Successor orders by President Richard M. Nixon in March 1972 and President Jimmy Carter in June 1978 built on this reform. For thirty years, these classification directives narrowed the bases and discretion for assigning official secrecy to executive branch documents and materials. Then, in April 1982, this trend was reversed by President Ronald Reagan with a new order, which expanded the categories of classifiable information, mandated that information falling within these categories be classified, authorized the reclassification of previously declassified documents, admonished classifiers to err on the side of classification, and eliminated automatic declassification arrangements.[50]

President William Clinton returned security classification policy and procedure to the reform trend of the Eisenhower, Nixon, and Carter administrations with Executive Order (E.O.) 12958 in April 1995.[51] Accountability and cost considerations were significant influences. In 1985, the temporary Department of Defense (DOD) Security Review Commission, chaired by retired general Richard G. Stilwell, declared that there were "no verifiable figures as to the amount of classified material produced in DOD and in defense industry each year." Nonetheless, it concluded that "too much information appears to be classified and much at higher levels than is warranted."[52] In October 1993, the cost of the security classification program became clearer when the General Accounting Office (GAO) reported that it was "able to identify government-wide costs directly applicable to national security information totaling over $350 million for 1992." After breaking this figure down—it included only $6 million for declassification work—the report added that "the U.S. government also spends additional billions of dollars annually to safeguard information, personnel, and property."[53] E.O. 12958, a new directive, set limits for the duration of classification, prohibited the reclassification of properly declassified records, authorized government employees to challenge the classification status of records, reestablished the balancing test of the Carter order weighing the need to protect information vis-à-vis the public interest in its disclosure, and created two review panels, one on classification and declassification actions and one to advise on policy and procedure.

In March 2003, President George W. Bush issued E.O. 13292 amending E.O. 12958.[54] Among the changes made by this directive were adding infrastructure vulnerabilities or capabilities, protection services relating to national security, and weapons of mass destruction to the categories of classifiable information; easing the reclassification of declassified records; postponing the automatic declassification of protected records twenty-five or more years old, beginning in mid-April 2003 to the end of December 2006; eliminating the requirement that agencies prepare plans for declassifying records; and permitting the director of central intelligence to block declassification actions of the Interagency Security Classification Appeals Panel, unless overruled by the president.[55]

Homeland Security Practice

There can be little doubt that the terrorist attacks of 9/11 prompted immediate actions and rethinking about various aspects of the domestic or homeland security of the United States, not the least of which included the public availability of information of potential value to the perpetrators of such assaults for either the commission of their acts or forewarning them of ways of their being detected. Among the policy consequences were the extension of security classification authority to federal health, environment, and agriculture leaders as a consequence of the important roles their entities would play in combating biological, chemical, radiological, and nuclear terrorism;[56] new controls on information concerning the location of, and research involving, certain biological agents and toxins;[57] and protection of voluntarily submitted critical infrastructure information and security-sensitive transportation information.[58]

New policy, however rushed into final form and implementation, usually provides some opportunity for public awareness of, and debate regarding, its formulation. A particularly disconcerting practice that occurred, with some frequency, in the aftermath of the 9/11 terrorist attacks was the disappearance of not only opportunities for public input but also government information previously available to the public. Oftentimes, no announcement of the suppression was made, and the extent of the excisions was not immediately apparent. Some losses, however, quickly became apparent: the Bureau of Transportation Statistics restricting access to its National Transportation Atlas Data Base; the Environmental Protection Agency removing from its Web site a database, developed from risk management plans filed with the agency, containing information on chemicals used at fifteen thousand industrial sites around the country; and the Nuclear Regulatory Commission closing its Web site briefly and returning with a "bare bones" version.[59] The GPO ordered federal depository librarians to destroy a CD-ROM containing government survey data on reservoirs and dams in the United States, and other depository holdings were reportedly under scrutiny for similar action.[60] After this initial phase of some previously public information products and services being curtailed by federal agencies owing to security concerns, speculation developed regarding the implications of such limiting actions for future Web site offerings and electronic reading-room holdings.

E-GOVERNMENT CONSIDERATIONS

In the late years of the twentieth century, the phenomenon of government information being increasingly collected, maintained, used, and disseminated in electronic form and formats signaled the coming of e-government in the United States. A pioneering, comprehensive assessment of the electronic collection and dissemination of information by federal agencies, produced by the House Committee on Government Operations (now the Committee on Government Reform) in the spring of 1986, offered a number of relevant and prescient findings.

- "Increasing amounts of information—both private and public—are being maintained in electronic data bases," and this "trend will both continue and accelerate."
- "Electronic collection, maintenance, and dissemination of information by Federal agencies can undermine the practical limitations and legal structures" governing public access to, as well as government collection, creation, and dissemination of, such information.
- "Electronic information systems offer the opportunity to make more government information readily available" to the public, and this same information "technology also permits government information to be used in ways that are not possible when the information is stored on paper records."
- "The development and installation of an electronic information system requires advanced planning and may require sizable capital expenditures."
- "The Federal Government must understand the consequences of electronic information systems and must recognize the need for new policies that will prevent these systems from being used in unintended ways."

- "There is little communication among Federal agencies about electronic information activities, and there is little central administrative guidance."[61]

These findings revealed a relatively new technology of growing use and application, one conveying considerable discretionary capability to federal agencies concerning
government information management, while simultaneously outstripping the existing
practical limitations and legal structures governing many aspects of the government
information life cycle.

An October 1988 report by the Office of Technology Assessment (OTA), a now
defunct congressional support agency, gave further testimony to the impact of the electronic information phenomenon upon existing government information policy and
practice. Among the "problems and challenges" identified in the OTA study were the
following:

- a blurring or elimination of "many distinctions between reports, publications,
databases, records, and the like, in ways not anticipated by existing statutes and
policies";
- electronic technology permitting "information dissemination on a decentralized
basis that is cost-effective at low levels of demand, but in ways that may challenge
traditional roles, responsibilities, and policies";
- electronic technology "eroding the institutional roles of government-wide
information dissemination agencies";
- electronic technology that "has outpaced the major government-wide statutes
that apply to Federal information dissemination."[62]

Calling explicitly for a defining of the "GPO's role in the dissemination of electronic formats" and the "GPO's role relative to the growth in agency desktop and high-
end electronic publishing systems," the report concluded:

> The government needs to set in motion a comprehensive planning process for creatively
> exploring the long-term future (e.g., 10 to 20 years from now) when the information
> infrastructure of the public and private sectors could be quite different. At the same time,
> the government needs to provide short-term direction to existing agencies and institutions
> with respect to electronic information dissemination.[63]

Thereafter, during the tenure of the Clinton administration (1993–2000),
e-government became realized within the federal establishment and continues to
evolve, although, arguably, at a somewhat slower pace during the initial years of the
current century than was initially experienced during the final decade of the past century. The two congressional reports noted above heralded not only its coming but also
some of the challenges it would pose.

The 1986 report of the House Committee on Government Operations on the
electronic information phenomenon was attentive to future management needs. Specifically, in view of the "sizable capital expenditures" that were thought to be required,
it foresaw the need for advanced planning in the development and installation of electronic information systems. It also seemed to consider existing central management
guidance on, and federal interagency communication about, electronic information

activities to be inadequate. These deficiencies came to be addressed in several policy pronouncements.

The Paperwork Reduction Act (PRA) of 1995, a recodification of a 1980 statute of the same name, specified a full range of responsibilities for the director of the Office of Management and Budget (OMB) for all government information, regardless of form or format, throughout its entire life cycle. Regarding information technology (IT), the director, among other duties, was tasked with (1) developing and overseeing the implementation of policies, principles, standards, and guidelines for federal IT functions and activities, including periodic evaluations of major information systems; (2) overseeing the development and implementation of certain statutorily specified technology standards; (3) monitoring the effectiveness of, and compliance with, certain statutorily authorized technology directives; (4) coordinating the development and review by the OMB Office of Information and Regulatory Affairs (OIRA) of policy associated with federal procurement and acquisition of IT with the OMB Office of Federal Procurement Policy; (5) ensuring, through the review of agency budget proposals, information resources management (IRM) plans, and other means, both (a) the integration of IRM plans with program plans and budgets for the acquisition and use of IT by each agency, and (b) the efficiency and effectiveness of interagency IT initiatives to improve agency performance and the accomplishment of agency missions; and (6) promoting agency use of IT to improve the productivity, efficiency, and effectiveness of federal programs, including through the dissemination of public information and the reduction of information collection burdens on the public. Similar responsibilities were specified for the agencies regarding government information throughout its life cycle.[64]

The following year, Congress enacted legislation that came to be denominated the Clinger-Cohen Act in honor of its principal sponsors. Among other provisions, the statute made each agency responsible for its own IT acquisitions, amended the PRA to establish a chief information officer (CIO) in each agency, and mandated capital and other planning responsibilities for both the OMB and the agencies regarding IT investment and applications.[65]

Thereafter, President Clinton issued E.O. 13011 of July 16, 1996, which mandated several IT management improvements and promoted a coordinated approach to IT applications across the executive branch. This included prescribing that executive agencies significantly improve the management of their information systems, including the acquisition of IT, by implementing the relevant provisions of the PRA and the Clinger-Cohen Act; refocus IT management to support directly their strategic missions; implement an investment review process that drove budget information and execution for information systems and rethought and restructured the way they performed their functions before investing in IT to support that work; establish clear accountability for IRM activities by creating agency CIOs with the visibility and management responsibilities necessary to advise agency heads on the design, development, and implementation of those information systems; and cooperate in the use of IT to improve the productivity of federal programs and to provide a coordinated, interoperable, secure, and shared government-wide infrastructure that was provided and supported by a diversity of private sector suppliers and a well-trained corps of IT professionals. Agencies were also directed to establish an interagency support structure that built on existing successful interagency efforts and provided expertise and advice to agencies; expanded the skill and career development opportunities of IT professionals; improved the management and use of

IT within and among agencies by developing IT procedures and standards and by identifying and sharing experiences, ideas, and promising practices; and provided innovative, multidisciplinary, project-specific support to agencies to enhance interoperability,
minimize unnecessary duplication of effort, and capitalize on agency successes. The
order detailed new responsibilities for agency heads, including effectively using IT to
improve mission performance and service to the public. It also mandated a Chief Information Officers Council to serve as the principal interagency forum to improve agency
practices regarding such matters as the design, modernization, use, sharing, and performance of agency information resources.[66]

Thus, in about three years, a considerable effort was made to address the management concerns expressed in the 1986 report of the House Committee on Government
Operations. A couple of additional features were dealt with in the E-Government Act
of 2002, which statutorily reestablished the CIO Council and created an Office of Electronic Government within the OMB.[67] The result was a better managerial superstruc-
ture for e-government in general and both access and security within it in particular.
The discussion below examines access and security developments in the context of
e-government.

E-access

The 1988 OTA report suggested that the electronic information phenomenon had particularly troubling implications for the GPO, which was beginning to experience various kinds of challenges to its virtually exclusive role as the printer for the federal
government. Among these were printing laws and regulations that were becoming out-
moded as a consequence of the emergence and employment of new IT; production
processes that were less efficient, economical, and effective than those resulting from
new IT applications; growing executive branch unhappiness, both for practical and
constitutional reasons, with the GPO's monopoly on printing production; and the
defanging of its watchdog over government printing, the Joint Committee on Printing,
at the hands of the Supreme Court.[68]

A subsequent congressional response to the OTA report regarding the GPO was
the Government Printing Office Electronic Information Access Enhancement Act of
1993.[69] This statute directed the superintendent of documents to provide a system of
online access to the *Congressional Record* and the *Federal Register* by June 1994. The
superintendent was given discretion to make available other appropriate publications
and responsibility for maintaining an electronic directory of federal electronic information, as well as for operating an electronic storage facility for federal electronic information. In addition to the online *Congressional Record* and *Federal Register,* the GPO also
created a legislation database containing all published versions of House and Senate bills
introduced since the 103rd Congress. The statute provided free online access for all
depository libraries and cost recovery based upon the marginal cost of dissemination for
all other users. Subsequently, in December 1995, the GPO announced that it was making the GPO Access service directly available over the Internet and was dropping the
subscription fee.

This legislation did not resolve the GPO's various other problems but did result in
greater attention being devoted to, and the success of, Internet distribution of government documents. This development, in turn, contributed to a reduction generally in

the number of copies of documents printed by the GPO; a reduction in sales of government documents by the GPO; the direct distribution of digitally formatted documents by agencies via the Internet, resulting in fugitive materials never indexed by the GPO or offered to depository libraries; and, to say the least, an uncertain future for the depository library system.[70] In April 2005, the OMB reported that, in FY 2004, 86 percent of all materials distributed through the depository program were available online.[71]

Another effort at harnessing the electronic information phenomenon was the Electronic Freedom of Information Amendments (E-FOIA) of 1996, which, among other changes, confirmed the statute's applicability to records in electronic forms or formats, required that responsive materials be provided in the form or format sought by the requester, and mandated so-called electronic reading rooms, which the public may access online to examine important and high-visibility agency records.[72] In a March 2001 report on the implementation of the E-FOIA, the GAO found that all of the twenty-five agencies it reviewed had established electronic reading rooms, but only sixteen agencies in the sample had posted guidance on agency-specific processing, only fifteen agencies had made available documents for all required categories of records, and only twelve agencies had provided reference material addressing all four areas specified by the amendments.[73] In an August 2002 follow-up report, the GAO indicated that agencies "have made progress in on-line availability of the materials required by e-FOIA as well as in using the Web to make materials publicly available," but "not all required materials were available on-line." The report also noted that "FOIA officials and requesters viewed the impacts of the post–September 11 environment on e-FOIA implementation differently." It proffered that "agency officials characterized the effects of the September 11 terrorist attacks on operations as relatively minor," but in doing so they were seen to focus on "specific changes in operations and compliance, rather than on general changes in their agencies' proactive information dissemination policies and practices." On the contrary, "requesters expressed considerably more concern, especially in a broader sense, about public access to government information" and "did not differentiate between specific concerns about FOIA compliance and their more general concerns about information dissemination and public access."[74]

Attention to the preservation of permanent, historically valuable government records in electronic forms and formats was begun at the National Archives and Records Administration (NARA) in 2001 with a survey of current record-keeping practices within the federal government.[75] The agency, however, had been advised to address the archiving of electronic records over a decade earlier.[76] A June 2002 evaluation of the Archives' efforts summarized the situation.

> In 2001, NARA completed an assessment of the current federal record-keeping environment; this study concluded that although agencies are creating and maintaining records appropriately, most electronic records (including databases of major federal information systems) remain unscheduled [for final disposition], and records of historical value are not being identified and provided to NARA for preservation in archives. As a result, valuable electronic records may be at risk of loss. Part of the problem is that records management guidance is inadequate in the current technological environment of decentralized systems producing large volumes of complex records. Another factor is the low priority often given to records management programs and the lack of technology tools to manage electronic records. Finally, NARA does not perform systematic inspections of agency records and records management programs, and so it does not have comprehensive information

allowing it to identify records management implementation issues and areas where its guidance needs to be strengthened. NARA plans to improve its guidance and to address technology issues. However, NARA's plans do not address the low priority generally given to records management programs nor the issue of systematic inspections.[77]

In planning for an electronic records archive (ERA), the Archives, at its request, was provided independent technical advice on the design of the ERA by the Computer Science and Telecommunications Board of the National Research Council, the principal operating agency of the National Academy of Sciences and National Academy of Engineering.[78]

In July 2003, a GAO representative acknowledged in testimony at a congressional committee hearing that "NARA has taken steps to improve its guidance and address the lack of technology tools" noted in an earlier assessment. Furthermore, "it has devised a comprehensive approach to improving agency records management that includes inspections and identification of risks and priorities, but its approach does not include provisions for using inspections to evaluate the efficiency of its government-wide guidance, and an implementation plan for the approach has yet to be established." Commenting that the Archives' acquisition of the ERA "presents significant challenges," the view was offered that "NARA is unable to objectively track the cost and schedule of the ERA project."[79] Despite these and other deficiencies, the ERA effort moved forward. In August 2004, the archivist announced the award of two design contracts for the ERA, valued at a little more than $20 million. At the end of the one-year design competition, one of the contractors receiving these awards will be selected by the National Archives to construct the ERA.

Finally, the E-Government Act of 2002 contains several provisions regarding information access. Section 202 directed agency heads, when promulgating policies and implementing programs regarding the provision of government information and services over the Internet, to consider the impact on persons without such access, and, "to the extent practicable, (1) ensure that the availability of Government information and services has not been diminished for individuals who lack access to the Internet; and (2) pursue alternate modes of delivery that make Government information and services more accessible to individuals who do not own computers or lack access to the Internet."[80] The heads of the OMB and General Services Administration and other agencies were directed in section 204 "to maintain and promote an integrated Internet-based system of providing the public with access to Government information and services."[81] In a recent report to Congress on the implementation of the E-Government Act, the OMB noted that FirstGov.gov, "the Executive branch's official Internet portal," which was launched on September 22, 2000, and subsequently upgraded, "meets statutory requirements, greatly simplifies the public's access to government information, and enables timely use of government services." The report proffered that "in FY2004 more than 78 million visitors (an increase of 24 percent over FY2003) viewed over 203 million pages on the FirstGov.gov website," and noted that, during FY2004, "the Federal government's official Spanish language web portal, FirstGov en Espanol," had been inaugurated.[82]

Web sites for all of the various federal courts were mandated by section 205, certain minimal information and access links for them were specified, and it was prescribed that "each website shall be updated regularly and kept reasonably current."[83] Federal regulatory agencies were similarly tasked in section 206 with ensuring that "a publicly accessible Federal Government website" included on it certain minimal information about their organization and operation that was otherwise required to be published in the *Federal Register*.[84]

Section 207 sought, in various ways, to improve the ways in which government information is organized, preserved, and made accessible to the public. "To accomplish these goals," a recent OMB implementation report explained, "the Act requires OMB to establish an interagency committee to recommend to OMB policies for agency public websites and indexing and categorizing government information." The committee, it continued, "is to recommend to OMB and the Archivist policies and procedures for applying the Federal Records Act to electronic records and government information on the Internet," and, guided by the committee's recommendations, the "OMB and the Archivist are to issue policies as necessary." Among the important issues to be addressed in the committee's work is better management of information on agency Web sites, such as its currency, time of availability, and preservation and subsequent retrieval from archival status through the Web sites. Established in June 2003, the committee included representatives from over twenty-five federal agencies in the executive and legislative branches, according to the OMB report, and organized four working groups, which began delivering recommendations to the OMB. Based in part on these recommendations, the OMB issued initial Web site management policy in December 2004, is continuing to review subsequent recommendations, and will issue such additional policy as thought to be necessary by December 2005.[85]

E-security

A foundation for the security of IT systems and subsequent e-government transactions was laid with the Computer Security Act of 1987.[86] The statute required each federal agency to develop security plans for its computer systems containing sensitive information. Such plans were subject to review by the National Institute of Standards and Technology (NIST) of the Department of Commerce, and a summary, together with overall budget plans for IT, was to be filed with the OMB. The NIST was authorized to set security standards for all federal computer systems, except those containing intelligence, cryptologic, or certain military information or information specifically authorized under criteria established by an executive order or statute to be kept secret in the interest of national defense or foreign policy. Each federal agency was directed to provide all employees involved with the management, use, or operation of its computer systems with mandatory periodic training in computer security awareness and accepted computer security practice.

As IT systems became more pervasive in the federal government and the realization of e-government made greater use of them, new security policy was adopted, each iteration building upon its predecessor(s). In late 2000, amendments to the PRA prescribed new government information and IT systems security requirements, which included OMB affirmative approval of agency security plans required by the legislation.[87] The director of OMB was made responsible for establishing government-wide policies for the management of programs that support the cost-effective security of federal information systems by promoting security as an integral part of each agency's business operations and was also tasked with overseeing and coordinating agency implementation of security policies, as well as coordinating with the NIST on the development of standards and guidelines for security controls for federal systems. Such standards were to be voluntary and consensus based and developed in consultation with industry. To enforce agency accountability, the director was authorized to take budgetary action with respect to an agency's information resources management allocations.

Agency heads or, by delegation, agency CIOs or comparable officials were made responsible for developing and implementing security policies, and each agency was required to develop and implement an agency-wide security program, which must include risk assessment considering internal and external threats; risk-based policies; security awareness training for personnel; periodic reviews of the effectiveness of security policies, including remedies to address deficiencies; and procedures for detecting, reporting, and responding to security incidents. The agencies were required to have an annual independent evaluation of their information security program and practices, conducted either by their inspector general, the GAO, or an independent external auditor, with the GAO then reviewing these evaluations and reporting annually to Congress regarding the adequacy of agency information programs and practices.

The Federal Information Security Act of 2002, enacted as Title III of the E-Government Act, superseded the 2000 government information security amendments to the PRA but did so by generally improving upon them with slight embellishment.[88] The director of OMB continued to be the central manager for federal information systems security. Agencies were required to inventory their major IT systems; to identify and provide appropriate security protections; and to develop, document, and implement an agency-wide information security program. The NIST was authorized to develop security standards and guidelines for federal systems, and the agencies continued to be obligated to have an annual, independent evaluation of the effectiveness of their security program, plans, practices, and compliance with the statute's requirements. The requirements of the statute, however, did not extend to national security systems involving defense, intelligence, cryptologic, or related matters, which were separately managed regarding their security.

Finally, with regard to personal security or privacy, two policy developments are relevant. The first concerns the facilitation of electronic transactions with the federal government. The Government Paperwork Elimination Act (GPEA) of 1998 amended the PRA to require federal agencies to make electronic versions of their forms available online and to allow individuals and businesses to use electronic signatures to file these forms electronically and securely.[89] The GPEA made the director of OMB responsible for providing government-wide direction and oversight regarding "the acquisition and use of information technology, including alternative information technologies that provide for electronic submission, maintenance, or disclosure of information as a substitute for paper and for the use and acceptance of electronic signatures."[90] In fulfilling this responsibility, the director, in consultation with the National Telecommunications and Information Administration (NTIA) of the Department of Commerce, was tasked with developing, in accordance with prescribed requirements, procedures for the use and acceptance of electronic signatures by the executive departments and agencies. A five-year deadline was prescribed for the agencies to implement these procedures.[91]

In cooperation with the NTIA, the director of OMB was directed to conduct an ongoing study of the use of electronic signatures under the GPEA, with attention to paperwork reduction and electronic commerce, individual privacy, and the security and authenticity of transactions, the results of which are to be reported periodically to Congress. The statute also specified that, unless otherwise provided by law, "information collected in the provision of electronic signature services for communications with an executive agency . . . shall only be used or disclosed by persons who obtain, collect, or maintain such information as a business or government practice, for the purpose of facilitating such communications, or with the prior affirmative consent of the person about whom the information pertains."[92]

The following year, a June 2, 1999, memorandum from the director of OMB to the heads of executive departments and agencies required the posting of clear privacy policies on federal Web sites, and provided guidance for this action. Such policies, it said, "must clearly and concisely inform visitors to the site what information the agency collects about individuals, why the agency collects it, and how the agency will use it." Also, they "must be clearly labeled and easily accessed when someone visits a web site," according to the memorandum. Agencies were reminded that, pursuant to the Privacy Act of 1974, they must protect an individual's right to privacy when they collect personal information.[93]

A June 22, 2000, follow-up memorandum was issued by the OMB after press disclosures that the National Drug Control Policy Office, an agency within the Executive Office of the President, was secretly tracking visitors to its Web site through the use of computer software known as "cookies."[94] Addressing this revelation, the second memorandum said:

> Particular privacy concerns may be raised when uses of web technology can track the activities of users over time and across different web sites. These concerns are especially great where individuals who have come to government web sites do not have clear and conspicuous notice of any such tracking activities. "Cookies"—small bits of software that are placed on a web user's hard drive—are a principal example of current web technology that can be used in this way. The guidance issued on June 2, 1999, provided that agencies could only use "cookies" or other automatic means of collecting information if they gave clear notice of those activities.

The memorandum concluded, saying that cookies should not be used at federal Web sites, or by contractors when operating Web sites on behalf of agencies, unless, in addition to clear and conspicuous notice, the following conditions are met: a compelling need to gather the data on the site; appropriate and publicly disclosed privacy safeguards for handling of information derived from 'cookies'; and personal approval by the head of the agency."[95]

CONCLUSION

The realization of e-government in the federal experience in the United States has occurred with awareness of, and attention to, various interests, including efforts at improved information access, information dissemination, records management, and information security. In some obvious regards, the relationship between information access and security is symbiotic within the e-government context. Policies are in place requiring agencies to inform visitors at their Web sites about their privacy policy and to not track visitors when they leave those Web sites, just as they are for secure transactions by persons with an agency using electronic forms and digital signatures, and limiting use of the resulting information to management of the immediate transaction.

The sharing of certain kinds of sensitive information among federal, state, and local governments in the United States for reasons of homeland security may be regarded as a realization of the government-to-government (G2G) dimension of e-government, and the inclusion of private enterprises in this sharing a realization of the government-to-business (G2B) dimension. There are, however, concerns regarding the government-to-citizen (G2C) sector. When, in the aftermath of the 9/11 terrorist attacks, previously accessible information suddenly disappeared, it was not always clear to what extent, if any, attempts were made to weigh citizen needs for information vis-à-vis denying its availability to terrorists, or if thoughtful consideration was given to alternative limits short of total restriction. "At the very least," commented the authors of a report from the conservative Heritage Foundation not long ago, "such wholesale withdrawal of information seems arbitrary and undermines important values of government openness, the development of electronic government (e-gov) to speed the delivery and lower the costs of government services, and public trust."[96] Then, after this cleansing process, the question arises as to what will be the offerings on agency Web sites and in their electronic reading rooms—information lite? There is, as well, the interesting prospect identified by GAO analysts who, having sought the views of FOIA requesters regarding the post-9/11 environment, proffered that "some portion of the long-term impact may be masked by as-yet-unknown (or never-known) changes in the mix of FOIA requests and by any perceived 'chilling effect' on requesters that results in some potential requests not being made."[97]

Long ago, in the early years of the Cold War, political scientist Harold D. Lasswell offered the following observation regarding security.

> Since all security policies entail risk, the public interest calls for the calculation of risk by a procedure that balances each policy against every policy and arrives at a judgment to which many minds have contributed. Only by developing proper procedures can public confidence be gained or vindicated in the long-run wisdom of the outcome. At any given moment well-informed persons may disagree as to whether defense expenditures are too high or too low, or whether the overall defense program is in balance or seriously unbalanced. The public must estimate the bias and competence of rival leaders. The public interest can be protected by the use of a procedure that takes conflicting views into account and subjects them to the discipline of debate and exposure to available knowledge.[98]

Such a procedure may be found in the lawmaking arrangements of legislatures or the less structured airing of opposing viewpoints in the mass media, including televised debates. What Lasswell's observation so importantly emphasizes, however, is that the procedure requires "well-informed persons" and "knowledge." The irony, in the case of attempting to arrive at a homeland security policy for government information, is that some likely would impair or subvert the procedure or process by restricting information essential for its successful occurrence, resulting in a diminished realization of e-government, if not a diminished democracy.

NOTES

1. 116 Stat. 2899 at 2901.

2. 116 Stat. 2899 at 2901.

3. See Harold C. Relyea, "Homeland Security and Information," *Government Information Quarterly* 19 (2002): 213–20.

4. The Homeland Security Act, which may be found at 116 Stat. 2135, does not define the homeland security concept; the quoted definition is from U.S. Office of Homeland Security, *National Strategy for Homeland Security* (Washington, DC: GPO, July 2002), 2.

5. 116 Stat. 2902.

6. 116 Stat. 2253.

7. 116 Stat. 2253–54.

8. See Jeffrey W. Seifert and Harold C. Relyea, "Considering E-government from the U.S. Federal Perspective: An Evolving Concept, a Developing Practice," *Journal of E-Government* 1 (2004): 7–15.

9. Evan Hill, "Some Thoughts on E-Democracy as an Evolving Concept," *Journal of E-Government* 1 (2004): 23.

10. David C. Wyld, "The 3 Ps: The Essential Elements of a Definition of E-government," *Journal of E-Government* 1 (2004): 20–21.

11. E-government also is the product of evolving technology and related vision and applications, which has a legacy, as well. See Harold C. Relyea and Henry B. Hogue, "A Brief History of the Emergence of Digital Government in the United States," in *Digital Government: Principles and Best Practices*, ed. Alexei Pavlichev and G. David Garson (Hershey, PA: Idea Group Publishing, 2004), 16–33.

12. See, e.g., 1 Stat. 68, 443, 519, 724; 2 Stat. 302; 3 Stat. 145, 439, 576.

13. See 1 Stat. 168.

14. See, e.g., 1 Stat. 28, 49, 65. These and similar provisions were consolidated in the *Revised Statutes of the United States* (1878) at sec. 161, which is presently located in the *United States Code* at 5 U.S.C. 301.

15. See 3 Stat. 140.

16. 13 Stat. 460.

17. 17 Stat. 510.

18. 9 Stat. 113.

19. 12 Stat. 117.

20. 28 Stat. 601.

21. 11 Stat. 253.

22. 28 Stat. 610. Current authority for the depository library program may be found at 44 U.S.C. 1901–1915.

23. 33 Stat. 584.

24. 42 Stat. 541.

25. 3 Stat. 376.

26. 42 Stat. 816.

27. John A. Fairlie, "Administrative Legislation," *Michigan Law Review* 18 (January 1920): 199.

28. Erwin N. Griswold, "Government in Ignorance of the Law: A Plea for Better Publication of Executive Legislation," *Harvard Law Review* 48 (December 1934): 199.

29. *United States v. Smith*, 292 U.S. 633 (1934), appeal dismissed on the motion of the appellant without consideration by the Court.

30. *Panama Refining Company v. Ryan*, 293 U.S. 388 (1935).

31. 49 Stat. 500.

32. 50 Stat. 304.

33. David Banisar, *Freedom of Information and Access to Government Records Around the World* (Free-dominfo.org; Washington, DC: George Washington University), updated May 12, 2004. Available at www.freedominfo.org/survey.htm, accessed June 7, 2005.

34. 48 Stat. 1122.

35. Donald R. McCoy, *The National Archives: America's Ministry of Documents, 1934–1968* (Chapel Hill: University of North Carolina Press, 1978), 5–6.

36. Drawn from Harold C. Relyea, "Life Cycle Management of Government Information: A Brief Overview of American Federal Experience" (prepared as background to remarks offered at the Shanghai Open Government Information Implementation Workshop, October 30, 2004).

37. William W. Moss, "Research Note: Dang'an, Contemporary Chinese Archives," *China Quarterly* 145 (March 1996): 116–18, 120, 122; also see James E. Nalen, "Private Archives in China," *Libri* 52 (December 2002): 241–62.

38. Moss, "Research Note: Dang'an," 123.

39. 80 Stat. 250.

40. *Administrator, FAA v. Robertson*, 422 U.S. 255 (1972).

41. 90 Stat. 1247.

42. 42 U.S.C. 2014(y).

43. See Harold C. Relyea, "Information, Secrecy, and Atomic Energy," *New York University Review of Law and Social Change* 10 (1980–1981): 265–91; A. DeVolpi, G. E. Marsh, T. A. Postal, and G. S. Stanford, *Born Secret: The H-Bomb, the* Progressive *Case, and National Security* (New York: Pergamon, 1981).

44. See Harold C. Relyea, *Silencing Science: National Security Controls and Scientific Communication* (Norwood, NJ: Ablex Publishing, 1994); Harold C. Relyea, ed., *Striking a Balance: National Security and Scientific Freedom—First Discussions* (Washington, DC: American Association for the Advancement of Science, 1985).

45. Timothy A. Gelatt, "The New Chinese State Secrets Law," *Cornell International Law Journal* 22 (1989): 255–56.

46. Gelatt, "New Chinese State Secrets Law," 257–59.

47. See Harold C. Relyea, "The Evolution of Government Information Security Classification Policy: A Brief Overview (1775–1973)," in U.S. Congress, House Committee on Government Operations, *Security Classification Reform*, hearings, 93rd Cong., 2nd sess. (Washington, DC: GPO, 1974), 505–97; Harold C. Relyea, "Appendix II: Government Information Security Classification Policy," in U.S. Congress, Senate Select Committee to Study Governmental Operations with Respect to Intelligence Activities, *Supplemental Reports on Intelligence Activities*, Book VI, S. Rept. 94-755, 94th Cong., 2nd sess. (Washington, DC: GPO, 1976), 313–52.

48. Anthony Cave Brown and Charles B. MacDonald, eds., *The Secret History of the Atomic Bomb* (New York: Dial Press/James Wade, 1977), 201.

49. In *Environmental Protection Agency v. Mink*, Supreme Court Associate Justice Byron White, delivering the majority opinion, proffered that "Congress could certainly have provided that the Executive Branch adopt new procedures" for the security classification of information, "or it could have established its own procedures—subject only to whatever limitations the Executive [or constitutional separation of powers] privilege may be held to impose upon such congressional ordering." 410 U.S. 73, 83 (1973).

50. See Richard C. Ehlke and Harold C. Relyea, "The Reagan Administration Order on Security Classification: A Critical Assessment," *Federal Bar News & Journal* 30 (February 1983): 91–97.

51. 3 C.F.R., 1995 Comp., pp. 333–56.

52. U.S. Department of Defense, Department of Defense Security Review Commission, *Keeping the Nation's Secrets* (Washington, DC: GPO, 1985), 48–49.

53. U.S. General Accounting Office (GAO), *Classified Information: Costs of Protection Are Integrated with Other Security Costs*, GAO/NSIAD-94-55 (Washington, DC: October 1993), 1.

54. 3 C.F.R., 2003 Comp., pp. 196–218.

55. While it is recognized that state secrets can be problematic for some litigating with a government, that issue is regarded to be somewhat outside of the scope of this chapter, particularly, at least within the American experience, since the arrival of e-government appears to have made no change in the conditions of this aspect of security policy. See James Zagel, "The State Secrets Privilege," *Minnesota Law Review* 50 (1966): 875–910.

56. See Alison Mitchell, "Classified Information: Bush Gives Secrecy Power to Public Health Secretary," *New York Times,* December 20, 2001, B6; *Federal Register* 66 (December 12, 2001): 64347; *Federal Register* 67 (May 9, 2002): 31109; *Federal Register* 67 (September 30, 2002): 61465.

57. 116 Stat. 637.

58. 16 Stat. 2150, 2312.

59. Guy Gugliotta, "Agencies Scrub Web Sites of Sensitive Chemical Data," *Washington Post,* October 4, 2001, A29; Robin Toner, ""Reconsidering Security, U.S. Clamps Down on Agency Web Sites," *New York Times,* October 28, 2001, B4.

60. Eric Lichtblau, "Response to Terror; Rising Fears That What We Can Do Can Hurt Us," *Los Angeles Times,* part A, part 1, November 18, 2001, 1; also see Saragail Runyon Lynch, "GPO Recalls of Depository Documents," *Journal of Government Information* 22 (January–February 1995): 23–31.

61. U.S. Congress, House Committee on Government Operations, *Electronic Collection and Dissemination of Information by Federal Agencies: A Policy Overview,* H. Rept. 99-560, 99th Cong., 2nd sess. (Washington, DC: GPO, 1986), 10–11.

62. U.S. Office of Technology Assessment (OTA), *Informing the Nation: Federal Information Dissemination in an Electronic Age* (Washington, DC: OTA, October 1988), 8.

63. OTA, *Informing the Nation,* 10–11.

64. 109 Stat. 163, 165-166; 44 U.S.C. 3501-3520; see David Plocher, "The Paperwork Reduction Act of 1995: A Second Chance for Information Resources Management," *Government Information Quarterly* 13 (1996): 35–50.

65. 110 Stat. 642; 110 Stat. 679; 110 Stat. 3009-393.

66. 3 C.F.R., 1996 Comp., pp. 202–209.

67. 116 Stat. 2901; 44 U.S.C. 3602-3603.

68. See *INS v. Chadha,* 462 U.S. 919 (1983), in which the Supreme Court ruled that, where legislative action has "the purpose and effect of altering legal rights, duties and relations of persons . . . outside the legislative branch," it must be effected through the constitutionally mandated lawmaking process. This determination greatly limited the manner in which the Joint Committee on Printing might exercise the remedial powers conferred by 44 U.S.C. 103, such as its issuance of printing regulations for federal agencies.

69. 107 Stat. 112; 44 U.S.C. 4101-4104.

70. See James A. Jacobs, James R. Jacobs, and Shinjoung Yeo, "Government Information in the Digital Age: The Once and Future Federal Depository Library Program," *Journal of Academic Librarianship* 31 (May 2005): 198–208.

71. U.S. Office of Management and Budget (OMB), *Section 213 of the E-Government Act, Report to Congress: Organizations Complementing Federal Agency Information Dissemination Programs* (Washington, DC: OMB, April 15, 2005), 4.

72. 110 Stat. 3048; 5 U.S.C. 552.

73. GAO, *Information Management: Progress in Implementing the 1966 Electronic Freedom of Information Act Amendments,* GAO-01-378 (Washington, DC: GAO, March 2001), 19–22.

74. GAO, *Information Management: Update on Implementation of the 1996 Electronic Freedom of Information Act Amendments,* GAO-02-493 (Washington, DC: GAO, August 2002), 45, 55.

75. See SRA International, *Report on Current Recordkeeping Practices within the Federal Government,* prepared for the National Archives and Records Administration (Arlington, VA: NARA, December 10, 2001).

76. See, e.g., Committee on the Records of Government, *Report,* sponsored by the American Council of Learned Societies, Social Science Research Council, and Council on Library Resources

(Washington, DC: March 1985); U.S. Congress, House Committee on Government Operations, *Taking a Byte out of History: The Archival Preservation of Federal Computer Records*, H. Rept. 101-978, 101st Cong., 2nd sess. (Washington, DC: GPO, 1990).

77. GAO, *Information Management: Challenges in Managing and Preserving Electronic Records*, GAO Report GAO-02-586 (Washington, DC: GAO, June 2002), 2–3.

78. See National Research Council, Computer Science and Telecommunications Board, Committee on Digital Archiving, *Building an Electronic Records Archive at the National Archives and Records Administration* (Washington, DC: National Academies Press, 2003).

79. GAO, *Electronic Records: Management and Preservation Pose Challenges*, GAO Testimony GAO-03-936T (Washington, DC: GAO, July 8, 2003), 3–4.

80. 116 Stat. 2911.

81. 118 Stat. 2913.

82. OMB, *FY 2004 Report to Congress on Implementation of the E-Government Act of 2002* (Washington, DC: OMB, March 1, 2005), 6–7.

83. 118 Stat. 2913.

84. 118 Stat. 2916.

85. OMB, *Implementation of the E-Government Act of 2002*, 8; also see OMB, "Policies for Federal Agency Public Websites," memorandum for the heads of executive departments and agencies, M-05-04 (Washington, DC: OMB, December 17, 2004).

86. 101 Stat. 1724.

87. 114 Stat. 1654A-266.

88. 116 Stat. 2946.

89. 112 Stat. 2681-749.

90. 44 U.S.C. 3504(a)(1)(B)(vi), as amended.

91. The final version of the OMB procedures and guidance for implementing the GPEA was published in *Federal Register* 65 (May 2, 2000): 25508–21.

92. 112 Stat. 2681–751.

93. OMB, "Privacy Policies on Federal Web Sites," memorandum for the heads of executive departments, M-99-18 (Washington, DC: OMB, June 2, 1999); the Privacy Act may be found at 5 U.S.C. 552a.

94. See John F. Harris and John Schwartz, "Anti-Drug Web Site Tracks Visitors," *Washington Post*, June 22, 2000, A23; Lance Gay, "White House Uses Drug-Message Site to Track Inquiries," *Washington Times*, June 21, 2000, A3.

95. OMB, "Privacy Policies and Data Collection on Federal Web Sites," memorandum for the heads of executive departments and agencies, M-00-13 (Washington, DC: OMB, June 22, 2000).

96. James Jay Carafano and David Heyman, "DHS 2.0: Rethinking the Department of Homeland Security," *Heritage Special Report* (Washington, DC: Heritage Foundation, December 13, 2004), 20.

97. GAO, *Information Management: Update on Implementation of the 1996 Electronic Freedom of Information Act Amendments,* 55.

98. Harold D. Lasswell, *National Security and Individual Freedom* (New York: McGraw-Hill, 1950), 56.

· 9 ·

Trends and Challenges in Archiving E-government Records

Rachel Lilburn

$\mathscr{T}$ypical e-government initiatives relate to improving access to information, to engaging in e-commerce, and to enabling public service delivery via the Internet; figure 1.1 identifies other initiatives. In the process of there being a transaction between a person and an agency Web site electronic records are created; for example, a log of site visitors, an e-mail message, a payment made, or a form that has been filled out online and transmitted to the agency. Web site–related records are public records and they are a subset of other electronic records created by government. These records, as with paper records, need to be maintained for as long as required by law and normal prudent business practice. Approval of the disposition of government records, paper and/or electronic, is usually mandated by statute to be the prerogative of the archives authority. The focus of this chapter on trends and challenges in archiving electronic records, in particular those created through e-government processes, will be on the profession coming to terms with major adjustments and adaptations to theory, the nature of the profession, and managerial practice when facing the ongoing problems of the management of these *born digital* electronic records and archives.

Worldwide, public institutions responsible for public sector records and archives management increasingly want to ensure that when e-government initiatives are launched sufficient regard is paid to issues involving the forms of electronic records created as a result, notably:

- e-mail messages;
- electronic documents;
- Web sites; and
- digitized documents.

The issues surrounding the definition of what is a record in an electronic environment, and how to capture and maintain it over time for as long as it is needed, predate many e-government initiatives. Archivists and records managers have grappled with the problems of electronic records for more than fifty years. The 1990s was the decade, however, in which the Internet matured, enabling information to be delivered online and then, more recently, electronic processes to be carried out online.[1]

164

The delivery of services through e-government has exacerbated the need for national/federal, state, and local archives and records agencies to take a proactive approach to creating policies, standards, and guidelines in order that government remains accountable through its records when transactions take place over the Internet as a delivery channel. The issue of accountability has never been more important to address, for otherwise there will be no history to pass on to future generations. A major challenge for such public sector bodies is to harness the expertise of appropriate agencies and employees to build and maintain a cooperative approach to dealing with the complex nature of electronic records created by e-government. Solutions, as will be dealt with later in this chapter, require new relationships and skills of archivists and records managers. Initially, it has required them to engage in considerable reexamination of basic professional precepts and principles.

This chapter first examines trends and challenges in electronic records and archives from a theoretical and professional viewpoint. It is of value to provide the context of the professional debate that has accompanied addressing the problems of electronic records and archives. Second, some of the practical and managerial initiatives being taken to address the issues of digital records and archives preservation will be reviewed. The difficult issue of custody of electronic records then necessitates a discussion of the debate about relationships between government and public sector archives and records agencies, and policy decision making and the theoretical frameworks within which those policies are determined. In so doing it is the intention that the broader context for policies, statements, and actions by archives authorities on public records created through e-government may be better understood.

The chapter concentrates primarily on Australasian public sector archives agency initiatives—that is, Australia and New Zealand, with some limited reference to developments in the United Kingdom and North America—and public Web sites used to conduct business and to provide services and products. It should be noted that the literature on the management and preservation of personal electronic records and archives is limited as yet and will not be discussed. Challenges for manuscript librarians include, for example, how to influence the creation of electronic records that are able to be preserved when, more often than not, they receive such records after a person's death.[2]

DEFINITIONS

There are three main debates in the development of the archival discourse in relation to electronic records in the 1990s, the first being the definition of a record; the second being definition of the professional responsibilities of those charged with the management and care of records and archives; and the third about what theoretical model will guide the profession through to the twenty-first century. The overall significance of such debates for e-government is that they have provided professional clarity and enhanced engagement by the record-keeping professions with others involved in designing, developing, and implementing Web sites and auditing e-government initiatives.

Surprisingly, despite the longevity of record keeping and the archives and records management professions, definition of what is a record and hence what is an archive emerged as a significant question.[3] Such definition in an electronic environment, including e-government, is paramount in order to establish the differences among records, data, documents, and information. The Society of American Archivists' glossary states that a record is a "document created or received and maintained by an agency, organization or individual in pursuance of legal obligations or in the transaction of business."[4] An archive was further defined as being the noncurrent records of an organization or institution "preserved because of their continuing value."[5]

The use of the word *document* has been considered insufficiently precise to distinguish the characteristics of a record that differentiated it from data, information, and documents, commonly used to describe what is found in electronic systems, namely, their transactional and evidential qualities. Ensuring evidentiality through processes and management systems to create and maintain reliable, authentic, and usable records is, therefore, just as important as whether the record is in paper or electronic form. As discussed later in this chapter, research into and definition of metadata requirements for electronic records and record-keeping systems have been in response to a renewed understanding of what is a record.

Implied also in such definitions was that a record had to be noncurrent to be deemed an archive, a problem further complicated by the information technology (IT) profession's use of the term *archive* to mean any noncurrent record, not just those of archival value. Arguably, a record may be deemed an archive from the time of creation. Thus, archival records do not have to cross an *archival threshold* (in terms of physical custody being passed over to an archives institution), and electronic systems should be designed therefore to manage not only data, documents, and information but also records in order to provide evidence of an action.[6] More recent definitions of records and archives, while often influenced by national legislation and conditions, are also all-encompassing in terms of format and medium. The International Council of Archives (ICA), for example, defines a record as "recorded information produced or received in the initiation, conduct or completion of an institutional or individual activity and that comprises content, context and structure sufficient to provide evidence of the activity."[7] The implications of the points made above, about archiving electronic records as soon as possible, and the importance of system design for effective record keeping, are fundamental for ensuring accountability by government when delivering services electronically.

Further to the discussion about what is a record and when it might become an archive has been the practical need to define what it is when in Web, intranet, and extranet environments. E-government is now enabling more services, and not simply information (found traditionally, for example, in printed brochures), to be delivered electronically, which is resulting in transactions needing to be recorded. National archives authorities in both Australia and New Zealand have published documents that define what a Web record is and how to manage it over time. At its simplest, Web records are "all documents or data that are published or transmitted by websites."[8] The National Archives of Australia defines a Web record as a record created and offered through a Web site, including public Web sites, virtual private networks (VPNs), extranets, intranets, individual Web-based documents and publications, and records of Web-enabled activity, including electronic commerce.[9]

Both institutions, National Archives of Australia and Archives New Zealand, make it very clear that all digital data created or received in the conduct of Australian or New Zealand government business are public records and covered by the Archives Act 1983 or the Public Records Act 2005, respectively. Ultimately, the definition of a record remains the same whether it is in paper or electronic form or created in an e-government environment. However, the definition enables a distinction to be made between a Web record and a Web publication, although in practice there are problems. For example, the National Archives of Australia's Web archives guidelines state that "web resources that are designed to publish and disseminate information, and are relatively static informational resources are to be treated as publications" for the purposes of disposition.[10] However, a Web site version of a publication that contains Web-based functionality that is not replicated in the printed version must be captured in the agency's record-keeping system. Definition of the difference between a Web site publication and a record also enables responsibilities and accountability for preservation to be allocated to the appropriate agency. In the case of Australia, the National Archives and the National Library have complementary roles and the latter collects the Web-based publications, including Commonwealth agency Web sites (on a selective basis) as part of its PANDORA project.[11]

THEORETICAL MODELS

Concomitant with reexamination of definitions of a record in the current hybrid electronic/paper records environment, of which e-government records are a part, has been the growing emergence of a new model in the 1980s and 1990s to depict the relationship between archives and records and their management, in a nonlinear and non-time-bound fashion. Until development of this continuum model the most common model utilized by archivists and records managers was the life cycle, a model criticized for being too linear, too paper-oriented, and professionally divisive. In the life cycle a record goes through a number of steps: it is born, it lives, it dies, and then it is resurrected as an archive. The archivist's contact with the records manager is said to be primarily at the time of the appraisal or choice of records of archival value. However, the continuum model does not prescribe roles in this manner and allows for records to fulfill roles of organizational and collective memory. To sum up,

> The dimensions in the continuum are not time-based, but represent different perspectives on the management of records. The circles move out from the creation of records of business activities, to ensuring that records are captured as evidence and to their inclusion in formal systems for records management within the organization, while the fourth dimension looks out towards the needs of society for collective memory.[12]

The continuum model has a strong emphasis on evidence, crucial to citizens placing trust in e-government, and hence to government accountability. According to Sue McKemmish, Head of the School of Information Management and Systems, Monash University, Melbourne, records continuum thinking defines

> the role of recordkeeping in relation to accountability as:
> - facilitating good governance;
> - underpinning accountability mechanisms;
> - constituting corporate, national and societal memory;

- constructing individual, community and national identity; [and]
- providing authoritative sources of information.[13]

The continuum model is also suited to an e-government environment because it has allowed for adaptation of practice by archivists and records managers for electronic records. It has most clearly influenced Australian and New Zealand practice: for example, Archives New Zealand has developed a suite of record-keeping standards and policies titled the *Continuum*.[14] A standard Australian records management text uses the continuum model[15] while a recent British text also is based on the model.[16] One could predict that the influence of the continuum will grow worldwide, for among other things it has led to vigorous discussion of the dual roles of archivist and records manager in the electronic records world.

PROFESSIONAL CONVERGENCE

A significant trend in the professional literature addressing the issues of managing electronic records and archives has been the question of "whose responsibility is it?" Is it the records manager, the archivist, the librarian, or the information technology specialist? For others involved in developing successful e-government delivery, this question about definition of roles and skills is relevant. Who is going to provide the answers to the record-keeping questions, including what to archive and how, posed by e-government?

The life cycle model, as previously discussed, has been said to separate the work of the archivist and the records manager, creating a disjunction between the shared roles that they fulfill in the management of the record over time. This debate is particularly pertinent to electronic records and archives for, to reiterate an earlier point, if they are not captured into record-keeping systems that maintain their *recordness,* enabling their effective disposal and ongoing management, including access, there will be no electronic archives. Of the shared roles of the professions it has been said that ongoing access is one of the most important. Charles Dollar, consultant, Cohasset Associates and author of the award-winning publication *Authentic Electronic Records: Strategies for Long-Term Access,* also notes the importance of maintaining records integrity and incorporating records disposition into systems design as being two other shared roles.[17]

The ICA, the leading policymaking body on archives, has articulated four principles for the management of electronic records. One of those principles is that

> the archives should be involved in the entire records life cycle (conception, creation, maintenance) to ensure both the creation and retention of records that are authentic, reliable and preservable and the capture, preservation and continued accessibility of records identified as having archival value.[18]

The ICA also clearly understands the professional challenges that archivists face in a complex electronic work environment and finding staff who can cope with these challenges. It advocates that "priority should be given to the development of education, training and recruitment programs and strategies to ensure the availability of staff with the required competencies."[19]

There are challenges with professional convergence, and there has been regular debate about whether the two roles can ever really become one, despite the electronic revolution being a potential catalyst. For example, even in Australia, where the continuum model is strong, there remain separate associations for archivists (the Australian Society of Archivists) and records managers (the RMAA, the Records Management Association of Australasia). Discussion about merging the two associations has not resulted in action. However, educational programs for future record keepers, such as at Monash University, are intended to produce a hybrid record-keeping paradigm specialist. Ann Pederson, currently visiting fellow in Recordkeeping Studies in the School of Information Systems, Technology and Management (SISTM) at the University of New South Wales, has conducted a research-based overview of the major strands of practice in the record-keeping professions and what will be required to create a reinvented professional and converged profession in terms of skill sets and competencies. She concludes that difficulties remain, not the least of which are the temperamental differences of record-keeping professionals.[20]

It is difficult to predict the level of convergence on an international basis, despite a developing trend in countries such as Australia and New Zealand. However, there seems to be greater clarity of understanding about what archivists and records managers need to do in terms of cooperation with each other and with other information professionals (e.g., lawyers, auditors, the records creators, Web site content authors and administrators, and information technology specialists) to achieve a common mission. Unlike much of the debate in the professional literature in the 1970s and 1980s from which one could infer considerable concern about the future of the records management professional in particular should they not metamorphose into an information manager/IT specialist, it now seems that the archivist/records manager's unique contribution to managing electronic records and the skills required can be defined. In so doing, says Philip Bantin, university archivist for Indiana University at Bloomington, we will be able "to speak the language of the technologist, understand how various data and information systems function, and be able to perform some basic tasks related to modeling and describing business processes."[21]

Luciana Duranti, professor/chair of the master of archival studies (SLIS), University of British Columbia, notes that just because records managers and archivists carry out functions that are not archival in nature (e.g., database design) the archival role has changed. Both groups should cooperate with members of allied professions to "foster common outcomes for the advancement of different but complementary interests."[22]

Record-keeping professionals, archivists, and records managers are seemingly far better equipped to engage with each other to work in partnership and to enter into new relationships with those involved with the processes of e-government. The continuum model also empowers them to also adopt nontraditional roles "as policy makers, standard setters, strategic planners, systems designers, educators, advocates and auditors."[23]

POLICIES AND STANDARDS

Having outlined debates over definitions, theory, and professional relationships, it is time to review the response of major archival institutions in Australasia to the increasingly complex issues created by the evolving electronic workplace. Many of the early electronic record-keeping systems utilized anywhere in the world would not have met today's standards for good record keeping. However, they often operated as transactional processing systems with records unlikely to be of long-term value (e.g., financial records).[24] As power to make and delete records devolved to the desktop and the newer products utilized enabled electronic production of documents in the form of correspondence, memos, spreadsheets, and so on, the name *the wild frontier* aptly describes their management and use.[25]

The first step that many Australasian national and state archives institutions took in the early 1990s, when the electronic workplace was recognized to be detrimental to effective record keeping and survival of an archival record, was to issue discussion papers, followed by policy statements to government agencies reminding them of their responsibilities to ensure an accountable public service through records of their actions.

The next trend in Australasia is the issuing of standards and statements on how to choose and/or design electronic record-keeping systems that conform to standards. These standards may have been generated by the archives institution, such as those found on the State Records Authority of New South Wales for electronic record keeping; for example, the *Standard on Recordkeeping in the Electronic Business Environment*, published in June 2000.[26] Or reference may have been made to an existing standard. Such standards might include the *Model Requirements for the Management of Electronic Records* (MoReq), issued by the Public Records Office in Britain (now the National Archives) in 2002, and the U. S. Department of Defense's *Design Criteria Standard for Electronic Records Management Software Applications* (DoD 5015.2-STD).[27] The basis for other documents frequently has been AS 4390-1996 Records Management published by Standards Australia, or ISO 15489, "2001 Information and Documentation–Records Management," which the International Standards Organization published.[28]

There has been a noticeable trend for the New Zealand national archives authority to avoid reinventing the wheel by adapting Australian products to the local environment. The Archives New Zealand *Guide to Developing Recordkeeping Strategies for Websites*, published in June 2004, acknowledges that it is based on work by the National Archives of Australia.[29]

Developers and vendors of electronic record-keeping products, particularly electronic document management systems that handle many forms of electronic objects, have not been slow to realize the importance of meeting not only market need, such as the vexatious problem of capturing e-mail as a record, but also such state, national, and international standards requirements. The trend in product development has definitely been to address these in order to obtain recognition that they comply with a standard(s) and therefore, in some instances, be endorsed by a national and/or state archives institution. This is the case in Australia but currently not New Zealand.

Another example of how Australasian archives authorities have heeded the advice of international professional bodies (e.g., the ICA) is their continuing to engage in influencing strategies by producing further documents to provide the frameworks for improved management of current records creation and management,[30] such as standards for developing a record-keeping policy.[31] Some research has revealed, however, that without the development of strong relationships between a national archives body and individual government records managers, and between those records managers and provision of support, standard setting will not be successful. Adam Stapleton, of the New

Zealand State Services Commission's E-government Unit, used diffusion of innovations theory[32] to examine how successfully the continuum model's use by Archives New Zealand in its standards and advice products had been adopted by New Zealand state sector records managers. He concluded that records managers for electronic information management did not perceive Archives New Zealand as the key influencing or leadership agency.[33]

In undertaking the aforementioned influencing actions, Australasian archives authorities are following an international trend to think and act strategically in relation to electronic records, as the ICA advocated in *Electronic Records: A Workbook for Archivists,*[34] which follows on from the 1997 *Guide for Managing Electronic Records from an Archival Perspective*.[35] Similar to institutions with records and archives management oversight elsewhere, there is an emphasis on steering rather than rowing;[36] that is, not being directly or operationally involved, for example, in the design and implementation of an electronic document management system. Few archives agencies worldwide are funded to oversee electronic records systems directly or, for that matter, to be involved at the grass roots with implementing solutions for e-government records. Nor are they likely to be in the near future. Standards are theoretically one way of achieving effective record-keeping outcomes in tight financial environments.

E-GOVERNMENT WEB SITE STANDARDS

In relation to e-government records, for example, both archives and records authorities in New Zealand and Australia have issued guidelines for their management and preservation. The guidelines emphasize capturing and managing Web transactional records within record-keeping systems, or advise that record-keeping functionality can be integrated into Web sites during their design or redevelopment. Assessment of business risk to a government agency leading to a lack of fulfillment of accountability, should Web records' authenticity and integrity be compromised in any way, and the need for risk mitigation, is reiterated also in the National Archives and Records Administration's (NARA) new guide to managing agency Web sites, released in January 2005.[37]

Given the variety of record-keeping hardware and software environments, it is a huge challenge for government archives and records authorities to prescribe a "one size fits all" strategy or solution. Some Web sites are static (i.e., they have a collection of static documents with little interactivity); some are static but have form-based interactivity; and then there are sites that are dynamic and enable the generation of pages on the fly on the basis of user queries. These are harder to preserve over time. Then there are the issues relating to Web portals and sites that are managed and jointly sponsored by multiple government agencies. NARA, despite spending almost seven years developing its guide, states that the unique Web issues this creates will be dealt with in a subsequent publication.[38] The accountability of public sector agencies for trustworthy e-government Web sites and record keeping in this situation has to be called into question. Which agency should be accountable for maintaining the shared e-government record over time?

There are several other challenges, the first being those related to the acquiring of soft skills. The ICA identifies the need for record-keeping professionals to demonstrate bold leadership and to improve their management and people skills in order to reposition the archives to address electronic records issues. They need to learn to work with others and to influence records creators.[39] The second set of challenges pertains to the credibility of electronic records programs, of which Web site records, created through e-government, will become an increasingly important focus. It will be essential, for example, for the standards issued to be workable for public sector agencies. Stapleton found, in the New Zealand context, that what public sector records managers wanted was not just standards and advice but the facilitation of real-world implementations through, for instance, the dissemination of examples of best practice.[40] Standards without follow-up and communication will not be the so-called silver bullet.

How to carry out the monitoring of agency compliance covered by these standards through audit processes will need to be carefully thought out. Ultimately cooperation may only be achieved through legislation that will enable mandatory rather than voluntary standards. The new Public Records Act passed in 2005 covering New Zealand government sector archives and records management enables just this.[41]

Perhaps New Zealand and Australian archives authorities could be considered unusual in terms of the level of cooperation that they are developing. In 2004, the Australasian Digital Recordkeeping Initiative (ADRI) was begun. It involves the National Archives of Australia, Archives New Zealand, and all the Australian state archives agencies. One of its aims is to foster a uniform Australasian approach to digital preservation and achieve, among other things, trans-tasman interoperability in the process. Strategically ADRI is about making the best possible use of limited collective resources.[42]

METADATA

One of the areas being considered for uniformity by the ADRI project is in metadata standards, which have been a significant challenge worldwide for the management of electronic records and archives, including those created in an e-government environment. Members of the profession believe that electronic records will not be trustworthy, authentic, and reliable without adequate metadata, nor will they be able to be preserved over time without this and possible additional metadata that describes the content, context, and structure of records and their management over time. Such standards need to accommodate different forms of digital objects, Web sites, publications, and records. In relation to e-government it must be recognized that metadata for records and record-keeping purposes has greater requirements than that for resource discovery. Web site record metadata also has to meet additional requirements; as the National Archives of Australia *Archiving Web Resources: Guidelines* points out, these include links to the universal resource indicator (URI) and information about version and date of link to a specified URI.[43] Some metadata about Web sites may only exist in paper form and, therefore, also need to be preserved (e.g., Web site administrative and operations records, and Web site system software-related records). The NARA guide on Web records states that a trustworthy Web site and records relies on such contextual data.[44]

It will be interesting to observe the future development of metadata standards in Australia and New Zealand, their adaptation for e-government records, and the achievement and maintenance of uniformity over time. There is still some disparity between various standards worldwide.

One of the most influential research projects worldwide into the metadata requirements for electronic records and archives was conducted by the University of Pittsburgh, closely followed by projects at the University of British Columbia (InterPARES), Indiana University, and Monash University (SPIRT). All these projects have had a significant impact on the development of metadata standards in the public sector and how they have been adapted for practical purposes.[45] The Victorian Electronic Records Strategy (VERS) project, run by the Public Record Office Victoria in order to pilot and develop a statewide solution for electronic records, revealed that the metadata set established by the Pittsburgh project was too complex to be implemented in its entirety.[46]

Undoubtedly, theoretical and applied metadata research will continue, but the challenge will be to develop cost-effective metadata systems that can accompany records from time of creation to their possible archiving that will enable effective electronic delivery modes for access purposes. The continuum model rather than the life cycle model emphasizes that capture of metadata to accompany the electronic archival record should not be retrospective. Involvement of archives authorities in e-government metadata initiatives, such as has occurred in Australia and New Zealand, will also enable the effective creation, capture, and maintenance of recorded transactions via the Web.[47]

ELECTRONIC RECORDS CUSTODY

Maintaining agreement over a uniform set of Australasian metadata and in approaches to digital/electronic records preservation may prove as difficult in the future as perhaps agreement over custodial arrangements for electronic records was in the past. Should they continue to reside with their creating or successor agency? In the 1990s, the Australian Archives was clearly not interested in establishing a custodial regime for electronic records, whereas Archives New Zealand (or National Archives as it was then known) chose to do the opposite. In a sense this was in theory, not in practice, for a digital repository remains to be established in New Zealand, and the fallback option of allowing government agencies to retain records under a contractual agreement with the chief archivist was never utilized.[48] Now it would seem that there is more trans-tasman agreement on the need for an archives authority to take custody of some, if not all, electronic records. This could be because digital repository solutions seem to be becoming available.

There will continue to be local and international debate over the appropriate custody of electronic records. The provision in the New Zealand Public Records Act 2005 for the chief archivist to be able to defer deposit of such records was, anecdotally, not popular with some members of the profession.[49] Should electronic records of archival value continue to be maintained by a government organization, then there are significant metadata and monitoring issues as well as the problem of developing effective public-sector-wide finding aids to ensure access. Who should pay for their upkeep? Why would agencies want to maintain their own electronic archives, including those resulting from e-government? Should government, citizens, or a third party be responsible for the long-term preservation of a public record created through an e-government interaction? The custodial issue for e-government electronic records will be increasingly influential in this debate as the new legislation and its deferred deposit provisions are tested.

POSTMODERNISM, ARCHIVAL THEORY, AND E-RECORDS

A strong trend in the archival discourse since the early 1990s has been to debate issues such as the custody of electronic records, among other archival management practices, through a postmodernist lens. Not all members of the profession agree that this is necessary. NARA's Linda Henry lambastes theorists who believe that it is futile to rely on "physical custodianship of records as a key means of assuring their preservation and ongoing accessibility."[50] Conceptually, electronic records can be managed by their creators and do not have to be in the custody of an archives institution, but Henry maintains that "shifting custodial responsibilities to creators 'would leave the Oliver Norths of this world in charge of their records.'"[51]

But how archives and records management professionals are attempting to address the preservation of the digital record, including that created by e-government, has been reenvisioned as a result of the influence of postmodernism on archival theory. As Terry Cook, adjunct professor, Department of History at the University of Manitoba, notes, "archival mindsets and solutions reflect generations of sound practice in a paper-based world." However, he asks, "How do we recast our 'paper minds' to deal with electronic realities?"[52]

In the use of postmodernist analysis, whereby the nature of meaning is seen to be contingent on context rather than universal and objective, it is suggested that archivists in the electronic age cannot afford to be the neutral, impartial, and trusted third-party guardians of archives and archival systems that they used to be (issues of neutrality and impartiality of historical analysis have, of course, also confronted historians). Mark Greene, director, American Heritage Center, University of Wyoming, states, "Whether we knew it or not, those of us who accepted the relativism of the archival paradigm were participating in a larger and seemingly esoteric discussion about what is named postmodernism."[53] He sees practical benefits to the subjective archival paradigm and "looking through the lens of postmodernism" for appraisal of electronic records, among other things.[54] Meanwhile, Henry would argue that there is no need to reenvision the archival paradigm for electronic records. Archivists, she says, should continue to use established archival principles and practices when dealing with electronic records. She criticizes the writing of advocates of a new paradigm, as seen through a postmodernist lens as having "little basis in archival theory and practice and [containing] alarmist language, unnecessary jargon, technobabble and unclear new ideas."[55]

While there is, therefore, more than one lens through which the resolution of electronic records management and preservation may be viewed, it would seem that use of a postmodernist theoretical framework to examine these problems has provided a professional mandate to many record-keeping practitioners to become involved, for example, in the design of electronic records systems, including Web sites. Furthermore, it is suggested that to ensure the archiving and preservation of electronic records, active intervention by an archivist and/or records manager is needed from time of the creation of the record, and archival processes should be integrated into record-keeping processes, particularly the creation of descriptive metadata and a disposal regime.

Whatever theoretical framework dominates archival methodologies and practice, electronic records enable us, as Cook says, quoting Frank Upward, senior lecturer, School of Information Management and Systems, Monash University, to refresh and renew the archival discourse, but not at the expense of abandoning traditional roles and sensibilities.[56]

CONCLUSION

The technical solutions for the management of digital/electronic records and archives for as long as they need to be accessible are going to change over time. This chapter, therefore, has explored some of the theoretical, professional, managerial, and technical issues, notably metadata, related to effective preservation of electronic records. By revisiting theoretical basics, it is possible for the professional discourse to focus on the unique characteristics of the record and archive, whether paper or electronic, and what record-keeping professionals can offer in terms of skills and knowledge for the preservation of electronic records and archives. The degree to which there is disciplinary convergence between records managers and archivists will be dictated in the future probably by general environmental factors (e.g., economic, political, social, and technological conditions) in local, state, national, and international general environments. Professional specializations (e.g., the systems records manager or archivist) may well become a reality.

The continuum model offers a powerful way to reenvision the relationship and to adapt archival practices for improved archiving of electronic records. The model tends to be associated with a postcustodial approach to their management (foreshadowed by a postmodernist analysis of the roles of the archivist and archives in an electronic online world). The task of definition of a technically and financially feasible set of metadata requirements is unlikely to be completed anytime soon, and continual change in response to developments in IT and record-keeping research means that this is inevitable. Of course, the professional discourse will need to continue accommodating the nonarchival and technical aspects of the archivist's and records manager's work, involving managerial and people skills, in particular the capacity to cooperate with other allied professionals to ensure the effective archiving of the electronic record. Noncustodial regimes for electronic archives may not be the end of the world for archival civilization. Strategic thinking and theoretical rethinking by leaders in the profession to address the many challenges (e.g., the issue of custody) are needed, that is, if electronic records, including those created through e-government, will survive to become archives.

NOTES

1. Philip Bantin, "Electronic Records Management: A Review of the Work of a Decade and a Reflection on Future Directions" (Bloomington, IN: University Archives), 2–3. *Encyclopedia of Library and Information Science* 71, supp. 34 (2002), 47–81. Available at www.indiana.edu/~libarch/ER/ency cloarticle9.doc, accessed June 24, 2005.

2. Janine Delaney, "Redefining the Role for Collecting Archives in an Electronic Paradigm," *Archifacts,* April 2000, 13–24; Adrian Cunningham, "The Archival Management of Personal Records in Electronic Form: Some Suggestions," *Archives and Manuscripts* 22, no. 1 (May 1994): 94–105; Adrian Cunningham, "Waiting for the Ghost Train: Strategies for Managing Electronic Personal Records Before It Is Too Late," *Archival Issues* 24, no. 1 (1999): 55–64.

3. According to the National Archives Australia (Canberra) Web site's Glossary of Record-keeping Terminology (2004), the description of record keeping is "the making and maintaining of complete, accurate and reliable evidence of business transactions in the form of recorded information. Recordkeeping includes: the creation of records in the course of business activity and the means to ensure the creation of adequate records; the design, establishment and operation of recordkeeping systems; and the management of records used in business (traditionally regarded as the domain of records management) and as archives (traditionally regarded as the domain of archives administration)." Available at www.naa.gov.au/recordkeeping/rkpubs/recordkeeping_glossary.html#R, accessed June 16, 2005.

4. Society of American Archivists, *A Glossary for Archivists, Manuscript Curators, and Records Managers* (Chicago: Society of American Archivists, 1992), 28.

5. Society of American Archivists, *A Glossary for Archivists,* 3.

6. Adrian Cunningham, "Archival Institutions," in *Archives: Recordkeeping in Society,* ed. Sue McKemmish, Michael Piggott, Barbara Reed, and Frank Upward (Wagga Wagga, Australia: Charles Sturt University, 2005), 45.

7. International Council of Archives, Committee on Electronic Records, *Guide for Managing Records from an Archival Perspective, February 1997* (Paris: International Council of Archives, 1997). Available at www.ica.org/biblio/cer/guide_eng.html, accessed June 25, 2005.

8. Archives New Zealand, *G20 Guide to Developing Recordkeeping Strategies for Websites* (Wellington: Archives New Zealand, June 2004). Available at www.archives.govt.nz/continuum/rkpublications.html, accessed June 3, 2005.

9. National Archives of Australia, "Archiving Web Resources: Guidelines" (Canberra: National Archives of Australia, 2000). Available at www.naa.gov.au/recordkeeping/er/web_records/guide_intro.html, accessed June 3, 2005; see also National Archives of Australia, "Archives Advice 43: Archiving Web Resources: A National Archives Policy, January 2001" (Canberra: National Archives of Australia, 2001). Available at www.naa.gov.au/recordkeeping/rkpubs/advices/advice43.html, accessed June 3, 2005.

10. National Archives of Australia, "Archiving Web Resources: Guidelines," sec. 3.3.

11. National Archives of Australia, "Archiving Web Resources: Guidelines," sec. 1.3.

12. Elizabeth Shepherd and Geoffrey Yeo, *Managing Records: A Handbook of Principles and Practices* (London: Facet, 2003), 9.

13. Sue McKemmish, "The Smoking Gun: Recordkeeping and Accountability," *Archifacts,* April 1999, 2.

14. The Archives New Zealand Continuum products are available at www.archives.govt.nz/continuum/index.html, accessed June 1, 2005.

15. Jay Kennedy and Cherryl Schauder, *Records Management: A Guide to Corporate Recordkeeping,* 2nd ed. (South Melbourne: Longman, 1999), 9–12.

16. See Shepherd and Yeo, *Managing Records,* 9. Another influential article in the United Kingdom is Sarah J. A. Flynn, "The Records Continuum Model in Context and Its Implications for Archival Practice," *Journal of Society of Archivists* 22, no. 1 (April 2001): 79–83.

17. Charles M. Dollar, "Archivists and Records Managers in the Information Age," *Archivaria* 36 (Autumn 1993): 47; for his award-winning book see Charles M. Dollar, *Authentic Electronic Records: Strategies for Long-Term Access* (Chicago: Cohasset Associates, 1999). This book won the Society of American Archivists' Waldo Gifford Leland Award in 2000 for a work of superior excellence and usefulness in the field of archival history, theory, or practice.

18. John McDonald, "Archives and Current Records: Towards a Set of Guiding Principles," *Janus* (1999): 111.

19. McDonald, "Archives and Current Records," 113.

20. Ann Pederson, "Professing Archives: A Very Human Enterprise," in *Archives: Recordkeeping in Society*, ed. Sue McKemmish, Michael Piggott, Barbara Reed, and Frank Upward (Wagga Wagga, Australia: Charles Sturt University, 2005), 71.

21. Philip Bantin, "The Indiana University Electronic Records Project: Lessons Learned," *Information Management Journal* 35 (January 2001): 18–20.

22. Luciana Duranti, "Meeting the Challenge of Contemporary Records: Does It Require a Role Change for the Archivist?" *American Archivist* 63 (Spring/Summer 2000): 12–13.

23. McKemmish, "The Smoking Gun," 11.

24. For a discussion of this, see Bantin, "Electronic Records Management," 3–7.

25. John McDonald. "Managing Records in the Modern Office: Taming the Wild Frontier," *Archivaria* 39 (Spring 1995): 70–87.

26. State Records Authority of New South Wales, *Standard on Recordkeeping in the Electronic Business Environment* (New South Wales: State Records Authority of New South Wales, 2004). Available at www.records.nsw.gov.au/publicsector/erk/electronic.htm, accessed June 24, 2005.

27. Marc Fresco and Martin Waldron, *Model Requirements for the Management of Electronic Records* (MoReq) (London: Cornwell Affiliates, 2001). Available at www.cornwell.co.uk/moreq, accessed June 27, 2005; Assistant Secretary of Defense for Command, Control, Communications and Intelligence, *Design Criteria Standard for Electronic Records Management Software Applications DoD 5015.2-STD* (Washington, DC: Department of Defense, June 19, 2002).

28. Standards Australia, *AS 4390:1996: Australian Standard for Records Management* (Homebush: Standards Australia, 1996); Standards Australia, *AS ISO 15489.1-2002: Records Management–Part 1: General* (Sydney: Standards Australia, 2001); Standards Australia, *AS ISO 15489.1-2002: Records Management–Part 2: Guidelines* (Sydney: Standards Australia, 2001).

29. Archives New Zealand, *G20 Guide to Developing Recordkeeping Strategies for Websites.*

30. See International Council on Archives (ICA), Committee on Current Records in an Electronic Environment, *Electronic Records: A Workbook for Archivists* (Paris: ICA, April 2005), chap. 3.

31. Archives New Zealand, *G6, A Standard for Developing a Recordkeeping Policy* (Wellington: Archives New Zealand, 2003). Available at www.archives.govt.nz/continuum/rkpublications.html, accessed June 16, 2005.

32. See E. Rogers, *Diffusion of Innovations,* 5th ed. (New York: Free Press, 2003).

33. See Adam Stapleton, "From Icons to Ideas: Archives New Zealand as the Change Agency for the Post-Custodial Paradigm" (M.A. thesis, Wellington, New Zealand, University of Victoria, 2005).

34. ICA, Committee on Current Records in an Electronic Environment, *Electronic Records.*

35. ICA, Committee on Managing Electronic Records, *Guide for Managing Electronic Records from an Archival Perspective.*

36. This saying was coined by David Osborne and Ted Gaebler in *Reinventing Government* (New York: Penguin, 1992).

37. National Archives and Records Administration, *Guidance on Managing Web Records, January 2005* (Washington, DC: National Archives and Records Administration, 2005). Available at www.archives.gov/records_management/policy_and_guidance/managing_web_records_index.html, accessed June 24, 2005.

38. National Archives and Records Administration, *Guidance on Managing Web Records,* 2.

39. ICA, Committee on Current Records in an Electronic Environment, *Electronic Records*, 20.

40. Stapleton, "From Icons to Ideas," 125.

41. Public Records Act 2005, sec. 27–28.

42. For a copy of the PowerPoint presentation given by National Archives of Australia representative Adrian Cunningham, director of recordkeeping standards and policy, see www.archives.govt.nz/continuum/previouspap.html#adri, accessed June 26, 2005.

43. National Archives of Australia, "Archiving Web Resources: Guidelines," sec. 3.4.

44. National Archives and Records Administration, *Guidance on Managing Web Records, January 2005*, sec. 9–10.

45. See InterPARES 2 Project, *International Research on Permanent Authentic Records in Electronic Systems* (Vancouver, Canada: InterPARES2 Project, 2002). Available at http://www.interpares.org/ip2.htm, accessed June 26, 2005; Philip Bantin, *Indiana University Electronic Records Project: Phase II, 2000–2002; Final Report to the National Historical Publications and Records Commission* (Bloomington, IN: University Archives, 2002). Available at www.indiana.edu/~libarch/ER/nhprcfinalreport.doc, accessed June 25, 2005; and Sue McKemmish et al., "Describing Records in Context in the Continuum: The Australian Recordkeeping Metadata Schema," *Archivaria* 48 (Fall 1999): 3–43.

46. See Public Record Office Victoria. *Victorian Electronic Records Strategy Final Report* (Melbourne: Public Record Office Victoria, 1998).

47. The management of the New Zealand Government Locator System (NZGLS) metadata standard is overseen by Archives New Zealand. The standard is available at www.e-government.govt.nz/nzgls/standard/index.asp, accessed April 6, 2005.

48. See Greg O'Shea and David Roberts, "Living in a Digital World: Recognizing the Electronic and Post-Custodial Realities," *Archives and Manuscripts* 24 (November 1996): 286–311; Michael Hoyle, "Developing an Electronic Records Policy for New Zealand," *Archifacts,* October 1997, 8–21.

49. Public Records Act 2005, sec. 22.

50. Sue McKemmish, Barbara Reed, and Michael Piggott, "The Archives," in *Archives: Recordkeeping in Society*, ed, Sue McKemmish, Michael Piggott, Barbara Reed, and Frank Upward (Wagga Wagga, Australia: Charles Sturt University, 2005), 164.

51. Linda J. Henry, "Schellenberg in Cyberspace," *American Archivist* 61 (Fall 1998): 320.

52. Terry Cook, "Electronic Records, Paper Minds: The Revolution in Information Management and Archives in the Post-custodial and Post-modernist Era," *Archives and Manuscripts* 22 (November 1994): 300.

53. Mark A. Greene, "The Power of Meaning: The Archival Mission in the Post-Modern Age," *American Archivist* 65 (Spring/Summer 2002): 53.

54. Greene, "The Power of Meaning," 54. Greene quotes Steven Connor, who posits the question "Instead of asking, what is postmodernism? We should ask . . . what is at stake in its debates? . . . not, what does postmodernism mean?, but what does it *do?*" See Steven Connor, *Postmodernist Culture: An Introduction to Theories of the Contemporary* (New York: Basil Blackwell, 1989), 10.

55. Henry, "Schellenberg in Cyberspace," 327.

56. Cook, "Electronic Records, Paper Minds," 320.

IV

AUDIENCE ISSUES

10

Citizens' Response to E-government

Rowena Cullen and Peter Hernon

$\mathcal{A}$lthough this chapter focuses on the citizens of one country—New Zealand—the issues examined are applicable to any country that wants the public and the business community to use its electronic government information and services. As a study prepared for the Benton Foundation notes, "information on most government Websites is skewed to the needs and abilities of highly educated English speakers. For low-literate populations, the Web remains an untapped resource. People with disabilities, such as those with visual impairments, continue to struggle with government Websites that do not address their needs."[1] This chapter and the next one address such issues. They also show how the public searches for government information and the channels they prefer to use in their pursuit of government information and in interacting with government departments and agencies. The insights provided in these chapters came from an extensive set of focus group interviews and asking some citizens to search government Web sites on predetermined topics.

BACKGROUND

Several studies (e.g., a 2001 report prepared by the Institute for Economic Research on e-government preparedness in the small coastal township of Levin, New Zealand[2] and Rowena Cullen's report on a series of focus group interviews with selected groups of citizens in and beyond the Wellington region[3]) have highlighted some of the motivators and barriers lying behind the use of government information on the Internet. Motivators that Cullen identified for using the Internet varied greatly among the groups interviewed, but they centered on convenience, rapid access to a wide range of up-to-date information, the ability to participate in policy debates, the ability to schedule appointments, the avoidance of difficulties in speaking and listening to English, anonymity, and the ability to contact government in a less personal and intrusive way. Each group encountered some barriers in its use of government on the Internet. Those barriers that

---

This chapter is drawn from *Wired for Well-Being: Citizens' Response to E-government*. A report presented to the E-government Unit, New Zealand State Services Commission, by Rowena Cullen and Peter Hernon (June 2004). Available at http://www.e-government.govt.nz/docs/vuw-report-200406.

related to the *digital divide*—the gap between those who have access to information technologies such as the Internet, and those who do not—include:

- physical access to information and communications technologies (ICT), ranging from competition for the one residential telephone line to poor connections in rural areas, to lack of time and money;
- the level of ICT skills and support, as well as the need to keep up-to-date with computer hardware and software;
- attitudes related to concerns about the safety of communication over the Internet, the lack of privacy for community access services, and a preference for human communication, either face-to-face or by telephone; and
- the relevance of content and contacts, as the public may find neither appropriate content nor personal contacts on government Web sites that are helpful in resolving their information needs.

Both of the reports highlight some key issues, in particular:

- the need for alternative channels of communication to cater to those who, for whatever reasons, lack access to government on the Internet, or who prefer a more interactive and personal form of communication;
- a lack of awareness of the general government portal and the need for greater promotion of it if the portal is to fulfill the vision of serving as a one-stop shop for e-government;
- the need for government departments and agencies to promote the information and services that they make available on the Internet and that are accessible through the portal;
- a widespread need for an education program to enable the public to be more effective and efficient in searching for, and gaining access to, government information and services through the Internet; and
- the need to build a culture of open communication between government and citizens, and a climate of trust to facilitate online transactions and other services.

While some of the above-mentioned issues are specific to groups that, in the past, have been considered to be disadvantaged in terms of the digital divide (e.g., rural groups, those from lower socioeconomic groups, those with either poor English-speaking skills or low education, those on public assistance, and Maori), the two studies indicate that response to e-government is more individualistic. That response is a complex mixture of external circumstances, opportunity, and personal and cognitive preferences. Thus, use of government on the Internet involves issues such as the digital divide, socioeconomic characteristics, and cultural and personal issues.

The success of e-government—whether government to government, government to citizen, or government to business—depends on a better understanding of the types of barriers that inhibit or prevent use, as well as the public's information-gathering preferences and past experiences in gathering information and dealing with particular government departments and agencies. Cullen and the Institute for Economic Research have identified a number of barriers related to the public's use of e-government. These barriers might be related to service, technology, agency, content, or level of education.

Because other barriers might exist, there is need to develop a taxonomy of different barriers (see the next chapter).

The technique of telephone interviewing limited the scope and depth of the survey for *Government Online*[4] because there was insufficient time to probe motivators and barriers to gathering government information. Regional perspectives and the highly selective coverage of groups limited the insights gained from the Institute for Economic Research and Cullen, both of which were qualitative studies. Clearly, there is a need for additional probing of the public's information-gathering behavior related to the use of government information and services, particularly those available over the Internet.

PURPOSE OF THE STUDY

This study, which builds on the previous reports, includes the perspectives of more individuals, and from different parts of New Zealand's North Island, but still predominantly the Wellington area. The study expands the knowledge base of citizen and business needs for government information and services through the Internet, and it contrasts Internet use with the use of other channels for gathering government information and for using government services. The study indicates what New Zealanders expect of the government information and services provided over the Internet as well as through more traditional channels. Equally important issues are the following:

- How do New Zealanders interact with government in their daily lives, either as individuals and citizens, or in relation to their roles in the workplace?
- What government information and services have they used, either online or through more traditional channels, and how do they view those experiences?
- How do they locate the government information and services they use?
- Has access to the Internet changed the way in which they seek government information and services?
- What barriers, if any, does the public encounter in seeking government information and services both online and through traditional channels?
- How might barriers be overcome?
- Do they consider the government portal (www.govt.nz) as a way to overcome obstacles to the receipt of government information and services?
- How much trust and confidence does the public place in the information and services that the government provides on the Internet?
- What factors affect their levels of trust and confidence?
- Do they distinguish between trust in the Internet as a secure means of accessing information and services in general and trust in government Web sites for the information and services provided?
- Do demographic characteristics (e.g., personal, educational, cultural, and geographic) influence responses to the previous questions?

The answers to these questions neither suggest nor imply that the government perceives the provision of information and services as the exclusive role of the Internet. Instead, the answers show how people interact with government and their preferred methods of that interaction, as well as suggest strategies for meeting the information needs and information-gathering preferences of the public through assorted channels, be they traditional or digital. In essence, as the percentage of the public using government on the Internet increases, has the public really become more dependent on the Internet for access to government information and services? Has increased Internet access resulted in a decrease in the use of other channels for gaining access to government information?

STUDY PROCEDURES

For data collection, the study used focus group interviews, but before the interview started each participant was asked to complete a general questionnaire. That questionnaire delved into participants' use of computers, the Internet, and government information and services, as well as perceptions about the availability of government on the Internet; the instrument also gathered background demographic information. Members of the E-government Unit, State Services Commission, reviewed the questionnaire and suggested new wording where appropriate and, at the request of the research team, conducted two separate pretests of the instrument. Based on the responses they received from their staff, the instrument was further revised.

The investigation was conducted in three stages. First, in March 2004, two focus group interviews explored, in some depth, the issues of security and trust. These interviews were conducted first because the E-government Unit needed the information quickly for a survey it was preparing. These focus groups contained people who were much more broadly defined demographically than the subsequent interviews, and the interviews were conducted in Wellington. The purpose was to gather a diverse set of perspectives; nonetheless, subsequent focus group interviews continued to probe the issues of security and trust.

From March through May 2004, ten focus group interviews were conducted in the Auckland, Hamilton, Taranaki, and Wellington areas with individuals representing the following groups:

1. disabled citizens, recruited from two local branches of the Disabled Persons Association;
2. maori, from rural and urban areas around Hawera;
3. pacific peoples, from the Pacific Island Advisory Committee of the Manukau City Council;
4. new immigrants attending English as a Second Language classes in Karori;
5. people in the business community (Auckland), recruited through Newmarket Rotary Club;
6. people in the business community (Wellington), recruited through Wellington Rotary Club;
7. residents of rural communities, recruited from a rural women's network outside Morrinsville;
8. senior citizens attending a senior social group at Miramar Community Center;
9. students attending Victoria University;
10. working professionals, all members of an amateur choir in Wellington.

Each interview lasted from one hour to ninety minutes. For consistency and reliability, the same investigator led the discussion in each focus group interview. The other investigator monitored the responses, taking careful notes and occasionally asking a follow-up question to clarify a response for the written record. The focus group interviews were taped and a written transcript produced.

As discussed in the next chapter, for a further dimension to data collection, participants in the early focus group interviews were invited to take part in a walkthrough—an observational technique to examine how they would go about answering a set of predetermined questions. During April and May, these observations were conducted at Victoria University in the office of one of the investigators. Participants sat at the computer but had access to a nearby telephone book. They were asked to verbalize and demonstrate their method of searching for the answers to preselected questions.

It also merits mention that many participants, especially the Pacific peoples, Maori, and disabled carefully reviewed their answers to the questionnaire before turning in the form. A typical comment was, "I feel I am representing all Maori, so I am taking great care in completing the survey."

A limitation of the study was that it was not possible in the time frame during which the study had to be completed to conduct additional focus group interviews across New Zealand and involve more people from each of the ten demographic groups. The Maori interviewed inserted a caution. They stressed that because "literacy is an issue for our people," future surveys should be cognizant of this fact and should involve Maori as the research team (or part of it).

FOCUS GROUP PARTICIPANTS

Altogether, sixty-five individuals[5] participated in the ten focus group interviews and the two additional ones that concentrated on the issue of "security and trust." Table 10.1 provides background information on them, and table 10.3 indicates their level of experience with computers and Internet use. (The information for both of these tables was taken from questionnaire responses.) During the focus group interviews, a number of those interviewed mentioned that they tended to confine their use of the Internet to work. Home use might center on doing e-mail and engaging in fun activities (e.g., playing games or helping children with projects). Some others disagreed and were more likely to search the Internet at home, including government Web sites. Whichever approach they used depended, in part, on (1) whether there was a single line for Internet access at home, and (2) the speed of modem access. In those instances in which participants found it too time-consuming to search at home, they were likely to contact government by phone.

Twenty-nine respondents were employed, whereas fourteen received a benefit or pension, and six a student loan or allowance. Another four were homemakers who shared their partner's income, and one was retired (self-funded); eleven respondents did not state a source of income (see table 10.2).

Overwhelmingly, English is the major language that participants used in their daily lives. They might, however, combine English with another language: Bengali; Chinese; Cook Island Maori; Dutch; Fijian; Japanese; Maori; Romanian; Samoan; Swedish; or Tamil. Two people indicated Maori or Tongan, and some listed sign language.

Table 10.1.   Background Information

Category	Number	Percent
Gender		
Female	36	55.4*
Male	28	43.1
Unidentified	1	1.5
Ethnic Group		
NZ European	46	70.8
Maori	8	12.3
Pacific peoples (Samoan, Tahitian, Tongan)	8	12.3
Asian (Chinese, Taiwanese) or Indian	3	4.6
Age		
15–19	2	3.1
20–24	6	9.2
25–29	4	6.2
30–34	6	9.2
35–39	7	10.8
40–44	5	7.7
45–49	7	10.8
50–54	6	9.2
55–59	5	7.7
60–64	5	7.7
65–69	7	10.8
70–74	2	3.1
75–79	1	1.5
80 or over	2	3.1
Highest Level of Formal Educational Qualification		
School certificate	6	9.7
6th form certificate/UE/Bursary	14	22.6
Trade/vocational certificate or diploma	11	17.7
Business diploma	2	3.2
Bachelor's degree	15	24.2
Postgraduate degree	10	16.1
Other	4	6.5
Household Income		
$0–9,999	3	4.6
$10,000–19,999	5	7.7
$20,000–29,999	5	7.7
$30,000–39,999	6	9.2
$40,000–49,999	4	6.2
$50,000–59,999	6	9.2
$60,000–69,999	6	9.2
$70,000–79,999	3	4.6
$80,000 or over	1	1.5
Did not answer	26	40

Note: Some participants did not answer all of the questions. In case of the new immigrants, we viewed the questionnaire as too complex for them to complete. The nine women came from Hong Kong, Japan, China, Romania, Indonesia, Sri Lanka, and Korea.

*All percentages subject to rounding.

Table 10.2.   Occupation of Respondents

Employment category	Number
Banking/finance	3
Business/consulting	3
Council employee	1
Farmer	6
Legal annotator	1
Lab technician	1
Librarian	1
Manager/administrator	2
Musician	1
Retail worker	1
Retired self-funded	1
Public servant	2
Scientist	1
Self-employed	4
Student	6
Teacher	2
Supported by partner	4
Benefit/pension	14
Not specified	11
Total	65

Table 10.3 indicates the respondents' level of experience with computers and Internet use. They tend to have "some experience" or to be "experienced" in their use of computers and the Internet, and their use often came from home, work, or school.

WEB USE AND NONUSE

Their responses to the survey question, "What kinds of things encourage you to use the Internet?" encompassed seven broad categories:

1. *Create a record.* The ability to create a paper trail or bookmark relevant home pages, Web pages, or information content
2. *Convenience of online activities.* Ability to engage in online activities (banking, purchasing products, and travel bookings)
3. *Ability to find information* (e.g., on a wide variety of topics, current and useful for the completion of assignments for school-age children)
4. *24/7/365 access.* Anytime/anywhere access to information and communication with others (communication is not limited to friends and colleagues)
5. *Convenience* (and being able to avoid being placed on hold, as when calling an organization by phone)
6. *Information content.* The ability to find high-quality information that reflects different views and perspectives, that is readily accessible, or that is germane to their information need
7. *Independent information gathering.* The ability to find information independently and anonymously, and the ease and serendipity of searching

Table 10.3. Level of Experience with Computers and Internet Use

Category	Number	Percent
Computer Use		
No experience	4	6.2*
Some experience (e.g., e-mail, basic word processing, and office computer)	31	47.7
Experienced (e.g., competent with a number of computer applications)	30	46.2
Internet Use (including e-mail and Web sites)		
No experience	4	6.2
Some experience (e.g., e-mail, online purchasing, games, and/or some searching for information)	39	60
Experienced (e.g., dedicated surfer)	22	33.9
*Use Internet from****		
Home	58	50
Work	32	27.6
School or place of study	10	8.6
Internet café	6	5.2
Library	5	4.3
Other (e.g., hotel/motel)	5	4.3

*Percents subject to rounding.
**Respondents could choose all that apply.

Participants in the focus group interviews reinforced the above-mentioned advantages, while suggesting some new ones related to general use of the Internet and Web. They mentioned the following:

- Access to contextual information. The background and detailed information provided enable them to understand issues better.
- Home use as an alternative to attending a meeting or visiting a government department or agency. Participants with an impairment limiting their mobility could gather information from home. If they were unable to attend a meeting, they could obtain information, perhaps related to that meeting, from the Internet.
- The Internet provides contact information. That contact information might be more detailed than the telephone book provides. When they contact a government department or agency, they like to know the name of an individual.
- An opportunity to be reflective. When they use the Web, they are not likely to be in a hurry. In contrast, when dealing with someone on the phone, they or the person at the other end may face time pressures. Clearly, use of the phone is a time-sensitive issue. Web use is not. In essence, Web use is more of a leisure activity.
- Flexibility. They can search for information at their own pace and from whatever location they choose.

Everyone in the rural group uses computers, but they have different levels of experience. Dairy farmers, for example, might use computers to help manage their business. Using specialized software, they maintain herd records, with information on each cow (e.g., milk yield, volume, content, parentage, and offspring), which adds to the value of the herd. They also expressed the view that "the Web has been a real boon for farmers." As one explained, "the Web provides access to information that otherwise might be time-consuming to collect. Still, it [the Web] can be slow and it can get frustrating when we are bounced back to the opening screen of the home page."

Many of those interviewed—regardless of citizen group—view the Internet as only one means by which they gain access to information. They were most emphatic that the Internet should not become the exclusive means of access to information or the sole channel for communication.

DISCOURAGEMENT FROM USING THE WEB

As for the kinds of things that discouraged their use of the Internet, questionnaire responses can be collapsed into four broad categories:

1. Computer use (cost, connectivity, security, and level of knowledge and searching)
2. Coping with online forms (they can be hard to download, as well as to complete and return online)
3. Information searching (distractions such as pop-up advertisements and finding new but interesting material unrelated to the subject of their original search, hard-to-navigate Web sites, and unsuccessful searching)
4. Information results (varied quality and relevance)

Focus group interviewees reinforced the above-mentioned points and noted some additional issues:

- People (e.g., the elderly, those with disabilities, and Maori) might lack the money to purchase a computer or upgrade an old computer that had limited capability. According to one person with a disability, "I have a computer with Windows 95 that lacks sufficient memory and is slow." Depending on the level of disability, a person on a modest income who does not receive government support would likely be unable to afford to purchase a new computer.
- People with disabilities may not have ready access to the necessary adaptive technologies. All the needed technologies, it was explained, are available, but individuals may not be able to afford to purchase them. While those in the workforce might have jobs in which the employer provides the technologies, such technologies might be too expensive for home purchase.
- Some people have no perceived critical need for a computer or Internet access. As one senior citizen mentioned, "I would love to get on the Internet and there're hundreds of things you find interesting, but they also tell you at our age you've got to be active and so I spend my time in the garden and looking after my house." Others in that focus group reinforced the need to be active at their age.
- Elderly persons were afraid of becoming "addicted" to the Internet (see previous bulleted item).

USE OF GOVERNMENT INFORMATION AND SERVICES

Of the sixty-five participants, forty-seven (72.3 percent) had contacted national or local government departments in the past year. Table 10.4, which is drawn from question-naire responses, identifies the broad topic about which they made contact, the number of mentions for each, and the relative position of the category in comparison to the other categories. They selected city council matters the most often and fisheries the least.

Figure 10.1, which offers another perspective on some of the data in that table, identifies the most frequently mentioned topics about which the members of the public participating in the focus group interviews contacted government. Ten topics produced at least sixteen responses. The chapter appendix expands on the figure and indicates the range of topics and subject matter for which they contacted government. Most likely, the search for some legislation (i.e., statutes) was through Knowledge Basket, a private sector database vendor.

Figure 10.2 identifies the method by which participants contacted government

Table 10.4.   Topics for Which Citizens Approached Government

Category	Number	Position
Births, deaths, and marriages	16	9
Benefits	15	12
Broadcasting	7	25.5
Business-related issues (e.g., grants and compliance)	16	9
Consumer affairs	7	25.5
Customs	4	30
Driver's licenses	15	12
Education	24	3
Elections	12	20.5
Employment	20	5.5
Environment	15	12
Farming	7	25.5
Fisheries	3	32
Funding agencies (e.g., social security)	9	22.5
Health	13	17.5
Housing/tenancy	6	28
Immigration/passport/citizenship	27	2
Legislation (laws and regulations)	20	5.5
Maps and land information	13	17.5
Occupational safety and health	4	30
Personal/family issues (e.g., child safety)	4	30
Police/justice	13	17.5
Policy and politics	13	17.5
Recreation and sport	7	25.5
Statistics	16	9
Tax and finance	22	4
Tourism	12	20.5
Transportation	14	14.5
Treaty issues	9	22.5
City council matters	29	1
Regional council matters	18	7
Other (e.g., conservation, defense, disability, food safety, and science)	14	14.5

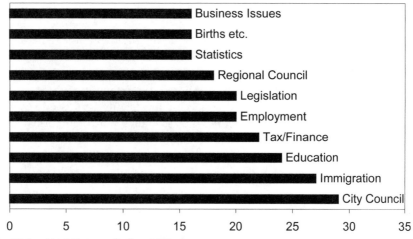

Figure 10.1. Most Frequently Sought Topics

departments or agencies. The most common method was by telephone, with Web sites in second position. Because e-mail constitutes part of the Internet, the combination of Web sites and e-mail strengthens the position of the Internet as an important means of contact. Viewed from another perspective, in-person visits to government departments and agencies are important but less so than contact by telephone and the Internet. Four respondents checked the "other" category, which included contact at meetings that government departments held for consultation and fax. Of the forty-seven people who had contacted government, forty-two (89.4 percent) used multiple means.

Use of Government on the Internet

Most of the focus group participants who had used government on the Internet—made contact through the Web or e-mail—indicated that their use was limited; only a few

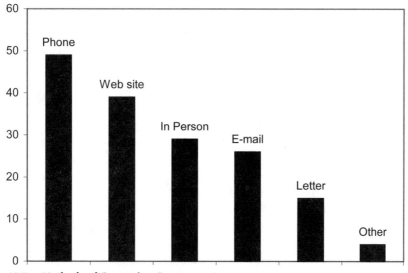

Figure 10.2. Methods of Contacting Government

individuals make frequent use (at least weekly).[6] Use tended to center on a search for information or the names of people to contact in departments or agencies.

When asked why they consult government on the Internet (either a departmental or agency Web site, or by e-mail), their questionnaire responses reinforced the previously mentioned reasons that either encourage or discourage their use of the Internet in general. Encouragement focused on issues such as anytime/anywhere access and information content (good background or specific information and good coverage of issues). They also mentioned new categories such as finding portable information (e.g., able to download and work on a spreadsheet) and their dislike of being placed on hold when they make a call. Likewise the reasons for nonuse paralleled those previously mentioned. However, some respondents noted (1) a preference to talk with someone (create and maintain a personal relationship); (2) the difficulties associated with downloading, reading, completing, and returning online forms (e.g., "I would use government forms if they were easier and more accessible to use"); and (3) the complexity of navigating government Web sites, especially if they did not regard themselves as good or highly competent searchers.

Use by Participant Groups

This section provides an overview of use of government Web sites by each of the ten groups.

Disabled Citizens   Those interviewed tended to be activists who need information on assorted topics but who also think it is important to be informed citizens. As one explained, "being informed enriches my life." They might use government on the Internet anywhere from infrequently to weekly. They gather government information on the Internet (e.g., legislation, policies, and general information, including bus schedules) at the local or national level for their advocacy, work, school, or personal needs or interests. One person uses government information on the Internet for work-related purposes (research and writing reports), as she works on government contracts. Personal use, which is limited (perhaps once or twice a year), focuses on passport regulations, travel advisories, or policy documents. An advantage of government sites for activists is that they can obtain the complete text of a speech (e.g., by the prime minister) or a policy document. Newspapers, on the other hand, only provide a synopsis.

Maori   Most of those interviewed use government on the Internet; that use ranged from weekly to monthly but is not increasing. They definitely like to search for information on the Internet owing to its convenience and the fact that they can do it anytime. When searching for information, they might not pay attention to Web addresses and did not always realize that a particular site might be government. Most of all, the group wanted to see Maori reflected in government Web sites—if not through use of Te Reo, at least through Maori news and events being prominently reported. They might seek government information on careers, education, the environment, legislation, statistics, and so on.

Regarding services, two of them use an electronic tendering service and receive e-mail announcements and go to different sites for more information about such opportunities. They might also apply for study grants.

Pacific Peoples   All of this group use computers and government on the Internet, but to varying degrees. Their use ranges from occasional to daily. They might seek information or contacts related to agriculture, education, health care, immigration, and so on. Regarding services, they did not engage in online booking. As one participant pointed out, "Who among Pacific peoples has a credit card?" He also commented, "I don't want to be on the phone forever calling Wellington [from Auckland]. So, I want to know what I want to talk about and to be informed before I place the call." He questioned the accuracy of the legislation online but realized that this issue is being resolved.

New Immigrants   The participants (two of whom were on temporary visitor permits) have been in New Zealand for a length of time ranging from four months to more than a decade. Those who have been in the country for a long time indicated they delayed learning English because they could rely on their husbands or children to find out what they wanted. For some, there is a strong desire to avoid contact with government, especially the police (an attitude possibly gained from experiences in the country from which they came). As a result, their contact with government, even through the Internet, is limited and relates to their daily lives.

All of them use computers, but some of their use focuses on retaining contact with their old country and its language. Eight have made contact with government through the Internet. Most use of government Web sites relates to seeking material to borrow from the city library. They have also used the home pages of the city council (for paying rates and other services), Ministry of Education (for school and general information), Land Transport Safety Authority (for obtaining a driver's license), and New Zealand Immigration Service (for visas, passports, and information on the quota for family entering the country).

People in the Business Community (Auckland)   Two focus group interviews were conducted with people in the business community, one in Auckland and the other in Wellington. The Wellington meeting is reported below.

Use of government on the Internet by the Auckland group was "project driven" and involved, for instance, the use of legislation and policy documents. Depending on the project, their use might be very frequent. As a general (crude) indicator, the use for some is monthly and for others less so. The participants believed their use is increasing.

People in the Business Community (Wellington)   With one exception (a retired individual), the group was familiar with government on the Internet, and many had served as consultants to various departments; such consultancies might involve extensive use of the departmental Web site. They also seek policy documents, recent reports, information related to funding opportunities, and other material from government Web sites. They find online forms and software that helps them complete those forms in a timely manner.

Their knowledge about and use of government on the Internet far exceeded the knowledge and use that other people have and make. Reinforcing this observation is the fact that they used government on the Internet "every day." They maintained that their use of government Web sites, which, like that of the members of the Auckland business community, is project driven, increased two years ago but has now flattened out. They tend to use the same sites repeatedly.

Residents of Rural Communities   Half of the group has searched government on the Internet for online forms, legislation, maps, tenancy information, and landlord rights, but use ranges from infrequently to monthly. The group had a good understanding of what government services are available through the Internet. One had filed her tax returns online. As she explained, "I did it because I was running late [the deadline was approaching]."

Senior Citizens   This group only made occasional use of government on the Internet, and that use centered on seeking tax information or forms—issues related to daily life rather than any specific interests, although some reported recreational use of the Web for travel, recipes, radio programs, and e-mail contact with family.

Students   University students were some of the more frequent users of government on the Internet. Their use ranged from weekly to several times a year. They thought that finding something relevant on government Web sites meant that in the future they would likely return to those sites. They distinguished between use for personal reasons and for course assignments. They were more likely to use government Web sites for course work, and in those instances they were more persistent in their search. Weekly use might pertain to seeking information for course research such as conservation, policy, and legislation. Their use for personal purposes might relate to obtaining a visa, renewing a driver's license, or seeking information about immigration or about a tax write-off for interest on a student loan. Some of their use was from overseas.

Regarding services, one student mentioned making a submission as part of a conservation public consultation process on the Waimangaroa Mine on the West Coast. Most had some experience of downloading and completing application forms for student loans and allowances from Work and Income New Zealand (WINZ) but commented that to complete the submission process, WINZ sent these forms by mail, for signature.

Working Professionals   All of these participants use government on the Internet[7] on a "sporadic" basis; by this, they meant between twice a month and six times per year. The purpose of their use related to funding opportunities for research; finding policy documents, legislation (statutes), and maps; looking for speeches of ministers and members of Parliament; and seeking advisories about travel abroad and information about music collections and immigration.

As for services, they might have signed up to receive e-mail announcements from a government department or agency. Those announcements might alert them to new publications in areas of interest. They also download forms, and one of them has filed her taxes online.

INFORMATION-GATHERING BEHAVIOR

Some Likes

The participants liked government to provide information on the Internet that they could browse at their leisure. A number of them thought that government sites were a "good source of *basic information*" and that the government's presence on the Internet would continue to develop. That presence, they suspected, would center on the increased availability of digital information. They also believed that government would become more responsive to the needs of the public as that presence matures.

Those interviewed liked government Web sites to identify contact people so that they had the name of someone they could call. This made the call more personal and provided a level of accountability in that they could also contact that person again. The

Web site of the Department of Conservation (www.doc.govt.nz) received the most praise for its layout, ease of use, and the high quality of the support staff who answer questions by telephone. Participants also liked the Web sites of the Ministry of Tourism (www.tourism.govt.nz); Inland Revenue Department (IRD; www.ird.govt.nz), except for having to negotiate forms; and Web sites of ministers of the Crown. However, they suspected the Web sites of ministers filter information and only tell part of the story, that part most favorable to the person.

The new immigrants were very selective in the Web sites they visited and the information they used. They found the forms related to visas and passport application easy to download. They also liked being able to reserve a public library book online.

Those in the rural community, especially, appreciated that their use of the Internet and government sites could be in the evening. Given their work schedule, they might be unable to call departments or agencies during daytime hours when an office is open.

Some members of the Wellington business community appreciated the availability of the online public access catalog (OPAC) of the National Library as well as the OPACs of other libraries. They liked those government Web sites that had good search engines and were well laid out and easy to use. As one stated, "I like the design of a Web site that enables a person to find the same information from different routes." They also like access to legislation without having to pay for that access.

Some Dislikes

Participants in different focus groups disagreed about whether they liked or disliked a particular Web site. They realized it was hard to compare sites, as their expectations differed, especially if they were work related or personal. Furthermore, they recognized that departments and agencies serve different audiences. The Ministry of Tourism, for example, wants to attract a broad international audience and promote New Zealand. IRD, on the other hand, involves compliance with domestic tax laws.

Those interviewed realized that the functionality of Web sites varied from department to department. Some sites require more search skills than others. Also, some sites are better developed than others—that is, they have better architecture and are easy to use. A number of those interviewed wanted more standardization across government Web sites. One member of the Wellington business community stated, "Every government department is learning on the go. They use different language but often mean the same thing. There is much they could do to achieve standardization of language." The others in the group agreed.

There was a feeling among many focus group participants that government Web sites "packed a lot of information content of varying quality" and that this resulted in sites that "looked cosmetic and not real." Another criticism was that government sites tend to rely on jargon and do not communicate with the public in plain language. The dislikes of the new immigrants relate to the language barrier. They did not want Web sites to contain too much information for them to navigate or read and text that is long and does not use simple language. (At those Web sites they used, they would prefer text where the content is bulleted.)

Maori participants felt strongly that the contents of Web sites were not always well presented, or retrievable, especially for Maori as an audience. The "arrangement may put [Maori people] off." In addition, the information appeared to them outdated.

When they go to the search option on a Web site and insert the word *Maori,* the information retrieved might be five to seven years old. Thus, they assume the site has nothing more recent. Or they find a document that covers Maori but the reference is only on one page—it merely states that Maori were consulted. Such experiences also impact on trust in government (see next chapter).

Members of the Wellington business community reiterated that not all departments and agencies share the same mission or serve the same general audience. They cautioned against making sweeping generalizations. Still, they thought that Web sites could be more user friendly and use plain language. They also thought that some sites were cumbersome to search. The example given was the Environmental Risk Management Authority (www.ermanz.govt.nz), where it might "take eight to nine clicks of the mouse to find what you need; this is too many [clicks]." Another limitation is that Web sites, such as that of the Department of Corrections (www.corrections.govt.nz), might take a defensive view ("be a spin machine") and try to "sell their view of the world. The result is that a Web site might lose its credibility."

Most of the dissatisfaction centered on WINZ, especially for the perceived low quality of service provided to those visiting it in person. A number of people commented that dealing with the department might result in an unpleasant experience.[8] Making contact via the Internet, they hoped, might reduce that unpleasantness. Some participants indicated that WINZ robustly encouraged their use of its Web site; they thought this was an effort to reduce the volume of people coming or calling in, or a reluctance to deal with them as an individual.

A number of participants complained about online forms and the fact that they frequently could not be completed and submitted electronically. Most were unaware of the difficulties in creating a reliable authentication system for handling electronic submissions, although the Wellington business people dismissed this issue as a legitimate reason for delaying the introduction of more online forms and service transactions using forms. The disabilities group noted that online forms could be difficult for people with poor sight to read. There was a consensus among those interviewed who had impairments that government was not trying to make it easier for them to navigate or complete online forms.

Those with disabilities also noted that some of the tables on the Web site of Statistics New Zealand (www.stats.govt.nz) could be hard to download. On the other hand, the Web site of the Office for Disability Issues (www.odi.govt.nz) "is very plain," which "is good for disabled access." However, even that site can be difficult to navigate: "It is hard to pick out contacts and move around [the site] easily."

People with disabilities prefer to use standard sites that have been designed with disabled-enabled access in mind. Some complained about sites that were "too bland" and alternative sites for disabled users that are very plain. "Those with disabilities want to 'go in the front door' with everyone else. Why should we have to go through the back door?" They favor universal access—just as wheelchair users should be able to make use of the same entry to a building, disabled Web users want to use the same Web page (with alternative text for graphics, and complying with World Wide Web Consortium [W3C] disability access guidelines) not a separate plain site. "'Accessible' does not have to mean 'boring'. For disabled users, accessing information on Web sites still needs to be a pleasurable and useful experience."

Observations

First, people want the content of the site to be well organized, permitting them to find relevant information with a degree of ease. Second, the Web site might have an icon or some instruction in a corner of the page, but that information may not show up on a smaller screen at home. They feel "stupid" when they call an agency and are told that the information was on the screen, but they could not see it. They want Web sites designed with their home computer in mind. Third, members of the public interviewed want Web pages to provide a date for the last time the information content was updated. The older the date, the more likely they are to assume the content is outdated. The lack of a date makes them feel very insecure about the information. Fourth, they believe that any set of frequently asked questions (FAQs) should be based on the most often asked questions and problems the public experiences in searching a particular Web site. Fifth, they dislike having to print a long document when they only need one page. They would like to be able to print more selectively. And, finally, they dislike trying to contact a Web site at busy times of the day and being unable to get through (much as they resent not being able to get through on the phone).

Search Patterns

As focus group participants explained, if they need to conduct a general search on a topic new to them, they are likely to search by:

- Google (www.google.com), which is the search engine they use most often;
- guessing the URL (uniform resource locator) of a department or inserting its name between "www." and ".govt.nz";
- checking a site they have previously used; or
- asking a friend or colleague for assistance.

There was great uncertainty about which government department did what, so even if they knew the name, they were unsure if it was the correct department. Some thought that their search behavior might change (become more sophisticated) if they searched for government information more often, although most disagreed. Almost all respondents combine searching for information on the Internet with use of the phone to make contact with a department or agency. Government on the Internet therefore provides valuable information on which to base an inquiry, or the names of contacts. One person, who is fairly typical of the users, banks online and cannot imagine doing things the old way, in person. Still, when it comes to using government Web sites, he continues to combine Web and phone use: "If I want to know how to file taxes online, I'd check the IRD site. If I still had a question, I'd use the phone."

Three other examples merit mention. First, many people commented, "When I know what I'm looking for, the Internet is fine, but I usually phone." They get the number from the phone book, most likely the white pages, not the blue pages. The white pages, however, are selective in their coverage of government departments and agencies. They might even use the white pages to locate Web addresses of government departments and agencies. The blue and white pages are far from complete in giving Web addresses for government departments and agencies.

Second, some students believed that government Web sites are usually harder to navigate than nongovernment sites. As a consequence, they might pose their question over the telephone. The problem, they felt, with the phone is that they might have to go through a long menu of choices before selecting the right one, and then they would be placed on hold; there was a strong dislike for being placed on hold, for any length of time.[9] One student said, "I will look for five minutes . . . and [if unsuccessful, I would] e-mail . . . [the department]." The department, however, might be "quite slow" in responding.

Third, a complication is that the information content on Web sites might be broad and detailed, but might not address specific questions. A number of those participating in the study stated that their particular query or problem did not fit the information outlines on Web sites, such as in FAQs. As one person noted, government on the Internet provides information but "my questions are very specific." He continued, "I do not find answers to them on the sites. I get my answers from calling people. I have contacts [by phone and e-mail] and through them I can build a relationship."

Those with disabilities have specific strategies for gathering the information they want (based on past experience). It seems that they are often part of a close-knit community or interpersonal network, one that shares information. Being less mobile, they have a high need for information and regard the Internet as a key resource. Still, unless they have a speech impairment, they tend to prefer oral communication and personal contact. Furthermore, sometimes they might order a printed, published document by phone; the print copy is often easier for someone with poor eyesight to read. The decision about whether to seek a printed or an online copy might depend on the urgency and type of need; the size, format, and so on of the document; and how hard it is to find online.

Most rural areas cope with poor telecommunication infrastructures and have to run their Internet connections on low bandwidth, and they encounter frequent interruptions due to interference. Those interviewed had mobile phone coverage, which is not universal in rural New Zealand, but which provides an alternative channel of communication when the phone line is tied up with Internet use or technical assistance is needed. In other rural areas, use of the one phone line becomes a hotly contested issue because a family cannot use the Internet and the phone simultaneously; the phone takes precedence.

Those people interviewed who live in a rural community use mobile phones when they are away from their home and need to contact someone to fix a problem that just arose. They expressed great dislike of calling a call center only to find that the person is in Wellington, Auckland, or Australia. They need someone local. In some instances, they might call an 800 number and ask where they should search on the home page for information. In some instances, when they cannot find the necessary information on government Web sites, they call the agency's information service, explain that they could not find the information on the site, and ask for guidance in locating it there. Participants in other focus groups confirmed that they might also call a department or agency and request assistance in locating something on that Web site.

Maori participants found it difficult to locate Web addresses and they preferred to make contact with government agencies through 800 numbers or to ask a friend or relative for help. However, like participants in all focus groups, they disliked calling a government department or agency and being placed on hold or encountering an extensive menu of options on the phone system. In either case, they might hang up. One explained that when IRD put him through "a lot of rigmarole, I hung up and called my tax accountant." A participant in another focus group explained that, for people in rural settings, it could be expensive to be placed on hold for a long period of time. The issue is not just one of money but time—time away from completing other tasks.

The Pacific peoples might be looking for information or contacts; contacts are important as they like to interact one-to-one, and they believe that government is more likely to listen if there is human interaction. The Internet is a channel for gathering information but not the best one for receiving answers. Government on the Internet uses "formal English" and the jargon of government; these limit its broad appeal. In their community, some people serve as gatekeepers and pass along information that the community needs. Others in the community might "ring us and we pass along the information to them." If those interviewed search for information on a topic new to them, they might call an agency and ask where to search on that agency's Web site, or they might "muddle through," using Ask Jeeves (www.ask.com) or "a search engine" (e.g., Google), or guess the name of an agency to insert in www.____.govt.nz. The last option for one of them who was familiar with the government portal would be to check it.

Because language is a definite barrier for new immigrants, information gathering has three facets: (1) finding information, (2) understanding it, and (3) checking on its accuracy or how it applies to them. First, to find general information, they might rely on an English-language search engine or use one in the language with which they are most comfortable. (For example, Empas [www.empas.com] provides information in Korean.) For New Zealand government information, they would often ask a family member for assistance. If that search proved unsuccessful, they would most likely go to Yahoo! or on occasion Google. A couple of them indicated they might even insert whatever term they are looking for into www.____.govt.nz or consult the blue pages of the phone book to ascertain a departmental or agency Web address. A number of them find the telephone threatening. The person on the other end might not understand their accent and have to repeat the information conveyed, but they still might not understand what they are told. It is easier for them to view written information so they can carefully formulate their question and be sure they understand what they read and hear. Second, to understand information content, they would print the material and check a dictionary for words they did not understand. Third, if the information found was not specific enough or they wondered if it covered their circumstance, they would visit in person, or perhaps call the department or agency.

Figure 10.3 summarizes how people find a government Web site, what they use, and the relationship between Web site and phone use. A large number of those interviewed do not consider themselves to be skilled searchers. This lack of skill, they felt, might explain why their searches may fail or be inefficient.

Exception to the General Pattern

The Wellington businesspeople do not follow the same pattern as the other people interviewed. They rely more extensively on e-mail and the Web. When they conduct a general search requiring information from a department not previously known to them, they rely on Google or try to guess the name of the department or agency con-

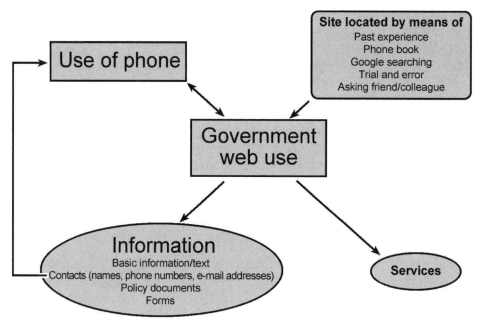

Figure 10.3.   Typical Use Patterns

cerned. If they have a complex question for which they need an answer, they turn to the telephone. They might also rely on the phone to develop and maintain relationships. As one explained, "every once in a while, I'll call a contact just to keep the relationship going." E-mail has become part of the way members of the Wellington business community do business; they often send their invoices by e-mail and receive contracts by that medium. E-mail has other advantages. First, people may not be in their office and "you can leave a detailed message. If you called, someone might only record that you called. No message is left." Second, e-mail saves time in addressing, stamping, and mailing a letter.

Use of the Basic Government Portal

Only twelve people (18.5 percent) had used the portal, although most of these did not find it very helpful. As one explained, "I found it quite slow [e.g., using the alphabetical list of departments and agencies to identify the correct Web address] and aesthetically old—it looks very traditional: very English." For another, knowledge about it has not altered his information gathering. He still relies on guessing a URL or asking someone where to search; he is "very people focused. As a last resort," he might try the portal. And three others indicated that they might use it to locate URLs, ones that are not easy to guess from the name of the department. As an example, one person mentioned the URL for the Ministry of Education (www.minedu.govt.nz). As three others noted, "the portal lists departments and agencies without providing information about their mission, role, or jurisdiction—if you place the cursor over the name of the government body such information does not pop up." Only two people (out of all participants) have used the search option on the portal.

Four individuals had stumbled across the portal, as each explained, by mistake: "I forgot to enter the name of the department and just put in 'www.govt.nz.'" Yet, their experience with the portal did not result in it being a natural place for them to begin or even use in their search for government information. Awareness of it did not alter their present method of gathering information. For instance, one person who had used the Web portal found it too complicated for someone with her disabilities to navigate. As she explained, "people with mental health issues find a lot of information hard to digest."

In addition to the previously mentioned twelve people, eight other people expressed some familiarity with the portal, and a few others had a faint recollection of hearing about it, but they still asked, "What is a portal?" One person, a farmer, had read about its launch, and she noted that she finds reference to it at other Web sites. Those sites might say, "If you want further information, go to www.govt.nz." Even so, she does not use the portal. Another person had used the portal without knowing what it was. It is interesting to note that one student said, "Estonia has one central site which leads to other government sites. From it, government Web sites branch out." Neither he nor the others in his focus group realized that New Zealand had something similar.

When the investigators explained the purpose of the portal, a typical remark was either, "Why doesn't the government rename it?" (they regarded the word *portal* as bureaucratic jargon), or "Why doesn't the government broadcast information about the portal?"—that is, call their attention to it. Yet, few of them jotted down the Web address or seemed to want to include it in future searches.

Another point merits mention. Given the reliance of those interviewed on Google, a number of those interviewed asked, "Why doesn't government link into Google, with Google providing the general search capability?" Members of the Wellington business community supported this view; they marveled at the quality of the Google search engine and dismissed the usefulness of the search engines on most government Web sites.

All of the Wellington businesspeople had used the portal, but none of them did so frequently. They might use it to locate a Web address so they can identify a contact person, but, because they prefer to rely on particular pages in a Web site, they find the portal to be too general. Instead of having government continue to invest in a general portal, some suggested the creation (or support) of specialty portals, such as one for science that marries government and nongovernment or quasi-government sites. "I often do not want to stop to think if this body is government or nongovernment," one person explained.

It would seem that someone would need to be familiar with government, its structure, and how it functions to use the portal effectively on a repeated basis. An important question arising from these comments is, Would they go (or return) to the portal in the future if the department or agency they needed to contact was unknown? The answer is likely to be no or very infrequently. The government portal obviously has not created a lasting or sustaining impression. The strongest negative opinion on the portal came from a Wellington businessman who had used it often. He compared the portal to fax, a technology he felt was more of the past than the present or future. He wanted government departments and agencies to join Google and "take advantage of a really good search engine."

CONCLUSION

Numerous public opinion polls conducted in other countries indicate that the public's use of computers, the Internet, and government Web sites is on the increase, as (in some countries) is their contacting government officials by means of e-mail. Still, even with those users, there is a desire that access to government not be confined to the Internet. The public, as figure 10.3 indicates, also wants traditional means of access (the telephone and in-person visits).[10] A number of people in New Zealand and elsewhere like to interact with others orally, and they are accustomed to dealing with others through the telephone. It is clear that many members of the public are satisfied with their present methods of gaining access to government information and are not about to change their present information-gathering behavior. Furthermore, " 'real time' interaction with government—the telephone or in-person visits—is preferred when people have urgent or complex problems to sort out with government,"[11] or if they cannot find an answer to the precise question online. Another point is that the public wants choice regarding how they contact government, and they are likely to use more than one means, perhaps government Web sites, e-mail, and the telephone.

The next chapter provides more insights gained from the research in New Zealand that have implications elsewhere. For example, in countries such as the United States, too much reliance on flash technology to present the contents of home pages may actually limit access to people with disabilities and others who rely on home computers that might not be able to cope with that technology.[12]

NOTES

1. Benton Foundation, *Achieving E-Government for All: Highlights from a National Survey,* prepared by Darrell M. West (Washington, DC: Benton Foundation, 2003), 2. Available at www.benton.org/publibrary/egov/access2003.doc, accessed October 12, 2003.

2. Institute for Economic Research, *As Seen from Levin: Improving Government Communications with Citizens; A Report from the Region* (Wellington: New Zealand State Services Commission, 2001).

3. Rowena Cullen, "E-government: A Citizen's Perspective," *Journal of E-Government* 1, no. 3 (2004). Available at www.haworthpress.com/store/toc/J399v01n03_TOC.pdf, accessed December 21, 2005.

4. *Government Online: A National Perspective,* a report prepared by TNS (Wellington: New Zealand State Services Commission, 2003).

5. Nine women made up the new immigrants' focus group, thereby raising the number of participants to seventy-four. However, we have separated them from tables 10.1 and 10.2 and the total number because we did not ask them to complete the questionnaire and we abbreviated the questions asked in the focus group interviews. We also provided extensive prompting. The different treatment was due to their limited English reading, writing, and oral communication skills.

6. The people who did not use government on the Internet either did not perceive a need for such information or they were satisfied with their current method of gathering information. A factor affecting nonuse for some participants was a lack of understanding about the types of information the government disseminates. As one elderly respondent commented, "I assume government sites just contain booklets." The desire "to stay away from government" was seldom mentioned; one member of the business community and a number of the new immigrants held that attitude.

7. One person stated on the questionnaire that he did not use government on the Internet. However, during the discussion, he realized his error. As others in the group noted, "you often don't pay

attention to the Web address and government has so many quasi-agencies that might or might not be government." Still, they asked if "such and such an agency was or was not part of government."

8. For example, students mentioned problems (on the WINZ site) such as the forms being hard to complete online, especially "if you had specific questions." They dislike going in person to a department and being told to go to the Web site for an answer to their question.

9. A number of participants in other focus groups made the same point.

10. See, e.g., Pew Internet and American Life Project, *How Americans Get in Touch with Government,* by John B. Horrigan (Washington, DC: Pew Internet and American Life Project, 2004). Available at www.pewinternet.org/, accessed June 1, 2004. This report shows that Americans shared the identical methods for contacting government.

11. Pew Internet and American Life Project, *How Americans Get in Touch with Government,* i.

12. For complementary coverage of the public's interaction with e-government—the American public—see Christopher G. Reddick, "Citizen Interaction with E-government: From the Streets to Servers?" *Government Information Quarterly* 22 (2005): 38–57.

Appendix: Specific Matters for Which Participants Contacted Government (Categories nominated by respondents)

Births, Deaths, and Marriages
   Apply for marriage licence
   Checking family history
   Copy of birth certificate
   Copy of marriage certificate
   Historic data and status of online research facilities
   New birth certificate
   Procedure for obtaining birth certificate

Benefits
   Application for student allowance
   Application for student allowance/loan while overseas
   Applications, problems with payment
   Availability of student allowance for myself, support for my partner
   Confirming date of superannuation
   Disability allowance
   Eligibility for grants and financial support while studying
   Find out benefit eligibility
   Inquiry about niece's requirements
   Proving level of income
   Requirements for disability allowance and sickness benefits
   Unemployment benefit

Broadcasting
   Iwi radio
   News
   Seeking program information

Business-Related Issues
   Environment Waikato grants for fencing waterways
   Grants
   New business funding
   Rules for incorporated societies

City Council Matters
   Building consents (e.g., extension of house)
   Bylaw information
   Drainage from house going down neighbor's land
   Liaising with council on issues affecting disabled students
   Meeting (minutes and policy)
   Te Ara ō nga Tupuna and information on history of area
   Paying rates
   Policy plans and statements of local council
   Safety and environmental regulations, building codes
   Street matters
   Summer events in Wellington
   Water supply and concern over trees in a local park

Consumer Affairs
   Issues related to vehicle ownership and use
   Ongoing work relationship
   Product recalls
   Things for sale

Customs
   Restrictions on what a traveler may take into New Zealand
   Visas
   What to declare

Driver's License
   Checking what my Australian girlfriend needs to do to change license
   Regulations for replacing lost items
   Reissue/renewal of driver's license

Education
   Consultation appointments
   Cost of university for foreigners in New Zealand
   Find out about learning sign language
   Find out entitlements as a returning student
   Funding for study
   Information about New Zealand Certificate of Educational Achievement (NZCEA)
   Information on student support for NZers
   List of university courses
   Looking at new school (e.g., Education Review Office [ERO] reports)
   Looking into private schooling
   Research grant applications
   Status of a tertiary project

Status of peer support programs
Teacher registration

Elections
Accurate electoral roll information
Polling booth
Time frame for next election, employment possibilities

Employment
Employment opportunities (e.g., for my partner)
Government jobs listings
Seeking research work
Staff recruitment
Where we stand with time off and wages for our workers

Environment
Find out about whale stranding
Issues related to technology, science in society, etc.
Lease conditions, buildings, etc.
Policies being introduced on environmental issues
Policy wording for a contract project
Resource management
Weather information

Farming
Dairy company issues
Looking at Fonterra (e.g., milk collection and weather)
Record keeping

Fisheries
Update law books fisheries

Funding Agencies
Information about research funding (from Ministry of Research, Science and Technology [MORST])
See what is going on

Health
Issues related to technology, science in society, etc.
A matter regarding compensation
Mental health issues and publications
Seeking a copy of a discussion document

Housing and Tenancy
Had bad tenant and wanted to know rights as landlords
Information on costs as a result of a dispute
Tenancy rights/agreement

Immigration, Passport, and Citizenship
Apply for, reissue, or renew passport
Changes in immigration policies that affected new immigrants
Details required about getting into New Zealand for a friend

Family overseas trip
Family passport problems
Immigration requirements for my partner
Information on costs as a result of a dispute
Migration information for parents
Residency status of my girlfriend
Rights of refugees
Rules for citizenship
Visa information (e.g., requirements for travel)

Legislation (Laws and Regulations)
Bills in the House
Copyright law
Employment law
Information for study
Information on NZCEA and New Zealand Qualifications Authority (NZQA)
Issues related to technology, science in society, GM debate, etc.
Legalities of paternity tests
Staff information
Statutes (contents of various acts)

Maps and Land Information
Boundaries of property
Finding streets
Finding the quickest routes
Information on a site for a geography project
Land information
Land title
LINZ data
Maps for holidays
Maps of Wellington
Toured New Zealand and relied exclusively on the Web for information

Occupational Safety and Health
Paying OSH

Personal/Family Issues
Accident Compensation Committee (ACC)
Reporting on an incident
Was pregnant and working with child, youth, and family

Police/Justice
America's Cup security
Handing in a law related to a burglary
Information on sexual abuse
Issues related to technology, science in society, GM debate, etc.
Prowler and car theft outside my gate
Reporting on an incident
Respond to a submission to law commission

Seeking clarification on facts or official interpretation of what I have read or heard
Statements by ministers

Policy and Politics
Concerns about a child
Latest policy and statements that the government has issued
Politics
Release from restricted security rating for thesis written while in the defense force
Reserve Bank exchange rates
Seeking general information and policies
Research work
Various government policies

Recreation and Sport
Book a play trailer for kindergarten
Grants for sports club
Results of rugby matches
What is occurring around Wellington?
Virtual Super 12

Regional Council Matters
Building permit for local marae (community meeting centers)
Installation of water meters
Permits and consents
Regional district plan information
Regional growth plan
Timetables
Treaty issues
Update law books regional council
Water supply information

Statistics
Copies of forms
Information on Maori population and language fluency
Seeking data (e.g., on research work or goods and services tax [GST] payment)
Seeking population and other online statistics

Tax and Finance
How to get an IRD number
Information about GST
Paying taxes
Personal income tax regulations
Refund of taxes on charity donation
Signed up online GST
Tax code
Tax forms
Tax refund
Tax return

Tourism
    Information about immigration
    Milford Sounds walk
    New Zealand referrals
    Tourism (general information)

Transportation
    Information on policy for accessing trains
    New trailer regulations
    Policies being introduced on transport issues
    Public transport (fares and timetables)
    Warrant of fitness regulations

Treaty Issues
    Information for study
    Information on specific issues or fact

Other
    Copies of submissions and commission pages
    Disability issues, strategies, and pertinent building codes
    Events: Date of birth of a friend's child that had been advertised
    Seeking career information
    Seeking information on a government department
    Updating myself: Finding out what is going on (especially in relationship to my key sectoral and personal interests)

11

More Citizen Perspectives on E-government

Rowena Cullen and Peter Hernon

$\mathcal{T}$his chapter continues the presentation of findings from focus group interviews and questionnaires, as well as the observation of citizen navigation of government Web sites. The findings continue to focus on issues relevant to an international audience, namely, their experiences, satisfaction, degree of trust in the content of government on the Internet, search behavior, and barriers encountered in their search. The chapter also summarizes the findings for the questions posed at the beginning of the previous chapter.

GOVERNMENT ON THE INTERNET

This section presents responses from both the questionnaire and focus group interviews. Of the forty-seven questionnaire respondents who ticked either "some experience" or "experienced" in their use of government Web sites, twenty-two (46.8 percent) had a negative experience and twenty-five (53.2 percent) did not. The negative experiences related to their degree of search expertise, limitations of search engines (e.g., the inability of the search engine to guess the right search term if the spelling is close but incorrect, slow response time, and poor or nonexistent instructions on how to search), the sending of e-mail but not receiving an acknowledgment or response, problems with Web sites (other than with search engines) (e.g., slow response, the use of language that they find difficult to understand, pages where the text moves past the screen too rapidly, and cluttered Web sites that pack too much information onto one screen), and problems with online forms—their downloading, completion, and electronic return.

Their use of government information on the Internet related to (arranged in descending order of most frequently mentioned):

- personal requirements and research/finding information (thirty-one ticks each);
- work (twenty-three ticks);

This chapter is drawn from *Wired for Well-Being: Citizens' Response to E-government*. A report presented to the E-government Unit, New Zealand State Services Commission, by Rowena Cullen and Peter Hernon (June 2004). Available at http://www.e-government.govt.nz/docs/vuw-report-200406.

- school/study (seven ticks); and
- other (i.e., volunteer work; one tick).

Questionnaire

Both questions depicted in table 11.1 used a seven-point scale common to many studies of customer satisfaction. The points on that scale ranged from -3 ("falls short of expectations") to $+3$ ("exceeds expectations"), with 0 representing "exactly meets." First, study participants were asked "whether government falls short of, exactly meets, or exceeds your expectations in protecting any personal information you provide face to face or over the phone." Next, using the same scale, the same question was repeated, but this time "face to face or over the phone" was replaced with "on the Internet (Web site or e-mail)."

A comparison of the findings to these two questions becomes difficult in part because there was substantial variation in the number of responses to each question (n = 42 and n = 29) and the expectations are not necessarily related to the actual problems participants experienced or the specific subject matter they sought. In other words, these questions lack a context. Nonetheless, the results are interesting. The mode for both rests with "exactly meets" and the numbers on both the plus and minus sides of the mode tend to be somewhat similar. In other words, both the phone and Internet met expectations but did not create a climate of the *delighted customer.* It merits mention that a number of participants provided a written comment about their expectations. They asked, "How are we to know what our expectation should be?" In other words, they had not given any thought to the issue, and the Web sites did not try to raise expectations.

The next question asked whether or not "government Web sites make it easier to find what you want." Respondents circled a number between 1 ("strongly disagree") to 7 ("strongly agree"). Of the forty-five respondents to the question, more than half (twenty-four, 53.3 percent) circled a number from 5 to 7. With the inclusion of the responses to 4, a neutral response, the percentage increases to 75.6. Thirteen people indicated a number between 1 and 3; however, only two people circled 1 or 2. On the other hand, only three circled 7. In effect, those participants completing the questionnaire believed that government Web sites make it easier to find the information they want (mode and median of 5).

Next, the participants were asked, "How important is it to you that government information/services are available on the Internet?" The seven-point scale ranged from 1 ("not at all important") to 7 ("extremely important"). Nobody circled 1 and six people marked 2 to 4. Viewed from the other end of the scale, twenty-one circled 7 and thirty-six circled either 6 or 7; forty-one people circled 5 to 7. Evidently, the availability

Table 11.1.   Extent of Satisfaction

	Falls short of expectations			Exactly meets expectations	Exceeds expectations		
	−3	−2	−1	0	1	2	3
Face-to-face or by phone	2	2	5	26	4	2	1
On the Internet	0	2	4	20	3	0	1

of government information and services on the Internet has some importance to them (mode of 7, median of 6).

To provide a better context for the answers to the above questions, one questionnaire item asked, "What do you like *most* about access to government information and services on the Internet?" The responses reinforced answers given to previous questions, namely, anytime/anywhere access, saving time, the breadth and depth of information available, and instant communication. Respondents also reiterated their dislike of being placed on hold when they call and for having to "battle the automated call service to find someone to talk to." They also mentioned they liked "reasonable anonymity."

On the other hand, they "least" liked coping with pdf files, trying to locate Web addresses for government departments and agencies, being unable to determine when a Web page or particular content was last updated, the confusing organization of different Web sites, the difficulty of reading and digesting the information provided, not finding the information sought, conducting a search that turned out to be time-consuming, poor search capabilities at numerous Web sites, loss of face-to-face contact, the uncertainty about whether or not e-mail communication was received, insufficient provision of contact information, and the presumption that if they could not find the information on a Web site, that information would otherwise be very difficult to obtain. One person commented, "There are a lot of statements saying that the information should not be taken as gospel. It is only advice. If it is government, shouldn't there be more facts?"

The final question in this section asked, "If the government could do *one* thing to improve its Internet services and communication with people, what should it be?" The students wanted the placement of kiosks around the country as well as better access to their financial records covering loans for university studies. Others favored the acknowledgment of e-mail messages, more contact information for departmental personnel, simplification of Web sites and the language used, the deployment of more and simpler electronic filing, provision of training in searching government Web sites, inclusion of all Web addresses in the phone book (both the white and blue pages), provision of free Internet access to government Web sites from places spread throughout the country, creation of some degree of uniformity for government Web sites (including the use of common language and good site design), enabling pages to load faster, improvement in the functionality of the government portal, creation of specialized (supplementary) portals, and advertisements explaining what government does on the Internet, informing people about the information and services available, and facilitation of communication directly with government through e-mail. Several people wanted the inclusion of more information—all except that which it is legitimate for government to withhold.

Impact of the Internet on Communication with Government

Three questions dealt with bringing the government and the public closer together by means of the Internet. The first two questions covered one-way communication—government to the public—and focused on the provision of government information and services. The final question covered two-way communication—government to the public and vice versa. The data displayed in table 11.2 support the comments made in focus group interviews. People readily recognized the value of one-way communication (particularly for information provision) but did not consider two-way communication as useful, although a few regarded e-mail as a means of communication with government. Of the forty-six respondents to each question, eleven people circled 4 or lower for finding information, whereas twenty-one circled 4 or lower for service provision and twenty-eight indicated 4 or lower for communication with government. Viewed from another perspective, only a small number strongly agreed with any of the statements. (The next section clarifies table 11.2 and the discussion provided here.)

DEMOCRATIC PROCESSES

Except for the Wellington businesspeople, the sixty-five participants were unfamiliar with e-government in New Zealand, its concept and purposes, as articulated in documents related to the government's vision and strategy (see www.e-government .govt.nz). They also were unfamiliar with the name "e-government" and assumed that e-government referred to online voting. As a result, they had no substantial knowledge upon which to base their answers to questions about the Internet and e-government promoting democratic processes. Nonetheless, the questions let them reflect on the Internet and the direction in which the government is proceeding.

When they thought about government on the Internet, they equated it with government's provision of information—current information—to the public. They did not see the process so much as involving services or communication from the public to government. In effect, they saw e-government and the promotion of democratic processes as a means of one-way, not two-way, communication. They liked the availability of legislation, policy documents, and other information on the Internet, but they saw great variation among departments and agencies in supplying such information in a way that the public—not sophisticated in information gathering—can find. One person summed up nicely her view of e-government: the government provides "information useful to me. That information informs me." It is the "citizen's duty to be informed and government's duty to inform the citizen." Some of the Maori interviewed liked it when government Web sites provided e-mail announcements that they could forward "to our people. The e-mail shows what government is doing to (not for) Maori!"

For some interviewees, e-mail constitutes a means of two-way communication and a means of generating a record of what is written. Some people may shy away from e-mail communication because they are unsure how to word the message or because the government department or agency may neither acknowledge receipt nor provide a

Table 11.2. Participants' Views on the Impact of the Internet on Relations with Government

Government on the Internet brings people closer to government by:							
Making it easier to find information	0	2	3	6	17	13	5
Providing better service (service that is convenient to use and reliable)	0	3	9	9	13	9	3
Making it easier for people to communicate their views to government	2	2	11	13	9	6	3

Note: Scale ranges from 1, strongly disagree, to 7, strongly agree.

written response. As two people remarked, "If the message doesn't bounce [back to you] you know it has arrived (unlike leaving a telephone message). It also provides a record" and "saves finding a stamp and envelope." For some participants, the creation of e-mail records, with prompt acknowledgment and a formal response, promotes democratic processes.[1] This type of communication, however, disadvantages those who do not have computers with Internet connectivity. One of the working professionals noted that the "Internet is a passive mechanism. You have to make the effort to gain access to the information. This requires time and access to computers." A few participants mentioned that solutions such as the availability of cybercafés and public libraries "don't work for . . . everyone."

Democracy is better served, some remarked, by not relying on only one channel for information provision and communication. "The government should not assume that if information is placed on the Web everyone will have seen, read, and understood it." The importance of human interaction should not be minimized. Such interaction is a critical means of maintaining democratic processes. One other example is informative. One of the Pacific people noted, "You can complain online. E-mail, though, is not as good as doing so by letter or in person. Face-to-face is the best." Still, this group will not engage in e-mail messaging unless they know the other party. Furthermore, "making a submission by e-mail does not carry weight like human interaction. I am always surprised when I get an e-mail response from a government department." They might look for opportunities to provide online feedback, but they still want to attend meetings and voice their opinions and concerns orally. Maori also supported face-to-face or telephone interaction. A businessperson added further clarification: he prefers to call people because he wants information right away and he favors personal contact, to build relationships.

The Maori and Pacific peoples interviewed did not see the availability of government information and services on the Internet as improving or promoting democracy. Some of those interviewed distrusted government. They saw newspapers as informing the public about what government does. Newspapers have the currency, they thought, that government on the Internet lacks. However, one of the Pacific people thought that online submissions for input into policy development promoted democracy.

The Exception

The Wellington businesspeople were familiar with e-government. They thought that e-government "has the potential to further democratic processes." To achieve that potential, they wanted all government information not subject to copyright or restrictive statutes placed on government Web sites. They also realized that advice given to a ministry should receive some protection (i.e., submissions or advice from industry should not be publicly available while policy is still being formed), although they still favored the release of submissions afterward. Publicly available information must be well organized and presented, and supported by a good archive for information removed from those sites.

For them, democracy is served when the public has input into policy development and refinement. They liked the widespread availability of policy documents, and they thought the real potential of e-government related to e-compliance. E-compliance, they said, would be a real boon for owners of small businesses. For instance, "they need not take off part of the day to go to Inland Revenue department (IRD). Instead, they can work on their compliance in the evenings and on weekends." If government provides more online transactions—does more of what the private sector does online—there is greater potential for government to serve the public through the Internet.

BARRIERS TO USE

General Barriers (Identified in the Questionnaires)

The study produced a list of barriers related to both general and government Internet use. The barriers identified on the questionnaires tended to match those mentioned during the focus group interviews (see the next section). Respondents in both instances distinguished between general Internet use and use of government Web sites. Regarding general Internet use, several participants mentioned that they encountered too many pop-ups and too much online advertising. Such distractions, they felt, were a nuisance. Other problems were that links on a site may not work and that it takes too long to download information. The time-consuming nature of downloading also pertains to the use of government Web sites as well as the fact that the public may not find the information it wants.

Interviewees also regarded computer use as time-consuming, especially when they are at home. They specifically mentioned the amount of time it takes to turn on the machine, to get it functional, search Web sites, and communicate by e-mail. One survey respondent considered the Internet as "a time waster." Many commented on the speed of the modem they used at home, which can be very slow. A further barrier noted in questionnaire responses is a dislike of reading extensive information and files on computer monitors.

General Barriers (Identified in the Focus Group Interviews)

The initial two focus groups, which examined the issues of security and trust, produced a list of barriers applicable to the Internet in general. The subsequent focus group interviews reinforced that list:

- Horror stories in the press about identity theft and other problems related to general use of the Internet: However, the typical attitude was that anyone using computers must be aware of and deal with these issues.
- Information on Web sites is often poorly presented: It might take too long to find what they seek, assuming they were using the correct Web site.
- Price/cost: If someone does not have a computer at home, he or she would have to pay for access (e.g., at a public library or Internet café). A number of focus group participants were concerned about the "high" cost of high-speed Internet access. They were also concerned that they were being limited to the use of these selected channels.
- Use of the Web can be a time waster: A person could easily spend too much time trying to find something on the Internet. This barrier fits within some of the other barriers, especially when there is a high level of comfort with how they currently search and find information, usually by telephone.

Barriers to Using Government on the Internet

In contrast to the previous section, this one focuses on barriers that respondents specifically associated with the use of government on the Internet. An issue that both the questionnaires and focus groups disclosed is that the public is uncertain about what comprises e-government.

The focus group interviews related to security and trust also generated a list of barriers associated with the use of government Web sites. Other focus group participants added to the list. Thus, the resulting barriers included the following:

- Comfort with existing methods of information gathering: Even if their methods are haphazard, they are comfortable with what they are doing. In other words, what worked for them in the past will guide future search behavior. Except for members of the Wellington business community, the participants tended to be unfamiliar with the government portal and are comfortable with their use of the phone book and the phone.
- Cost: Internet use, including in libraries, costs money. Cost issues also extend to the purchase of computer hardware and software, as well as one's time.
- Currency of content: The participants seek current, up-to-date information and, when they use government Web sites, they want those sites to provide the date of last revision of content—that date should be no longer than the past week. For them, *currency is a key trust issue.* They noted instances where the date on a Web site was not current.
- A faster means of access: If someone has a computer at home or work but does not have it turned on all day, it takes too much time to turn it on just to access a government (or nongovernment) Web site. It is much faster to make a phone call. If a phone number and contact person were unknown, the person needing the information might use the Web to locate such information. Most likely, he or she would then make a phone call. The first choice would be to check the phone book but if that consultation failed, the Web became an alternative source for providing similar information.
- Government Web sites are "text heavy": A common perception is that it is very time-consuming to navigate an overwhelming amount of information on a Web site to find what the person is seeking.
- Information overload: As one participant explained, "People are overinformed now. So much information is coming in, and the computer only adds to information availability."
- Lack of computer skills: Some were still learning to use computers and suspected that their skills would improve over time. Others had limited search skills. It cannot be determined that if they do indeed improve their search skills, they will automatically use, or increase their use of, government Web sites.
- Limited broadband impacts use: This is definitely true for numerous rural residents and for groups such as Pacific peoples.
- Perception that government Web sites provide information—nothing more: A number of participants were unaware that government Web sites provide services and might have a role in promoting democratic processes. (The most likely service used by participants other than those from the Wellington business community was to book a reservation at a campground.)

- No perceived need and lack of prior experience: Many participants had approached government online, but those who had not felt that they were unlikely to do so, especially if they lacked a perceived need, had not used government on the Internet before, and could find the needed information in other ways. Those who had not used government on the Internet could not think of an instance in which they might do so.
- Preference for oral communication: This barrier intersects with the next one. The participants liked person-to-person contact; they considered Internet use as impersonal and preferred to know the person with whom they were dealing.
- Presentation of Web site content: Not all of the material may fit on the screen—the person needs to scroll vertically or horizontally (this may present a problem for people with older computers). Furthermore, a screen might contain too much information. Poor presentation interferes with information access.
- Presentation of the Web site itself: Lack of easy navigation and differentiation of headings using color and various fonts were criticized. People easily got lost on Web sites and felt they compared poorly in design and architecture with commercial sites. Furthermore, as was noted, Web sites may not comply with disability guidelines and standards. There is a need for alternative text to be used with graphics.
- Reliance on the phone: Except for the Wellington business community, those interviewed rely on this method for the following reasons:
  - Fast and timely (saves time): However, it can be frustrating to encounter a menu choice (e.g., press 1 for __, 2 for __, etc.), then be placed in a long queue to get the desired information or to speak to a person, and sometimes have to go through it all again.
  - More personal ("easier to talk with someone; . . . the phone is instant gratification"): "If you get the name of the person and call again, a *trust relationship* might emerge." E-mail, on the other hand, is more impersonal and others might read your message—not a secure communication. With e-mail, you can save and track messages. If there is no response, you can follow up. However, the process of getting an answer becomes longer and "you might forget the question you [originally] asked" (back to *fast and timely*). Furthermore, e-mail may require a number of exchanges to get the desired information.
  - Able to judge the person at other end (e.g., does that person take you seriously?) and clarify unclear answers: If the public servant to whom you speak makes a mistake, it is taken as an honest mistake—no intention of deliberately providing misleading information.
  - Extremely comfortable (and satisfied) with phone use: Receipt of the right information via phone is a *trust* issue. This is especially true if the information sought relates to you or your family.
  - Come from a generation that communicates by phone: As one person noted, "I am a telephone person."
- Web sites might not use plain language: Many respondents considered that government Web sites contain a lot of jargon and do not communicate directly to them. They thought that government Web sites frequently used confusing language.

A number of the above-mentioned barriers overlap or intersect; they are not all discrete or independent of each other.

Disability Issues

Those with disabilities suggested additional barriers, in particular:

- Inadequate compliance with the disability guidelines, especially the use of alternative text: A site might contain a lot of graphics, which would be difficult for sight-impaired people to navigate. Graphics and use of color contrast on the site might also present problems for people who are color-blind; careful attention to color contrasts and shading is necessary.
- There might be too many colors around words: People may not be able to see all of the colors on a page. It may be hard for them to discriminate among colors. (This is a separate issue from color blindness.)
- Some Web sites seemed to focus on appearance and not functionality—need to focus on communication.
- There might be insufficient explanation on the site (in simple language) about how to navigate it and find the information sought.
- Information organization: It may be difficult to follow all of the information presented on a Web page and to sort out the relevant from the not so relevant (that part that meets their information need).
- Creation of a mirror site: The temptation might be to establish a mirror site for people with disabilities to use. Some of those interviewed rejected such a consideration.
- People with disabilities find the Internet time-consuming to search, and, depending on their disability, it may be difficult for them to sit or concentrate for long periods of time. They find it hard to navigate some sites. They believed that "sites are competitive—each trying to look better than the others." Web sites might assume a sophisticated look whereas people with disabilities may need something simpler. They also noted that downloading material from the Web could pose problems. People with a visual disability may be unable to access and use pdf files. Furthermore, downloading and printing are time-consuming, and they may tie up the one telephone line in the home for a long time. Also, some files may be too large to e-mail from the person's computer.

One person with a disability wanted those constructing and maintaining Web sites to remember that the use of those sites might be equated to "climbing Mt. Everest; the more difficult it is the more likely I'd try later" or find a different way to gather the information. "Disability," she explained, "means time limitations—someone with a disability may not have the same length of time in a day as someone without a disability."

For a number of the problems identified, the disability group participants suggested some general solutions, namely:

- provide clear directions to show how to navigate the site;
- use plain language (avoid jargon and long words);
- provide information in a straightforward manner;

- avoid the placement of color on color;
- focus on information provision (provide shortcuts);
- avoid the use of a small font size; and
- do not mix font sizes, do not use italics, and do not use small print with text underlined.

Taxonomy of Barriers

Based on the oral and written comments from the participants, we developed a taxonomy of barriers. The taxonomy represented the four main categories noted in the introduction and a fifth issue related to information architecture. That taxonomy included the following barriers:

1. Physical
    Limited domestic access—competition for computer, phone line, computer not always on, low bandwidth, etc.
    Limited access in rural communities—low bandwidth, interference, etc.
    Public kiosks not always suitable for task of contacting government
    Charges at public libraries
    Cost of computer and software
    Telecommunications costs
2. Skill-based
    Unable to determine which department needed
    Lack of knowledge of how government functions
    Lack of search skills
    Lack of navigation skills
    Not familiar with jargon of government agencies
    Unfamiliar with portal
3. Attitudinal
    Preference for oral contact
    Preference for personal contact
    Reluctance to spend time/waste time
    No perceived need for contact
    Comfort with existing methods of contact, especially phone
    Concerns over security of information exchange
    Concerns over confidentiality of personal information
    Concerns over confidentiality of e-mail address
4. Content-based
    Concerns over currency of content
    Lack of links between government agencies to assist users to find information from an alternative department or agency
    Not all information needed found
    Information generalized, not personal to user
    Sites have poor online assistance
5. Information architecture
    Poor navigation aids
    Text on sites dense and hard to read

Language used difficult to follow

Problems with site design (e.g., use of color and labels)

Overall arrangement of site dependent on agency perspective, not user-focused

Problems with font size and type

The participants in the various focus groups believe that government could greatly improve its Web sites. The one Web site that they tended to praise was that of the Department of Conservation because it is well laid out and easy to navigate. Some recommendations of the participants for Web site improvements include segmenting the information presented by different audiences (e.g., the general public, but perhaps further refining that category). Online forms should be easy to download and complete. People want to be able to submit them electronically. A related problem is that people may not be used to the online completion of forms and find it irritating that they might have missed a box and cannot proceed without completing it, or that they cannot go back and correct something without losing all their earlier effort. The print may be so small that it is easy to miss an item.

It is important for government to remember, as one of the Pacific peoples pointed out, "government [Web sites] should . . . [adopt] the perspective of what people want and not the perspective of government wanting to just get information out." As well, the above-mentioned suggestions of the disability group should also guide Web site design and presentation.

TRUST IN GOVERNMENT

Trust in government is a complex issue that includes cultural, political, socioeconomic, and other factors. Trust includes the public's perspective on how well government is performing and the issues of the day that dominate public discussion. Because this study did not focus exclusively on trust, all of these issues were not raised in each focus group meeting. Thus, the following provides a general overview, one that highlights confidence in government, the intrusion of government in people's lives, privacy, and security. The examination of these factors, however, does not directly look at or compare the public's trust in government in general but looks at trust in government as represented by the Internet.

A further complication is that there is a global dimension to the trust issue. Some governments, as a few focus group participants mentioned, have more of a trust problem with their public. That problem relates to government in general and to the perceived use of government Web sites to promote a political party's political, economic, military, and social agenda. Overt conformity by a government agency and on its Web site to a government's political agenda may result in a loss of confidence. One participant, who was born in the United Kingdom and lived there until recently, commented that the public there was "losing confidence in the government and therefore placing less trust in government Web sites." He noted that he had heard the same was occurring in the United States. The other participants in that focus group did not share his distrust of government Web sites in New Zealand. However, they pointed out that if a significant problem of trust in government arose, their level of trust in New Zealand government Web sites could change.

An advantage that New Zealand has over many other countries is its size. Members of the public tend to feel a closeness to, or connection with, government. They can interact directly with government officials, and they might see these people, for instance, in their city or suburb, on airplanes and in airports.

The Internet

Focus group participants distinguished between trust in the Internet in general and in government on the Internet. They maintained that the general problems commonly associated with Internet use (e.g., identity theft, pornography, spam, and viruses) do not apply to government Web sites. For instance, they viewed spam and viruses as general problems that every computer user faces. They did not consider these as issues related exclusively to use of government Web sites. As one participant stated, "Why would government send me spam?" and another queried, "Why would government send me unwanted e-mail?" They could not imagine government selling e-mail addresses to the private sector.

Confidence in Government

Focus group interviewees interpreted confidence as relating to the quality of the information provided, the currentness of information, and the recency of the publication date on a Web page. Some members of the Auckland business community distinguished among types of government information; they saw some (e.g., press releases and statements by ministers) as likely to be self-serving and less trustworthy than other types of government information. The working professionals agreed; government information on the Internet might reflect the "official line." They were the only group to question the version of the information they examined—"Is it in draft or final form?" Furthermore, "Which version has been archived, and can the public tell the difference?" "Where is the authoritative version if the pdf version is not a faithful rendition of the actual document?" One working professional added, "If I see typos and other errors in proofreading, I assume the document is half-finished and not the final report."

Most respondents were willing to supply information via the Internet to the extent that they would do so by post, telephone, or face-to-face. Those who took the view "I have nothing to hide" also applied this to Internet-based exchanges. Those who were more sensitive about personal information applied this to their use of the Internet.

Related to this was the widespread belief that government will not misuse the information provided—whether that information relates to their work or personal lives. Confidence would be eroded if they found out that the government cross-matched data or extensively engaged in data mining—sharing data among departments and agencies and culling information from assorted databases to learn more about the public. The Maori group, however, were sensitive to information about their iwi (tribes) not being broadly shared.

Another aspect of confidence is that government provides some incentives for providing information through the Internet while properly protecting the security of the information provided. The information supplied might be business information, and the incentive is a cost reduction for supplying the information online as opposed to offline. Such incentives (such as that applied by the Companies Office to the ability to register a company online) were broadly approved. Some commented that such incentives could be applied across other departments and agencies.

It merits mention that the members of the public interviewed do not always trust the information supplied by phone. Because the person on the phone might make a mistake, they might ask for the name of the person to whom they speak. One participant added, "If the question is simple and there is not much at stake (cost, time, etc.), then I'd use the Web site."

Intrusion of Government in Daily Lives

Intrusion has different aspects. One aspect occurred in the interview with members of the business community (Auckland) and the working professionals. That aspect related to the belief that government was becoming Orwellian in its adoption of "Big Brother." The number of people who mentioned this term, however, was small.

Privacy

The members of the public interviewed believed that personal information "is out there. What can I do about it?" An area of limited concern relates to the handling of personal information that the public might be asked to provide online. One person asked, "How secure is personal information in filing cabinets of a department?" Obviously, information can never be entirely secure. However, if a government Web site claimed that the information provided was secure, focus group participants would believe it. Still, they would like government Web sites to indicate (1) that they protect information provided and (2) how they protect it. Nobody interviewed mentioned either the Privacy Act or the Office of the Privacy Commissioner when they discussed government's handling of personal information that they supplied to government. (However, we did not insert a prompt in the discussion to refer to either the commissioner or the act.)

Security

Those interviewed assumed that government blocks viruses and that computer hacking of government sites has not yet presented a problem in New Zealand. However, if someone were to create a mirror site that involved a scam and that sought credit card information, their response to trust in government sites might change. There is a definite belief that any site address containing ".govt" is official and therefore is trustworthy. Furthermore, if a government Web site promises secure transactions, the public is likely to believe it.

An area of limited concern, but a concern that might grow in the future, related to the security of e-mail messages. A number of focus group participants wondered, "How well would government protect e-mail messages they might send?" They realized that recipients can forward messages, perhaps to large groups. Forwarding capability relates to the content of a message but also the protection of one's e-mail address. They definitely wanted their e-mail address protected and not shared without their permission. If government Web sites use cookies, both the type and use must be carefully explained on the opening screen of the home page. Cookie use could lead to a level of distrust in government Web sites.

The members of the Auckland business community thought that the quality of security varied from department to department. For them consistency and standardization promoted a sense of security in their dealings with government on the Internet. An element of security for the Wellington business community is that government could preserve e-mail correspondence. Even if departmental personnel deleted e-mail messages, they still reside on the hard drive and could be accessed. Still, the question for them is, How significant is the risk if staff passed a computer to someone else in (or outside) the department?

Major Areas of Distrust

Although many groups placed trust in New Zealand government on the Internet, five groups were less trustful. These were the working professionals, students, some of the people with disabilities, Pacific peoples, and the Maori interviewed. Maori were very vocal about their distrust. They distinguished between government as "politicking" and as "governing." The two may overlap and government bureaucrats may not be responsive to the needs of the people, they explained. "Government," as one stated, "does not communicate well with us." She continued, "We are used to being watched!" Their distrust is related more to government itself than to the information provided. Nonetheless, before using government information, they wanted to know who wrote the document, when it was written, and, in the case of Web sites, when pages were last updated. Furthermore, if their search of a government Web site did not turn up current information, they assumed the fault rests with the department. They also commented that there could be great variation in content among types of government information. Press releases, for example, might not be accurate; they might be self-serving. If government asks for advice only from Internet users, such requests do not instill much confidence in government. There is no evidence that the advice given feeds into policy development and refinement. Finally, they discussed trust as relationship building and maintenance. Without such a relationship, they believed trust was impossible. The discussion ended with one person saying, "He who has the gold makes the rules."

The students, the working professionals, the Maori, and the Pacific peoples referred to government as "Big Brother" engaged in surveillance of them and their Internet use. Students and some people in other focus groups distrusted the service that WINZ provided them. As one of them explained,

> If I complete any WINZ form I want to get a receipt saying that I've handed something in to them. If I don't get a receipt and they say that they've never got it—then I have to go back to the start. *So you physically go down there?* Well, if it's just the form—I give it to them and say look would you mind just signing so I've got something to stand on if they say they've lost it. Since they lose so much I don't trust them.

Finally, despite the view of some with disabilities that government on the Internet promoted trust, there were others who disagreed. The major points regarding distrust for this group were:

- "The Ministry of Health does not provide up-to-date information about drugs. It passes along drug company information. [That] information is not independent. [It reflects] what drug companies say."
- Government serves some of the population on the Internet but not everyone. This perceived selectivity raised a concern about trust in government itself.
- They felt that if government sites claimed they were "secure," they would not believe it. They do not provide personal information online and seemed unlikely to ever do so.
- Trust involves easy-to-find and up-to-date information. Government should not mislead or misinform. This is a reference to the previously mentioned drug information on the Ministry of Health Web site.
- They thought that government departments shared personal information, such as health information.

The group thought that some of the questions that government asks on numerous forms reflected a stereotyped image of people with disabilities. They might ask for a declaration of the specific disability. To them, this is "personal information." Insensitivity of people is an aspect of trust to them; "If I don't reveal my disability, they won't do what I want." This perceived insensitivity has trust implications.

The public interviewed saw the Internet currently as means of one-way dialogue: government to the people rather than the people to government. Trust issues focus on the accuracy and objectivity of the information supplied and on the availability of policy documents for their examination and use. Once e-government evolves and emphasizes two-way dialogue, trust issues might become more significant, depending on how government responds to two-way communication. Those interviewed did not associate government on the Internet with e-commerce; they could not imagine government ever trying to sell them anything. They also did not think that departments and agencies such as the Department of Inland Revenue and Statistics New Zealand would ask for personal information online. Such bodies, they thought, were more likely to request such information through other channels.

Once the public identifies e-government with the provision of services and people make more use of those services, service performance will become another factor influencing trust. For small businesses, once they can engage in e-compliance on a larger scale, their use will also have trust implications.

Trust can relate to one's patterns of past experience with a department. Repeated use of government Web sites, with each experience being positive, promotes trust. Trust is reinforced when government personnel are responsive to public inquiries. Those with disabilities complimented the New Zealand Office for Disability Issues because their dealings with it have all been satisfactory.

OBSERVATION OF SEARCH BEHAVIOR

Six participants in the series of observed walk-throughs searched for information on a set of preselected topics on government Web sites and indicated how they would go about answering the question. The tasks involved finding information on the following:

1. the justification and risks of spraying areas in Auckland for the painted apple moth (this information was available on the MAF site);
2. information and necessary forms that must be completed by landlords and tenants as part of setting up a rental agreement (this information was available on the Tenancy Services Web site, which is linked from the Ministry of Housing);
3. information for the participant's (fictional) recently widowed mother about how much she will receive on the single pension, with a living-alone allowance, and how much additional income she can have without penalty (this information is on the Work and Income Web site, under the heading Get financial assistance/Main benefits/New Zealand Superannuation);
4. information about facilities and whether you can make a booking for the Department of Conservation (DOC) campsite at Elaine Bay, in Pelorus Sounds (information is available on the DOC Web site, but the campsite is not bookable);
5. information behind a recent news announcement that Maori life expectancy had increased slightly, and recent figures on Maori health status (a number of sources are needed to compile this information).

None of the six participants, who ranged from a young male computer expert to a retired female civil servant, were able to complete all of the tasks fully and completely, although some got much further than others. Some only managed to tackle three tasks in the allotted time for the walk-through sessions (one hour). Participants used a range of search strategies, but the approach of each individual to each of the set of tasks was relatively consistent.

Most participants in the walk-throughs started their search in one of two ways: if they knew or could guess the URL of the Web site, they would enter that directly into the address box. Once they reached the Web site of the agency, they would then search by navigating through the site, using headings, menus, or textual links. Although some used a search box on a government Web site, this was later in the search. Alternatively, they would employ a search engine—either Google or MSN, www.msn.com (MSN search was the more obvious option on the PC being used, although some participants were less familiar with it). Once they had opened a search engine, participants did one of two things: they would enter the department name, or what they thought was part of its URL, or the topic they wished to search for (a small number of searches combined the two—name and topic). In total ten of the searches started with MSN; six used the department name and four focused on the topic; five started with Google (two using the department name, and three the topic); and eleven started with the URL (ten then proceeded to navigation through headings and links, and one employed a search engine). Table 11.3 shows how effective participants were in their search strategies.

On many occasions participants had reached the right part of a Web site to retrieve the information they were searching for but did not fully recognize this. On ten out of twenty-six occasions participants indicated they would phone the department in question, whether or not they had retrieved the required information. Their reasons for this were largely uncertainty that they could now act on the information retrieved and a reluctance to trust an online booking. Two out of the six participants had heard of the

Table 11.3.   Number of Clicks Taken to Reach Target Information in Walk-Through Observations (Compared with the Number Needed)

Participant	Task 1 *(No. of clicks needed = 6)*	Task 2 *(No. of clicks needed = 4)*	Task 3 *(No. of clicks needed = 5)*	Task 4 *(No. of clicks needed = 4)*	Task 5 *(No. of clicks needed = 6)*
One	15 + FC	10 FC	10 FC	15 + C/P	NA
Two	NA	9 FC	15 + NC	12 C/P	NA
Three	6 C	4 FC	12 NC/P	12 C/P	3 E
Four	4 C	4 FC	4 NC/P	6 C	7 NC
Five	10 NC	6 C/P	6 NC/P	9 C/P	NA
Six	8 FC	6 FC/P	13 NC/P	NA	11

NA = Task not attempted
NC = Task not completed
C = Task essentially completed, although participant has not identified information exactly
FC = Task fully completed—participant can identify relevant information
E = Task ended for other reasons
P = Participant would phone at this point

government portal, but they would not use it for this kind of search. Some would arrive at it as part of their search but showed no recognition of what it was.

The chapter appendix provides a full account of the tasks, the ideal solution, and how each participant coped with the tasks tackled.

Problems Participants Encountered

The sorts of problems participants encountered as they attempted to complete the tasks were that they were:

- not sure which agency Web site would contain the information, and if they knew which one it might be, what its URL was;
- not sure which agencies were parts of which department, or the structure of a department, and "who does what";
- not sure whether a particular heading would take them where they wanted to go on the site, or how information on the site was categorized;
- lacking skill in being able to interpret the results of a search by Google or MSN, or to read the keywords or URLs given in annotations on search results;
- lacking some basic knowledge of Web navigation and protocols (e.g., links changing color once activated);
- unskilled in using search engines (e.g., in choice of search terms, or restriction to New Zealand sources);
- failing to read all the information on the page that would answer a question, especially if it was a lengthy pdf file (as in the DOC campsite information brochure);

- not employing the same language as agencies (e.g., many people continued to search for the commonly used term *pension,* although the information they sought required them to recognize that it was found under the heading "New Zealand superannuation");
- not pleased with the size of fonts (especially on the portal, if they ended up there);
- not always seeing links or important headings that required scrolling vertically or horizontally;
- stymied by a lack of live links to critical information within Web sites, and especially from parts of the portal (an exception was the Tenancy site, where forms are well linked and labeled);
- wanting more links to have explanatory notes of what they linked to, and terms and headings to be more clearly defined; and
- failing to link to critical information on other government Web sites (e.g., the failure of the Ministry of Health site to suggest users also check the Statistics NZ site for life tables).

Searching was often a question of hit and miss, going backward and forward, sometimes over the same territory, often with a rising sense of frustration, resulting in "at this point I would call the department." The problems listed above can be attributed to two main causes. The first is lack of user skills. Agencies need to take this into account and provide more support for unskilled users of their Web sites. The second cause is poor design and lack of user-friendly Web site organization and navigation, and the fact that the language is not focused on the needs of those approaching the site. In some cases brochures put on the Web as pdf files do not permit links out to useful information, and internal Web site search engines do not search contents of pdf files very well. Many online brochures in pdf format need to be redesigned for Web use, and taking into account the habits of Web users, in order to relinquish their information more easily. An example is the difficulty for Web users in putting two separate pieces of information together (as in the case of the Department of Conservation booklet on South Island conservation camp sites, which explained in one place that standard campsites are not bookable and then, several pages further on, that the Elaine Bay site is a standard campsite. What users quickly see in print, they do not see on a computer screen.) By contrast, users were able to get tenancy information in pdf format or printable files and link from information pages to forms. This was the task most successfully completed by participants.

SUMMARY

The questions posed in the introduction to chapter 10 underpin the entire project. Given the extent of coverage in the body of the report, they need only summarizing here.

How do New Zealanders interact with government in their daily lives, either as individuals and citizens, or in relation to their roles in the workplace?

A wide range of New Zealanders from different socioeconomic backgrounds and from many different sectors in society were interviewed for the study. The amount of contact they had with government depended on their personal circumstances, and their role in society. For most people not dependent on benefits, their contact is limited to routine tasks motivated by compliance with government regulations—filing tax returns; licensing of motor vehicles, animals, drivers, firearms, and so on—or prompted by temporary issues in their daily lives (e.g., travel plans, children's school projects, or current events). If they have a personal interest in social issues (such as education or conservation), they are more likely to seek information about these issues online, looking for information and policy documents. People with a deeper concern about such issues, who see themselves as *advocates* for a particular cause, are even more active in seeking this kind of information. Such groups include the disabilities groups, the Maori, and Pacific people we interviewed. Students, superannuitants, sickness and other beneficiaries have an additional need to contact WINZ, but their other contact with government agencies is little different from the dominant patterns. Two other main groups have higher use than average of government Web sites. These are business groups (especially the Wellington business group) and students, whose studies may give rise to the need to find government information.

What government information and services have they used, either online or through more traditional channels, and how do they view those experiences?

All those interviewed, whether they are experienced computer users and high users of government information or have little contact with government, used a variety of channels for that contact, relying on the telephone as well as face-to-face contact to supplement any use of Web sites. All channels interact; phone use might lead to following instructions to locate information on the Web, or Web site use might lead to a phone contact or a need for personal contact to follow up. Their information seeking is based on their preferences and experiences. Use of government sites has not altered their information seeking or understanding of what is available through these sites.

Apart from the Wellington business community, which was in daily contact with government and uses government Web sites to exchange data and tender for contracts (as well as some other individuals who were also contractors tendering on the Web; or people isolated in some way by distance), few respondents had much knowledge of services on the Web or much interest in taking up any services available. They are unaware of the full potential of e-government and all (or even much) that the government provides on Web sites. They think of the sites as only providing contact and basic information, which they may need to confirm or supplement through other channels.

How they felt about their experiences of contacting government was dependent on a number of factors: their success in accessing the information sought, the time and difficulty of accessing it, and the extent to which they felt "valued" in the process. The focus on personal contact suggests a view of government as a collection of public servants rather than an impersonal entity or a monolithic portal. While the Web per se does not add value to their interaction with government, they are appreciative of the convenience of being able to access information at any time and from anywhere and of the amount of information that is now available to them. This favorable view is greatly enhanced in the case of those with special needs, such as rural people, the business community with its daily contact with government, and people with disabilities.

How do they locate the government information and services they use?

Unless they had regular contact with a particular government agency—for work, study, or personal reasons—the majority of respondents have little idea of which agency they might need to contact or how the department is internally structured. If they have some idea of the likely URL, they will try it, but the majority find which department they want, or the information they want, by using a search engine. Google was the most commonly used, although MSN featured more in the observed walk-throughs because of the home page from which the exercise started. The telephone directory (blue or white pages) is also a common way of identifying which agency they might need, or which section of a department.

Has access to the Internet changed the way in which they seek government information and services?

Most respondents did not make high use of government Web sites and felt their use was not increasing at present, largely because they had no increasing need to contact government. Only in the high-use groups was there a dramatic change in the way they made contact and interacted with government, as a result of the advent of the Internet. However, there were some cases in which agencies use incentives (Companies Office) or persuasion (WINZ) to get people to make more use of their Web sites, and there was some interest among respondents in greater use of financial incentives for this purpose.

What barriers, if any, does the public encounter in seeking government information and services both online and through traditional channels?

Barriers to the use of government information online have been defined in five categories: physical (i.e., technical and infrastructure), skills-based, attitudinal, content-based, and Web page design and architecture. In addition, lack of knowledge that the information is there, and where to seek it, inhibits use.

How might barriers be overcome?

There are several measures that respondents suggested, or that emerged in other ways from the study, to overcome these barriers. These are best addressed under the five categories:

- Physical infrastructure: Participants believed that the government could do much more to promote access to the Internet for geographically isolated or socially or economically deprived communities, helping fund groups or individuals to get computers, eliminating charges in libraries for Internet access when people were only accessing government sites, doing more to develop broadband access in rural areas, and finding some way for access to government sites to be on some form of free access code, as with 800 telephone numbers.
- Skills-based: Respondents suggested that as well as Web sites being better designed for ease of use, with user needs to the fore, these sites could also contain more online assistance and guidance. They would welcome more publicity on government on the Web, more information about the portal, and more generally available assistance on search skills, and the best way to access government on the Web. Attention could also be paid to the role the phone book plays in helping people identify which government department does what, what part of the

department they need to contact, and what e-mail and Web addresses of various sections are.

- Attitudinal: This was not an area where one might expect much change. Given the preference of many for a mixture of channels through which to communicate with government, the best strategy might be to accept the Internet as one among many channels and take care not to place too heavy a reliance on online information at the expense of telephone-based information services or print-based alternatives. Measures to reassure people that information provided (or even the fact of their accessing a Web site) was treated as confidential would be welcomed, and awareness among agencies that they should use techniques such as blind carbon copy to send out messages to groups could be fostered.
- Content-based: Protocols that required all information on a Web site to be dated would assure users of the currency of content. The desire for links between agencies (if necessary to sites outside government) would be helpful and lead to less of an impression that departments are "buried in their silos," as one participant commented, and not part of "the whole of government." Polling users to establish what information they seek (especially capturing the views of those who leave without finding what they want) would help agencies focus their Web site development on user needs.
- Information architecture: Users overwhelmingly wanted cleaner, clearer sites with better navigation aids, simple language, and fewer large chunks of text. They seek better use of color to help distinguish major navigation points, headings, and larger font sizes. They would prefer text to be in HTML, scannable, and searchable rather than in pdf format. They want forms that are easier to fill in online, and they want to be able to submit them online. Overall, they wanted a user perspective built into the site and not a site arranged and using language based on the departmental priorities. Better compliance with the W3C and New Zealand Government Web Guidelines (see www.e-government.govt.nz/docs/ Web-guidelines-2-1/index.html), with more understanding of the difficulties that people with disabilities face, would remove some additional barriers for the disabled community. Sites that attract approval from users (e.g., the DOC or MAF [Ministry of Agriculture and Fisheries] sites) could be used as examples of good Web site design. A method to identify problems with architecture and navigation would be transactional log analysis of user behavior while searching a site.

Do they consider the government portal (www.govt.nz) as a way to overcome obstacles to the receipt of government information and services?

The majority of users simply do not know of or make use of the portal, and those that have tried it do not return to it, or build it into their search strategy. Those who accidentally alight on it are unaware where they are, and do not find it easy to get from the portal to the site they want because of the lack of live links and the tendency of the portal to try to provide information directly, and duplicate information on agency Web sites. When the idea is explained to people they approve of the concept, but the portal clearly does not meet needs in the way that was intended. Consequently, the portal therefore needs to be re-examined and probably redesigned.

How much trust and confidence do the public place in the information and services that the government provides on the Internet?

The public does not seem to have any lower perception of trust and confidence in government information and services than they do of either government information and services generally, or the Internet itself. Although responses on this issue were generally positive, those who have suspicions of how government manages their personal information transfer those suspicions to Internet-based services. Only in certain groups, with particular grounds for suspecting lack of attention to their cultural needs (e.g., Maori and Pacific peoples) were additional concerns raised.

What factors affect their levels of trust and confidence?

Trust and confidence were dependent on general levels of trust in the "bureaucracy" independent of a person's judgment of the government in power. Most people put mistakes in information supplied down to human error and incompetence, rather than anything more sinister. Assurances over the currentness of information and a willingness to indicate who could be contacted raised levels of trust and confidence about information sought. Being treated courteously and having their individuality respected was an important factor in building confidence in people's relations with government agencies (this is shown clearly in negative statements made about WINZ services both on and offline).

Do they distinguish between trust in the Internet as a secure means of accessing information and services in general and trust in government Web sites for the information and services provided?

Positive perceptions of government in terms of integrity of transactions affected responses on this issue. People do not believe the government agencies would send spam, or willingly allow private information to be sold to a third party. However, they were more inclined to believe that through naïveté or incompetence there might be breaches of privacy or security at times. This was not a major concern. Some concern was expressed about the need to know the authority behind information on the Web, and whether print formats took precedence over Web material. A related issue concerned the need to find outdated material that might be evidence supporting a past decision. The lack of any established process for archiving material removed from government Web pages or any accessible public archive was a concern to many.

Do demographic characteristics (e.g., personal, educational, cultural, and geographic) influence responses to the previous questions?

To the extent that people in different occupations and in different socioeconomic groups, or with different levels of dependency through disability, sickness, or lack of employment opportunities, have different needs of government, this is reflected in the use shown. From those with minimal contact to the business group with daily contact with government, there are clear differences in frequency of use, need for specific content and services, and expertise and confidence in accessing and using government on the Web. The major motivators emerging from this study are therefore the role(s) that a person is currently playing: as taxpayer, parent, business person, advocate, activist, Maori, contractor or consultant to government, and so forth, rather than the more obvious demographic differences (see figure 11.1). The second major motivator is personal preference for certain styles of communication, and lifestyle choices.

Figure 11.1 also shows that the public identifies government on the Internet largely with information provision. However, some realized a service role, and only the Wellington business community advocated e-compliance. Finally, the public is unfamiliar with the term *e-government* and looks to government on the Internet largely for policy documents and other information.

It is evident from figures 10.3 and 11.1 that generating greater and more effective use of government on the Internet, including the government portal, will be more difficult than merely promoting its presence. The public needs to relate information-gathering from these sites to specific information needs and to determine that the information found is preferable to what they can obtain elsewhere. Furthermore, it will need to be evident to them that they can gather information with ease and understand and apply it. They also need to understand the concept of e-government, realize that it does not displace other means of access but offers more information, and that it can provide useful services, such as helping small business owners with e-compliance.

CONCLUSION

The literature on the effectiveness and efficiency of government Web sites tends to focus on performance metrics that are output based (focus on productivity, including the number served) and outcomes based (typically here the focus is on results). One type of outcome considers customer satisfaction. The marketing literature focuses extensively on service quality and often examines the match between customer expec-

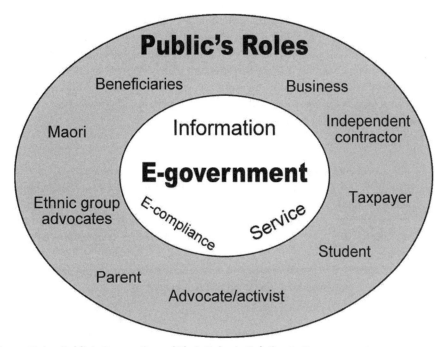

Figure 11.1. Public's Perspectives of Their Roles in Relation to E-government

tations and the service actually provided. Attention to service quality should be a central concern when government evaluates the effectiveness of its services, including the dissemination of information and services through the Internet (see chapter 13).

A key tenet of service quality is the need to understand and respond to the different markets, or audiences, for a product or service. In the case of e-government, as well as the expressed preferences of the majority of respondents, the role(s) they play in society is the primary determinant of their use of government on the Internet. Use of high-quality e-government information and services will increasingly depend on an understanding of these roles.

NOTE

1. With an e-mail submission, one businessperson mentioned that he sent an e-mail message to a minister. Presumably, a secretary logged it in and acknowledged the message. Within five weeks, he received a complete reply from the minister. Such a service provided him with a receipt and the detailed information sought. Such services "make life easier."

Appendix: Description and Transcripts of Walk-Throughs

Participants in early focus group interviews were invited to take part in an observed walk-through, searching for information on a set of preselected topics on government Web sites, to indicate how they would go about answering the questions. During April and May, these observations were conducted at Victoria University of Wellington (New Zealand) in the office of one of the investigators. Participants sat at a computer opened to a neutral Web home page and had a telephone book nearby. They were asked to show how they would go about a search to answer the preselected questions and to explain their strategy and the reasons for selecting particular options. Participants were allowed approximately ten minutes for each task (some took longer), and not all completed all five tasks within the hour allotted to each person. The tasks were developed after consultation with staff at the E-government Unit.

The tasks were:

1. The controversy over painted apple moth is in the news again. Your married daughter and grandchildren have moved into the spray zone, and you heard recently on the radio that there were new concerns over the safety of the chemicals used. You are keen to find out more about the issue, and to find MAF's reasons for doing the spraying and why they think it is safe. Where would you look?

2. You have to manage the renting out of a family property. You have some idea that there are forms that the tenant and landlord fill in as part of this process and that a bond (against damage, etc.) is sent somewhere, but you have not done this before. See if you can find the necessary information and forms on the appropriate government Web site.

3. Your recently widowed mother will have to have her pension adjusted to a

single pension, with a living-alone allowance. You think she may be entitled to some other benefits because of her declining health. What can you find out about her entitlement to these additional benefits and the living-alone allowance and how much private income she can have before losing these?

4. A friend has told you of a wonderful DOC campsite at Elaine Bay, in Pelorus Sound. You are interested in including it in your planned summer tour of the South Island. See if you can find out what facilities the site has, and if you can make a booking for the campsite for early December.

5. For research purposes you need to find the report that was issued recently stating that Maori life expectancy had increased slightly and compare this with the most recent figures on Maori health status. You thought these were issued by the Ministry of Health, and decide to start there.

Each of these tasks, except for the final one, which required some knowledge of the authors of the report, could be found by a skilled searcher by retrieving readily available sources on a government Web site. Even if the last task could not be satisfactorily completed on government Web sites, related and useful information on Maori life expectancy could be found by a skilled searcher.

The participants were:

1. A young male professional, who was experienced with computer software and applications, but his experience with government Web sites was limited. He completed four tasks in the allotted time. He had not heard of the portal, and after being told about it, stated he would not have a use for it.

2. A retired female civil servant with experience of the Web and specialized software but little general experience of government Web sites. She attempted three tasks and had used the portal in the past but did not do so after retirement.

3. A middle-aged female familiar with the Internet through personal use and as a mother, supervising children's homework, projects, and so forth. She attempted all five tasks and completed four of them.

4. A female working in an administrative/secretarial role, with good computing and general Web experience. She did not know about the portal and had never seen it. She thought it would be a good tool to use but noted the small writing on it when shown it. She commented that she likes to look at things anonymously on the Web. She attempted the five tasks and completed three of them.

5. A professional musician and mother with school-age children. She attempted three tasks and completed one.

6. A young female graduate in her mid-twenties engaged in contract work across several agencies, including government departments from time to time. She knew of the portal, which she had used to locate jobs in relation to a human resources contract, but stated she would not otherwise use it "because I know the URLs." She attempted five tasks and completed four.

SOLUTIONS TO THE TASKS

Task 1. Painted Apple Moth

On the Ministry of Agriculture home page, the major heading "Pests and Diseases" lists "painted apple moth" in its subheadings. (This is well down the page, and on most computers the user would need to scroll down to find it.) Clicking on either subheading takes the user to a page dedicated to the painted apple moth, and the user can scroll down and click on either "Answers to frequently asked questions about the painted apple moth" or "Answers to frequently asked questions by painted apple moth zone residents."

Under the "Aerial spraying" heading, the user can click on a subheading "What is involved in aerial operations" to find the information:

> An environmental impact report was prepared in 1996 when Foray 48B was used to eradicate the white spotted tussock moth. The report concluded that it is unlikely to have any long-term adverse effects on New Zealand's soils, waters, plants, food sources, mammals, birds, and fish. A publicly available independent health risk assessment carried out by the Auckland District Health Board in 2002 concluded that Foray 48B has never been implicated in any significant health effects on humans in 35 years of use.

Readers are invited to e-mail for further information.

On the main page for painted apple moth, there is also reference to an Environmental Impact Assessment of Aerial Spraying Btk in NZ for painted apple moth, with the explanatory note, "MAF is planning an eradication programme for painted apple moth using the biological insecticide based on *Bacillusthuringiensis kurstaki* (Btk)," with a link to a more detailed explanation of the chemicals used in the spray. The page also contains a phone helpline number for residents to call.

Using the portal, a search on "painted apple moth" gives a list of links, the first three of which are press releases; the fourth is a direct link to the MAF painted apple moth pages (described above). The report on health risks of these chemicals, prepared by the Ministry of Health, that gave rise to the news item was not made available on the MOH Web site until near the end of the walk-throughs. It still does not appear on the first page of results from a search on "painted apple moth" on the portal.

Task 2. Tenancy Information and Forms

This information is accessible through the Ministry of Housing Web site, but the user needs to know a URL or find some other way of accessing the site, since "Ministry of housing" does not find it. (The URL is www.minhousing.govt.nz.) On the Ministry of Housing home page there is a large notice headed "Tenancy Services," which asks "Are you a tenant or a landlord?" Clicking on the sign or the statement "Enter Tenancy Services" takes the user to a dedicated Web site. A prominent notice on the right-hand side (and a small sidebar menu) contains the headings "Tenancy Forms" and "Tenancy Information." The URL www.tenancy.govt.nz also finds the Ministry of Housing home page and the link to Tenancy Services.

On the portal, clicking on the top link, "Services," offers a page of services, on which, well down, is found the heading/link "housing, property & local environment." On the page linked from here twelve items are available. and a sidebar lists a heading for "Rental Housing" under the general heading "Housing." Clicking on this takes the searcher to another page, with another twelve miscellaneous items on it, some of the lower ones of which suggest links to Tenancy services to resolve problems that arise with tenancies. A small heading on the sidebar "Tenancy" links to a further page that has some helpful links to appropriate parts of the Tenancy Services site. Typing "tenancy" in the search box on the home page of govt.nz produces a similar set of relevant links.

Task 3. Single Superannuation and Allowances

This information is on the WINZ (Work and Income New Zealand) site. WINZ is a division of the Ministry of Social Development (MSD; at www.msd.govt.nz), which has a link to "Work and Income" in the text of its first paragraph (but no navigation link). On a sidebar menu the fourth heading links to the page "Get Financial Assistance." On this page, there is a right-hand menu bar, which includes the heading "Main benefit information." The second paragraph in the center of this page has a heading "New Zealand Superannuation" and the explanation "New Zealand Superannuation gives people a retirement income once they reach the qualifying age of 65." Further down the page are listed other benefits: invalids benefit, widows benefit, and so on. Clicking on "New Zealand Superannuation" takes the user to a long document, with structured headings at the top. Either scrolling down or clicking on "How much will I get?" the user arrives at a table that shows the "the maximum fortnightly payments for Super" and includes the category "Single (living alone)." Further down there is additional information about other benefits available to those under sixty-five and information about the amount of additional income that can be received before personal tax is levied.

Using the portal and entering the term "superannuation," the searcher is taken to a portal page on benefits, with links to information on pensions and a link further down to additional information on superannuation, and the WINZ 800 number. A large number of information documents in pdf format are listed, along with the MSD Web site.

Task 4. DOC Camp Site

(The DOC home page has been redesigned since this exercise was conducted.) On the DOC home page, there is a subheading "huts, cabins and campsites," under the major category "Explore." On the "huts, cabins and campsites" page, there are two small text links on the sidebar menu (which are also noted in the text on the page). Clicking on the heading "Conservation campsites" takes the user to a site with two further headings on the central panel: "North Island conservation campsites" and "South Island conservation campsites" (which note that they are pdf files—there is also a link to information about pdf files). More items also appear on the sidebar, notably the names of provinces where such campsites can be found.

Clicking on Nelson-Marlborough on the left-hand menu takes the user to a further Web page with a map of the region, and two further items on the sidebar, including "List of Nelson-Marlborough camp sites." Clicking on this (or the appropriate part of the map) takes the user to a page with another set of links in the center panel: five locations, of which Pelorus Sound is one. Clicking on this link takes the user further down the same page, where information about the Elaine Bay campsite is found. It is a "standard" campsite, which has a water supply, picnic tables, and toilets. Its location is given and the fact that it is accessible by road and boat.

Information well down on the "Conservation campsites" page (several pages back) states that standard campsites "generally do not have booking arrangements and operate on a first come first served basis." The same information can be found on the pdf file on South Island camp sites. The same information is available on a panel on the first page of the pamphlet (the pdf file), which also has a map, and a list of sites and facilities.

Task 5. Maori Life Expectancy

On the Ministry of Health Web site there is a heading "Maori health" in the central panel, which takes the user to the MOH Maori health pages, and a link to the separate Maori Health Web pages. However, the needed information is only available under "Publications" and is most easily found by searching MOH publications using the terms "Maori" and "life expectancy." The most recent report available is the Health and Independence Report 2002, released December 23, 2002. The user would need to search outside the site to find more recent data, available in the New Zealand Life Tables (2000–2002) on the Statistics New Zealand site, and research carried out by the staff at the Wellington Medical School, which was the source of the press release that prompted the question.

TASK COMPLETION

1. Painted Apple Moth (completed by four participants)

The first participant opened the MSN search engine, searched for MAF, and selected the home page for MAF from the resulting top hits. On the MAF home page he entered "apple" into the search box, which produced one media report. He then went back to the home page and clicked on the "Pests & Diseases" link, and on that page the sub-heading "painted apple moth," which linked to the painted apple moth page. He scanned through that page and clicked on the "Environmental Impact Report 2003" and scanned through that report. Satisfied with the information on impacts in the report and that it was commissioned by MAF, he then searched further for any updated information on the effects of spraying. He clicked on "Recent releases" and, still in search of recent reports, returned to the MSN site and searched for "apple moth + MAF," trying several links offered by the search, some of which were to MAF pages and some of which included press releases by other bodies or political parties. He finally tried the NZoom.co.nz news Web site but could not identify the press report in question. He had found all information about the spraying program that was currently on the MAF Web site.

Participant 3 also started with MSN and entered "MAF." Looking at the search results, the participant stated that she was unsure if she was looking for an official report or a newspaper report. She clicked into the MAF Web site from a link from her search, and through the "Pests & Diseases" link to the "painted apple moth" page. Scrolling though the information, she clicked on "FAQs by residents" and "Are there viable alternatives?" and finally, returning to the painted apple moth page, clicked on "Where can residents get more information?" where she found contact details for MAF and some explanation of why spraying was necessary. She was satisfied with this.

Participant 4 typed "www.MAF.govt.nz" into the address bar (stating that she usually does this if she knows or can guess the URL, otherwise she will use Google to get there). She clicked on a link to the painted apple moth pages from the MAF home page and scrolled down to "FAQs by residents," checked the task, and stated that she could click into any of the links on this page for the necessary information. She confirmed this by clicking on "What should you do if you live in or near?" and indicated that she had completed the search.

Participant 5 opened Google and entered "MAF," with a resulting set of news reports and links to the MAF Web site. Scrolling down, she rejected a page labeled "Ministry of Agriculture and Fisheries" and selected the "MAF Quarantine" page. After trying a few links here—"General enquiries" and "Border control"—she decided she was getting too far from the topic and returned to a general search page, ending up by accident on the MSN search page. Entering "painted apple moth" she got eight relevant hits listing MAF and scrolled down, reading carefully, stating that she was looking for something that mentioned health. Selecting an Auckland city site, she found she was reading a Green Party press release on the issue. She stated that she needed to look up MAF and went back to the list of hits from her search, clicking on a link to a MAF index of items on the painted apple moth. This took her to a list of press releases on the MAF Web site, so she went to the side menu bar on the left, and clicked on "research," which took her to a list of recent MAF research reports, which she scanned for a while before ending her search.

Participant 6 typed "www.maf.govt.nz" in the address bar, and on the MAF Web site, clicked on the direct "painted apple moth" link. On the painted apple moth site she clicked on several FAQ links on general topics, and the "FAQs by residents." She scrolled up and down the site and, not finding anything about health and the chemicals used, went to Google and entered "painted apple moth" and "Ministry of Health" restricting to New Zealand, and found the report, which had just been released by the Ministry of Health and was on that site.

2. Tenancy Forms

Using MSN search, participant 1 entered "tenant" and, on getting a large number of hits, amended the search to "tenant + New Zealand." Finding still a large number of hits that did not seem exactly relevant, he then entered "tenant + New Zealand + govt" and got a link to the Ministry of Housing's Tenancy Services high on the list. On this site, he clicked on "Tenancy Services" and "Tenancy Forms," then "Quick Information," which described the forms needed. He then clicked on the pdf file "Renting and you," which also describes the forms. After trying the link "Starting a tenancy," which still did not provide the link to the forms needed, he eventually identified the correct link to the tenancy forms and identified the correct form for registering a bond and a tenancy, including the property inspection form at the end of that. He commented that the link to the forms did not have an adequate explanation and that there was no direct link to the forms from several points where they were mentioned (in fact, this was not so).

Participant 2 started her search with Google, entering "Tenancy govt NZ," and selected the fourth hit in the resulting list, which was to tenancy information on the govt.nz portal. She complained that the small typeface was hard to read but did find that the portal listed a www.tenancy.govt.nz Web site, but this was not a live link. She returned to her Google search results, paused at the second link to the Ministry of Housing Web site (which she then rejected as not relevant), and continued scrolling through her original search results. She finally clicked on a link to the brochure "Renting and you" in pdf format, which she scanned before returning to the Google search list and clicking a second time on "Tenancy Agreements" (although the color of the link had changed, she was unaware that this indicated she had visited that link). The link took her to the Tenancy Services site of the Ministry of Housing, which she now realized had relevant information, and scrolled down the page to the link "Tenancy Agreements." She clicked on this and found information but no form, reexamined the site, and found the link to the tenancy forms. She commented that key links are not clear—she had passed it by because it was not obvious.

Participant 3 started with MSN, entering "tenancy/law/NZ," and clicked on the link to "Tenancy Services" that came up in the resulting list. She found the link to "Tenancy Agreements" and scanned the file looking for the relevant forms. She found the link she needed under the heading "Tenancy Forms" and retrieved the correct forms in pdf format.

Participant 4 typed "www.tenancy.govt.nz" in the address bar, which took her straight to the Tenancy Services site, where she found the tenancy forms she needed and the brochure "Renting and you." She stated that she had done this before.

Participant 5 brought up Google and entered "tenant and landlord forms in rental properties." This brought up sites from the United Kingdom and the United States, which she scrolled down, trying a site for commercial landlords in the United States. She then commented that she needed a government site and that she had maybe typed in too much information. She thought she should have put in "bond and tenants" and returned to Google to type in "bond form for tenant and landlord," which retrieved links to two Ministry of Housing Web sites. After some hesitation, she selected the first link, which retrieved the brochure "Renting and you" on the Tenancy Services site, and shortly after, she discovered the heading "Tenancy Information" and finally the "Tenancy Forms" link on the left. She was happy to find that phone numbers are also provided in this set of links.

Participant 6 knew how to find the Ministry of Housing Web site through the address "minhousing" and once there clicked on "Tenancy Services." On this page she quickly found the links "Tenancy Forms," "Tenancy Agreements," and "Tenancy Information," although she thought this was not really aimed at landlords. She knew she needed a tenancy bond form, and had found all the needed forms, but would now call them.

Task 3. Changing to Single Superannuation

Participant 1 started with an MSN search on "pension + New Zealand," and the first search result was a link to the WINZ site. Using the WINZ search box he entered the word "pension" and got an extensive list of links to war veterans' pensions. He returned to the WINZ home page and selected the heading "Get financial assistance." This listed services (but no live links, he complained), and the participant chose the heading "New Zealand superannuation." From a variety of headings he then chose "What if I need extra assistance," but this did not contain the wanted information, so he clicked on

"Living alone allowance" and scrolled up and down the pdf file at this point, finding the Table of Allowances, including the living-alone supplement. Looking for information on other income allowed, he tried "How can I get it?" and finally the heading "Receiving other income," which provided the information sought.

Participant 2 started with a Google search on "WINZ pension widow" and, on finding no relevant hits, amended this to "WINZ NZ." She clicked on the first search result, a link to the WINZ home page, stating she was not sure if this was the right place. She then looked for the site map, noting that there is a lot of information on the site, and chose a link to "Financial assistance—widows benefits." She looked at the question again, noted that the widow in the task question already had the pension, and so scrolled down through information about widow's benefits, noting the WINZ helpline. She then returned to the link in the top menu bar "What other help can I get," noting that this includes information about the community services card. She returned again to the top menu bar, selecting "Part time temporary work," which provides information about how much those on the widows benefit can earn, and then tried "What other help can I get," looking for information on the living-alone allowance. After trying the "Checklist of information" link, she went back to "Get financial assistance" by using the scroll bar at the top of the page but decided this was not helpful. She went back to Google and entered "WINZ NZ" and then amended this to "WINZ NZ living alone." From the search results list, she selected SSA.gov (a U.S. site summarizing benefits around the world), but seeing nothing of relevance to widows, she tried another link from the search results and clicked on a link to a pdf file on census information. Finally, she tried another Google search "NZ widow living allowance." Initial results from this search are to information about Irish benefits. The participant gave up at this point but in later discussion pointed out that none of the links she looked at explained that the term used for an old age pension is *superannuation,* and that widows of sixty-five and over are on this benefit.

Participant 3 searched on "widows benefit in NZ," using the MSN search facility, which resulted in a number of hits and news items. She amended the search to "benefits and allowances in NZ" and selected a link to the govt.nz portal. She scrolled through the portal (noting that it was hard to read because of the color of the text), clicking on a link to "social services," stating she was not sure she was in the right place. She went back and clicked on the "benefits and allowances" link in the portal, which provided three headings, and of these chose "retirement benefits and allowances." This also resulted in a number of results, of which she chose "Get work and income assistance," commenting again that it was hard to read the page and there were a lot of services to choose from. She clicked into a pdf file, which was a booklet entitled "How can we help you?" This did not appear to contain the needed information, but she scrolled down to a section on the widow's benefit, with the heading "Your partner has died." Commenting that there are no live links in this pdf file, she then scrolled down the page to find a number to call. Finally, she clicked back to the portal and clicked on a link on the disability allowance and declining health and then "Extra financial assistance—a guide for people on super," which is another booklet. Stating that she was not getting the information she wanted from the booklet, she said she would make a phone call at this stage.

Participant 4 typed in the URL "www.WINZ.govt.nz," to get to the WINZ home page, and clicked on "Get financial assistance." She then clicked on "Main benefit information" thinking "the lady might be able to get the sickness benefit," and when that did not look promising, the heading "Widows benefit." At this stage, not finding an answer, she said she would call the WINZ 0800 number displayed but would do so reluctantly because "you get ten different answers and it's unreliable."

Participant 5 began with the statement, "I need to know what these things are called." She then used the Google search engine and entered "single pension," searching the New Zealand pages only. Initial search results include a link to the pages headed "Get a surviving spouse pension" on the govt.nz portal and other information about superannuation and war veterans' pensions. She clicked on the first item, which took her into a pdf pamphlet-style file entitled "Extra Financial Assistance: a guide for people receiving superannuation or a war veteran's pension." She scrolled down this and found instructions about applying and a 0800 number to call. She returned to the portal and, clicking on the heading "Things to know when" on the top menu bar, selected "There's a death in the family" but decided "it's of no help. . . ."

Participant 6 typed in the address of the Ministry of Social Development (as www.msd.govt.nz) and on that site clicked on "Work and Income," a link in the central text. Looking for an index (her usual approach), she opened the site map. Under the heading "Get Financial assistance," she clicked on the subheading "Domestic purposes and widows benefits" and then, within that page, on "What other help can I get?" Within the first paragraph on that page is a reference to Family Support, which she clicked on. Finding that mainly details additional support for children under fifteen, she returned to "What other help," scrolling up and down the screen and stopping to read the tables called "How does income affect my benefit?" Nothing here seemed to answer the question, so she continued scrolling, then went back to the site map to check "Extra help," the third major heading under the "Get financial assistance" option. Rejecting this, she clicked on the alternative heading "Sickness benefits" before giving up, saying, "I don't have much patience. If I don't get it quickly, I'd call."

Task 4. DOC Campsite at Elaine Bay

Participant 1 used the MSN search tool and typed in "DOC + camp," which pulled up a wide range of information about camping in New Zealand. He then redefined his search to include quote marks around the statement, which produced an alternative range of headings. Several other search attempts were made using "DOC + campsites" and "DOC." Finally, he clicked on a link to the DOC Web site and entered "Elaine Bay" in the DOC search engine. He did not identify Elaine Bay in the resulting list of hits but clicked into a file with campsite names and prices. He tried the search again using "camp site +Elaine bay," which reduced the number of hits to seven, from which he chose "Nelson/Marlborough." Pelorus Sound came up, and a list of facilities at Elaine Bay campsites. Searching for booking information, he then went to the main DOC page and clicked on the heading "Huts/cabins/campsites," and from the left-hand menu link accessed the heading "Conservation camp sites" and on the following page "Conservation camp sites—South island," which opened a pdf file booklet, scrolling up and down looking for information on bookings. At this point the participant stated that he would call the DOC visitor center, noted at the top of the booklet. He also scanned the map showing where sites were but again stated he would call DOC.

Participant 2 used the MSN search tool and typed in "DOC NZ," which brought up several pages of links, which she scanned. She amended her search to "DOC NZ Elaine Bay" and clicked on a link about holiday homes to rent. She tried another link, which led to tourist information about Pelorus Sound and which listed a link to the DOC site. She clicked on the link, which contained information about the Elaine Bay campsite, but no booking information was found. She returned to the MSN search site and redefined the search as "DOC NZ Elaine bay bookings." This produced a number of hits, including one titled "Marlborough Sounds accommodation," which she opened, searching for accommodation in Pelorus Sound. She found a link to a DOC hut and cottage in the sound, then went back to the MSN search site, and after scanning more search results, entered "DOC NZ Elaine Bay campsites." She again found the DOC information on Elaine Bay and stated that that was the best she could do. She would call DOC at this point. She realized afterward that she had missed the main DOC site in her first search results, the search results not being very easy to read.

The third participant also opened MSN search, typed in "DOC," and went straight to the DOC Web site, where she clicked on "Explore" and found the link to "Huts, cabins and campsites." Using the left-hand menu link to "Conservation camp sites" and the link to "Conservation campsites—South Island," she opened the pdf brochure. Clicking on the map, she found Elaine Bay and Pelorus Sound. She scrolled to the end of the file without success, looking for the necessary information on bookings, and then went back to "Huts, cabins and campsites," looking for the same information without success, and decided to enter the word "bookings" in the DOC search box. Although the word appeared in lots of files, no search results appeared relevant. She tried the links "About DOC" and "Explore" again, and "Huts, cabins and campsites" without finding the information. She looked at the brochure again and found the nearest DOC visitor center, which she said she would call.

Participant 4 entered "www.DOC.govt.nz" in the address bar and on the DOC home page clicked on "Huts, cabins and campsites," under the heading "Explore." On the left-hand menu she chose "Conservation campsites—South Island," and "Nelson-Marlborough," then the map, and the link to Pelorus Sound through the map. She scrolled down through the brochure without finding any booking information, trying to click on sections to see if they were live. She returned to "Huts, cabins and campsites" before giving up, stating that the information was "too ambiguous."

Participant 5 entered "www.DOC.govt.nz" in the address bar and on the DOC home page looked for a search box and entered "Elaine Bay." One of the resulting documents lists Elaine Bay with an address, but, unsatisfied, the participant went back to Google, searching on "Elaine Bay Pelorus Sound," scrolled through the first screen of several pages of resulting search results, and added "Bookings" to the search. She scanned the resulting documents, and then decided to go back to the DOC site via its URL. She searched on "Elaine Bay book" and from several options chose the pdf brochure. She scanned the brochure and found a contact for the DOC visitor center in Nelson. After a further search on Pelorus Sound looking for a nearer visitor center, she found the Pelorus Sound center and phone number. At this point she said she would prefer to call and would not normally book online. She commented that the site is "not presented for quick information."

Task 5. Maori Life Expectancy

Participant 3 searched for "Ministry of Health" using the MSN search engine and clicked on the first result to reach the Ministry of Health Web site, where she clicked on the link to "Maori health." Server problems made continuation of the search difficult, and it was ended.

Participant 4 typed the URL "www.moh.govt.nz" into the address bar and on the Ministry of Health Web site clicked on the "Maori health" link. She clicked on "News and Issues" and scrolled through the information. She returned to the main Maori health page and tried the link "Media and Publications" but noted that there were no recent reports and no search engine on the page. Returning to the Maori health page, she tried the link "Maori health strategy" and a list of media releases without success and ended the search.

Participant 6 entered the URL for the Ministry of Health into the address bar and clicked on "Maori Health," scrolling down the page to the link for "Maori health publications," without finding anything that appeared relevant. She then entered the URL for Statistics New Zealand, saying that she knew where the life tables are found. On the Statistics site she selected the link on the left-hand menu "People and Society" and then "Maori" from the "Communities" listed on that page, and "Maori Population" from the page on Maori statistics. Scrolling down to New Zealand Life Tables she found statistics for 1995–1997. She clicked into some sections "to see what's there" and returned to the main New Zealand Life Tables, commenting "I should be in the right thing. . . . I would have thought the answer would be more obvious." She found an article under the heading "Life expectancy and death rates," which is part of the report "New Zealand Now Maori (1998)." "I knew it would be in Stats—looking for something specific, they would direct me to a Web page, so I'd persevere. I wouldn't use Google for factual information. But I'm usually impatient and will call if I need things quickly. I write down the name of whom I've spoken to, and the time, for a record."

V

RESULTS AND EVALUATION

• 12 •

Government Portals

Rowena Cullen

*M*ost commentators see the use of a gateway or portal Web site as a means of providing a one-stop-shop entry point to government information and services as a significant advancement in the maturity of e-government. Many countries include the development of such a portal in their e-government objectives and base one measure of e-government success on the effectiveness of their portal. However, the concept of a portal has not yet been standardized, and government portals around the world address the task of creating a central gateway to government information and services in a variety of ways. This chapter examines some of the definitions of *portal* in the general Web literature and the emergent e-government literature, proposes key elements for a definition and criteria for evaluation, and applies some of these elements to selected, but representative, government portals. The chapter also discusses some of the ways in which new technologies enable portals to achieve better functionality; these technologies will lead to additional advances in achieving the universal vision of seamless access and one-stop-shop access.

As the United Nations' *Global E-Government Readiness Report 2004* notes, "countries need to develop their e-government portals keeping in mind outreach, delivery and usability. Whereas a move towards specialized portals is commendable it should also be integrated within the official government portal."[1] The report commends a number of countries for their best-practice approaches to the use of integrated portals, noting the many variants. The report lists some specialized portals as examples but only identifies a few as a true e-service, one-stop-shop, or integrated portal (i.e., Singapore's e-citizen.gov.sg site, Chile's gobiernodechile.cl site, and New Zealand's www.govt.nz).

The integrated information/service portals that this chapter will examine include the following:

- Australian Commonwealth Government Entry point, www.Australia.gov.au;
- New Zealand government portal, www.govt.nz;
- United Kingdom's Directgov, www.direct.gov.uk, which provides access to the widest range of information and services; www.gateway.gov.uk is the URL for the portal to services. It requires user identification and authentication;
- U.S. official portal FirstGov, www.firstgov.gov.

Each site brings a remarkably different approach to the task of providing universal or one-stop-shop access to government information and services, and each has different strengths and weaknesses.

PORTALS: AN OVERVIEW

As yet, there is no generally accepted definition of a portal, and the definition and characteristics of a government portal are even less well specified; no existing definition fits the unique requirements of a government portal. Government portals are not the same as public portals that have a strong commercial aspect and that provide structured access to Web sites across the whole of the World Wide Web (e.g., GNN or Yahoo!—two of the earliest Web portals). They are not vertical portals that attempt to provide comprehensive access to information on a defined topic or function to a defined audience, even though there are vertical specialist portals in the government sector. Although they may focus exclusively on government information and services, government has much broader scope than does the normal range of a specialist portal. They are not corporate or education portals with a set range of tasks and functionality for well-defined user groups. Nor can they be categorized as enterprise portals, focused on a specific and authorized user group—employees, customers, or members with a defined set of roles and requiring a number of levels of access. They have a challenging and unique mission, focused on public access, for an unknown group of users who vary greatly in terms of the information and services they seek, as well as their education, background, and access to technology. Within this context government portals must try to channel users and inquiries through hundreds of thousands, and in some cases millions, of Web pages, with maximum efficiency and with maximum user satisfaction. A new definition of *information portal* seems to best capture their purpose,[2] but what is needed most of all is an understanding of the very specific requirements of government portals and the unique range of roles they play.

Wikipedia, an online encyclopedia, simply defines a portal as "a web site that provides a starting point, a gateway, or portal, to other resources on the Internet or an intranet." It also states, "They are designed to use distributed applications, different numbers and types of middleware, and hardware to provide services from a number of different sources," but adds further characteristics that may form part of a definition. "Portals typically provide personalized capabilities to their users," and "in addition, business portals are designed to share collaboration in workplaces."[3] The Open Directory Project proposes a further set of criteria and applications that are mandatory for a portal; these include: "search engine/directory," "groupware and collaboration," "knowledge management," "content management," "work flow," "multi-channel facilities," "single sign on," "business intelligence and integration of applications," "identity management integration," and "infrastructure functionality."[4] Some of these clearly refer more to an intranet environment ("groupware and collaboration," and "work flow"), but the rest are reasonable requirements for an open portal.

A number of commentators endorse these criteria; there is general consensus that the defining criteria for a portal center on the concept that "portals constitute a critical layer of middleware that enable users to customize, personalize and tailor resources and services to their unique needs and preferences."[5] Definitions of portals should "specifically include customization and personalization functions. It is these features that, inter alia, distinguish the portal from the present intranet or a general, corporate, and institutional web site."[6] Thus, a working definition of a portal is "an information infrastructure providing secure, customizable, personalizable, integrated access to dynamic content from a variety of sources, in a variety of source formats."[7] While government portals do not share the same closed and fee-paying user group as campus or enterprise portals, they are still within the same broad category of information portals, which contain these key building blocks.[8]

William Graves, co-founder of Educause's National Learning Infrastructure Initiative, the University Corporation for Advanced Internet, and the Internet 2 project, defines a portal less as a technology than as "a means to unify three aspects of a quality service environment: (1) the horizontal integration of a comprehensive set of services, (2) the personal customization of those services at the discretion of the receiver, and (3) self-service."

While portals enable the integration of services in an online self-service environment, they also can help improve customer satisfaction through the personal customization of those services. However, as Graves observes,

> self-service and personalized service have heretofore been more in opposition than not. On the one hand, "self-service" has typically described a service environment in which there is little or no human mediation . . . on the other hand, "personalized service" has typically implied a high degree of human mediation.[9]

In contrast with enterprise and educational portals, government portals, with their insistence on the one-stop-shop approach, have focused, to date, on horizontal integration rather than customization. However,

- Are customization and personal service in conflict?
- Is vertical integration a more effective approach to the unique challenges of the government portal than customization or horizontal integration?
- Does it, in this context, offer an adequate level of self-service?

If both horizontal and vertical integration are key components of a functional government portal and may, in fact, be definitional, this does not imply that all portals achieve this. True horizontal and vertical integration will require a more transformational approach to e-government, a degree of integration of services across all government agencies that is beyond the level of achievement reached by any one jurisdiction at this point in time. As William H. Graves and Kristen Hale note,

> There is only cosmetic gain in bolting a portal technology onto existing service processes because most of these service processes have been designed in a vertical, departmental paradigm that neglect the customer's desire for an integrated one-stop shop process. . . . In a portal implementation, there will be no cost efficiencies unless most service processes are redesigned and streamlined to drive out unnecessary expenses while integrating service islands.[10]

Finally, just as there are emerging levels, or stages, of e-government that jurisdictions pass through, so there may be levels or stages of government portals. The U.S.

National Electronic Commerce Coordinating Council (NEC3) has defined five levels of e-government portals:

- The first-level portal provides information and services within relatively few mouse clicks. It is functional, hiding organizational complexity and showing government as the citizen wants to see it.
- The second level offers online transactions such as vehicle registration, business licensing, tax filing, and bill payment.
- The third-level portal lets people jump from one service to the next without having to authenticate themselves again. . . .
- The fourth-level portal draws out data needed for a transaction from all available government sources. . . .
- The fifth- and highest-level portal adds value and allows people to interact with government on their own terms, providing aggregated and customized information and services in subject areas corresponding to the citizen's own particular circumstance.[11]

For example, instead of simply logging on to a motor vehicle registration Web site, users could go to a government portal, click on "my car," which would give them access to their vehicle registration and a list of their traffic citations, and they could request traffic updates for their area. A level 5 portal of this kind "will be a complex, growing organism, rich in data, transactions and multimedia—it will almost replicate society," according to P. K. Arwal, past chair of the NEC3.[12]

IMPORTANT CRITERIA FOR EFFECTIVE PORTALS (NONDEFINITIONAL)

A number of other considerations relevant to the effectiveness of portals have an impact on government portals. Critical to functionality and the achievement of the criteria above are some common Web criteria (clearly defined strategy, good architecture and design principles, usability and accessibility, interoperability, scalability, user support, compliance with standards, and evaluation). These are discussed below, with particular focus on the concept of the portal and on government portals in particular.

Portal Strategy

Critical to effective design and usability of a government portal is the overall vision it is intended to fulfill and the goals it is trying to achieve. Such a high-level plan might range from a simple marketing strategy, directed at nonresidents, to promote international business and tourism, to a primarily business focus that would reduce the costs of compliance with regulations, to making all government information available online as the primary point of access for citizens. To achieve the goal of making the government portal a one-stop shop or single gateway to government information and services, countries have adopted various strategies. These strategies are dependent on the way that portal developers define the portal concept and their understanding of how citizens will use the portal to access information and services. These decisions will determine the architecture, design, and functionality of the site. For example, will users be able to gain access to information on other government Web sites directly from the portal, or will the portal be conceived as a high-level directory, telling users what information there is on a topic and where that information can be found, before inviting them to "click through," as in the case of the New Zealand portal (www.govt.nz)?

A portal that is intended to provide access to several hundred thousands, if not millions, of individual government agency pages must be very carefully designed in terms of technical infrastructure, architecture, and design, as well as placing rigorous requirements on all linked agency sites. In many jurisdictions, the authority to demand compliance with such requirements does not exist. One such technical requirement that central governments are beginning to demand of agency sites is the quality and structure of metadata used on the Web sites of individual agencies, and the establishment of links between agency Web sites and the portal site. Creating a metadata standard applicable across a government sector, and managing its application and use, is an arduous and labor-intensive process. However, it is the only way to ensure the seamless linking of the portal to agency sites that provide the information and services to which the portal provides access. Global standards are emerging that support the application of appropriate metadata on government Web sites to enable a central portal to discover information resources, and in many countries these metadata are mandatory across government agencies. The Dublin Core Metadata Element Set version 1.1 (now also ISO Standard 15836-2003) is the most commonly used standard, with individual variations or applications created for use in individual countries (e.g., the Australian Government Locator Service [AGLS], the New Zealand Government Locator Service [NZGLS]). By contrast, the United Kingdom's E-Government Metadata Standard is an XML schema, which is related to, but is not an application of, the Dublin Core.[13]

One design approach that some government portal designers take is to define a limited number of key links, based on defined user groups, activities, and commonly asked questions, and to define these as user *channels*. These channels will generally not be the only way of accessing agency sites and services, but, in the event the user does not identify an appropriate "channel" for an inquiry, they will also be accompanied by an alphabetical index to all linked government agencies. In addition, a search facility is normally offered as a third access option to take care of inquiries where the user is not able to identify which agency he or she wants. (As noted above, effective searching across agency Web sites is still highly dependent on high-quality metadata.) Channels are emerging as a major way of providing access to information and services on government portals. Jameson Watkins, leader of the Educause portal group, endorses this approach when he states, "Channels that streamline your institution's business processes will be the most valuable parts of your portal." He defines effective use of channels as the "killer application" that will bring people to the portal.[14]

At the same time, Watkins stresses the need for portal developers to spend time at the strategy and design phase assessing and identifying the content that users will be seeking on the site. They can do this, for instance, through focus groups and pilot Web sites, so that they make the right choices about content for the limited links available on the main portal site. Such procedures assist in grouping content according to the preferences of users. In the case of government portals, the grouping might be by specific user groups or by type of information: news and media releases, policy documents, online forms, or information about entitlements in relation to the various roles of the citizen (e.g., as taxpayer, student, parent, and property owner). As part of this process the preferred language of users—the way in which they frame their requests (rather than the formal language of agencies)—needs to be identified. Content choice should also address the dominant pattern of information demands, the 80/20 rule, or Pareto effect, observed in most information systems that 80 percent of use comes from 20 percent of collection. Thus, the most-sought-after and most-used information or services, the 20 percent that will meet the needs of 80 percent of users, must be the main focus of the site, although the less used 80 percent of information/services must still be readily accessible. Channels are designed to do exactly this, but access to the less used 80 percent of material is dependent on high-quality indexing, metadata, and full and accurate directory-type services. The problem for developers is how to define the core 20 percent.

The design aspect of government portals must also be based on a careful and consultative analysis of user needs. As Christopher Rusay, a senior consultant and information architect at global portal developer Roundarch, notes:

> Citizens expect to find public information and services online. They'd like to renew drivers' licenses, file their taxes, and make their lives easier. Citizens generally do not understand the bureaucratic and organizational landscape. When looking for a permit to cut down a tree in front of his or her property, a citizen may have no idea which government agency would handle such a permit. Many government sites are difficult to use, preventing users from finding information and services because they follow their own internal structure and language instead of speaking the language of citizens.[15]

The architecture and design problems that need to be resolved in order to achieve this expectation are more complex for developers of government portals than for developers of enterprise or vertical portals because of the large number of agencies being linked and the great variety in agency structures and agency activities. Designers of government portals have a challenging task, therefore, in attempting to "balance the needs of citizens with government goals and objectives."[16] Strategic decisions about the placement of content need to be integrated with decisions about metadata structure, along with any other classification system or taxonomy used to identify the various topics/activities that can adequately represent the scope of government. Indexes based on a well-developed taxonomy need to be integrated into the search and help facilities of the portal. A highly developed, ongoing content management system should be in place to ensure that these indexes are constantly updated. Site architecture and infrastructure also need to provide for scalability as the scope of the portal broadens to include more facets of government.

To achieve a seamless integration of central portal and core agency sites requires:

- uniform look and feel (visual appearance and layout, and standardized navigation aids) of all agency sites as well as the portal;
- navigation pathways that lead back to the portal when the citizen does not find the required information or wishes to start another task;
- uniform metadata structures and taxonomies; and
- language, channels, and choices that reflect the citizen's understanding of government.

To achieve seamless integration requires a high level of centralized control of agency sites.

The development of effective portals depends on extensive research into user needs and an ability and political willingness to portray a citizen's (or a business or a marketing) perspective of government on a government portal, rather than purely a government's perspective. This is a challenge for governments and for the design of government portals and is possibly only ever partially achievable, owing to the nature of government. However, the more that government portals make the architecture of the portal site transparently clear, the more easily users will be able to find the information they seek. If government portals cannot reflect the mental models that users bring to the site, they can at least make clear the mental model lying behind the site, in the architecture, design, and even the metadata used, so that users can make their own translation into the world of government. Simple techniques of Web site architecture, navigation, and design, the use of site maps, good labeling, and mouse-over explanations of headings and links can reveal the mental model to users, but these basics of good Web practice are not always observed.

Customization versus Channels to Meet Citizens' Needs

Distinctions need to be made at the design stage among content that will reside on the portal site, content that will be linked from the portal site, and content that users will be able to find through a dedicated search engine on the site. Key decisions might focus on strategies such as leading certain major audiences away from the main site to other specialist or channel sites, such as a business interface with vertical integration or a service interface with a single authentication procedure (e.g., the United Kingdom's Gateway site). However, a strategic decision also needs to be made about whether vertical integration of related information and services (say, for business users meeting compliance requirements, or international students seeking study visas at the same time as enrolling for courses) should be maintained at portal level, on individual subportals, or at agency level.

Portal strategy also needs to determine whether customization will be supported or whether approaches to the site, and its content, will be defined by predetermined audiences, and how these will be defined: through channels, roles, or life events. Customization, which is used in a small number of sites, enables users to create their own preferred and maintained channels through the portal's offerings. If customization is a major feature of the site, there always needs to be a prominent facility to override the customization in case users need to go beyond the preselected channel. In relation to central government, citizens play many roles; on one day, they may need information to solve a business problem or to complete a business compliance requirement. That same day they may make an inquiry about educational opportunities for themselves or a dependent.

Portal software vendors continue to advocate strongly for customization for government as well as enterprise portals, and some government portals have attempted to introduce an element of customization (e.g., Singapore, Canada, U.S. state governments such as Virginia, and smaller city Web sites). For example, Singapore's main government portal offers four user channels—"Government," "Citizens and Residents," "Businesses," and "Non-residents." The "Citizens and Residents" channel offers a

"My eCitizen" customization facility and personalized services. Following an authentication process, citizens can then complete tasks such as "renewal of road tax; passport renewal notifications; library book reminders; season parking reminders; Parliament notices and alerts."[17] One important opportunity for using customization to meet user needs is the ability of customization to enable the user to make choices about presentation, rather than content. Henrike Gappa and Gabriele Nordbrock see customization as important in allowing users with disabilities to customize their access to frequently sought information according to their own particular needs.[18] However, in general, customization is not the preferred way for government portals to streamline their services; most agencies prefer channel strategies. As Web usability guru Jakob Nielsen notes, it is better to design sites for ease of access to the information contained in them than to require customers to spend time personalizing and customizing sites, with the necessary exchange of information this entails.[19] It remains to be seen whether customization will reappear as a key strategy for government portals as more of them reach the fourth and fifth levels defined by Holmes.

The European Community's e-government project, eGOV, which focuses on the concept of "an integrated platform for realizing online one-stop government," also includes personalization and customization in its objectives, alongside a channel approach based on life events and business situations.[20] The definition of life events is, in itself, a complex aspect of government portal development. Should it be focused around user-based research and definitions or a technical standard? The eGOV project follows a technical standard—the Government Markup Language (GovML) format for XML documents, which describes public services and life events and which is a form of an RDF or XML metadata set.[21] This approach, linked with unified modeling language (UML) modeling of life events, supports citizens' portals at national and local government levels. The UK portal, Directgov, has adopted a life-events approach to its portal strategy and design. Eleven life events were defined in its first life-events portal, which included: "Having a baby," "Your choices at 16 +," "Looking for a job," "Going away," "Dealing with crime," "Death and bereavement," "Starting a new school," "Learning to drive," "Pensions and retirement," "Moving home," and "Looking after someone."[22] In more recent versions of Directgov these events are dispersed among a variety of user categories and topics, as increasing numbers of life events are added and as the portal attempts to reflect the complexity of twenty-first century life and the impossibility of defining the core 20 percent of uses in such oversimplified terms. If they are to work, models of life events must be carefully designed to be user- or citizen-centric.

Usability

Usability issues for government portals differ little from standard usability criteria for Web sites. Screen design and color, the use of white space, navigation aids, managing links, designing with style sheets to preserve the look and feel on all platforms, avoiding frames, and using text designed for the Web not for A4 pages are all important criteria; they are well covered in any standard treatise on Web usability.[23] Additional usability features related to portals include designing for the novice user, the length of time it takes to load portal pages, access links, authentication, single-click shortcuts back to the main portal page, enhanced browser and platform compatibility because of the complex tasks carried out by the site, and the level of personalization.[24] Usability is not the same as accessibility. All developed government portals attempt to comply with Web accessibility guidelines based on the W3C Web Accessibility Initiative. However, since portals are more complex than Web sites, they are often less successful in applying Web accessibility principles.[25]

Technical issues also have a considerable impact on the usability of government portals and the degree to which they achieve interoperability between agency sites. Although few standards have been established, several international working groups have been created to define appropriate standards for the government sector. Through projects such as eGOV and the work of various government agencies overseeing e-government within each jurisdiction (e.g., the Office of Management and Budget in the United States and the E-government Unit in New Zealand), technical standards are slowly being developed. The Office of Management and Budget, for example, requires agencies to consider a range of interoperability standards, including Java 2 Enterprise edition for distributed application code: Java Specification Request for portlet development;[26] section 508 for disability access; triple DES FIPS 140 security; and Web-services standards: Web Services Description Language, Web Services for Remote Portals, and Simple Object Access Protocol.[27]

Even with national and international standards in place, interoperability presents one of the major technical problems that portals face, and many e-government programs address it (e.g., the New Zealand e-GIF program). Portals necessarily bring in, group, and organize content from a variety of information sources or legacy systems such as Word documents, Web pages, or databases in a variety of software. A problem is that portal providers may not have portlets suitable to integrate with every legacy system, and portlets from one portal provider may not integrate with or interoperate with another portal's specification. For example, portlets written with Java Server Page technology do not interact with Active Server Page portlets. That means that portal providers or integrators must adapt content to a format the portal understands—using HTML, XML, or Wireless Mark-up Language. This task can be labor-intensive, and it can affect functionality by reducing the portal server's ability to leverage personalization services.[28]

EVALUATION

Evaluations of government portals, if judged by some of the major reports on e-government ratings and success, provide little guidance as to how to determine portal effectiveness. The United Nations' *Global e-Government Readiness Report 2004* makes a number of relatively superficial judgments about the effectiveness of individual portals, and it considers the existence of a national portal as one measure in e-government readiness rankings,[29] although the report does not really measure the effectiveness, scope, and functionality of such a portal. FirstGov in the United States is highlighted as a "best practice model,"[30] Korea's portal is described as "a model approach to an integrated online portal,"[31] the multilingual capabilities of the Canadian and the Belgian portals are praised,[32] and Singapore's many specialist portals are described as "innovative."[33] However, these judgments do not appear to be based on any clear criteria or analysis of how well these portals work; research evidence suggests that these portals may not be as successful as the rhetoric implies.[34]

One set of criteria that has been applied to educational portals defines the attributes that can be expected in any well-developed proprietary portal software: ease of use, maintainability, potential for personalization, availability of single-sign-on authentication, ease of customization, ease of integration with existing services, platform independence, performance, expandability (scalability), and conformity to open standards.[35] To these could be added the usability and accessibility criteria noted above and evidence of use and value to citizens. Some measures of content scope and the advancement of open government might also be appropriate, if portals are to serve as a way to make government decision making more open and ensure accountability; in other words, a government portal might be judged on more than just its effectiveness in providing core information and services. This approach might suggest a more useful list of criteria for evaluating government portals, especially if personalization and customization have not necessarily been accepted as the preferred option over the clear definitions of user channels.

CASE STUDIES OF GOVERNMENT PORTALS

This section discusses four government portals that illustrate the range of policies and strategies, architecture, and design approaches being used in the sector. The examples are not comprehensive, but they highlight aspects of these sites to demonstrate the present understanding of best practice at this stage of government portal development.

FirstGov

The U.S. federal government's portal, FirstGov (www.firstgov.gov), considers itself as "the Official U.S. gateway to all government information" and claims "whatever you want or need from the U.S. government, it's here on FirstGov." FirstGov provides links to "millions of pages from federal and state agencies," has an alternative Spanish-language portal, and provides for multichannel access to government by offering "to help you find and do business with government online, on the phone, by mail, or in person." It has cross-agency subportals focused on particular groups of users (e.g., students, people with disabilities, and exporters) and customer gateways based on specific user roles (e.g., citizens, businesses and nonprofits, and federal employees). The Spanish version of the portal carries very much the same information on its home page, and at least two levels of information below this is in Spanish in the majority of cases, but for other languages users are directed toward the site of the Federal Citizen Information Center of the General Services Administration, which has links to fairly limited information in twenty-four other languages.

The FirstGov home page is relatively compact, with clear tabs to indicate where information for each category of user is available—creating effectively four basic homepages, or user channels although the user is always offered the citizens' homepage on re-entering the site. This is not surprising since OMB do not permit the use of persistent cookies (necessary to track users activities, and permit a level of personalization on a recurring basis) on federal Web sites unless stringent privacy conditions are met.[36]

FirstGov has a privacy policy, accessible by clicking on a button in the bottom navigation bar, which states that "we will collect no personal information about you when you visit our site unless you choose to provide that information to us." FirstGov uses only per-session cookies that collect information that does not personally identify a user.[37]

On design and usability the site performs well on standard criteria. Good design factors include the use of color to mark key information categories, clear navigation aids, and no information hidden below the fold since it is clear that the user should scroll down. The look and feel of the site are welcoming without being too official and busy, and the site has a very patriotic U.S. look in its strong red, white, and blue theme. Usability is possibly more open to criticism—although the language (apart from the term "cross agency portals") is clear and succinct, there are so many ways offered to the user to access information that confusion rather than clarity could be the end result, and the choice of which is the appropriate one is not always easy. The major user groups are identified by page-top tabs ("for citizens," "for businesses and nonprofits," "for federal employees," and "government to government"), but sidebars on both sides of the page offer options by type of information (although not all users would know that the Reference Center is the place to look for information on public holidays or how to contact government, etc.). The center of the page offers a well-crafted set of topics leading to more options on similar topics, and right-hand sidebar options, below news and events, offer an additional breakdown of audiences (e.g., kids, parents, and seniors), although these end up rather hidden below the fold. Other important links ("about us," "Site index," "frequent questions," "help," "Español," and "other languages") are on the top navigation bar. A search engine offers options for narrowing the scope of the search (searching federal or state sites only) and advanced search. There is a site map, and the search facility is powerful and offers search tips.

While the user is still on the portal's pages, breadcrumbs[38] help with orientation on this complex site. However, many links on the home page take the user immediately into the site of an other agency, and navigating out of and back into a portal is more difficult than navigating Web pages belonging to one agency. Few agency sites provide a quick link back to FirstGov for the user who has left the portal site and wants to return. Accessibility issues are highlighted on some agency sites but are not at all evident on others. FirstGov itself is by no means fully compliant with standard accessibility criteria, when tested by the Watchfire WebXACT Web site, which applies the W3C Web Accessibility Initiative criteria.[39] Customization and personalization for routine access to specific content, or for formatting text for users with disabilities, are not possible. Only individual agency sites offer authentication to support protected information or transactions, so there is no attempt made at single-sign-on. There were a large number of broken (or at least temporarily unavailable) links, perhaps not surprising among so many.

A key principle of the FirstGov portal since its early days has been the three-clicks principle, based on the Implementation Plan for e-Government Act of 2002, which remains as a plank in the Bush administration's e-government strategy, and which is used as a measure of success. The three-clicks strategy has increased "the number of unique site visitors dramatically, from 5 million in FY01 to over 28 million in FY02."[40] However, there is no evidence provided that the policy was responsible for this increase in use of the site. Nor is there any general research data supporting the claim that if users cannot find what they are looking for within three clicks, they are likely to get frustrated and leave a site. As Josh Porter, a researcher at Usability Interface Engineering, notes:

> Our analysis showed that there wasn't any more likelihood of a user quitting after three clicks than after 12 clicks. When we compared the successful tasks to the unsuccessful ones, we found no differences in the distributions of task lengths. Hardly anybody gave up after three clicks. . . . For both successful and unsuccessful clickstreams, we see it isn't until 15 clicks that we see 80% of our tasks completed. Successful clickstreams have the same distribution as unsuccessful clickstreams—the number of clicks doesn't predict task success or failure.[41]

While core information can be readily found through FirstGov, and often within three clicks, the site does not yet meet its claim of providing "whatever you want or need from the U.S. government." Although all agencies are required to participate with FirstGov, they do not include all of their information and records here. Important information sources such as the *Congressional Record* and other "serials" are not indexed by content. Distinctions between different kinds, and the authority, of information found are not made, for example, reports versus press releases. The site is immense, and although it makes a worthy attempt to explain the structure of the U.S. government to users, assistance to users is not entirely adequate. For example, "cross-agency portals," one of the key features of FirstGov, and critical to the achievement of its three-clicks policy, is buried among the links to federal and state agencies, and the label is not instinctively meaningful for uninitiated users. The opportunity to use a more user-friendly mouse roll-over explanation of its meaning and purpose is not taken.

The United Kingdom's Directgov

The United Kingdom's portal, Directgov, which was completely redesigned in 2005, has a very different approach to the provision of access to government information and services from FirstGov. The site has a primarily informational and educational focus, providing explanations about government agencies and entitlements and how citizens register for various services. It provides advice on parenting, money management, getting tax reductions, and staying healthy and highlights topical chat rooms for citizens' participation. It is a colorful site, dominated by bands of bright orange and yellow, with the style of a popular newspaper or magazine. It is aimed at citizens, although there is a link at the bottom of the page to links for business, which eventually lead to the companion business portal Business Link. A life-events approach is preferred to a channel approach, although, among the many options for citizens on the home page, certain categories of citizens (e.g., parents, disabled, and over fifties Britons living abroad) are highlighted. Topics featured center page include "education," "motoring," "employment," "health," "leisure," "travel," and "crime," and a prominent right-hand sidebar features additional topics (e.g., "car tax," "disability living allowance," and "electoral roll"). Navigational aids at the top of the screen are to: "Directories," which links to alphabetical lists of central government agencies, as well as local and regional bodies, and is the place where policies on which the government is currently consulting the public are found; "Guide to Govt," which describes the structure of the UK government, the monarchy, the judiciary, and the European Union and Parliament; "Do it online," which links to a range of services and online transactions from reporting crime to registering to vote or filing a tax return; and "Newsroom" (government press releases). Wherever possible, detailed information is provided before links and addresses to external agencies are provided.

High on the page are a few standard tools—"helpdesk," "site index," "contacts," and a link to the accessibility statement. The helpdesk focuses on advice on downloading Webcasts and pdf files, as well as frequently asked questions (FAQs) based on popular topics and advice on how to use the search engine. (This does not explain, however, that default search is for terms to be combined with OR, the opposite of what happens on Google and other commonly used search engines.) Side displays show users where they are in relation to the main topic selected and the link to the nearby home page.

A full privacy statement, referring to the Data Protection Act, is available through a button at the bottom of the page. It acknowledges that cookies are used but does not state whether this relates to per session or permanent cookies. The privacy page has links to the E-Govt Unit, Freedom of Information Act, and the Parliamentary and Health Service ombudsman's office where complaints about government agencies are made. The home page has no high-level accessibility errors, when tested by the Watchfire WebXACT Web site.

A parallel vertical portal, Business Link, offers an extensive range of information about doing business in the United Kingdom, online forms, and a few online transactions (e.g., filing and paying tax), which require registration and user authentication. Authentication is obtained from a third site, the Government Gateway, which operates as a single-sign-on portal to, at present, a limited range of government services online (at both national and local-body levels). The clear intent of both Business Link and the Government Gateway is to increase the number of online transactions substantially as these become available from individual agencies. Neither of these is easily accessible from the main portal site.

The new United Kingdom portal has focused on citizens' immediate needs for information about their interactions with government in their daily lives. It does not appear to attempt to provide access to government information in the form of policies, legislation, regulations, and other documents relating to the democratic process. In this way it virtually changes the definition of a government portal from one of access to government information to a form of online citizens' advice bureau.

The Australian Government Entry Point

The Australian government portal (www.Australia.gov.au), by contrast, has a clean and simple look, which on lower-level browsers converts rather too quickly to text only. The site provides links to "over 700 Australian Government web sites, indexes more than 5,000,000 pages and uses both metadata and full text indexing to ensure it is a comprehensive government portal."[1] The site has three main tabs: "Information for,"

"Browse by subject," and "Online services." The site employs a channel strategy as its main way of providing access to information, and under the main tab "Information for" offers a range of channels: "Australians travelling," "businesses," "communities," "families," "indigenous peoples," "jobseekers," etc. Subject headings under "Browse by subject" are clear, user-friendly, and comprehensive. Quicklinks are provided on a left side menu to key government information, all departments and agencies, and state and territory web sites. There is also a link to the separate Business portal, where businesses are directed to topics such as "start up a business," "invest in Australia," "business information," "employer responsibilities," and "grants & financial assistance." Clicking on any of these might take the user to a specialized Web site or portal, or another set of links on an Australia.gov.au page. It is rare to go more than two or three clicks without getting an agency page. The key channels remain visible on a new side menu one the subpages of the main portal.

Although design is uncluttered, the site makes use of standard navigation aids, using breadcrumbs to assist users in moving backward and forward through the layers of the site, until they leave the site. There is a key to the symbols beside links that warn the user whether a folder or a link to a new site is being offered. There is a prominent search box, which also offers an advanced search facility. Important government notices (travel advisories and health warnings) are central on the page, and news releases well-placed on a right-hand menu. Key issues on which the government is inviting citizens to "have your say" are also featured on the home page. The page is spacious, attractive, and informative and combines a range of types of access to information, by channel or topic, through effective design and architecture. Its simplicity, however, does not mean it meets all Watchfire WebXACT criteria for accessibility. Standard links (privacy, copyright, disclaimer, copyright, accessibility, and a site map) are provided at the bottom of the page; the privacy statement explains that although server addresses and browser types are recorded, e-mail addresses are not captured. Furthermore, the statement indicates that the site does not use cookies or web bugs.

New Zealand's "Classic Portal" Site

The New Zealand government portal (www.govt.nz), which was until recently almost as minimal in design as the Australian portal, has been recently relaunched with more color, style, and functionality. Like the UK site, it is less a gateway to government than an information service about government. Describing itself as "your front door to New Zealand Government online," the portal offers access to information and services on a range of selected topics. The two main access points are "government services," which links to services listed alphabetically under common subject headings (e.g., "arts and culture," "employment,' "licences, certificates, permits," and "social welfare and services"), each of which has supplementary links underneath to subcategories of the topic; and "A-Z government," another alphabetical list on a linked page, with built-in cross-referencing from commonly used names to the proper name used in the portal; this is a very helpful feature. Beneath these primary access points, links to "things to know when . . . ," "Maori," "participate in government . . . ," and "about New Zealand" offer commonly sought information and services and subpages of the portal considered to have special significance or value. The band beneath this level offers current items of news from government, and on the bottom band (rather inconspicuously) are the necessary statements about privacy, security, and copyright, as well as "about govt.nz," and a link to online "government jobs."

A brief privacy statement indicates that the Privacy Act governs the collection of use data and that no personally identifying information is collected—only statistics used to improve the site and its content. The search button (basic search only) offers the user a search of services or organizations, a strategic decision about the scope of information available on the site. However, not all user inquiries necessarily fit into one of these two categories, and this may be one reason for the high rate of failure of users to find information, as reported in chapter 11. The scope of the site does not yet match user expectations. A site map is not offered on the home page.

The design is clean and functional with an attractive color scheme shading from light orange through to dark brown. Lettering on the bottom bar is in a rather small font, but the home page sits well on one screen with very little below the fold on most browsers. Breadcrumbs offer users a clear indication of where they are on the site once they have left the home page, and on these secondary pages all major navigation links are visible on the top menu bar. While the portal links out to agency sites, not all agency sites have a link back to the portal. All text on the home page is in English with Maori versions in smaller type underneath. On the Maori subpage, headings are in Maori with English translation, but there is no actual content in Maori. The site does not appear to use a design concept focused on audiences or channels the way the U.S., U.K., and Australian pages are. Rather, it is focused on tasks that users might want to carry out, and a view of what kind of information or services might be needed, although the "What to know when . . ." pages are designed around a concept of life events that give rise to a need for specific information and services. Watchfire WebXACT reported no high-level errors of accessibility.

The New Zealand portal takes a different approach to how best to help citizens gain access to government information and services. Unlike the three-click approach, its pages are focused on giving basic information and describing what services are available, before indicating where the information is held, or how to contact the specific agency that provides a service. Thus, users who click on "things to know when," and then on the following page select "appearing in court," and then decide that the link "speak Maori in your courtcase" covers the information and service they need, are linked to a further page (still part of the portal itself), which explains their right to do so and informs them that they will need to write for a brochure and an application form. The address of the Ministry of Justice and its phone and e-mail access details are noted. Thus, the third or fourth page that users find provides information about the agency they must contact online or off-line for the service or information they want. Although this policy fits the multichannel (phone, online, or face-to-face) policy of the New Zealand e-government strategy, it can lead to user frustration, since on longer agency pages, with several different physical addresses listed, the URL address of the agency Web site is not visible. It can be difficult to exit the site and reach the desired agency. The portal seems to hold users longer than necessary, before linking them to the agency site that contains full information.

In summary, the four portals use a variety of strategies to help citizens gain access to government information and services. Two portals (FirstGov and the Australian government entry point) use a channel strategy to define similar key user groups (business, citizens, nonresidents, and government to government), and two (DirectGov and the

New Zealand portal) approach the task as an information service that may or may not require the user actually to gain access to the relevant agency Web site. In this approach life events and tasks that users might want to complete play a more dominant role, but these features are also part of FirstGov. All four portals take very different approaches to basic design issues, the strategy by which they will link users to the information they seek, and the importance of linking users directly and as early as possible with agencies. They all have well-developed infrastructure and rely on highly developed metadata standards and taxonomies, but none provides a very effective search capability, suggesting that these are not yet well mapped to user-defined language. None provides universal access to government information in all formats. They have made choices of what to present to users, although this is not always clear to users. None is able to make clear to users the mental model informing the portal.

Surprisingly, after substantial investment and several iterations, the four sites barely represent the first three levels of the NEC3's five levels. Although some have related vertical portal sites supported by government, primarily in the business sector, the portals themselves remain at a fairly low level. The U.S. portal offers a large number of forms online, but agency-based authentication is needed to file a form online. This is also true of the Australian and New Zealand sites. None therefore reaches full level 2 status and certainly none meet the criteria of providing "secure, customizable, personalizable, integrated access to dynamic content from a variety of sources, in a variety of source formats," which would equate to the NEC3's level 4. While they would all claim to offer horizontal integration of a comprehensive set of services, they have opted for self-service rather than customization and in some cases favor advice over direct access.

FUTURE DEVELOPMENTS

It is generally accepted that portal development is in its infancy, and those working in the field predict a new generation of portals with enhanced capabilities. As portal developer and editor Ali Jafari notes:

> We need the next generation of portals to have some level of autonomy, making informed, logical decisions and performing useful tasks. We need to consider the use of artificial intelligence in framing the next generation of portals, and in developing their capabilities for learning about their users. And finally, we would like future portals to have some learning ability.[43]

This is a vision primarily focused on education portals, and it would be a significant undertaking for government portals, with their extensive range of contributing agencies, millions of pages, and potentially billions of users worldwide. However, the vision of future government portals could well include these concepts of autonomy, trainability, and expertise.[44]

Such developments are dependent on technologies that are already available and that are starting to be used in some of the most advanced commercial, educational, and enterprise-based portals; they are being tentatively applied to government portals. Some of the more sophisticated portal software packages are capable of generating taxonomies based on metadata using a dynamic-reasoning engine and would fit this model of an autonomous, trainable portal based on artificial intelligence.[45] However, their success will also be dependent on advances in metadata technology.

Tools and techniques of the Semantic Web,[46] especially the use of ontologies and Topic Maps, will be a critical technology in providing better access to content and greater relevance in information retrieval.[47] Ontologies and Topic Maps extend the value of the taxonomies, thesauri, and controlled vocabularies currently used in metadata systems to identify and link relevant material on agency Web sites to a central portal, such as the government locator systems used in Australia[48] and New Zealand,[49] Canada,[50] and the United States.[51] Taxonomies and thesauri relate classes and subclasses of objects but do not express any more complex relationships between terms and concepts used. Ontologies and Topic Maps, by contrast, extend these somewhat linear relationships between concepts by capturing the relationships not only between classes of things but also between instances of that class of things; relationships, properties, and values of those things; functions and processes involving those things; and constraints on and rules involving those things.[52] Topic Maps, which is an emerging Web standard for organizing information, represent a technology

> that has arisen in recent years to address the issue of semantically characterizing and categorizing documents and sections of documents on the Web with respect to their *content*—in other words, what topics, or subject areas those documents actually address. . . . Topic Maps provide a content-oriented index into a set of documents, much like the index of a book, but with this qualification: an index of a book does not typically characterize that book as a set of linked topics, but rather as a set of mostly isolated references with occasional cross-references to other subjects.[53]

Topic Maps and ontologies can be developed with specific reference to aspects of government activity to support a vertical or specialized portal. For example, access to legislation and regulations is the focus for an annual conference, sponsored by the International Federation of Library Associations, the International Workshop on Regulatory Ontologies, which centers on modeling regulatory and legal knowledge and the parsing of legal texts.[54]

Topic Maps have been developed extensively in Norway and are used to support a number of specialist or vertical government portals, such as the Norwegian Research Council site for popular science and research information (see www.forskning.no) based on ZTM (Zope content management software combined with Topic Map technology in an open-source software).[55] These are not yet integrated into a single government portal, although Topic Maps, "the building blocks of seamless knowledge," are usually constructed with the capacity for integration with each other and are rapidly leading the way toward true superhighways of knowledge, as the Norwegian portals become more and more extensive. The European Parliament has also adopted the Semantic Web and Topic Maps technology to support its visions of high-level information and service access based on the principles of logical rather than physical object identification, "no wrong door" for users, and a multilingual approach to content.

According to Peter Brown, information resource manager for the European Parliament, Topic Maps are "more abstract and complex but better supported and more powerful" than resource descriptor frameworks, based on XML technology, used by most portals.[56] Standards for Topic Maps (ISO/IEC JTC 1/SC34) are found on the

U.S. Department of Energy's National Nuclear Security site (www.y12.doe.gov/sgml/sc34/) but do not appear to be applied to any U.S. federal Web sites.[57]

There is a growing recognition that the Semantic Web, with its focus on identifying and capturing the semantic relationships between various ways of describing information/services within agencies, is the essential tool that will bring the next stage in portal development, the stage that will put into effect the concept of seamless access and a true one-stop shop for citizens. The Semantic Web has the ability to create and capture metadata in a variety of languages—Spanish, French, Chinese, English, Maori, and so on—as well as the differences between technical, agency-based, and citizens' preferred terms. It also has the capacity to capture the relationships among government agencies and some of the entities, or *logical objects* that represent their activities, responsibilities, and roles. Thus, an ontology of government, unique to each jurisdiction, can be created that will provide the infrastructure necessary to achieve the vision of seamless interoperability.

Some jurisdictions have already begun this challenging task. The team behind the New Zealand government portal, for example, is using techniques of the Semantic Web to develop new elements in the NZ Government Locator Service metadata. For example, the metadata element "mandate" allows for a link to be created from an agency to the legislation that empowers that agency and its activities, or that the agency administers, and a new record type ("role") allows the metadata to express the relationship between the prime minister and the monarch's representative, the governor-general, or between a minister and government agencies for which he or she is responsible. This will enable a picture of government in New Zealand to be created through relationship-based metadata.

CONCLUSION

Two questions remain unanswered:

1. Do these forward-looking technologies present the solution to the present incompletely achieved vision of one-stop-shop access to government information and services?
2. Would customization provide a better solution than the current channel strategies in use, the life-events approach, or the citizens' advice bureau approach?

The examples discussed in this chapter do not represent a vision of complete access to government information in the way envisaged in the early days of e-government. Many of the documents that were part of the initial impetus—the policy papers, critical reports, and access to legislation and regulations—have become lost in trying to meet the information needs of the average citizen and to provide the core 20 percent of information that is most in demand. Government publications should not be buried in the deep or invisible Web;[58] they should be openly accessible. Perhaps a vertical portal approach, where official publications are treated as a separate channel, as important to democracy as the business channel is to economic growth, will emerge as the main government portal becomes more and more focused on the routine interactions of government and citizens. Participation in e-government requires more than online access to these routine interactions and the limited range of issues highlighted for citizen consultation on a government portal Web site.

Portals are clearly a key element in the achievement of e-government, and in the implementation of the vision of e-government within most jurisdictions. They are critical to the achievement of the goal of the seamless, one-stop-shop access to government information and services. In achieving this they have an immense task to do in identifying the core information and services sought by citizens in a multiplicity of roles, in identifying the various activities and services in agencies that correspond to these information and service needs, and in establishing and maintaining the infrastructure necessary to the management of access. At the same time, they have an equally important part to play in ensuring that they do not obscure access to the vital policy reports and instruments of government decision making to which citizens also need seamless access.

While there are some notable examples of portal development in the government sector, these fall far behind some of the standards and benchmarks being set in other sectors. To move toward the higher levels of government portals, as defined by Douglas Holmes, the fourth and fifth levels of truly integrated information and services will require an investment in the new technologies of the Web, a political commitment to break down the existing barriers between agencies, and an ability to span the full range of government information in whatever format it is found. It will require closer attention to, and the development of, further internationally agreed standards; constant attention to site strategy, architecture, and design; ongoing and more intensive research into user needs; and an adoption of ontologies that can capture the world of government that the portal is trying to portray to users. If these are attended to, the government portal of the future may become the "complex growing organism, rich in data, transactions and multimedia [that will] almost replicate society."[59]

NOTES

1. Australia. "Australia.gov.au: About This Site." Available at http://www.Australia.gov.au/index.php?about, accessed May 19, 2005.

2. Pieter van Brakel, "Information Portals: A Strategy for Importing External Content," *The Electronic Library* 21 (2003): 591–601.

3. Wikipedia: The Free Encyclopedia is available at http://en.wikipedia.org/wiki/Main_Page, accessed May 13, 2005.

4. The Open Directory Project, also known as DMoz, is a multilingual, open-content directory of World Wide Web links owned by Time Warner. A community of volunteer editors constructed and continues to maintain it. The directory is generally considered to present consensus knowledge on Web matters.

5. R. N. Katz and L. Goldstein, "Portals: Summing up" in *Web Portals and Higher Education: Technologies to Make IT Personal,* ed. R. N. Katz (San Francisco: Jossey Bass, 2002), 152–62.

6. van Brakel, "Information Portals," 594.

7. Michael Alan Smith, "Portals: Toward an Application Framework for Interoperability," *Communications of the ACM* 47, no. 10 (October 2004): 93–97.

8. Smith, "Portals."

9. William H. Graves and Kirsten Hale, "Portals: Your Institution's Reputation Depends on Them," in *Designing Portals: Opportunities and Challenges*, ed. Ali Jafari and Mark Sheehan (Hershey, PA: Information Science Publishing, 2003), 37.

10. Graves and Hale, "Portals: Your Institution's Reputation," 38.

11. Douglas Holmes, *eGov: eBusiness Strategies for Government* (London: Nicholas Brealey, 2001), 23.

12. Holmes, *eGov,* 24.

13. UK GovTalk, "Metadata" (London: Cabinet Office, n.d.). Available at www.govtalk.gov.uk/schemasstandards/metadata.asp, accessed May 30, 2005. An XML schema is a set of rules for defining the structure, content, and semantics (vocabulary) used in the XML documents that constitute the UK government Web pages.

14. Jameson Watkins, "Developing a Portal Channel Strategy" in *Designing Portals: Opportunities and Challenges,* ed. Ali Jafari and Mark Sheehan (Hershey, PA: Information Science Publishing, 2003), 51.

15. Christopher Rusay, "User-Centered Design for Large Government Portals," *Digital Web Magazine* (January 16, 2003). Available at http://digital-web.com/articles/user_centered_design_for_large_government_portals/, accessed May 18, 2005.

16. Rusay, "User-Centered Design," 2.

17. My e.Citizen: Personalized services for you, available at http://my.ecitizen.gov.sg/portal/dt, accessed June 1, 2005.

18. Henrike Gappa and Gabriele Nordbrock, "Applying Web Accessibility to Internet Portals," *Universal Access in the Information Society* 3 (2004), 85.

19. Jakob Nielsen, "Personalization Is Over-rated," *Alertbox* [an irregularly issued column at useit .com: Jakob Nielsen's Web site] (October 4, 1998). Available at www.useit.com/alertbox/981004.html, accessed May 18, 2005.

20. Maria A. Wimmer, "A European Perspective towards Online One-Stop Government: The eGOV Project," *Electronic Commerce Research and Applications, 2002.* Available at www.egov-project.org/egovsite/wimmer_icec2001.pdf, accessed May 19, 2005.

21. Gregory Kavadias and Efthimios Tambouris, "GovML: A Markup Language for Describing Public Services and Life Events," *Lecture Notes in Computer Science* 2645 (2003): 106–13.

22. Archived at the E-envoy site at http://archive.cabinetoffice.gov.uk/e-envoy/about-servicetransformations-dooline/$file/uk_online_portal.htm.

23. See, e.g., Jakob Nielsen, *Designing Web Usability* (Indianapolis, IN: New Riders, 2000) or his usability heuristics available on his Web site, www.useit.com.

24. Ali Jafari, "The ABCs of Designing Campus Portals," in *Designing Portals*, 7–27.

25. Gappa and Nordbrock, "Applying Web Accessibility to Internet Portals."

26. Portlets are reusable Web components that display relevant information to portal users. Portlet standards enable developers to create portlets that can be plugged in any portal supporting the standards. Portlet specifications enable interoperability between portlets and portals, e.g., in relation to the areas of aggregation, personalization, presentation, and security.

27. Bruce Boardman and Sean Doherty, "Portals: Agencies through the Looking Glass," *Government Enterprise,* June 2, 2002. Available at www.governmententerprise.com/showArticle.jhtml?article ID = 17501644, accessed June 13, 2005.

28. Boardman and Doherty, "Portals: Agencies through the Looking Glass," 3.

29. United Nations, *Global E-Government Readiness Report 2004*, 164.

30. United Nations, *Global E-Government Readiness Report 2004*, 28.

31. United Nations, *Global E-Government Readiness Report 2004*, 32.

32. United Nations, *Global E-Government Readiness Report 2004*, 29–30.

33. United Nations, *Global E-Government Readiness Report 2004*, 33.

34. Rowena Cullen and Peter Hernon, *Wired for Well-Being: Citizens' Response to E-Government* (Wellington: State Services Commission, 2004), 60. Available at www.e.govt.n2/resources/research/vuw-report-200406, accessed May 13, 2005.

35. Jafari, "The ABCs of Designing Campus Portals."

36. Office of Management and Budget (OMB), Memorandum 00-13: "Privacy Policies and Data Collection on Federal Web Sites" (Washington, DC: OMB, 2000).

37. Accessible on the FirstGov home page or at www.firstgov.gov/About/Privacy_Security .shtml.

38. Breadcrumbs are linked headings across the top of a Web page, for instance, Home> Agencies>A-Z Index, that show users which subsite they are on in relation to the homepage.

39. See Watchfire, WebXACT Home page. "WebXACT is a free online service that lets you test single pages of web content for quality, accessibility, and privacy issues." Available at http://webxact .watchfire.com/scanform.aspx, accessed June 12, 2005.

40. FirstGov, E-government strategy, E-Gov, My government, My terms (April 2003), 11. Available at www.firstgov.gov/Topics/Includes/Reference/egov_strategy.pdf.

41. Joshua Porter, "Testing the Three-Click Rule." Available from home page of User Interface Engineering (Middleton, MA), www.uie.com/articles/three_click_rule/, accessed June 12, 2005.

42. Australia, "Australia.gov.au: About This Site." Available at www.australia.gov/about-this-site, accessed May 19, 2005

43. Ali Jafari, "The Next Generation of Internet Portals," in *Designing Portals,* 89–100, quote on 90.

44. Jafari, "Next Generation of Internet Portals," 92–93.

45. Boardman and Doherty, "Portals: Agencies through the Looking Glass," 3.

46. The Semantic Web is a World Wide Web Consortium project that intends to create a universal medium for information exchange by giving meaning (semantics), in a manner understandable by machines, to the content of documents on the Web.

47. Anne V. Zhdanova, "The People's Portal: Ontology Management on Community Portals" (paper presented at the First Workshop on Friend of a Friend, Social Networking and the Semantic Web, September 1–2, 2004, Galway, Ireland). Available at www.w3.org/2001/sw//Europe/events/ foaf/galway/papers/fp/peoples_portal, accessed May 30, 2005.

48. National Archives of Australia, "AGLS [Australian Government Locator Service] Metadata Standard." Available at www.naa.gov.au/recordkeeping/gov_online/agls/summary.html, accessed June 13, 2005.

49. State Services Commission, E-government Unit, *NZGLS Metadata and Thesauri—Home* (Wellington: State Services Commission, 2001). Available at www.e.govt.nz/standards/nzgls-intro-e.html, accessed May 28, 2005.

50. Government of Canada, "Core Subject Thesaurus" (Ottawa: Depository Services Program, 2004). Available at http://en.thesaurus.gc.ca/intro_e.html, accessed June 13, 2005.

51. U.S. Department of Agriculture, "Government Information Locator Service@USDA" (Washington, DC: Department of Agriculture). Available at www.usda.gov/gils/usdagils.htm, accessed May 24, 2005.

52. Michael C. Daconta, Leo J. Obrst, and Kevin T. Smith, *The Semantic Web: A Guide to the Future of XML, Web Services, and Knowledge Management* (Indianapolis, IN: Wiley, 2003).

53. Daconta, Obrst, and Smith, *The Semantic Web,* 67.

54. The Third International Workshop on Regulatory Ontologies. See STARLab: Semantics Technology and Applications Research Laboratory (Brussels). Available at www.starlab.vub.ac.be/ staff/mustafa/WORM_2005.htm, accessed June 12, 2005.

55. Steve Pepper, "Towards a Seamless Knowledge: Integrating Public Sector Portals in Norway," Semantic Web Seminar, Oslo, January 17, 2003. Available at www.ontopia.net/topicmaps/materials/ Towards%20Seamless%20Knowledge.ppt, accessed May 24, 2005.

56. Peter Brown, "European Parliament and Topic Maps" (paper presented at the Real World Topic Maps seminar held by XMLuk.org, Duxford, Cambridge, November 2003). Available at www .xmluk.org/slides/duxford_2003/2003-11-05-Peter-Brown.pdf, accessed May 24, 2005.

57. Steve Pepper and Motomu Naito, *Topic Maps: Overview and Basic Concepts, JTC1 / SC34* (Oakridge, TN: Y-12 National Security Complex, 2003). Available at www.y12.doe.gov/sgml/SC34/doc ument/0446.htm, accessed June 13, 2005.

58. The "deep Web" is a term used to describe the information held in electronic databases, catalogs, and repositories that is inaccessible to search engines such as Google, either because of the bibliographic structures within which it is held, or because it is not freely available to searchers but is available only through vendor services.

59. P. K. Agarwal, cited in Douglas Holmes, *eGov,* 2.

· 13 ·

Performance Metrics—Not the Only Way to Frame Evaluation Results

Peter Hernon and Robert E. Dugan

$\mathscr{P}$icture an evening with each star in the sky visible to the naked eye. Now pretend that each star represents the Web site of a different government body, regardless of branch of government. If we really want to make the picture more complex, now consider that we cannot tell the level of government or country to which that Web site belongs. As our eyes adjust to the fact that some stars appear brighter and larger than others, we expect to see some connection among different stars; more likely that connection, if it exists, would be within a country rather than globally. Any connection, however, might be more imaginary than real. The driving force behind creating a connection might be a portal such as FirstGov in the United States (see chapter 12) and/or an agency that might (or might not) have oversight over different departments and agencies (e.g., the Office of Management and Budget [OMB] in the United States or elsewhere perhaps in an e-government unit that is part of a larger agency).

To complicate the picture even more, imagine that, if we were to view each star (Web site) from a telescope, we would see something different depending on the lens through which we view the sky. Let us assume that there are three lenses: one for the general public, another for the business community, and the third for other government bodies. As a further complication, the picture constantly changes, presumably as the Web sites become more sophisticated over time.

Now, as we look at the sky, we might wonder how any sane person could navigate the various sites and discern a connection. With government's presence on the Internet increasing, we realize we cannot ignore the opportunities and challenges posed by the heaven of stars. At the same time, government realizes that, with its commitment to e-government evolving and diversion of resources to its furtherance, issues of accountability, effectiveness, efficiency, and meeting the needs and expectations of the groups reflected in those lenses become more critical to document and address through the planning process. Any documentation should be linked to planning and decision-making processes to ensure government bodies meet their stated mission.

Against this vision of e-government, it is important for any government entity that has a Web site and for those bodies that exercise government-wide oversight to ensure that adequate documentation exists to support claims of success, to monitor performance over time, and to engage in benchmarking. Benchmarks apply within departments and agencies and can be used to compare performance to that of their so-called peer departments and agencies. The purpose of this chapter is to provide a framework showing the key concepts that governments should explore as they serve different audiences and to discuss different performance metrics, as well as to identify other ways to collect relevant data to improve Web site effectiveness and to ensure continuous quality improvement. In examining performance metrics and other means of data collection for different countries, it might be argued that the focus is typically on one lens—that of government itself. However, the perspectives represented through the other lenses (the citizen and businessperson) cannot be ignored. Data collection should deal with all perspectives, including those of subpopulations (e.g., a nation's elderly, youth, and student body).

POLICY CONTEXT

Within a country, various policy instruments set the stage for both assessment and evaluation. For example, in the United States, the E-Government Act of 2002 (P. L. 107-347) established an Office of Electronic Government (OEG) within OMB and charged it to work with the Office of Information and Regulatory Affairs and other offices within OMB. OEG has a role in ensuring "access to, dissemination of, and preservation of Government information" (section 3602(e)(5)) and in providing "overall leadership and direction to the executive branch on electronic Government" (section 3602(f)(3)).

President George W. Bush's fiscal year 2002 management agenda envisioned e-government as a way to serve better the public (including persons with disabilities); make government more efficient and effective; reduce government operating costs as well as the expense and difficulty of doing business with the government; and enable the government to become more transparent and accountable.[1] To achieve these goals, the Bush administration envisioned an expansion of e-government as part of its government-wide reform effort and as being guided by three principles: the federal government should be citizen centered, results oriented, and market based.[2] Citizen centered addresses four segments:

1. individuals: "Building easy to find one-stop shops for citizens—creating single points of easy entry to access high quality government services [and information]";
2. businesses: "Reduce burden on businesses through use of Internet protocols and by consolidating myriad redundant reporting requirements";
3. intergovernmental: "Make it easier for states to meet reporting requirements, while enabling better performance measurement and results, especially for grants";
4. internal efficiency and effectiveness: "Reduce costs for federal government administration by using best practices in areas such as supply chain management and financial management, and knowledge management."[3]

EVALUATION CONCEPTS RELATED TO
E-GOVERNMENT

As shown in figure 13.1, four concepts appear to be central to accountability and continuous quality improvement. Effectiveness and efficiency, which fall on the vertical edges of the figure, are factors of critical importance to government. It seems that governments focus largely on one or both of them. However, service quality and satisfaction, which rest on the horizontal edges of the figure, cannot be ignored, that is, if government bodies want to address and meet the expectations of the audiences served by their Web sites.

Effectiveness

Effectiveness deals with "goodness, achieving success, and the quality of performance," and it addresses four questions:

1. "To what extent does the organization achieve its goals (input, process, output, or outcome goals)?"
2. "To what extent is the organization a *healthy operating unit?*"

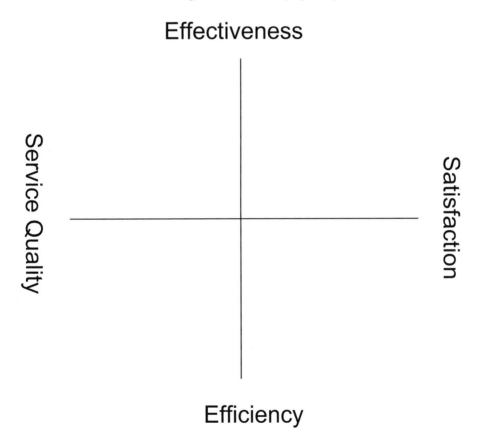

Figure 13.1. Concepts for Performance Metrics to Address

3. "To what extent can the organization capture from the external environment the resources needed to survive or thrive?"
4. "To what extent are the various stakeholders' priorities met?"[4]

The management literature offers four perspectives on effectiveness: *goal,* the achievement of specific ends; *process,* the internal health of the organization; *systems resource,* the organization's need to take resources from its environment; and *multiple constituencies,* the constituency groups of the organization. The perspectives "emphasize different aspects of the organization's effectiveness. They should be seen as overlapping rather than contradictory."[5]

J. Richard Hackman and Richard E. Walton see effectiveness as multidimensional and not confined to organizational outputs and results. They advance two other dimensions: the degree to which people work together *(a social aspect)* and grow professionally *(a personal aspect).*[6] These dimensions become important when e-government encourages collaboration within a department or agency and across departments and agencies. E-government asks for public servants to cooperate in new ways, to be service focused, and to anticipate the near future. In a separate work, Hackman expands on the conditions essential for organizations making extensive use of teams to be effective or enhance "the social processes essential to collective work," build "shared commitment, skills, and task-appropriate coordination strategies," help "members troubleshoot problems and spot emerging opportunities," and capture "experiences and . . . [translate] them into shared knowledge."[7]

Efficiency

Efficiency deals with the appropriateness of resource allocations. Both cost-benefit and cost-effectiveness analyses relate costs to program results. Cost-benefit analyses measure program inputs and outcomes in monetary terms, whereas cost-effectiveness estimates inputs in monetary terms and outcomes in terms of actual outcomes. Cost-effectiveness covers the accomplishment of objectives expressed in terms of cost.[8]

Service Quality

Service quality has been defined from at least four perspectives:

1. Excellence: The attributes associated with excellence may change dramatically and rapidly. Excellence is often externally defined.
2. Value: It incorporates multiple attributes, but quality and value are different constructs—one is the perception of meeting or exceeding expectations and the other stresses benefit to the recipient.
3. Conformance to specifications: It facilitates precise measurement, but users of a service may not know or care about internal specifications.
4. Meeting and/or exceeding expectations: This definition is all-encompassing and applies across service industries, but expectations change and may be shaped by experiences with other service providers.[9]

Most marketing researchers have concentrated on the last perspective. The gaps model of service quality reflects that perspective and offers service organizations a framework to identify services in the form of the gaps that exceed (or fail to meet) customers' expectations. The model posits five gaps that reflect a discrepancy between

- customers' expectations and management's perceptions of these expectations (gap 1);
- management's perceptions of customers' expectations and service quality specifications (gap 2);
- service quality specifications and actual service delivery (gap 3);
- actual service delivery and what is communicated to customers about it (gap 4); and
- customers' perceptions of expected services and of the service already delivered (gap 5).[10]

Although all five gaps may hinder an organization in providing high-quality service, the fifth gap is the basis of a customer-oriented definition of service quality that examines the discrepancy between customers' expectations for excellence and their perceptions of the actual service delivered. Expectations are *desired* wants—the extent to which customers believe a particular attribute is *essential* for an excellent service provider,[11] and perceptions are a judgment of service performance.

Jeffrey E. Disend correlates the gaps model with the concept of service quality. He maintains that poor service results if the gap, or difference, is large between what is expected and what is delivered. When what is delivered matches what is expected, customers find the service acceptable. If the service provided is better than what they expected, exceptional service materializes.[12]

The definition of service quality presented in the gaps model recognizes that expectations are subjective and are neither static nor predictable.[13] The model's designers were influenced by the confirmation/disconfirmation theory, which involves a comparison between expectations and performance. Before using a service, a customer has certain expectations about it. These expectations become a basis against which to compare actual performance. After having some experience with a service, the customer can compare any expectations with actual performance, and his or her perception is confirmed (if they match), negatively disconfirmed (if expectations exceed perceptions), or positively disconfirmed (if perceptions exceed expectations).[14]

Satisfaction

Both service quality and satisfaction can be an end in themselves; each differs and is worthy of examination as a framework for evaluating customer expectations of their use of Web sites. Service quality is an evaluation of specific attributes of some importance to the organization, and this judgment is cognitive. However, satisfaction focuses on a specific transaction, or, in the case of overall satisfaction, it is a cumulate judgment based on collective encounters with a service provider over time. Satisfaction judgments are more affective and are emotional reactions to an experience or a collection of experiences. "Simply put, satisfaction is a sense of contentment that arises from an actual experience in relation to an expected experience."[15]

Because service quality as a means of evaluation probes precise statements on which the organization seeks customer input, it serves as a planning tool. Judgments about satisfaction, on the other hand, tend to be global in the types of questions asked.

Unlike service quality, satisfaction focuses less on specific statements and relies more on open-ended questions. In satisfaction studies, there can be a probing of how customers rate the organization or Web site in a few specific areas, though the list is much shorter and more general than found in a service quality questionnaire. The intention of satisfaction studies is to identify if some general areas require scrutiny, whereas service quality studies offer data to examine specific problem areas for improvement. Satisfaction surveys offer organizations the opportunity to gauge the temperature of customers on an array of services they use (or have used). A service quality questionnaire might ask for "any other expectations that you consider important" and let respondents insert whatever they want and rate it on a seven- or ten-point scale.[16] Finally, the temptation is to compile an output measure showing among all of the respondents those expressing some degree of satisfaction. Such a compilation ignores the concept of *delighted* customers, those indicating complete satisfaction. Thus, the revised measure is the percentage of all the satisfied customers who were completely satisfied. The purpose is to concentrate on increasing that percentage.

PERFORMANCE METRICS

Figure 13.2 relates performance metrics to the concepts presented in figure 13.1. The perspectives of the department or agency, any oversight body, and the customers or citizens should be addressed. It is critical that whatever measures government departments and agencies use reflect a mixture of those perspectives. It cannot be assumed that one perspective adequately covers the other.

Overview

Input measures deal with resource allocation or what departments and agencies "put in" to e-government. They address the questions of How much? or How economical? Output measures, on the other hand, depict the results of the applied inputs; these mea-

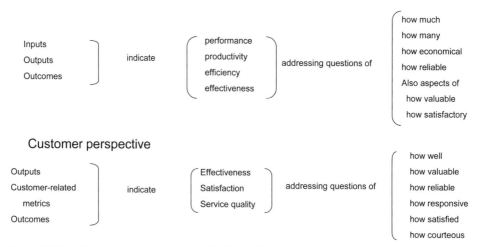

Figure 13.2.   Conceptual Framework for Metrics Relating to Service

sures are usually expressed in quantitative terms that focus on questions of How many? Neither input nor output measures deal satisfactorily with questions of

- How prompt?
- How accurate?
- How responsive?
- How well?
- How valuable?
- How reliable?
- How courteous?
- How satisfied?[17]

Expressed another way, input and output measures have an organizational perspective. The public, for example, is not so interested in How much? although taxpayers care about How economical? However, inputs are infrequently presented in terms of what matters to taxpayers: cost-effectiveness or cost-benefit. The public is often concerned about performance metrics that relate to their interests and experiences, namely,

- the speed in completing processes, functions, or transactions (How prompt?);
- the quality of the information they receive (How accurate?);
- how well the organization anticipates their questions and problems and works to eliminate or ameliorate them (How responsive?);
- how their experience compares to cost (time, effort, or money) in navigating government Web sites (How valuable?);
- how well the Web site provided what they want (expressed in terms of dependability and reliability) (How reliable?);
- any interaction with the staff, including use of the Web site itself (broadly this point deals with How courteous?); and
- how satisfied they are with a particular experience or overall use of government Web sites (How satisfied?).

Indicators of satisfaction include a willingness to return or use a Web site repeatedly, to recommend a site to others, or to continue to support a service or advocate its support to others. Satisfaction and courteousness cannot be divorced from service quality.

The only remaining question—How well?—views results in terms of outcomes. More specifically, the question examines the impact of the information gained or the service used on peoples' lives—work or personal. A type of educational outcome involves student learning outcomes and the ability of educators and institutions of higher education to answer, What do students know that they did not know before? and What can they do that they could not do before? Clearly, the question of How well? is the most difficult to answer, but that answer can be partially inferred from answers to the other questions.

In summary, departments and agencies could be held accountable for their ability to answer different questions and to factor those answers into continuous quality improvement. Returning to figure 13.1, departments and agencies should examine all four perspectives while continuing to address the question of How well? Such a focus on outcomes requires evidence that the mission of the department and agency has been met.

Evaluation Framework

Figure 13.3 shows that organizations have choices about which types of performance metrics they gather. Not all of these metrics, especially those related to outcomes and impacts, can be reduced to a ratio with a nominator and denominator. Furthermore, a popular impression is that inputs lead to outputs and that outcomes result from outputs and related activities. However, in the case of student learning outcomes, there is no progression from outputs to outcomes. In fact, such outcomes proceed from inputs directly to outcomes. The figure illustrates that organizations have choices about which metrics they gather and how often they do so. However, as this chapter illustrates, not all data collected can (or should) be reduced to a simple metric.

Some Applications

This section provides four examples in an effort to illustrate the application of the previously mentioned measures. First, because "at least 70 percent of FirstGov visitors are citizens, and most of these visitors are looking for help with services such as applying for social security or changing an address," the portal has the citizen tab as its default home page.[18] This change to the portal reflects the administration's *three clicks to service or information strategy*, which stipulates that users of FirstGov should only have to follow three links to find the information or service they seek, or to make a transaction. Some

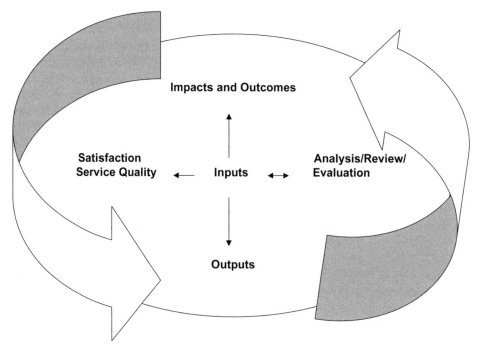

Figure 13.3. Organizational Effectiveness and Improvement

government agencies have now adopted either two- or three-click access to the content on their home page.[19]

Any attempt to quantify a number of clicks of the mouse comprises an output measure. It is not a customer measure in that there is as yet no evidence that any specified number of clicks by itself is important to the public; in fact, some research indicates that as long as people find relevant information with any click, they are satisfied and willing to proceed with their search.[20]

As the second example, the Small Business Administration (SBA), which launched its home page in 1992, has served more than 1.2 million visitors on its site each week; this site offers more than fifty thousand publications! This example indicates that a meaningful output measure, one gathered repeatedly over time, might be the number of downloads per a particular time frame (e.g., for a fiscal year).

Third, in 2003, the SBA redesigned its home page and removed "excessive jargon and confusing terminology" while "adding tutorials and training to help users learn how to do business with the federal government," and creating specific "information categories designed to guide users through the small-business process: starting a business, financing a business, managing and growing a business, business opportunities, and disaster assistance."[21] Customer-oriented measures, for example, might focus on the extent to which the public is delighted with the navigability of the site and the outcome of their search.

Fourth, some government Web sites have scored high on user satisfaction surveys. The National Women's Health Information Center of the Department of Health and Human Services (www.4women.gov/), for example, scored the highest among government sites on one satisfaction survey. In fact, that site "scored higher than several prominent private sites and on a par with Amazon.com."[22] Here is a good example of something that could be expressed as a customer-oriented measure.

A KEY GAO REPORT

In congressional testimony, Linda D. Koontz, director of information management issues, General Accounting Office (GAO), discussed performance metrics, targets (goals), and progress in achieving those targets. The list complements the metrics discussed in the previous section. Some of the metrics and targets listed include the following:

- Number of visitors to a Web site per month: For this output measure, the target might be, let us assume, thirty-five thousand hits or users. Progress refers to what number of users or hits has been achieved thus far and how the agency proposes to meet the target.
- Median time for agency processing of electronic records: For this input measure, the time period might be set in terms of workdays. It is important that a realistic target number be available, against which progress can be measured.
- Number of electronic comments submitted via e-mail: This output measure is important where e-government involves e-compliance, e-procurement, e-democracy, or even access to information and services. If the target became, say, two hundred thousand within a specified time period, what number has

been achieved, and is that number higher or lower since it was last calculated? Does the target look realistic in terms of where those numbers (past and present) stand? If the numbers are unrealistic, what changes are necessary to achieve that target?

- Time savings for business compliance and filing: This input really has direct customer implications and would be important where e-government involves e-compliance. A key question is, What is the target?
- Number of downloads (of laws): This output also has customer implications. Again, what is the target?
- Number of datasets posted to a government portal: For this input measure, what is the target, and how close is it to being met?
- Number of departments posting datasets to that portal: This input measure has benchmarking implications.
- The percentage of users expressing "complete satisfaction" with a Web site, Web page, or service: For these customer outcomes, what is the target and how close is it to being achieved?
- Number of grant applications received online: For this output, what is the target, how close is it to being met, and what does benchmarking reveal?
- Percentage of taxpayers who file their tax returns online: For this output, what is the target, how close is it to being met, and what does benchmarking reveal?
- Number of dataset hits: For this output, what is the target, how close is it to being met, and what does benchmarking reveal?[23]

As her testimony reveals, the examples given tend to be inputs or outputs that only cover certain aspects of effectiveness and efficiency. Missing is coverage of effectiveness from the vantage point of outcomes and impacts, efficiency as reflected in terms of cost-effectiveness and cost-benefit, and customer expectations, especially as seen through service quality.

EXAMPLES FROM OTHER COUNTRIES

In its e-government strategy, New Zealand's e-Government Unit notes that "the Government wants agencies to deliver 'outcomes' as well as outputs and achieve better results for people. This will involve agencies working more effectively across their traditional boundaries and collaborating with other agencies, stakeholders and their customers."[24] Outcomes might focus on convenience, collaboration, satisfaction, integration, and efficiency. Clearly, all four points in figure 13.1 should be addressed, as the metrics partially indicate the extent to which the organizational culture embraces e-government.

The strategic framework developed in the United Kingdom highlights "four guiding principles" for e-government:

1. building services around citizens' choices;
2. making government and its services more accessible;

3. social inclusion;
4. using information better.[25]

Each of these principles could be recast in terms of performance metrics.

STANDARD INDICES

This section describes two frameworks for viewing public sector outcomes and customer satisfaction. Although these frameworks have received widespread attention, there are other ways to evaluate programs and services; again, not all results can (or should) be reduced to a simple metric.

Accenture Public Sector Value Model

The Accenture Public Sector Value Model is designed to provide long-term, politically neutral accountability information to government officials in an effort to determine how effectively applied resources yield value for their identified clientele. In this specific model, public sector value is equated with citizen-focused outcomes and the necessary direct cost-effectiveness of the service delivery. Outcomes are determined by consensus as driven by the stated mission of the agency and the expectations of the agency's users, and other stakeholders, such as legislators. The model measures outcomes as weighed social achievements and then compared to the components of cost-effectiveness focusing on known annual expenditures and capital funding considerations.

Greater value is created when either outcomes are increased or indicators of cost-effectiveness reflect an improvement. However, if there is a decrease, the public sector agency needs to make a trade-off based upon input factors, such as available funding or staffing levels. A reduction in both outcomes and cost-effectiveness results in a decrease in delivered, perceived, and received value.

While the model cannot be used to evaluate the agency's day-to-day performance, the baseline and subsequent annually compiled and analyzed data can be applied to determine if the agency is improving, and as a comparative measure with similar agencies. Furthermore, the data from the year-to-year measures are designed to help the agency identify which factors positively or negatively influence value, highlight problem areas, and suggest activities that can be implemented resulting in improvements.

Research discovered during the model's creation identified seven characteristics of high-performance government agencies. Each is

- relentlessly outcome and value focused;
- highly efficient;
- exceptionally aware of changes in its environment, and able to translate insight into action;
- highly focused on its core capabilities, and adopts outsourcing strategies to improve efficiencies in noncore activities;
- highly agile;
- committed to the growth and development of its employees; and
- headed by courageous leaders.

In its simplest application, this model seeks to provide the government agency with objective information to determine if the consensus-derived outcomes are worth the expenditure of the taxpayer resources and, if so desired, how to improve citizen-focused value.[26] Nonetheless, the next step is to develop a set of metrics representing customer outcomes and to supplement that list with other insights into service quality and satisfaction.

American Customer Satisfaction Index

Established in 1994, the American Customer Satisfaction Index—a partnership among the University of Michigan Business School, the American Society for Quality, and CFI Group, an international consulting firm—views satisfaction in terms of perceived (experienced) quality, expectations, and perceived value. It also presupposes that satisfaction influences complaining (or complimenting) behavior, as well as customer loyalty. Based on econometric modeling of data received from telephone interviews with customers, the index covers participating companies, industry trade associations, and federal and local government agencies. On a scale ranging from zero to one hundred, it provides them on a quarterly basis with agency- or company-specific information and benchmarking data relating to satisfaction (see www.theacsi.org/overview.htm for benchmarking scores for e-government participants). As an illustration, for the second quarter of 2004, Medline Plus (http://medlineplus.gov) of the National Library of Medicine (National Institutes of Health, Department of Health and Human Services) scored the highest (85) and the MapFinder Web site of the National Ocean Service (http://oceanservice.noaa.gov/dataexplorer) scored the lowest (48). Scores for U.S. government sites can also be compared to the performance of selected private sector organizations and of similar agencies in other countries, assuming the focus is on Web site performance.

With quarterly benchmarking data, the departments and agencies can address questions such as, Are we performing better than we did in the past? and How do we compare in relationship to some other government or private sector Web sites? Benchmarking comparisons are usually based on time, cost, and quality as measured against previous performance or the best in that class.[27] However, the entire focus of satisfaction studies should not be on benchmarking. It is important that the evaluation process provides relevant and timely information that has utility—generates feasible recommendations that can lead to change or improvement in the presentation of the information or in services offered. Carol H. Weiss and Michael J. Bucuvalas expect data collection to meet two tests. The first—the *truth test*—asks, Is the research trustworthy? Can I rely on it? and Will it hold up under attack? The second—the *utility test*—queries, Does the research provide direction? and Does it yield guidance—either for immediate action or for considering alternative approaches to problems?[28]

METHODS OF DATA COLLECTION

The tool chest of methodologies available to explore various facets of figure 13.1 exists; however, the methodologies do not all lead to simply stated performance metrics. In other words, those concepts are richer than any set of performance metrics can capture.

Table 13.1 identifies eight methods of data collection that go beyond performance metrics; many of these methods could be used in combination. In addition, Web sites often have the ability to compile a record of, How many? (e.g., hits of that site). Such simple outputs do not need to rely on any of the methods; however, such simple counts should not be a substitute for generating a combination of data elements useful for continuous quality improvement. Departments and agencies might also have electronic complaint and compliment systems or e-mail communication that they can monitor and conduct content analysis of the responses.

Observation

Observation is not limited to watching people and being undetected. It also involves the use of videotaping searches, most likely with people aware that they are being watched. Observation might also occur in a controlled setting and be used in combination with other methods. Chapter 11, which documents selected participants' involvement in a walk-through, presents a type of observation, one where they searched government Web sites to answer predetermined questions.

Because it is impossible to observe people for any prolonged length of time, compilation of a diary might be a suitable means of data collection. Key questions relate to the length of time for maintaining the diary, the reliability and internal validity of the data collected, and how the data will be analyzed.

Surveys

Surveys become a way to listen to customers and to factor the insights gained into improved service. It is not necessary to accept everything they say; surveys, especially when used on a repeated basis, provide an ongoing dialogue with the public. Surveys might be conducted in a proactive way (e.g., in person, by telephone, contacting people by e-mail, or distributing questionnaires to people in a certain setting) or passively (e.g., placement on a home page). Each method has certain advantages and disadvantages. Typically, service quality studies (on gap 5) involve questionnaires distributed to a sample taken from a specific population. Satisfaction studies might follow the same pattern but they need not. Any government department or agency preparing to conduct a customer satisfaction survey should explore readings, such as *State Agency Use of Customer Satisfaction Surveys*.[29]

The problem with a number of the research studies related to service quality and satisfaction is that the focus might not be on expectations related to Web site use. Nonetheless, recent studies have begun to explore e-service quality, a multidimensional construct.[30]

One type of survey is a focus group interview in which six to ten people get together and interact with each other. Five to seven general questions guide such interviews. Prior to conducting one of these interviews, a department or agency might provide a demonstration and then concentrate those general questions on that experience.

Testing

Such testing might be conducted obtrusively (participants are aware that they are being tested) or unobtrusively (those people tested are unaware that they are participating in

Table 13.1.   Evaluation Methodologies

Methodology	What it measures	What it indicates	Limitations
Observation	User search behavior and thinking	Yields insights into what users actually do	It might be difficult to observe performance without people being aware. If they are aware, do they alter their normal search behavior?
Survey	User perceptions or expectations	Indicates how well customer expectations (service quality and satisfaction) are met	Provides self-reports or what people want to reveal. May not be possible to follow up on responses. People may not want to participate
Focus group interview	User perceptions	Shows how users view and experience a Web site	Limited generalizability of findings; does not reflect actual user behavior; requires a skilled moderator to be objective in data collection
Testing (obtrusive or unobtrusive)	User performance	Focuses on the results that users receive—accuracy and how long it takes to answer questions	The questions may not reflect real-life situations and testing may lack broad generalizability. Awareness of the testing situation may influence the results
Transactional log analysis	User performance and site analysis	Examines records of Web server activity (evidence of Web site use)	Cannot determine what motivated user actions. Only certain aspects of user behavior are revealed
Usability testing	Site analysis and user navigation behavior	Shows how users go about performing tasks	Does not provide detailed insights into user search behavior
Verbal protocols	User perceptions and search behavior	Indicates how users react as they perform specified tasks (e.g., their reaction to three-click access)	People may not be good at articulating their search behavior and expectations
Web metrics	User performance and volume of use	Reflects overall traffic (hits and page views), volume of use, click stream, and exit route	Does not provide detailed insights into user search behavior

a test). Obtrusive testing focuses on factors such as the receipt of a correct answer, question negotiation, and how long it took to answer questions. Unobtrusive testing examines the same factors as well, for instance, the offering of referral, the accuracy of any referral, and the number of staff involved in answering the question. With so many governments including e-mail service as part of their e-government menu of offerings, the following questions arise:

- What types of questions do departments and agencies receive? (content analysis)
- How long does it take to answer questions? (transactional log analysis, obtrusive testing, and unobtrusive testing)
- Was the question answered correctly? (obtrusive testing and unobtrusive testing)
- What were the expectations of the customers asking the questions? (satisfaction and service quality)
- Were those expectations met? (satisfaction and service quality)

If those public servants answering e-mail questions maintain a log of the questions and their answers, those logs might be retained and a sample of them explored to learn more about the quality of service received and to consider methods for improving staff training.

Transactional Log Analysis

An examination of the actual records of Web server activity provides insights into the domain name of users (e.g., .gov, .com., .org, and .edu); the number of site hits; the length of time spent at the site or page; which Web pages received the longest use; the number of clicks to reach those pages; which items were downloaded and how long downloading took; which browser they used; and whether any errors or problems were encountered (e.g., dead links). Government departments and agencies might use cookies to complement (or as an alternate means of) data collection. However, government policies most likely guide the use of a cookie.

Usability Studies

Usability testing evaluates the effectiveness and ease of use of Web sites. It assists in identifying architecture, navigation, and design problems and in developing ways to attack those problems. Usability studies might examine the extent to which some customers can navigate a Web site easily and efficiently; usability of Web sites examines navigation of the site, page design, content layout, accessibility of the site and its pages, use of media, interactivity, and consistency. Customer satisfaction might focus on customers' comfort; whether they become tired or frustrated in navigating the site, and if so, what is their response; and the personal effort they make to answer questions.

The intent of data collection and evaluation might be to provide continuous quality improvement in making government Web sites and Web pages more user friendly and retrieval of items more efficient; to document the effectiveness of government Web sites and the delivery of their content; to aid in the oversight of e-government; to record the volume of activity and encourage agencies to increase that volume on a monthly or annual basis; and to benchmark performance with comparable agencies. A number of agencies already engage in usability testing, for instance, to examine:

- navigation (e.g, menus, buttons, and site maps);
- links (e.g., their relevance, accuracy, and annotations);
- load times (e.g., browsers, output devices, and pdf documents);
- scannability, readability, and printability;
- screen design (layout, style sheets, and no frames); and
- searchability (metadata, language, labels, and facets).

Webmasters might also engage in heuristic evaluation, which provides a way to locate problems in a user interface, as they conduct tests against an agreed set of principles. Such testing usually relies on a set of predetermined tasks that individual experts carry out. These individuals repeat the tests looking for specific usability principles. Agency personnel might also observe selected individuals searching the Web site to answer specific questions (e.g., the walk-through of chapter 11), conduct focus group interviews, and monitor, for instance, the

- amount of time to complete a task;
- percentage of tasks completed;
- navigation paths that indicate poor directional instructions;
- number of commands and pathways ignored; and
- possibility of a mismatch between search terms and content.

For each facet of e-government that a government pursues (see figure 1.1), there needs to be a method (or methods) for evaluating the success and efficiency of an agency in providing that aspect. The intent is to document and improve, as e-government continues to mature and be responsive to the customers it serves and those providing oversight.

One method focuses on Web content accessibility and the extent of compliance with the Web Accessibility Initiative (WAI) to increase universal access to everyone regardless of disability (e.g., see www.w3.org/WAI/). It is important to remember, however, that those with disabilities may prefer to enter Web sites the same as everyone else and not to encounter mirror sites. They do not want to be perceived as different from others. Clearly, not all disabilities are physical. Web site managers need to be familiar with learning disabilities and, for example, be aware of problems such disabilities present. Three-click access presumably is intended to reduce the amount of time that people spend searching for information. The problem is to present all the information available on a home page in a way that permits simple access. Because many people may be unfamiliar with government terminology, site navigation is an important area on which to concentrate. However, as this section shows, it is not the only one.

Verbal Protocol

Think-aloud protocol is a type of verbal protocol analysis that seeks information about participants' cognitive thoughts using verbal reports. These reports occur during data collection and should be compared with verbal reports given after completion of the task. The subsequent reports, known as "think afters," are important because some participants might not be able to articulate their thoughts or actions well as they carry out a task that involves complex cognitive processing. Think afters can produce pertinent insights in such a situation, but they might be influenced by forgetting and fabrication.[31]

Other

Government Web sites are often expected to meet accepted criteria of usability and to be efficient in terms of the investment made. In fact, there are instances in which oversight bodies are unwilling to make more of a commitment to improving government Web sites and portals. Therefore, it might be critical to identify the return on investment for usability. Such an analysis examines inputs and projects the cost of usability engineering activities throughout the project life cycle. Such information might be useful if a department or agency needs to conduct an analysis based on cost-effectiveness. Return on investment, which is a financial ratio, can also be viewed as the incremental gain from an action divided by the cost of that action. Because business investments produce financial consequences extending for several years, the metric has meaning only when the time period has been clearly specified.

Those departments and agencies that engage in e-commerce might also be interested in return on investment, which examines the following equation: $ revenue generated by the Web site (per month) ÷ No. of visitors to the site (per month) = $ value of each visitor to the Web site

Naturally, the amount purchased and the number of visitors, as well as the total amount of money taken in, become important Web metrics. Still, the goal is improved customer service, reduced administrative and customer service time, increased use of the Web site, and reduced costs (e.g., printing and advertising/marketing).

ADDITIONAL INSIGHTS: AN EXAMPLE OF RESEARCH GOING BEYOND MERE METRICS

Government entities within all three branches of government place large quantities of statistical data on their Web sites as electronic tables in column format. Educators Gary Marchionini and Xiangming Mu examined how people use "highly compressed and highly structured" e-tables, and they designed and tested a Web-based browser to assist the public in using these tables. Figures 2–7 of their article plot eye movement for tasking a simple lookup, a comparison, and trend analysis.[32] Eye movement studies, as well as other types of data collection, could be applied more broadly to electronic tables and to help people navigate government portals. If they encounter page after page of screen listings presumably relevant to their search, how do they decide which items to select? Do they use only the first screen (e.g., of a government portal), do they know how to read all of the entries (even if five hundred to a thousand items are listed), or do they know how to separate perishable (e.g., press releases) from other kinds of information resources (e.g., reports)? Also, what prototype interface tools can be developed to simplify information identification, retrieval, and use?

CONCLUSION

It is impossible to have one all-encompassing data-collection activity that answers completely any and all questions that might arise in coping with figures 1.1 and 13.1, as well as the assorted issues discussed in this chapter. Complicating matters, almost everything can be subjected to evaluation and measurement; measurement is a tool for the collection and analysis of data on which evaluators judge the performance of government Web sites against yardsticks that reflect effectiveness, efficiency, service quality, and satisfaction, as well as the different types of performance metrics. Clearly, individual departments and agencies, and those bodies exercising oversight, must decide what is important to know and how the data gathered contribute to continuous quality assessment. In this context, customers should be neither ignored nor slighted; their opinions are worthy of recognition, that is, if the concept of e-citizen is to materialize. Clearly, government has choices in its representation of each of the three lenses mentioned at the beginning of the chapter. Whatever choices—metrics or nonmetrics—the goal is to improve the quality of the image gained, add to accountability, and engage in continuous quality improvement.

NOTES

1. Joel C. Willemssen, managing director, information technology issues, "Electronic Government: Success of the Office of Management and Budget's 25 Initiatives Depends on Effective Management and Oversight," testimony before the Subcommittee on Technology, Information Policy, Intergovernmental Relations and the Census, House Committee on Government Reform, GAO-03-495T (Washington, DC: General Accounting Office [GAO], 2003), 4. For policy instruments of the Office of Management and Budget, see "Information Policy, IT & E-Gov" (Washington, DC: Office of Management and Budget [OMB]). Available at www.whitehouse.gov/omb/inforeg/infopoltech .html, accessed June 12, 2005.

2. "Presidential Memo: The Importance of E-Government," Egov: The Official Web Site of the President's E-Government. Available at www.whitehouse.gov/omb/egov/pres_memo.htm, accessed May 29, 2003. For additional discussion of e-government as "a critical element in the management framework," see sec. 2, E-Government Act 2002 (116 Stat. 2899).

3. Mark A. Forman, associate director for IT and e-government, "Achieving the Vision of E-government" (Washington, DC: OMB, October 1, 2001), 4. Available at www.hpcc.gov/pitac/ pitac-25sep011format.pdf, accessed November 14, 2003.

4. Thomas A. Childers and Nancy A. Van House, *What's Good? Describing Your Public Library's Effectiveness* (Chicago: American Library Association, 1993), 7.

5. Childers and Van House, *What's Good?* 7.

6. J. Richard Hackman and Richard E. Walton, "Leading Groups in Organizations," in *Designing Effective Work Groups,* ed. Paul S. Goodman and Associates (San Francisco: Jossey-Bass, 1986), 72–120.

7. J. Richard Hackman, *Leading Teams: Setting the Stage for Great Performances* (Boston: Harvard Business School Press, 2002), back cover jacket.

8. For a more detailed discussion, see Peter H. Rossi, Mark W. Lipsey, and Howard E. Freeman, *Evaluation: A Systematic Approach* (Thousand Oaks, CA: Sage, 2004).

9. Adapted from C. A. Reeves and D. A. Bednar, "Defining Quality: Alternatives and Implications," *Academy of Management Review* 19, no. 3 (1994), 419–45.

10. Valarie A. Zeithhaml, A. Parasuraman, and Leonard L. Berry, *Delivering Quality Service: Balancing Customer Perceptions and Expectations* (New York: Free Press, 1990).

11. A. Parasuraman, Leonard L. Berry, and Valarie A. Zeithaml, "Refinement and Reassessment of the SERVQUAL Scale," *Journal of Retailing* 67, no. 4 (1991): 420–50.

12. Jeffrey E. Disend, *How to Provide Excellent Service in Any Organization* (Radnor, PA: Chilton, 1991), 108.

13. R. F. Blanchard and R. L. Galloway, "Quality in Retail Banking," *International Journal of Service Industry Management* 5, no. 4 (1994): 5–23.

14. See R. L. Oliver, *Satisfaction: A Behavioral Perspective on the Consumer* (New York: McGraw-Hill, 1997); R. L. Oliver and W. S. DeSarbo, "Response Determinants in Satisfaction Judgments," *Journal of Consumer Research* 14 (1998): 495–507.

15. Peter Hernon and John R. Whitman, *Delivering Satisfaction and Service Quality: A Customer-Based Approach for Libraries* (Chicago: American Library Association, 2001), 32.

16. Danuta Nitecki and Peter Hernon, "Measuring Service Quality at Yale University's Libraries," *Journal of Academic Librarianship* 26, no. 4 (July 2000): 271.

17. Peter Hernon and Ellen Altman, *Assessing Service Quality: Satisfying the Expectations of Library Customers* (Chicago: American Library Association, 1998), 51–54.

18. Diane Frank, "Online Feng Shui," *Federal Computer Week,* May 19, 2003, 40.

19. See White House, The President's Management Agenda: "Expanded Electronic Government: E-Gov Challenges and Solutions" (Washington, DC: White House, 2004). Available at www.results.gov/agenda/fiveinitatives10.html, accessed September 19, 2004; Department of Transportation, Federal Transit Administration, "President's Management Agenda (PMA) and E-Grants, Number C-14-03, 08-04-03" (Washington, DC: Federal Transit Administration, 2004). Available at www.fta.dot.gov/legal/guidance/dear_colleague/2003/178_12145_ENG…HTML.htm, accessed September 19, 2004. Borrowing the three-clicks-to-service approach used by FirstGov, GovBenefits takes each user through a three-step screening process and then presents a list of benefits for which the user may qualify; see http://govbenefits.gov/govbenefits/index.jhtml, accessed September 19, 2004; Joshua Dean, "Daily Briefing: GovBenefits Debut Marks Bush Administration's First E-gov Success," *GOVEXEC.com* (Washington, DC: GOVEXEC, April 29, 2002). Available at www.govexec.com/dailyfed/0402/042902j2.htm, accessed September 19, 2004.

The Bureau of Economic Analysis promises two-click access to resources on its Web site. See Patricia Daukantas, "It's All Within Two Clicks on New BEA Site," *Government Computer News,* August 4, 2003, 14.

20. Steve Krug, *Don't Make Me Think! A Common Sense Approach to Web Usability* (Indianapolis, IN: New Riders Publishing, 2000), 41.

21. Margaret A. T. Reed, "SBA: Web Simplicity Is a Virtue," *Federal Computer Week,* June 30, 2003, 36.

22. Patricia Daukantas, "E-gov Sites Score High on User Satisfaction Survey," *Government Computer News,* September 22, 2003, 68.

23. Linda D. Koontz, "Electronic Government: Initiatives Sponsored by the Office of Management and Budget Have Made Mixed Progress. Testimony before the Subcommittee on Technology, Information Policy, Intergovernmental Relations and the Census, Committee on Government Reform, House of Representatives, GAO-04-561T (Washington, DC: GAO, 2004).

24. New Zealand, State Services Commission, e-Government Unit, "A Summary of the E-Government Strategy" (Wellington: State Services Commission, 2003). Available at www.e-government.govt.nz/docs/e-gov-strategy-june-2003/, accessed August 6, 2004.

25. United Kingdom, Cabinet Office, e-Government Unit, *Strategic Framework for Public Services* (London: e-Government Unit, n.d.). Available at http://e-government.cabinetoffice.gov.uk/EStrategy/StrategicFrameworkArticle/fs/en?CON . . . , accessed August 6, 2004.

26. Accenture, *A Value Model for the Public Sector* (New York: Accenture, 2004). Available at www.accenture.com/xd/xd.asp?it = enweb&xd = ideas\outlook\1_2004\hp_gov.xml (html), accessed September 17, 2004.

27. For a discussion of the different types of benchmarking, see Hernon and Altman, *Assessing Service Quality*, 63–65.

28. Carol H. Weiss and Michael J. Bucuvalas, "Truth Tests and Utility Tests: Decision-Makers' Frames of Reference for Social Science Research," *American Sociological Review* 45 (April 1980): 311.

29. Minnesota, Office of the Legislative Auditor, Program Evaluation Division, *State Agency Use of Customer Satisfaction Surveys* (St. Paul, MN: Program Evaluation Division, 1995). See also Terry G. Vavra, *Improving Your Measurement of Customer Satisfaction: A Guide to Creating, Conducting, Analyzing, and Reporting Customer Satisfaction Measurement Programs* (Milwaukee, WI: ASQ Quality Press, 1997).

30. See, e.g., Valarie A. Zeithaml, A. Parasuraman, and Arvind Malhotra, *A Conceptual Framework for Understanding e-Service Quality: Implications for Future Research and Managerial Practice* (Cambridge, MA: Marketing Science Institute, 2000); Yi-Shun Wang and Tzung-I Tang, "Assessing Customer Perceptions of Website Service Quality in Digital Marketing Environments," *Journal of End User Computing* 15, no. 3 (July–September 2003): 14–31; Jessica Santos, "E-service Quality: A Model of Virtual Service Quality Dimensions," *Managing Service Quality* 13, no. 3 (2003): 232–46; Valarie A. Zeithaml, A. Parasuraman, and Arvind Malhotra, "Service Quality Delivery through Web Sites: A Critical Review of Extant Knowledge," *Journal of the Academy of Marketing Science* 30, no. 4 (Fall 2002): 362–75.

31. See Jennifer L. Branch, "Investigating the Information-Seeking Processes of Adolescents: The Value of Using Think Alouds and Think Afters," *Library & Information Science Research* 22, no. 4 (2000): 371–92.

32. Gary Marchionini and Xiangming Mu, "User Studies Informing E-table Interfaces," *Information Processing & Management* 39 (2003): 561–79.

VI

CONSEQUENCES

• *14* •

E-government and the Digital Divide

Rowena Cullen

$\mathscr{T}$he digital divide, which concerns the lack of access to information and communications technologies (ICTs) in both developed and developing nations, inevitably impacts on the accessibility and uptake of e-government in all communities. This chapter, which investigates the problem in both the developed and the developing world, addresses different factors that affect access to and use of ICTs in all societies. It then estimates ICT and Internet access in various countries and regions of the world, and relates these to global studies of "e-government readiness," development, and uptake. The chapter also raises issues that particularly impact on citizens' participation in e-government (e.g., civic engagement and trust) and discusses measures used to estimate the development of e-government in the global community and the various rankings produced. Some proposed solutions to both the global and the national digital divide are outlined.

Perspectives on the digital divide are dependent on the source of information. The International Telecommunications Union and the global telecommunications industry primarily focus on the uptake of technology in various countries. The public administration literature, on the other hand, is more likely to address issues such as social inclusion, the nature of government and governance, and the relationship between citizens and government. In a field as new as e-government, it is important to combine different perspectives to gain an overall understanding of the complexity of the issue and to develop appropriate measures and policies that address the social, political, economic, and cultural context of each country.

Government policies in most Western nations attempt to ensure that all citizens have the opportunity to access and use effectively ICTs so that they can participate fully in the educational, social, and economic activities that depend on these technologies. As increasing amounts of government information and transactions are made available on the Internet, lack of access to ICTs, especially the Internet, impact severely on the ability of citizens to access information and services from government and to participate in democratic processes. Studies of citizens' involvement with e-government to date have shown that the digital divide—the lack of access to, or the lack of interest in using ICTs—has as much if not more impact on effective communication between citizens and government than it does in relation to general Internet use.[1] Thus, governments are refocusing their endeavors to ensure the equity of access to e-government, as well as access to the Internet for other educational and social purposes. They are achieving this refocus through policies such as the Bush administration's effort to make broadband spectrum more widely available[2] and the New Zealand government's Digital Strategy,[3] and through active promotion of broadband networks in rural areas, in initiatives such as Project Probe.[4]

There is an important digital divide between the state of ICTs and levels of access to and utilization of the Internet in developed nations and in less developed countries. Dramatic differences in access to the Internet are now becoming evident as usage reaches 30–40 percent of the population in most Western countries and exceeds 65 percent in the most advanced Internet nations (e.g., the United States and Scandinavia). In contrast the poorest developing nations have rates of access ranging from less than 1 percent to 5 percent. While some developing nations are increasing rates of access, others are not keeping pace with the rates of increase in developing nations. An increase in Internet use from 15 percent to 30 percent of the population in many developed countries is of an order of magnitude greater than an increase from 1.5 percent to 3 percent of the online population in a developing country. It seems, therefore, that the majority of the world's population is excluded from both the vast information resources of the Internet and information about their own government's activities, policies, regulations, and processes. As e-government practice brings benefits of enhanced openness and accountability to the government sector, these benefits are not available to the world's poorest and least developed nations. This double deprivation signifies a growing digital divide between the developed and the developing world.

The digital divide focuses on the higher end of information and communications technologies involving the electronic transfer of information using digital formats that may themselves be replaced by new technologies within the next decade. The digital divide assumes that the benefits of these technologies and access to the world of information that is contained within them is a benefit that no citizen in the twenty-first century should be without, certainly not, at least, in the developed world. However, two key points about the impact of technology on human civilization should be remembered:

1. Technology does not in itself solve social and economic discrepancies within societies, and can often exacerbate them. Massive growth in the use of ICTs in India, for example, has had no impact at all on what has been described as the highest concentration of poverty in the world.
2. New technologies do not always replace the old. They may coexist and in doing so enhance the range of human experience without necessarily diminishing the experience of those who do not use them or who must rely on older technologies to achieve the same ends.

It is important, therefore, not to assume that ICTs are essential to social inclusion in either the developed or developing world. The very concept of the digital divide oversimplifies the nature of human society and the complex social and economic factors that lie behind the adoption or otherwise of ICTs. For the majority of the world's population telephones are a technology beyond the reach of many people; food, sanitation, and literacy are more urgent needs. There may be problems in bringing the Internet to an African village, or communities may have to rely on battery- or solar-operated computers. As the *Economist* notes in an editorial strongly critical of the recently launched United Nation's Digital Solidarity Fund, "even if it were possible to wave a magic wand and cause a computer to appear in every household on earth, it would not achieve very much: a computer is not useful if you have no food and electricity and cannot read."[5] The Internet requires highly developed skills to access and interpret the information found. A better solution to the problem of limited access to information for many communities still lies in the use of basic technologies to promote traditional forms of education, enhance the delivery of health care, and improve animal husbandry and crop management. The debate engaged in by the *Economist*, that mobile telephones bring more economic advantage to impoverished communities, reemerges later in this chapter as part of the debate over solutions to the digital divide.

There is undoubtedly a significant contribution to be made by the Internet to the poorest nations of the world, even within the constraints of the very limited access to ICTs, which is found primarily in government agencies, universities, and some businesses in the most deprived communities. The Internet has dramatically increased the rate, and reduced costs, in both the improvement of communications and the transfer of knowledge from North to South. (Most of the world's poorest nations are in the Southern Hemisphere, and the richest in the Northern Hemisphere.) The contribution of ICTs to the developed part of the economy in each developing nation shows the same benefits from the application of ICTs as in developed nations. Benefits are therefore likely to include:

- better communication with trading partners through e-commerce;
- the ability to market tourism and trade opportunities through the World Wide Web;
- the use of a low-wage economy and different time zones to process outsourced transactions globally (e.g., data processing, call centers, and help desks);
- the sharing of global knowledge and expertise to help support their initiatives against poverty and disease.

The benefits of knowledge transfer are seen not only in the wide accessibility through the Internet of reports by government agencies but also of information from nongovernmental and intragovernmental agencies (e.g., the United Nations and the World Bank). New initiatives to make formerly charged-for print-based information available online and at no or low cost through the Open Access movement have enhanced the availability of medical and scientific knowledge. (The Budapest Open Access Initiative and several other initiatives to make scientific and scholarly information available to the global community are listed at www.soros.org/openaccess/initiatives.shtml.) Similarly the availability of medical research through journal articles on PubMed Central significantly enhances the value of Internet-based access to the National Library of Medicine's database of medical research. Other open-access biomedical services, such as free access to online medical journals to users from developing countries, and dedicated networks such as the African Health Network (AHILA) and the Health Internetwork Access to Research Initiatives (HINARI) project make significant contributions to health care in developing nations. These networks are global e-government initiatives, to the extent that many of the participating agencies and promoters of the initiatives are government agencies in the developed world.

WHO IS EXCLUDED BY THE DIGITAL DIVIDE?

Research over the past decade has identified specific groups of people as being especially disadvantaged in their uptake of ICTs and the Internet. These include people on low incomes, people with few educational qualifications or with low literacy levels, the unemployed, elderly people, people in isolated or rural areas, people with disabilities, sole parents, and, in some communities, women and girls. Because they are often already disadvantaged in terms of education, income, and health status, and also because of their profound cultural differences from the dominant Western culture of the developed world, many indigenous peoples and some migrant and ethnic minority groups are identified as having a very low uptake of ICTs.

There is, however, an ongoing debate as to whether this alienation from the Internet culture is primarily due to the factors such as low income, low rates of literacy, or isolation or to socioeconomic disadvantage. The Gartner Group report *The Digital Divide and American Society*[6] argues that there is a very strong correlation between socioeconomic status and participation in the digital economy that suggests cause and effect. The report argues that, while it can be shown that minority groups are at a disadvantage when it comes to having Internet access, they still value the acquisition of computer skills and place value on having access to the Internet. The reason for their lack of access is not that they are minorities but that they are at a socioeconomic disadvantage due to lower education levels and poorer incomes. This is a powerful argument in relation to developing nations and poverty, and one that will be discussed later in this chapter.

BARRIERS TO USE OF THE INTERNET

Among the many known barriers that the Gartner Group report subsumes under socioeconomic status are four key issues that need much more research, and which are not dependent on socioeconomic status alone. Any attempt to address the digital divide must take these potential barriers into account if it is to succeed. These four key issues are:

1. physical access to ICTs;
2. ICT skills and support;
3. attitudes; and
4. content.

Physical Access

The main barriers identified under physical access are lack of a robust telecommunications infrastructure with sufficient reliable bandwidth for Internet connections; cost; and the inability to purchase or rent the necessary equipment without financial hardship. Affordable routine access is essential for participation in the new information age, as well as for participation in e-government. Most measures of ICT and Internet access are not confined to home-based access and include workplace, educational, and community-based access. However, in many instances the types of activities that can be carried out in the workplace are severely constrained; there are also constraints on the type of activity that can be carried out in the public environment of a community access center or cybercafé.

At present landline telephone connectivity dominates Internet access, although routine Internet access through mobile telephony is growing, and widespread access through cable and digital TV is predicted.[7] Economically depressed communities and households with low per capita income have lower rates of access to telephones. Given that Internet access is likely to incur additional costs for households, the impact of charges is even more marked in the poorest communities. For example, in the New Zealand 2001 census, the lowest rates of Internet access (less than one in four households) are in economically depressed areas, and less than one in nine households on the lowest income level reported access to the Internet. Rural communities beyond the reach of landline or good cell phone reach also have considerably reduced access, as is shown in the census figures: rates of household Internet access were around 25 percent in rural areas and rural townships. Even affluent rural communities suffer from geographic isolation, low bandwidth, unreliable connections, and interference from agricultural equipment such as electric fences.

Rapidly developing mobile telephone technology is likely to improve Internet access to some rural communities but only those in areas that are already better served in terms of landline services and bandwidth. More-remote areas remain outside normal mobile telephone service, and development of mobile services in remote areas is regarded as prohibitively expensive in many countries. Satellite services, also promoted as a solution, solve only part of the problem because, although they allow high-bandwidth traffic inward, they are unlikely to support a very high level of outward connectivity. Other technical solutions on the horizon (e.g., Internet access through cable TV) are likely to exclude those in the lowest socioeconomic groups, since all these technical solutions carry costs that must either be borne by users or by central government or local authorities and passed on through taxes. In countries where the telecommunications industry is privately owned, the industry is quite open about its reluctance to make a substantial investment in markets that represent a tiny percentage of the revenue stream. This is a key point in the recent World Bank discussion document on ways of financing the ICT needs of the developing world.[8] Technical problems are likely to continue to inhibit access in rural communities for some time to come, while cost of both the equipment and monthly charges remain an issue with lower socioeconomic groups in both rural and urban areas.

Physical access also includes provision of access for people with disabilities. The importance of making the Internet accessible to allow all people in the community full participation in communications systems, education, employment, and other economic opportunities regardless of their physical capacity is a high priority for many governments. Indeed, one of the strengths of the Internet is that it opens up channels of communication and access to information for people who have previously been excluded from full participation in the economic and social life of the country. Demand for access to the Internet by people with disabilities is steadily increasing and is now seen as a human rights issue in some countries. Physical disabilities inhibit keyboard use, visual impairment inhibits screen use, and learning disabilities prevent large numbers of users from participating in the benefits of the Internet and its rich resources. Web developers in the public and private sectors are increasingly aware of the need to comply with the requirements of the Web Accessibility Initiative of the World Wide Web Consortium (W3C),[9] which is now incorporated in many government Web standards worldwide.

Lack of ICT Skills and Support

Lack of ICT skills and support is another significant factor in preventing certain groups of users from using the Internet. People in many disadvantaged groups are often prevented from making use of ICTs because of low levels of computing and technology skills and literacy skills. Where people in business or professional occupations acquire skills as part of their employment, manual workers and the unemployed are less likely to be exposed to such opportunities.

Measures to introduce computing skills into primary and secondary schools address a skill deficit in the adult population as time goes by, but the need to keep up with hardware and software developments disadvantages those who after leaving school have little access to ICT support. The interaction of factors (e.g., cost restricted access to equipment; low educational achievement; and cultural, age, or gender-based exclusion from literacy and computing skills) counteracts the dissemination of such skills in disadvantaged communities. Educational programs intended to bring these skills to such groups must overcome a range of such barriers.

Attitudinal Barriers

Closely aligned with lack of skill and support are cultural and behavioral attitudes toward the technology (e.g., that computers are for "brainy" people, for males, for the young, are difficult to use, or belong to a middle-class Caucasian culture). There might be concern over the lack of security of personal information or that computers are unsafe for families because of the amount of unsuitable material on the Internet. Attitudinal barriers are also culturally based. In many communities that place a high value on oral culture, personal communication, and strong family and kinship networks, the use of computers for communication purposes will not be a high priority. Such barriers may apply to the lowest socioeconomic groups of developed nations, to strongly networked cultural minorities, indigenous groups emerging from an oral culture, and nonliterate rural communities throughout the world.

Content

One significant reason why some groups choose not to access the Internet is that the content is not relevant or interesting to them. This may apply to specific groups in society (e.g., the elderly, women, or cultural or ethnic groups outside the predominantly Western culture of the Internet). In some countries digitization of heritage collections is proceeding at a considerable pace, and these projects often include rare and highly valued records of indigenous peoples, but they also raise complex issues of ownership and access. Equally important, the contemporary content of these records is relevant to these communities; that content is in their own language and addresses the concerns of their daily life. For example, the National Congress of American Indians lists access, content, and sovereignty as key issues. Economic investment and education are essential to the development of the Web as a resource for economic development, and for use in Native American schools as a teaching/learning resource.[10] It is not always clear who should take responsibility for this investment, especially in the most deprived communities, unless the government sees it as a social and educational investment; the UN *Global E-government Readiness Report* provides several examples.[11]

Language is a major barrier to Internet use for many people. Although other major world languages are beginning to emerge in terms of Internet use/users, English has been the dominant language of the Internet since its inception. Although that is changing rapidly, the English language still dominates the Internet with 283 million (34.7 percent) users. By contrast, Chinese, the next-most-used language on the Internet is used by 112 million or 13.8 percent of Internet users. Some 706 million Internet users used the top 10 languages of the Internet: English, Chinese, Japanese, Spanish, German, French, Korean, Italian, Portuguese, and Dutch. Other languages account for 111 million or 13.6 percent of users. Unicode has so far coded for use on the Web only 450 languages out of the estimated more than 6,000 languages spoken in the world today. Thus, many minority cultures are still excluded from using the Internet in their own languages. The Internet can play no part in the processes of government for most of these people.

GENDER AND INTERNET USE

Although in the United States, the United Kingdom, Australia, and New Zealand the disparities in access to the Internet by gender appear to have been eliminated (figures from a variety of sources range from 50 percent males/females to a slight preponderance of females in the United States), in other developed countries they are still evident, with ratios ranging from 75 percent male to 25 percent female users in parts of Western Europe, to 62 percent male/38 percent female in Latin America, 78 percent male/22 percent female in Asia, and 94 percent male/6 percent female in the Middle East.[12]

Disparities between male and female use of ICTs, and therefore access to the Internet, are much greater in developing countries. Reliable statistics are difficult to determine, but estimates of the involvement of women in Internet use range from 12 percent in Senegal and as high as 37.5 percent in Zambia[13] to estimates as low as 5 percent in some other developing nations, reflecting the fact that women make up 75 percent of the world's illiterates and have the lowest incomes, especially in countries where monthly access rates to the Internet may be equivalent to a year's wages. These figures have serious implications for women's participation in a growing global economy and in any developments in e-government that occur within their societies.

Women's access to the Internet is higher in countries with higher per capita incomes, and this may depend partly on location. In developed nations, access may be available in the workplace or at home, and rates of use by women have increased along with a general increase in rates of access. In countries with low per capita income, where home access is unaffordable and women are primarily employed in unskilled labor, Internet access is only available in public arenas such as cybercafés, which women may not frequent. Overall, therefore, women's use of the Internet is seen to be a result of lower per capita income and lower literacy rates, as well as exclusion from some male-oriented social activities in some cultures.[14]

Another issue concerns some disparity in the width and depth of Internet use by men and women (i.e., the length of time online, the variety of activities, and types of sites visited), even in countries where disparities between men and women in terms of actual use have been eliminated. Lack of interest in technology and of willingness to persist in mastering technology, as well as women's greater role in maintaining and enhancing family communications, may have some impact on overall use made of the Internet.

INTERNATIONAL CONCERNS ABOUT
THE GLOBAL DIGITAL DIVIDE

A high level UN-sponsored meeting of government ministers and leaders in technology from developed and developing nations around the world was held in New York in April 2000 to discuss the role of ICT programs, to share experiences, and to look for ways in which the poorer nations could extract early and tangible benefits from ICT and globalization rather than, as they put it, "watch globalization extract benefits from them."[15] The participants called on all parties to unite to provide access to the Internet for the world's population presently without it by the end of 2004 and proposed as action points for reaching this goal that the United Nations should proclaim the universal right of access to ICTs (e.g., the Internet) as an important new component of UN principles and conventions on human rights. The United Nations has so far declined to do so, but the Secretary General's statement subsequent to this report acknowledges the Internet as having a significant role to play in achieving human rights for all people.

The goal of universal access to the Internet was to be achieved by the establishment of an ICT Task Force, an establishment fund of $500 million to which the private sector and foundations would also be invited to contribute, and the writing off of 1 percent of debt for each developing country that would allocate the equivalent to ICT development. The United Nations was to arrange for international financing for ICT development for countries that met certain targets in their carbon-fixing activities.

Twelve national reports focus on the very real benefits and the substantial growth in the sector that planned development of ICTs has brought to a number of countries in Europe, South America, and Africa. One notable development was the Small Island Developing States Network, which links forty-two island nations in the Caribbean, Indian, Atlantic, and Pacific Oceans, giving them vital links with the wider world from which they have traditionally been very isolated; the possibility of joint educational, health, and business initiatives; and some combined clout in their attempts to break some of the monopolistic telecommunications practices that keep connectivity charges prohibitively high.[16] Such monopolistic practices have generally been outlawed in developed nations. The irony of globalization is that the smaller and less developed the nation, the lower the average national income, the higher telecommunications charges seem to be.

The first meeting of the World Summit on the Information Society made the first moves toward an international commitment to equity of access to the Internet in both the developed and the developing world. Participants were invited to endorse the commitment of the global community to the use of ICTs to promote the developmental goals of the United Nations' Millennium Declaration and foster a "people-centred, inclusive and development-oriented information society." Some participants undertook to commit to the Digital Solidarity Agenda and Digital Solidarity Fund and a plan of action intended to "bridge the digital divide" through such measures as regional integration, the provision of financial and technical assistance, and creation of "an environment conducive to technology transfer."[17] The Digital Solidarity Fund, a plan for wealthy nations to contribute a digital tax to provide high-tech tools for poor nations, was officially launched in Geneva on March 15, 2005. Geneva was the first city, and France, Nigeria, Algeria, and Senegal were the first countries to join.

INTERNET ADOPTION RATES AROUND THE WORLD

What figures are available for national rates of access to the Internet (gleaned from a wide variety of sources) indicate a huge disparity between nations and between world regions. A recent World Bank study found that 90 percent of the world's Internet subscribers are from countries that represent only 15 percent of the world's population.[18] Patterns of Internet use reflect commonplace variables (e.g., gross domestic product [GDP], culture, the balance between rural and urban economies, and levels of literacy). The figures presented in tables 14.1 and 14.2 are compiled by the Internet World Stats Web site from data published by sources such as ACNielsen/NetRatings and the International Telecommunications Union. ACNielsen figures normally include all users, adults and children, who have accessed the Internet in the past three months or, where this figure is not available, in the past six months or earlier. The figures include all people who have accessed the Internet and are not specific to Internet account holders. Where only data on Internet service provider (ISP) account holders is available, this has been multiplied by a factor of three.

These figures mask significant differences within continents and regions and highlight the dominance of North America in the online global community and, more importantly, in the global Internet economy. Table 14.2 includes a further breakdown by country (including selected countries only).

Rates of adoption range from less than 1 percent of population with access to the Internet (Nigeria, Bangladesh, in common with other African nations not listed here) to countries with around two-thirds or more of their population online, such as Sweden (74.6 percent), Hong Kong (69.9 percent), the United States (66.8 percent), and Australia (65.4 percent). (A number of countries will reach or have reached this target in 2005, notably Canada, Singapore, and the United Kingdom.) Highest rates of growth

Table 14.1.   Rates of Internet Use in World Regions

World region	No. of Internet users	% of world Internet users	Population (est.)	% of world population
Africa	16,174,600	1.7	896,721,874	14.0
Asia	323,756,956	34.5	3,622,994,130	56.4
Europe	269,036,096	36.8	731,018,523	11.4
Middle East	21,770,700	2.3	260,814,179	4.1
North America	218,400,380	66.0	328,387,059	5.1
Latin America/Caribbean	68,130,804	12.5	546,723,509	8.5
Oceania/Australia	16,448,966	1.8	33,443,448	0.5

Source: Internet World Stats home page, http://www.internetworldstats.com/ (updated July 23, 2005), accessed August 3, 2005.

Table 14.2.   Rates of Internet Use in Selected Countries

Country	Number of Internet users	Population No.	% of population	Date
Australia	13,410,816	20,507,264	65.4	Dec 2004
Bangladesh	243,000	134,792,167	0.02	Dec 2003
Botswana	60,000	1,820,498	3.3	Dec 2002
Brazil	19,311,854	181,823,645	10.8	Aug 2004
Canada	20,450,000	32,050,369	63.8	Dec 2003
Chile	4,000,000	15,514,014	25.8	Sept 2004
China	87,000,000	1,282,491,508	7.3	Dec 2004
Egypt	2,700,000	69,954,717	3.9	Dec 2003
France	24,352,521	60,293,927	40.6	Aug 2004
Germany	47,182,628	82,726,188	57.1	Aug 2004
Hong Kong	4,878,713	6,727,900	69.9	Dec 2002
India	18,481,000	1,094,870,677	1.7	Dec 2003
Indonesia	8,080,000	219,307,147	3.7	Dec 2002
Ireland	1,319,608	4,027,303	32.8	June 2002
Israel	2,000,000	6,986,639	29.1	Dec 2002
Japan	67,677,944	128,137,485	52.8	Nov 2004
Jordan	457,000	788,340	8.1	Dec 2003
Malaysia	8,692,100	26,500,699	32.8	Dec 2003
New Zealand	2,110,000	4,122,609	51.2	Dec 2003
Nigeria	750,000	156,488,571	0.5	Dec 2003
Pakistan	1,500,000	160,166,742	4.2	Dec 2002
Poland	8,970,000	38,133,691	23.5	Dec 2003
Singapore	2,135,000	3,547,809	60.2	Sept 2004
South Africa	3,523,000	48,051,581	7.4	Aug 2004
Spain	14,332,763	43,435,136	34.2	Aug 2004
Sweden	6,722,576	9,043,990	74.6	Aug 2004
Thailand	6,971,500	65,699,545	10.6	Sept 2004
United Kingdom	34,874,469	59,889,407	58.5	Aug 2004
United States	197,895,880	296,208,476	66.8	Nov 2004

Source: Internet World Stats home page, http://www.internetworldstats.com/stats/htm, accessed March 30, 2005. (These figures have since been updated.)

between 2000 and 2005 (over 200 percent), according to the Internet WorldStats Web site, are in the Middle East and Latin American regions, with Africa not far behind. However, increases of 200 percent from 1 to 3 percent mean that such countries will still take many years to come anywhere near the rates of adoption of the developed world. Given that these regions start so far behind the leading developed nations and, apart from Latin America, do not represent the major populations of the world, the Asian region is expected to see the most growth over the next few years and to redress the imbalance in access to the Internet between North and South.[19]

THE RELATIONSHIP BETWEEN INTERNET ACCESS AND ECONOMIC GROWTH

A report on the link between Internet use and economic growth highlights the potential for developing as well as developed countries to exploit the potential of ICTs to promote economic growth through the diffusion of information and technical know-how and enhanced communication and human interactions. The ability to engage in global commerce, gain access to and compete in global markets, and reduce transactions costs is potentially open to all countries. However, that this ability is reducing disparities between countries is not borne out by the evidence. Over half the global CEOs in thirty-six countries polled by Antoninu Esperitu of the Hawaii Pacific University did not believe that the Internet would decrease the economic disparity between the developed and the developing world and considered that, to the extent that there is a link between Internet use and growth in income, this benefit is being exploited more by industrialized and developed nations than by the less developed.[20]

One group well placed to benefit from the use of ICTs and contribute to economic growth in developing nations is small or medium enterprises (SMEs); however, even here the benefit is not being maximized. A recent study by the United Nations Conference on Trade and Development (UNCTAD) found that most small businesses surveyed used the Internet for research (which may have included government information and regulations as well as market information) and e-mail. The study found that although Internet access is "relatively high" among enterprises, even among some of the least connected countries in Africa, the adoption of e-business is low. In countries in which over 90 percent of SMEs surveyed had Internet access, barely a third of these had a Web presence, and involvement in full two-way e-commerce ranged from a low of 2 percent (Colombia) to 30 percent (Costa Rica).[21] The World Bank Report of 2004 details some of the ways in which SMEs benefit from access to telecommunications, through direct income to local village telecom providers (service agencies taking a discount of fees); expansion of contact with family expatriate workers, leading to increased repatriation of earnings; and increased revenues for farmers who can get price and other market information without relying on middlemen.[22] The report concludes that "poor households value telecom services so highly that rapid expansion is possible at relatively low cost to the public sector," that "access promotion would yield substantial benefits for poor households," and that "cost-effective intervention strategies are available."

This is also the view taken by a recent report in the *Economist Technology Quarterly,* which acknowledges that Internet technologies often have little to do with the lives of the world's poor, whose need for food, shelter, health care, and education overrides any other considerations. However, the report does outline ways in which a combination of technologies—information from an Internet hub, relayed to a village by mobile technology, and broadcast around a village in leaflet form or via a loudspeaker—may provide critical and relevant Internet-based information through low-technology channels.[23] Similarly, the market information that assists the illiterate rural farmer may well be dependent on Internet access to government-owned or government-sponsored producer and marketing boards.

The conduct of e-business rather than just access to information underlies the real value of the Internet to economic growth. Online information itself enhances knowledge of markets, and hence competitiveness, but online transactions enhance business opportunity. Engaging in a global market requires, at the very least, a Web presence and ideally is supported by the capacity for transactions from business to business (B2B) and businesses to potential customers (B2C). Both Esperitu's and the World Bank's studies mentioned above show a correlation between telecommunications/Internet use and growth in income, but it is still not proven that this growth is the result of Internet use and the opportunities it offers and not related to the factors outlined by the Gartner report, that is, the link is that income level is the critical factor in Internet adoption, and not vice versa. Other reports also attempt to demonstrate the link between Internet use and economic growth. While Scott Wallsten of the American Enterprise Institute–Brookings Joint Center admits that some industry commentators have "oversold the potential benefits of IT to developing countries," he also claims there is some research that shows that IT can improve productivity and economic growth. He cites examples of export-oriented firms in Eastern Europe and auto components firms in India.[24]

Wallsten's analysis focuses on telecommunications infrastructure as the critical factor in Internet use, rather than IT per se, citing the World Bank Report of 2004, which demonstrates the close link between mainline telecommunications and Internet subscriptions.[25] Wallsten therefore investigates the role of regulations, and specifically ISP regulations, in the countries studied, concluding that the net effect of telecommunications regulation in developing countries is unclear. On one hand, regulatory agencies may be crucial in encouraging entry and investment in the face of a dominant incumbent. On the other hand, the track record is not good. Recent research finds that regulations in developing countries are costly and create high barriers to entry.[26]

Even in the United States, he points out, regulators have often rejected requests by the dominant firm to introduce new features. Wallsten's data on the regulation of ISPs compared with Internet penetration from sixteen developing countries in 2001 suggest that ISP regulation produces worse outcomes, that countries that require ISPs to get formal approval to provide services have lower Internet use, and that ISP price regulation is correlated with higher ISP service prices. In particular, Wallsten suggests that "a country's regulatory approach to the Internet and ICTs can have a large impact on its ubiquity throughout the country,"[27] thus contributing to the internal rural/urban digital divide that holds back a number of countries with low adoption rates.

INTERNET ACCESS AND E-GOVERNMENT

Self-evidently, rates of ICT adoption and access to the Internet, whether through home or work-based computers, cybercafés, mobile telephony, or the multiple channels described by the *Economist*, are critical to the development of e-government within a community. The most recent and most reliable study of "e-government readiness" is the United Nations' *Global E-government Readiness Report 2004*. The report assesses the Web sites of 178 member states with a Web presence (from a total of 191 members of the United Nations), using the E-government Readiness Index. This index presents a comparative ranking of the countries of the world based on two primary indicators: the state of e-government readiness, and the extent of e-participation. E-government readiness, the report states, "is a composite measurement of the *capacity* and *willingness* of countries to use e-government for ICT-led development . . . [and the] ICT opportunity for national, economic, social and cultural empowerment of its people."[28]

The E-government Readiness Index combines the Web Measure Index, the Telecommunication Infrastructure Index, and the Human Capital Index. The Web Measure Index, which was developed largely from the UN E-government survey 2003, applies a set of measures to selected government Web pages, including the home page and main portal and pages from other key agencies according to defined stages of development represented by the following:

- emerging presence: limited and basic information;
- enhanced presence: sources of current and archived information on public policy and governance;
- interactive presence: downloadable forms and contacts with government officials;
- transactional presence: allowing two-way interaction between the citizen and his/her government;
- networked presence: characterized by the integration of government to government (G2G), government to citizen (G2C), and citizen to government (C2G). "The government encourages participatory deliberative decision-making, and is able to involve the society in a two-way dialogue."[29]

The Telecommunications Infrastructure Index, based largely on data from the ITU and UN Statistics Division, aggregates measures such as personal computers, Internet users, telephone lines, mobile phones, and TVs per thousand persons. The Human Capital Index is based on the UNDP Education Index, which is a weighted composite of the adult literacy rate and a combined primary, secondary, and tertiary education enrollment. The E-participation Index is a qualitative measure of the quantitative measures used in the Web Measure Survey, which explores how relevant and useful the features that offered consultation and involvement in decision making on government Web sites actually were and "how well they were deployed by government." This assessment, although adding considerable value to the statistical data, was still based only on information available on the relevant Web sites.

The 2004 survey results indicated substantial progress in the past year: five more countries were online, and the report records a notable increase in use of portals as a one-stop-shop point of entry to a country's government Web sites, as well as an increase in the amount and types of information offered. Not surprisingly, North America and Europe were the leading regions in e-government readiness, with the United States scoring the highest, followed by Denmark, the United Kingdom, Sweden, the Republic of Korea, Australia, Canada, Singapore, Finland, and Norway. On the E-participation Index, the United Kingdom led by a considerable margin, followed by the United States, Canada, Singapore, the Netherlands, Mexico, New Zealand, the Republic of Korea, Denmark, and Australia. Fewer than 25 percent of the countries with a Web presence encouraged citizens to participate in public policy making, and only 11 percent had actual provision for user feedback on citizen participation. A large number of tables in the report rank countries according to specific information/services offered, and while these sorts of rankings can help individual countries to assess their progress in e-government and perhaps acquire more resources to further develop e-government services, they are to some extent invidious and open to challenge. The real value of the report lies in its commentary on individual countries' Web sites and services and its discussion of the broader issues facing developing countries. Thus, the second half of the report, *Part Two: Access-for-Opportunity Framework,* is the more insightful and useful. It highlights the reality of the digital divide, the fact that many undeveloped nations are falling further and further behind the developed nations, and acknowledged that many, advisedly, set their priorities on issues other than e-government and e-participation. The Access-for-Opportunity Framework identifies the critical factors necessary for ICT access and e-government readiness: ICT infrastructure, penetration of technology tools, government leadership supportive of technology, education directly related to technology, incorporation of an emerging global culture of technology, and incorporation of an emerging language of technology (English).[30] At the same time, the report highlights initiatives where governments have made strenuous efforts to build infrastructure and/or local content. The fundamental problems of the digital divide emerge as clearly from this report as from any other—the barriers to e-government are the same as those to Internet use generally. They are primarily economic, exacerbated by lack of telecommunications infrastructure, low education rates, and lack of content in the vernacular. The report's recommendations focus on the benefits of ICT and e-government development, within the official policy of the United Nations to build an "inclusive Information Society."

In contrast, the UNCTAD 2004 report reemphasizes the view of earlier reports on e-government, citing the view of the I-Ways (2002) report that "e-government is not a short cut to economic development or savings, but rather a tool for achieving these." The report highlights the factors that may inhibit the governments of developing countries, such as insufficient planning within the organization; shortage of professional skills required; underestimation of funds needed, or lack of funds; lack of technical support; and limited or inappropriate hardware and software. It points out that moving from the provision of government information online to online transactions requires a number of changes in the IT infrastructure systems of government agencies to enable information provided online by citizens to be stored in databases, rather than forms being available online that are then printed and processed in a paper-based system. Similarly, for financial transactions to be online requires Internet-enabled electronic banking, dependent on individuals' having bank accounts, credit cards, and so on. However, the report also indicates that governments in many developing countries may decide not to invest heavily in e-government information and services, despite the apparent efficiencies and cost-savings, for a variety of reasons. These may include unwillingness to commit expenditure to e-government to build skills and infrastructure when there are other, more pressing developmental needs, such as poverty alleviation, health, housing, and basic literacy; the reluctance to engage in the business process reengineering that underpins a shift to e-government; and concerns over the small numbers of citizens who have access to the Internet. The township of Tshwane Metro, South Africa, is an example of ways in which communities can get around some of these issues, at least through the use of government Internet kiosks and so on. A key point in the report relates to ways in which e-government can promote transparency in government, noting that this is a major issue in many developing countries, through providing access to information but also through the use of simple e-procurement systems and placing government contracts on public Web sites for open tender.

An independent study was conducted over the same period of time at Brown University, using a different set of criteria. In the Fourth Annual Global E-government Study, several developing countries score high on the measures used. The measures focus on information availability, service delivery, and public access and rate sites for features such as online publications, online databases, audio and video clips, and language translation as well as provision of information in English, commercial advertising, premium fees and user payments, disability access, privacy policy, security features, ability to use credit cards and digital signatures, e-mail contacts, Web page personalization, and access through PDAs (personal digital assistants) or other hand-held devices. This results in a score between 0 and 50. Apart from the top 4 countries, which have scores of 40 or more (Taiwan, Singapore, the United States, and Canada), most countries fall between 20 and 30, and only 24 out of 198 countries have scores below 20. Among some of the highest-rating countries (in the top quartile of scores) lie countries such as Togo, which rates eighth (in the Internet WorldStats tables Togo is listed as having only 210,000 Internet users, representing 4 percent of the population), and Bolivia at twenty-third, with 270,000 users (3 percent of the population). On the other hand, Uruguay, with 34.5 percent of the population having access, and St. Kitts and Nevis (with 25 percent access) scored respectively forty-eighth and twentieth from the bottom in terms of e-government development. These findings suggest that either the measures of online-government *presence* used in the Brown study are not measuring e-government activity adequately, or that governments in developing countries are making different judgments about the role of e-government in relation to development and economic growth.

A comparison of the United Nations *Global E-government Readiness Report 2004* and the Brown University scores makes interesting reading (see table 14.3). The Web Measure Index rankings from the UN report have also been included, since the criteria used for these may correlate more directly with the Brown criteria. Only three countries appear in the top ten of both the E-Government Readiness Index and the Brown study, and four countries appear in the top ten of both the E-Government Readiness project's Web Measure Index and the Brown study. Positive (and high) correlations between the E-Government Readiness Index ranking and the Web Measure Index ranking are expected because the Web measure score is incorporated into the E-government Readiness Index. Of the remaining six countries in the Web Measure Index, only the United Kingdom makes it into the top twenty of the Brown rankings, with Denmark coming in around thirtieth. Sweden, which is fourth in e-government readiness, gains its higher ranking through its high Telecommunications and Human Capital Index scores. The value of incorporating technology penetration and human capital factors into the picture is obvious.

The comparison between rankings does call into question the validity of the criteria used and the way they are applied in the assessment of e-government capability. The UN report on e-government readiness uses subjective criteria for gauging the ability of Web sites to judge the variables of *readiness* and *participation*. In particular, and especially

Table 14.3.   Comparison in Rankings: UN E-government Readiness Report, Brown University Study, and Web Measure Index

UN E-Government Readiness ranking	Brown University Ranking	Web Measure Index ranking
United States	Taiwan	United States
Denmark	Singapore	United Kingdom
United Kingdom	United States	Singapore
Sweden	Canada	Republic of Korea
Republic of Korea	Monaco	Denmark
Australia	China	Chile
Canada	Australia	Canada
Singapore	Togo	Australia
Finland	Germany	Finland
Norway	Iraq	Germany

in relation to the digital divide, it seems important not to bias criteria too much toward the developed world and the North American/European domination of the telecommunications industry. For example, one criterion used in applying the Web Measure Index was, "Is there any homeland/security/terrorism related information on the home page, either as an alert or a link to such information?"[31] This criterion disadvantages many countries not willing to engage with the United States on its own terms in the so-called war on terror, whatever their stance on terrorism and the strength of their internal security measures might be. In fact, it is the only criterion that makes specific reference to content, rather than to process and general principles of access to information, which are contained in criteria such as "Are laws, and policy documents available online?" and "Are downloadable statistics available from databases?"

In addition, both the Brown study and the UN report on e-government readiness use judgments based on what is stated on government Web sites. Statements inviting contact by e-mail, with assurances that the citizen's inquiry will be dealt with within a certain time frame, or Web sites inviting users to post comments or contribute to a chat-room discussion, are used in both studies as indicators of, in the case of the E-Government Readiness Web Measure Index, the fifth, or networked presence, stage, and in the case of the Brown University study, "public outreach." Such apparent online interactivity is also used to measure e-participation in the E-Government Readiness report, especially e-consultation and e–decision making. The problem is that such statements are taken at face value and do not appear to be independently tested. Earlier studies have shown that contact with government officials through publicly posted e-mail addresses does not always result in a response,[32] and that the process of consultation over policy, through a Web interface, chat room, or the more traditional forums for citizen input does not lead to better government decision making.

Measures of the impact of the Internet on government and on the relations between government and citizens that have been proposed by practitioners of other disciplines are more able to take such considerations into account. M. Kent Jennings, professor of political science at the University of California, Santa Barbara, applies a model of *civic engagement* to assess the likely impact of the Internet on citizens' involvement with government and tests assertions that the Internet will simply "perpetuate and reinforce existing inequalities in civic engagement" or even that the other activities and distractions available on the Internet, such as e-shopping and entertainment, will "diminish involvement with civic matters."[33] An additional assumption that the Internet depersonalizes relationships, depresses the stock of social capital, and possibly impacts on the level of trust in government because of the inadequacy of e-mail and online chat compared with face-to-face discourse is also examined. Rather, the research to date suggests, Internet users have higher levels of civic engagement, as a result of two factors: the apparent relationship between socioeconomic status and Internet use, and the relationship between socioeconomic status and engagement with government shown in previous research.

In a survey designed to overcome limitations of previous studies due to intergenerational variation (the difference in Internet use between younger people and older generations) and limitations caused by the measures of civic engagement used (as in the studies discussed above), this well-designed study of specific cohort studies over three generations between 1965 and 1997 reached four main conclusions. First, the gap between those engaged in civic activities remained, and "the Internet would map onto or exacerbate already existing inequalities in civic engagement,"[34] although the assertion that the Internet would lead to a decline in civic engagement was not warranted. Previous and current levels of civic engagement correlated strongly with use of the Internet for political engagement. However, the depersonalizing impact of Internet use, as represented in interpersonal trust, was not evident in the older generations surveyed, although there was some evidence of this in younger generations. The paper concludes that access to and use of the Internet for political communication "did not foster greater levels of political distrust," a finding that transcended generations. However, it does conclude that the effects of the Internet differ between upcoming and contemporary adult generations, and that it is difficult to predict the impact of the Internet on a generation that has simply incorporated the Internet into its media repertory.[35]

EMERGING ISSUES IN E-GOVERNMENT AND BARRIERS TO PARTICIPATION

Linking the concept of civic engagement to the assessment of e-government readiness and e-government participation suggests that the framework for investigation needs to be broadened beyond the one-dimensional evaluation of government Web sites to include the perceptions of citizens. Once the construct of e-government on which world rankings and judgments are based depends on measures related to participatory democracy, and not just the use of the Internet for exchange of information between government and citizens or routine transactions and compliance with regulations, a complex set of judgments about the nature of government, and especially the nature of good government, starts to intrude. A construct of e-government based on the transformational model of e-government or full citizen participation in government through the Internet, rather than a more relaxed multichannel model, will continue to disadvantage those in developed or developing countries alike without access to ICTs or the desire to use them. In addition the model risks becoming rather too entrenched with Western concepts of democracy. A broad range of measures that reflect a global perspective would perhaps provide a more helpful framework for evaluation at the global level.

There are many concerns of this kind that are emerging as more countries, cultures, and disciplines join the debate. There are also many models of civic engagement, or models of the relationship between citizens and government, that must be incorporated into a global understanding of e-government. These are not only dependent on cultural, religious, and historical factors, but they are also impacted by issues such as trust and the nature of the relationship that citizens *want* with government and with other citizens.

Trust is emerging as a critical factor in the digital divide. Countries of low trust, often also countries of low and middle income, and countries where various ethnic groups must interact in business transactions show the impact of trust on economic growth through higher transaction costs and slower uptake of technology. Investigating this problem in relation to the Internet, Hai Huang et al. suggest that not only are low-trust countries disadvantaged economically but also that the disparity is exacerbated by the degree of trust: "Differences in trust between countries will promote an increasing digital divide among them. To the extent that contributions the Internet makes to economic growth accrue disproportionately to high trust countries, this digital divide will translate into a developmental divide."[36] Although the study does not directly address the question of trust in government and adoption of e-government, there is some evidence that the *degree of political openness,* an index measuring how democratic different countries are in terms of elective government and constitutional constraints on political power, positively influences Internet penetration and therefore uptake of e-government. The authors conclude that "it seems reasonable to expect that people in societies characterized by 'fair' institutions will be more willing to trust than people living in societies in which the government is less accountable."[37]

SOLUTIONS

There are no quick or easy solutions to the problem of the digital divide, either within nations or between nations. The disadvantaged in both rich and poor nations have too little cash to attract the attention of multinational computer and telecom giants for long, and profit lies in higher bandwidth and new technologies. However, in the plethora of UN, government, and commercial reports concerning the digital divide, a range of solutions are proposed, some of which specifically address the barriers to Internet use (e.g., the lack of physical access to ICTs, the lack of ICT skills and support, the lack of relevant content, and negative attitudes).

In a report to the UN Economic and Social Council[38] in 2000 the Secretary General of the United Nations focused on some key points that need to be addressed in order to assist developing nations increase their adoption of the Internet and enhance their participation in the global economy. Many of these involve international development initiatives and collaborative efforts between governments, donor organizations, and nongovernmental organizations (NGOs). The Secretary General called for a more effective transfer of knowledge from the rich Northern Hemisphere to the South and noted the increasing number of scientific and research publications appearing on the World Wide Web, a development that brings more benefits to the developing South than to researchers in the North, who would have other forms of access. The importance of information flows South–South and South–North should also be recognized and fostered, so that expertise in successful planning and implementation of ICT development projects can be shared and resources are not wasted.

The Secretary General's report noted that lack of physical telecommunications infrastructure is not the key problem in many parts of the developing world where mobile technology is already well developed. The UN has set a goal of 50 percent access to mobile telephony by 2015, and a recent World Bank reports suggests that 77 percent of the world's population already lives within range of a mobile network.[39] As the cost of mobile phones able to access Web sites and support e-mail and the costs of connectivity continue to come down, it is not too far-fetched to suggest that a very substantial proportion of Internet use will by mobile technology or via PCs with mobile connectivity in the near future. Despite major improvements in infrastructure in the developing world in recent years, the most recent World Bank report considers ways to achieve the necessary investment needed to develop that infrastructure further, in particular to finance the extension of basic backbone facilities, including those that cross borders, in areas where the return on investment is likely to be low. Financing this development is seen as being best supported by competitive, well-regulated private investment and a regulatory environment that fosters private investment and public–private partnerships.[40]

Another issue that is less openly addressed in such reports is the fact that 98 percent of Internet Protocol bandwidth globally connects to and from North America. The United States operates as the hub of Internet traffic, and countries must make payments for traffic exchange and connectivity to U.S. telecommunications carriers. Not only does this require foreign exchange payments in prohibitively high U.S. dollars, which developing countries can barely afford, it also reverses the accounting system for telephone traffic where the cash flow has traditionally been from the developed to the developing world. As more users transfer land telephone systems to the Internet, not only do developing nations lose cash income, they also must pay increased charges for this connectivity. Careful renegotiation of existing global telecommunications agreements and a restructuring of the World Wide Web, a difficult task when the Web has no formal governance structure, will be needed to address these issues.

At the country level one of the most important issues raised in the UN report is the success that has been achieved in developing local community access centers, whether these are established in existing community centers, schools, meeting houses, and so forth, or brought to the community in mobile units. This involves a shift from the concept of individual connectivity to community connectivity, contrary to the thrust of the Gartner report, which recommends domestic access to ensure maximum advantage of the technology. However, it has to be recognized that for much of the world individual connectivity is an unachievable, and not necessarily a relevant, goal and that therefore models of community connectivity need to be seriously explored. Thus, mobile technology will have a large part to play in linking communities with the Internet and with government.

For example, the Secretary General's report in 2000 refers to an example, cited in the accompanying report of an expert panel, of mobile Internet units in Costa Rica known as LINCOs (Little Intelligent Communities), which are multipurpose multimedia mobile units housed in cargo containers and powered by a generator. LINCOs offer Internet access, e-mail, and training in ICT as well as banking facilities, telemedicine, soil testing, and FM radio and TV in a small theatrette. Cargo containers have been used for telephone centers in Africa for some years, and container-based multipurpose community telecenters are being set up in several African states on a trial basis as part of an African Information Society Initiative.[41] This is perhaps a solution for the poorest communities across Africa, which has the lowest levels of connectivity in the world, but only where existing literacy levels are adequate for advantage to be taken of the rich resource being offered.

While content development is not often seen as a primary factor in Internet uptake, inappropriate or inaccessible content continues to be a major deterrent. The use of English as the lingua franca of the Internet is far more inhibiting than English speakers realize. However, despite efforts to educate Internet users in English because of its dominance as the emerging language of technology,[42] English is in fact declining in terms of the number of speakers, as cultures using other languages grow more rapidly. The development of local content and more widespread use of automatic translation systems are necessary to address this issue. The example of China is often given, and the fact that only when the Internet in China was developed in Chinese characters did the 95 percent of the population who do not read English show any interest in connecting to the Internet. Usage multiplied immediately tenfold and continues to grow at the same rate. The same rapid expansion was experienced in Russia after the introduction of Cyrillic letters to the Web interface. Relevant content in the vernacular, or language of each community, is a key issue in persuading users of the relative advantage of the technology and reducing the complexity involved in its use.

Solutions within Developed Nations

Addressing the problem, the Clinton administration proposed a seven-point scheme to eliminate the digital divide within America. It included:

1. tax incentives to encourage private sector donation of computers, and sponsorship of community technology centres and training centers;
2. funds to train all new teachers in the effective use of IT;
3. funding for community technology centers in low-income rural and urban areas;
4. public–private partnership to expand home access to the Internet for low-income families;
5. promotion of innovative use of technology for underserved communities;
6. subsidies to accelerate private sector extensions of broadband networks in underserved communities;
7. funding to help prepare Native Americans for careers in IT.

Not all of these initiatives are suitable for other countries, although they are carefully targeted at what were perceived as the key problems in the United States. Among them are some key points—solutions at least for developed nations attempting to reach the disadvantaged sectors of the community and assist indigenous peoples to become involved in the ICT economy. The Clinton initiatives address two of the four basic issues that affect uptake of the new technologies and focus primarily on physical access (i.e., supplying the hardware and enhancing networks and infrastructure; and ICT skills training in both schools and communities). Certain benefits may flow on from addressing these two fundamental tasks. Once the skills and access to the technology are in place, perhaps it is easier to change attitudes and encourage the development of relevant content, created by the groups who find existing content irrelevant or unsympathetic.

The focus in the United States on digital divide issues has shifted under the Bush administration to the question of access to broadband networks, which are fundamental to widespread adoption of voice over IP (the routing of voice conversations over the Internet or a dedicated Internet Protocol [IP] network instead of dedicated voice transmission lines), high-quality video, as well as more advanced forms of e-commerce. The U.S. Telecommunications Act of 1996 (110 Stat. 56) raises the issue of intervention by the federal government to prevent a digital divide in broadband access and requires the Federal Communications Commission to take action to ensure broadband infrastructure is made available by removing barriers to investment and promoting competition (see chapter 15). The Bush administration has made this its top priority in addressing the digital divide, endorsing the goal of universal broadband access by 2007, and it announced a broadband initiative in April 2004, supporting legislation that would permanently prohibit broadband taxes, make part of the wireless spectrum available for broadband use, and simplify federal procedures to acquire rights of way on federal land for broadband providers.[43]

Solutions to the problem of broadband access throughout the community are highly dependent on the structure of the telecommunications sector in each country. Deregulation of the industry is perceived to be the best solution, but competition will not necessarily bring higher bandwidths to more-remote areas. Competition alone will not resolve this question; legislation, pressure, and some subsidy may be necessary, and rural communities are already exploring building their own telecommunications networks to get around this problem. In an announcement on May 7, 2000, from the Cabinet Office, the British government signaled its intention to speed up the rollout of broadband services to rural areas that individual suppliers did not see as commercial by aggregating public sector procurement of broadband services (i.e., combining demand from schools, libraries, hospitals, etc.) and sharing with industry partners the commercial risk of rolling out broadband networks in rural areas. A similar New Zealand initiative was launched in 2002.[44]

A key feature of the Clinton plan was the allocation of $100 million to establish one thousand community technology centers. This initiative parallels the emphasis on community access centers noted by the UN report as having considerable success in isolated or otherwise disadvantaged communities. This model has been strongly promoted in Canada as the Community Access Program (CAP),[45] and many other countries have observed and learned and decided to follow suit. CAP, administered by Industry Canada, was designed to provide Canadians wherever they live with affordable public access to the Internet and the skills to use it. CAP is a combined effort of federal and provincial governments, schools, libraries, business, and community agencies. The program, which began in small rural communities in 1994, is now extended to larger urban communities and offers beginners courses in basic computing and Internet skills, including creating Web pages, as well as advanced industrial skills and advice on how to identify and enroll in online education programs.

Community access centers can also be based in schools, churches, job training centers, or community centers. In New Zealand some are based on marae—traditional Maori community centers focused on an elaborately carved meetinghouse that is used for formal meetings and communal accommodation of visitors; the marae are the center of Maori community life.[46] A different, but very successful, community training model, SeniorNet, has also been developed in New Zealand. This is a loose network of local societies, each of which is formed in its own community and incorporated as a non-profit-making society. Members receive initial training and then pass on skills to other members, who pay minimal fees for training and access. Most SeniorNet members eventually acquire and rely on their own Internet access at home and use the society for training purposes only.

A report commissioned by the New Zealand government looked at several community access models around the world, analyzing the potential of each to address the problems of rural communities in New Zealand. The models identified were the social service model, the free-market model, the extension model (based on existing community services in schools and libraries), the SeniorNet model, and the mobile model.[47] Several examples of free-market model community access programs were identified in both urban and rural areas across North America and Europe, known either as telecenters or telecottages. These are usually based on the concept of a salaried manager offering access and training within the community on a semicommercial, self-sustaining basis. Few of these have had the major success of the Canadian initiative and are often not sustainable beyond the expiration of their initial subsidy. The success of the Canadian model is attributed to visionary leadership, a highly effective national coordinating committee aligned with strong community participation, a successful sustainable strategy that combines financial and training incentives for communities and community leaders, and effective utilization of technology to maximize resources and minimize bureaucracy.

The Botha report's analysis of the success and failure of a large number of initiatives around the world in sustaining such community access centers reaches the following conclusions:

- Financially self-sustaining access centers seem to be unworkable in rural areas. The failure rate in most parts of the world is high.
- Coordinating teams promoting such ventures nationally should ideally be independent of any one government agency but should act as a catalyst among government agencies, business, and the community.
- Community access centers need to be community driven, have high community participation, and focus on community needs rather than the technology.
- Training in valued ICT and other skills that people value is essential for community involvement.
- Clear incentives are required to foster the development of such centers and cooperation among community groups, businesses, and schools.[48]

In 2001, the International Trade Forum identified a wider range of critical success factors in addressing the digital divide. The five-step framework to make countries e-competitive comprised the legal framework, e-government, financial access, education and training, and Internet access.[49] The International Trade Forum recommends a legal framework that reinforces several of the factors identified above for successful uptake of ICTs and the development of e-government as well as e-commerce. These include the creation of trust in the mechanics of e-trade (electronic signatures, copyrights, consumer protection, consumer privacy, and dispute resolution), the reinforcement of international competitiveness (e.g., through tax laws and the reduction of regulation), and the international harmonization of laws (e.g., on telecommunications regulation and e-commerce). In the field of e-government, the International Trade Forum recommends that governments emphasize online government services for exports in addition to providing routine online information and transaction services. The benefits of e-government include greater public sector efficiency and transparency; and faster, more accessible services for business that induce firms to become e-competent and to benefit from online procurement, export information, and more efficient compliance administrative requirements. However, access to development finance is seen as critical for the public sector, to develop telecommunications infrastructure and to provide initial working capital for digital start-ups.

The International Trade Forum also stresses the need to focus on Internet access and government intervention for the provision of basic telecommunications services and Internet access, low or no tax on hardware and software imports in order to promote access, and "technology that does the job not necessarily the latest technology . . .

Leverage your resources: find ways to maximize the number of users per connection. Combine Internet access and training, for example, by setting up community telecentres."[50] Finally, education and training are identified as critical success factors. If governments do not have the resources to invest single-handedly in necessary changes, public–private initiatives should be explored (e.g., IT corporations, ISPs, and even Internet cafés and community centers can be used). The forum advises "bring technology into the classroom at an early stage, and . . . keep it there."

CONCLUSION

Many of the recommendations proposed in the literature and discussed in this chapter are crucial to the development of e-government at the most fundamental level. However, many of them are beyond the reach of communities in the poorest and least developed nations. They are also beyond the most disadvantaged groups in developed nations, often the poorest, most marginalized groups in terms of socioeconomic indicators, health, housing, and literacy. If such communities are not to become increasingly excluded from any form of participation in government, let alone e-government, communications between governments and citizens must continue to employ as many channels as possible, while governments continue to seek ways to engage all their citizens in the digital information age.

NOTES

1. John Clayton Thomas and Gregory Streib, "The New Face of Government: Citizen Initiated Contacts in the Era of E-government," *Journal of Public Administration Research and Theory* 13 (January 2003): 83–102; Rowena Cullen, "E-government: A Citizens' Perspective," *Journal of E-government* 1, no. 3 (2004). Available at www.haworthpress.com/store/toc/J399v01n03_TOC.pdf, retrieved December 21, 2005.

2. Angele A. Gilroy and Lennard G. Kruger, *Broadband Internet Access: Background and Issues*, CRS Issue Brief (Washington, DC: Library of Congress, Congressional Research Service, 2004). Available at www.ipmall.info/hosted_resources/crs/IB10045_040622.pdf, accessed April 15, 2005.

3. New Zealand, Ministry for Economic Development, *The Digital Strategy: Creating Our Digital Future* (Wellington: Ministry of Economic Development, June 2004). Available at www.digital strategy.gov.nz, accessed January 8, 2006.

4. See Ministry of Education, Project Probe, www.probe.govt.nz, accessed April 15, 2005.

5. "The Real Digital Divide," *Economist*, March 12, 2005, 11.

6. Mark Smolenski, *The Digital Divide and American Society*, Report to the House Subcommittee on Government Management, Information and Technology (Stamford, CT: Gartner Group, 2000).

7. Organisation for Economic Co-operation and Development (OECD), *Understanding the Digital Divide* (Paris: OECD, 2001).

8. World Bank, Global Information and Communication Technologies Department, *Financing Information and Communications Needs in the Developing World: Public and Private Roles*, Draft for Discussion (Washington, DC: World Bank, 2005). Available at http://lnweb18.worldbank.org/ict/resources .nsf/InfoResources/04C3CE1B933921A58 5256FB60051B8F5, accessed April 15, 2005.

9. W3C, Web Accessibility Initiative (Cambridge, MA: MIT, n.d.). Available at www.W3C .org/WAI, accessed April 15, 2005.

10. National Congress of American Indians, *American Indians and the Digital Divide* (Washington,

DC: National Congress of American Indians, 2000). Available at the Internet Archive Wayback Machine, http://web.archive.org/web/20000620214426/ncai.org/indianissues/DigitalDivide/digitaldiv.htm, accessed April 15, 2005.

11. United Nations, *Global E-government Readiness Report 2004: Towards Access for Opportunity* (New York: United Nations, 2004).

12. Ruby Roy Dholakia, Nikhilesh Dholakia, and Nir Kshetri, "Gender and Internet Usage," in *The Internet Encyclopedia*, ed. Hossein Bidgoli (New York: Wiley, 2003), 2:12–22.

13. Nancy Hafkin and Nancy Taggart, *Gender, Information Technology, and Developing Countries: An Analytic Study* (Washington, DC: Academy for Educational Development, for the Office of Women in Development, Bureau for Global Programs, Field Support and Research, Agency for International Development, 2001).

14. Dholakia, Dholakia, and Kshetri, "Gender and Internet Usage."

15. United Nations, *Report of the Meeting of a High Level Panel of Experts on Information and Communication Technology, New York, 17–20 April, 2000.* A/55/75 (New York: United Nations, April 2000).

16. Small Island Developing States Network, Home page (New York: United Nations). Available at www.sidsnet.org, accessed April 1, 2005.

17. World Summit on the Information Society, *Declaration of Principles* (Geneva: United Nations, 2003). Available at www.itu.int/wsis/docs/geneva/official/dop.html, accessed March 30, 2005.

18. Susmita Dasgupta, Somik Lall, and David Wheeler, *Policy Reform, Economic Growth, and the Digital Divide: An Econometric Analysis* (Washington, DC: World Bank, Development Research Group, 2004). Available at www.econ.worldbank.org/files/1615_wps2567.pdf, accessed March 31, 2005.

19. Pippa Norris, "The World-wide Digital Divide: Information Poverty, the Internet, and Development" (paper presented at the Annual Meeting of the Political Studies Association of the United Kingdom, London School of Economics and Political Science, April 2000). Available at www.pippanorris.com/, accessed March 15, 2001.

20. Antoninu Esperitu, "Digital Divide and Implications on Growth: Cross-country Analysis," *Journal of the American Academy of Business* 2, no. 2 (March 2003): 450–53.

21. United Nations Conference on Trade and Development, *E-Commerce and Development Report* (Geneva: United Nations Conference on Trade and Development, 2004). Available at www.unctad.org/Templates/WebFlyer.asp?intItemID=3356&lang=1, accessed April 1, 2005.

22. Dasgupta, Lall, and Wheeler, *Policy Reform, Economic Growth, and the Digital Divide.*

23. "Behind the Digital Divide," *Economist Technology Quarterly,* March 12, 2005, 16.

24. Scott Wallsten, "Regulation and Internet Use in Developing Countries," *Economic Development and Cultural Change* 53, no. 2 (January 2005): 501–24.

25. Dasgupta, Lall, and Wheeler, *Policy Reform, Economic Growth, and the Digital Divide.*

26. Wallsten, "Regulation and Internet Use in Developing Countries," 504.

27. Wallsten, "Regulation and Internet Use in Developing Countries," 519.

28. United Nations, *Global E-Government Readiness Report 2004.*

29. United Nations, *Global E-Government Readiness Report 2004,* 17.

30. United Nations, *Global E-Government Readiness Report 2004,* 81.

31. Gregory G. Curtin and Christopher J. Walker, "A Comparative Analysis of E-government in Latin America: Applied Findings from United Nations E-government Readiness Reports," in *Latin America On-line: Cases, Successes, and Pitfalls,* ed. Mila Gasco (Hershey, PA: Idea Group, in press).

32. Rowena Cullen and Caroline Houghton, "Democracy On-line: An Assessment of New Zealand Government Web Sites," *Government Information Quarterly* 17 (July 2000): 243–67; Rowena Cullen, Deborah O'Connor, and Anna Veritt, "An Evaluation of Local Government Web Sites in New Zealand," *Journal of Political Marketing* (special issue on e-government) 2, no. 3/4 (2003): 185–211.

33. M. Kent Jennings and Vicki Zeitner, "Internet Use and Civic Engagement," *Public Opinion Quarterly* 67 (Fall 2003): 311–26.

34. Jennings and Zeitner, "Internet Use and Civic Engagement," 322.

35. Jennings and Zeitner, "Internet Use and Civic Engagement."

36. Hai Huang, Claudia Keser, Jonathon W. Leland, and Jason Shachat, "Trust, the Internet, and the Digital Divide," *IBM Systems Journal* 42 (2003): 507–19.

37. Hai Huang, Keser, Leland, and Shachat, "Trust, the Internet, and the Digital Divide," 513.

38. United Nations, Economic and Social Council, *Development and International Cooperation in the Twenty-first Century: The Role of Information Technology in the Context of a Knowledge-Based Global Economy. A Report of the Secretary General 16 May 2000.* ECOSOC 2000/52 (New York: United Nations, 2000).

39. World Bank, Global Information and Communication Technologies Department, *Financing Information and Communication Infrastructure Needs in the Developing World* (Washington, DC: World Bank, 2005).

40. World Bank, *Financing Information and Communication Infrastructure Needs.*

41. African Information Society Initiative, Home page (Addis Ababa, Ethiopia: Economic Commission for Africa). Available at www.uneca.org/aisi/, accessed April 1, 2005.

42. United Nations, *Global E-government Readiness Report 2004*, 86.

43. White House, *A New Generation of American Innovation* (Washington, DC: White House, 2004). Available at www.whitehouse.gov/infocus/technology/economic_policy200404/chap4.html, accessed March 30, 2005.

44. See Project Probe, home page.

45. Industry Canada, Community Access Program. Available at http://cap.ic.gc.ca, accessed April 15, 2005.

46. N. Botha, B. Small, and P. Crutchley, *Addressing the Rural Digital Divide in New Zealand*, Client report (Wellington: Ministry of Agriculture, 2001).

47. Botha, Small, and Crutchley, *Addressing the Rural Digital Divide.*

48. Botha, Small, and Crutchley, *Addressing the Rural Digital Divide.*

49. "Bridging the Digital Divide," *International Trade Forum* 1 (January 2001): 20–21. Available at www.tradeforum.org/news/fullstory.php/aid/260/Bridging_the_Digital_Divide.html, accessed March 30, 2005.

50. "Bridging the Digital Divide."

• 15 •

Broadband Internet Access and the Digital Divide in the United States

Lennard G. Kruger

Digital divide is a term that describes a gap between "information haves and have-nots," or, in other words, between those Americans who use or have access to telecommunications technologies (e.g., telephones, computers, and the Internet) and those who do not.[1] Whether or not individuals or communities fall into the "information haves" category depends on a number of factors, ranging from the presence of computers in the home, to training and education, to the availability of affordable Internet access. A widely cited series of reports issued by the Department of Commerce (DOC) during the Clinton administration argued that a digital divide exists,[2] with many rural citizens, certain minority groups, and low-income Americans tending to have less access to telecommunications technology than other Americans.[3]

In February 2002, the Bush administration's DOC released its first survey report on Internet use, entitled *A Nation Online: How Americans Are Expanding Their Use of the Internet.*[4] While acknowledging a disparity in usage between information haves and have-nots, the report focused on the increasing rates of Internet usage among traditionally underserved groups:

> In every income bracket, at every level of education, in every age group, for people of every race and among people of Hispanic origin, among both men and women, many more people use computers and the Internet now than did so in the recent past. Some people are still more likely to be Internet users than others. Individuals living in low-income households or having little education still trail the national average. However, broad measures of Internet use in the United States suggest that over time Internet use has become more equitable.[5]

One important subset of the digital divide debate concerns high-speed Internet access, also known as broadband. Broadband is provided by a series of technologies (e.g. cable, telephone wire, satellite, and wireless) that give users the ability to send and receive data at volumes and speeds far greater than current "dial-up" Internet access over traditional telephone lines. In addition to offering speed, broadband access provides a continuous, "always on" connection (no need to dial up) and a "two-way" capability, that is, the ability to both receive (download) and transmit (upload) data at high speeds.

According to the latest data from the Federal Communications Commission (FCC) on the deployment of high-speed Internet connections (released July 7, 2005), as of December 31, 2004, there were 37.9 million high-speed lines connecting homes and businesses (both large and small) to the Internet in the United States, a growth rate of 17 percent during the first half of 2004. Of the 37.9 million high-speed lines reported by the FCC, 35.3 million serve homes and small businesses.[6] While broadband adoption stands at roughly 35 percent of U.S. households, broadband availability is much higher. As of June 30, 2004, the FCC found at least one high-speed subscriber in 94 percent of all zip codes in the United States. The FCC estimates that "roughly 20 percent of consumers with access to advanced telecommunications capability do subscribe to such services." According to the FCC, possible reasons for the gap between broadband availability and subscribership include the lack of computers in some homes, price of broadband service, lack of content, and the availability of broadband at work.[7]

BROADBAND IN RURAL AND LOW-INCOME AREAS

While the number of new broadband subscribers continues to grow, the rate of broadband deployment in urban and high-income areas appears to be outpacing deployment in rural and low-income areas. In response to a request by ten senators, the Departments of Commerce and Agriculture released a report on April 26, 2000, concluding that rural areas lag behind urban areas in access to broadband technology. The report found that fewer than 5 percent of towns with populations of 10,000 or less have access to broadband, while broadband over cable has been deployed in more than 65 percent of all cities with populations over 250,000, and broadband over the telephone network has been deployed in 56 percent of all cities with populations over 100,000.[8] Similarly, the February 2002 report from the DOC found that 12.2 percent of Internet users in rural areas had high-speed connections, as opposed to 21.2 percent of Internet users in urban areas. The report's survey also found, not surprisingly, that individuals in high-income households have higher broadband subscribership rates than individuals in lower-income households.[9]

A study released in February 2004 by the Pew Internet & American Life Project found that while broadband adoption is growing in urban, suburban, and rural areas, broadband users make up larger percentages of urban and suburban users than rural users. Between 2000 and 2003, the study found that while the number of home broadband users grew from 8 percent to 36 percent of the online population in urban communities, and from 7 percent to 32 percent in suburban communities, the number of home broadband users in rural communities grew from 3 percent to 19 percent.[10]

According to FCC data on the deployment of high-speed Internet connections (released December 22, 2004), high-speed subscribers were reported in 99 percent of the most densely populated zip codes, as opposed to 73 percent of zip codes with the lowest population densities. Similarly, for zip codes ranked by median family income, high-speed subscribers were reported present in 99 percent of the top one-tenth of zip codes, as compared to 81 percent of the bottom one-tenth of zip codes.[11] On the other hand, the FCC's *Fourth Report,* while acknowledging that disparities in broadband deployment exist, asserts that the gap between the broadband haves and have-nots is narrowing:

> The *Fourth Report* also documents the continuation of a positive trend that first emerged in our last report: namely, the increasing availability of advanced telecommunications capability to certain groups of consumers—those in rural areas, those with low incomes, and those with disabilities—who stand in particular need of advanced services. Consumers in these groups are of special concern to the Commission in that [while] they are most in need of access to advanced telecommunications capability to overcome economic, educational, and other limitations, they are also the most likely to lack access precisely *because* of these limitations. The *Fourth Report* demonstrates that we are making substantial progress in closing the gaps in access that these groups traditionally have experienced.[12]

The September 2004 DOC report *A Nation Online: Entering the Broadband Age* found that a lower percentage of Internet households have broadband in rural areas (24.7) than in urban areas (40.4), and that "while broadband usage has grown significantly in all areas since the previous survey, the rural-urban differential continues."[13] The report also noted that broadband penetration rates are higher in the West and Northeast than in the South and Midwest.[14] Race and ethnicity were also found to be significant determinants of broadband use, with 25.7 percent of white Americans living in broadband households, as opposed to 14.2 percent of African Americans and 12.6 percent of Hispanic Americans.[15]

Some policymakers believe that disparities in broadband access across American society could have adverse consequences on those left behind. While a minority of American homes today subscribe to broadband, many believe that advanced Internet applications of the future (e.g., voice over the Internet protocol [VoIP] or high-quality video) and the resulting ability for businesses and consumers to engage in e-commerce may increasingly depend on high-speed broadband connections to the Internet. Thus, some say, communities and individuals without access to broadband could be at risk to the extent that e-commerce becomes a critical factor in determining future economic development and prosperity. A 2003 study conducted by Criterion Economics found that ubiquitous adoption of current-generation broadband technologies would result in a cumulative increase in gross domestic product of $179.7 billion, while sustaining an additional 61,000 jobs per year over the next nineteen years. The study projected that 1.2 million jobs could be created if next-generation broadband technology is rapidly and ubiquitously deployed.[16]

Some also argue that broadband is an important contributor to U.S. future economic strength with respect to the rest of the world. According to the International Telecommunications Union, the United States ranks sixteenth worldwide in broadband penetration (subscriptions per one hundred inhabitants as of December 2004).[17] Similarly, data from the Organization for Economic Co-operation and Development (OECD) found the United States ranking eleventh among OECD nations in broadband access per one hundred inhabitants as of June 2004.[18] By contrast, in 2001 an OECD study found the United States ranking fourth in broadband subscribership per one hundred inhabitants (after Korea, Sweden, and Canada).[19]

The Telecommunications Act of 1996 (P.L. 104-104) addresses the issue of whether the federal government should intervene to prevent a digital divide in broadband access. Section 706 requires the FCC to determine whether "advanced telecommunications capability [i.e., broadband or high-speed access] is being deployed to all Americans in a reasonable and timely fashion." If this is not the case, the act directs the FCC to "take immediate action to accelerate deployment of such capability by removing barriers to infrastructure investment and by promoting competition in the telecommunications market."

On January 28, 1999, the FCC adopted its first report (FCC 99-5) pursuant to section 706. The report concluded that "the consumer broadband market is in the early stages of development, and that, while it is too early to reach definitive conclusions, aggregate data suggests that broadband is being deployed in a reasonable and timely fashion."[20] The FCC announced that it would continue to monitor closely the deployment of broadband capability in annual reports and that, where necessary, it would "not hesitate to reduce barriers to competition and infrastructure investment to ensure that market conditions are conducive to investment, innovation, and meeting the needs of all consumers."

The FCC's second section 706 report was adopted on August 3, 2000. On the basis of more extensive data than in the first report, the FCC similarly concluded that notwithstanding risks faced by some vulnerable populations, broadband is being deployed in a reasonable and timely fashion overall:

> Recognizing that the development of advanced services infrastructure remains in its early stages, we conclude that, overall, deployment of advanced telecommunications capability is proceeding in a reasonable and timely fashion. Specifically, competition is emerging, rapid build-out of necessary infrastructure continues, and extensive investment is pouring into this segment of the economy.[21]

The FCC's third section 706 report was adopted on February 6, 2002. Again, the FCC concluded, "the deployment of advanced telecommunications capability to all Americans is reasonable and timely."[22] The FCC added:

> We are encouraged by the expansion of advanced services to many regions of the nation, and growing number of subscribers. We also conclude that investment in infrastructure for most advanced services markets remains strong, even though the pace of investment trends has generally slowed. This may be due in part to the general economic slowdown in the nation. In addition, we find that emerging technologies continue to stimulate competition and create new alternatives and choices for consumers.[23]

On September 9, 2004, the FCC adopted and released its *Fourth Report* pursuant to section 706. As in the previous three reports, the FCC concludes that "the overall goal of section 706 is being met, and that advanced telecommunications capability is indeed being deployed on a reasonable and timely basis to all Americans."[24] The FCC notes the emergence of new services such as VoIP and the significant development of new broadband access technologies such as unlicensed wireless (WiFi and broadband over power lines). The FCC notes the future promise of emerging multiple advanced broadband networks that can complement one another:

> For example, in urban and suburban areas, wireless broadband services may "fill in the gaps" in wireline broadband coverage, while wireless and satellite services may bring high-speed broadband to remote areas where wireline deployment may be costly. Having mul-

tiple advanced networks will also promote competition in price, features, and quality-of-service among broadband-access providers.[25]

Two FCC commissioners (Michael Copps and Jonathan Adelstein) dissented from the *Fourth Report* conclusion that broadband deployment is reasonable and timely. They argued that relatively poor world ranking of U.S. broadband penetration indicates that deployment is insufficient, that the FCC's continuing definition of broadband as 200 kilobits per second is outdated and is not comparable to the much higher speeds available to consumers in other countries, and that the use of zip code data (measuring the presence of at least one broadband subscriber within a zip code area) does not sufficiently characterize the availability of broadband across geographic areas.[26]

While the FCC is currently implementing or actively considering regulatory activities related to broadband,[27] no major regulatory intervention pursuant to section 706 of the Telecommunications Act of 1996 has been deemed necessary by the FCC at this time. Meanwhile, DOC's National Telecommunications and Information Administration (NTIA) was tasked with developing the Bush administration's broadband policy.[28] Statements from administration officials indicated that much of the policy would focus on removing regulatory roadblocks to investment in broadband deployment.[29] On June 13, 2002, in a speech at the Twenty-first Century High Tech Forum, President Bush declared that the nation must be aggressive about the expansion of broadband and cited ongoing activities at the FCC as important in eliminating hurdles and barriers to get broadband implemented. President Bush made similar remarks citing the economic importance of broadband deployment at the August 13, 2002, economic forum in Waco, Texas.

Subsequently, a more formal administration broadband policy was unveiled in March and April of 2004. On March 26, President Bush endorsed the goal of universal broadband access by 2007. Then on April 26, 2004, he announced a broadband initiative that includes promoting legislation that would permanently prohibit all broadband taxes, making spectrum available for wireless broadband and creating technical standards for broadband over power lines, and simplifying rights-of-way processes on federal lands for broadband providers.[30]

The Bush administration has also emphasized the importance of encouraging demand for broadband services. On September 23, 2002, the DOC's Office of Technology Policy released a report, *Understanding Broadband Demand: A Review of Critical Issues,*[31] that argues that national governments can accelerate broadband demand by taking a number of steps, including protecting intellectual property, supporting business investment, developing e-government applications, promoting efficient radio spectrum management, and others. Similarly, the President's Council of Advisers on Science and Technology (PCAST) was tasked with studying "demand-side" broadband issues and suggesting policies to stimulate broadband deployment and economic recovery. The PCAST report, *Building out Broadband,* released in December 2002, concludes that while government should not intervene in the telecommunications marketplace, it should apply existing policies and work with the private sector to promote broadband applications and usage. Specific initiatives include increasing e-government broadband applications (including homeland security); promoting telework, distance learning, and telemedicine; pursuing broadband-friendly spectrum policies; and ensuring access to public rights of way for broadband infrastructure.[32] Meanwhile, "high-tech" organizations such as TechNet,[33] the Computer Systems Policy Project (CSPP),[34] and the Semi-conductor Industry Association (SIA),[35] have called on the federal government to adopt policies toward a goal of 100 megabits per second to 100 million homes by the end of the decade.

Some policymakers in Congress assert that the federal government should play a more active role to avoid a digital divide in broadband access and that legislation is necessary to ensure fair competition and timely broadband deployment. To accomplish this goal, bills have been introduced into the 109th Congress that seek to provide federal financial assistance for broadband deployment in the form of grants, loans, subsidies, and/or tax credits.

FEDERAL TELECOMMUNICATIONS DEVELOPMENT PROGRAMS

The *Catalog of Federal Domestic Assistance* lists federal domestic assistance programs that can be associated with telecommunications development. Many (if not most) of these programs relate, if not necessarily to the deployment of broadband technologies in particular, then to telecommunications and the digital divide issue generally.

The Universal Service Concept and the FCC

Since its creation in 1934 the FCC has been tasked with "mak[ing] available, so far as possible, to all the people of the United States, . . . a rapid, efficient, Nation-wide, and world-wide wire and radio communications service with adequate facilities at reasonable charges."[36] This mandate led to the development of what has come to be known as the universal service concept.

The universal service concept, as originally designed, called for the establishment of policies to ensure that telecommunications services are available to all Americans, including those in rural, insular, and high-cost areas, by ensuring that rates remain affordable. Over the years this concept fostered the development of various FCC policies and programs to meet this goal. The FCC offers universal service support through a number of direct mechanisms that target both providers of and subscribers to telecommunications services.[37]

The development of the federal universal service high-cost fund is an example of provider-targeted support. Under the high-cost fund, eligible telecommunications carriers, usually those serving rural, insular, and high-cost areas, are able to obtain funds to help offset the higher-than-average costs of providing telephone service.[38] This mechanism has been particularly important to rural America, where the lack of subscriber density leads to significant costs. FCC universal service policies have also been expanded to target individual users. Such federal programs include two income-based programs, Link Up and Lifeline, established in the mid-1980s to assist economically needy individuals. The Link Up program helps low-income subscribers pay the costs associated with the initiation of telephone service, and the Lifeline program helps low-

Angele Gilroy, specialist in Telecommunications Policy, Resources, Science and Industry Division, Congressional Research Service, prepared this section on universal service.

income subscribers pay the recurring monthly service charges. Funding to assist carriers providing service to individuals with speech and/or hearing disabilities is also provided through the Telecommunications Relay Service Fund. Effective January 1, 1998, schools, libraries, and rural health care providers also qualified for universal service support.

Universal Service and the Telecommunications Act of 1996

Passage of the Telecommunications Act of 1996 codified the long-standing commitment by U.S. policymakers to ensure universal service in the provision of telecommunications services. Through that act, Congress not only codified but also expanded the concept of universal service to include, among other principles, that elementary and secondary schools and classrooms, libraries, and rural health care providers have access to telecommunications services for specific purposes at discounted rates.[39] Under universal service provisions contained in the act, elementary and secondary schools and classrooms and libraries are designated as beneficiaries of universal service discounts. Universal service principles detailed in section 254(b)(6) state, "Elementary and secondary schools and classrooms . . . and libraries should have access to advanced telecommunications services." The act further requires in section 254(h)(1)(B) that services within the definition of universal service be provided to elementary and secondary schools and libraries for education purposes at discounts, that is, at "rates less than the amounts charged for similar services to other parties."

The FCC established the Schools and Libraries Division within the Universal Service Administrative Company (USAC) to administer the schools and libraries or "E (education)-rate" program to comply with these provisions. Under this program, eligible schools and libraries receive discounts ranging from 20 to 90 percent for telecommunications services depending on the poverty level of the school's (or school district's) population and its location in a high-cost telecommunications area. Three categories of services are eligible for discounts: internal connections (e.g., wiring, routers, and servers); Internet access; and telecommunications and dedicated services, with the third category receiving funding priority. According to data released by program administrators, $12.9 billion in funding has been committed over the first six years of the program with funding released to all states, the District of Columbia, and all territories. Funding commitments for funding year 2004, the seventh and current year of the program, totaled $1.1 billion as of December 3, 2004.

Turning now to the Rural Health Care Program, section 254(h) of the 1996 act requires that public and nonprofit rural health care providers have access to telecommunications services necessary for the provision of health care services at rates comparable to those paid for similar services in urban areas. Subsection 254(h)(1) further specifies that "to the extent technically feasible and economically reasonable" health care providers should have access to advanced telecommunications and information services. The FCC established the Rural Health Care Division (RHCD) within the USAC to administer the universal support program to comply with these provisions. Under FCC-established rules only public or nonprofit health care providers are eligible to receive funding. Eligible health care providers, with the exception of those requesting only access to the Internet, must also be located in a rural area.[40] The funding ceiling, or cap, for this support was established at $400 million annually. The funding level for year 1 of the program (January 1998–June 30, 1999) was set at $100 million. Owing to less-than-anticipated demand, the FCC established a $12 million funding level for the second year (July 1, 1999–June 30, 2000) of the program but has returned to a $400 million cap for the three most recent years. As of December 3, 2004, covering the first seven years of the program, a total of $89.7 million has been committed to 2,327 rural health care providers. The primary use of the funding is to provide reduced rates for telecommunications services necessary for the provision of health care.[41]

The Telecommunications Development Fund

Section 714 of the 1996 act created the Telecommunications Development Fund (TDF), which is a private, nongovernmental, venture capital corporation overseen by a seven-member board of directors and fund management. The purpose of the TDF is to promote access to capital for small businesses in order to enhance competition in the telecommunications industry, stimulate new technology development and promote employment and training, and support universal service and enhance the delivery of telecommunications services to rural and underserved areas. The TDF is authorized to provide financing to eligible small businesses in the telecommunications industry through loans and investment capital. At this time the TDF focuses on providing financing in the form of equity investments ranging from $375,000 to $1 million per investment.[42] Initial funding for the program is derived from the interest earned from the up-front payments bidders submit to participate in FCC auctions. The availability of funds for future investments is dependent on earning a successful return on the fund's portfolio. As of March 11, 2004, the TDF had $50 million under management, of which approximately $13–15 million is committed to thirteen portfolio companies.[43]

Universal Service and Broadband

One of the policy debates surrounding universal service is whether access to advanced telecommunications services (i.e., broadband) should be incorporated into universal service objectives. The term *universal service,* when applied to telecommunications, refers to the ability to make available a basket of telecommunications services to the public, across the nation, at a reasonable price. As directed in the 1996 Telecommunications Act (section 254[c]), a federal-state joint board was tasked with defining the services that should be included in the basket of services to be eligible for federal universal service support, in effect using and defining the term *universal service* for the first time. The joint board's recommendation, which was subsequently adopted by the FCC in May 1997, included the following in its universal services package: voice-grade access to and some usage of the public switched network; single-line service; dual-tone signaling; access to directory assistance; emergency service such as 911; operator services; and access and interexchange (long-distance) service.

Some policymakers expressed concern that the FCC-adopted definition is too limited and does not take into consideration the importance and growing acceptance of advanced services such as broadband and Internet access. They point to a number of provisions contained in the Universal Service section of the 1996 act to support their claim. Universal service principles contained in section 254(b)(2) state, "Access to advanced telecommunications services should be provided to all regions of the Nation."

The subsequent principle (b)(3) calls for consumers in all regions of the nation, including "low-income" and those in "rural, insular, and high cost areas," to have access to telecommunications and information services including "advanced services" at a comparable level and a comparable rate charged for similar services in urban areas. Such provisions, they state, dictate that the FCC expand its universal service definition.

Others caution that a more modest approach is appropriate given the "universal mandate" associated with this definition and the uncertainty and costs associated with mandating nationwide deployment of such advanced services as a universal service policy goal. Furthermore, they state that the 1996 act does take into consideration the changing nature of the telecommunications sector and allows for the universal service definition to be modified if future conditions warrant. Section 254(c) of the act states that "universal service is an evolving level of telecommunications services" and the FCC is tasked with "periodically" reevaluating this definition, "taking into account advances in telecommunications and information technologies and services." The joint board is given specific authority to recommend "from time to time" to the FCC modification in the definition of the services to be included for federal universal service support. The joint board, in July 2002, concluded such an inquiry and recommended that at this time no changes be made in the current list of services eligible for universal service support. The FCC, in a July 10, 2003, order (FCC 03-170) adopted the joint board's recommendation, thereby leaving unchanged the list of services supported by federal universal service.

Rural Utilities Service

The Rural Electrification Administration (REA), subsequently renamed the Rural Utilities Service (RUS), was established by the Roosevelt administration in 1935. Initially, it was established to provide credit assistance for the development of rural electric systems. In 1949, the mission of REA was expanded to include rural telephone providers. Congress further amended the Rural Electrification Act in 1971 to establish within REA a Rural Telephone Account and the Rural Telephone Bank (RTB). The RTB is described as a public–private partnership intended to provide additional sources of capital that will supplement loans made directly by RUS. Another program, the Distance Learning and Telemedicine Program, specifically addresses the needs engendered by passage of the Telecommunications Act of 1996. Its passage has contributed to an increase in demand for telecommunications loans. Currently, the RUS implements two programs specifically targeted at providing assistance for broadband deployment in rural areas: the Rural Broadband Access Loan and Loan Guarantee Program, and Community Connect Broadband Grants.

Rural Broadband Access Loan and Loan Guarantee Program   The Farm Security and Rural Investment Act of 2002 (P.L. 107-171) authorized a loan and loan guarantee program to eligible entities for facilities and equipment providing broadband service in rural communities. Section 6103 makes available, from the funds of the Commodity Credit Corporation, a total of $100 million through FY 2007 ($20 million for each of fiscal years 2002 through 2005, and $10 million for each of fiscal years 2006 and 2007). The 2002 act also authorizes any other funds appropriated for the broadband loan program. On January 30, 2003, the RUS published in the *Federal Register* amended regulations establishing the Rural Broadband Access Loan and Loan Guarantee Program, as authorized by the 2002 act.[44] For FY 2003, loans totaling $1.455 billion were made available. Of this total, $1.295 billion was for direct cost-of-money loans, $80 million for direct 4 percent loans, and $80 million for loan guarantees.[45] For FY 2003, the RUS received over eighty applications requesting loans totaling $1 billion.

In its FY 2004 budget request, the administration proposed canceling the mandatory $20 million from the Commodity Credit Corporation (as provided in P.L. 107-171), while providing $9.1 million in discretionary funding through the FY 2004 appropriations process. The $9.1 million in discretionary budget authority would support almost $200 million in loans during FY 2004. In addition, the administration proposed $2 million for broadband grants in FY 2004. The FY 2004 House agriculture appropriations bill, passed by the House on July 14, 2003, also cancels the mandatory $20 million from the Commodity Credit Corporation, while providing $9.1 million in loan subsidies and $8 million for broadband grants. The Senate agriculture appropriations bill, as passed by the Senate on November 6, 2003, while also blocking the $20 million from the Commodity Credit Corporation, provides $15.1 million in loan subsidies and $10 million in broadband grants. The conference agreement on the FY 2004 Consolidated Appropriations Act provides $13.1 million in loan subsidies (which will support a loan level of $602 million) and $9 million for broadband grants. The FY 2004 Consolidated Appropriations Act was signed into law on January 23, 2004 (P.L. 108-199).

For FY 2004, $38.8 million (mandatory budget authority) is carried over from prior years and is available to support a direct and guaranteed loan level of $1.6 billion. Additionally, the $13.1 million of discretionary budget authority (appropriated for FY 2004) supports a loan level of $600 million. Therefore, the total loan level available for FY 2004 is about $2.2 billion. On March 29, 2004, RUS announced the availability of $2.211 billion, consisting of $2.051 billion in direct cost-of-money loans, $80 million for direct 4 percent loans, and $80 billion for loan guarantees.[46]

The administration's FY 2005 budget proposal requests $9.9 million in discretionary authority, which would support about $331 million in loan levels. The mandatory funding provided by the farm bill for 2004 and 2005, a total of $40 million, would be rescinded. The FY 2005 House agriculture appropriations bill, passed by the House on July 13, 2004, provides $9.9 million (representing approximately $464 million in lending authority) for the cost of broadband loans. The FY 2005 Senate agriculture appropriations bill, approved by the Senate Appropriations Committee on September 14, 2004, provides $12.78 million for the cost of broadband treasury rate loans (representing $600 million in lending authority). The FY 2005 Consolidated Appropriations Act (P.L. 108-447) provides $11.715 million for the cost of broadband loans, representing $550 million in lending authority.

The administration's FY 2006 budget proposal requests $10 million in discretionary authority, which would support about $359 million in loan levels (includes direct treasury rate loans, direct 4 percent loans, and guaranteed loans). The budget proposal would cancel mandatory funding for FY 2006 ($10 million) as well as canceling unobligated carryover balances from FY 2004 and FY 2005.

Community Connect Broadband Grants   Complementing the broadband loan program, the RUS has established a broadband pilot grant program that issues grants to applicants proposing to provide broadband service on a "community-oriented connectivity" basis to rural communities of fewer than twenty thousand inhabitants. The program targets rural, economically challenged communities by providing support for broadband service to schools, libraries, education centers, health care providers, law enforcement agencies, public safety organizations, residents, and businesses. In the program's initial year, FY 2002, $20 million was made available; RUS received more than three hundred applications requesting a total of $185 million. On May 15, 2003, RUS announced forty awards totaling $20 million for the FY 2002 program. On July 18, 2003, RUS announced the availability of $10 million for the FY 2003 program; thirty-four FY 2003 grant awards totaling $11.3 million were announced on September 24, 2003. The FY 2004 Consolidated Appropriations Act (P.L. 108-199) provides $9 million for broadband grants in FY 2004. On July 28, 2004, the secretary of agriculture announced the availability of FY 2004 funds for broadband grants. The application period closed on September 13, 2004. Awards were announced on October 29, 2004.

The administration's FY 2005 budget proposal requests no funding for broadband grants. The FY 2005 House agriculture appropriations bill, passed by the House on July 13, 2004, provides $9 million for broadband grants. The FY 2005 Senate agriculture appropriations bill (S. 2803) also provides $9 million for broadband grants. The FY 2005 Consolidated Appropriations Act provides $9 million for broadband grants, and the administration's FY 2006 budget proposal requests no funding for broadband grants.

POLICY ISSUES

Legislation introduced into the 109th Congress seeks to provide federal financial assistance for broadband deployment in rural and underserved areas. In assessing this legislation, several policy issues arise.

Is Broadband Deployment Data Adequate?

Obtaining an accurate snapshot of the status of broadband deployment is problematic. Anecdotes abound of rural and low-income areas that do not have adequate Internet access, as well as those that are receiving access to high-speed, state-of-the-art connections. Rapidly evolving technologies, the constant flux of the telecommunications industry, the uncertainty of consumer wants and needs, and the sheer diversity and size of the nation's economy and geography make the status of broadband deployment difficult to characterize. The FCC periodically collects broadband deployment data from the private sector via FCC Form 477, a standardized information-gathering survey. Statistics derived from the Form 477 survey are published every six months. Additionally, data from Form 477 are used as the basis of the FCC's four broadband deployment reports. The FCC is working to refine the data used in future reports in order to provide an increasingly accurate portrayal. In its March 17, 2004, Notice of Inquiry for the Fourth Report, the FCC sought comments on specific proposals to improve the FCC Form 477 data-gathering program.[47]

On November 9, 2004, the FCC voted to expand its data-collection program by requiring reports from all facilities-based carriers, regardless of size, to track better rural and underserved markets; by requiring broadband providers to offer more information on the speed and nature of their service; and by establishing broadband–over–power line as a separate category in order to track its development and deployment. The FCC

Form 477 data-gathering program is extended for five years beyond its March 2005 expiration date.[48]

Is Federal Assistance for Broadband Deployment Premature or Inappropriate?

Related to the data issue is the argument that government intervention in the broadband marketplace would be premature or inappropriate. Some argue that financial assistance for broadband deployment could distort private sector investment decisions in a dynamic and rapidly evolving marketplace, and question whether federal tax dollars should support a technology that has not yet matured and whose societal benefits have not yet been demonstrated.[49] On the other hand, proponents of financial assistance counter that the available data show, in general, that the private sector will invest in areas where it expects the greatest return: areas of high population density and income. Without some governmental assistance in underserved areas, they argue, it is reasonable to conclude that broadband deployment will lag behind in many rural and low-income areas.[50]

Which Approach Is Best?

If one assumes that governmental action is appropriate to spur broadband deployment in underserved areas, which specific approaches, either separately or in combination, would likely be most effective? Targeted grants and loans from several existing federal programs have been proposed, as well as tax credits for companies deploying broadband systems in rural and low-income areas. How might the impact of federal assistance compare with the effects of regulatory or deregulatory actions? And, finally, how might any federal assistance programs best complement existing digital divide initiatives by the states, localities, and private sector?[51]

CONCLUSION

One important subset of the digital divide debate concerns broadband—high-speed Internet access. Broadband is provided by a series of technologies (e.g., cable, telephone wire, satellite, and wireless) that give users the ability to send and receive data at volumes and speeds far greater than current dial-up Internet access over traditional telephone lines. Broadband technologies are currently being deployed by the private sector throughout the United States. While the numbers of new broadband subscribers continue to grow, studies conducted by the FCC, DOC, and the Department of Agriculture suggest that the rate of broadband deployment in urban and high-income areas may be outpacing deployment in rural and low-income areas.

Some policymakers, believing that disparities in broadband access across American society could have adverse economic and social consequences on those left behind, assert that the federal government should play a more active role to avoid a digital divide in broadband access. One approach is for the federal government to provide financial assistance to support broadband deployment in underserved areas. Others, however, believe that federal assistance for broadband deployment is not appropriate. Some opponents question the reality of the digital divide and argue that federal intervention in the broadband marketplace would be premature and, in some cases, counterproductive.

NOTES

1. The term *digital divide* can also refer to international disparities in access to information technology. This chapter only focuses on domestic issues.

2. See Department of Commerce (DOC), *Falling through the Net: Toward Digital Inclusion* (Washington, DC: DOC, October 2000).

3. Not all observers agree that a digital divide exists. See, e.g., Adam D. Thierer, *Divided over the Digital Divide* (Washington, DC: Heritage Foundation, March 2000). Available at www.heritage.org/Press/Commentary/ED030100.cfm, accessed September 9, 2004.

4. DOC, *A Nation Online: Experiencing the Broadband Age* (Washington, DC: DOC, 2004). Available at www.ntia.doc.gov/ntiahome/dn/index.html, accessed September 9, 2004.

5. DOC, *A Nation Online,* 10–11.

6. Federal Communications Commission (FCC), *High-Speed Services for Internet Access: Status as of December 31, 2004* (Washington, DC: FCC, July 7, 2005). Available at www.fcc.gov/Bureaus/Common_Carrier/Reports/FCC-State_Link/IAD/hspd0705.pdf, accessed August 2, 2005.

7. FCC, *Fourth Report to Congress: Availability of Advanced Telecommunications Capacity in the United States,* GN Docket No. 04-54, FCC 04-208 (Washington, DC: FCC, 2004), 38. Available at http://hraunfoss.fcc.gov/edocs_public/attachment/FCC-04-208A1.pdf, accessed September 14, 2004.

8. See DOC, National Telecommunications and Information Administration (NTIA), *Advanced Telecommunications in Rural America: The Challenge of Bringing Broadband Service to All Americans* (Washington, DC: DOC and Department of Agriculture, April 2000). Available at www.ntia.doc.gov/reports/ruralbb42600.pdf, accessed September 9, 2004.

9. DOC, *A Nation Online,* 40–41.

10. Pew Internet & American Life Project, *Rural Areas and the Internet* (Washington, DC: Pew Internet & American Life Project, 2004), 14. Available at www.pewinternet.org/reports/pdfs/PIP_Rural_Report.pdf, accessed September 9, 2004.

11. FCC, *High-Speed Services for Internet Access,* 4–5.

12. FCC, *Fourth Report to Congress,* 8–9.

13. DOC, *A Nation Online,* 12–13.

14. DOC, *A Nation Online,* 12.

15. DOC, *A Nation Online,* A-1.

16. Robert W. Crandall, Charles L. Jackson, and Hal J. Singer, *The Effect of Ubiquitous Broadband Adoption on Investment, Jobs, and the U.S. Economy.* Conducted by Criterion Economics, LLC for the New Millennium Research Council (Washington, DC: New Millennium Research Council, September 2003). Available at www.newmillenniumresearch.org/archive/bbstudyreport_091703.pdf, accessed September 9, 2004.

17. International Telecommunications Union, *Birth of Broadband* (Executive Summary) (Geneva, Switzerland: International Telecommunications Union, September 2003), 5.

18. Organization for Economic Co-operation and Development (OECD), *Broadband Access in OECD Countries per 100 inhabitants* (Paris: OECD, June 2003; released November 18, 2003). Available at www.oecd.org/document/60/0,2340,en_2825_495656_2496764_1_ 1_ 1_1,00.html, accessed September 9, 2004.

19. OECD, Directorate for Science, Technology and Industry, *The Development of Broadband Access in OECD Countries* (Paris: OECD, October 29, 2001). For a comparison of government broadband policies, also see OECD, Directorate for Science, Technology and Industry, *Broadband Infrastructure Deployment: The Role of Government Assistance* (Paris: OECD, May 22, 2002).

20. FCC, News Release, "FCC Issues Report on the Deployment of Advanced Telecommunications Capability to All Americans" (Washington, DC: FCC, January 28, 1999).

21. FCC, *Deployment of Advanced Telecommunications Capability: Second Report* (Washington, DC: FCC, 2000), 6.

22. FCC, *Third Report: Inquiry Concerning the Deployment of Advanced Telecommunications Capability to All Americans in a Reasonable and Timely Fashion, and Possible Steps to Accelerate Such Deployment Pursuant to Section 706 of the Telecommunications Act of 1996*, CC Docket 98-146 (February 6, 2002), 5. Available at www.fcc.gov/broadband/706.html, accessed September 9, 2004.

23. FCC, *Third Report,* 5–6.

24. FCC, *Fourth Report to Congress,* 8.

25. FCC, *Fourth Report to Congress,* 9.

26. FCC, *Fourth Report to Congress,* 5, 7.

27. See app. C FCC, *Fourth Report to Congress,* 54–56.

28. DOC, NTIA, Speech by Nancy Victory, assistant secretary for communications and information, before the National Summit on Broadband Deployment, October 25, 2001 (Washington, DC: NTIA, 2002). Available at www.ntia.doc.gov/ntiahome/speeches/2001/broadband_102501.htm, accessed September 9, 2004.

29. DOC, NTIA, Address by Nancy Victory, NTIA administrator, before the Alliance for Public Technology Broadband Symposium, February 8, 2002 (Washington, DC: NTIA, 2002). Available at www.ntia.doc.gov/ntiahome/speeches/2002/apt_020802.htm, accessed September 9, 2004.

30. See White House, *A New Generation of American Innovation* (Washington, DC: White House, April 2004). Available at www.whitehouse.gov/infocus/technology/economic_policy200404/innovation.pdf, accessed September 9, 2004.

31. DOC, Technology Administration, *Understanding Broadband Demand* (Washington, DC: Technology Administration, 2002). Available at www.ta.doc.gov/reports/TechPolicy/Broadband_020921.pdf, accessed September 9, 2004.

32. President's Council of Advisers on Science and Technology, Office of Science and Technology Policy, *Building Out Broadband* (Washington, DC: Office of Science and Technology Policy, December 2002).

33. TechNet represents over three hundred senior executives from companies in the fields of information technology, biotechnology, venture capital, investment banking, and law. TechNet's policy document, "A National Imperative: Universal Availability of Broadband by 2010" (Palo Alto, CA: TechNet, 2002), is available at www.technet.org/news/newsreleases/2002-01-15.64.pdf, accessed September 9, 2004.

34. CSPP is composed of nine CEOs from computer hardware and information technology companies. See CSPP, "A Vision for 21st Century Wired & Wireless Broadband: Building the Foundation of the Networked World" (Washington, DC: CSPP, n.d.). Available at www.cspp.org/reports/networkedworld.pdf, accessed September 9, 2004.

35. See Semiconductor Industry Association, "Removing Barriers to Broadband Deployment" (San Jose, CA: Semiconductor Industry Association, 2001). Available at http://sia-online.org/downloads/Broadband_Combined.pdf, accessed September 9, 2004.

36. Communications Act of 1934, As Amended, Title I sec. 1 (47 U.S.C. 151).

37. Many states participate in or have programs that mirror FCC universal service mechanisms to help promote universal service goals within their states.

38. Additional FCC policies such as rate averaging and pooling have also been implemented to assist high-cost carriers.

39. See sec. 254(b)(6) and 254(h) of the 1996 Telecommunications Act, 47 U.S.C. 254.

40. Any health care provider that does not have toll-free access to the Internet can receive the lesser of $180 in toll charges per month or the toll charges incurred for thirty hours of access to the Internet per month. To obtain this support the health care provider does not have to be located in a rural area but must show that it lacks toll-free Internet access and that it is an eligible health care provider.

41. For additional information on this program including funding commitments, see the Rural Health Care Division Web site, www.rhc.universalservice.org.

42. The TDF also provides management and technical assistance to the companies in which it invests.

43. For additional information on this program, see the Telecommunications Development Fund Web site, www.tdfund.com.

44. Department of Agriculture, Rural Utilities Service, "Rural Broadband Access Loans and Loan Guarantees Program," *Federal Register* 68, no. 20 (January 30, 2003), 4684–92.

45. Department of Agriculture, Rural Utilities Service, "Rural Broadband Access Loans and Loan Guarantees Program," *Federal Register* 68, no. 20 (January 30, 2003), 4753–55.

46. Department of Agriculture, Rural Utilities Service, "Rural Broadband Access Loans and Loan Guarantees Program," *Federal Register* 69, no. 60 (March 29, 2004), 16231–32.

47. FCC, Notice of Inquiry, "Concerning the Deployment of Advanced Telecommunications Capability to All Americans in a Reasonable and Timely Fashion, and Possible Steps to Accelerate Such Deployment Pursuant to Section 706 of the Telecommunications Act of 1996, FCC 04-55 (Washington, DC: FCC, March 17, 2004), 6.

48. FCC, "FCC Improves Data Collection to Monitor Nationwide Broadband Rollout" (Washington, DC: FCC, November 9, 2004). Available at http://hraunfoss.fcc.gov/edocs_public/attach ment/DOC-254115A1.pdf, accessed May 2, 2005.

49. See Wayne A. Leighton, *Broadband Deployment and the Digital Divide: A Primer,* Cato Institute Policy Analysis no. 410 (Washington, DC: Cato Institute, 2001). Available at www.cato.org/pubs/ pas/pa410.pdf, accessed September 9, 2004. See also Adam Thierer, *Broadband Tax Credits, the High-Tech Pork Barrel Begins* (Washington, DC: Cato Institute, 2001). Available at www.cato .org/tech/tk/010713-tk.html, accessed September 9, 2004.

50. See, e.g., Mark Cooper, *Expanding the Digital Divide and Falling Behind at Broadband* (New York: Consumer Federation of America and Consumers Union, October 2004). Available at www.consu mersunion.org/pub/ddnewbook.pdf, accessed May 2, 2004.

51. For more information on state, local, and private sector initiatives, see Benton Foundation, Digital Divide Network (Washington, DC: Benton Foundation), www.digitaldividenetwork.org, accessed September 9, 2004.

VII

CONCLUSION AND IMPROVEMENTS IN E-GOVERNMENT

•16•

The Internet, the Government, and E-governance

Kenneth Flamm, Anindya Chaudhuri, and Associates

$\mathcal{T}$he logic behind the detailed Web sites offered by governmental bodies is that citizens, when they have convenient access to information and services twenty-four hours a day, are more likely to utilize them. With people constantly searching for new ways to multitask and save time, their use and expectations of the contents and online services offered through Web portals should also increase. If this tenet holds true, government agencies have a strong incentive to update their Internet content and provide user-friendly applications.

Historically, e-government has followed the path paved by e-commerce, with initial e-government Web sites often limited to providing static information, rather than dynamic interactive environments. The benefits of streamlining applications, transactions, and general information exchanges soon became apparent to all business entities and those in government. The general consensus is that by implementing e-government, the notoriously tedious bureaucratic processes can be simplified for all concerned.

Although the richer nations typically have much stronger programs that offer online services, some developing nations are trying to catch up within their financial means. Some of the benefits expected from e-government are simplicity, lower costs, smoother and more efficient operation, reduction of bureaucracy, and less opportunity for corruption. All these have immense significance, especially for the less developed countries where traditional channels of government–citizen transactions are invariably cumbersome and corrupt. Unfortunately, these countries also face financial and infrastructural constraints. On the other hand, Korea is an outstanding illustration of the fact that even middle-income countries can lead the world in e-government, if the political will is present. The recent and exciting developments in the online provision of governmental services seem here to stay.

This chapter is divided into two parts. The first part provides an overview of gov-

Soumya Bhat, Maile Broccoli-Hickey, Margaret Bresnahan, Ji-Hye Chae, Michelle Christ, Robert Gilbert, Christy Hall, Jingli Jiang, Kristi Katsanis, Dorie Pickle, Tiffany Turner, Jessica Wozniak, Jaime Carlson, Ji Hye Chae, Hyo Jung Chang, Mehmet Darakcioglu, Meredith Despain, F. J. Elorrieta Puente, Shazia Faruqui, Sharmistha Ghosh, Brian Kelsey, Kirby Kornegay, Dawei Liu, Marianne Mahaffey, Loulia Mahmassani, Jie Qiu, and Qingchuan Zhong

ernment initiatives around the world in providing online services. It discusses both proactive measures to enhance e-government and barriers that can hinder development, and it identifies the more successful countries. The chapter concludes with an analysis of e-education as an application with tremendous potential for socioeconomic progress. Part 2 mainly discusses legislative issues in the United States but discusses telemedicine as an application that is already providing huge benefits, with potential for many more in the future.

PART 1: E-GOVERNMENT AROUND THE WORLD

Countries around the world offer a wide range of online governmental services. Government Web portals enable users to submit forms, look for jobs, purchase licenses, pay parking fines, apply for social benefits, and so on. Web portals also allow citizens to perform routine transactions electronically (e.g., driver's license renewal), to execute sales of government assets, and to issue grants and loans for student financial assistance and other government-provided aid.

When people want to start a business, they usually have to apply for a license or inform the government about their business. This procedure is often time-consuming and requires a significant amount of paperwork; both time and paperwork can be effectively reduced online. For instance, the city of Vienna, Austria, provides an online application for this administrative procedure.[1] This service is quite efficient for both the applicants and the government agency. In addition, this site offers several language options such as English, French, and Hungarian to facilitate navigation for people who cannot speak German.

The Korean e-government site is a good example of the successful application of newer developments of online service offerings.[2] It offers some four thousand services classified under twelve headings including, for instance, real estate, business, tax, transportation, home, education, and environment. The site uses a secure system that requires people to log in and out, thus enabling them to verify and track their own service processes.

Ranking E-governments

It is difficult to rank countries according to the level of e-government services they provide; no matter how encompassing the set of criteria, the resultant ranking is necessarily subjective. A very comprehensive effort was made by the World Market Research Centre in its *Global E-government Survey* in 2001, in which were analyzed 2,288 government Web sites in 196 countries.[3] It created an index between 0 and 100 based on the availability of twenty-two features. Perhaps its very comprehensiveness proved to be overly stringent, since even the top-ranked nation, the United States, scored only 57.2 points, implying that the portal had less than 60 percent of the features thought critical for success.

In contrast, *Benchmarking E-government: A Global Perspective*, a collaboration in the same year between the United Nations Division for Public Economics and Public Administration (UNDPEPA) and the American Society for Public Administration

(ASPA) considered ten measures grouped under "Web Presence," "Telecommunication," and "Human Capital" (see table 16.1).[4]

The countries in the UN system were classified as "high," "medium," "minimal," or "deficient" (see table 16.2). Sixty-one (42 percent) countries were ranked above the global mean of 1.62. Thirty-six countries (25 percent of the 144) have high e-government capacity; they exceed the value of 2.00. Twenty-six countries (18 percent) have medium e-government capacity and are scored between 1.60 and 1.99. Thirty-six countries (25 percent) demonstrated a minimal e-government capacity, indexing 1.00–1.59. Thirty-five countries (24.3 percent) have deficient e-government capacities, indexing below 1.00. Of the thirty-five countries, thirty-one are among the world's least developed nations with twenty-five from sub-Saharan Africa.[5] Lack of basic information communications technology (ICT) infrastructure (e.g., personal computers [PCs], inadequate number of telephone lines, and incomplete Internet access) is one of the reasons behind minimal and deficient e-government capabilities. Limited economic resources, poor educational systems, and inadequate human resources are other factors influencing basic Internet development in certain countries.

Singapore provides an excellent example of the possibilities of e-government. The civil services of Singapore are famous for being technology-savvy, and the country is always ranked among the top in the world in terms of e-government. Singapore, which was one of the first countries to recognize the importance of digital signatures, enacted the Electronic Transactions Act in 1998. To support the programs in the e-government action plan, the Singapore government set aside $1.5 billion between 2001 and 2003.

Table 16.1.   Key Indicators of UNDPEPA/ASPA E-government Index

Web Presence Measure	Stages of Online Development	
Telecommunication Measure	PCs Internet Hosts	Primary device for getting online Measures Internet penetration
	% of a nation's population online	Estimates how many citizens are using the Web
	Telephone lines Mobile phones	Basic infrastructure measure Indicates a country's potential for wireless capacity
	Television sets	Cable and satellite TV potentially offer the highest rates of access
Human Capital Measure	Human Capital Measure	Measures a society's well-being, including level of education, economic viability, and health care
	Information Access index	Draws on two annual surveys: http://www.transparency.org http://www.freedomhouse.org
	Urban/rural population ratio	Gives an indication of Internet service patterns and how access may be prioritized

Source: United Nations. Division for Public Economics and Public Administration. *Benchmarking E-government: A Global Perspective.* Prepared with the American Society for Public Administration (New York: United Nations, 2001). Available at http://pti.nw.dc.us/links/docs/ASPA_UN_egov_survey.pdf, accessed on August 3, 2005.

Table 16.2. UNDPEPA/ASPA E-government Ranking

Global Index: 1.62

High E-gov Capacity (2.00–3.25)		Medium E-gov Capacity (1.60–1.99)		Minimal E-gov Capacity (1.00–1.59)		Deficient E-gov Capacity (Below 1.00)	
USA	3.11	Poland	1.96	Armenia	1.59	Cameroon	0.99
Australia	2.6	Venezuela	1.92	Brunei	1.59	Central African Rep.	0.98
New Zealand	2.59	Russian Federation	1.89	South Africa	1.56	Ghana	0.98
Singapore	2.58	Colombia	1.88	Paraguay	1.5	Nepal	0.94
Norway	2.55	Latvia	1.88	Cuba	1.49	Thailand	0.94
Canada	2.52	Saudi Arabia	1.86	Philippines	1.44	Congo	0.94
UK	2.52	Turkey	1.83	Costa Rica	1.42	Maldives	0.93
Netherlands	2.51	Qatar	1.81	Panama	1.38	Sri Lanka	0.92
Denmark	2.47	Lithuania	1.81	Nicaragua	1.35	Mauritania	0.91
Germany	2.46	Ukraine	1.8	Djibouti	1.35	Bangladesh	0.9
Sweden	2.45	Bahamas	1.79	Dominican Republic	1.34	Kenya	0.9
Belgium	2.39	Hungary	1.79	Trinidad & Tobago	1.34	Laos	0.88
Finland	2.33	Greece	1.77	Indonesia	1.34	Angola	0.85
France	2.33	Jordan	1.75	Jamaica	1.31	Haiti	0.84
Republic of Korea	2.3	Bolivia	1.73	Iran	1.31	Mauritius	0.84
Spain	2.3	Egypt	1.73	Azerbaijan	1.3	Tanzania	0.83
Israel	2.26	Slovakia	1.71	India	1.29	Senegal	0.8

Country	Index	Country	Index	Country	Index	Country	Index
Brazil	2.24	Slovenia	1.66	Kazakhstan	1.28	Madagascar	0.79
Italy	2.21	Mongolia	1.64	Belize	1.26	Zimbabwe	0.76
Luxembourg	2.2	Oman	1.64	Barbados	1.25	Burkina Faso	0.75
United Arab Emirates	2.17	Ecuador	1.63	Guyana	1.22	Zambia	0.75
Mexico	2.16	Suriname	1.63	Honduras	1.2	Mozambique	0.71
Ireland	2.16	Malaysia	1.63	El Salvador	1.19	Sierra Leone	0.68
Portugal	2.15	Romania	1.63	Guatemala	1.17	Cambodia	0.67
Austria	2.14	Belarus	1.62	Gabon	1.17	Comoros	0.65
Kuwait	2.12	Peru	1.6	Turkmenistan	1.15	Guinea	0.65
Japan	2.12			Uzbekistan	1.1	Namibia	0.65
Malta	2.11			Vietnam	1.1	Togo	0.65
Iceland	2.1			Samoa (Western)	1.09	Gambia	0.64
Czech Republic	2.09			Cote d'Ivoire	1.05	Malawi	0.64
Argentina	2.09			China	1.04	Mali	0.62
Estonia	2.05			Pakistan	1.04	Ethiopia	0.57
Bahrain	2.04			Nigeria	1.02	Chad	0.55
Uruguay	2.03			Kyrgyzstan	1.01	Niger	0.53
Chile	2.03			Botswana	1.01	Uganda	0.46
Lebanon	2			Tajikistan	1		

Source: United Nations, Division for Public Economics and Public Administration, *Benchmarking E-government: A Global Perspective.* Prepared with the American Society for Public Administration (New York: United Nations, 2001). Available at http://pti.nw.dc.us/links/docs/ASPA_UN_egov_survey.pdf, accessed on August 3, 2005.

Currently, 132 government services are available online to Singapore citizens. In 1999, Singapore started the E-Citizen Center, a common portal to all services that emphasizes ease of use.[6] Using this portal, citizens, for instance, can renew their driver's licenses online. The site has been a tremendous success, not least because of easy access—approximately 59 percent of homes have computers and about 42 percent of them are online. Table 16.3 offers a complete listing of the services available.

Topical Issues

Owing to the disparity that exists in the ability to connect to technology, many individuals and businesses may not be able to access e-services. Geographical isolation (e.g., rural and inaccessible areas), low incomes, and linguistic barriers contribute to this disparity. This is a growing concern in intergovernment operations because governments prioritize program development based on limited or contracting resources. Consequently they target sectors that are more likely to use e-government.[7]

Speed and Quality   The goal of e-government is to improve the features of the preexisting physical government organization and to provide citizens and businesses with access to services with a few clicks of the mouse. Improving the speed and quality of e-government services is paramount to achieving this, as well as for meeting the high expectations of people from these new technologies. As the number of people who are aware of e-government increases, the demand for better quality and faster access to online services will grow. In order to encourage people to make more active use of e-government portals, governments should work on changing people's poor perception of public services and improving their confidence in e-government. For example, South Korea's Cyber Korea 21 projects developed a country-wide high-speed network by 2001 so that anyone could have access to multimedia services anytime and from anywhere.

Privacy and Security   The two most important issues for e-government are privacy and security. If government online services do not address these concerns, there might be a negative impact on usage. Displaying visible statements outlining what the site is doing regarding privacy for personal information and security is a valuable means for reassuring citizens and encouraging them to make use of these services. However, only a few e-government sites offer explicit policy statements that deal with such issues. Only 6 percent of the sites provide some form of privacy protection, and only 3 percent have a visible security policy.[8] To establish security and trust in e-government systems, the concrete development of encryption and authentication technologies is absolutely essential.

The lack of cyber laws is also a problem in the realm of privacy and security. Strong legislation is needed in order to prevent the gratuitous sharing of personal information and to give people confidence in using e-government services. In cases of government-to-business transactions, the system must be securely protected so that private businesses can access, provide, and exchange information in various fields with ease.

Cost-Effectiveness   E-government seeks to deliver cheaper services that are accessible regardless of time and place. It is estimated that in Australia an online service can cost as little as $1–7. This compares with costs of $2–200 incurred to deliver the same services over the counter, by mail, by telephone, or by sending out a brochure.[9] However, the convenience of e-government services requires attention to the cost of hard-

Table 16.3.   Services Available on eCitizen Center of Singapore

Topic	Representative Services	Government Agencies
Arts and heritage	*An Explorer's Guide to Heritage Trails* Exhibitions and festivals, arts and heritage education, funding and support	National Heritage Board National Arts Council
Business	Business assistance and financing Business registration, licenses, and permits eCommerce Market research Taxation	Ministry of Trade & Industry Insolvency & Public Trustee's Office Intellectual Property Office of Singapore Singapore Tourism Board Registry of Companies
Defense	Register for national service Notify Singapore Armed Forces of overseas travel Apply for exit permit	Ministry of Defence Ministry of Foreign Affairs Ministry of Home Affairs
Education	Attend kindergarten Preschool teacher qualification Attend primary school Attend secondary school Place overseas Singaporeans in local school	Ministry of Education Ministry of Manpower National University of Singapore National Institute of Education Nanyang Polytechnic
Elections	Check names of electors	Elections Department
Employment	Information on managing workforce, recruiting and training workers and individuals Job searching facilities	Ministry of Manpower Central Provident Fund Board
Family	Register birth Experience youth Find your soul mate Respite care (someone else who does the caring for a short period of time to give the full-time carer a vacation)	Ministry of Community Development and Sports Singapore Immigration and Registration Registry of Marriages Ministry of Health
Health	Care for the elderly Seek dental care Seek hospital services Seek healthy lifestyle	Ministry of Health Ministry of Community Development and Sports Health Promotion Board Health Sciences Authority
Housing	Buying property Look for property Selling property	Ministry of National Development Housing Development Board Urban Redevelopment Authority

(continues)

Table 16.3.   Continued

Town	Representative Services	Government Agencies
Law	The Singapore legal system Fire codes Legal aid and advice Court-related information Bankruptcy and winding up	Ministry of Law Singapore Civil Defence Force Singapore Land Authority; Prisons Department Infocomm Development Authority of Singapore Intellectual Property Office of Singapore
Library	eLibrary hub	National Library Board
Recreation	Park recreation activities Park and greenery Book a facility at community center	National Parks Board People's Association See "Community Centres" at http://app.sgdi.gov.sg/listing_others.asp?t_category=COMMUNITY_CENTRE
Safety and security	Applying for a passport Seeking crime statistics Facility for checking identity card Electronic Police Centre	Ministry of Home Affairs Singapore Police Force Singapore Civil Defence Force Singapore Police Force
Sports	Getting started Staying fit	Singapore Sports Council National Sports Association
Transportation	Buy a new vehicle Driving/riding in Singapore Pay parking fines	Ministry of Information, Communications and the Arts
Travel	Registration with Singapore embassy Questions about importing goods Visa and entry requirements Apply for exit permit from Singapore Armed Forces, Civil Defense Force, Police Force	Ministry of Foreign Affairs Singapore Customs Ministry of Foreign Affairs Singapore Civil Defence Force

Source: Singapore, Ministry of Finance, eCitizen. This portal is available at http://www.ecitizen.gov.sg/.

ware and software, training citizens to access the e-services, and retraining government employees.

Since e-government service facilities have economies of scale, the number of citizens using the online service is an important factor to be taken into consideration in order to increase cost-effectiveness. Logically, the unit cost of Web-based services should decline as the level of citizen use increases.[10] E-government systems do reduce service costs compared to costs incurred by traditional (physical) government transactions. In the United States, state governments are saving up to 70 percent by moving their services online, compared to the cost of providing the same services over the counter. Online license renewal in the state of Arizona costs $2 per transaction, versus $7 over the counter. As far as developing countries are concerned, the government of Brazil saved $10 million after 11 million citizens paid their income taxes online. The

Chilean government expects to save $200 million, from a total of $4 billion in bids tendered annually, after the introduction of a procurement Web site.[11]

Transparency and Anticorruption For the successful implementation of e-government, issues of transparency and anticorruption are perhaps even more important than efficiency. There is a need for the construction and impartial operation of a transparent system so that the government cannot manipulate it in favor of certain stakeholders. For example, with the inauguration of Mayor Goh in 1998, Seoul, the capital of the Republic of Korea, declared an all-out war on corruption. The Seoul municipal government created an Internet portal, Online Procedures Enhancement for Civil Applications, which explains the various administrative procedures to the public.[12]

Barriers to E-government

A lack of qualified human resources, at both the technical and management levels, can ultimately slow down the transition to e-government. There also exists the problem of a lack of resources for training citizens about e-government applications. Leadership should be one of the important components of the overall technology strategy for e-government. Leadership ingredients for e-government include better-informed citizens, businesses, and nonprofits, as well as a government officer at the level of the chief executive (e.g., governor, mayor, president, or premier).[13]

To overcome the shortage of human resources, governments should invest more to support education in IT areas. To promote more active use of e-services, governments should train people on how to use electronic applications (e.g., Internet, e-mail, and word processing). In addition, keeping up with rapidly changing information technology requires substantial financial resources. The limitations of funding and investment are major hurdles for e-government enhancement in both developing and developed countries. Effective funding and investment strategies need to be developed in order to ensure a sustainable model for sophisticated service delivery to an increasing number of customers.

Cultural barriers may also hinder the development of e-government. The tools of e-government (e.g., Web site) have created a new technological environment for both citizens and governments. Different institutions and societal groups with different organizational cultures could have different responses to the possibilities offered by these new technologies.[14] Fixed mind-sets, a chronic problem in organizations, is one of the serious cultural barriers. To illustrate, budget processes and agency cultures often perpetuate obsolete bureaucratic divisions that are resistant to change. Budgeting processes have not provided a mechanism for investing in cross-agency information technology (IT). Moreover, agency cultures and fear of reorganization create resistance to integrating work and sharing use of systems across several agencies.[15] Finally, some government employees resist change because they view e-government as a threat to their jobs.

Applications: E-education

Perhaps one of the most desirable and beneficial applications of Internet technology with the highest potential for improving overall long-term societal welfare is educational access, for all ages and sectors of society, with few prerequisites aside from basic literacy skills. In an educational capacity Internet access serves as an enabling tool, not a teaching mechanism in itself. The power of technology to open gateways to information resources cannot replace the verbal and physical interactions that make learning a shared experience. The Internet provides some conduits, such as newsgroups and forums, through which ideas may be shared, debated, and reconstituted by users. It thus effectively becomes a remote communication device between students and teachers.

Distance education is gaining acceptance as a practical means for acquiring general knowledge as well as specialized skills in nontechnical fields. While distance learning may be made available to the general public and most actively sought by tertiary-level students, the techniques are particularly useful for disabled persons, people living in remote rural areas, and migrant workers and their children.

Impacts   E-education has made its impact on society in various ways. It has aided the spread of cultural and social learning. With the help of the Web, it is easier to learn about the various cultures and customs around the world without actually traveling to those places. Various forums and chat rooms also help in the expression of different ideas and arguments. The Internet also helps a student to communicate with a teacher outside classroom hours. It also facilitates communication between parents and teachers.

Barriers   Developing countries face various obstacles on the path of developing e-education. First, the expenses associated with introducing new technology in the field of education are very high. Governments in developing countries often spend a greater portion of their revenue on food and defense, with little left over for education. The projects can be quite expensive for the poorer nations. For example, two such projects in India and Morocco are expected to cost approximately $850,000 (US) to $950,000 (US) at the initial stage.[16]

Second, before any new technology is to be successfully implemented, it is necessary to have the infrastructure required to support the technology in place. In many of these developing countries, people in rural areas—sometimes also in urban areas—may not have electricity or access to a telephone. It would be difficult to expand e-education in such places without developing the infrastructure. Also, usually younger people are more adept in using new technologies. This may result in students having greater knowledge about the Internet than do their teachers.

Another issue that has been a cause of concern in these countries is that there may be no way of judging the quality of education offered online by foreign universities. The people who take these courses have no way of knowing how the university is ranked in its own home country, whether the degree it offers is really of any credit, and even whether the fees charged are fairly assessed.

In the classroom, investing in proper teacher training in computer and Internet basics, in addition to adopting best teaching practices, is critical to achieving a sound balance of progressive and traditional academic curricula. Connectedness to the Internet and the unique attractiveness of this new technology may keep some otherwise listless or restless students from losing interest in classroom activities and may actually contribute to reduced dropout rates.

However, application of technology to traditional education has not always been warmly embraced, particularly in primary education settings where close contact between teachers and children is highly encouraged, and both educators and parents support development through interactive group play and the creative use of physical objects (blocks, art colors, toys, and writing implements) to build cognitive, writing, and motor skills. In developed countries educators are resisting the introduction of PCs to classrooms with children under age eleven, favoring reinstatement of underfunded programs in the arts, dance, and physical education. In developing countries public–private sector partnerships have put computers in some classrooms. However, they remain unconnected and soon become obsolete owing to lack of infrastructure (electricity) or trained instructors.

Physical requirements include installation of electric and telephone lines, work surfaces, and temperature-moderating devices in addition to the basic PC hardware, software, and qualified instructors. Quality of content is equally important. Educators must also devote personal and school resources to help students and themselves climb the technical learning curve.

As with all Internet access initiatives, stable financing, focused initiatives, and sustained commitment separate the success stories from the failures. The greatest value realized from distance learning programs and general access is direct, on-demand individual command of academic and informational resources, to "share and build intellectual capital."[17] Internet access will not promote greater intelligence or productivity by osmosis. As with any resource, the manner in which technology is used will determine the degree of benefit extracted and future effects—both positive and negative.

PART 2: THE INTERNET IN THE UNITED STATES (LEGISLATION AND REGULATION)

Unsolicited Commercial E-mail (Spam)

As Internet access and usage increase, so does the sending of unsolicited commercial e-mail, also known as spam. For some, spam is simply an annoyance that is easily removed by pressing the delete key. Unfortunately, the problem is much more complex. The Coalition against Unsolicited Commercial E-Mail outlines how spam is "a threat to the viability of Internet e-mail and a danger to Internet commerce."[18] One issue is that the organizations that send spam market products are rarely reputable. Second, while sending spam is extremely inexpensive for the sender, costs are incurred along various points on the distribution and transmittal chain. Spam consumes bandwidth and forces Internet service providers (ISPs) to provide slower access to their customers or to increase prices to cover the cost of purchasing more bandwidth.[19]

Recognizing the negative effects that spam has on the Internet, Congress passed the Controlling the Assault of Non-Solicited Pornography and Marketing Act (CAN-SPAM Act). President Bush signed it into law on December 16, 2003, and the law took effect on January 1, 2004. This law (P.L. 108-187) takes precedence over state spam laws except for the states that have laws that require labeling of spam or prohibit spam altogether.[20]

As of April 2004, thirty-six states have laws regulating spam. The states that have yet to pass any spam regulation laws include Alabama, Florida, Georgia, Hawaii, Kentucky, Massachusetts, Mississippi, Montana, Nebraska, New Hampshire, New Jersey, New York, South Carolina, and Vermont. States differ in how they choose to regulate spam, but in general state laws contain at least one of the following components:

- Contact information in the form of a valid e-mail address or the sender's name and mailing address must be included so that the recipient can communicate with the sender.

- Opt-out information must be included, and requests opting for no further e-mail solicitations must be honored.
- Spam must contain accurate header and routing information so that recipients can identify the sender's identity and location.
- Subject lines should contain information that accurately reflects the e-mail's content. E-mail solicitations must contain "ADV:" in the first part of the subject line, and if the solicitation promotes adult products or services, "ADV: ADLT" is required.
- If a third-party domain name is used to send spam, the sender must have that party's authorization.[21]

In September 2003, California adopted the strictest spam law in the country. This law makes it illegal to send spam from the state or to an e-mail address based in the state. Instead of giving spam recipients the chance to opt out, they must opt in to receive spam. This law imposes fines of $1,000 for each spam e-mail sent in violation of this law and up to $1 million for each incident.[22]

Broadband Parity

As a result of the 1996 Telecommunications Act (P.L. 104-104), most local telecommunication companies have had to open their lines for use by competitors. The act stipulates that the lines and services be made available in unbundled network elements, which allows competing local exchange carriers (CLECs) to purchase only the services they need (e.g., switches and/or transmission lines). "Although the Act did not identify competition in broadband services as a specific goal, the rapid growth of Internet use and widespread interest in broadband networks intersected the broader move toward enhancing new carriers' opportunities to develop the marketplace."[23] The large incumbent telecommunication companies (e.g., the Regional Bell Operating Carriers [RBOC], SBC, and Verizon) have asked for "regulatory relief" saying "it was too expensive for incumbents to share their facilities . . . [arguing that] they cannot invest in new fiber-based networks if they are to share them with competitors at below-cost rates."[24] In an attempt to remove the pro-competitive regulations on broadband services, the regional Bells have introduced broadband-parity bills in many states.

In many areas across the country, the telecommunication companies providing DSL service compete with cable broadband, satellite, and fixed wireless broadband ISPs.[25] The regulations requiring line sharing and unbundling of services for use by competitors apply only to telecommunication companies; cable companies are excluded from these types of regulations. By eliminating these competitive access and resale requirements, the telephone companies' DSL services would no longer be regulated by the states' public utilities commissions. The telecom companies argue that this would allow them to compete more with cable companies. The small CLECs maintain that without the regulation, the RBOCs would have monopoly power to set the rates for leasing part or all of their network to competitors, if they chose to allow smaller competitors access at all.

In 2003, eight states introduced broadband-parity bills. Most of the bills, such as those in the Texas legislature (HB 1658 and SB 377), propose the elimination of unbundling requirements for telecommunications companies' broadband services to create parity with cable companies, which are not subject to the pro-competition unbundling requirements. "Such bills represent a way to bypass the federal layer of authority on regulating high-speed Internet services. Most of these bills are extremely brief (and many are identical). They generally prohibit any regulation of high-speed Internet services."[26]

Five states have laws prohibiting the regulation of broadband services, particularly the requirement of opening lines for use by competitors (with both bundled and unbundled services). On February 21, 2003, the Federal Communications Commission exempted the telecom companies from being required to provide access to competitors to utilize the new high-speed fiber-based networks.[27] However, according to a May 2003 report from the Telecommunications and Information Policy Institute, "Consumer price data suggests that rural location may be less important in determining broadband prices than is the presence of competition. As the data [from Texas, Kansas, and Missouri] suggest, prices will be lower where there is choice."[28]

Broadband Deployment

Broadband deployment has become a matter of public policy owing to the lack of competitive market forces in rural and traditionally underserved areas. High-speed or broadband access is considered essential for having equal access opportunities in all communities. Many factors contribute to closing the gap between areas that have broadband technologies and those that do not. However, many of those efforts are receiving less funding as the economy has weakened in recent years.

Some federal programs have tried to address the problem of broadband inequities:

- The E-rate program: Founded through the Telecommunications Act of 1996, this program provided a structure for schools and libraries to receive substantial discounts on telecommunications services, internal wiring, and communications technologies as a result of a Universal Service Fund (USF). Many remote areas, such as northern Alaska, have high-speed Internet access due solely to this investment.
- No Child Left Behind: This program provides a number of technology-based programs as a part of educational reform.
- The NTIA Technology Opportunity Program (TOPS): This program under the Department of Commerce's National Telecommunications and Information Administration has provided grants to community-based initiatives totaling $218.9 million and has helped attract over $297 million in matching funds. This program has been scheduled for elimination under the Bush administration.
- Competitive forces may be able to provide broadband services equitably. Theoretically, with the existence of a competitive market, broadband services will be offered at an affordable price. However, in many rural areas, competition is not present in the telecommunications industries. The 1996 Telecommunications Act attempts to correct market forces to provide for more competition. Many people believe that the digital divide should and will be solved through the competitive private market rather than government intervention.
- Philanthropic groups, such as the Gates Foundation, provide grants, subsidies,

and loans for technology hardware, software, and training to local organizations such as libraries, schools, and senior centers. These groups are helping to address the lack of broadband access as well, but they are more focused on peripheral supplies and not actually building out broadband access.

• State and local government initiatives also help to address the broadband dilemma. Most states and many local governments have programs that address the inequities in technology. Many state governments have a state technology office and educational programs that research and fund programs to help close the gap for rural and traditionally underserved citizens.

The efforts of many states have been tracked in certain broadband- and network-related surveys and studies. In 2003, TechNet, an association of more than 150 chief executive officers and senior partners from several industries, released a study on broadband-deployment state policies that identified the (1) ways that states can encourage the rapid deployment of broadband services and (2) states that are conducting best practices. The report of the study focuses on three main policy areas: roadblocks to broadband deployment, supply-side policies, and demand-side policies.[29]

In terms of roadblocks to deployment policies, the main area of evaluation in the report is right-of-way barriers. Broadband providers often face high fees and bureaucracy in many states because of right-of-way barriers. Defining right-of-way fees and policies is often the responsibility of municipalities, but many municipalities set policies that will maximize their income rather than broadband deployment. However, many states have passed regulations for right-of-way fees and procedures to reduce the burden on broadband providers.[30]

In addition to encouraging industry to invest in broadband networks, state policies can encourage both the public and the private sector to use broadband. Policies that increase broadband demand include financial incentives, increasing e-government services, and increasing public sector demand by implementing programs that require broadband, such as telemedicine or online education programs.[31] Most states have implemented distance learning and telemedicine programs.

It is surprising, however, that the states outlined by TechNet to be actively pursuing broadband deployment neither rank among the highest in broadband deployment nor have they received high levels of federal funding from the USF. The American Electronics Association released a report, *Broadband in the States 2003,* that ranks all fifty states and the District of Columbia in four categories: broadband subscribers, broadband growth rate, broadband subscribers per one thousand households, and all types of Internet access.[32]

While the report provides good recommendations on broadband deployment strategies, there does not yet appear to be any correlation between those states that pursue those strategies and their level of broadband subscribers. It is important to note that the broadband-subscribers ranking does not portray the availability of broadband access but just the number of consumers using that access.

Taxing Internet Services

As of April 27, 2004, Congress was debating whether or not to enact a permanent ban on Internet access taxes. The original moratorium on Internet access taxes was established in 1998 by the Internet Tax Freedom Act (ITFA; P.L. 105-277) and was renewed through November 1, 2003. Those who oppose a permanent ban claim that a moratorium "will cost state and local governments billions of dollars in revenue and force them to raise local taxes" to compensate for what some believe to be an already well-subsidized industry.[33] Those who support a permanent tax ban believe that decreasing the cost of Internet services will enable more people to afford broadband.

Prior to the passage of ITFA, eleven states were charging state and local taxes on Internet access, and the ITFA included a grandfather clause that allowed these states to continue taxing all types of Internet access. These states include Colorado, Hawaii, New Hampshire, New Mexico, North Dakota, Ohio, South Dakota, Tennessee, Texas, Washington, and Wisconsin. If Congress decides to permanently extend the tax moratorium, these states could lose between $80 million and $120 million in annual revenue. At least twenty-seven states, including the eleven states that have grandfathered laws, collect taxes on DSL service. The loss of revenue to these states would be approximately $70 million annually.[34]

Applications: Telemedicine

Telemedicine, which is the use of electronic communication and information technologies to provide or support clinical care at a distance, is a growing field for health care and Internet technology. At the federal level, support for telemedicine programs has come from a variety of programs including the Office for the Advancement of Telehealth (OAT), the Department of Commerce, Technology Opportunities Program (TOPS) grants, the Rural Utilities Service, the Office of Rural Health Policy, the National Library of Medicine, and the Centers for Medicare and Medicaid Services. The OAT grant program has funded nearly $180 million in telemedicine programs since 1989.[35] Since the inception of the TOPS grant program, over $19 million has been distributed to states and organizations for creating and expanding their innovative health care programs. Telemedicine can reduce costs and provide the ability to increase greatly the quality of health care and life in rural and urban areas.

In 1999, Congress passed the Healthcare Research and Quality Act (P.L. 106-129), which required the Department of Health and Human Services (HHS) to report on telemedicine in 2001. HHS and the Office for the Advancement of Telehealth submitted the report to Congress in March 2001. That report details a number of current trends of telemedicine as well as barriers to its continued growth. It also identifies the following key issues affecting the growth of the telemedicine field: lack of reimbursement, legal issues, safety and standards, privacy, security and confidentiality, and the telecommunications infrastructure. Finally, the report comments on the importance of telemedicine, given new emerging technologies and the aging of America's population.[36]

The technology for telemedicine varies widely from simple consolidated databases of patient information to store-and-forward, video conferencing, and interactive digital video. Telemedicine appears to be primarily provided in two types of situations. The majority of programs target the needs of rural residents. Even though the U.S. population continues to grow, many states persist in having significant rural populations. Telemedicine is a useful tool, along with programs that boost community health clinic funding and pay doctors to move to medically underserved areas. Telemedicine may turn out to be more cost-effective in many cases. For example, the Center for Health and Technology in California, which provides quality care to eighty rural facilities and which began working in the telemedicine field in 1996, has brought specialties such as mental health care and endocrinology to rural California regions. Second, many telemedicine programs are in place to expand the coverage of specialty physicians. General practitioners will always be in high demand as primary health care providers. However, in many cases, the services of specialty providers are needed. With telemedicine, hospitals have access to specialists in cardiology, mental health, and radiology. These needs will likely be in rural areas, but urban areas face shortages of specialty providers as well.

In many cases, university medical schools have created telemedicine programs as a way to provide training and teaching opportunities for students. Medical schools rely heavily on the hands-on training their students undergo in hospitals across the country. Telemedicine programs broaden these training opportunities. In addition, medical schools generally have access to federal and state research funding and can direct these dollars toward telemedicine. For these reasons, many universities have partnered with private hospitals and health carriers to create telemedicine networks in their states. A final trend across telemedicine programs is multistate programs that have been created to fulfill telemedicine needs.

CONCLUSION

E-government can be looked at from two diametrically opposite viewpoints. The first is that it is a completely new interface between the government and citizens, using technologies that did not exist even a decade ago. The other is that it is simply a better way of conducting governance, using technologies that have been evolving—though at a very rapid pace—through the near past. Both viewpoints are valid, depending on the context. What is undoubtedly true is that it is making lives easier for both government and citizens and hence needs to be encouraged whenever and wherever possible.

The biggest benefit of e-government is that it makes services available to the public in a manner impossible to replicate in a brick-and-mortar setting. In essence, the services are delivered right to the homes of the citizens, when it is most convenient for them to attend to the matter. So a person does not have to rush to the local branch of the Department of Public Safety—or the equivalent organization in other countries—after work, before it closes, to renew a driver's license. Nor does that person have to stand in line at the post office to file tax returns. The individual can do these at leisure, right at home—provided access to the Internet is available.

This convenience, though not the only benefit to the public, is certainly the biggest. The increased accessibility and better understanding of the processes involved invariably translates to lower chances of corruption by public servants. This happens in two ways. First, e-services simply cut out the many intermediaries—the infamous "file pushers"—from the process, the transactions generally being one-point affairs. Second, the process allows those public personnel who remain involved to be better scrutinized. This is especially beneficial for developing countries, where corruption is invariably endemic. The government officials of these countries, who are now enthusiastically climbing on to the trendy e-government bandwagon, may in the near future regretfully discover that their scope for fleecing the public has become much lower.

Unfortunately, progress does not come cheap. Many e-government projects are financially challenging even for the richer nations. For the poorer countries, faced usually with the much more pressing concerns of ensuring food, clothing, shelter, education, and health services for the maximum number of people, reluctance to embrace this new interface is both understandable and realistic. However, it may well be that the benefits in the long run far outweigh the initially daunting investment required. Distance education and telemedicine, in particular, may yield benefits in a very short time. As a mass communications medium, the Internet is still extremely young, and the rapidity with which it has become a global phenomenon points to potential yet to be imagined. Governance, too, is sure to be transformed by this new technology in the future.

NOTES

1. Elektronische Abwicklung von Gewerbeangelegenheiten (Vienna, Austria). Available at www .wien.gv.at/wgrweb, accessed February 10, 2005.

2. Republic of Korea, E-government. Available at www.egov.go.kr, accessed February 10, 2005.

3. World Markets Research Centre, *Global E-government Survey* (Singapore: World Markets Research Centre, 2003). Available at www.worldmarketsanalysis.com/pdf/e-govreport.pdf, accessed June 4, 2003.

4. United Nations, Division for Public Economics and Public Administration, *Benchmarking E-government: A Global Perspective*. Prepared with the American Society for Public Administration (New York: United Nations, 2001). Available at http://pti.nw.dc.us/links/docs/ASPA_UN_egov _survey.pdf, accessed on August 3, 2005.

5. United Nations, Division for Public Economics and Public Administration, *Benchmarking E-government*, 27–33.

6. Singapore, E-Citizen: Your Gateway to All Government Services. Available at www .ecitizen.gov.sg/, accessed February 10, 2005.

7. United Nations, Division for Public Economics and Public Administration, *Benchmarking E-government*, 27–33.

8. World Markets Research Centre, *Global E-government Survey*.

9. New Zealand, State Services Commission, E-Government Unit, *FAQs* (Wellington: State Services Commission, n.d.). Available at www.E-government.govt.nz/programme/faqs.asp, accessed September 30, 2004.

10. United Nations, Division for Public Economics and Public Administration, *Benchmarking E-government*, 53.

11. Chile, E-Government: Government Procurement E-System. Available at www1.world bank.org/publicsector/egov/eprocurement_chile.htm, accessed January 28, 2005.

12. World Bank Group, OPEN: Seoul's Anticorruption Project. Available at www1 .worldbank.org/publicsector/egov/seoulcs.htm, accessed September 30, 2004.

13. Janet Caldow, director, Institute for Electronic Government, *The Quest for Electronic Government: A Defining Vision* (White Plains, NY: IBM Corporation, 1999). Available at www1.ibm.com/ industries/government/ieg/pdf/egovvision.pdf, accessed September 30, 2004.

14. United Kingdom, National Audit Office, *Cultural Barriers to E-government*, by Helen Margetts and Patrick Dunleavy (London: National Audit Office, 2002). Available at www.nao.org.uk/, accessed September 30, 2004.

15. Office of Management and Budget (OMB), *E-government Strategy* (Washington, DC: OMB, 2002), 5. Available at www.whitehouse.gov/omb/inforeg/infopoltech.html, accessed September 30, 2004.

16. *Internet and Education: Virtual Classrooms for Everyone?* (Geneva, Switzerland: International Tele-

communications Organization, 2001). Available at www.itu.int/newsarchive/wtd/2001/FeatureEdu cation.html, accessed September 30, 2004.

17. Bridges.org, Home page (Washington, DC: Bridges.org). Available at www.bridges.org/case studies/bridgebuilders/builder_schoolnet.html, accessed September 30, 2004.

18. Coalition against Unsolicited Commercial Email, About the Problem. Available at www .cauce.org/about/problem.shtml, accessed April 26, 2004.

19. Coalition against Unsolicited Commercial Email, About the Problem.

20. "Spam Law: United States: Federal Laws: 108th Congress: Summary." Available at www.spam laws.com/federal/summ108.html#s877, accessed April 26, 2004.

21. Mondaq, *United States: Anti-Spam Laws: Navigating the Web of Compliance* (New York: Latham & Watkins, 2004). Available at www.mondaq.com/i_article.asp_Q_articleid_E_23763, accessed April 27, 2004.

22. "Spam Laws: United States: State Laws: California." Available at www.spamlaws.com/state/ ca1.html, accessed April 27, 2004.

23. University of Texas at Austin, Telecommunications and Information Policy Institute, *Local Services and Broadband Telecommunications Competition in Texas, Missouri and Kansas* (Austin, TX: Telecommunications and Information Policy Institute, n.d.), 3. Available at www.utexas.edu/research/tipi/ reports2/loc_services.pdf, accessed April 21, 2004.

24. University of Texas at Austin, Telecommunications and Information Policy Institute, *Local Services and Broadband Telecommunications Competition,* 4.

25. University of Texas at Austin, Telecommunications and Information Policy Institute, *Local Services and Broadband Telecommunications Competition,* 5.

26. E-mail communication with Sharon Strover, professor, Department of Radio-Television and Film, University of Texas at Austin.

27. University of Texas at Austin, Telecommunications and Information Policy Institute. *Local Services and Broadband Telecommunications Competition,* 5.

28. University of Texas at Austin, Telecommunications and Information Policy Institute, *Local Services and Broadband Telecommunications Competition,* 2.

29. TechNet, *The State Broadband Index* (Palo Alto, CA: TechNet, n.d.). Available at www.Tech net.org/resources/State_Broadband_Index.pdf, accessed April 16, 2004.

30. TechNet, *The State Broadband Index.*

31. TechNet, *The State Broadband Index.*

32. American Electronics Association, *Broadband in the States: A State-by-State of U.S. Broadband Deployment, 2003* (Washington, DC: American Electronics Association, 2003).

33. Carl Hulse, "Senate Votes to Consider Ban on Taxes on Net Access," *New York Times,* April 27, 2004.

34. Michael Mazerov, "Making the Internet Tax Freedom Act Permanent in the Form Currently Proposed Would Lead to a Substantial Revenue Loss for States and Localities" (Washington, DC: Center on Budget and Policy Priorities, 2003).

35. Office for the Advancement of Telehealth, *Telehealth Funding Guide* (Rockville, MD: Office for the Advancement of Telehealth, 2004). Available at http://telehealth.hrsa.gov/grants/funds.htm, accessed April 26, 2004.

36. Office for the Advancement of Telehealth, *2001 Telemedicine Report to Congress* (Rockville, MD: Office for the Advancement of Telehealth, 2001). Available at http://telehealth.hrsa.gov/pubs/ report2001/2001REPO.PDF/, accessed April 26, 2004. See also Office for the Advancement of Telehealth, *1997 Telemedicine Report to Congress* (Rockville, MD: Office for the Advancement of Telehealth, 1997). Available at www.ntia.doc.gov/reports/telemed/index.htm, accessed March 9, 2004.

Advancing E-government

Peter Hernon and Rowena Cullen

$\mathcal{A}$lthough the term *e-government* has existed since the 1990s, what e-government actually is, and should be, is still evolving and is not fully understood. The term e-government, or e-gov in the United States, and how the concept is converted into practice, remains unknown to most of the people of the countries discussed in this book. Nonetheless, e-government is slowly becoming incorporated into the very fabric of government. This chapter reiterates some of the themes that emerge from this book and from the implementation of e-government in the five countries profiled in detail. It looks at how far governments have come in terms of developmental stages outlined in chapter 1, the varying paths that e-government is starting to take in different jurisdictions, and some of the challenges for e-government over the next few years. The model depicted in figure 1.1 represents a composite of many of the possible directions that e-government might take but does not reflect the priorities of any individual government. Some governments through their e-government programs stress efficiency and cost-effectiveness, others highlight the benefits of online services, and others emphasize information access. Each direction involves an evolutionary process, and depending on their priorities, individual governments may have moved further on one direction or dimension than others.

Chapter 1 outlines several models to describe e-government development. Darrell M. West, for example, advances four stages: (1) the billboard stage; (2) the partial service delivery stage; (3) the portal stage, with fully executable and integrated service delivery; and (4) interactive democracy with public outreach and accountability enhancing features.[1] The equivalent stages developed by Accenture to evaluate and support e-government ventures comprise a series of plateaus reached in the effort to transform government from an agency-centric to a citizen-centric (or customer-focused) operation. These stages move from "online presence . . . a passive presentation of general information," which equates with West's billboard stage; through the intermediate stages of "basic capability" and "service availability," which equate to West's partial service delivery; to "mature delivery," or the portal stage.[2] However, where West conceives of the final stage of e-government as interactive democracy, which has a political dimension, Accenture's final stage of "service transformation," which transforms "how government functions are conceived, organized, and executed," has an administrative focus. This model highlights the goals of efficiency and cost reduction for both government and citizens. E-government policy in many countries, and the degree and nature of the transformation sought and achieved, may endorse both models, but in some instances the development and delivery of e-government focus more on serving the business community than fulfilling the democratic model.

In many countries, e-government is moving toward a clearer definition of the multiple constituencies interacting with government, through their channel approach to portal development and the use of vertical portals for interactive service delivery to the business and education sectors. These developments seem to reflect Chadwick and May's third level of e-government, the multiple constituency participatory model. But in reality, the interaction with these groups rarely moves beyond Chadwick and May's first, managerial model of information transfer to citizens as customers, with some interactions available through a limited range of online consultative procedures. There is little focus on the availability of the core information to inform the citizens or to foster their involvement in policy development.

ACCESS TO GOVERNMENT
INFORMATION AND SERVICES

One of the key issues that have emerged in this book is the need for governments to provide transparent access to information and services. However, the citizens of a country may be unfamiliar with the structure of their own national government and the roles and functions of individual departments and agencies. When they first approach e-government, they might discover that there are more subunits of departments and more agencies than they had realized. If they approach the home pages of other governments, they are likely to be unfamiliar with the structure of those governments, the functions of departments and agencies, and the terminology (e.g., covering different types of publications). Thus, it becomes essential that government on the Web is transparent and the public can rely on government portals that provide access to a range of government sites and services. While many governments endorse this with a one-stop-shopping access policy, the existence of a government portal may not be widely known, and it may not adequately meet citizens' needs. Research to date (see chapters 10 and 11) suggests that there is a need for a major marketing exercise to publicize the existence and the concept of government portals as a primary access tool, to ensure that they can easily be found and that the public identifies portals as the most efficient way of finding government information or services on the Web.

The roles and scope of specialized portals should also be proactively marketed. They play a critical part in offering more specialized services. For example, while the United States has FirstGov as its main portal, other government information portals that relate more specialized information (e.g., FedStats, and GPO Access) are linked from FirstGov's pages. Specialized portals that assist citizens to access and participate in government, such as Regulations.gov, which is a U.S. federal e-rulemaking site that enables citizens to search, retrieve, and comment on proposed regulations from approximately 160 federal agencies, or Singapore's Government Consultation Portal (http://app.feed back.gov.sg/asp/index.asp), which also poses questions to help citizens focus on key policy issues, are important agents in fostering e-participation.

MARKETING E-GOVERNMENT

As chapters 10 and 11 point out, members of the public might visit government Web sites, but the extent of their use varies greatly, from infrequently to frequently. A number of people do not use the Internet, or government Web sites, and prefer to deal with government in person or by telephone. A public opinion poll conducted in 2003 in the United States by Hart-Teeter suggested that "a majority of Americans are online, knowledgeable about e-government and exploring its uses."[3] The accuracy of these assertions might be questioned. Users may know about and rely on a few sites. However, even if sites are known, governments may change Web page addresses (if only because agency names change, often with changes of government). Many government Web site addresses are not intuitive. Even when an official Web site can be easily found, the public may prefer to rely on nonofficial sites unless, for whatever reason, they need an *official* copy. Clearly, many members of the public want information about politics, government, and policies, activities, and accountability. Evidence of the interest in interacting directly with government or candidates for office is found in the following example in which the public bypassed the media and its coverage:

> In the hour block during which Kerry [US presidential candidate] delivered his speech, his campaign Web site drew approximately 50,000 visitors—far exceeding the average of 40,000 visitors per day in June [2004]. . . . President Bush's official re-election site [www .georgewbush.com] saw increased traffic as well, drawing approximately 30,000 visitors during Kerry's acceptance speech.[4]

Despite the Hart-Teeter poll, two questions remain unresolved. To what degree are members of the public in their respective countries aware of the extent to which their government(s) has an e-government component? and To what degree do they associate government Web sites with their daily work- and non-work-related information needs? Instead of going directly to a government site, they might (or might not) consult a government portal. If they visit a portal, most likely it is a general, not a specialized, one. The question here is, Does the public factor portal use into their everyday information gathering from government Web sites? If, as we suggested earlier, the public is unaware of the structure of government, the various components (departments, agencies, and committees) of government, their various roles and responsibilities, as well as the types of information and services they provide, portals must make a concerted effort to meet that need and to market their services extensively.

There is a need for government in each country to promote its concept of e-government to the public and to help people access government sites for the information and services provided there. Promotion is more than the assumption that if the government builds a Web site, the public will come and fully use available services and information. Successful promotion requires more than simply pointing out the existence of sites, search engines, and portals. Entities, such as Congress in the United States, have been reluctant to fund e-government efforts that are not linked to a planning document. The Office of Management and Budget (OMB) promises that it will produce such plans. In response to OMB's inaction, Congress limits funds where discretionary spending is involved.

As Philip Kotler discusses, the basic steps for a marketing program or plan include:

- conceptualizing the market;
- analyzing the market;
- determining the market programs and services;
- administering those programs and services.[5]

These steps are interrelated and also include evaluating the extent to which goals, targets, and objectives have been met. Conceptualization and market analysis include awareness of and expanding market penetration—conducting market segmentation analyses. Who are the customers, for example, of a government Web site? How are those customers informed about the site? How do the developers of the site link the content to specific customers' information needs? How convenient is it to find information and use government services? In instances where e-commerce exists, how well do the sites protect personal information that customers provide? How easy is it to navigate the site(s)? Depending on the aspect of figure 1.1 on which a government is focusing, how well does e-government strengthen:

- public interactions with departments, agencies, and elected officials;
- information access;
- service delivery;
- e-commerce; or
- e-compliance?

How does a government inform its citizens about its online capability for emergency response? The United States, for instance, has a portal for homeland security (www .dhs.gov/dhspublic/), and Singapore maintains a portal on bird flu (www.flu.gov.sg/). How well known are such sites?

Marketing needs to address the types of issues that focus group participants raised in chapter 11. Web sites "must also give users information about security testing and risks." Furthermore, Web developers need to resist "looking at service delivery and interaction with the public from the inside out."[6] As the Maori participating in the focus groups for chapters 10 and 11 noted, government should hold public forums around the country and speak about e-government in jargon-free language. It is critical to develop a dialogue with the public and not lecture to people. Other venues for alerting the public to Web site content and altering information-gathering behavior should be included as part of a marketing plan. Still, countries may have legal restrictions about marketing government information and services.

Marketing also needs to make clear to citizens the added value to be gained from accessing information on the Internet or through government Web sites. Portals such as E-rulemaking broaden the concept and acceptance of e-government as well as ensure that e-democracy is not an abstraction. As the General Accounting Office noted,

> Each year, federal agencies publish thousands of regulations that can affect almost every aspect of citizens' lives—from allowing a fireworks display over the Columbia River in Vancouver, Wash., to registering food facilities in light of the potential for bioterrorism. The public can play a role in the rules that affect them through the notice and comment provisions of the Administrative Procedure Act of 1946, as amended. In fact, involvement of the public in rulemaking has been described as possibly "the most complex and impor-

tant form of political action in the contemporary American political system." However, in order to be involved in rulemaking effectively, the public must be able to (1) know whether proposed rules are open for public comment, (2) prepare and submit comments to relevant decisionmakers, and (3) access regulatory supporting materials (e.g., agencies' economic analyses) and the comments of others so that their comments can be more informed and useful.[7]

In January 2005, the portal (www.regulations.gov) was revamped and the features related to the federal docket management system were added, namely Web access to open-rule dockets, public comments posted online within twenty-four hours of electronic submission, e-mail notification sent when rule dockets are modified, Boolean and compound search engines, an expanded character limit for public comment (up from four thousand characters), and access to related nonrulemaking documents (e.g., agency information collection requests).[8] The changes are in line with the E-Government Act of 2002 (P.L. 107-347), which requires federal departments and agencies to have an online docket system. This added value brings this aspect of e-government in the United States to the level of Chadwick and May's third, multiconstituency participatory level. At the same time, however, it may create conflicts and tensions within government, as it seeks to reconcile public/private conflicts and efficiency with public participation.

FREEDOM OF INFORMATION

The level of information routinely provided on government portals and Web sites may be described as equivalent to printed brochures outlining policies or services, and even the services themselves; this information is not difficult for governments to provide online. The potential of the Internet to make *all* government information freely available does pose problems for some governments. For example, e-government within the United States is taking place in the post-9/11 period in which the focus is on homeland security, combating terrorism, and information protection. There is discussion within government of the public's right to know and the extent to which there can be open government, but that discussion has not yet produced a dialogue between government and its citizenry. The Bush administration expects agencies to remove broad categories of so-called sensitive information from their Web sites. As a report from the Heritage Foundation noted, "At the very least, such wholesale withdrawal of information seems arbitrary and undermines important values of government openness, the development of electronic government . . . to speed the delivery and lower the costs of government services, and public trust."[9]

The war on terrorism has had a profound impact on e-government in the United States, on the categories of information provided, and on how this information should be protected from misuse. As e-government becomes more and more a channel for intergovernmental cooperation and resource sharing, conceivably e-government and its infrastructure might become a terrorist target. As a result, "safeguarding e-government has been one of the [U.S.] government's priorities."[10] Yet, as L. Elaine Halchin of the Congressional Research Service notes, "What is missing today is a debate, or deliberation, on what is 'too public' as the agencies unilaterally alter their Web sites. Changing, removing, and withholding information has implications for e-government as a means of fostering democratic government."[11] It may also impact on the achievement of a fully developed and integrated model of e-government, as outlined in figure 1.1.

Good information management within government creates a balance between security and access (many countries have freedom of information or similar legislation that requires agencies to specify a threat if they wish to withhold information) and between the collection, security, and scrutiny of vast amounts of personally identifiable information.[12] Government needs to manage both carefully, to legislate safeguards for the protection of democracy, and to hire privacy and civil liberties officers. However, the U.S. Freedom of Information Act is no longer the "centerpiece of access policy. . . . The long-standing fissures between providing the right of access to federal government information (by 'any person,' 'on request') and the responsibility to protect personal privacy have become a gaping chasm."[13] Countries such as New Zealand have privacy acts that prohibit data mining and produce better individual protection than found in U.S. legislation and have freedom of information legislation to enable citizens to obtain government records that have not been made freely available on the Internet, unless privacy or commercial issues prevent their release. However, not all countries envision the Web as a means to release and provide access to declassified records. As a result, e-government might fail to balance protection against access. Each country needs to articulate its vision of e-government and to ensure that government alone does not arbitrarily set that vision. Currently, there seems to be a lack of public debate on these issues in countries such as New Zealand and the United States.

CITIZEN OR CUSTOMER EXPECTATIONS

If the purpose of e-government in a country is to provide more and improved information and service to the citizens of a country or a larger population—e-citizens worldwide—this provision must be evaluated in terms of service quality and satisfaction. The public, regardless of whether people are known as customers or citizens, visit a department or agency through its Web site, and that experience has both content and context. Content refers to obtaining the thing that prompted the visit to the Web site—any aspect of figure 1.1. Context covers the experience itself: ease or difficulty in navigating the site, interaction with public servants, and so on. That experience results in the public forming expectations about the service they encountered. Those expectations may or may not match what the department or agency thinks appropriate, but nevertheless they represent reality for the customer. Expectations focus on two interrelated but different concepts: *service quality* and *satisfaction*. Service quality has several dimensions beyond content/context and the performance/performance-expectations gap (see chapter 13). Service quality is both personal to individuals and collective among many customers. Each individual who interacts with a government department or agency forms an opinion about the service and information provided. When the collective opinions of many customers become known and seem to agree, those opinions create a reputation for the department or agency and for the quality of its service.

Satisfaction, which implies a filling or fulfillment, can be viewed as a consumer's fulfillment response. It is a personal, emotional reaction to a government service or product, or a sense of contentment that arises from an *actual* experience in relation to an *expected* experience. The degree to which expectations conform to or deviate from experience is the pivotal determinant of satisfaction. Satisfaction measures a customer's immediate and subjective experience with a specific service encounter—a uniquely personal and internalized experience that generates a spontaneous perception based, consciously or subconsciously, on expectations.

Government departments and agencies express a willingness to listen to customers through comments expressed on satisfaction surveys. However, how much customer input is *valued*—what results from that input, and whether it leads to continuous quality improvement—is difficult to discern. Service quality may be an aspect of expectations that governments fail to address. As a perusal of chapters 10 and 11 suggests, governments could do much more in the area of customer expectations to improve the layout and content of Web sites and the delivery of information and services to all segments of the public. Reinforcing this assumption is an e-government survey in the United States that showed some federal government Web sites and portals received a higher satisfaction rating over time, whereas others dropped in their satisfaction rating.[14]

It should not be assumed that increased demand for information or a service from year to year is a sufficient substitute for gathering insights into service quality and satisfaction and then using those insights to make improvements in the delivery of that information or those services. A much greater investment in research in the various user communities is needed to determine the expectations of citizens in terms of content (information and services) and the process of accessing and interacting on sites. As noted in chapter 12, ongoing user research is needed to define the content and the services that citizens most want, whether this relates to a core 20 percent of most-used information and services, or the less used, but for those users no less important, 80 percent of content. In addition, user research is needed to identify the mental models that citizens apply to government and its resources, in order to reflect these in the language, labels, navigation, and any indexes or taxonomies pertaining to a site and to bridge the gap between government's representation of itself on the Web and the citizens' own perception of it.

An example of this is found in the Singapore Government Consultation portal (http://app.feedback.gov.sg), where questions are put to citizens to help them grasp the kind of comment that is sought from them in the consultation process and letters from citizens thought to make a valuable contribution to the debate are highlighted. User research is also needed to define the life events most meaningful to citizens of a particular country, if a life-events approach underpins the architecture of a government portal or Web site. User research and feedback, as well as service quality and satisfaction research, could define the needs that various channels best meet or suggest portals that might be created to serve a specific audience. In this way, by utilizing research to match service delivery to customers' needs and expectations, the public is served more effectively and efficiently.

POPULAR WEB SITES AND WHY ARE NOT MORE SITES POPULAR?

Different public opinion polls and satisfaction studies have identified popular government Web sites, but these works tend to ignore the purposes for which the public visits those sites and whether they use services such as e-mail alert services that announce new media releases, publications, or changes in regulations. The quarterly American Customer Satisfaction Index, which was established in 1994, is produced through a partnership of the Stephen M. Ross Business School at the University of Michigan, the American Society for Quality, and the CFI Group, an international consulting firm.[15] In the scores dated December 14, 2004, the public's average satisfaction with U.S. federal government Web sites was 72.1 percent, which is a 1.2 percent increase from fourth-quarter results the previous year.[16] Of the few sites covered, services of three agencies aimed at retirees (Social Security Administration, Office of Personnel Management, and the Pension Benefit Guaranty Corporation) showed no increase from the previous year. On the other hand, buyers of numismatic and commemorative coins showed less satisfaction with the U.S. Mint in 2004—a 3 percent decrease from the previous year.

The first quarterly poll for 2005 showed a reduction in public satisfaction with federal Web sites. The rating was now 71.9 percent. That percentage reflected lower scores for government search engines and Web site navigability,[17] and it is suggested that lower scores relate to dissatisfaction with the search engines available at the sites. Furthermore, the number of people visiting government Web sites may be increasing, but "first-time users are unfamiliar with the virtual organization and thus more likely to use keyword searches."[18] This may partially explain why the Bush administration has advanced the idea of retrieval within three clicks of a mouse. As well, the Office of Management and Budget, in a memorandum dated December 17, 2004, has required all government Web sites to have search engines by the end of 2005. In some instances, mostly for small Web sites, agencies may still rely on site maps or subject indexes. If the government expects agencies to develop better search engines, this recognizes the fact that if good site architecture and navigation do not lead people to the information they seek, search engines constitute the primary means by which the public finds relevant sites and information. In fact, as discussed in earlier chapters, the public may rely extensively on Google, especially since it enhances its search capability.

There might be other reasons for lower satisfaction. Government Web sites might contain information that is accessible only if the public has the right software package. For instance, some U.S. government Web sites (e.g., some court sites and the Department of Justice)[19] contain word-processed reports available only in WordPerfect, which is not necessarily easily converted into other formats. Users with disabilities also have specific demands regarding the format of documents. As noted in chapter 11, they may not favor pdf files since such files are not easily enlarged for viewing by the sight disabled.

GOVERNMENT WEB SITES ARE PUBLIC RECORDS

Government information online comprises government Web pages, documents available for downloading as Web pages, html pages, or pdf files, as well as a vast array of information advising users on how to access a service, offering forms for citizens to complete, and providing information that would have in the past been sent in the form of a letter or conveyed by telephone or face to face. Online information might also include reports to government, legislation, regulations, and records of government activity and policy. There is now an expectation that the entire range of information resources should be available on government Web sites under principles of open government and accountability. Thus, government Web sites, and especially government portals, need to make citizens aware of how they can gain access to policy documents and government records alongside the descriptive information about services, and the brochureware that is available on many government Web sites. In many cases, this need has given way to the promotion of services.

In addition, much of this information forms a public record of government. The public may be unfamiliar with the difference between *information* and *record* and may fail to realize that records provide evidence of decision making and the development, implementation, and execution of policy. Government Web sites and portals need to help citizens make these distinctions and to deepen their understanding of the workings of government in order to make the government decision-making process more accountable. The New Zealand e-government site (www.e-government.govt.nz) is an example of a site that offers a range from simple explanations of the government's vision and implementation of e-government, and what citizens can expect to find, to a full account of the development of policies, decisions, debates, and minutes of Cabinet decisions, and so forth that underpin its current activities and authority.

Electronic evidence of decisions is now also part of the government's record—this includes e-mail messages, memos sent electronically, and other electronic records (e.g., minutes of meetings and decisions made by statutory and other entities). This requires governmental and quasi-governmental offices to make decisions about whether to archive all such electronic material. To create an archive denotes that value has been assigned to a record, but not all records, electronic or paper, are of value. Policy must be established (through a national government archive or a local body) to guide agencies in making critical decisions about whether a record is in the public interest and does not contravene privacy and other commercial constraints. (The decision often involves political considerations.) Records that meet both tests merit retention in publicly available electronic archives. Material not deemed to be sufficiently important or suitable to be publicly available may be retained in the more secure environment of a government intranet.

Also critical is the archiving of Web sites that carry government information pertinent at a particular time. Already in this book several earlier versions of Web sites (the Native American Web sites referred to in chapter 14 on the digital divide, and the earliest New Zealand portal, in chapter 6) were only available through the Wayback Machine's Web archive (www.archive.org/web/web.php). The archiving of government Web sites, while it may be the responsibility of each government agency, must have official oversight, with sufficient authority to ensure that the public interest is protected in this way. Archived Web sites, and the information they contain, need to be well indexed and should have public pointers to them (on an agency site or the main portal) so that the public can access them either out of historical interest, when in pursuit of the development of a policy, or because they affect the legitimacy of actions or decisions made at that time on the basis of that information (e.g., as in tax regulations promoted on a Web site at a certain time, which may impact on the legality of a citizen's tax transactions made at that time). Principles governing the archiving of Web pages and records of transactions conducted via the Web are now being adopted in a number of jurisdictions that specifically define government Web pages as government records[20] (see chapter 9 for a more detailed discussion of this issue).

Once administrations leave office, their records must be archived, whether in print or electronic format. In the United States, there are significant exceptions to this generalization. The National Archives and Records Administration has "received more electronic files from the Clinton administration than it had in the previous thirty years from all of the federal government."[21] How many of these records are accessible? How many will be so over time? Does the technology exist to preserve and read all of the files? How many of those records, along with e-mail messages and word-processed documents that show how decisions were made, provide information unavailable elsewhere? "Preserving the public record . . . ensures a measure of accountability that is a linchpin of democracy."[22] The assumption, however, is that what has been preserved becomes part of the collective memory or the public record. While such papers may not be available for a stipulated period of years (in most countries this may be twenty or thirty or as many as fifty years), it is critical that someone is responsible for the archiving of these informal electronic records throughout each administration.

MAKING GOVERNMENT STATISTICS AVAILABLE ON THE WEB

Countries such as Australia, Canada, the United Kingdom, and the United States, as well as members of the European Union, have extensive and broad statistical systems that have captured a substantial amount of highly specialized data for years. There is a concerted effort in these countries to develop comprehensive key indicator systems that cast these activities in a broader framework to aid policymakers, researchers, and others in gaining a broader perspective. Such data, termed key indicators, key measures, or key statistics, provide a snapshot of a nation's or a region's progress "in addressing and resolving key issues and concerns."[23] They should also be used to "clarify problems and opportunities, and track progress towards achieving results."[24] As the Government Accountability Office (GAO), formerly the General Accounting Office, noted in a major report entitled *Informing Our Nation:*

> To be a leading democracy in the information age may very well mean producing unique public sources of objective, independent, scientifically grounded, and widely shared quality information so that we know where the United States stands now and how we are trending, on both an absolute and relative basis—including comparisons with other nations. By ensuring that the best facts are made more accessible and usable by the many different members of our society, we increase the probability of well-framed problems, good decisions, and effective solutions.[25]

Those comprehensive key indicator systems might cover the *economy* (consumers and employment, transportation and infrastructure, finance and money, business and markets, government, and the world economy), the *environment* (the earth [ecosystems], land, water, life, air, and national resources), and *society and culture* (health and housing; communities and citizenship; education and innovation; security and safety; crime and justice; children, families, and aging; democracy and governance; and values and culture).

The GAO defines an indicator as "a quantitative measure that describes an economic, environmental, social or cultural condition over time. The unemployment rate, infant mortality rates, and air quality indexes are a few examples." The GAO then defines an indicator system as "an organized effort to assemble and disseminate a group of indicators that together tell a story about the position and progress of a jurisdiction or jurisdictions, such as the City of Boston, the State of Oregon, or the United States of America." These "systems collect information from suppliers (individuals who respond to surveys or institutions that provide data they have collected), which providers (e.g., the Census Bureau) then package into products and services for the benefit of users."[26] Furthermore, indicator systems might be topical (cover, e.g., health, education, or public safety) or comprehensive (pull together only the most essential indicators on a range of economic, environmental, and social and cultural issues).

Canada dedicates several portals to disseminating key indicators, two of the main ones being Statistics Canada (www.statcan.ca/) and Canadian Economy Online (www.canadianeconomy.gc.ca), as well as private statistical aggregator GDSourcing (Government data sourcing; www.gdsourcing.ca). Australia's Commonwealth Bureau of Statistics presents key national indicators (primarily economic and social) on a page updated daily. It links to other industrial and environmental statistics data and a "web-based information service," Ausstats (www.abs.gov.au/), to provide free summary information and a subscription service to aggregated and annotated data across a number of sectors. The Key National Indicators Initiative (www.keyindicators.org) is a multinational forum that investigates the methods for data collection and analysis across a full range of social and economic statistics as used in a wide range of OECD (Organisation for Economic Co-operation and Development) countries. There are links to institutes of social policy as well as national sites. This initiative marks a global advance in the use of statistics to measure national progress toward predetermined goals, and it encourages standardization in data collection and analysis.

The "GAO found that comprehensive key indicator systems are primarily but not exclusively, either learning-oriented or outcome-oriented. . . . The term outcome-oriented refers to a general concern with impacts on the conditions of society."[27] Furthermore, "these indicator systems are used to monitor and encourage progress toward a vision for the future—or in some cases a specific set of goals—which have been established by the people and institutions within a jurisdiction."[28]

Although the GAO report does not address the question of key indicators for e-government, a comprehensive indicator system might be developed to cover it. Government Webmasters, for example, already capture a range of input and output metrics that reflect the government body's perspective and user satisfaction. They could also gauge service quality, such as the precise expectations of those customers using government home pages for gaining access to information or services. Of course, decisions would have to be made about the most relevant indicators and the story they collectively tell. That story could then be compared to the one told by other jurisdictions within a country and globally. Herein might be a productive direction for measurement and evaluation of e-government to turn, leading to international standards that could form the basis for further global analyses by bodies such as the United Nations, eliminating some of the limited acceptability of the criteria used in the *Global E-Government Readiness Report 2004*.[29]

PARTICIPATION

An Accenture report defined five principles of e-democracy, which is composed of e-participation and e-voting:

1. inclusion: a voice for all;
2. openness: electronic provision of information;
3. security and privacy: a safe place;
4. responsiveness: listening and responding to people;
5. deliberation: making the most of people's ideas.[30]

Despite many government vision statements supporting and advocating greater citizen participation in government through e-government, this is one area where there has been little measurement, and possibly less progress than in many others. There are a variety of reasons for this.

First, participation in government at the level of contributing to policymaking is limited in most countries to those individuals with sufficient interest and the ability to do so. Government policy on a specific issue will attract the attention of groups with an interest in that specific issue, but these groups vary from issue to issue. While political activists may have an interest across a wide spectrum of issues, on most issues there is a limited range of professional associations, social agencies, recreational and environmental organizations, lobbyists, and others wishing to comment. These groups and individuals contribute to policymaking through a variety of channels. They may use online forums or may choose other more formal or less formal approaches (e.g., lobbying individual politicians). A multichannel policy must continue to support citizen input, as well as government information and services, in a variety of formats.

Second, although the number of citizens accessing government information and services is increasing, this tends to focus on a core set of activities—those most in demand. Although some government Web pages highlight issues that they are "currently consulting on," as the Singapore and New Zealand main portals do, and the U.S. feedback portal does, the issues are not always ones on which lobbyists wish to comment. As more government information and policy come online, it is increasingly difficult to maintain an overview of what is available and to keep citizens informed on a wide range of issues. Thus, while ready access to online government initiatives, reports, and policies can supplement other media used for dissemination of government information, the Internet cannot function as the sole channel to alert citizens to issues and solicit feedback, while at the same time functioning as a highly structured information repository and archive.

Governments are selective in what they put forward for debate and the information they provide to support public debate. Citizens with an interest in social and political issues will be unlikely to be satisfied with the information provided by a government in power and will want access to the reports and analyses underlying political decisions, not just the justification for the decisions themselves. The example cited by British Prime Minister Tony Blair, dealing with the dossier on Iraq on the Web site of No. 10 Downing Street, which was accessed by "one million people from all over the world . . . within hours of its release"[31] may not be, as Blair asserts, an example of democracy in action but rather government propaganda that not all visitors to the site would take at face value. The question of the extent to which the need for openness and account-ability in government is met by overtly political statements on the Internet is debatable. The kind of openness and accountability that citizens call for may not be the same as the commitment made in various governments' vision statements concerning e-government and e-participation (see chapter 7 for further discussion of this issue).

It is unlikely that governments intend to extend the political process beyond cur-rent levels of citizen input to decision making through well-established procedures, whether or not these are online. In countries where committees of the legislature con-sider legislation, there are procedures for citizens to follow when they make submis-sions; these may be available online. In other countries, lobbying of politicians is seen as the most effective way to influence political decisions and legislation, and these pro-cedures can also be translated to the online environment. E-government may increase the number of channels used to facilitate these activities, but it does not necessarily in itself enhance citizen participation in government decision making. As noted in a New Zealand government paper on participation, "increased participation by public and businesses is not intended to replace our representative system. The government is still expected to take the initiative and to lead."[32] The real meaning of, and the parameters for, e-participation need further research and investigation. The vision of e-participation as the next stage of transformational e-government, or multichannel participatory government, as advocated by Chadwick and May[33] would require trans-formation of the political process and the nature of government itself.

THE FUTURE OF E-GOVERNMENT

In 2004, Accenture's *eGovernment Leadership: High Performance, Maximum Value* indi-cated that much work remains to be done, because progress in the maturity of e-government is "slowing down."[34] The goal remains twofold: first, the achievement of service transformation as the public, businesses, and government itself rely more on e-services, and, second, better performance, which depends on the achievement of specified outcomes in a more cost-effective manner.[35]

Furthermore, as chapters 10 and 11 of this book indicate, there is a wide gap between what government provides on the Web and what the public realizes is available and can access. "Until that gap is bridged, governments will never get all of the value possible out of their eGovernment investments."[36] Closing the gap will require inter-agency cooperation and the implementation of effective portals that provide ready access to a wide range of information and personalized services—addressing more of the components of figure 1.1. A key finding of the Accenture report was that the United Kingdom "seems to be ahead of many countries in its use of marketing," although the report noted that much work remained in order to gain broad penetration of market segments (citizens, businesses, and government itself). Service to these groups has been the focus of the new UK government portal, under the leadership of Ian Watmore, a former director of Accenture. In most countries, the public continues to view e-government in terms of information, not service, provision.

In the various country profiles in this book, there are perceptible differences in key issues that have determined progress to date and define the next stages identified for development. The differences focus especially on governance, and formal procedures for monitoring progress, to encourage e-government accountability. The country profiles also reveal that, within the general framework of e-government, there are wide variations in how individual jurisdictions may go about implementing e-government, the priorities each sets, and how each addresses the future. Observed differences center on channels used for delivery; the degree of authority of central government over state, provincial, or local governments; the extent to which a government ensures access through subsidized information and communications technology (ICT) connectivity for citizens; and whether the focus of e-government policy is on meeting citizens' needs, on efficiency and cost-effectiveness, or on greater participation.

In the United Kingdom, there is a deliberate policy of forging strong links between the two tiers of national and local e-government. The newly created e-Government Unit (eGU, replacing the Office of the e–Envoy) within the Cabinet Office has an appointed high-profile head with authority to enforce regulations and to oversee e-government development at national and local levels. The eGU's mission is to ensure that "IT supports the transformation of government itself, so that [it] can provide better, more efficient public services."[37] Much government effort is going into basic literacy and ICT literacy skills among the population, with an emphasis on access to ICT for all citizens to support e-government and the UK economy. The new government portal highlights online services for citizens, and specific government service areas have been prioritized for full e-service delivery: welfare benefits, education, health care, and personal tax.

E-government in the United Kingdom has a new framework, with a focus on data structures, standardization, and Web guidelines to support interoperability and seamless access across agencies of central and local government; digital signatures and authentication to support single sign-on online service delivery; and call centers, supporting a multichannel access to government, which include digital TV as a channel for accessing government services.

The British government is a major advocate of e-government and expresses strong support for better communication and participation through e-government. However, lower-than-expected rates of uptake in the business community and society at large suggest that progress toward implementing the government's vision of e-government has slowed, and the question remains as to whether the newly created head of the eGU can reinvigorate the program.

Australia's three-tier system of government (federal, state, and local), as in Canada and the United States, makes uniform advancement of e-government throughout the entire public sector more of a challenge. Australian e-government policy focuses on providing leadership in the use of ICTs across public and business communities, to improve the efficiency of information management within and across government agencies at all levels, to deliver fast and appropriate information and services to business and other communities, and to allow for greater citizen interaction with government through e-participation and e-democracy. The Australian government is also very concerned with overcoming the digital divide and with getting appropriate services out to citizens across a large continent with many remote rural communities. This endeavor is supported by community access programs and the National Communications Fund.

The current state of development appears to show that the first two objectives are closer to achievement than the latter two. ICT enablement within government and the community is strongly supported through two central agencies, the Office for Information Economy (in the community) and the Australian Government Information Management Office (AGIMO; government delivery of programs). A third agency, the Information Management Strategy Committee, integrates information and services through the standardization of data and systems among agencies and between federal and state government. There is some focus also on cost-effectiveness and return on investment, which has led to a greater focus on measurement.

There is considerable discussion in government reports on greater citizen participation and e-democracy, but in the main this consists primarily of making government information available and seeking/accepting submissions online, although Sue Burgess and Jan Houghton see some emerging initiatives that will foster a dialogue (see chapter 5). The recent incorporation of AGIMO into the Department of Finance and Administration gives greater authority to the office to enforce interoperability and transformation of business process in government. However, Burgess and Houghton see the rate of progress slowing as the early achievements become operationalized and more complex problems emerge that need to be addressed. They also comment on the potential for conflict between the goals of further government efficiency and the government's goals for greater citizen interaction.

Canada's three tier-system of government impacts on its progress in adopting e-government. Canada promoted and funded ICT for business, education, and economic growth. The Canadian Treasury Board was involved early in the Canadian Government Online (GOL) strategy, with its dual focus on the needs and expectations of citizens and a centrally coordinated whole-of-government approach to e-government, providing services across all government agencies. Canada has placed considerable emphasis on overcoming the digital divide and achieving broadband access across rural and remote communities. Progress toward e-government has been systematically evaluated through auditor general's reports, the latest of which saw a shift of responsibility for GOL to Public Works and Government Service Canada.

Canada has made significant investment in authentication for online transactions and has developed clear guiding principles for delivery of information and services to Canadian citizens, focused on access regardless of language and location, emphasizing ease of use of government Web sites, including uniform appearance and navigation. At the same time, Canadian e-government policy emphasizes choice of channel for access (through Web or telephone, or face-to-face), although this policy faces the criticism that recent emphasis on getting more people online works against choice. The policy emphasizes the dual goals of cost-efficiency for government and in service delivery and exemplary use of citizens' feedback and input to improve e-services. As the Government Online project comes to an end, its responsibilities are picked up by Service Canada, a completely separate agency charged with achieving better coordination of services at less cost, with outcomes focused on citizen satisfaction, cost savings, and accountability. As Kirsti Nilsen notes (chapter 4), although GOL was unsuccessful in achieving a true transformation of government, Service Canada has a major challenge to face in developing a new system of e-government governance at the same time that it promotes enhanced service delivery, information dissemination, and e-commerce for Canada.

In the United States, e-government initiatives must also span the three-tier system of government. At the federal level, the U.S. e-government initiative is the largest and most complex in the world and often sets the benchmark for other jurisdictions. The

Bush administration's e-government agenda has several key focuses: the improvement of services to citizens, the improvement of the internal management procedures of the federal government and its agencies, the development and application of performance metrics to stimulate the further expansion of e-government, the promotion of ICT and broadband connectivity to the benefit of the U.S. economy, and the enhancement of federal and state IT security. The president's Expanding Electronic Government initiative,[38] based in the White House, depends on the authority of the CIO Council, the Office of Electronic Government in the OMB, and the archivist of the United States to ensure good management of electronic information, services, and records. The E-Government Act and other related acts, such as the Paperwork Reduction Act, give these entities considerable centralized power in relation to the implementation of e-government in the United States. Enhancement of online services through the federal projects on e-authentication and agency enterprise architecture (for greater interoperability) is intended to improve the already wide range of online services to citizens, business, and state and local governments. Increasing amounts of information are available through specialist portals (e.g., FedStats and GPO Access) linked from the highly effective main government portal, FirstGov. With these advances to the third level in both the democratic and business transformative models, the United States continues to set the benchmark for the development of e-government. At the same time, restrictions on information available on the Web imposed by the Bush administration call into question its real commitment to freedom of information.

New Zealand has a simple two-tier layer of government, like the United Kingdom, but implementation of e-government was impeded by competition in the government in the early years of e-government. Impetus toward e-government has been as much about establishing a whole-of-government approach and greater cooperation and collaboration in the public sector as service to users. Critical to the development of e-government in New Zealand was the establishment of a centralized unit with some authority to oversee the implementation of e-government practices in agencies. The E-Government Unit in the State Services Commission, with oversight of central government agencies in key areas, has used its authority to establish guidelines for government Web sites, foster interoperability through the use of standards, and support one-stop access to government information and services. A small number of services are available online, through vertical portals targeted at specific groups (e.g., business and education).

The E-Government Unit's activities have been focused on the goals of better access to information and services, cost-effective services, improved national reputation, greater participation by citizens, and leadership in the uptake of ICT through the example set by the public sector. There is awareness of the digital divide—which is perceived in New Zealand to be a cultural as well as a technological issue—and government investment in ICT and broadband access is made through public–private partnership investments in rural schools and communities. Government policy continues to support a multichannel strategy to enable citizens to choose how to gain access to government information and services.

Availability of government information and policy documents is supported in principle and endorsed by the Freedom of Information Act and has been a stronger focus than online services. Progress in e-government at the local government level is supported by the central government but is mainly on the initiative of local government entities themselves. While accessibility, interagency cooperation, and interoperability are major elements in the e-government strategy, authentication for single sign-on is still in development, and this impedes the further development of e-services. Measurement of progress so far is through informal procedures, reports commissioned by the E-Government Unit in the form of independent evaluation of Web sites and qualitative and quantitative studies of user participation. Significant advances have been made in e-government infrastructure, and there are some examples of highly effective online service delivery, but use of e-government by citizens has been slower than might have been expected in a fairly small, well-wired community. The recent extension of the State Services Commission's e-government authority across the wider state sector continues efforts to standardize support access. Authentication should extend the reach of e-government further, but the recently adopted policy of mainstreaming e-government back to agencies may reduce the impetus to greater service delivery and enhanced citizen participation when these developments conflict with other departmental demands.

In summary, most of the countries profiled in this book have reached a similar level of development in terms of the Accenture model outlined above and have addressed some of the key components of the model in figure 1.1. In most jurisdictions, there is a sense that the next stage must be a transformation of government at the level of the agency, with a number of general and specialized (vertical) portals providing the necessary integration among agencies and services that will lead to the vision of seamless access to information and services. Although many challenges lie ahead, these are challenges of political will and cooperative enterprise rather than of technology. If the transformation is truly achieved, it will perhaps signify that e-government has simply become government—the way the modern state carries out its business and interacts with its citizens. As John Sindlar of the U.S. Office of Governmentwide Policy noted recently, "The goal of e-gov is to basically end breaking initiatives into the business of government, drop the 'e' from the initiatives . . . and once we've integrated our solution into our business lines . . . we won't take everything to OMB when there's a problem."[39]

A number of governments now articulate the vision of mainstreaming or dropping the e from e-government. With this devolvement of authority to agencies, the sense that the major task has been completed and that the transformation is under way may be misleading. There are still problems with legacy systems not interacting among agencies and with divergent data-collection policies that act against interoperability and seamless access to services. Most countries are still grappling with interoperability issues, have not completed their authentication projects, and have limited services available online and limited numbers of citizens accessing these. Consultation online is channeled along existing pathways or focused on issues carefully selected by governments. There is a long way to go before either the transformative business model or the transformative participatory model has been achieved.

CONCLUSION

Although governments have made an extensive commitment to the development of e-government, the global public tends not to be familiar with the concept of e-government, especially as defined in figure 1.1. In fact, governments may have contributed to the confusion on occasion by expecting the public to obtain government information services and information only or largely online, despite a range of multichannel policies. Undoubtedly, governments need to explain better what they mean by e-government and to view it as one means of communicating and interacting with the public. E-government refers to those aspects of figure 1.1 delivered over the Internet, but there are other avenues involving technology that the public might choose. Let us not forget that the telephone and the fax machine are also forms of technology. Within the context of that figure, e-government will continue to evolve. Its name may change, but its functions will remain as the public deals directly with government and relies less on intermediaries, such as depository libraries, for access to government information.

The information environment for anyone with access to a computer and the Internet will continue to expand. National governments only constitute a portion of that environment. One factor that might inhibit the extent to which the public turns to e-government would materialize if the public questions the messages that government disseminates through the Internet. Many people in countries such as the United States are concerned that the growing incidents of Internet hacking, viruses, worms, spam, spyware, phishing, and data mining and the loss of privacy[40] will undermine the credibility and utility of the Internet so that people will not want to use it, or will use it minimally for e-government and e-commerce transactions. Indeed, some experts are contemplating a new version of the Internet. Experiments are under way with Internet 2, which apparently is extremely fast and allows some user authentication.

NOTES

1. Darrell M. West, "E-Government and the Transformation of Service Delivery and Citizen Attitudes," *Public Administration Review* 64, no. 1 (January–February 2004), 15–17.

2. Accenture, *eGovernment Leadership: Engaging the Customer,* Government Executive Series no. 3 (New York: Accenture, 2004). Available at www.accenture.com, accessed July 15, 2004.

3. David Perera, "Campaigning Enters the Internet Age," *Federal Computer Week* 18, no. 28 (August 16, 2004): 12.

4. Perera, "Campaigning Enters the Internet Age," 12.

5. See, e.g., Philip Kotler, *Marketing for Nonprofit Organizations* (Englewood Cliffs, NJ: Prentice-Hall, 1975, 1982).

6. Patricia McGinnis, "Poll Reveals the Next E-government Challenge," *Government Computer News,* May 19, 2003, 29.

7. General Accounting Office (GAO), *Electronic Rulemaking: Efforts to Facilitate Public Participation Can Be Improved,* GAO-03-901. Report to the Senate Committee on Governmental Affairs (Washington, DC: GAO, 2003), 1.

8. GAO, *Electronic Rulemaking,* 1.

9. James Jay Carafiano and David Heyman, *DHS 2.0: Rethinking the Department of Homeland Security,* Heritage Special Report (Washington, DC: Heritage Foundation, December 13, 2004), 20.

10. David Perera, "OMB's Rule: Pay As You Go," *Federal Computer Week,* September 20, 2004, 12.

11. L. Elaine Halchin, "Electronic Government: Government Capability and Terrorist Response," *Government Information Quarterly* 21 (2004): 416.

12. Harold C. Relyea, "Statement: Emerging Threats: Overclassification and Pseudo-Classification," before the House Government Reform Subcommittee on National Security (March 2, 2005), 1.

13. Lotte E. Feinberg, "FOIA, Federal Information Policy, and Information Availability in a Post-9-11 World," *Government Information Quarterly* 21 (2004): 440.

14. For the quarterly American Customer Satisfaction Index for federal Web sites, see third-quarter

(September 2004) results. Available at www.theacsi.org/government.htm, accessed September 29, 2004. Chap. 13 of this book discusses the index.

15. American Customer Satisfaction Index (Ann Arbor: University of Michigan, 2004). Available at www.theacsi.org/, accessed January 1, 2005.

16. "ACSI Overall Federal Government Scores with Historic Scores of Agencies Measured 1999–2004" (see n. 14 and 15). Available at www.theacsi.org/government/govt-all-04.html, accessed June 20, 2005.

17. David Perera, "Web Satisfaction Dips," *FCW.com* [*Federal Computer Week* online], March 16, 2005. Available at www.fcw.com/print.asp, accessed March 16, 2004. See also David Perera. "Fed Sites Satisfy," *FCW.com,* December 18, 2004. Available at www.fcw.com/fcw/articles/2004/1213/web-asci-12-14-04.asp, accessed December 18, 2004.

18. McGinnis, "Poll Reveals the Next E-government Challenge," 29.

19. Allya Stemstein, "Justice Sticks with WordPerfect," *FCW.com,* March 7, 2005. Available at www.fcw.com/fcw/articles/2005/0307/web-wordperfect-03-07-05.asp, accessed March 16, 2004. See also "Justice Extends WordPerfect," *Federal Computer Week,* March 14, 2005, 11.

20. National Archives of Australia, Archives Advice 43: Archiving Web Resources: A National Archives Policy (January 2001). Available at www.naa.gov.au/recordkeeping/rkpubs/advices/advice/advice43.html, accessed June 3, 2005.

21. Jason Miller, "Digital Records Swamp NARA," *Government Computer News,* February 10, 2003, 1.

22. "E-records: Hope Is Not Lost," *Federal Computer Week,* June 16, 2003, 3.

23. United States, Key National Indicators Initiative. Available at www.keyindicators.org/, accessed June 17, 2005.

24. Halchin, "Electronic Government: Government Capability and Terrorist Response," 417.

25. GAO, *Informing Our Nation: Improving How to Understand and Assess the USA's Position and Progress,* GAO-0501 (Washington, DC: GAO, November 2004), 2.

26. GAO, *Informing Our Nation,* 2.

27. GAO, *Informing Our Nation,* 11.

28. GAO, *Informing Our Nation,* 12.

29. United Nations, *Global E-Government Readiness Report 2004* (New York: United Nations, 2004). Available at www.unpan.org/egovernment4.asp, accessed April 1, 2005.

30. Accenture, *eGovernment Leadership: High Performance, Maximum Value* (New York: Accenture, 2004). Available at www.accenture.com, accessed June 20, 2004.

31. "Prime Minister's Keynote Speech to e-Summit" (London: Prime Minister's Office, 2004), 2. Available at www.number10.gov.uk/output/Page1734.asp, accessed July 8, 2004.

32. E-Government Unit, *Participation through E-Government: The Context* (Wellington: State Services Commission, 2004), 4. Available at www.e.govt.nz/docs/participation-0305/index.html, accessed April 20, 2005.

33. Andrew Chadwick and Christopher May, "Interaction between States and Citizens in the Age of the Internet: 'e-Government' in the United States, Britain, and the European Union," *Governance: An International Journal of Policy, Administration and Institutions* 16 (April 2003): 271–300.

34. Accenture, *eGovernment Leadership,* 2.

35. Accenture, *eGovernment Leadership,* 39.

36. Accenture, *eGovernment Leadership,* 2.

37. United Kingdom, Cabinet Office, "eGU's mission." Available at www.cabinetoffice.gov.uk/e-government, accessed June 20, 2005.

38. White House, "Expanding Electronic Government Initiative" (Washington, DC: White House, 2005). Available at www.whitehouse.gov/omb/egov/, accessed June 22, 2005.

39. David Perera, "E-gov Aims to Lose the 'E,'" *FCW.com,* May 24, 2005. Available at www.fcw.com/articlee88957-05-24-05-Web, accessed May 30, 2005.

40. For coverage of privacy in the United States and the European Union, see "Privacy," *Federal Computer Week,* June 27, 2005, 3, 16–18, 21–22, 24–25, 34.

Bibliography

ARTICLES

Allan, Barbara, Ann Luc Juillet, Gilles Paquet, and Jeffrey Roy. "E-Governance & Government On-line in Canada: Partnerships, People, and Prospects." *Government Information Quarterly* 18 (2001): 93–104.

Anderson, Christopher J., and Andrew J. LoTemplo. "Winning, Losing, and Political Trust in America." *British Journal of Political Science* 32 (April 2002): 335–52.

Bantin, Philip. "The Indiana University Electronic Records Project: Lessons Learned." *Information Management Journal* 35 (January 2001): 18–20.

Barr, Stephen. "President Searching for a Few Good E-Government Ideas." *Washington Post,* August 10, 2001, B2.

Basu, Subhajit. "E-Government and Developing Countries: An Overview." *International Review of Law Computers & Technology* 18 (March 2004): 109–32.

"Behind the Digital Divide." *Economist Technology Quarterly,* March 12, 2005, 16.

Blanchard, R. F., and R. L. Galloway. "Quality in Retail Banking." *International Journal of Service Industry Management* 5, no. 4 (1994): 5–23.

Branch, Jennifer L. "Investigating the Information-Seeking Processes of Adolescents: The Value of Using Think Alouds and Think Afters." *Library & Information Science Research* 22, no. 4 (2000): 371–92.

Chadwick, Andrew, and Christopher May. "Interaction between States and Citizens in the Age of the Internet: 'e-Government' in the United States, Britain, and the European Union." *Governance: An International Journal of Policy, Administration, and Institutions* 16, no. 2 (April 2003): 271–300.

Cheshire, William P. "Hoaxing along the Infobahn." *Arizona Republic,* October 30, 1994, E1.

Chu, Pin-Yu, Naiyi Hsiao, Fung-Wu Lee, and Chun-Wei Chen. "Exploring Success Factors for Taiwan's Government Electronic Tendering System: Behavioral Perspectives from End Users." *Government Information Quarterly* 21, no. 2 (2004): 219–34.

Coles, Clifton. "Britons Distrust Government on Key Risk Issues: Providing Technical Information Is Not Enough to Instill Trust." *The Futurist* 37 (July–August 2003): 10.

Cook, Terry. "Electronic Records, Paper Minds: The Revolution in Information Management and Archives in the Post-custodial and Post-modernist Era." *Archives and Manuscripts* 22 (November 1994): 300–328.

Cullen, Rowena. "E-government: A Citizen's Perspective." *Journal of E-Government* 1, no. 3 (2004). Available at http://www.haworthpress.com/store/toc/J399v01n03_TOC.pdf, retrieved December 21, 2005.

Cullen, Rowena, and Caroline Houghton. "Democracy On-line: An Assessment of New Zealand Government Web Sites." *Government Information Quarterly* 17 (July 2000): 243–67.

Cullen, Rowena, Deborah O'Connor, and Anna Veritt. "An Evaluation of Local Government Web

Sites in New Zealand." Special issue on e-government, *Journal of Political Marketing* 2, no. 3/4 (2003): 185–211.

Cunningham, Adrian. "The Archival Management of Personal Records in Electronic Form: Some Suggestions." *Archives and Manuscripts* 22, no. 1 (May 1994): 94–105.

———. "Waiting for the Ghost Train: Strategies for Managing Electronic Personal Records before It Is Too Late." *Archival Issues* 24, no. 1 (1999): 55–64.

Daukantas, Patricia. "E-gov Sites Score High on User Satisfaction Survey." *Government Computer News,* September 22, 2003, 68.

———. "It's All Within Two Clicks on New BEA Site." *Government Computer News,* August 4, 2003, 14.

Delaney, Janine. "Redefining the Role for Collecting Archives in an Electronic Paradigm." *Archifacts,* April 2000, 13–24.

Dollar, Charles M. "Archivists and Records Managers in the Information Age." *Archivaria* 36 (Autumn 1993): 37–52.

Duranti, Luciana. "Meeting the Challenge of Contemporary Records: Does It Require a Role Change for the Archivist?" *American Archivist* 63 (Spring/Summer 2000): 12–13.

Edwards, Meredith. "Public Sector Governance: Future Issues for Australia." *Australian Journal of Public Administration* 61, no. 2 (June 2002): 51–61.

Ehlke, Richard C., and Harold C. Relyea. "The Reagan Administration Order on Security Classification: A Critical Assessment." *Federal Bar News & Journal* 30 (February 1983): 91–97.

"E-records: Hope Is Not Lost." *Federal Computer Week,* June 16, 2003, 3.

Esperitu, Antonina. "Digital Divide and Implications on Growth: Cross-country Analysis." *Journal of the American Academy of Business* 2, no. 2 (March 2003): 450–53.

Fairlie, John A. "Administrative Legislation." *Michigan Law Review* 18 (January 1920): 181–200.

Feinberg, Lotte E. "FOIA, Federal Information Policy, and Information Availability in a Post-9-11 World." *Government Information Quarterly* 21 (2004): 439–60.

Flynn, Sarah J. A. "The Records Continuum Model in Context and Its Implications for Archival Practice." *Journal of Society of Archivists* 22, no. 1 (April 2001): 79–83.

Frank, Diane. "Online Feng Shui." *Federal Computer Week,* May 19, 2003, 40.

Gappa, Henrike, and Gabriele Nordbrock. "Applying Web Accessibility to Internet Portals." *Universal Access in the Information Society* 3 (2004): 80–87.

Gay, Lance. "White House Uses Drug-Message Site to Track Inquiries." *Washington Times,* June 21, 2000, A3.

Gelatt, Timothy A. "The New Chinese State Secrets Law." *Cornell International Law Journal* 22 (1989): 255–68.

Griswold, Erwin N. "Government in Ignorance of the Law—A Plea for Better Publication of Executive Legislation." *Harvard Law Review* 48 (December 1934): 198–213.

Gugliotta, Guy. "Agencies Scrub Web Sites of Sensitive Chemical Data." *Washington Post,* October 4, 2001, A29.

Halchin, L. Elaine. "Electronic Government: Government Capability and Terrorist Response." *Government Information Quarterly* 21 (2004): 406–19.

Harris, John F., and John Schwartz. "Anti-Drug Web Site Tracks Visitors." *Washington Post,* June 22, 2000, A23.

Hernon, Peter. "Disinformation and Misinformation through the Internet: Findings of an Exploratory Study." *Government Information Quarterly* 12, no. 2 (1995): 133–39.

———. "Government Information Policy in New Zealand: Businesslike but Evolving?" *Government Information Quarterly* 13, no. 3 (1996): 215–28.

Hill, Evan. "Some Thoughts on E-democracy as an Evolving Concept." *Journal of E-Government* 1 (2004): 23–39.

Holliday, Ian, and Rebecca C. W. Kwok. "Governance in the Information Age: Building E-Government in Hong Kong." *New Media & Society* 6, no. 4 (August 2004): 549–70.

Hoyle, Michael. "Developing an Electronic Records Policy for New Zealand." *Archifacts,* October 1997, 8–21.

Huang, Hai, Claudia Keser, Jonathon W. Leland, and Jason Shachat. "Trust, the Internet, and the Digital Divide." *IBM Systems Journal* 42 (2003): 507–19.

Hulse, Carl. "Senate Votes to Consider Ban on Taxes on Net Access." *New York Times,* April 27, 2004.

Jacobs, James A., James R. Jacobs, and Shinjoung Yeo. "Government Information in the Digital Age: The Once and Future Federal Depository Library Program." *Journal of Academic Librarianship* 31 (May 2005): 198–208.

Jennings, M. Kent, and Vicki Zeitner. "Internet Use and Civic Engagement." *Public Opinion Quarterly* 67 (Fall 2003): 311–26.

"Justice Extends WordPerfect." *Federal Computer Week* 19, no. 6 (March 14, 2000): 11.

Kavadias, Gregory, and Efthimios Tambouris. "GovML: A Markup Language for Describing Public Services and Life Events." *Lecture Notes in Computer Science* 2645 (2003): 106–13.

Ke, Weiling, and Kwok Kee Wei. "Successful E-government in Singapore." *Communications of the ACM* 47, no. 6 (June 2004): 95–99.

Koga, Takashi. "Access to Government Information in Japan: A Long Way toward Electronic Government?" *Government Information Quarterly* 20 (2003): 47–62.

Kuk, George. "The Digital Divide and the Quality of Electronic Service Delivery in Local Government in the United Kingdom." *Government Information Quarterly* 20, no. 4 (2003): 353–63.

Laurent, Anne. "Revamping Reinvention." *Government Executive,* April 1998, 31–32.

Lichtblau, Eric. "Response to Terror: Rising Fears That What We Can Do Can Hurt Us." *Los Angeles Times,* November 18, 2001, part A, part 1: 1.

Licklinder, J. C. R. "Man-Computer Symbiosis." *IRE Transactions on Human Factors in Electronics* 1 (1960): 4–11.

Licklinder, J. C. R., and W. E. Clark. "On-line Man-Computer Communication." *Proceedings of the American Federation of Information Processing Societies* 21 (1962): 113–28.

Licklinder, J. C. R., and Robert W. Taylor. "The Computer as a Communication Device." *Science and Technology* 76 (1968): 21–31.

Lynch, Saragail Runyon. "GPO Recalls of Depository Documents." *Journal of Government Information* 22 (January–February 1995): 23–31.

Marche, Sunny, and James D. McNiven. "E-government and E-governance: The Future Isn't What It Used to Be." *Canadian Journal of Administrative Sciences* 20 (2003): 74–86.

Marchionini, Gary, and Xiangming Mu. "User Studies Informing E-table Interfaces." *Information Processing & Management* 39 (2003): 561–79.

Matthews, William. "FirstGov to Add State Links." *Federal Computer Week,* May 21, 2001, 13.

McGinnis, Patricia. "Poll Reveals the Next E-government Challenge." *Government Computer News,* May 19, 2003, 29.

McDonald, John. "Archives and Current Records: Towards a Set of Guiding Principles." *Janus* (1999): 108–15.

———. "Managing Records in the Modern Office: Taming the Wild Frontier." *Archivaria* 39 (Spring 1995): 70–87.

McKemmish, Sue. "The Smoking Gun: Recordkeeping and Accountability." *Archifacts,* April 1999, 2.

McKemmish, Sue, Glenda Acland, Nigel Ward, and Barbara Reed. "Describing Records in Context in the Continuum: The Australian Recordkeeping Metadata Schema." *Archivaria* 48 (Fall 1999): 3–43.

Michael, Sara. "Do Your Project Managers Measure Up?" *Federal Computer Week,* November 3, 2003, 28.

Miller, Jason. "Digital Records Swamp NARA." *Government Computer News,* February 10, 2003, 1, 8.

Mitchell, Alison. "Classified Information: Bush Gives Secrecy Power to Public Health Secretary." *New York Times,* December 20, 2001, B6.

Mitchell, William J. "When Is Seeing Believing?" *Scientific American,* February 1994, 68–73.

Moss, William W. "Research Note—Dang'an: Contemporary Chinese Archives." *China Quarterly* 145 (March 1996): 112–29.

Muir, Adrienne, and Charles Oppenheim. "National Information Policy Developments World-wide 1: Electronic Government." *Journal of Information Science* 28, no. 3 (2002): 173–86.

Nalen, James E. "Private Archives in China." *Libri* 52 (December 2002): 241–62.

Nitecki, Danuta, and Peter Hernon. "Measuring Service Quality at Yale University's Libraries." *Journal of Academic Librarianship* 26, no. 4 (July 2000): 259–73.

Oliver, R. L., and W. S. DeSarbo. "Response Determinants in Satisfaction Judgments." *Journal of Consumer Research* 14 (1998): 495–507.

Olsen, Florence. "GAO Web Site Redesign Improves Efficiency." *Federal Computer Week,* July 19, 2004, 44.

O'Shea, Greg, and David Roberts. "Living in a Digital World: Recognizing the Electronic and Post-custodial Realities." *Archives and Manuscripts* 24 (November 1996): 286–311.

Parasuraman, A., Leonard L. Berry, and Valarie A. Zeithaml. "Refinement and Reassessment of the SERVQUAL Scale." *Journal of Retailing* 67, no. 4 (1991): 420–50.

Perera, David. "Campaigning Enters the Internet Age." *Federal Computer Week,* August 16, 2004, 12–13.

———. "OMB's Rule: Pay As You Go." *Federal Computer Week,* September 20, 2004, 12.

Ploucher, David. "The Paperwork Reduction Act of 1995: A Second Chance for Information Resources Management." *Government Information Quarterly* 13 (1996): 35–50.

"Privacy." *Federal Computer Week* 19, no. 21 (June 27, 2005): 3, 16–18, 21–22, 24–25, 34.

Raum, Tom. "Memo Tests Honesty as Best Policy." *Middlesex News* (Framingham, MA), February 11, 1994, A4.

"The Real Digital Divide." *Economist,* March 12, 2005, 11.

Reddick, Christopher G. "Citizen Interaction with E-government: From the Streets to Servers?" *Government Information Quarterly* 22 (2005): 38–57.

Reed, Margaret A. T. "SBA: Web Simplicity Is a Virtue." *Federal Computer Week,* June 30, 2003, 36.

Reeves, C. A., and D. A. Bednar. "Defining Quality: Alternatives and Implications." *Academy of Management Review* 19, no. 3 (1994): 419–45.

Relyea, Harold C. "Homeland Security and Information." *Government Information Quarterly* 19 (2002): 213–23.

———. "Information, Secrecy, and Atomic Energy." *New York University Review of Law and Social Change* 10 (1980–1981): 265–91.

Rose, Meithya. "Democratizing Information and Communication by Implementing E-government in Indonesian Regional Government." *International Information & Library Review* 36 (2004): 219–26.

Sadik, Hasan. "Introducing E-Government in Bangladesh: Problems and Prospects." *International Social Science Review* 78, nos. 3 and 4 (2003): 111–26.

Santos, Jessica. "E-service Quality: A Model of Virtual Service Quality Dimensions." *Managing Service Quality* 13, no. 3 (2003): 232–46.

Seifert, Jeffrey W., and Harold C. Relyea. "Considering E-government from the U.S. Federal Perspective: An Evolving Concept, a Developing Practice." *Journal of E-Government* 1 (2004): 7–15.

Smith, Michael Alan. "Portals: Toward an Application Framework for Interoperability." *Communications of the ACM* 47, no. 10 (October 2004): 93–97.

"Survey Finds Many Government Web Sites Are Inaccessible." *Disability Compliance for Higher Education* 9, no. 4 (November 2003): 9.

Swartz, Nick. "E-government around the World." *Information Management Journal* 38 (January/February 2004): 12.

Thomas, John Clayton, and Gregory Streib. "The New Face of Government: Citizen Initiated Contacts in the Era of E-government." *Journal of Public Administration Research and Theory* 13 (January 2003): 83–102.

Toner, Robin. "Reconsidering Security, U.S. Clamps Down on Agency Web Sites." *New York Times,* October 28, 2001, B4.

Turner, Steven. "The HEP Test for Grading Web Site Usability." *Computers in Libraries* 22, no. 10 (November/December 2002): 37–39.

van Brakel, Pieter. "Information Portals: A Strategy for Importing External Content." *Electronic Library* 21 (2003): 591–601.

Wallsten, Scott. "Regulation and Internet Use in Developing Countries." *Economic Development and Cultural Change* 53, no. 2 (January 2005): 501–24.

Wang, Yi-Shun, and Tzung-I Tang. "Assessing Customer Perceptions of Website Service Quality in Digital Marketing Environments." *Journal of End User Computing* 15, no. 3 (July–September 2003): 14–31.

Weiss, Carol H., and Michael J. Bucuvalas. "Truth Tests and Utility Tests: Decision-Makers' Frames of Reference for Social Science Research." *American Sociological Review* 45 (April 1980): 302–13.

West, Darrell M. "E-government and the Transformation of Service Delivery and Citizen Attitudes." *Public Administration Review* 64, no. 1 (January/February 2004): 15–27.

"What Americans Think: Trust in Government." *Spectrum* 73, no. 2 (Spring 2000): 19.

Wong, Wilson, and Eric Welch. "Does E-Government Promote Accountability? A Comparative Analysis of Website Openness and Government Accountability." *Governance: An International Journal of Policy, Administration, and Institutions* 17, no. 2 (April 2004): 275–97.

Wyld, David C. "The 3 Ps: The Essential Elements of a Definition of E-government." *Journal of E-Government* 1 (2004): 17–22.

Zachman, J. A. "A Framework for Information Systems Architecture." *IBM Systems Journal* 26, no. 3 (1987): 276–92.

Zagel, James. "The State Secrets Privilege." *Minnesota Law Review* 50 (1966): 875–910.

Zeithaml, Valarie A., A. Parasuraman, and Arvind Malhotra. "Service Quality Delivery through Web Sites: A Critical Review of Extant Knowledge." *Journal of the Academy of Marketing Science* 30, no. 4 (Fall 2002): 362–75.

BOOKS

Brown, Anthony Cave, and Charles B. MacDonald, eds. *The Secret History of the Atomic Bomb.* New York: Dial Press/James Wade, 1977.

Braithwaite, Valerie, and Margaret Levi, eds. *Trust and Governance.* New York: Russell Sage Foundation, 1998.

Casson, Herbert N. *The History of the Telephone.* Chicago: A. C. McClurg, 1910.

Childers, Thomas A., and Nancy A. Van House. *What's Good? Describing Your Public Library's Effectiveness.* Chicago: American Library Association, 1993.

Clarke, Richard A. *Against All Enemies: Inside America's War on Terror.* New York: Free Press, 2004.

Daconta, Michael C., Leo J. Obrst, and Kevin T. Smith. *The Semantic Web: A Guide to the Future of XML, Web Services, and Knowledge Management.* Indianapolis: Wiley, 2003.

DeVolpi, A., G. E. Marsh, T. A. Postal, and G. S. Stanford. *Born Secret: The H-Bomb, the Progressive Case, and National Security.* New York: Pergamon, 1981.

Disend, Jeffrey E. *How to Provide Excellent Service in Any Organization.* Radnor, PA: Chilton, 1991.

Dollar, Charles M. *Authentic Electronic Records: Strategies for Long-Term Access.* Chicago: Cohasset Associates, 1999.

Donnelly, Vanessa. *Designing Easy-to-Use Web Sites: A Hands-On Approach to Structuring Successful Web Sites.* Harlow, UK: Addison-Wesley, 2001.

Hackman, J. Richard. *Leading Teams: Setting the Stage for Great Performances*. Boston: Harvard Business School Press, 2002.

Hernon, Peter, and Ellen Altman. *Assessing Service Quality: Satisfying the Expectations of Library Customers*. Chicago: American Library Association, 1998.

Hernon, Peter, and John R. Whitman. *Delivering Satisfaction and Service Quality: A Customer-Based Approach for Libraries*. Chicago: American Library Association, 2001.

Hernon, Peter, Robert E. Dugan, and John A. Shuler, eds. *U.S. Government on the Web: Getting the Information You Need*. 3rd ed. Westport, CT: Libraries Unlimited, 2003.

Holmes, Douglas. *eGov: eBusiness Strategies for Government*. London: Nicholas Brealey, 2001.

Kennedy, Jay, and Cheryl Schauder. *Records Management: A Guide to Corporate Recordkeeping*. 2nd ed. South Melbourne: Longman, 1999.

Kotler, Philip. *Marketing for Nonprofit Organizations*. Englewood Cliffs, NJ: Prentice-Hall, 1975, 1982.

Krug, Steve. *Don't Make Me Think! A Common Sense Approach to Web Usability*. Indianapolis: New Riders Publishing, 2000.

Lasswell, Harold D. *National Security and Individual Freedom*. New York: McGraw-Hill, 1950.

McCoy, Donald R. *The National Archives: America's Ministry of Documents, 1934–1968*. Chapel Hill: University of North Carolina Press, 1978.

Mintz, Anne P., ed. *Web of Deception: Misinformation on the Internet*. Medford, NJ: Information Today, 2002.

National Research Council. Computer Science and Telecommunications Board. Committee on Digital Archiving. *Building an Electronic Records Archive at the National Archives and Records Administration*. Washington, DC: National Academies Press, 2003.

Nielsen, Jakob. *Designing Web Usability*. Indianapolis: New Riders, 2000.

Nye, Joseph S., Jr., Philip D. Zelikow, and David C. King. *Why People Don't Trust Government*. Cambridge, MA: Harvard University Press, 1997.

Oliver, R. L. *Satisfaction: A Behavioral Perspective on the Consumer*. New York: McGraw-Hill, 1997.

Orwell, George. *1984*. New York: New American Library, 1950.

Osborne, David, and Ted Gaebler. *Reinventing Government*. New York: Penguin, 1992.

Relyea, Harold C. *Silencing Science: National Security Controls and Scientific Communication*. Norwood, NJ: Ablex, 1994.

———, ed. *Striking a Balance: National Security and Scientific Freedom—First Discussions*. Washington, DC: American Association for the Advancement of Science, 1985.

Rogers, E.. *Diffusion of Innovations*. 5th ed. New York: Free Press, 2003.

Rossi, Peter H., Mark W. Lipsey, and Howard E. Freeman. *Evaluation: A Systematic Approach*. Thousand Oaks, CA: Sage, 2004.

Shepherd, Elizabeth, and Geoffrey Yeo. *Managing Records: A Handbook of Principles and Practices*. London: Facet, 2003.

Society of American Archivists. *A Glossary for Archivists, Manuscript Curators, and Records Managers*. Chicago: Society of American Archivists, 1992.

Vavra, Terry G. *Improving Your Measurement of Customer Satisfaction: A Guide to Creating, Conducting, Analyzing, and Reporting Customer Satisfaction Measurement Programs*. Milwaukee, WI: ASQ Quality Press, 1997.

Zeithaml, Valarie A., A. Parasuraman, and Arvind Malhotra. *A Conceptual Framework for Understanding e-Service Quality: Implications for Future Research and Managerial Practice*. Cambridge, MA: Marketing Science Institute, 2000.

Zeithaml, Valarie A., A. Parasuraman, and Leonard L. Berry. *Delivering Quality Service: Balancing Customer Perceptions and Expectations*. New York: Free Press, 1990.

BOOK CHAPTERS

Capron, William M. "The Executive Branch in the Year 2000." 299–308 in *The Future of the U.S. Government: Toward the Year 2000,* edited by Harvey S. Perloff. New York: George Brazziller, 1971.

Cunningham, Adrian. "Archival Institutions." 20–50 in *Archives: Recordkeeping in Society*, edited by Sue McKemmish, Michael Piggott, Barbara Reed, and Frank Upward. Wagga Wagga, Australia: Charles Sturt University, 2005.

Curtin, Gregory G., and Christopher J. Walker. "A Comparative Analysis of E-government in Latin America: Applied Findings from United Nations E-government Readiness Reports." In *Latin America On-line: Cases, Successes, and Pitfalls*, edited by Mila Gasco. Hershey, PA: Idea Group, in press.

Dholakia, Ruby Roy, Nikhilesh Dholakia, and Nir Kshetri. "Gender and Internet Usage." 12–22 in *The Internet Encyclopedia*, vol. 2, edited by Hossein Bidgoli. New York: Wiley, 2003.

E-Government Policy Network. "Transforming Government and Governance for the 21st Century: A Conceptual Framework." 3–31 in *E-Government Reconsidered: Renewal of Governance for the Knowledge Age*, edited by E. Lynn Oliver and Larry Sanders. Regina: Canadian Plains Research Center, University of Regina and Saskatchewan Institute of Public Policy, 2004.

Gibbins, Roger. "Federalism and the Challenge of Electronic Portals." 33–42 in *E-government Reconsidered: Renewal of Governance for the Knowledge Age*, edited by E. Lynn Oliver and Larry Sanders. Regina: Canadian Plains Research Center, University of Regina and Saskatchewan Institute of Public Policy, 2004.

Graves, William H., and Kirsten Hale. "Portals: Your Institution's Reputation Depends on Them." 37–50 in *Designing Portals: Opportunities and Challenges*, edited by Ali Jafari and Mark Sheehan. Hershey, PA: Information Science Publishing, 2003.

Hackman, J. Richard, and Richard E. Walton. "Leading Groups in Organizations." 72–120 in *Designing Effective Work Groups*, edited by Paul S. Goodman and Associates. San Francisco: Jossey-Bass, 1986.

Holzer, Marc, Lung-Teng Hu, and Seok-Hwi Song. "Digital Government and Citizen Participation in the United States." 306–19 in *Digital Government: Principles and Best Practices*, edited by D. G. Garson and A. Pavlichev. Hershey, PA: Ideas Group, 2004.

Jafari. Ali. "The ABCs of Designing Campus Portals." 7–27 in *Designing Portals*, edited by Jakob Nielsen. Indianapolis: New Riders, 2000.

———. "The Next Generation of Internet Portals." 89–100 in *Designing Portals*, edited by Jakob Nielsen. Indianapolis: New Riders, 2000.

Katz, R. N., and L. Goldstein. "Portals: Summing up." 152–62 in *Web Portals and Higher Education: Technologies to Make IT Personal*, edited by R. N. Katz. San Francisco: Jossey-Bass, 2002.

Longford, Graham. "Rethinking the Virtual State: A Critical Perspective on E-Government." 109–40 in *Seeking Convergence in Policy and Practice: Communications in the Public Interest*, vol. 2, edited by Marita Moll and Leslie Regan Shade. Ottawa: Canadian Centre for Policy Alternatives, 2004.

McKemmish, Sue, Barbara Reed, and Michael Piggott. "The Archives." 1158–95 in *Archives: Recordkeeping in Society*, edited by Sue McKemmish, Michael Piggott, Barbara Reed, and Frank Upward. Wagga Wagga, Australia: Charles Sturt University, 2005.

Millar, Laurence. "Connected Government: The New Zealand Story." 25–41 in *Connected Government: Thought Leaders; Essays from Innovators*, edited by Willi Kaczorowski. London: Premium Publishing, 2004.

Mitchinson, Tom, and Mark Ratner. "Promoting Transparency through the Electronic Dissemination of Information." 89–105 in *E-Government Reconsidered: Renewal of Governance for the Knowledge Age*, edited by E. Lynn Oliver and Larry Sanders. Regina: Canadian Plains Research Center, University of Regina and Saskatchewan Institute of Public Policy, 2004.

Paquet, Gilles. "There is More to Governance than Public Candelabras: E-governance and Canada's Public Service." 181–203 in *E-Government Reconsidered: Renewal of Governance for the Knowledge Age*, edited by E. Lynn Oliver and Larry Sanders. Regina: Canadian Plains Research Center, University of Regina and Saskatchewan Institute of Public Policy, 2004.

Pederson, Ann. "Professing Archives: A Very Human Enterprise." 51–74 in *Archives: Recordkeeping in*

Society, edited by Sue McKemmish, Michael Piggott, Barbara Reed, and Frank Upward. Wagga Wagga, Australia: Charles Sturt University, 2005.

Poelmans, Matt. "Making E-government Work: The Content and Significance of an e-Citizens' Charter." 78–89 in *Connected Government: Thought Leaders; Essays from Innovators,* edited by Willi Kaczorowski. London: Premium Publishing, 2004.

Relyea, Harold C. "E-Gov Comes to the Federal Government." 379–401 in *U.S. Government on the Web: Getting the Information You Need,* edited by Peter Hernon, Robert E. Dugan, and John A. Shuler. Westport, CT: Libraries Unlimited, 2003.

Relyea, Harold C., and Henry B. Hogue. "A Brief History of the Emergence of Digital Government in the United States." 16–33 in *Digital Government: Principles and Best Practices,* edited by Alexei Pavlichev and G. David Garson. Hershey, PA: Idea Group Publishing, 2004.

Watkins, Jameson. "Developing a Portal Channel Strategy." 51–67 in *Designing Portals: Opportunities and Challenges,* edited by Ali Jafari and Mark Sheehan. Hershey, PA: Information Science Publishing, 2003.

REPORTS

American Electronics Association. *Broadband in the States: A State-by-State of U.S. Broadband Deployment, 2003.* Washington, DC: American Electronics Association, 2003.

Baum, Christopher, and Andrea Di Maio. *Gartner's Four Phases of E-Government Model.* Stamford, CT: Gartner Group, November 21, 2000.

Carafiano, James Jay, and David Heyman. *DHS 2.0: Rethinking the Department of Homeland Security.* Heritage Special Report. Washington, DC: Heritage Foundation, December 13, 2004.

Committee on the Records of Government. *Report,* sponsored by the American Council of Learned Societies, Social Science Research Council, and Council on Library Resources. Washington, DC: Committee on the Records of Government, 1985.

Gartner Group. "Key Issues in E-Government Strategy and Management." *Research Notes, Key Issues.* Stamford, CT: Gartner Group, May 23, 2000.

International Council on Archives. Committee on Current Records in an Electronic Environment. *Electronic Records: A Workbook for Archivists.* Paris: International Council on Archives, April 2005.

InterPARES 2 Project. *International Research on Permanent Authentic Records in Electronic Systems.* Vancouver, Canada: InterPARES2 Project, 2002. Available at http://www.interpares.org/ipz.htm, accessed June 26, 2005.

Mulgan, Richard. *Public Sector Reform in New Zealand—Issues of Public Accountability.* Asia Pacific School of Economics and Government Discussion Papers. Canberra: Asia Pacific School of Economics and Government, Australian National University, 2004.

Report on Canadian Government On-Line Activities. Country report presented by Christine Poirier at the Government On-Line International Network meeting in Leiden, October 8–11, 2000. Available at http://www.governments-online.org/documents/Canada_Leiden.pdf, accessed April 11, 2005.

Smolenski, Mark. *The Digital Divide and American Society.* Report to the House Subcommittee on Government Management, Information and Technology. Stamford, CT: Gartner Group, 2000.

SRA International. *Report on Current Recordkeeping Practices within the Federal Government.* Prepared for the National Archives and Records Administration. Arlington, VA: SRA International, 2001.

GOVERNMENT DOCUMENTS (NONWEB RESOURCES)

Australia

Arch, Andrew, and Brian Hardy. "E-government Accessible to All." In *Future Challenges for E-government,* vol. 2. Canberra: Australian Government Information Management Office, 2004.

Australian Government Information Management Office and Institute of Public Administration. ICT Division. *Future Challenges for E-government.* 2 vols. Canberra: Australian Government Information Management Office, 2004.

Australian National Audit Office. *Electronic Service Delivery, Including Internet Use, by Commonwealth Government Agencies.* ANAO Report No.18, 1999/2000. Canberra: Australian National Audit Office 1999.

Broadband Services Expert Group. *Networking Australia's Future, Final Report.* Canberra: Australian Government Publishing Service, 1995.

Department of Communications, Information Technology and the Arts. *A Strategic Framework for the Information Economy: Identifying Priorities for Action.* Canberra: Department of Communications, Information Technology and the Arts, 1998.

Fahey, John. *Media Release: Towards an Australian Strategy for the Information Economy.* Canberra: Minister for Finance and Administration, 1998.

Management Advisory Committee. *Australian Government Use of Information and Communication Technology.* Canberra: Management Advisory Committee, 2002.

National Office of the Information Economy. *Guide to Minimum Website Standards, April 2003.* Canberra: National Office of the Information Economy, 2003.

New South Wales Office of Information and Communications Technology. *Connect NSW: An Internet Strategy for NSW.* Sydney: Office of Information and Communications Technology, 1997.

Public Record Office Victoria. *Victorian Electronic Records Strategy Final Report.* Melbourne: Public Record Office Victoria, 1998.

Standards Australia. AS 4390–1996: Australian Standard for Records Management. Homebush, NSW: Standards Australia, 1996.

———. AS ISO 15489.1-2002: Records Management–Part 1: General. Sydney, NSW: Standards Australia, 2001.

———. AS ISO 15489.1-2002: Records Management–Part 2: Guidelines. Sydney, NSW: Standards Australia, 2001.

Vivian, Raelene. "Elements of Good Government Community Collaboration." 27–46 in *Future Challenges for E-government,* vol. 1. Canberra: Australian Government Information Management Office, 2004.

Western Australia. *E-government Strategy for the Western Australian Public Sector.* Perth: Office of E-government, 2004.

Williams, Daryl. News Release: Maximising the Benefits of the Information Economy. Canberra: Minister for Communications, Information Technology and the Arts, 2004.

———. News Release: Strategic Framework for the Information Economy. Canberra: Minister for Communications, Information Technology and the Arts, 2004.

Canada

Canada. Treasury Board Secretariat. "Government of Canada's Internet Strategy." In *Government of Canada Internet Guide.* Ottawa: Treasury Board, 1995.

New Zealand

Botha, N., B. Small, and P. Crutchley. *Addressing the Rural Digital Divide in New Zealand.* Client report. Wellington: Ministry of Agriculture, 2001.

Cabinet Minute, May 2000. Cab (00)M14 1F(1).

Crib, Jo, and Tom Berthold. *Roles of Central and Local Government in Joint Problems.* Working Papers no 1. Wellington: State Services Commission, 1999.

Crown Entities Act 2004.

Electronic Transactions Act 2002.

Government Online: A National Perspective. A report prepared by TNS. Wellington: New Zealand State Services Commission, 2003.

Institute for Economic Research. *As Seen from Levin: Improving Government Communications with Citizens. A Report from the Region.* Wellington: New Zealand State Services Commission, 2001.

United States

Boyd, Eugene, and Michael K. Fauntroy. *American Federalism, 1776 to 2000: Significant Events.* CRS Report RL31057. Washington, DC: Congressional Research Service, November 30, 2000.

Communications Act 1934 (47 U.S.C. 151).

Congress. House. Committee on Government Operations. *Electronic Collection and Dissemination of Information by Federal Agencies: A Policy Overview,* H. Rept. 99-560, 99th Cong., 2nd sess. Washington, DC: GPO, 1986.

————. *Taking a Byte out of History: The Archival Preservation of Federal Computer Records,* H. Rept. 101-978, 101st Cong., 2nd sess. Washington, DC: GPO, 1990.

Department of Agriculture. Rural Utilities Service. "Rural Broadband Access Loans and Loan Guarantees." *Federal Register* 68, no. 20 (January 30, 2003): 4684–92.

————. "Rural Broadband Access Loans and Loan Guarantees Program." *Federal Register* 68, no. 20 (January 30, 2003), 4753–55.

————. "Rural Broadband Access Loans and Loan Guarantees Program." *Federal Register* 69, no. 60 (March 29, 2004): 16231–32.

Department of Commerce. *Falling through the Net: Toward Digital Inclusion.* Washington, DC: Department of Commerce, October 2000.

Department of Defense. Assistant Secretary of Defense for Command, Control, Communications and Intelligence. *Design Criteria Standard for Electronic Records Management Software Applications DoD 5015.2-STD.* Washington, DC: Department of Defense, June 19 2002.

Department of Defense Security Review Commission. *Keeping the Nation's Secrets.* Washington, DC: GPO, 1985.

E-Government Act 2002. P. L. 107-347 (116 Stat. 2899).

Environmental Protection Agency v. Mink, 410 U.S. 73 (1973).

Executive Order 13011, *Federal Information Technology.* Washington, DC: White House (President Clinton), July 16, 1996.

Federal Communications Commission. *Deployment of Advanced Telecommunications Capability: Second Report.* Washington, DC: Federal Communications Commission, 2000.

————. News Release, "FCC Issues Report on the Deployment of Advanced Telecommunications Capability to All Americans." Washington, DC: Federal Communications Commission, January 28, 1999.

————. Notice of Inquiry, "Concerning the Deployment of Advanced Telecommunications Capability to All Americans in a Reasonable and Timely Fashion, and Possible Steps to Accelerate Such Deployment Pursuant to Section 706 of the Telecommunications Act of 1996." FCC 04-55. Washington, DC: Federal Communications Commission, March 17, 2004.

General Accounting Office. *Classified Information: Costs of Protection Are Integrated with Other Security Costs,* GAO/NSIAD-94-55. Washington, DC: General Accounting Office, 1993.

————. *Electronic Government: Challenges Must Be Addressed with Effective Leadership and Management,* GAO-01-959T. Washington, DC: General Accounting Office, 2001.

————. *Electronic Government: Selection and Implementation of the Office of Management and Budget's 24 Initiatives,* GAO Report GAO-03-229. Washington, DC: General Accounting Office, November 2002.

————. *Electronic Records: Management and Preservation Pose Challenges,* testimony, GAO-03-936T. Washington, DC: General Accounting Office, 2003.

————. *Electronic Rulemaking: Efforts to Facilitate Public Participation Can Be Improved*, GAO-03-901. Washington, DC: General Accounting Office, 2003.

————. *Information Management: Challenges in Managing and Preserving Electronic Records*, GAO-02-586. Washington, DC: General Accounting Office, 2002.

————. *Information Management: Progress in Implementing the 1996 Electronic Freedom of Information Act Amendments*, GAO-01-378. Washington, DC: General Accounting Office, 2001.

————. *Information Management: Update on Implementation of the 1996 Electronic Freedom of Information Act Amendments*, GAO-02-493. Washington, DC: General Accounting Office, 2002.

————. *Information Security: Continued Efforts Needed to Fully Implement Statutory Requirements*, GAO Testimony GAO-03-852T. Washington, DC: General Accounting Office, June 24, 2003.

————. *Information Technology: The Federal Enterprise Architecture and Agencies' Enterprise Architectures are Still Maturing,* GAO Testimony GAO-04-798T. Washington, DC: General Accounting Office, May 19, 2004.

Government Accountability Office. *Informing Our Nation: Improving How to Understand and Assess the USA's Position and Progress*, GAO-05-1. Washington, DC: Government Accountability Office, November 2004.

Hafkin, Nancy, and Nancy Taggart. *Gender, Information Technology, and Developing Countries: An Analytic Study.* Washington, DC: Academy for Educational Development, for the Office of Women in Development, Bureau for Global Programs, Field Support and Research, Agency for International Development, 2001.

INS v. Chadha, 462 U.S. 919 (1983).

Koontz, Linda D. "Electronic Government: Initiatives Sponsored by the Office of Management and Budget Have Made Mixed Progress." Testimony before the Subcommittee on Technology, Information Policy, Intergovernmental Relations and the Census, Committee on Government Reform, House of Representatives. GAO-04-561T. Washington, DC: General Accounting Office, 2004.

McMurty, Virginia A. *The President's Management Agenda: A Brief Introduction,* CRS Report RS21416. Washington, DC: Congressional Research Service, February 14, 2005.

Minnesota. Office of the Legislative Auditor, Program Evaluation Division. *State Agency Use of Customer Satisfaction Surveys.* Saint Paul, MN: Program Evaluation Division, 1995.

Office of Homeland Security. *National Strategy for Homeland Security.* Washington, DC: Office of Homeland Security, 2002.

Office of Management and Budget. "Citizen-Centered E-government: Developing the Action Plan." Memorandum for the heads of executive departments and agencies, M-01-28. Washington, DC: Office of Management and Budget, July 18, 2001.

————. *Enabling Citizen-Centered Electronic Government 2005-2006 FEA PMO Action Plan.* Washington, DC: Office of Management and Budget, March 2005.

————. *FY2004 Report to Congress on Implementation of the E-Government Act of 2002.* Washington, DC: Office of Management and Budget, 2005.

————. "Policies for Federal Agency Public Websites." Memorandum for the heads of executive departments and agencies, M-05-04. Washington, DC: Office of Management and Budget, 2004.

————. *The President's Management Agenda, FY2002.* Washington, DC: Office of Management and Budget, 2001.

————. "Privacy Policies on Federal Websites." Memorandum for the heads of executive departments and agencies, M-99-18. Washington, DC: Office of Management and Budget, 1999.

————. "Privacy Policies on Federal Websites." Memorandum for the heads of executive departments and agencies, M-00-13. Washington, DC: Office of Management and Budget, 2000.

————. *Section 213 9f the E-Government Act, Report to Congress: Organizations Complementing Federal Agency Information Dissemination Programs.* Washington, DC: Office of Management and Budget, 2005.

Office of Technology Assessment. *Accessibility and Integrity of Networked Information Collections,* background paper. Washington, DC: Office of Technology Assessment, 1993.

————. *Informing the Nation: Federal Information Dissemination in an Electronic Age*. Washington, DC: Office of Technology Assessment, 1988.

Office of the Vice President. *Access America: Reengineering through Information Technology, Report of the National Partnership for Reinventing Government and the Government Information Technology Services Board*. Washington, DC: Office of the Vice President, 1997.

————. *Creating a Government That Works Better and Costs Less, Status Report September, 1994, Report of the National Performance Review*. Washington, DC: Office of the Vice President, 1994.

————. *From Red Tape to Results: Creating a Government That Works Better and Costs Less, Report of the National Performance Review*. Washington, DC: Office of the Vice President, 1993.

Panama Refining Company v. Ryan, 293 U.S. 388 (1935).

President's Council of Advisors on Science and Technology. Office of Science and Technology Policy. *Building Out Broadband*. Washington, DC: Office of Science and Technology Policy, December 2002.

Privacy Act. 5 U.S.C. 552a.

Relyea, Harold C. "Appendix II: Government Information Security Classification Policy." 313–352 in Congress. Senate. Select Committee to Study Governmental Operations with Respect to Intelligence Activities. *Supplemental Reports on Intelligence Activities*, Book VI, S. Rept. 94-755, 94th Cong., 2nd sess. Washington, DC: GPO, 1976.

————. "The Evolution of Government Information Security Classification Policy: A Brief Overview (1775–1873)." 505–97 in Congress. House. Committee on Government Operations. *Security Classification Reform*, hearings 93rd Cong., 2nd sess. Washington, DC: GPO, 1974.

Relyea, Harold C., Maricele J. Cornejo, and Henry B. Hogue. *The National Performance Review and Other Government Initiatives: An Overview, 1993–2001*. CRS Report RL30596. Washington, DC: Congressional Research Service, June 4, 2001.

Seifert, Jeffrey W. *Government Information Technology Management: Past and Future Issues (The Clinger-Cohen Act)*. CRS Report RL30661. Washington, DC: Congressional Research Service, January 15, 2002.

Telecommunications Act of 1996, P.L. 104-104.

United States Code. Available at GPO Access, http://www.gpoaccess.gov; THOMAS, http://thomas.loc.gov.

United States v. Smith, 292 U.S. 633 (1934).

White House. *Electronic Government*. Memorandum for the heads of executive departments and agencies. Washington, DC: White House, December 17, 1999.

International Organizations

Organisation for Economic Co-operation and Development (OECD). *E-Government Imperative*. Paris: OECD, 2003.

————. *Understanding the Digital Divide*. Paris: OECD, 2001.

————. Directorate for Science. Technology and Industry. *Broadband Infrastructure Deployment: The Role of Government Assistance*. Paris: Organization for Economic Co-operation and Development, May 22, 2002.

————. *The Development of Broadband Access in OECD Countries*. Paris: OECD, October 29, 2001.

United Nations. *Global E-Government Readiness Report 2004: Towards Access for Opportunity*. New York: United Nations, 2004.

————. *Report of the Meeting of a High Level Panel of Experts on Information and Communication Technology, New York, 17–20 April, 2000*. A/55/75. New York: United Nations, April 2000.

United Nations. Economic & Social Council. *Development and International Cooperation in the Twenty-first Century: The Role of Information Technology in the Context of a Knowledge-Based Global Economy. A Report of the Secretary General 16 May 2000*. ECOSOC 2000/52. New York: United Nations, 2000.

WEB RESOURCES

Australia

Australian Bureau of Statistics. *Household Use of Information Technology, Australia 2003*. ABS Catalog No. 8146.0. Canberra: Australian Bureau of Statistics, 2004. Available at http://www.abs.gov.au/ Ausstats/abs@.nsf/0/acc2d18cc958bc7bca2568a9001393ae?OpenDocument, accessed February 10, 2005.

Australian Capital Territory Electoral Commission. *The 2001 ACT General Assembly Election Electronic Voting and Counting System Review*. Canberra: Australian Capital Territory, 2002. Available at http://www.elections.act.gov.au/CompExecSumm.htm, accessed March 25, 2005.

Australian Government Information Management Office. *Access and Equity Issues for Websites. Better Practice Checklist 19*. Canberra: Australian Government Information Management Office, 2004. Available at http://www.agimo.gov.au/practice/delivery/checklists/web_access, accessed March 9, 2005.

————. *Annual Report 2003–2004*. Canberra: Australian Government Information Management Office, 2004. Available at http://www.agimo.gov.au/publications/2004/10/annrep03-04, accessed December 10, 2004.

————. *Online Policy Consultation: Better Practice Checklist 12*. Canberra: Australian Government Information Management Office, 2004. Available at http://www.agimo.gov.au/practice/delivery/ checklists/online_policy, accessed March 5, 2005.

Australian National Audit Office. *Internet Delivery Decisions: A Government Program Manager's Guide*. Canberra: Australian National Audit Office, 2001. Available at http://www.anao.gov .au/WebSite.nsf/Publications/4A256AE90015F69B4A256A3E0025D82A, accessed December 1, 2004.

————. *Quality Internet Services for Government Clients: Monitoring and Evaluation by Government Agencies*. Report No. 30. Canberra: Australian National Audit Office, 2004. Available at http://www .anao.gov.au/WebSite.nsf/Publications/2A51AE59FB11AA5ECA256E40000DCC32, accessed March 5, 2005.

Australian Portal. "Australia.gov.au: About This Site." Available at http://www.Australia.gov.au/ index.php?about, accessed May 19, 2005.

Australian Public Service Commission. *State of the Service Report, 2003–2004*. Canberra: Australian Public Service Commission, 2004. Available at http://www.apsc.gov.au/stateoftheservice/0304/ chaper4.pdf, accessed March 20, 2005.

Brumby, John. *Connecting Victoria*. Melbourne: Minister for State and Regional Development, 1999. Available at http://www.mmv.vic.gov.au/connectingvictoria, accessed January 20, 2005.

Burgess, Sue, and Jan Houghton. "Evaluation of Selected NSW Government Websites: A User Perspective." 23–46 in *Performance Audit Report: E-government: User-friendliness of Websites*. Sydney: Audit Office of New South Wales, 2002. Available at http://www.audit.nsw.gov.au/perfaud-rep/ Websites-June2002/Websites-Contents.html, accessed March 20, 2005.

Cooper, Mark. *Expanding the Digital Divide and Falling behind at Broadband*. New York: Consumer Federation of America and Consumers Union, October 2004. Available at http://www.consumers union.org/pub/ddnewbook.pdf, accessed May 2, 2004.

Croger Associates. *TIGERS Report: Program Summary*. Canberra: National Office of the Information Economy, 2003. Available at http://www.agimo.gov.au/publications/2003/09/tigers_report/ case_studies, accessed March 10, 2005.

Department of Communications, Information Technology and the Arts. *Australia's Strategic Framework for the Information Economy, 2004–2006*. Canberra: Department of Communications, Information Technology and the Arts, 2004. Available at http://www.dcita.gov.au/ie/framework, accessed March 10, 2005.

————. *Current State of Play 2004*. Canberra: Department of Communications, Information Technology and the Arts, 2004. Available at http://www.dcita.gov.au/ie, accessed March 10, 2005.

———. *Customer Focussed Portals Framework.* Canberra: Department of Communications, Information Technology and the Arts, 2000. Available at http://www.agimo.gov.au/services/portals, accessed February 1, 2005.

———. *Government Online: The Commonwealth Government's Strategy.* Canberra: Department of Communications, Information Technology and the Arts, 2000. Available at http://www.agimo.gov.au/publications/2000/04/govonline, accessed February 1, 2005.

———. *Information Economy Index.* Canberra: Department of Communications, Information Technology and the Arts, 2004. Available at http://www.dcita.gov.au/__data/assets/pdf_file/23454/IE_Index_2004.pdf, accessed March 10, 2005.

———. *Tel: Info: The Regional Landscape.* Canberra: Department of Communications, Information Technology and the Arts, 2004. Available at http://www.telinfo.gov.au/, accessed March 25, 2005.

Dugdale, Anni, Anne Daly, Franco Papandrea, and Maria Maley. "Connecting the Dots: Accessing E-government." 75–91 in *Future Challenges for E-government,* vol. 2. Canberra: Australian Government Information Management Office, 2004. Available at http://www.agimo.gov.au/publications/2004/05/egovt_challenges/, accessed April 15, 2005.

Howard, John. *Investing for Growth: The Howard Government's Plan for Industry.* Canberra: Department of the Prime Minister, 1997. Available at http://www1.industry.gov.au/archive/growth/html/statement.html, accessed March 19, 2005.

———. *Media Release: Fourth Howard Ministry.* Canberra: Office of the Prime Minister, 2004. Available at http://www.pm.gov.au/news/media_releases/media_Release1134.html, accessed March 1, 2005.

Lloyd, Rachel, and Anthea Bill. *Australia Online: How Australians Are Using Computers and the Internet 2001.* ABS Catalog No. 2056.0. Canberra: Australian Bureau of Statistics, Australian Census Analytic Program, 2004. Available at http://www.abs.gov.au, accessed February 10, 2005.

Management Advisory Committee. *Connecting Government: Whole of Government Responses to Australia's Priority Challenges.* Canberra: Management Advisory Committee 2004. Available at http://www.apsc.gov.au/mac/connectinggovernment.htm, accessed February 8, 2005.

National Archives of Australia. "AGLS [Australian Government Locator Service] Metadata Standard." Available at http://www.naa.gov.au/recordkeeping/gov_online/agls/summary.html, accessed June 13, 2005.

———. "Archives Advice 43: Archiving Web Resources: A National Archives Policy" (January 2001). Available at http://www.naa.gov.au/recordkeeping/rkpubs/advices/advice/advice43.html, accessed June 3, 2005.

———. "Archiving Web Resources: Guidelines." Canberra: National Archives of Australia, 2000. Available at http://www.naa.gov.au/recordkeeping/er/web_records/guide_intro.html, accessed June 3, 2005.

———. *Glossary of Record-keeping Terminology.* Canberra: National Archives Australia, 2004. Available at http://www.naa.gov.au/recordkeeping/rkpubs/recordkeeping_glossary.html#R, accessed June 16, 2005.

———. PowerPoint slides: Adrian Cunningham, Director of Recordkeeping Standards and Policy. Available at http://www.archives.govt.nz/continuum/previouspap.html#adri, accessed June 26, 2005.

National Office of the Information Economy. *Advancing Australia: The Information Economy Progress Report.* Canberra: National Office of the Information Economy, July 1999, May 2000, November 2002. Available at http://www.dcita.gov.au/ie/publications/2002/november/advancing_australia__the_information_economy_progress_report_2002, accessed March 15, 2005; http://www.dcita.gov.au/ie/publications/2000/may/strategic_framework_forethe_information_economy_second_progress_report, accessed March 10, 2005.

———. "Australian Taxation Office." 8–13 in *E-government Benefits: Agency Case Studies.* Canberra: National Office of the Information Economy 2003. Available at http://www.agimo.gov.au/publications/2003/05/e-govt_case_studies/ato, accessed March 15, 2005.

———. *Better Services, Better Government.* Canberra: National Office of the Information Economy, 2002. Available at http://www.agimo.gov.au/__data/assets/pdf_file/35503/Better_Services-Bet ter_Gov.pdf, accessed January 30, 2005.

———. *Interoperability Technical Framework for the Australian Government.* Canberra: National Office of the Information Economy, 2003. Available at http://www.agimo.gov.au/publications/2003/08/ framework, accessed February 10, 2005.

New South Wales Office of Information and Communications Technology. *Information Management and Technology Blueprint.* Sydney: Office of Information and Communications Technology, 1997. Available at http://www.gcio.nsw.gov.au/content/1.2.4.content.asp, accessed January 5, 2005.

Queensland Government. "Get Involved" Web site. Brisbane: Department of Communities, Community Engagement & Development Policy Unit. Available at http://www.getinvolved.qld.gov.au, accessed March 10, 2005.

State Records Authority of New South Wales. *Standard on Recordkeeping in the Electronic Business Environment.* New South Wales: State Records Authority of New South Wales, 2004. Available at http://www.records.nsw.gov.au/publicsector/erk/electronic.htm, accessed June 24, 2005.

Trinitas Proprietary Limited. *Inquiry into Electronic Democracy: Scrutiny of Acts and Regulations Committee: Discussion Paper.* Melbourne: Parliament of Victoria, 2002. Available at http://www.parliament.vic .gov.au/sarc/E-Democracy/Discussion%20Paper.htm, accessed March 1, 2005.

Austria

Vienna. Elektronische Abwicklung von Gewerbeangelegenheiten. Available at http://www.wien .gv.at/wgrweb, accessed February 10, 2005.

Canada

Auditor General. *E Commerce: Conducting Government Business via the Internet.* Ottawa: Auditor General, 1998. Available at http://www.oag-bvg.gc.ca/domino/reports.nsf/html/9819ce.html, accessed May 7, 2005.

———. *Information Technology: Government On-Line,* Report of the Auditor General. Ottawa: Auditor General, 2003. Available at http://www.oag-bvg.gc.ca/domino/reports.nsf/html/20031101ce .html, accessed May 1, 2005.

———. *Information Technology Security.* Chap. 1 of 2005 Status Report. Ottawa: Auditor General, February 2005. Available at http://www.oag-bvg.gc.ca/domino/reports.nsf/html/05menu_e.html, accessed May 1, 2005.

———. Web site. Available at http://www.oag-bvg.gc.ca/domino/oag-bvg.nsf/html/menue.html, accessed May 9, 2005.

Canada Site [portal]. Available at http://www.canada.gc.ca, accessed May 7, 2005.

Department of Finance. *Budget 2003—Budget Plan.* Chap. 5, "Investing in a More Productive, Sustainable Economy." Ottawa: Department of Finance, February 2003. Available at http://www.fin .gc.ca/budget03/bp/bpc5e.htm, accessed May 7, 2005.

———. *Expenditure Review for Sound Financial Management.* Ottawa: Department of Finance, February 23, 2005. Available at http://www.fin.gc.ca/budget05/booklets/bkexpe.htm, accessed May 6, 2005.

Government of Canada. "Core Subject Thesaurus." Ottawa: Depository Services Program, 2004. Available at http://en.thesaurus.gc.ca/new_e.html, accessed June 13, 2005.

Government On-Line: Serving Canadians Better [Web site]. Ottawa, 2004. Available at http://www .gol-ged.gc.ca/index_e.asp, accessed April 10, 2005.

Government On-Line and Canadians (1st annual report). Ottawa, March 2002. Available at http://www.gol-ged.gc.ca/rpt/2002rpt_e.asp, accessed April 30, 2005.

Government On-Line 2003 (2nd annual report). Ottawa, March 2003. Available at http://www
.gol-ged.gc.ca/rpt2003/rpt03_e.asp, accessed April 30, 2005.

Government On-Line 2004: "This Report: What's Next" (3rd annual report). Ottawa, March 2004.
Available at http://www.gol-ged.gc.ca/rpt2004/rpttb_e.asp, accessed April 30, 2005.

Government On-Line 2005: From Vision to Reality and Beyond (4th annual report). Ottawa, March 2005.
Available at http://www.gol-ged.gc.ca/rpt2005/rpttb_e.asp, accessed April 30, 2005.

Government On-Line Advisory Panel. *Connecting with Canadians: Pursuing Service Transformation.* Final
Report to the President of the Treasury Board of Canada. Ottawa: Treasury Board, December
2003. Available at http://www.gol-ged.gc.ca/pnl-grp/reports/final/final00_e.asp, accessed May 4,
2005.

———. *Transforming Government to Serve Canadians Better.* Report to the President of the Treasury
Board of Canada. Ottawa: Treasury Board, December 2002. Available at http://www.gol-ged.gc
.ca/pnl-grp/reports/second/transform/transform00_e.asp, accessed May 4, 2005.

Industry Canada. *Evaluation Study of the Community Access Program.* Ottawa: Industry Canada, January
16, 2004. Available at http://www.ic.gc.ca/cmb/welcomeic.nsf/0/ffd2e3755d7f251585256e
9800510b66?OpenDocument, accessed May 7, 2005.

———. *Industry Canada: Making a Difference.* Ottawa: Industry Canada, October 2003. Available at
http://www.ic.gc.ca/cmb/welcomeic.nsf/532340a8523f33718525649d006b119d/012bffa29fcb
623885256dc200424073!OpenDocument, accessed May 7, 2005.

———. "Minister Emerson Appoints Members of Telecommunications Policy Review Panel," Backgrounder. News Release. Ottawa: Industry Canada, April 11, 2005. Available at http://www.ic.gc
.ca/cmb/welcomeic.nsf/0/85256a5d006b972085256fe0005b8149?OpenDocument, accessed April
11, 2005.

———. Community Access Program. Available at: http://cap.ic.gc.ca, accessed April 15, 2005.

Industry Canada. Electronic Commerce Branch. *The Digital Economy in Canada.* Ottawa: Industry
Canada, 2005. Available at http://e-com.ic.gc.ca/epic/internet/inecicceac.nsf/en/home, accessed
May 4, 2005.

Industry Canada. Electronic Commerce Task Force. *Canadian Electronic Commerce Strategy.* Ottawa:
Industry Canada, 1998. Available at http://strategis.ic.gc.ca/epic/internet/inecic-ceac.nsf/vwapj/
ecom_eng.pdf/$file/ecom_eng.pdf, accessed May 7, 2005.

Information Highway Advisory Council. *Building the Information Society: Moving Canada into the 21st
Century.* Ottawa: Supply and Services, 1996. Available at http://www.ifla.org/documents/info
pol/canada/ihac9601.pdf, accessed May 9, 2005.

———. *Connection, Community, Content: The Challenge of the Information Highway,* Final Report (Phase
1). Ottawa: Industry Canada, 1995. Available at http://www.hc-sc.gc.ca/ohih-bsi/pubs/
1995_connect/rpt_e.html, accessed May 7, 2005.

———. *Preparing Canada for a Digital World,* Final Report (Phase 2). Ottawa: Industry Canada, 1997.
Available at http://www.iigr.ca/pdf/documents/768_Preparing_Canada_for_a_D.pdf, accessed
May 7, 2005.

National Broadband Task Force. *The New National Dream: Networking the Nation for Broadband Access.*
Ottawa: Industry Canada, 2001. Available at http://broadband.gc.ca/pub/program/NBTF/broad
band.pdf, accessed May 7, 2005.

Parliament. Speech from the Throne to Open the First Session of the Thirty-seventh Parliament of
Canada. Ottawa: Parliament, January 30, 2001. Available at http://www.parl.gc.ca/information
/about/process/info/throne/index.asp?lang = E&parl = 37&sess = 1, accessed May 7, 2005.

———. Speech from the Throne to Open the First Session of the Thirty-sixth Parliament of Canada.
Ottawa: Parliament, September 23, 1997. Available at http://www.parl.gc.ca/information/about/
process/info/throne/index.asp?lang = E&parl = 36&sess = 1, accessed May 7, 2005.

———. Speech from the Throne to Open the Second Session of the Thirty-sixth Parliament of Canada. Ottawa: Parliament, October 12, 1999. Available at http://www.parl.gc.ca/information
/about/process/info/throne/index.asp?lang = E&parl = 36&sess = 2, accessed May 7, 2005.

Privy Council. *Getting Government Right: A Progress Report.* Ottawa: Privy Council Office, 1996. Available at http://www.tbs-sct.gc.ca/est-pre/19961997/gettinge.pdf, accessed May 7, 2005.

———. *Seventh Annual Report to the Prime Minister on the Public Service of Canada,* by Mel Cappe, Clerk of the Privy Council and Secretary to the Cabinet. Ottawa: Privy Council Office, March 31 2000. Available at http://www.pco-bcp.gc.ca/default.asp?Page = Publications&Language = E&doc = 7r ept2000/7rept2000cover_e.htm, accessed April 11, 2005.

———. *Twelfth Annual Report to the Prime Minister on the Public Service of Canada,* by Alex Himmelfarb, Clerk of the Privy Council and Secretary to the Cabinet. Ottawa: Privy Council Office, March 31, 2005. Available at http://www.pco-bcp.gc.ca/docs/Report/12_report-rapport_e.pdf, accessed May 17, 2005.

Public Works and Government Services Canada. Government On-Line [Web site], *Priorities.* Ottawa: Public Works and Government Services Canada, 2004. Available at http://www.communication. gc.ca/gol_ged/gol_overview.html, accessed May 7, 2005.

———. *Report on Plans and Priorities: 2005–2006 Estimates,* "Information Technology: Government On-Line." Ottawa: Public Works and Government Services Canada, March 2005. Available at http://www.pwgsc.gc.ca/reports/text/rpp_2005-2006_complete-e.html, accessed May 6, 2005.

———. *Report on Plans and Priorities: 2005–2006 Estimates.* Sec. III, Supplementary Information, Horizontal Initiative C. "Government On-Line." Ottawa: Public Works and Government Services Canada, 2005. Available at http://www.pwgsc.gc.ca/reports/text/rpp_2005-2006_sct3_tbl20_c-e .html, accessed May 6, 2005.

———. "What Is Government On-Line?" (and its Fact Sheet, "Secure Channel"). Ottawa: Public Works and Government Services Canada, 2004, 2005. Available at http://www.pwgsc.gc.ca/text/ factsheets/secure_channel-e.html, accessed April 17, 2005; http://www.pwgsc.gc.ca/text/facts heets/what_is_gov-e.html, accessed May 1, 2005.

Treasury Board. "Crossing Boundaries Conference: When E-government Becomes Simply Government: Making the Case for Radical Incrementalism in Public Service Governance." Speech by Lucienne Robillard, President of the Treasury Board. Ottawa: Treasury Board, May 8, 2003. Available at http://www.tbs-sct.gc.ca/media/ps-dp/2003/0508_e.asp, accessed May 16, 2005.

———. Serving Canadians Better: Moving Forward with Service Transformation at the Enterprise Level [Web site]: "Canada's Strategic Approach to e-Government." Ottawa: Treasury Board, 2004. Available at http://www.cio-dpi.gc.ca/cio-dpi/2004/canada/canadatb_e.asp, accessed May 16, 2005.

———. Speaking Notes for The Honourable Lucienne Robillard, President of the Treasury Board, to the International Council for Information Technology in Government Administration. Ottawa: Treasury Board, September 18, 2000. Available at http://www.tbs-sct.gc.ca/media/ps-dp/2000/ 0918_e.asp, accessed May 16, 2005.

Treasury Board Secretariat. *Blueprint for Renewing Government Services Using Information Technology.* Ottawa: Treasury Board, 2004. Available at http://www.tbs-sct.gc.ca/pubs_pol/ciopubs/tb_ oimp/uit-ati/uit-ati_e.asp, accessed May 7, 2005.

———. *Government of Canada Internet Guide.* Ottawa: Treasury Board, March 2004. Available at http://www.cio-dpi.gc.ca/ig-gi/index_e.asp, accessed April 8, 2005.

———. *Government On-Line: Serving Canadians in a Digital World.* Ottawa: Treasury Board, February 2004. Available at http://www.gol-ged.gc.ca/pub/serv-can/serv-can00_e.asp, accessed May 7, 2005.

———. *Strategic Directions for Information Management and Information Technology: Enabling 21st Century Service to Canadians.* Ottawa: Treasury Board, 1999. Available at http://www.tbs-sct.gc.ca/pubs_ pol/ciopubs/TB_OIMP/sdimit_e.asp, accessed May 7, 2005.

Treasury Board Secretariat. Chief Information Officer Branch. Common Look and Feel for the Internet [Web site]. Ottawa: Treasury Board, 2004. Available at http://www.cio-dpi.gc.ca/clf-nsi/ index_e.asp, accessed May 7, 2005.

———. "Our Responsibilities Have Changed!" Ottawa: Treasury Board, March 29, 2004. Available at http://www.cio-dpi.gc.ca/cio-dpi/resp_e.asp, accessed April 12, 2005.

———. *Performance Measurement for the Government On-Line Initiative: Performance Measurement Methodology: Expected Outcomes.* Ottawa: Treasury Board, October 2004. Available at http://www.cio-dpi.gc.ca/si-as/performance/performance00_e.asp, accessed April 12, 2005.

Chile

Chile. E-government: Government Procurement E-system. Available at http://www1.worldbank.org/publicsector/egov/eprocurement_chile.htm, accessed January 28, 2005.

New Zealand

All of Government Project—the Big Ask Project. Wellington: Local Government New Zealand. Available at http://www.lgnz.co.nz/projects/big-ask/index.html, accessed April 10, 2005.

Archives New Zealand. *Continuum Products.* Wellington: Archives New Zealand, n.d. Available at http://www.archives.govt.nz/continuum/index.html, accessed June 1, 2005.

———. *G6 A Standard for Developing a Recordkeeping Policy.* Wellington: Archives New Zealand, 2003. Available at http://www.archives.govt.nz/continuum/rkpublications.html, accessed June 16, 2005.

———. *G20 Guide to Developing Recordkeeping Strategies for Websites.* Wellington: Archives New Zealand, June 2004. Available at http://www.archives.govt.nz/continuum/rkpublications.html, accessed June 3, 2005.

Chief Executives' Group on Information Management and Technology. *Electronic Government: Briefing to Minister of State Services and Minister of Information Technology, December 1999.* Wellington: Chief Executives' Group on Information Management and Technology, 1999. Available at http://www.e-government.govt.nz/docs/info-tech-briefing, accessed April 11, 2005.

Cullen, Rowena, and Peter Hernon. *Wired for Well-Being: Citizens' Response to E-government.* Wellington: State Services Commission, E-government Unit, June 2004. Available at http://www.e-government.govt.nz/docs/vuw-report-200406, accessed April 12, 2005.

Curtis, Cate, Jack Vowles, and Bruce Curtis. *Channel-Surfing: How New Zealanders Access Government.* Wellington: State Services Commission, 2004. Available at http://www.e-government.govt.nz/docs/channel-surfing-200409/index.html, accessed April 10, 2005.

District Health Boards New Zealand. Available at http://www.dhbnz.org.nz, accessed April 27, 2005.

GOVIS Web site. Wellington: GOVIS. Available at http://www.govis.org.nz, accessed April 16, 2005.

Ministry for Economic Development. *The Digital Strategy: Creating Our Digital Future.* Wellington: Ministry for Economic Development, 2005. Available at http://www.digitalstrategy.govt.nz/, accessed May 16, 2005.

———. *Digital Strategy: A Draft New Zealand Digital Strategy for Consultation.* Wellington: Ministry for Economic Development, June 2004. Available at http://www.med.govt.nz/pbt/infotech/digital-strategy/index.html, accessed April 15, 2005.

Ministry of Education. Project Probe. Available at http://www.probe.govt.nz, accessed April 15, 2005.

Ministry of Health. Health Information Standards Organization. Wellington: Ministry of Health. Available at http://www.moh.govt.nz/hiso, accessed April 11, 2005.

Ministry of Housing. Tenancy Services. Wellington: Ministry of Housing. Available at http://www.tenancy.govt.nz.

Ministry of Social Development. Office for Disability Issues. Wellington: Office for Disability Issues. Available at http://www.odi.govt.nz, accessed April 21, 2005.

Sofres, Taylor Nelson. *GO2003 9.* Wellington: State Services Commission, December 2003. Available at www.e-government.govt.nz/docs/go-survey-2003, accessed April 15, 2005.

State Services Commission. "Development Goals for the State Services." Wellington: State Services Commission, 2005. Available at http://www.ssc.govt.nz/display/document.asp?navid = 242, accessed April 28, 2005.

———. "NZGLS Metadata Standard." Wellington: State Services Commission, n.d. Available at http://www.e-government.govt.nz/nzgls/standard/index.asp, accessed April 6, 2005.

———. "NZGLS Thesaurus (FONZ and SONZ)." Wellington: State Services Commission, n.d. Available at http://www.e-government.govt.nz/nzgls/thesauri/index.asp, accessed April 6, 2005.

———. *Policy Framework for Government-Held Information.* Wellington: State Services Commission, 1997. Available at http://www.ssc.govt.nz/display/document.asp?NavID = 222, accessed April 18, 2005.

State Services Commission. E-government Unit. *Achieving E-government 2004: A Report on Progress towards the New Zealand E-government Strategy.* Wellington: State Services Commission, 2004. Available at http://www.e-government.govt.nz/docs/ready-access-2004/index.html, accessed April 20, 2005.

———. *@your.service: Updated E-government Strategy Incorporates Service Delivery Architecture.* Wellington: State Services Commission, n.d. Available at http://www.e-government.govt.news/200309 1902, accessed April 12, 2005.

———. Authentication Fact Sheet. Wellington: State Services Commission, April 2005. Available (as a pdf file) at http://www.e-government.govt.nz/authentication/index.asp, accessed April 12, 2005.

———. *Channel Strategy: Scoping Study.* Wellington: State Services Commission, June 2004. Available at http://www.e-government.govt.nz/docs/cs-scoping-0104/index.html, accessed April 10, 2005.

———. *e-Government in New Zealand.* Wellington: e-Government Unit, n.d. Available at http://www.e-government.govt.nz.

———. "E-government Vision, Mission, Goals and Outcome." Wellington: State Services Commission, 2003. Available at http://www.e-government.govt.nz/docs/e-gov-strategyjune-2003, accessed April 10, 2005.

———. *E-services: Electronic Service Delivery.* Wellington: State Services Commission, n.d. Available at http://www.e-government.govt.nz/e-services/index.asp, accessed April 10, 2005.

———. FAQs. Wellington: State Services Commission, n.d. Available at http://www.e-government.govt.nz/programme/faqs.asp, accessed September 30, 2004.

———. *Government@your.service: E-government Strategy.* Wellington: State Services Commission, April 2001. Available at http://www.e-government.govt.nz/docs/e-gov-strategy-apr-01/index.html, accessed April 8, 2005.

———. *The New Zealand Government Locator Service (NZGLS) Metadata Standard and Reference Manual.* Wellington: State Services Commission, 2001. Available at http://www.egovernment.govt.nz /docs/nzglsv2/index.html, accessed May 28, 2005.

———. *New Zealand Government Portal Strategy for a Customer-Centric Portal:* Part B, High-Level Implementation Plan, 2001–2004. Wellington: State Services Commission, 2000. Available at http://www.e-government.govt.nz/docs/nz-gov-portal-strategy-b/index.html, accessed October 18, 2004; April 6, 2005.

———. *Overview.* Wellington: State Services Commission, 2000. Available at http://www.e-govern ment.govt.nz/programme/index.asp, accessed April 9, 2005.

———. *Participation through E-government: The Context.* Wellington: State Services Commission, 2004. Available at http://www.e.govt.nz/docs/participation-0305/index.html, accessed April 20, 2005.

———. "A Summary of the E-Government Strategy." Wellington: E-Government Unit, 2003. Available at http://www.e-government.govt.nz/docs/e-gov-strategy-june-2003/, accessed August 6, 2004.

———. *Trust and Security of the Internet: Keeping the Internet Safe for E-government in New Zealand.* Wellington: State Services Commission, E-government Unit, November 24, 2004. Available at http://www.e-government.govt.nz/docs/trust-security-2004/index.html, accessed April 15, 2005.

Statistics New Zealand. Home page. Wellington: Statistics New Zealand. Available at http://www
.stats.govt.nz.

Strategic Plan for E-Local Government. Wellington: Local Government New Zealand, 2003. Available
(as a pdf file) at http://www.lgnz.co.nz/news/pr1080274637.html, accessed April 11, 2005.

WAVE Advisory Board to Director-General of Health. *From Strategy to Reality: The WAVE Project. Kia
Hopu te Ngaru.* Wellington: Ministry of Health, 2001. Available at: http://www.moh.govt.nz/
publications, accessed April 12, 2005.

Williamson, Maurice. *Vision Statement: Electronic Government for New Zealand.* Wellington: Parliament,
1999. Available at http://www.executive.govt.nz/96-99/minister/williamson/egovernment/vis
ion.html, accessed April 10, 2005.

Republic of Korea

E-government home page. Available at http://www.egov.go.kr.

Singapore

Ministry of Finance. E-Citizen: Your Gateway to All Government Services. Available at http://www
.ecitizen.gov.sg/index.htm, accessed February 10, 2005.

My e.Citizen (personalized services). Available at http://my.ecitizen.gov.sg/portal/dt, accessed June
1, 2005.

United Kingdom

Cabinet Office. *eGU's Mission.* London: Cabinet Office, n.d. Available at http://www.cabinet
office.gov.uk/e-government, accessed June 20, 2005.

———. *In the Search of Democracy.* London: Cabinet Office, 2004. Available at http://www.democ
racy.gov.uk, accessed July 10, 2004.

———. *Measurement Framework for the e-Economy.* London: Cabinet Office, 2004. Available at
http://e-government.cabinetoffice.gov.uk/Resources/EStatmap/fs/en, accessed July 9, 2004.

———. *Web Handbook Checklist.* London: Cabinet Office, n.d. Available at http://e-gov
ernment.cabinetoffice.gov.uk/Resources/WebHandbookIndex1Article/fs/en?. . . . , accessed July
12, 2004.

Cabinet Office. e-Government Unit. Directgov. London: e-Government Unit. Available at http://
www.direct.gov.uk, accessed July 12, 2004.

———. *The Government Gateway.* London: Cabinet Office, 2004. Available at http://www
.iagchampions.gov/uk/Briefings/BriefingsArticle/fs/en?CONTENT_ID = 40000 . . . , accessed
July 12, 2004.

———. *Illustrated Handbook for Web Management Teams.* London: Cabinet Office, 2004. Available at
http://e-government.cabinetoffice.gov.uk?resources/WebGuidelinesArticle/fs/en? CONTE . . . .
Accessed July 12, 2004.

———. *Index of Web Guidelines Related Publications.* London: Cabinet Office, n.d. Available at
http://e-government.cabinetoffice.gov.ukl/Resources/WebGuidelines/fs/en, accessed July 9,
2004.

———. "Information Age Government." In *Modernising Government White Paper.* London: Cabinet
Office, e-Government Unit, 1999. Available at http://www.archive.official-documents.co.uk/
document/cm43/4310/4310-05.htm, accessed July 9, 2004.

———. "Our Responsibilities." London: e-Government Unit, n.d. Available at http://e-govern
ment.cabinetoffice.gov.ul/Home/Homepage/fs/en, accessed July 8, 2004.

———. "Responsibilities." London: Cabinet Office, 2005. Available at http://www.cabinetoffice
.gov.uk/e-government/responsibilities/, accessed June 11, 2005.

————. *Strategic Framework for Public Services*. London: Cabinet Office, 2004. Available at http://e-government.cabinetoffice.gov.uk/Estrategy/StrategicFrameworkArticle/fs/en?CO . . . , accessed July 12, 2004.

Cabinet Office. Office of the e-Envoy. *UK Online: Annual Report* 2003. London: Office of the e-Envoy, 2003. Available at http://www.e-envoy.gov.uk, accessed July 8, 2004.

Freedom of Information Page. London: Department for Constitutional Affairs. Available at http://www.foi.gov.uk.

Government Gateway. London. Available at http://www.gateway.gov.uk/.

GovTalk. London: Cabinet Office. Available at http://www.govtalk.gov.talk.

National Audit Office. *Cultural Barriers to E-government,* by Helen Margetts and Patrick Dunleavy. London: National Audit Office, 2002. Available at http://www.nao.org.uk/, accessed September 30, 2004.

————. Home page. Available at http://www.nao.org.uk/.

Office of Government Commerce. Home page. London: Office of Government Commerce. Available at http://www.ogc.gov.uk.

————. "What Is eProcurement?" London: Office of Government Commerce, 2004. Available at http://www.ogc.gov.uk/index.asp?id = 2363, accessed July 12, 2004.

Office of the Deputy Prime Minister. Home page. London: Office of the Deputy Prime Minister. Available at http://www.localgov.gov.uk/page.cfm?pageID = 74&Language = eng.

————. News Release. London: Office of the Deputy Prime Minister, April 2004. Available at http://www.odm.gov.uk/pns/DisplayPN.cgi?pn_id = 2004_0112, accessed July 12, 2004.

"Prime Minister's Keynote Speech to e-Summit." London: Prime Minister's Office, 2004. Available at http://www.number10.gov.ukl/output/Page1734.asp, accessed July 8, 2004.

UKGovTalk. *e-Services Documents: e-Government Schema Guidelines for XML*. London: Cabinet Office, 2004. Available at http://www.govtalk.gov.uk/schemasstandards/eservices_document2.asp?doc num = 859, accessed July 9, 2004.

————. "Metadata." London: Cabinet Office, n.d. Available at http://www.govtalk.gov.uk /schemasstandards/metadata.asp, accessed May 30, 2005.

United States

Access Board. *Access Board Issues New Guidelines for Accessible Design*. Washington, DC: Access Board, 2004. Available at http://www.access-board.gov/ada-aba.htm, accessed August 27, 2004.

Administrator, FAA v. Robertson, 422 U.S. 255 (1972).

Department of Agriculture. "Government Information Locator Service@USDA." Washington, DC: Department of Agriculture. Available at http://www.usda.gov/gils/usdagils.htm, accessed May 24, 2005.

Department of Commerce. *A Nation Online: How Americans Are Expanding Their Use of the Internet*. Washington, DC: Department of Commerce, February 2002. Available at http://www.ntia.doc .gov/ntiahome/dn/index.html, accessed September 9, 2004.

Department of Commerce. National Telecommunications and Information Administration. Address by Nancy Victory, NTIA Administrator, before the Alliance for Public Technology Broadband Symposium, February 8, 2002. Washington, DC: National Telecommunications and Information Administration, 2002. Available at http://www.ntia.doc.gov/ntiahome/speeches/2002/apt_020 802.htm, accessed September 9, 2004.

————. *Advanced Telecommunications in Rural America: The Challenge of Bringing Broadband Service to All Americans*. Washington, DC: Department of Commerce and Department of Agriculture, April 2000. Available at http://www.ntia.doc.gov/reports/ruralbb42600.pdf, accessed September 9, 2004.

————. Speech by Nancy Victory, Assistant Secretary for Communications and Information, before the National Summit on Broadband Deployment, October 25, 2001. Washington, DC: National

Telecommunications and Information Administration, 2002. Available at http://www.ntia.doc
.gov/ntiahome/speeches/2001/broadband_102501.htm, accessed September 9, 2004.

Department of Commerce. Technology Administration. *Understanding Broadband Demand.* Washington, DC: Technology Administration, 2002. Available at http://www.ta.doc.gov/reports/TechPol
icy/Broadband_020921.pdf, accessed September 9, 2004.

Department of Energy. Roadmap. Washington, DC: Department of Energy, n.d. Available at
http://www.eh.doe.gov/ohre/roadmap/whitehouse/part1.html, accessed October 17, 2004.

———. Human Radiation Experiment. Home page. Washington, DC: Department of Energy. Available at http://hrex.dis.anl.gov/, accessed October 17, 2004

Department of Transportation. Federal Transit Administration. "President's Management Agenda
(PMA) and E-Grants, Number C-14-03, 08-04-03." Washington, DC: Federal Transit Administration, 2004. Available at http://www.fta.dot.gov/legal/guidance/dear_colleague/2003/
178_12145_ENG_HTML.htm, accessed September 19, 2004.

E-authentication Web site. Available at http://www.cio.gov/eauthentication.

Federal Communications Commission. "FCC Improves Data Collection to Monitor Nationwide
Broadband Rollout." Washington, DC: Federal Communications Commission, November 9,
2004. Available at http://hraunfoss.fcc.gov/edocs_public/attachment/DOC-254115A1.pdf,
accessed May 2, 2005.

———. *Fourth Report to Congress: Availability of Advanced Telecommunications Capacity in the United
States.* GN Docket No. 04-54, FCC 04-208. Washington, DC: Federal Communications Commission, 2004. Available at http://hraunfoss.fcc.gov/edocs_public/attachment/FCC-04-208A1.pdf,
accessed September 14, 2004.

———. *High-Speed Services for Internet Access: Status as of June 30, 2003.* Washington, DC: Federal
Communications Commission, December 22, 2003. Available at http://www.fcc.gov/Bureaus/
Common_Carrier/Reports/FCC-State_Link/IAD/hspd1 203.pdf, accessed September 9, 2004.

———. *Third Report: Inquiry Concerning the Deployment of Advanced Telecommunications Capability to All
Americans in a Reasonable and Timely Fashion, and Possible Steps to Accelerate Such Deployment Pursuant
to Section 706 of the Telecommunications Act of 1996.* CC Docket 98-146, February 6, 2002. Available
at http://www.fcc.gov/broadband/706.html, accessed September 9, 2004.

Federal Election Commission. Home page. Washington, DC: Federal Election Commission. Available
at http://www.fec.gov, accessed August 7, 2004.

FirstGov. Home page. Available at http://www.firstgov.gov.

———. "About FirstGov." Available at http://www.firstgov.gov/About.shtml, accessed July 1, 2005.

Forman, Mark A. "Achieving the Vision of E-government." Washington, DC: Office of Management and Budget, October 1, 2001. Available at http://www.hpcc.gov/pitac/pitac-25sep01lfor
mat.pdf, accessed November 14, 2003.

Geospatial One-Stop Web Site. Available at http://www.geo-one-stop.gov/.

Gilroy, Angele A., and Lennard G. Kruger. *Broadband Internet Access: Background and Issues.* CRS Issue
Brief. Washington, DC: Library of Congress, Congressional Research Service, 2004. Available at
www.ipmall.info/hosted_resources/crs/IB10045_040622.pdf, accessed April 15, 2005.

GovBenefits. Home page. Available at http://govbenefits.gov/govbenefits/index.jhtml, accessed September 19, 2004.

Government Accountability Office. *Financial Management: Challenges in Meeting Requirements of the
Improper Payments Information Act,* GAO-05-417. Washington, DC: Government Accountability
Office, March 2005. Available at http://www.gao.gov/new.items/d05417.pdf, accessed July 1,
2005.

GPO Access. "Budget of the United States Government: Main Page: Fiscal Year 2006 Budget
(FY06)." Washington, DC: GPO, 2005. Available at http://www.gpoaccess.gov/usbudget/fy06/
pdf/ap_cd_rom/9_3.pdf, accessed July 1, 2005.

Healthfinder. Washington, DC: Department of Health and Human Services. Available at http://
www.healthfinder.gov, accessed August 7, 2004.

Levi, Michael D., and Frederick G. Conrad. *Usability Testing of World Wide Web Sites.* Washington, DC: Department of Labor, Bureau of Labor Statistics, 2002. Available at http://stats.bls.gov/ore/htm_papers/st960150.htm, accessed October 18, 2004.

National Archives and Records Administration. *Guidance on Managing Web Records January 2005.* Washington, DC: National Archives and Records Administration, 2005. Available at http://www.archives.gov/records_management/policy_and_guidance/managing_web_records_index.html, accessed June 24, 2005.

Office of Management and Budget. *Budget of the United States Government, Fiscal Year 2006: Analytical Perspectives.* Washington, DC: Office of Management and Budget, 2005. Available at http://www.whitehouse.gov/omb/budget/fy2004/sheets/itspending.xls, http://www.whitehouse.gov/omb/budget/fy2006/spec.html, and http://www.whitehouse.gov/omb/budget/fy2006/, accessed July 1, 2005.

———. "E-GOV: About E-GOV." Washington, DC: Office of Management and Budget, n.d. Available at http://www.whitehouse.gov/omb/egov/c-presidential.html, accessed July 1, 2005.

———. "E-GOV: Business Reference Model." Washington, DC: Office of Management and Budget, n.d. Available at http://www.whitehouse.gov/omb/egov/a-3-brm.html, accessed July 1, 2005.

———. "E-GOV: Case Management." Washington, DC: Office of Management and Budget, n.d. Available at http://www.whitehouse.gov/omb/egov/c-6-1-case.html, accessed July 1, 2005.

———. "E-GOV: Data Reference Model." Washington, DC: Office of Management and Budget, n.d. Available at http://www.whitehouse.gov/omb/egov/a-5-drm.html, accessed July 1, 2005.

———. "E-GOV: Federal Health Architecture." Washington, DC: Office of Management and Budget, n.d. Available at http://www.whitehouse.gov/omb/egov/c-6-5-federal.html, accessed July 1, 2005.

———. "E-GOV: Financial Management." Washington, DC: Office of Management and Budget, n.d. Available at http://www.whitehouse.gov/omb/egov/c-6-2-financial.html, accessed July 1, 2005.

———. "E-GOV: Grants Management." Washington, DC: Office of Management and Budget, n.d. Available at http://www.whitehouse.gov/omb/egov/c-6-3-grants.html, accessed July 1, 2005.

———. "E-GOV: Human Resources Management." Washington, DC: Office of Management and Budget, n.d. Available at http://www.whitehouse.gov/omb/egov/c-6-4-human.html, accessed July 1, 2005.

———. "E-GOV: Performance Reference Model." Washington, DC: Office of Management and Budget, n.d. Available at http://www.whitehouse.gov/omb/egov/a-2-prm.html, accessed July 1, 2005.

———. "E-GOV: Service Components Reference Model." Washington, DC: Office of Management and Budget, n.d. Available at http://www.whitehouse.gov/omb/egov/a-4-srm.html, accessed July 1, 2005.

———. "E-GOV: Technical Reference Model." Washington, DC: Office of Management and Budget, n.d. Available at http://www.whitehouse.gov/omb/egov/a-6-trm.html, accessed July 1, 2005.

———. *E-government Strategy.* Washington, DC: Office of Management and Budget, 2002. Available at http://www.whitehouse.gov/omb/inforeg/infopoltech.html, accessed September 30, 2004.

———. "Expanding Electronic Government Initiative." Washington, DC: White House. Available at http://www.whitehouse.gov/omb/egov/, accessed June 22, 2005.

———. *The Federal Government Is Results-Oriented: A Report to Federal Employees.* Washington, DC: Office of Management and Budget, August 2004. Available at http://www.whitehouse.gov/omb/pma/2004_pma_report.pdf, accessed July 1, 2005.

———. *Implementing the President's Management Agenda for E-Government, E-Government Strategy, Simplified Delivery of Services to Citizens.* Washington, DC: Office of Management and Budget, February 2002. Available at http://www.whitehouse.gov/omb/inforeg/egovstrategy.pdf, accessed July 1, 2005.

———. *Implementing the President's Management Agenda for E-Government, E-Government Strategy, Sim-*

plified Delivery of Services to Citizens. Washington, DC: Office of Management and Budget, April 2003. Available at http://www.whitehouse.gov/omb/egov/2003egov_strat.pdf, accessed July 1, 2005.

————. *Information Policy, IT & E-Gov.* Washington, DC: Office of Management and Budget, n.d. Available at http://www.whitehouse.gov/omb/inforeg/infopoltech.html, accessed August 7, 2004.

————. Memorandum 00-13: "Privacy Policies and Data Collection on Federal Web Sites." Washington, DC: Office of Management and Budget, 2000.

————. Presidential Memo: The Importance of E-Government. Egov: The Official Web Site of the President's E-Government. Available at http://www.whitehouse.gov/omb/egov/pres_memo.htm, accessed May 29, 2003.

White House. *A New Generation of American Innovation.* Washington, DC: White House, April 2004. Available at http://www.whitehouse.gov/infocus/technology/economic_policy200404/innovation .pdf, accessed September 9, 2004.

————. *The President's Management Agenda: Expanded Electronic Government: E-Gov Challenges and Solutions.* Washington, DC: White House, 2004. Available at http://www.results.gov/agenda/ fiveinitiatives10.html, accessed September 19, 2004.

Willemssen, Joel C. "Electronic Government: Success of the Office of Management and Budget's 25 Initiatives Depends on Effective Management and Oversight." Testimony before the Subcommittee on Technology, Information Policy, Intergovernmental Relations and the Census, House Committee on Government Reform, GAO-03-495T. Washington, DC: General Accounting Office, 2003.

International Organizations

Dasgupta, Susmita, Somik Lall, and David Wheeler. *Policy Reform, Economic Growth, and the Digital Divide: An Econometric Analysis.* Washington, DC: World Bank, Development Research Group, 2004. Available at http://www.econ.worldbank.org/files/1615_wps2567.pdf, accessed March 31, 2005.

International Telecommunications Union. *Birth of Broadband.* Executive summary. Geneva, Switzerland: International Telecommunications Union, September 2003. http://hrex.dis.anl.gov/, accessed October 17, 2004.

Internet and Education: Virtual Classrooms for Everyone? Geneva, Switzerland: International Telecommunications Organization, 2001. Available at http://www.itu.int/newsarchive/wtd/2001/FeatureEd ucation.html, accessed September 30, 2004.

Organisation for Economic Co-operation and Development. *Broadband Access in OECD Countries per 100 inhabitants.* Paris: OECD, June 2003; released November 18, 2003. Available at http://www .oecd.org/document/60/0,2340,en_2825_495656_2496764_1_1_ 1_1,00.html, accessed September 9, 2004.

————. *The Hidden Threat to E-Government: Avoiding Large Government IT Failures.* OECD Public Management Policy Brief No. 8. Paris: OECD, 2001. Available at http://www.oecd.org/dataoecd /19/12/1901677.pdf, accessed July 19, 2004.

————. "Policy Brief: Checklist for e-Government Leaders." *OECD Observer*, 2003. Available at http://www.oecd.org/dataoecd/62/58/11923037.pdf, accessed July 20, 2004.

————. "Policy Brief: E-Government in Finland: An Assessment." *OECD Observer*, 2003. Available at http://www.oecd.org/dataoecd/20/50/13314420.pdf, accessed July 20, 2004.

————. *Trust in Government: Ethics Measures in OECD Countries.* Paris: OECD, 2000. Available at http://217.26.192.119/cgi-bin/OECDBookShop,storefront/4106839700edf940273fc0a8 011 . . . , accessed July 28, 2004.

Small Island Developing States Network. Home page. New York: United Nations. Available at http://www.sidsnet.org, accessed April 1, 2005.

Turner, Michael, and Christine Desloges. "Strategies and Framework for Government On-Line: A Canadian Experience." PowerPoint presentation, June 18, 2002, Washington DC: World Bank e-Government Learning Workshop. Available at http://www.comnet-it.org/e-government/cdn experience.pdf, accessed May 7, 2005.

United Nations. Conference on Trade and Development. *E-Commerce and Development Report.* Geneva: United Nations Conference on Trade and Development, 2004. Available at http://www .unctad.org/Templates/WebFlyer.asp?intItemID = 3356&lang = 1, accessed April 1, 2005.

United Nations. Division for Public Economics and Public Administration. *Benchmarking E-government: A Global Perspective.* Prepared with the American Society for Public Administration. New York: United Nations, 2001. Available at http://www.unpan.org/e-government/Benchmar king%20E- gov%202001.pdf, accessed September 29, 2004.

————. *Global E-Government Readiness Report 2004: Towards Access for Opportunity.* UNPAN 2004/11. New York: United Nations, 2004. Available at http://www.unpan.org/egovernment4.asp, accessed March 1, 2005.

World Bank. Global Information and Communication Technologies Department. *Financing Information and Communications Needs in the Developing World: Public and Private Roles.* Draft for discussion. Washington, DC: World Bank, 2005. Available at http://lnweb18.worldbank.org/ict/resources .nsf/InfoResources/04C3CE1B933921A585256FB60051B8F5, accessed 15 April, 2005.

World Bank Group. E★Government: A Definition of E★Government. Washington, DC: World Bank, n.d. Available at www1.worldbank.org/publicsector/egov/definition.htm, accessed July 15, 2004.

————. The Anticorruption Home Page: "Anticorruption." Washington, DC: World Bank, n.d. Available at http://www.worldbank.org/anticorruption, accessed July 20, 2004.

————. *OPEN: Seoul's Anticorruption Project.* Available at http://www1.worldbank.org/publicsector /egov/seoulcs.htm, accessed September 30, 2004.

World Summit on the Information Society. *Declaration of Principles.* Geneva: United Nations, 2003. Available at http://www.itu.int/wsis/docs/geneva/official/dop.html, accessed March 30, 2005.

Regional Organizations

African Information Society Initiative. Home page. Addis Ababa, Ethiopia: Economic Commission for Africa. Available at http://www.uneca.org/aisi/, accessed April 1, 2005.

Nongovernment

Accenture. *eGovernment Leadership: Engaging the Customer.* Government Executive Series. New York: Accenture, 2004. Available at http://www.accenture.com, accessed July 15, 2004.

————. *eGovernment Leadership: High Performance, Maximum Value.* New York: Accenture, 2004. Available at http://www.accenture.com, accessed July 15, 2004.

————. *e-Government Leadership: Rhetoric vs Reality—Closing the Gap.* New York: Accenture, 2001. Available at http://www.accenture.com/xdoc/en/industries/government/2001FullReport.pdf, accessed May 16, 2005.

————. *Leadership in Customer Service: New Expectations, New Experiences.* New York: Accenture, 2005. Available at http://www.accenture.com/xdoc/en/industries/government/insights/leadership_ customerservice.pdf, accessed May 16, 2005.

————. *A Value Model for the Public Sector.* New York: Accenture, 2004. Available at http://www.ac centure.com/xd/xd/asp?it = enweb&xd = ideas\outlook_2004\hp_gov.xml (html), accessed September 17, 2004.

American Customer Satisfaction Index. Home page. Ann Arbor: University of Michigan. Available at http://www.theacsi.org/government.htm, accessed August 6, 2004; January 1, 2005.

————. "ACSI Overall Federal Government Scores with Historic Scores of Agencies Measured 1999-2004." Ann Arbor: University of Michigan, 2004. Available at http://www.theacsi.org/gov ernment/govt-all-04.html, accessed January 1, 2005.

Ask Jeeves. Home page. Available at http://www.ask.com.

Banisar, David. *Freedom of Information and Access to Government Records around the World.* Freedominfo.org. Washington, DC: George Washington University. Available at http://www.freedominfo.org/survey.htm, accessed May 12, 2004.

Bantin, Philip. "Electronic Records Management: A Review of the Work of a Decade and a Reflection on Future Directions." Bloomington, IN: University Archives, 2–3. *Encyclopedia of Library and Information Science* 71, supp. 34 (2002), 47–81. Available at http://www.indiana.edu/~libarch/ER/encycloarticle9.doc, accessed June 24, 2005.

———. *Indiana University Electronic Records Project—Phase II, 2000–2002. Final Report to the National Historical Publications and Records Commission (NHPRC).* Bloomington, IN: University Archives, 2002. Available at http://www.indiana.edu/~libarch/ER/nhprcfinalreport.doc, accessed June 25, 2005.

Benton Foundation. *Achieving E-Government for All: Highlights from a National Survey.* Prepared by Darrell M. West. Washington, DC: Benton Foundation, 2003. Available at http://www.benton.org/publibrary/egov/access2003.doc, accessed October 12, 2003.

———. Digital Divide Network. Washington, DC: Benton Foundation. Available at http://www.digitaldividenetwork.org, accessed September 9, 2004.

Boardman, Bruce, and Sean Doherty. "Portals—Agencies through the Looking Glass." *Government Enterprise,* June 2, 2002. Available at http://www.governmententerprise.com/showArticle.jhtml?articleID=17501644, accessed Jun 13, 2005.

Bonham, G. Matthew, Jeffrey W. Seifert, and Stuart J. Thorson. "The Transformational Potential of e-Government: The Role of Political Leadership." Paper presented at the panel on Electronic Governance and Information Policy, Fourth Pan European International Relations Conference of the European Consortium for Political Research, held at the University of Kent, Canterbury, UK, September 9, 2001. Available at http://www.maxwell.syr.edu/maxpages/faculty/gmbonham/ecpr.htm, accessed July 20, 2004.

Bridges.org. Home page. Washington, DC: Bridges.org. Available at http://www.bridges.org/casestudies/bridgebuilders/builder_schoolnet.html, accessed September 30, 2004.

"Bridging the Digital Divide." *International Trade Forum* 1 (January 2001): 20–21. Available at http://www.tradeforum.org/news/fullstory.php/aid/260/Bridging_the_Digital . . . Divide.html, accessed March 30, 2005.

Brown, Peter. "European Parliament and Topic Maps." Paper presented at the Real World Topic Maps seminar held by XMLuk.org, Duxford, Cambridge, November 2003. Available at www.xmluk.org/slides/duxford_2003/ 2003-11-05-Peter-Brown.pdf, accessed May 24, 2005.

Center for Digital Government. Government Technology International. "Ian Watmore to Become UK's New Head of E-Government." Folsom, CA: Center for Digital Government, June 2004. Available at http://www.centerdigitalgov.com/international/arenastory.php?docid=90579, accessed September 13, 2004.

Coalition Against Unsolicited Commercial Email. *About the Problem.* Available at http://www.cauce.org/about/problem.shtml, accessed April 26, 2004.

Conference Board of Canada. "Canada Still Holds Second Place in Connectedness Index—But Slipping." News Release 04-23. Toronto: Conference Board of Canada, April 27, 2004. Available at http://www.conferenceboard.ca/press/2004/connectedness.asp, accessed May 7, 2005.

Cooper, Mark. *Expanding the Digital Divide and Falling Behind at Broadband.* New York: Consumer Federation of America and Consumers Union, October 2004. Available at http://www.consumersunion.org/pub/ddnewbook.pdf, accessed May 2, 2004.

Council for Excellence in Government. *Partnership for Trust in Government.* A project with the Ford Foundation. Washington, DC: Council for Excellence in Government, n.d. Available at http://www.trustingov.org/, accessed October 17, 2004.

Crandall, Robert W., Charles L. Jackson, and Hal J. Singer. *The Effect of Ubiquitous Broadband Adoption on Investment, Jobs, and the U.S. Economy.* Conducted by Criterion Economics, LLC, for the New

Millennium Research Council. Washington, DC: New Millennium Research Council, September 2003. Available at http://www.newmillenniumresearch.org/archive/bbstudyreport_091703.pdf, accessed September 9, 2004.

CSPP. "A Vision for 21st Century Wired & Wireless Broadband: Building the Foundation of the Networked World." Washington, DC: CSPP, n.d. Available at http://www.cspp.org/reports/networkedworld.pdf, accessed September 9, 2004.

Cuddihey, Alden. "'No. 1 with a But': E-government Legal and Policy Issues." *IT World Canada* [Web site], May 5, 2005. Available at http://www.itworldcanada.com, accessed May 6, 2005.

Dean, Joshua. "Daily Briefing: GovBenefits Debut Marks Bush Administration's First E-gov Success." *GOVEXEC.com* (Washington, DC), 2004. Available at http://www.govexec.com/dailyfed/0402/042902j2.htm, accessed September 19, 2004.

Fresco, Marc, and Martin Waldron, *Model Requirements for the Management of Electronic Records* (MoReq). London: Cornwell Affiliates, 2001. Available at http://www.cornwell.co.uk/moreq, accessed June 27, 2005.

Google. "The Google Timeline." Available at http://www.google.com/intl/en/corporate/timeline.html, accessed July 1, 2005

Government: The Next American Revolution. Reports Based on Findings of Surveys Conducted by Hart-Teeter. Washington, DC: Council for Excellence in Government, 2004. Available at http://www.excelgov.org, accessed June 1, 2004.

Health Level Seven. Available at http://www.hl7.org/, accessed April 13, 2005.

Hiser Group. *The User Experience of Government Online: Recommendations for a Citizen-centric Future.* Melbourne: Hiser Group, 2002. Available at http://www.egov.vic.gov.au/pdfs/HiserUsability Report.pdf, accessed March 10, 2005.

Hogan, Michael, Natalie Cook, and Monika Henderson. "The Queensland Government's E-democracy Agenda." Paper presented at the Australian Electronic Governance Conference 2004, Melbourne: University of Melbourne, Centre for Public Policy, April 2004. Available at http://www.public-policy.unimelb.edu.au/egovernance/ConferenceContent.html#michaelhogan, accessed March 1, 2005.

International Council of Archives. Committee on Electronic Records. *Guide for Managing Records from an Archival Perspective, February 1997.* Paris: International Council of Archives, 1997. Available at http://www.ica.org/biblio/cer/guide_eng.html, accessed June 25, 2005.

The Internet Archive. Available at http://www.archive.org, accessed April 10, 2005.

Jones, Jeffrey M. "Congressional Approval: Better or Worse with Age?" *Gallup Poll: Tuesday Briefing,* 2004. Available at http://www.gallup.com/content/login.aspx?ci=11731, accessed July 28, 2004.

Kaye, Barbara K., and Thomas J. Johnson. "Online and in the Know: Uses and Gratifications of the Web for Political Information." *Journal of Broadcasting & Electronic Media* 46 (March 2002): 54–72 (18 pages of digital text). Available in Expanded Academic ASAP, retrieved July 28, 2004.

Leighton, Wayne A. *Broadband Deployment and the Digital Divide: A Primer.* Cato Institute Policy Analysis no. 410. Washington, DC: Cato Institute, 2001. Available at http://www.cato.org/pubs/pas/pa410.pdf, accessed September 9, 2004.

Mazerow, Michael. "Making the Internet Tax Freedom Act Permanent in the Form Currently Proposed Would Lead to a Substantial Revenue Loss for States and Localities." Washington, DC: Center on Budget and Policy Priorities, 2003. Available at http://www.cbpp.org/10-20-03sfp.pdf, accessed April 27, 2004.

Michael. Sara. "Execs Call for Full-Time Project Managers." *Federal Computer Week,* November 5, 2003. Available at http://www.fcw.com/fcw/articles/2003/1103/web-egov-11-05-03.asp, accessed July 1, 2005.

Miller, Jason. "Next Wave of Egov Projects Coming Soon." *Government Computer News,* December 18, 2003. Available at http://www.washingtontechnology.com/news/1_1/daily_news/22380-1.html, accessed July 1, 2005.

Mondaq. *United States: Anti-Spam Laws: Navigating the Web of Compliance.* New York: Latham & Watkins, 2004. Available at http://www.mondaq.com/i_article.asp_Q_articleid_E_23763, accessed April 27, 2004.

National Congress of American Indians. *American Indians and the Digital Divide.* Washington, DC: National Congress of American Indians, 2000. Available at the Internet Archive Wayback Machine, http://web.archive.org/web/20000620214226/ncai.org/indianissues/DigitalDivide/digitaldiv .htm, accessed April 15, 2005.

Nielsen, Jakob. "Personalization Is Over-rated." *Alertbox* [an irregularly issued column at useit.com: Jakob Nielsen's Web site], October 4, 1998. Available at http://www.useit.com/alertbox/981004. html, accessed May 18, 2005.

———. "Usability Heuristics." Useit.com: Jakob Nielsen's Web site, n.d. Available at http://www .useit.com, accessed June 12, 2005.

Norris, Pippa. "The World-wide Digital Divide: Information Poverty, the Internet, and Develop-ment." Paper presented at the Annual Meeting of the Political Studies Association of the United Kingdom, London School of Economics and Political Science, April 2000. Available at http://ww w.pippanorris.com/, accessed March 15, 2001.

Oakes, Kerrie. "The Impact of Electronic Governance on the Public Sector." Paper presented at the Australian Electronic Governance Conference 2004, University of Melbourne, Centre for Public Policy, 2004. Available at http://www.public-policy.unimelb.edu.au/egovernance/Conference Content.html#kerrieoakes, accessed March 1, 2005.

"Office of Special Counsel Scrubs Website." *OMB Watcher,* February 23, 2004. Available at http:// www.ombwatch.org/article/articleview/2060/1/208, accessed March 9, 2004.

Pepper, Steve. "Towards a Seamless Knowledge: Integrating Public Sector Portals in Norway." Paper presented at Semantic Web Seminar, Oslo, January 17, 2003. Available at www.ontopia.net/topic maps/materials/Towards%20Seamless%20Knowledge.ppt, accessed May 24, 2005.

Pepper, Steve, and Motomu Naito. *Topic Maps—Overview and Basic Concepts, JTC1 / SC34.* Oakridge, TN: Y-12 National Security Complex, 2003. Available at http://www.y12.doe.gov/sgml/SC34/ document/0446.htm, accessed June 13, 2005.

Perera, David. "E-gov Aims to Lose the 'E.'" *FCW.com* [*Federal Computer Week* online], May 24, 2005. Available at http://www.fcw.com/articlee88957-05-24-05-Web, accessed May 30, 2005.

———. "Fed Sites Satisfy." *FCW.com,* December 18, 2004. Available at http://www.fcw.com/fcw/ articles/2004/1213/web-asci-12-14-04.asp, accessed December 18, 2004.

———. "Web Satisfaction Dips." *FCW.com,* March 16, 2005. Available at http://www.fcw.com/ print.asp, accessed March 16, 2004.

Pew Internet & American Life Project. *Dot-gov Goes Retail.* Washington, DC: Pew Internet & Ameri-can Life Project, 2004. Available at http://www.pewinternet.org, accessed July 28, 2004.

———. *How Americans Get in Touch with Government,* by John B. Horrigan. Washington, DC: Pew Internet & American Life Project, 2004. Available at http://www.pewinternet.org/, accessed June 1, 2004.

———. *The Rise of the E-Citizen: How People Use Government Agencies' Web Sites.* Washington, DC: Pew Internet & American Life Project, 2004. Available at http://www.pewinternet.org, accessed July 28, 2004.

———. *Rural Areas and the Internet.* Washington, DC: Pew Internet & American Life Project, 2004. Available at http://www.pewinternet.org/reports/pdfs/PIP_Rural_Report.pdf, accessed Septem-ber 9, 2004.

Porter, Joshua. "Testing the Three-Click Rule," 2003. Available from home page of User Interface Engineering (Middleton, MA), http://www.uie.com/articles/three_clikc_rule/, accessed June 12, 2005.

"Public Should Benefit from E-government Savings." *ZDNet UK News,* April 5, 2002. Available at http://news.zdnet.co.uk/internet/0,39020369,2107816,00.htm, accessed September 13, 2004.

The Quest for Electronic Government: A Defining Vision, by Janet Caldow. White Plains, NY: IBM Corp.,

1999. Available at http://www1.ibm.com/industries/government/ieg/pdf/egovvision.pdf, accessed September 30, 2004.

RAND Europe. *Benchmarking e-Government in Europe and the US.* Prepared in cooperation with SIBIS [Statistical Indicators Benchmarking the Information Society]. Bonn, Germany, 2003. Available at http://www.sibis-eu.org, accessed July 8, 2004.

Rural Health Care Division. Home page. Available at http://www.rhc.universalservice.org.

Rusay, Christopher. "User-Centered Design for Large Government Portals." *Digital Web Magazine,* January 16, 2003. Available at http://digital-web.com/articles/user_centered_design_for_large_government_portals/, accessed May 18, 2005.

Sarkar, Dibya. "E-gov Grows Down Under." *FCW.com,* June 21, 2005. Available at http://www.fcw.com/print.asp, accessed June 22, 2005.

Semiconductor Industry Association. *Removing Barriers to Broadband Deployment.* San Jose, CA: Semiconductor Industry Association, 2001. Available at http://sia-online.org/downloads/Broadband_Combined.pdf, accessed September 9, 2004.

"Spam Law: United States: Federal Laws: 108th Congress: Summary." Available at http://www.spamlaws.com/federal/summ108.html#s877, accessed April 26, 2004.

"Spam Laws: United States: State Laws: California." Available at http://www.spamlaws.com/state/ca1.html, accessed April 27, 2004.

Stemstein, Allya. "Justice Sticks with WordPerfect." *FCW.com,* March 7, 2005. Available at http://www.fcw.com/fcw/articles/2005/0307/web-wordperfect-03-07-05.asp, accessed March 16, 2004.

TechNet. *A National Imperative: Universal Availability of Broadband by 2010.* Palo Alto, CA: TechNet, 2002. Available at http://www.technet.org/news/newsreleases/2002-01-15.64.pdf, accessed September 9, 2004.

Telecommunications Development Fund. Home page. Available at http://www.tdfund.com.

Thierer, Adam D. *Broadband Tax Credits, the High-Tech Pork Barrel Begins.* Washington, DC: Cato Institute, 2001. Available at http://www.cato.org/tech/tk/010713-tk.html, accessed September 9, 2004.

———. *Divided over the Digital Divide.* Washington, DC: Heritage Foundation, March 2000. Available at http://www.heritage.org/Press/Commentary/ED030100.cfm, accessed September 9, 2004.

Third International Workshop on Regulatory Ontologies. [STARLab: Semantics Technology and Applications Research Laboratory, Brussels]. Available at http://www.starlab.vub.ac.be/staff/mustafa/WORM_2005.htm, accessed June 12, 2005.

United States of America. Key National Indicators Initiative. Available at http://www.keyindicators.org/, accessed June 17, 2005.

University of North Texas. CyberCemetery. Denton: University of North Texas Libraries, 2005. Available at http://govinfo.library.unt.edu/npr/library/review.html, accessed July 1, 2005.

University of Texas at Austin. Telecommunications and Information Policy Institute. *Local Services and Broadband Telecommunications Competition in Texas, Missouri, and Kansas.* Austin, TX: Telecommunications and Information Policy Institute, n.d. Available at http://www.utexas.edu/research/tipi/reports2/loc_services.pdf, accessed April 21, 2004.

Watchfire. WebXACT. Home page. Available at http://webxact.watchfire.com/scanform.aspx, accessed June 12, 2005.

West, Darrell. "Global E-government, 2003." Providence, RI: Brown University, Center for Public Policy, 2003. Available at http://www.insidepolitics.org/egovt03int.pdf, accessed September 26, 2004.

Wikipedia: The Free Encyclopedia. Available at http://en.wikipedia.org/wiki/Main_Page, accessed May 13, 2005.

Wimmer, Maria A. "A European Perspective towards Online One-stop Government: The eGOV Project." *Electronic Commerce Research and Applications, 2002,* 2002. Available at http://falcon.ifs.uni-linz.ac.at:8080/eGOV/publications/wimmer_icec2001.pdf, accessed May 19, 2005.

World Markets Research Centre. *Global E-government Survey*. Singapore: World Markets Research Centre, 2003. Available at http://www.worldmarketsanalysis.com/pdf/e-govreport.pdf, accessed on June 4, 2003.

World Wide Web Consortium. *Web Content Accessibility Guidelines*. Cambridge, MA: W3C, 1999. Available at http://www.w3.org/TR/WAI-WEBCONTENT/, accessed March 1, 2005.

W3C. Web Accessibility Initiative. Cambridge, MA: MIT, n.d. Available at http://www.W3C.org/WAI, accessed April 15, 2005; April 18, 2005.

Zhdanova, Anne V. "The People's Portal: Ontology Management on Community Portals." Paper presented at the First Workshop on Friend of a Friend, Social Networking and the Semantic Web, September 1–2, 2004, Galway, Ireland. Available at http://www.w3.org/2001/sw//Europe/eventsfoaf-galway/papers/fp/peoples_portal, accessed May 30, 2005.

UNPUBLISHED SOURCES

Relyea, Harold C. "Life Cycle Management of Government Information: A Brief Overview of American Federal Experience." Prepared as background to remarks offered at the Shanghai Open Government Information Implementation Workshop, Shanghai, 2004.

———. "Statement: Emerging Threats: Overclassification and Pseudo-Classification." Before the House Government Reform Subcommittee on National Security, March 2, 2005.

Stapleton, Adam. "From Icons to Ideas: Archives New Zealand as the Change Agency for the Post-Custodial Paradigm." M.A. paper, University of Victoria (Wellington, New Zealand), 2005.

Index

About the Editors and Contributors

Sue Burgess (sue.burgess@uts.edu.au) is the coordinator of, and a senior lecturer in, the Information and Knowledge Management Program at the Faculty of Humanities and Social Sciences, University of Technology, Sydney (PO Box 123, Broadway 2007, Sydney, Australia). Her teaching is mainly in information resources and the supervision of professional information management projects at undergraduate and graduate levels. Her particular research and consultancy interests are in access to government and legal information, and the evaluation of services and information resources. With Jan Houghton, she is the author of several papers on electronic government and has conducted an evaluation of the user friendliness of New South Wales government Web sites for the Audit Office of NSW.

Anindya Chaudhuri (anindya_chaudhuri@mail.utexas.edu) joined the doctoral program at the Lyndon B. Johnson School of Public Affairs at the University of Texas at Austin (Box Y, Austin, Texas 78713-8925) in 1999, after obtaining an MA in economics from Jadavpur University, India, where he specialized in international trade. In 1997, he was an honors graduate in economics from the same institution, with a minor in mathematics.

At the LBJ School, he worked with James Galbraith for the University of Texas Inequality Project from 1999 to 2001, researching global income inequality. Since 2001, he has been working with and under Kenneth Flamm on analyzing Internet access and use in the United States and around the world. His doctoral dissertation, parts of which have been presented at the Telecommunication Policy Research Conference (2004) and the Association of Public Policy Analysis and Management (2003, 2004), deals with Internet demand, public access, and federal and state policies. His research interests include telecommunications, international trade, and research methodology.

Rowena Cullen (rowena.cullen@vuw.ac.nz) is an associate professor in the School of Information Management at Victoria University of Wellington (PO Box 600, Wellington, New Zealand), where she teaches in the Master of Information Management and Master of Library and Information Studies programs. She has a PhD from Victoria University of Wellington and an MLitt from the University of Edinburgh. Her current research work focuses on health informatics, government information on the Internet, and the evaluation of information services. She is on the editorial boards of the *Journal* *of E-Government, Health Information and Libraries Journal, The Journal of Academic Librarianship, Performance Measurement and Metrics, Education for Information,* and *LibRes*. She has been a keynote speaker at several international conferences and has published over one hundred articles, book chapters, and conference papers. She is also the author of a monograph on health information on the Internet.

Robert E. Dugan (rdugan@suffolk.edu) is the director of the Mildred F. Sawyer Library at Suffolk University (8 Ashburton Place, Boston, Massachusetts 02108). In a career in librarianship of more than thirty years, he has been a reference librarian, director of public libraries, head of statewide library development, a state librarian, an associate university librarian, and college library director. He has coauthored seven books and more than fifty articles on topics such as information policy, technology, outcomes assessment, and library management and operations.

Kenneth Flamm (kflamm@mail.utexas.edu) is director, Technology and Public Policy Program, and Dean Rusk Chair in International Affairs, at the Lyndon B. Johnson School of Public Affairs, University of Texas at Austin (Box Y, Austin, Texas 78713-8925). He joined the LBJ School in fall 1998, is an expert on international trade and the high technology industry, and teaches classes in microeconomic theory, international trade, and defense economics.

He is a 1973 honors graduate of Stanford University and received a PhD in economics from MIT in 1979. From 1993 to 1995, he served as principal deputy assistant secretary of defense for economic security and special assistant to the deputy secretary of defense for dual use technology policy. He was awarded the department's Distinguished Public Service Medal in 1995 by Defense Secretary William J. Perry. Prior to his service at the Defense Department, he spent eleven years as a Senior Fellow in the Foreign Policy Studies Program at Brookings.

He has been a professor of economics at the Instituto Tecnológico A. de México in Mexico City, the University of Massachusetts, and George Washington University. Dr. Flamm has also been an adviser to the director general of income policy in the Mexican Ministry of Finance and a consultant to the Organisation for Economic Cooperation and Development, the World Bank, the National Academy of Sciences, the Latin American Economic System, the U.S. Department of Defense, the U.S. Department of Justice, the U.S Agency for International Development, and the Office of Technology Assessment of the U.S. Congress.

Among his publications are *Mismanaged Trade? Strategic Policy and the Semiconductor Industry* (1996), *Changing the Rules: Technological Change, International Competition, and Regulation in Communications* (ed., with Robert Crandell, 1989), *Creating the Computer* (1988), and *Targeting the Computer* (1987). He is currently working on an analytical study of the post–Cold War defense industrial base.

Peter Hernon (peter.hernon@simmons.edu) is a professor at Simmons College, Graduate School of Library and Information Science (300 The Fenway, Boston, Massachusetts 02115-5898), where he teaches courses on government information policy and resources, evaluation of information services, research methods, and academic librarianship. He received his PhD from Indiana University in 1978 and has taught at Simmons College, the University of Arizona, and Victoria University of Wellington (New

Zealand). He is the coeditor of *Library & Information Science Research*, founding editor of *Government Information Quarterly*, and past editor of *The Journal of Academic Librarianship*. He is the author of approximately 240 publications, 41 of which are books. Among these are *Outcomes Assessment in Higher Education* (2004), *The Next Library Leadership* (2003), *United States Government Information* (2002), and *Assessing Service Quality* (1998).

Jan Houghton (jan.houghton@uts.edu.au) is a senior lecturer in the Information and Knowledge Management Program, Faculty of Humanities and Social Sciences, the University of Technology, Sydney (PO Box 123, Broadway 2007, Sydney, Australia). She teaches information society and information policy in undergraduate and graduate programs. Her main research and consulting interests are public information and communications policies, access to government information, and e-government and e-democracy. With Sue Burgess, she is the author of several papers on electronic government and has conducted an evaluation of the user friendliness of New South Wales government Web sites for the Audit Office of NSW.

Lennard G. Kruger (LKRUGER@crs.loc.gov) is a specialist in science and technology at the Congressional Research Service of the Library of Congress (101 Independence Avenue, SE, Washington, D.C. 20540-7450). He holds bachelor of applied science and bachelor of arts degrees from the University of Pennsylvania and a master of science degree in national resource strategy from the Industrial College of the Armed Forces. His areas of expertise include broadband, digital television, and other telecommunications/Internet issues.

Rachel Lilburn (Rachel.Lilburn@vuw.ac.nz) is a lecturer in the School of Information Management, Victoria University (PO Box 600, Wellington, New Zealand). She has twenty years' experience in the field of archives and records management and, in the last thirteen years, has specialized in the teaching of these subjects. Much of her experience is in the public sector, in particular National Archives (now Archives New Zealand). Before she left to join the School of Information Management in 1992, she was head appraisal archivist at the Wellington Head Office. Ms. Lilburn was also the first National Archives advisory archivist in the Auckland region from 1984 to 1987. During this period she was a consultant to many local authorities and private companies. She holds an MA in history (archives/records management) from Western Washington University, Bellingham. She is a member of the Archives New Zealand Consultative Group, the National Preservation Office Client Input Group, the Archives and Records Association of New Zealand, Wellington Branch, and is a past member of the National Council of the Archives and Records Association of New Zealand. She is currently enrolled in the PhD program at Victoria University.

Kirsti Nilsen (knilsen@uwo.ca) recently retired from the Faculty of Information and Media Studies at the University of Western Ontario. She continues to research and write in the areas of information policy, reference services, and multiculturalism and to teach as an adjunct professor both at Western and at the University of Toronto's Faculty of Information Studies. She is the author of *The Impact of Information Policy* (2001) and coauthor of *Conducting the Reference Interview* (2002) and has produced articles and contributions to conference proceedings in her areas of interest. A graduate of Emerson

College and Simmons College in Boston, she received her PhD from the University of Toronto and may be contacted at 641 Millwood Road, Toronto, Ontario, M4S 1L1, Canada.

Harold C. Relyea (HRELYEA@crs.loc.gov) is a specialist in American national government with the Congressional Research Service (CRS) of the Library of Congress (101 Independence Avenue, SE, Washington, D.C. 20540-7450). A member of the CRS staff since 1971, he has held both managerial and research positions during his career. His principal areas of research responsibility include the presidential office and powers, executive branch organization and management, executive–congressional relations, congressional oversight, and various aspects of government information policy and practice. He has testified before congressional panels on various occasions and has served as an expert resource for other organizations.

In addition to his CRS duties, Dr. Relyea has authored numerous articles for scholarly and professional publications in the United States and abroad. He is currently preparing a book on national emergency powers. His recently published titles include *Silencing Science: National Security Controls and Scientific Communication* (1994), *Federal Information Policies in the 1990s* (1996), *The Executive Office of the President* (1997), and *United States Government Information: Policies and Sources* (2002). He serves on the editorial board of *Government Information Quarterly*, the *International Journal of Electronic Government Research*, and the *Journal of E-Government* and has held similar positions with several other journals in the past. He was recently named to the Advisory and Development Board of the College of Information Studies of the University of Maryland. An undergraduate of Drew University, he received his doctoral degree in government from American University. His biography appears in *Who's Who in America* and *Who's Who in the World*.

Jeffrey W. Seifert (jseifert@crs.loc.gov) is a specialist in information science and technology policy at the Congressional Research Service (CRS; Library of Congress, 101 Independence Avenue, SE, Washington, D.C. 20540-7450). He is also a visiting instructor in the Department of Political Science at Virginia Tech. At CRS he provides congressional member and staff briefings and writes reports and other materials on a variety of information technology policy issues including electronic government, homeland security, information sharing, data mining, critical information infrastructure protection, federal information technology management, cybersecurity, and continuity of operations planning. At Virginia Tech he teaches courses focusing on information technology issues and international politics.

Dr. Seifert is a frequent presenter at national and international conferences, and his articles have appeared in the *Journal of E-Government*, *International Studies Perspectives*, *Government Information Quarterly*, *Journal of Conflict Studies*, and *Perspectives on Global Development and Technology*. He currently serves on the editorial boards of *Government Information Quarterly* and the *Journal of E-Government* and is the president of the Information Technology Policy section of the American Political Science Association (APSA). He received his PhD in political science from the Maxwell School at Syracuse University.